ADDITIONAL COOKBOOKS AND DVD SETS AVAILABLE FROM THE PUBLISHERS OF *COOK'S COUNTRY* INCLUDE:

The *Cook's Country* Series

The *Cook's Country* Cookbook
Cook's Country Best Lost Suppers
America's Best Lost Recipes
Cook's Country Best Grilling Recipes
Cook's Country 2008 Annual Edition
Cook's Country 2007 Annual Edition
Cook's Country 2006 Annual Edition
Cook's Country 2005 Annual Edition

From the Editors of *Cook's Illustrated*

More Best Recipes
The Best Skillet Recipes
The Best Slow and Easy Recipes
The Best Chicken Recipes
The Best International Recipe
The Best Make-Ahead Recipe
The Best 30-Minute Recipe
The Best Light Recipe
The *Cook's Illustrated* Guide to
Grilling and Barbecue
Best American Side Dishes
Cover & Bake
The New Best Recipe
Steaks, Chops, Roasts, and Ribs
Baking Illustrated
Perfect Vegetables
The Quick Recipe
Italian Classics
The Best American Classics
The Best Soups & Stews
The *Cook's Illustrated* Complete Book of
Pasta and Noodles
The Kitchen Detective
834 Kitchen Quick Tips
1993–2009 *Cook's Illustrated* Master Index
Cook's Illustrated Annual Editions
from each year of publication (1993–2009)

America's Test Kitchen

Cooking for Two 2009
The *America's Test Kitchen* Family Baking Book
The *America's Test Kitchen* Family Cookbook
The Best of *America's Test Kitchen* 2010
The Best of *America's Test Kitchen* 2009
The Best of *America's Test Kitchen* 2008
The Best of *America's Test Kitchen* 2007

The *America's Test Kitchen* TV Series
(companion cookbooks and DVD sets
to our hit public television series)

America's Test Kitchen:
The Complete TV Show Cookbook

America's Test Kitchen:
2009 season companion cookbook

Behind the Scenes with *America's Test Kitchen:*
2008 season companion cookbook

Test Kitchen Favorites:
2007 season companion cookbook

Cooking at Home with *America's Test Kitchen:*
2006 season companion cookbook

America's Test Kitchen Live!
2005 season companion cookbook

Inside *America's Test Kitchen:*
2004 season companion cookbook

Here in *America's Test Kitchen:*
2003 season companion cookbook

The *America's Test Kitchen* Cookbook:
2002 season companion cookbook

The *America's Test Kitchen*
2009 season 4-DVD boxed set

The *America's Test Kitchen*
2008 season 4-DVD boxed set

The *America's Test Kitchen*
2007 season 4-DVD boxed set

The *America's Test Kitchen*
2006 season 4-DVD boxed set

The *America's Test Kitchen*
2005 season 4-DVD boxed set

The *America's Test Kitchen*
2004 season 4-DVD boxed set

The *America's Test Kitchen*
2003 season 4-DVD boxed set

The *America's Test Kitchen*
2002 season 4-DVD boxed set

The *America's Test Kitchen*
2001 season 2-DVD boxed set

To order any of our cookbooks listed above, give us a call at 800-611-0759 inside the U.S., or at 515-246-6911 if calling from outside the U.S.
You can order subscriptions, gift subscriptions, and any of our books by visiting our online store at www.cookscountry.com.

$35.00

Published by America's Test Kitchen, 17 Station Street, Brookline, MA 02445
ISBN-13: 978-1-933615-37-0 ISSN: 1552-1990

To get home delivery of *Cook's Country*, call 800-526-8447 inside the U.S., or 515-247-7571 if calling from outside the U.S., or subscribe online at www.cookscountry.com.

2009 Recipe Index

RC = Recipe card
IBC = Inside back cover

Cook's Country

FEBRUARY/MARCH 2009

Glazed Meat Loaf
Better Than Mom's Recipe!

Chicken in a Pot
Rediscover an American Classic

Smoky BBQ Brisket
Presto! Slow-Cooker Magic

Make-Ahead Pizza
All-New Crust Freezes Well

Boneless Buffalo Chicken
Spicy, Extra-Crunchy Coating

Pan-Fried Pork Chops
Double Dip for Double Duty

Eggs Benedict at Home
A 1944 Recipe Saves the Day

New Mexico Pork Chili
With Coffee and Raisins, Really!

Chocolate Silk Pie
With Creamy No-Bake Filling

Best Smashed Potatoes
Sour Cream and Scallions

Rating Plastic Wraps
Which Brands Really Stick?

Oatmeal Raisin Cookies
Cut the Fat, Boost the Flavor

Watch Our New Show on Public Television!
Cook's Country from America's Test Kitchen debuted last fall on public television stations across the country. The show relies on the same practical, no-nonsense recipes that have made *Cook's Country* magazine an indispensable resource for the home cook. Watch us develop recipes, test equipment, and taste supermarket ingredients in our brand-new test kitchen. Go to **CooksCountryTV.com** to learn more.

$4.95 U.S./$6.95 CANADA

0 74470 05251 7

03>

Cook's Country

Dear Country Cook,

The story told in our small Vermont town about anadama bread was that a farmer had come home one evening to find his wife gone and nothing ready for dinner. He quickly threw together a loaf of bread, including molasses and cornmeal, and then shouted, "Anna, damn her!" As a kid, I thought that this was purely a local tale, but other expressions such as, "I'm neither sugar nor salt, I won't melt," turned out to be common country sayings too. (I actually did hear an old Vermont farmer utter "neither sugar nor salt" as he walked slowly through the pouring rain towards the hay barn.)

I learned to bake bread on a green, wood-fired Kalamazoo cookstove in a small, yellow farmhouse occupied by the town baker, Marie Briggs. Marie was short and stocky, wore braided hair in a bun, sensible black shoes, round glasses, and worked dawn to dusk baking white, whole wheat, and anadama breads, molasses cookies as big as saucers, the occasional pie, baking powder biscuits, raisin-specked hermits, and her famous nutmeg doughnuts sold bagged by the dozen down at the Wayside Country Store.

Some things are local, yet others are universal, like walking out of the stinging cold of a dark winter's afternoon to a small, warm kitchen ripe with the smell of yeast, wet dog, and molasses. You'd step over the threshold into the front parlor and Marie sat you down with a thick slice of freshly baked bread slathered with homemade butter. No matter how bad the weather outside, here was a standing invitation to come home where the stove was hot, the bread was warm, and farmhands told and retold the stories we all knew and loved. Try it yourself. Bake a loaf of bread, sit back, and see who walks in the kitchen door.

Christopher Kimball

Christopher Kimball
Founder and Editor, Cook's Country Magazine

Young girl discovers the magic of baking.
Photographer: Evans/Three Lions/Getty Images

Cook's Country

Founder and Editor Christopher Kimball
Editorial Director Jack Bishop
Executive Editor Peggy Grodinsky
Deputy Editor Bridget Lancaster
Senior Editors Scott Kathan, Lisa McManus, Jeremy Sauer
Test Kitchen Director Erin McMurrer
Associate Editors Cali Rich, Diane Unger
Test Cooks Kelley Baker, Lynn Clark, Kris Widican
Assistant Editors Meredith Butcher, Peggy Chung
Assistant Test Cooks Meghan Erwin, María del Mar Sacasa
Assistant Test Kitchen Director Matthew Herron
Copy Editor Amy Graves

Online Managing Editor David Tytell
Online Editor Kate Mason
Online Assistant Editor Leaya Lee
Executive Assistant Meredith Smith
Senior Kitchen Assistant Nadia Domeq
Kitchen Assistants Maria Elena Delgado, Ena Gudiel
TV Producer Melissa Baldino
Contributing Editor Eva Katz
Consulting Editors Guy Crosby, Meg Ragland

Design Director Amy Klee
Art Director, Magazines Julie Bozzo
Senior Designer Christine Vo
Designers Jay Layman, Lindsey Timko
Staff Photographer Daniel J. van Ackere

Systems Administrator S. Paddi McHugh
Web Production Coordinator Evan Davis
IT Support Technician Brandon Lynch

Chief Financial Officer Sharyn Chabot
Human Resources Director Adele Shapiro
Controller Mandy Shito
Senior Accountant Aaron Goranson
Staff Accountant Connie Forbes
Accounts Payable Specialist Steven Kasha
Office Manager Tasha Bere
Receptionist Henrietta Murray

Production Director Guy Rochford
Traffic & Projects Manager Alice Carpenter
Production & Imaging Specialists Judy Blomquist, Lauren Pettapiece
Color & Imaging Specialist Andrew Mannone

Vice President Marketing David Mack
Circulation Director Doug Wicinski
Fulfillment & Circulation Manager Carrie Horan
Partnership Marketing Manager Pamela Putprush
Marketing Assistant Megan Cooley
Direct Mail Director Adam Perry
Marketing Database Analyst Ariel Gilbert-Knight
Products Director Steven Browall
Product Promotions Director Randi Lawrence
E-Commerce Marketing Director Hugh Buchan
Associate Marketing Manager Laurel Zeidman
Marketing Copywriter David Goldberg
Customer Service Manager Jacqueline Valerio
Customer Service Representatives Jillian Nannicelli, Kate Sokol

Sponsorship Sales Director Marcy McCreary
Retail Sales & Marketing Manager Emily Logan
Corporate Marketing Associate Bailey Vatalaro
Publicity Deborah Broide

COLOR FOOD PHOTOGRAPHY: Keller + Keller
STYLING: Mary Jane Sawyer

ILLUSTRATION: Russell Brocklehurst
Greg Stevenson (cover illustration)

Cook's Country magazine (ISSN 1552-1990), number 25, is published bimonthly by Boston Common Press Limited Partnership, 17 Station Street, Brookline, MA 02445. Copyright 2009 Boston Common Press Limited Partnership. Periodicals Postage paid at Boston, Mass., and additional mailing offices. Publications Mail Agreement No. 40020778. Return undeliverable Canadian addresses to P.O. Box 875, Station A, Windsor, Ontario N9A 6P2. POSTMASTER: Send address changes to Cook's Country, P.O. Box 8382, Red Oak, IA 51591-1382. **Customer Service:** It's easy to subscribe, give a gift subscription, change your address, and manage your subscription online. Visit www.americastestkitchen.com/customerservice for all of your customer service needs or write to us at Cook's Country, P.O. Box 8382, Red Oak, IA 51591-1382.

PRINTED IN THE USA

Contents

GLAZED MEAT LOAF

FRENCH SILK CHOCOLATE PIE

NEW MEXICO PORK CHILI

Featured Stories

In Every Issue

Watch our new show on public television!

Cook's Country from America's Test Kitchen debuted last fall on public television stations across the country. The show relies on the same practical, no-nonsense recipes that have made *Cook's Country* magazine an indispensable resource for the home cook. Watch us develop recipes, test equipment, and taste supermarket ingredients in our brand-new test kitchen. Go to CooksCountryTV.com to learn more.

Kitchen Shortcuts

EASY CLEAN-UP
Wrap That Lid
Andrea Wilhelm
Webster Groves, Mo.

Since it's difficult to clean the nooks and crannies of my food processor lid, I came up with a trick to keep the lid clean: Fill the workbowl with your ingredients, then stretch a piece of plastic wrap over the top. Replace the lid and lock it in place, securing both it and the plastic wrap, and process away. When finished, discard the spattered plastic and put the lid away. No cleanup needed.

DOUBLE DUTY
Breading Becomes Meatballs
Sun-Young Hendrick

Aurora, Colo.

When making chicken Parmesan, it always seems that I have leftover egg wash and bread crumbs. Now, instead of throwing it all out, I immediately make meatballs with the leftovers. I add the egg wash and bread crumbs to the meatball ingredients. It's perfect for the next night's dinner, especially if you make a double batch of marinara

BETTER BAKING
Quick Cookies, Cool Kitchen
Maureen Glatzmaier
Helena, Mont.

I discovered a great way to make cookies without having to turn on the oven (especially in the summer heat). Use your favorite cookie dough (or a premade, refrigerated roll) and griddle it! I heat my griddle to medium-high, lightly coat it with cooking spray, and cook ¼-inch-thick slices of dough (or mounds flattened to ¼ inch) until brown, about 5 minutes on each side. The cookies have two "bottoms," but you get warm cookies without warming up the kitchen.

SMART PREP
No-Peel Hard-Cooked Eggs
Darlene Lewis
Lander, Wyo.

Whenever I need hard-cooked eggs for salad, rather than boiling the eggs, I crack them into my egg-poaching pan. I let the eggs cook until I can see that the yolks have set and then simply slide them out and chop as needed. The eggs are perfectly done every time—no peeling required.

SMART PREP
Vegetable Revival
Kristen Sansoni
Pittsburgh, Pa.

To keep bagged salad greens or carrots from getting slimy, I place a folded paper towel in the bag immediately after opening it. The paper towel absorbs the excess water and keeps the greens fresh and long lasting.

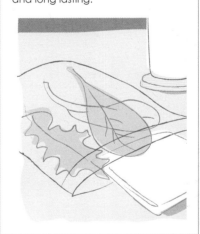

KITCHEN EFFICIENCY
Storing Garlic Neatly
Pamela Berube
Columbus, Ohio

I love to use fresh garlic in my cooking and often buy several heads at a time but have a hard time storing it without a mess of papery skins. I purchased a small mesh laundry bag and use that to store the garlic. There is plenty of airflow through the holes in the bag to keep the garlic fresh, and the skins are neatly contained.

HANDY TIP
Toasty Tortillas
Teo McIntosh
Philadelphia, Pa.

I like to use up leftover meat by eating it in tacos, but corn tortillas need to be warmed for the right texture and flavor. To quickly heat tortillas, I just drop them into the slots of my toaster. In about 30 seconds the tortilla is ready to be filled.

MAKE AHEAD
Ground Beef in a Flash
Carol Canfield
St. Paul, Minn.

When any type of ground meat I use regularly is on sale, I buy a lot, and rather than freeze the meat raw, I fry it in batches first. Once the cooked meat is drained, I spread it out on a large rimmed baking sheet and freeze it until firm. Then I dump premeasured amounts into smaller freezer zipper-lock bags and store them in the freezer. It is so fast and easy to add a measured amount of cooked meat to dishes I am making without the fuss of defrosting and cooking it first.

Ask Cook's Country

Why does chocolate sometimes form a white film on its surface?

Hilary Dent
Charlestown, Mass.

This harmless white substance is called bloom and is caused by extreme temperature changes, most commonly on chocolate that has been refrigerated or frozen. Although bloomed chocolate is safe to use, its appearance is off-putting (although the bloom is reabsorbed and disappears when the chocolate is melted).

When chocolate goes from a warm, humid environment to a cooler one, moisture forms on its surface, dissolving the sugar it comes in contact with. After the moisture evaporates, the sugar crystallizes and leaves behind the white film. Similarly, if kept in an environment that's too warm, the fat in the chocolate changes to a different crystal structure, which looks gray. For bloom-free storage, milk and white chocolate will last six months, and darker chocolate will last as long as a year when wrapped tightly in plastic wrap and stored at room temperature in a cool pantry.

NO BLOOM, BLOOM
To avoid this harmless—but unappetizing—white bloom (right), always store chocolate at room temperature.

Sun-Maid now makes Baking Raisins. What are they, and are they worth buying?

Audrey Littlejohn
Winston-Salem, N.C.

Raisins that have been in the cupboard too long can dry out and become tough. Some recipes call for softening raisins by plumping them with a liquid soak (typically water, tea, or liqueur) before the fruit is stirred into the batter. Sun-Maid has gone one step further by introducing "Baking Raisins" that have been presoaked in water, drained, and packaged dry. To test this new product, we baked oatmeal cookies and bran muffins with the new Baking Raisins, ordinary boxed raisins, and ordinary boxed raisins that we had soaked in hot tap water for 5 minutes and then drained. In both applications, the Baking Raisins and our soaked raisins were noticeably more moist and tender than the unsoaked ones. Sun-Maid's baking raisins cost about twice as much as regular raisins, and you can't add flavor by choosing a plumping liquid. We'll plump our own raisins until the price comes down.

Can plain and toasted sesame oil be used interchangeably?

Ben Sessions
Advance, N.C.

Plain and toasted sesame oil cannot be used interchangeably. The plain (or cold-pressed) variety is made from raw sesame seeds and has very little color, smell, or flavor. Its neutral taste and high smoke point make it a good oil for cooking. It also keeps for months at room temperature. Toasted (or roasted) sesame oil, on the other hand, is made from toasted seeds—toasting draws out rich flavor and aroma from the seeds. Toasted sesame oil has a deep brown color, a lower smoke point, and less shelf stability than plain sesame oil. In fact, toasted sesame oil should be stored in the refrigerator to keep it from going rancid. We like toasted sesame oil in vinaigrettes and cold salads, and we sometimes add a few drops to stir-fries off-heat at the very end of cooking. It should not be used as a cooking medium.

What is Indian sugar?

Beth Anderson
El Paso, Texas

Indian sugar is crystallized maple sugar made by boiling maple sap past the syrup stage until most of the liquid has evaporated; the native Americans of the Northeast U.S. are believed to be the first people to use this sugar.

This sugar, which is similar in texture to brown sugar (and can be substituted for light or dark brown sugar in most applications), is available in many supermarkets—but we prefer our moister, more flavorful homemade version. To make Indian sugar, boil 1 cup of good quality (grade A) maple syrup over medium-high heat until it reaches 237 degrees. Transfer the syrup to a large bowl and stir constantly until it dries and forms clumps, which takes approximately 10 minutes. Scatter the clumps onto a plate to cool, and then store the sugar in an airtight container. We like to combine Indian sugar with other sugars to add flavor to baked goods.

Do you recommend frozen shrimp, and what is the best way to defrost them?

Eric Beek
Burlington, Vt.

Almost all shrimp are frozen after being harvested, so the "fresh" shrimp you see at the market have very likely been frozen and then thawed by your fishmonger. Since there's no way to know for certain when these "fresh" shrimp were defrosted, quality varies dramatically. In the test kitchen, we find that buying frozen shrimp and defrosting them at home yields superior results. To defrost shrimp, place them in a colander under cold running water; they will be thawed and ready to cook in a few minutes (always thoroughly dry them first). Make sure to buy frozen shrimp with their shells on; shelled shrimp don't survive the freezing and thawing process very well and will surely be mushy (and the shrimp shells can be used to make a quick and flavorful shrimp stock).

Do angel food cakes have to be cooled upside down?

Kim Vinnakota
New York, N.Y.

Most cakes rely on baking powder and/or soda for leavening and structure, but angel food cakes get their lift from whipped egg whites alone (usually about one dozen whites) that are stabilized by the addition of cream of tartar. Once the cake emerges from the oven, high and golden, popular practice dictates inverting and resting the cake pan on the neck of a bottle to cool. The thinking is that a cake leavened by just egg whites is so delicate it could collapse during the time it takes it to cool.

To see if this inversion is truly necessary, we baked two cakes and cooled one upside down and the other right-side up. The cake that was left to cool right-side up deflated and caved in within minutes, demonstrating that upside down cooling is indeed necessary. Resting the tube pan on the neck of a bottle works fine, but the test kitchen's favorite tube pan, the Chicago Metallic Angel Food Cake pan, has feet that support the inverted pan during cooling.

RIGHT-SIDE UP
Gravity took its toll on this featherweight cake, weighing it down in no time.

UPSIDE DOWN
Cooling the cake upside down helped retain its structural integrity.

What's the best way to store asparagus?

Dave Stebbins
Charlottesville, Va.

To determine how to best maintain asparagus' bright color and crisp texture, we tested refrigerating spears in the plastic bag we'd bought them in, enclosed in a paper bag, wrapped in a damp paper towel, and with the stalk ends trimmed and standing up in a small amount of water. After three days the results were clear. Those left in the plastic bag had become slimy, while the paper bag and towel bunches had shriveled tips and limp stalks. However, the bunch stored in water looked as good as fresh and retained its firm texture.

To store asparagus this way, trim the bottom ½ inch of the stalks and stand the spears upright in a glass. Add enough water to cover the bottom of the stalks by 1 inch and place the glass in the refrigerator. Asparagus stored this way should remain relatively fresh for about four days; you may need to add a little more water every few days. Retrim the very bottom of the stalks before using.

VEGETABLE BOUQUET
Store cut asparagus in water to keep it fresh longer.

Can corn oil be substituted for vegetable oil?

Gordon Walker
Anaheim, Calif.

Oil that is labeled "vegetable oil" is typically made from soybeans and is called for in recipes where additional flavor isn't desired. Corn oil is, obviously, made from corn. Both oils have a high smoke point, which makes them suitable for frying.

To see how these oils stack up against one another, we deep-fried drop doughnuts, shallow-fried pork cutlets, and whisked vinaigrettes with each. We detected no flavor differences between the doughnuts and cutlets. The vinaigrettes, however, were another story, as the corn oil lent a pronounced unpleasant flavor to the vinaigrette. In sum, corn and vegetable oils can be used interchangeably when frying, but avoid corn oil in uncooked applications.

To ask us a cooking question, visit **CooksCountry. com/emailus.** You can also write to Ask Cook's Country, P.O. Box 470739, Brookline, MA 02447. See if you can stump us!

Recipe Makeover Oatmeal Raisin Cookies

Most reduced-calorie oatmeal cookies are as dry and tasteless as hardtack. How do you cut calories while keeping flavor and chew? BY KRIS WIDICAN

To get more flavor out of less butter, we brown it in a skillet to draw out the butter's nutty quality.

I used to give myself a pat on the back for choosing an oatmeal raisin cookie over other sweets, figuring the oatmeal and raisins made it a "healthy" choice. That was before learning that some cookies weigh in at close to 400 calories and 13 grams of fat. Many supermarkets sell "low-cal" versions, but when they replace real butter and sugar with engineered fat and artificial sugar, the chewy texture and natural oat flavor disappear, too.

The homemade low-fat cookies I tried were equally disappointing. One recipe used nonfat sour cream instead of butter and produced pale cookies with a lingering chemical aftertaste. Another replaced fat and sugar with applesauce for a gruesome, cottony cookie. Batch after batch of low-fat cookies sat uneaten in the test kitchen. Clearly, for good color, flavor, and texture, some fat was necessary. Changing my approach, I baked a batch of the test kitchen's favorite full-fat cookies to see where I could trim and whittle.

Reducing the amount of butter from 16 tablespoons to 6 and using a single egg instead of two substantially cut the amount of fat, but compared to the full-fat version, these cookies were nothing to brag about. While these cookies didn't have the cloying artificial taste of other diet recipes, they didn't have the seductive butter flavor or chew of full-fat, either. Wanting more butter flavor without the fat, I tried browning the butter, which intensifies butter's nuttiness. Tasters loved the pronounced buttery taste.

But reducing the fat in the original recipe had done more than affect flavor; it had changed the texture, too. The oats, pleasantly chewy yet tender in the full-fat version, had turned tough, as if they barely cooked during baking. Maybe I'd have to precook them before proceeding with the recipe. I tried dry-toasting the oats in the oven, in the microwave, and in a stovetop skillet before admitting defeat. In every case the finished cookies were leathery. A colleague suggested that the oats might benefit from sautéing with the butter as it browned. That did it. The oats cooked, losing toughness and gaining a welcome butter-toasted flavor.

To cut even more calories, I tried reducing the amount of sugar, but the cookies became brittle. I should have known: Sugar adds moisture as well as sweetness. To compensate, I tried adding water to the reduced-sugar batter, but even a drizzle made the cookies damp and fragile. I thought back to another test kitchen low-fat cookie recipe that used a puree of softened dried dates to add moisture. Since these were oatmeal raisin cookies, I reached for the box of raisins instead. After a few tries, I got the best results by simmering chopped raisins on the stovetop with ¾ cup water until the fruit was plump and the pan almost dry. I stirred the raisin "pulp" into the dough with the whole raisins.

These cookies baked up supple and chewy, with a caramel-y backdrop of raisin flavor. Amazingly, although I'd cut the fat per cookie by 9.5 grams and the calories by 220, in a side-by-side test of the original and reduced-fat-and-calorie versions, no one could tell which was which.

REDUCED-FAT OATMEAL RAISIN COOKIES Makes 20 cookies
The cooled cookies can be stored in an airtight container at room temperature for 3 days.

- 1 cup raisins; ½ cup chopped fine, ½ cup left whole
- ¾ cup water
- 6 tablespoons unsalted butter
- 1¾ cups old-fashioned oats
- 1½ teaspoons ground cinnamon
- 1 cup all-purpose flour
- ¼ teaspoon baking powder
- ¼ teaspoon baking soda
- ½ teaspoon salt
- 1½ cups packed light brown sugar
- 1 large egg
- 2 teaspoons vanilla extract

1. PLUMP RAISINS Adjust oven racks to upper-middle and lower-middle positions and heat oven to 350 degrees. Line 2 baking sheets with parchment paper. Combine chopped raisins and water in saucepan and bring to boil over medium-high heat. Reduce heat and simmer until water has evaporated and raisins are plump, about 15 minutes; let cool.

2. TOAST OATS Melt butter in large skillet over medium heat. Cook oats, stirring constantly, until just golden, about 5 minutes. Stir in cinnamon and cook until fragrant, about 30 seconds; let cool.

3. MIX Combine flour, baking powder, baking soda, and salt in bowl. In large bowl, whisk sugar, egg, and vanilla until smooth. Stir in whole and plumped raisins, oat mixture, and flour mixture until just combined.

4. BAKE Roll 2 tablespoons dough into 1½-inch balls and place 2 inches apart on prepared baking sheets. Gently press balls with measuring cup until ½ inch thick. Bake cookies until edges are light golden and centers are just set, 13 to 16 minutes, switching and rotating baking sheets halfway through baking. Cool 10 minutes on sheets, then transfer to wire rack. Serve warm or at room temperature.

Test Kitchen Secret Same Old Ingredients, Brand New Techniques
Simply reducing the amount of butter and sugar in oatmeal cookies will leave you with tough, flavorless cookies. While some recipes rely on strange stir-ins like applesauce or fat-free sour cream, we found a better approach:

RAISINS
To keep the cookies moist and chewy, we add a raisin paste (made by stewing chopped raisins and water) to the dough.

OATMEAL
To enhance the flavor of the cookies, we toast the oats in butter until they turn golden brown and fragrant.

Slow Cooking Barbecued Beef Brisket

To get good barbecued brisket, most people head outside to the grill. So how on earth do you make good brisket inside, in a slow cooker? BY DIANE UNGER

Barbecued brisket should be tender and moist, with a deep brown crust and robust spice and smoke flavor. That's hard enough to pull off on a backyard grill, but try translating it to the slow cooker and the problems seem insurmountable. Most recipes throw a slab of brisket in the slow cooker, cover it with bottled barbecue sauce, and hope for the best. But even the best recipes I tried turned out awful stuff. The problem was the large volume of moisture that brisket releases as it cooks. These recipes produced meat with a boiled, stringy exterior and an interior so dry (despite the juice it was floating in) that no amount of sauce could salvage it. Was I expecting too much from a slow cooker?

First up was a simple spice rub, often the hallmark of great barbecue. I combined salt, pepper, brown sugar, cumin, and paprika. To bump up the flavor and start building the smoky component, I added chipotle chiles. I scored the fat to allow the flavor to permeate and rubbed the mixture all over the brisket. I put the brisket in the slow cooker with just a little barbecue sauce (to minimize the liquid the meat would cook in) and waited. The test kitchen smelled great—but that was as good as it got. The brisket was bobbing in more than two cups of liquid that had been forced out of the meat as it cooked; this made it taste more like pot roast than barbecue (which traditionally isn't cooked directly in liquid).

Elevating the meat off the bottom of the slow cooker so that it wasn't sitting in any accumulated juices seemed worth a try. So for my next test, I balled up some aluminum foil and set the brisket on top. It was crude, but it served the purpose. Seven hours later, the results were promising: Half of the meat was out of the pool. The other half was listing precariously. I needed something sturdier to support the brisket's weight. Scanning the test kitchen's supply room, I spied a loaf pan. I inverted it in the slow cooker like a pedestal and placed the brisket on top. So far, so good.

I couldn't check the meat because opening the lid allows too much heat to escape. And condensation blocked my view through the lid, so when I took the lid off seven hours later, I did a double take. The brisket looked great: dark brown with a caramelized exterior. What really threw me, though, was instead of the usual couple of inches of juice in the slow cooker, there was barely any. Where had it gone? I lifted up the loaf pan and got my answer: Out came a flood of thin but concentrated beef juice, which had been drawn into the pan by a vacuum effect. What a brilliant accident! Containing the liquid under the loaf pan made the cooking environment even drier, which is closer to how real barbecue is cooked. To bump up the flavor of the juice, I sautéed onion, garlic, tomato paste, and more of the chipotle that I'd put in the rub and added that to the slow cooker, under the loaf pan, to cook along with the brisket. Adding a little water to the pan provided protection against scorching.

After the brisket rested for 30 minutes, I sliced it thinly against the grain and poured half of the flavorful, thin sauce over the meat. I turned the remaining juices into a thicker serving sauce by adding ketchup, vinegar, and a few drops of liquid smoke to drive home the outdoor flavor. One bite of this brisket and I knew I'd hit the mark. The meat was moist and tender; the sauce was spicy, a bit smoky, and packed with concentrated flavor. I expected more from my slow cooker and I got it!

This tender, spicy, smoky brisket tastes like real pit-smoked barbecue.

SLOW COOKER BBQ BEEF BRISKET Serves 8 to 10

Scoring the fat on the brisket at ½-inch intervals will allow the rub to penetrate the meat. Two disposable aluminum loaf pans stacked inside one another can substitute for the metal loaf pan.

SPICE RUB AND BRISKET
- ½ cup packed dark brown sugar
- 2 tablespoons minced canned chipotle chiles in adobo
- 1 tablespoon ground cumin
- 1 tablespoon paprika
- 1 teaspoon salt
- 2 teaspoons pepper
- 1 (4- to 5-pound) brisket roast, fat trimmed to ¼ inch thick and scored lightly

AROMATICS AND SAUCE
- 3 tablespoons vegetable oil
- 1 onion, chopped fine
- 2 tablespoons tomato paste
- 1 tablespoon chili powder
- 1 tablespoon minced canned chipotle chiles in adobo
- 2 garlic cloves, minced
- ½ cup water
- ¼ cup ketchup
- 1 tablespoon cider vinegar
- ¼ teaspoon liquid smoke

1. RUB Combine sugar, chipotle, cumin, paprika, salt, and pepper in bowl. Rub sugar mixture all over brisket. Cover with plastic wrap and let sit at room temperature for 1 hour or refrigerate for up to 24 hours.

2. COOK Heat oil in large skillet over medium-high heat until shimmering. Cook onion until softened, about 5 minutes. Add tomato paste and cook until beginning to brown, about 1 minute. Stir in chili powder, chipotle, and garlic

and cook until fragrant, about 30 seconds. Following photos at left, mound onion mixture in center of slow cooker, arrange inverted metal loaf pan over onion mixture, and place brisket, fat-side up, on top of loaf pan. Add water to slow cooker, cover, and cook on high until fork inserted into brisket can be removed with no resistance, 7 to 8 hours (or cook on low for 10 to 12 hours).

3. REST Transfer brisket to 13- by 9-inch baking dish, cover with foil, and let rest 30 minutes. Carefully remove loaf pan from slow cooker. Pour onion mixture and accumulated juices into large bowl and skim fat. (You should have about 2 cups defatted juices; if you have less, supplement with water.)

4. SAUCE Transfer brisket to cutting board, slice thinly across grain, and return to baking dish. Pour 1 cup reserved defatted juices over sliced brisket. Whisk ketchup, vinegar, and liquid smoke into remaining juices. Season with salt and pepper. Serve, passing sauce at table.

MAKE AHEAD In step 3, wrap brisket tightly in foil and refrigerate for up to 3 days. (Refrigerate juices separately in airtight container.) To serve, transfer foil-wrapped brisket to baking dish and heat in 350-degree oven and cook until brisket is heated through, about 1 hour. Reheat juices in microwave or saucepan set over medium heat. Continue with recipe as directed.

THE SLOW DISCOVERY **A Magic Trick That Really Works**
To minimize the moisture absorbed by the brisket, we place the meat on top of a loaf pan. The juices exuded by the meat are drawn under the pan by a vacuum effect, creating less moisture directly below the meat.

1. Pile onion mixture in the bottom of the slow cooker and top with an inverted loaf pan.

2. Keep the brisket dry by elevating it on top of the loaf pan.

3. Remove the loaf pan to release the juices, which make a flavorful base for barbecue sauce.

Make Ahead Pizza

Most store-bought frozen pizza tastes like the cardboard box it came in. We wanted the convenience of frozen but the taste of homemade. BY LYNN CLARK

Mixing half-and-half into the cheese keeps it from drying out in the freezer.

I love the idea of brightening my workweek with homemade pizza for dinner. But on an average weeknight, who has time for a big cooking project? No problem; I could make my usual homemade pie over a leisurely weekend and pop it in the freezer for later. I was looking for the ease of commercial frozen pizza with the flavor and texture—cheesy, crisp, and gooey—of fresh-baked.

I set to work making the test kitchen's pizza dough (flour, salt, sugar, yeast, olive oil, and water). I topped the crust with sauce and cheese, wrapped it in plastic, and into the freezer it went. A few days later, I baked it on a pizza stone—the test kitchen's preferred method. To my dismay, this homemade pizza was as ghastly as a commercial frozen pie. The cheese had dried out. The sauce had lost its vibrancy. The crust was tough and brittle on the outside, and gummy and dense on the inside. Freezing, I found out, equals loss of moisture and flavor. Manufacturers use gums, protein film formers, extra leaveners, and surfactants (wetting agents) to address those problems—not very successfully, judging by the way the stuff tastes—but what's a home cook to do?

I started with the crust. None among the slew of recipes I tried had a crust that even approached my ideal of soft and light on the inside, crisp and chewy on the outside. Tackling the gummy interior first, it was obvious that the yeast was being weakened by its time in the freezer. A quick review of science explained why: Ice crystals that form in dough in the freezer puncture the yeast cells, inhibiting their ability to form carbon dioxide, which is what causes the dough to rise. I decided to try to bolster the dough's rising power by adding baking powder, and was pleased to find that this also eliminated the problem of a wet interior.

But the crust was still a bit tough. To solve this problem I turned to a test kitchen pizza dough recipe that uses milk. The dairy acts as a tenderizer, making for rich, soft dough—think of the difference between rustic bread made with water and tender sandwich bread made with milk. Half-and-half turned out to be even better than milk, adding extra richness that my tasters appreciated. At the same time I replaced some of the flour with cornstarch to further tenderize the dough. (Cornstarch has less protein than flour does: the weaker the protein, the softer the dough.)

I was happy with the inside of the crust, but a crisp and chewy exterior eluded me. Most pizza dough recipes have a 60 percent water-to-flour ratio. Would wetter dough that took into account the inevitable moisture loss that occurs in the freezer produce the crisp-chewy crust I was seeking? I mixed up dough with a higher proportion of liquid to flour (4 cups flour, ¼ cup cornstarch, and 2 cups half-and-half for two pizzas). Unfortunately, the extra half-and-half made the crust taste like a biscuit. Next, I substituted water for ½ cup of the half-and-half. I gave the pizza a few days in the freezer and then baked it. The good news? The floppy, wet dough produced a lovely crust with a crisp shell and tender interior. The bad? The dough had been so sticky, it was a major hassle to handle. A colleague suggested I pat it out into disposable aluminum pizza pans (which I would remove before baking) instead of rolling it, and this let me shape the otherwise unruly dough.

With relief, I turned my attention to toppings. I started with the test kitchen's favorite pizza sauce recipe, but it became dull when frozen. Ultimately, switching from fresh to dried herbs and doubling the amounts normally called for compensated for the dulling capacity of the freezer. After the pies baked, the cheese (mozzarella and Parmesan) peeled off in tough, rubbery sheets. They, too, were drying out in the freezer. I tried test after test to moisten them, mixing the cheese with oil, water, milk, half-and-half, and ricotta. In the end, as with the crust, half-and-half worked best.

Even to me, the final recipe looked downright weird. Who'd ever heard of a pizza crust calling for half-and-half, cornstarch, and baking powder? Who would think to stir half-and-half into cheese? But the proof was in the pizza, which had freezer-to-oven ease without freezer taste.

MAKE-AHEAD PIZZA
Makes two 12-inch pizzas

You will need two 12-inch disposable aluminum pizza pans and a baking stone for this recipe. See page 30 for the test kitchen's recommended baking stone.

DOUGH
- 1½ cups half-and-half, heated to 110 degrees
- ½ cup water, heated to 110 degrees
- 2 tablespoons extra-virgin olive oil
- 4 cups all-purpose flour
- ¼ cup cornstarch
- 1 envelope (2¼ teaspoons) rapid-rise or instant yeast
- ½ teaspoon baking powder
- ½ teaspoon sugar
- 1½ teaspoons salt

SAUCE AND TOPPINGS
- 1 (14.5-ounce) can diced tomatoes
- 1 tablespoon extra-virgin olive oil, plus additional for brushing
- 1 tablespoon tomato paste
- 2 garlic cloves, minced
- 1 tablespoon dried basil
- 1 teaspoon dried oregano
- ¼ teaspoon red pepper flakes
  Salt
- 3 cups shredded mozzarella cheese
- ¼ cup grated Parmesan cheese
- ¼ cup half-and-half

1. MAKE DOUGH Adjust oven rack to lowest position and heat oven to 200 degrees. When oven reaches 200 degrees,

---

FREEZE WITH EASE Keys to Frozen Pizza Dough

The best pizza dough bakes up crisp on the outside and chewy on the inside. But if you place pizza dough in the freezer, it dries out, yielding a crust as tough as leather. Here are a few tricks to ensure great homemade frozen pizza.

1. The ultra-hydrated dough is ready when it forms sticky strands around the outside, but the center is uniform, after about 5 minutes of mixing.

2. To keep the loose, almost pourable dough contained, we pat it into disposable pizza pans.

3. To prevent moisture loss, we wrap the assembled pizzas twice, first with plastic wrap and then aluminum foil.

4. For easier transfer in and out of the oven, we place the frozen pizza on a sheet of parchment paper when ready to bake.

5 Easy Recipes Red Wine Pan Sauces for Steak

Stop! Don't wash that pan! Use the browned bits stuck to the skillet to create a restaurant-quality sauce in less than 10 minutes. BY KELLEY BAKER

shut it off. Grease large bowl. Combine half-and-half, water, and oil in liquid measuring cup. In bowl of stand mixer fitted with dough hook, mix flour, cornstarch, yeast, baking powder, sugar, and salt until combined. With mixer on medium-low speed, add half-and-half mixture in steady stream and mix until dough comes together, about 1 minute. Continue mixing until sticky strands form around exterior but center of dough is uniform in texture, about 5 minutes. Transfer dough to prepared bowl, coat lightly with cooking spray, cover with plastic wrap, and place in warm oven. Let rise until doubled in size, about 1 hour.

2. MAKE SAUCE Pulse tomatoes in food processor until coarsely ground. Heat 1 tablespoon oil in large saucepan over medium heat until shimmering. Cook tomato paste until just beginning to brown, about 2 minutes. Stir in garlic, basil, oregano, and pepper flakes and cook until fragrant, about 30 seconds. Add pulsed tomatoes and simmer until reduced to 1½ cups, about 10 minutes. Season with salt and let cool.

3. CONSTRUCT PIZZA Remove dough from oven and divide in half. Transfer each half to 12-inch disposable aluminum pizza pan and, using oiled hands, press dough to cover pan. Combine mozzarella, Parmesan, and half-and-half in large bowl and stir with rubber spatula until well combined. Top each pizza evenly with half of sauce and half of cheese, leaving ½-inch border around edges. Wrap each pizza tightly with plastic, then aluminum foil. Freeze up to 1 month.

4. BAKE PIZZA Adjust oven rack to lowest position, place pizza stone on rack, and heat oven to 500 degrees. Discard foil and plastic and remove frozen pizza from aluminum pan. Place pizza on large square of parchment paper and brush edges of dough lightly with oil. Transfer parchment and pizza to hot pizza stone. Cover pizza loosely with greased aluminum foil and bake until underside is golden brown and cheese is starting to melt, about 25 minutes. Discard foil and bake until crust is golden brown and cheese is completely melted, about 5 more minutes. Serve.

A thick, juicy steak served straight from the skillet, seasoned with nothing but salt and pepper, is a marvelous thing. Still, sometimes you want embellishment or, in kitchen terminology, sauce. At those times, turn to the browned bits left on the bottom of the pan after the steak has been removed. Known by their French name—fond—those little bits add big flavor. With a splash of red wine, some thoughtful additions, and a few minutes, you can transform them into a rich pan sauce.

First, transfer the steaks to a platter and tent them with foil; they'll stay warm while you make the sauce. We're fond of fond, but not of fat, so to start these sauces, pour off the excess fat from the skillet you used to sear the steaks. Melt 1 tablespoon butter in the pan and sauté the aromatics until softened. We like mild shallots here.

Draw out the flavors of the red wine by reducing it with a scant amount of sugar before you add the other ingredients. As soon as the half cup of wine hits the hot pan, scrape up the fond with a wooden spoon, and then simmer the mixture over medium heat until it has reduced to a jammy glaze. Stir in beef broth, once again letting the sauce simmer for a few minutes.

Herbs and butter are typically used to finish pan sauces. They add, respectively, flavor and body. For a wider range of sauces, use mustard, horseradish, sour cream, heavy cream, or Gorgonzola or Boursin cheese in place of the butter.

BASIC RED WINE PAN SAUCE
Makes enough sauce for 4 steaks
Use low-sodium broth and unsalted butter in this recipe or the reduced sauce may be too salty. See page 31 for a Cooking Lesson on pan-searing steak.

4 tablespoons unsalted butter, cut into 4 pieces and chilled
1 shallot, minced
½ cup red wine
1 teaspoon brown sugar
½ cup low-sodium beef broth
¼ teaspoon minced fresh thyme
Salt and pepper

1. COOK AROMATICS Once steaks are cooked, transfer them to platter, tent with foil, and pour off excess fat

Once you master these easy steak pan sauces, you can apply the same technique to make sauces for almost any cut of meat or poultry.

from skillet. Melt 1 tablespoon butter in empty skillet over medium-low heat. Cook shallot until softened, about 2 minutes.

2. REDUCE LIQUIDS Add wine and sugar to skillet and simmer over medium heat, scraping up any browned bits, until reduced to about 1 tablespoon, about 3 minutes. Add broth and any juices on plate with resting steaks and simmer until liquid is reduced to ⅓ cup, about 3 minutes.

3. ADD FLAVORINGS Off heat, whisk in thyme and remaining 3 tablespoons butter. Season with salt and pepper. Spoon sauce over steaks.

BOURSIN-PARSLEY PAN SAUCE
Prepare Basic Red Wine Pan Sauce, replacing thyme with 1 teaspoon minced fresh parsley and replacing 3 tablespoons butter used in step 3 with 3 tablespoons crumbled Boursin cheese. (Use either herb or cracked black pepper variety of this cheese.)

MUSTARD CREAM PAN SAUCE
Prepare Basic Red Wine Pan Sauce, replacing thyme with ¼ teaspoon minced tarragon and replacing 3 tablespoons butter used in step 3 with 2 tablespoons heavy cream and 1 tablespoon wholegrain or Dijon mustard.

ROSEMARY-GORGONZOLA PAN SAUCE
Prepare Basic Red Wine Pan Sauce, replacing thyme with ¼ teaspoon minced fresh rosemary and replacing 2 tablespoons of butter used in step 3 with 2 tablespoons crumbled Gorgonzola cheese.

HORSERADISH-CHIVE CREAM SAUCE
Prepare Basic Red Wine Pan Sauce, replacing thyme with 1 teaspoon minced fresh chives and replacing 3 tablespoons butter used in step 3 with 2 tablespoons sour cream and 1 tablespoon prepared horseradish. (Use 2 tablespoons horseradish for spicier sauce.)

Glazed Meat Loaf

Say meat loaf and most Americans think 1950s comfort food and Mom, but this humble recipe has surprisingly elegant roots in a now-forgotten dish called "cannelon." A typical cannelon recipe from the "Fannie Farmer Original 1896 Boston Cooking-School Cook Book" calls for chopping and seasoning beef, shaping it into a log, and basting with melted butter as it bakes. It's easy to imagine cannelon served in the finest homes in Victorian-era America, along with Fannie Farmer's recommended Brown Mushroom Sauce. The wide availability of meat grinders and the advent of reliable refrigeration made ground beef a household staple in the early 20th century and meat loaf recipes gained wide circulation. But popularity rarely translates into perfection. My goal was to make meat loaf special again. BY KRIS WIDICAN

Over the years, meat loaves have been dressed up and down every which way. I tested recipes that used a range of ingredients and cooking methods. Some were OK, but none had everything my tasters and I wanted: moist meat, brawny beef flavor, classic seasonings, and a well-browned crust enhanced with a simple ketchup-based glaze. The one thing these early trials reaffirmed is the test kitchen's technique of cooking the meat loaf free-form; one and all, meat loaves baked in pans emerged with greasy, mushy undersides.

Many recipes rely on meat loaf mix, a blend of ground chuck, pork, and veal available in most supermarkets. Loaves made from this blend can be good, but because the mix varies from store to store, it yields inconsistent results. I wanted something more reliable, so I tried an all-beef meat loaf made from ground sirloin. This loaf had good meaty flavor—so good

that it now tasted too much like a burger. Cutting the ground beef with an equal portion of sweet ground pork (ground veal isn't as readily available) balanced the beefy flavor. The traditional seasonings of salt, pepper, Dijon mustard, Worcestershire sauce, and parsley emerged as clear favorites—especially when mixed with sautéed onion and garlic.

The meat loaf now had great flavor, but it was dry and crumbly. Eggs were the obvious binder; two eggs, plus an extra yolk for richness, proved perfect. We sometimes use a panade (a paste of milk and bread or crackers) to add moisture to meat loaves and meatballs, so I tested different versions. My tasters preferred the mild saltiness of the panade made with milk and saltines to those that contained bread, bread crumbs, or raw oats. Combining the panade in a food processor and then pulsing it with the meat gave the

loaf the most cohesive, tender texture.

I had been following test kitchen protocol, letting the meat loaf bake to near doneness before turning on the broiler and brushing on an easy glaze of brown sugar and ketchup. But the top and sides of the loaf beaded with moisture in the oven, preventing a flavorful crust from forming. And without a dry, textured crust, the glaze slid off before it could caramelize and thicken. After several fruitless tests fiddling with baking and broiling specifics, a colleague suggested I broil the meat loaf before glazing and baking, to evaporate the surface moisture that was inhibiting the formation of a crust. This worked beautifully, and the browned crust gave the glaze—applied twice for extra effect—something to hang onto. Combined with the tender, flavorful meat, this made for one heck of a meat loaf.

GLAZED MEAT LOAF Serves 6 to 8

Both ground sirloin and ground chuck work well here, but avoid ground round—it is gristly and bland.

GLAZE
- 1 cup ketchup
- ¼ cup packed brown sugar
- 2½ tablespoons cider vinegar
- ½ teaspoon hot sauce

MEAT LOAF
- 2 teaspoons vegetable oil
- 1 onion, chopped fine
- 2 garlic cloves, minced
- ⅔ cup crushed saltine crackers (about 17 crackers)
- ⅓ cup whole milk
- 1 pound 90 percent lean ground beef (see note)
- 1 pound ground pork
- 2 large eggs plus 1 large yolk
- 2 teaspoons Dijon mustard
- 2 teaspoons Worcestershire sauce
- ½ teaspoon dried thyme
- ⅓ cup finely chopped fresh parsley
  Salt and pepper

1. MAKE GLAZE Whisk all ingredients in saucepan until sugar dissolves. Reserve ¼ cup glaze mixture, then simmer remaining glaze over medium heat until slightly thickened, about 5 minutes. Cover and keep warm.

2. COOK VEGETABLES Line rimmed baking sheet with foil and coat lightly with cooking spray. Heat oil in nonstick skillet over medium heat until shimmering. Cook onion until golden, about 8 minutes. Add garlic and cook until fragrant, about 30 seconds. Transfer to large bowl.

3. PROCESS MEAT Process saltines and milk in food processor until smooth. Add beef and pork and pulse until well combined, about ten 1-second pulses. Transfer meat mixture to bowl with cooled onion mixture. Add eggs and yolk, mustard, Worcestershire, thyme, parsley, 1 teaspoon salt, and ¾ teaspoon pepper to bowl and mix with hands until combined.

4. BROIL Adjust oven racks to upper (about 4 inches away from broiler element) and middle positions and heat broiler. Transfer meat mixture to prepared baking sheet and shape into 9- by 5-inch loaf. Broil on upper rack until well browned, about 5 minutes. Brush 2 tablespoons uncooked glaze over top and sides of loaf and then return to oven and broil until glaze begins to brown, about 2 minutes.

5. BAKE Transfer meat loaf to middle rack and brush with remaining uncooked glaze. Reduce oven temperature to 350 degrees and bake until meat loaf registers 160 degrees, 40 to 45 minutes. Transfer to carving board, tent with foil, and let rest 20 minutes. Slice and serve, passing cooked glaze at table.

Troubleshooting Meat Loaf

The beauty of meat loaf is that you can just stir together some meat and vegetables, pack the mixture into a pan, and pop it into the oven until suppertime. Right? Wrong. Meat loaf has its challenges, but a bit of know-how can fix them.

PROBLEM: Distractingly Crunchy Vegetables
SOLUTION: Trim Options, Then Sauté
We bypass crunchy vegetables like celery and carrots and stick with assertive onions and garlic. Chop the onions fine and cook them a good 8 minutes over medium heat to ensure that they are soft and sweet.

PROBLEM: Coarse, Hamburger-y Texture
SOLUTION: Break Out the Food Processor
Giving the meat mixture a quick spin in the food processor breaks it down for a smooth, finely textured loaf instead of a shaggy, coarse one.

PROBLEM: Greasy, Pale Loaf
SOLUTION: Bake the Loaf Free-Form
Skip the loaf pan. Baking the loaf on a rimmed baking sheet allows the fat and juices to drain and exposes more surface area for a better crust.

PROBLEM: Watery Glaze
SOLUTION: Glaze from the Get-Go
If the meat loaf is glazed toward the end of cooking, the juices from the loaf cause the glaze to drip off. We broil the meat loaf right away to create a crusty exterior, then use a double-glaze technique for a thick, lacquered finish.

ON THE SIDE
Sour Cream and Onion Smashed Potatoes

Sour cream and onion go hand-in-glove with potatoes, so why do they make a mess out of smashed spuds?

BY MARÍA DEL MAR SACASA

We use the scallion whites and greens, but we handle each a little differently.

You'd think adding sour cream and onion to smashed potatoes would be a smash-dunk: Plunk in sour cream, add onions, and call it a day. Unfortunately, the handful of recipes I tried featured harsh or cloying onion flavor, and their texture resembled spackle. My goal was clear: Develop bold yet balanced sour cream and onion flavor while maintaining the signature texture of this rustic dish.

I started with the test kitchen's technique for smashed potatoes, which calls for boiling small, unpeeled red potatoes until tender, draining them, breaking them up with a rubber spatula, then folding in melted butter and half-and-half until a chunky-yet-creamy puree is achieved. But when I added the sour cream, the potatoes had turned gluey by the time I'd fully incorporated it. After several tests, I found that stirring the sour cream directly into the melted butter and the other dairy (my tasters preferred half-and-half to cream or milk) before adding the mixture to the cooked potatoes meant less stirring together, which eliminated the glueyness caused by overworking. This technique also helped to meld the flavors.

As for the onion, minced chives proved too discreet, no matter how much I added. Seeking bolder onion flavor, I tried caramelized onions, but they were far too sweet. I had better results with sliced scallions, especially when I sautéed the whites in butter before mixing them with the warmed half-and-half and sour cream, and added the scallion greens raw for crunch and bite.

SOUR CREAM AND ONION SMASHED POTATOES Serves 4 to 6

If the potatoes are too thick after folding in the sour cream in step 3, stir in additional half-and-half, 1 tablespoon at a time, until they reach the desired consistency. This recipe can be doubled.

- 2 pounds small red potatoes, scrubbed
- 4 tablespoons unsalted butter
- 4 scallions, white parts minced, green parts sliced thin
- 1 cup sour cream
- ½ cup half-and-half
  Salt and pepper

1. COOK POTATOES Bring potatoes and enough water to cover by 1 inch to boil in large pot over high heat. Reduce heat to medium and simmer until potatoes are tender, about 30 minutes.

2. SAUTÉ SCALLIONS Meanwhile, melt butter in medium saucepan over medium-low heat. Cook scallion whites until translucent, about 5 minutes. Whisk in sour cream, half-and-half, 1 teaspoon salt, and ¼ teaspoon pepper until smooth. Remove from heat, cover, and keep warm.

3. SMASH Drain potatoes in colander and return to dry pot; let stand 5 minutes. Using rubber spatula, break potatoes into large chunks. Fold in sour cream mixture until incorporated and only small chunks of potato remain. Stir in scallion greens and season with salt and pepper. Serve.

Cheesy Broccoli and Rice Casserole

Recipes using condensed soup and frozen broccoli may move products off supermarket shelves, but they turn this dish into a gluey mess. We set out to revive what ought to be an irresistible casserole. BY MEGHAN ERWIN

Replacing the usual creamy condensed soup (or heavy cream) with a combination of half-and-half and chicken broth makes for a lighter, fresher casserole.

Close your eyes and take a bite of the typical back-of-the-can recipe for cheesy broccoli and rice casserole. Bet you wouldn't know what you were eating. Gloppy canned soup, shelf-stable "cheese food," and lifeless frozen broccoli combine into a stodgy mass of weak, muddled flavors. I wanted a livelier casserole with tender rice, fresh broccoli flavor, and sharp cheddar bite.

I started with a half-dozen recipes that skipped the canned soup and made the casserole from scratch. They all worked similarly: Butter and flour were stirred together on the stovetop to make a roux; heavy cream was poured in and reduced; and cheese, fresh broccoli florets, and cooked rice were folded in before baking. These casseroles put the canned soup/frozen broccoli version to shame, but they were still weak on flavor and couldn't seem to get the broccoli (too crunchy) or rice (overcooked and blown out) cooked right.

Addressing the flavor first, I suspected that the fatty heavy cream was masking the other ingredients, so I tested versions that replaced it with milk and half-and-half.

Milk was a little too lean and thin, but half-and-half was an improvement, especially when I cut it with chicken broth to add flavor. While some recipes call for American cheese, my tasters much preferred the bold bite of extra-sharp cheddar paired with nutty Parmesan.

Fresh broccoli was definitely better than frozen, but I knew I'd need finesse to get the most out of it. In the test kitchen, we've learned that broccoli stalks have just as much flavor as the florets, but they take longer to cook. This time I started my sauce by sautéing chopped broccoli stalks in butter with onion, then adding the flour, the liquids, and finally, broccoli florets that I'd precooked in the microwave to ensure they'd be tender in the baked casserole. With twice as much broccoli as most recipes, my casserole now had plenty of fresh broccoli flavor.

To avoid overcooked rice, I tried adding raw rice to the simmering cream sauce (instead of stirring in cooked rice just before baking). Unfortunately, the starch released from the rice as it cooked overthickened the sauce and produced a heavy, dense casserole. I was discouraged,

until a colleague suggested I try making the starch from the rice work to my advantage. I tested reducing the flour (originally 4 tablespoons) 1 tablespoon at a time, and ultimately discovered I could eliminate the flour altogether; the natural starch from the rice was enough of a thickener.

Some recipes simply top this style of casserole with more cheese, while recipes closer to the back-of-the-can version sometimes opt for canned fried onions. Wanting something fresher and more substantial, I made garlicky fresh bread crumbs enriched with more Parmesan. This topping baked up brown and crisp, adding a final layer of flavor and texture to my casserole.

CHEESY BROCCOLI AND RICE CASSEROLE Serves 8 to 10

Three to four medium heads of broccoli will yield roughly 2 pounds.

- 2 slices hearty white sandwich bread, torn into pieces
- ¾ cup grated Parmesan cheese
- 4 tablespoons unsalted butter, melted; plus 2 tablespoons, chilled
- 1 garlic clove, minced
- 2 pounds broccoli, florets cut into 1-inch pieces, stems peeled and chopped
- 1 onion, chopped fine
- 1¼ cups long grain white rice
- 4 cups low-sodium chicken broth
- 1¼ cups half-and-half
- 1 teaspoon salt
- 2 cups shredded extra-sharp cheddar cheese
- ⅛ teaspoon cayenne pepper

1. PREPARE TOPPING Adjust oven rack to middle position and heat oven to 400 degrees. Grease 13- by 9-inch baking dish. Pulse bread, ¼ cup Parmesan, and melted butter in food processor until coarsely ground. Add garlic.

2. MAKE FILLING Microwave broccoli florets, covered, in large bowl until bright green and tender, 2 to 4 minutes;

set aside. Melt remaining butter in Dutch oven over medium heat. Cook onion and broccoli stems until softened, 8 to 10 minutes. Add rice and cook, stirring constantly, until rice is translucent, about 1 minute. Stir in broth, half-and-half, and salt and bring to boil. Reduce heat to medium-low and cook, stirring often, until rice is tender, 20 to 25 minutes. Off heat, stir in cheddar, cayenne, remaining Parmesan, and broccoli florets.

3. TOP AND BAKE Pour mixture into prepared baking dish and top with bread crumb mixture. Bake until sauce is bubbling around edges and top is golden brown, about 15 minutes. Cool 5 minutes. Serve.

MAKE AHEAD Filling can be prepared, placed in greased baking dish, covered with plastic wrap, and refrigerated for 1 day. Refrigerate topping separately. Bring filling to room temperature before adding bread crumbs and baking as directed.

TEST KITCHEN TIP
Maximizing Broccoli Flavor
Broccoli stems are full of broccoli flavor, but because they're tough they require longer cooking than the florets.

SAVE YOUR STEMS

We sauté the chopped broccoli stems with onion to create a savory base of vegetable flavor. We microwave the quicker-cooking broccoli florets and stir them into the casserole right before baking.

Cornmeal Biscuits

We were after tender biscuits with hearty cornmeal taste—a simple goal that proved surprisingly tough to pull off. BY CALI RICH

These biscuits have plenty of corn flavor without the dry, gritty texture of cornmeal.

As biscuits go, cornmeal ranks as one of my favorites. Ideally, they have a tender crumb, a cheerful yellow hue, and the sweetness and subtle crunch of cornmeal. But how much cornmeal is right? The amount in recipes ranges from as little as 2 tablespoons (an afterthought) to as much as 1½ cups for a dozen biscuits (overkill)—enough to befuddle even the experienced biscuit maker.

Not surprisingly, such recipes delivered vastly different results. Biscuits with just a sprinkling of cornmeal had a tender, fluffy crumb but scant corn flavor. Those made with a lot of cornmeal offered lots of flavor, but were dry and leaden. I was looking for a biscuit that combined the advantages of both—tall and tender yet with distinct cornmeal flavor.

Since none of these recipes was very promising, I decided to start with the test kitchen's stamped buttermilk biscuit recipe and figure out how to add the cornmeal from there. This recipe calls for pulsing cubes of chilled butter with the dry ingredients (flour, baking powder and soda, and salt) in a food processor until only pea-sized pieces remain. The baker stirs in buttermilk, pats out the dough, stamps out the rounds, and bakes. For my first test, I substituted cornmeal for half the flour.

The biscuits looked promising coming out of the oven, but my hopes were soon deflated—they tasted dry and were overwhelmingly gritty. Working with the same recipe, I ran through a gamut of tests comparing different ratios. In the end, my work yielded mixed results. Tasters agreed that twice as much flour as cornmeal supplied the right cornmeal flavor, but they remained dissatisfied with the texture. Give us a little cornmeal crunch, they said, but show some restraint.

To soften the cornmeal grit, I first tried increasing the buttermilk. This dough was too wet to handle. Some recipes for cornbread suggest softening cornmeal in hot water; I wondered if that approach might lead to success here. Since my liquid ingredient was buttermilk, I microwaved that with the cornmeal. Alas, this worked too well, yielding a heavy biscuit with zero crunch. Next, I tried soaking the cornmeal in the buttermilk without applying any heat. Sometimes—this time—the simplest solution is the best one. A mere 10-minute soak produced the just-soft crumb tasters were after.

As I watched a group of fans drizzling honey onto their biscuits, it occurred to me to add honey directly to the dough. Sure enough, just a tablespoon provided a subtle sweetness that drew out even more of the cornmeal's sweet corn flavor.

CORNMEAL BISCUITS
Makes 12 biscuits

If you don't have buttermilk, whisk 1 tablespoon lemon juice into 1¼ cups of milk and let it stand until slightly thickened, about 10 minutes. Avoid coarsely ground cornmeal, which makes gritty biscuits.

- 1 cup cornmeal
- 1¼ cups buttermilk
- 1 tablespoon honey
- 2 cups all-purpose flour
- 1 tablespoon baking powder
- ½ teaspoon baking soda
- 1 teaspoon salt
- 12 tablespoons (1½ sticks) unsalted butter, cut into ½-inch pieces and chilled

1. SOAK CORNMEAL Adjust oven rack to middle position and heat oven to 450 degrees. Line baking sheet with parchment paper. Whisk cornmeal, buttermilk, and honey in large bowl; let sit 10 minutes.

2. PROCESS DOUGH Pulse flour, baking powder, baking soda, salt, and butter in food processor until mixture resembles coarse meal. Add to bowl with buttermilk mixture and stir until dough forms.

3. KNEAD Turn dough out onto lightly floured surface and knead until smooth, 8 to 10 times. Pat dough into 9-inch circle, about ¾ inch thick. Using 2½-inch biscuit cutter dipped in flour, cut out rounds (dipping cutter in flour after each cut) and transfer to prepared baking sheet. Gather remaining dough and pat into ¾-inch-thick circle. Cut rounds from dough and transfer to baking sheet.

4. BAKE Bake until biscuits begin to rise, about 5 minutes, and then reduce oven temperature to 400 degrees and bake until golden brown, 8 to 12 minutes more. Let cool 5 minutes on sheet, then transfer to wire rack. Serve warm or let cool to room temperature. (Biscuits can be stored in airtight container at room temperature for 2 days.)

STEP-BY-STEP Soft, Stately Biscuits

Our cornmeal biscuits have the moist, flavor-packed crumb of cornbread and the fluffy stature of a stamped biscuit.

1. For softer crumb without too much cornmeal grit, soak cornmeal in buttermilk.

2. Transfer dough to lightly floured surface and knead briefly before patting into 9-inch circle.

3. Use biscuit cutter to cut dough into rounds, dipping cutter into flour between cuts.

TEST KITCHEN SECRET
Need to Knead

It's an adage as old as biscuit making: Light hands make tender biscuits. So why do we instruct you to knead our cornmeal biscuit dough "until smooth, 8 to 10 times"? When biscuit recipes warn you not to overhandle the dough, they are cautioning against the development of gluten. It's desirable for chewy doughs (say, for bagels), but gluten is typically the enemy of tender, flaky biscuits. Our Cornmeal Biscuits replace some of the flour with 1 cup cornmeal, which has no gluten, so gluten development poses less of a risk. Also, our recipe calls for 1¼ cups buttermilk, an acidic ingredient that helps break down gluten. Kneading our cornmeal biscuit dough briefly ensures evenly textured biscuits that rise high instead of spreading.

Bringing Eggs Benedict Home

Who ate the first eggs Benedict? Was it Wall Street broker Lemuel Benedict, said to have cobbled the dish together from a poached egg, toast, ham, and hollandaise at the breakfast buffet at the Waldorf-Astoria? Other sources trace the recipe to New York City's famed Delmonico's restaurant and a loyal customer named Mrs. LeGrand Benedict. The notion of combining hollandaise sauce and poached eggs is a venerable one, probably dating back to a traditional French recipe, oeufs benedictine, where brandade (salt cod and potatoes) replaces the ham. Eggs Benedict is easy enough for a restaurant—it is just a question of last-minute assembly—but the home cook needs to master both perfect timing as well as two classic—and, yes, fickle—French recipes.

BY DIANE UNGER

Even seasoned cooks grow anxious at the idea of tackling this multi-component dish, especially if they want to cook it for a crowd—and I was after a recipe that would serve six people. After a few stabs at eggs Benedict, I shared their anxieties. My first attempts turned out poached eggs that spun into skeins of congealed egg white, barely holding on to overcooked yolks. The hollandaise sauce came together as recipes promised, but would suddenly separate beyond repair with one moment too long on the stove. Finally, the English muffins and Canadian bacon were stone cold by the time I was ready to assemble my first serving.

I started with the notoriously unstable hollandaise, hoping to solve my biggest challenge first. Like mayonnaise, hollandaise is an emulsified sauce (egg yolks do the emulsifying) that depends on the proper suspension of fat in liquid. If the balance goes out of whack, or if the mixture overheats, the sauce breaks into a puddle of oily melted butter and scrambled egg. The classic preparation is to whisk yolks with lemon juice and a small amount of water over a double boiler until thickened. You slowly drizzle in melted butter, whisking briskly all the while, and finish it with more lemon juice. If all goes well—a big if, I quickly realized—a thick, smooth emulsion forms. After a few frustrating attempts, I sought a more reliable method.

Newer recipes I tested make hollandaise in a food processor or blender by pouring hot melted butter onto the yolks, to ensure an emulsified sauce without the tedious whisking. These methods usually worked, but only if I served the sauce immediately—not very practical if you're also trying to poach eggs, toast English muffins, and crisp Canadian bacon. In the test kitchen library, I uncovered an unconventional method that intrigued me. Far from some newfangled technique that required yet another kitchen appliance, it was a recipe from the *Toll House Tried and True Recipes* cookbook, printed in 1944! It called for softened butter in place of melted butter, and for a lot more water than is in the standard recipes.

I whisked one stick of butter with four egg yolks and slowly poured in half a cup of boiling water (conventional hollandaise recipes call for 1 or 2 tablespoons water). At first, the mixture was a watery, lumpy mess, but I pressed on, cooking it over a

STEP-BY-STEP **Easier by the Dozen**

Getting 12 eggs into, and then out of, a skillet at precisely the right degree of doneness is no easy feat. Unless, that is, you follow these simple steps.

1. Crack the eggs into four teacups (three eggs per cup) and tip the cups simultaneously into the simmering water.

2. Cover the pan and remove it from the heat. The residual heat of the water will poach the eggs in about five minutes.

3. Use a slotted spoon to move the eggs from the pan to a paper towel–lined plate.

double boiler "until thick," as directed. I added the lemon juice off of the heat and was happily surprised with the result. The sauce was foamier than a classic hollandaise, and it tasted a little lean, yet it held without breaking for as long as an hour. In further tests, I tweaked the amounts of butter and yolks to bring back the classic richness (it took 4 more tablespoons of butter and two additional yolks). Satisfied with the sauce, I turned to the eggs.

Cookbooks suggest several classic methods for poaching eggs. I cracked them into a vat of boiling water, but they sank and were tough to remove without breaking. I "swirl(ed) the water into a mad vortex," as the 1931 edition of *Joy of Cooking* instructs, counting on the spinning water to "round the egg." Instead the whites spun into streamers. Anyway, the technique was impractical for cooking 12 eggs at once. I tried cooking the eggs in simmering water, but the temperature wasn't constant, and the agitating water threatened to break the yolks. In the end I solved those problems and managed to make a dozen eggs at once by "cooking" them off of the heat. First, I brought water to a simmer in a large skillet. While it was heating, I cracked the eggs into teacups, using each cup to hold three eggs at a time. I added vinegar and salt to the water, turned off the heat, and slipped the eggs in to cook in residual heat. I covered the skillet and waited

about five minutes before I removed the eggs with a slotted spoon. The method consistently produced restaurant-worthy poached eggs with soft, runny yolks and perfectly formed, round whites.

Now I could concentrate on the logistics of toasting. I didn't want to fuss with toasting 12 muffin halves in my toaster while poaching eggs and whisking hollandaise. So I lined up the muffins on a baking sheet and tried broiling them. In one go, all 12 halves turned golden brown, and it was so easy, it occurred to me to use the broiler for the Canadian bacon. (I had been frying it in a skillet.) I laid the bacon on the toasted muffins and slid the tray back under the broiler. Because Canadian bacon is precooked, all I needed to do was warm it through. Further testing established that I could do this step 20 minutes in advance. Then, when the poached eggs were nearly done, I reheated the muffins and bacon.

Before hanging up my apron, I reread the recipe for hollandaise and noticed something I'd overlooked: The sauce could be served cold, which implied it could be made ahead. I made one final batch and refrigerated it. The next day, I gently reheated it in the microwave, and then spooned it over poached eggs. It looked, tasted, and stayed together as though I had taken it off the stove only moments before. Not one taster could tell it was a day old, nor did anyone believe such a thing was even possible!

DON'T MAKE THIS MISTAKE
Smooth Eggs' Ruffled Feathers

One of the least appealing characteristics of poorly poached eggs is uneven, feathery whites instead of a beautifully round, domed egg. We've found that we can solve the problem by adding a few tablespoons of vinegar to the poaching water. The vinegar lowers the water's pH, which ensures that the egg whites stay intact during cooking. Plus, the eggs taste even better.

BAD EGG

GOOD EGG

EGGS BENEDICT Serves 6

The test kitchen's favorite Canadian bacon is Applegate Farms. If you like, you can toast the English muffins and warm the bacon 20 minutes in advance. Reheat them in a 200-degree oven just before serving.

- 2 tablespoons white vinegar
- 1 teaspoon salt
- 12 large eggs
- 6 English muffins, split
- 12 slices Canadian bacon (see note)
- 1 recipe Foolproof Hollandaise (recipe follows)

1. POACH EGGS Adjust oven rack to upper-middle position and heat broiler. Fill large skillet nearly to rim with water. Add vinegar and salt and bring to boil over high heat. Following photos at left, crack 3 eggs each into 4 teacups and carefully pour eggs into skillet. Cover pan, remove from heat, and poach eggs until whites are set but yolks are still slightly runny, 5 to 7 minutes. Using slotted spoon, transfer eggs to paper towel–lined plate.

2. TOAST MUFFINS While eggs are poaching, arrange English muffins, split side–up, on baking sheet and broil until golden brown, 2 to 4 minutes. Place 1 slice bacon on each English muffin and broil until beginning to brown, about 1 minute.

3. SAUCE AND SERVE Arrange 1 poached egg on top of each English muffin. Spoon 1 to 2 tablespoons hollandaise over each egg. Serve, passing remaining hollandaise at table.

FOOLPROOF HOLLANDAISE
Makes about 2 cups

The hollandaise can be refrigerated in an airtight container for 3 days. Reheat in the microwave on 50 percent power, stirring every 10 seconds, until heated through, about 1 minute. You will need an instant-read thermometer to make this recipe.

- 12 tablespoons (1½ sticks) unsalted butter, softened
- 6 large egg yolks
- ½ cup boiling water
- 2 teaspoons lemon juice
- ⅛ teaspoon cayenne pepper
   Salt

Whisk butter and egg yolks in large heat-resistant bowl set over medium saucepan filled with ½ inch of barely simmering water (don't let bowl touch water). Slowly add boiling water and cook, whisking constantly, until thickened and sauce registers 160 degrees, 7 to 10 minutes. Off heat, stir in lemon juice and cayenne. Season with salt. Serve.

RATING ENGLISH MUFFINS

Are there real differences among the four major national brands of English muffins? To find out, we got busy toasting and invited our tasters to the table. We were looking for slightly yeasty, slightly sweet flavor and a texture—once toasted—that was crisp and craggy on top and soft and chewy inside. Although we liked all four muffins, Bays English muffins were our favorite. Interestingly, this brand had more salt than the competition, which brought out the sweetness of the muffins. The muffins are listed in order of preference.

RECOMMENDED		TASTER'S NOTES
BAYS English Muffins **Price:** $2.39 per package (6 muffins)		**Comments:** Tasters picked this muffin as their favorite for its soft interior and slightly chewy exterior. They praised its "fresh and buttery" flavor; one picked up a hint of sweet corn.
PEPPERIDGE FARM English Muffins **Price:** $2.99 per package (6 muffins)		**Comments:** This muffin was "subtly sweet" and had a mild, pleasant sourdough tang. Its even crumb and crunchy exterior provided an excellent surface for spreading butter.
THOMAS' English Muffins **Price:** $3.39 per package (6 muffins)		**Comments:** This muffin's surface had the most nooks and crannies. When toasted, Thomas' were crisp with a "shattered" texture. Tasters described the muffin as flavorful with a strong yeasty aftertaste.
WOLFERMAN'S English Muffins **Price:** $4.74 per package (4 muffins)		**Comments:** This muffin, the most expensive in our tasting, had the grainy texture and "earthy" flavor of whole wheat bread, which was unpopular with some tasters.

ON THE SIDE Cajun Greens

Tender greens can't take tough treatment, but could they handle forceful flavors? BY DIANE UNGER

Cooking the aromatics, and then the greens, in sausage drippings ensures a deeply seasoned dish.

Stalwart kale, collards, and mustard greens hold up well to boiling, but tender chard, curly-leaf spinach, and beet greens need a kinder touch. We've found that a short spell in a covered hot skillet works best for these greens, but even this approach can yield army-issue mush if they are overcooked. I wanted to find the best way to cook these delicate greens and give them a kick of piquant Cajun flavor to boot.

The shortest route to bayou flavor was to first render some spicy andouille sausage in my skillet. For heartiness, onion and garlic were a must. However, tasters deemed as superfluous the bell pepper and celery called for in some recipes.

It was time to add the greens. After much trial and error, I determined that the greens needed some added moisture to quickly (about 5 minutes over medium heat) and evenly steam. Adding the washed—but not dried—greens worked fine, but to brighten their flavor I dried the greens and added a splash of cider vinegar instead.

As I plated the greens, I noticed a pool of flavorful liquid left behind in the pan. To harness that flavor, I reduced the initial cooking time to 3 minutes. Then I removed the lid, cranked up the heat, and simmered the liquid down to a potent glaze, which took only a few more minutes. These greens were simultaneously tender, tangy, smoky, and spicy.

GARLICKY GREENS WITH ANDOUILLE AND ONION Serves 4

If you can't find andouille, an equal amount of chorizo or kielbasa may be substituted. Swiss chard, curly-leaf spinach, or even beet greens work well in this recipe.

- 1 tablespoon vegetable oil
- 3 ounces andouille sausage, halved lengthwise and cut into ¼-inch half-moons (see note)
- ½ red onion, sliced thin
- 3 garlic cloves, minced
- 2 pounds tender greens (see note), stemmed (see page 30) and chopped rough
- 2 tablespoons cider vinegar
  Salt and pepper

1. BROWN SAUSAGE Heat oil in Dutch oven over medium heat until just smoking. Cook sausage until well browned, about 5 minutes. Add onion and cook until softened, about 3 minutes. Stir in garlic and cook until fragrant, about 30 seconds.

2. COOK GREENS Add greens and vinegar to pot and cook covered, stirring occasionally, until greens are wilted and have released their juices, about 3 minutes. Remove lid and increase heat to high. Cook until liquid evaporates, 2 to 3 minutes. Season with salt and pepper. Serve.

ON THE SIDE Lowcountry Red Rice

Our tasters told us to lighten up! We hoped to pare down this hearty classic without sacrificing flavor. BY CALI RICH

A popular side dish in the Lowcountry coastal region of South Carolina and Georgia, red rice is named for the brick-red color imparted by its main ingredient: tomatoes. Most recipes start by sautéing onion, celery, bell pepper, and often some ham or sausage in a good bit of bacon drippings before stirring in canned tomatoes, rice, and a generous amount of fresh parsley or scallions. From here, the mixture is simmered on the stovetop until the rice is tender. It's a comforting and flavorful dish, but with all those ingredients (and all that bacon fat) it's awfully heavy for a side dish. What's more, with so much liquid in the pot, the rice becomes stodgy and gluey.

My first step toward a lighter dish was to eliminate the meat and bacon fat altogether. Next I'd follow the test kitchen's method for rice pilaf: I softened the vegetables and toasted the rice in oil (to add flavor and ensure distinct, tender rice) before adding a combination of crushed tomatoes and chicken broth (for a liquid-to-rice ratio of about 1½ to 1). After 20 minutes at a gentle, covered simmer, I let the rice steam off heat for 10 minutes to ensure each grain was evenly cooked.

The rice was fluffy, but the crushed tomatoes might as well have been red dye for all the flavor they added. Meaty diced tomatoes (first drained) had more tomato presence, but not enough. For more concentrated tomato flavor, I added a concentrated tomato product: tomato paste. Just 1 tablespoon quickly sautéed

with the vegetables provided deep tomato flavor—and color. For the finishing touches, cayenne added welcome heat, and a handful of chopped fresh parsley freshened the dish.

RED RICE Serves 4 to 6
For a slightly sweeter flavor, substitute a red bell pepper for the green.

- 1 tablespoon vegetable oil
- 1 onion, chopped fine
- 1 green bell pepper, seeded and chopped fine (see note)
- 1 celery rib, chopped fine
- 1½ cups long-grain rice
- 1 tablespoon tomato paste
- 4 garlic cloves, minced
- 1 (14.5-ounce) can diced tomatoes, drained
- 2 cups low-sodium chicken broth
- 1½ teaspoons salt
- ¼ teaspoon cayenne pepper
- ¼ cup finely chopped fresh parsley

1. COOK VEGETABLES Heat oil in large saucepan over medium-high heat until shimmering. Cook onion, bell pepper, and celery until softened, about 5 minutes. Add rice and cook, stirring frequently, until edges begin to turn translucent, about 2 minutes. Stir in tomato paste and garlic and cook until fragrant, about 30 seconds.

2. ADD TOMATOES Stir in tomatoes, broth, salt, and cayenne and bring to boil. Cover, reduce heat to low, and cook until liquid is absorbed and rice is tender, about 20 minutes. Remove from heat and let stand, covered, for 10 minutes. Fluff rice with fork. Stir in parsley. Serve.

Tomatoes give this southern staple its signature color.

New Orleans Barbecue Shrimp

Who cares if the name is wrong? Made well, this bold, buttery skillet dish sure tastes right.

BY CALI RICH

New Orleans Barbecue Shrimp originated in the early 1950s at Pascal's Manale, a restaurant known for its Italian-inspired Creole cooking. The dish is now ubiquitous throughout the Louisiana coast.

Barbecue shrimp is a delicious misnomer. It is not grilled or barbecued, not smoky, and you won't see this particular recipe on the BBQ circuit anytime soon. It is, instead, a uniquely New Orleans skillet dish that sauces peel-on shrimp in a velvety mixture of butter and seafood stock fortified with cayenne, herbs, garlic, and Worcestershire. This dish is named for its "barbecue" kick and color, and like barbecued ribs, the messy peel-and-eat shrimp are best served with a stack of napkins—plus a hunk of soft French bread to sop up the sauce.

I turned to recipes from regional cookbooks as a starting point. Most begin by cooking shrimp in melted butter (up to two entire sticks!) seasoned with Worcestershire, red pepper flakes, cayenne, thyme, rosemary, oregano, and garlic. The liquids—some combination of fish or shrimp stock, beer, and white wine—are reduced in the shrimp-filled skillet, and the sauce is finished with even more butter to thicken. It sounds tasty and easy, but the shrimp were overcooked and rubbery, and the wallop of butter dulled the other flavors and made the sauce greasy.

Working on the cooking method first, I tested fully cooking the shrimp in plain butter and removing them from the pan. Then I sautéed the garlic, herbs, and Worcestershire in the empty skillet, poured in the liquid (a bottle of beer for now), and returned the shrimp to the sauce to warm through. This gave me more control over the texture of the shrimp, but their flavor suffered from spending so little time in the sauce. For my next test, I just seared the shrimp—removing them from the pan before they were fully cooked—before sautéing the aromatics, adding the liquid, and then finally returning the shrimp to gently finish cooking in the rich sauce. These shrimp were tender and just cooked through, and much more flavorful than before.

Now I could work on perfecting the sauce, starting with the liquid base. The test kitchen has had good results replacing seafood stocks with bottled clam juice, and sure enough, it worked well here, too. To round out the liquid, my tasters preferred mellow beer to acidic wine, hands down. I added tomato paste to the sautéing aromatics to enrich the sauce—it also reinforced the "barbecue" color. Cutting the amount of butter from two sticks to less than one helped the other flavors shine through and reduced the greasiness, but it also created a new problem. The sauce was now so thin, it ran right off the shrimp. I turned to a classic New Orleans technique for thickening: starting the sauce with a roux. Adding 2 teaspoons of flour to the sautéing aromatics created a sauce that was thick enough to coat the shrimp. Armed with a bowlful of the shrimp and a mug of cold beer, I could have been in the Crescent City.

NEW ORLEANS BARBECUE SHRIMP Serves 4

Although authentic barbecue shrimp is always made with shell-on shrimp, peeled and deveined shrimp may be used. Light- or medium-bodied beers work best here. Serve with Tabasco sauce and French bread, if desired.

- 2 pounds extra-large (21–25 per pound) shrimp (see note)
- ½ teaspoon salt
- ½ teaspoon cayenne pepper
- 2 tablespoons vegetable oil
- 6 tablespoons unsalted butter, cut into 6 pieces
- 2 teaspoons all-purpose flour
- 1 teaspoon tomato paste
- 1 teaspoon minced fresh rosemary
- 1 teaspoon minced fresh thyme
- ½ teaspoon dried oregano
- 3 garlic cloves, minced
- ¾ cup bottled clam juice
- ½ cup beer
- 1 tablespoon Worcestershire sauce

1. SEAR SHRIMP Pat shrimp dry with paper towels and sprinkle with salt and cayenne. Heat 1 tablespoon oil in large skillet over medium-high heat until just smoking. Cook half of shrimp, without moving, until spotty brown on one side, about 1 minute; transfer to large plate. Repeat with remaining oil and shrimp.

2. MAKE SAUCE Melt 1 tablespoon butter in empty skillet over medium heat. Add flour, tomato paste, rosemary, thyme, oregano, and garlic and cook until fragrant, about 30 seconds. Stir in clam juice, beer, and Worcestershire, scraping up any browned bits, and bring to boil. Return shrimp and any accumulated juices to skillet. Reduce heat to medium-low and simmer, covered, until shrimp are cooked through, about 2 minutes. Off heat, stir in remaining butter until incorporated. Serve.

KEY INGREDIENTS **Not Your Average Barbecue Sauce**

Barbecue sauce conjures up an image of a thick, sticky tomato-based mop, but New Orleans Barbecue Shrimp is bathed in a spicy herbed butter sauce made with these ingredients.

| CLAM JUICE | BEER | WORCESTERSHIRE | BUTTER |
| Briny bite. | Hit of hops. | Bold, tangy flavor. | Satiny finish. |

Getting to Know Rice

Go crazy—there is a rainbow of rice beyond Uncle Ben's. Here are 12 varieties, with our tasting notes on each.

Basmati
NEAR-EAST BOUQUET

In Hindi, basmati means "fragrant one." Basmati is usually aged (making it more expensive than un-aged rices) to reduce its natural moisture and to accentuate its "intensely floral," "nutty" aroma. The thin, extra-long grains cook up firm and very dry, making them a favorite for pilafs and other preparations where starchier rices fail. Steam or boil. Jasmine rice is an acceptable substitute.

Carolina Gold
THE COMEBACK KID

Carolina Gold, named for the region where it grows and for the stalk's golden color, was once at the center of a thriving U.S. rice industry. It disappeared after the Depression when growers replaced it with hardier (less flavorful) varieties. Some farmers today are replanting the historic grain, which has a "full, oatmeal-y" flavor and a "chewy" texture. It's firm enough for pilafs yet starchy enough for risotto.

Purple Sticky Grain
PURPLE REIGN

This gourmet whole-grain rice (its bran has not been removed) looks black when raw and turns a stunning purple when cooked. Because of its very high starch content, it clumps together when cooked, yet it maintains a firm, "pop-in-the-mouth" texture "reminiscent of wild rice." Tasters described the flavor as "inky" and "slightly tannic." Soak the rice in water for four to six hours before cooking, then drain, and steam or boil.

Jasmine
THAI KING

The long, slender grains and "assertive, popcorn-y" flavor of this Thai rice make it similar to basmati—minus the hefty price tag. For fluffy grains, quickly rinse jasmine rice (to remove any loose chaff), then steam or boil. For a stickier texture, soak it in water for six hours before cooking. Thai cooks make a memorable, fragrant rice pudding from jasmine rice, coconut milk, and sugar.

Arborio
PEARL OF ITALY

This Italian medium-grain variety plays a starring role in risotto. Arborio grains are pearly white, plump, and chock-full of starch. While an abundance of starch spells disaster for a fluffy pilaf, it's just what risotto needs. Stir constantly while cooking to bring out the grain's "luxuriously creamy" texture and "refined, milky-sweet" flavor. Arborio rice is also good in paella, Spain's famous rice-based dish.

Wild
THE PRETENDER

In Minnesota, Native Americans still use canoes to hand-harvest authentic wild rice, the seeds of a marsh grass native to the Great Lakes region. The test kitchen prefers the cultivated variety from California for its more resilient texture and lower price. Tasters liked its "nutty, earthy" flavor, but not its texture, like "chewing a mouthful of twigs." Boil it until tender, as long as an hour, or add directly to long-simmered soups or stews.

Brown
THE SLOWPOKE

Brown rice is a whole grain, meaning its exterior bran has not been removed. That bran accounts for its color and "wheaty" flavor and makes the rice prone to turning rancid; store it in a dark, dry area for no more than 6 months. Both brown rice and long-grain white rice require the same ratio of liquid to raw rice (1¼ to 1½ cups liquid to 1 cup raw rice) for cooking, but brown rice takes roughly twice as long. Cooking it in the oven brings out the best in its "dense, chewy" texture.

Himalayan Red
DIRTY RICE

This long-grain rice was once grown only in the foothills of the Himalayas. Now France cultivates it, too. Its red color comes from its intact bran, which gives it a "pleasantly chewy" texture and a distinct "mineral" taste with a hint of "shale or clay." Rinse Himalayan Red well to remove any loose chaff and carefully examine before cooking: Our sample included many pebbles. Prepare it as you would brown rice and use in rice salads or as a side dish.

Rosematta
PORRIDGE PICK

Easy to spot for its pale coral color and reddish-brown "pinstripes," Rosematta tastes "assertive and earthy" with a noticeable "iron-y" aftertaste. It cooks up fluffy, tender, and less starchy than most other medium-grain rices. In India, its native land, it's often sold parboiled. Many Indian recipes call for Rosematta in highly spiced porridges or stews, but it can also be used in rice salads, pilafs, or as a simple side dish.

Kokuho Rose
SUSHI SWEETHEART

This medium-grain rice was developed in the late 1950s in central California and is one of the most popular sushi rices grown in the U.S. Tasters praised Kokuho Rose (the name means "treasure of the country" in Japanese) as "sticky, but not too sticky" and "sweet and mild." Rinse it under running water until the water runs clear, then steam, boil, or cook in a rice cooker. Serve as a sticky side dish or season with sweetened rice vinegar to use in sushi.

Carnaroli
CHEF'S DARLING

This medium-grain rice is grown primarily in the Piedmont and Lombardy regions of Italy. Americans may not know it as well as Arborio, but many chefs, Italian and otherwise, prize its "firm texture," "rotund grains," and "creamy starches" above all other risotto rices. Tasters favorably compared its "buttery, earthy" flavor to Yukon Gold potatoes.

Calrose
JACK-OF-ALL-TRADES

This medium-grain rice was developed in California in the 1970s and is especially prized in Hawaii, Guam, and Australia for its slightly sticky texture. It has a "mild, neutral" flavor. Although "fairly starchy," the kernels retain some "chew," making Calrose suitable for dishes ranging from sushi to sticky rice to arroz con pollo. Steam or boil it until tender.

PASTA WITH PAN-ROASTED VEGETABLES

CARIBBEAN PORK TENDERLOIN

EASY STUFFED FILLETS OF SOLE

BAKED PORK CHOPS WITH PARMESAN-SAGE CRUST

CARIBBEAN PORK TENDERLOIN Serves 4

WHY THIS RECIPE WORKS: Using prepared mango chutney adds flavor and cling to this sweet-sour glaze.

 2 pork tenderloins (1½ to 2 pounds total), cut crosswise into 1-inch pieces
   Salt and pepper
 3 tablespoons vegetable oil
 1 onion, chopped fine
 1 red bell pepper, seeded and chopped fine
 1 jalapeño chile, seeded and minced
 1 teaspoon ground cumin
 ¼ teaspoon ground allspice
 1 (9-ounce) jar mango chutney, such as Major Grey's
 1 teaspoon grated zest and 3 tablespoons juice from 2 limes

1. Pat pork dry with paper towels and season with salt and pepper. Heat 2 tablespoons oil in large skillet over medium-high heat until just smoking. Add pork and cook until well browned and meat registers 145 degrees, about 4 minutes per side.

2. Add remaining oil, onion, bell pepper, and jalapeño to empty skillet and cook until lightly browned, about 5 minutes. Stir in cumin and allspice and cook until fragrant, about 30 seconds.

3. Add chutney, lime zest, lime juice, and any accumulated pork juices to pan and cook until thickened, about 3 minutes. Season with salt and pepper. Spoon sauce over pork. Serve.

TEST KITCHEN NOTE: Serve over white rice if desired.

PASTA WITH PAN-ROASTED VEGETABLES Serves 4

WHY THIS RECIPE WORKS: Cooking the vegetables on the stovetop over medium-high heat concentrates their flavor.

 5 tablespoons extra-virgin olive oil
 4 large portobello mushroom caps, halved and cut into ½-inch slices
 2 red bell peppers, seeded and chopped
 1 red onion, chopped
 5 tablespoons balsamic vinegar
   Salt and pepper
 2 garlic cloves, minced
 1 pound campanelle, fusilli, or penne
 1 pint cherry tomatoes, halved
 1 cup chopped fresh basil

1. Bring 4 quarts water to boil in large pot. Heat 3 tablespoons oil in large skillet over medium-high heat until shimmering. Add mushrooms, peppers, onion, 3 tablespoons vinegar, 1 teaspoon salt, and ½ teaspoon pepper to skillet and cook covered, stirring occasionally, until vegetables begin to soften, about 5 minutes. Uncover and continue to cook, stirring occasionally, until vegetables are tender and browned around edges, 10 to 12 minutes. Stir in garlic and cook until fragrant, about 30 seconds.

2. While vegetables are cooking, add 1 tablespoon salt and pasta to boiling water and cook until al dente. Reserve ½ cup cooking water, drain pasta, and return to pot. Add cooked vegetables, remaining oil, and remaining vinegar to pot with pasta and toss to combine, adding reserved pasta water as needed. Stir in tomatoes and basil and season with salt and pepper. Serve.

TEST KITCHEN NOTE: One pound of quartered white or cremini mushrooms can be substituted for the portobellos.

BAKED PORK CHOPS WITH PARMESAN-SAGE CRUST Serves 4

WHY THIS RECIPE WORKS: Adding 2 tablespoons mayonnaise to the crumb coating gives these baked chops a pan-fried crunch, minus the mess.

 1 (5-ounce) box Melba toast, broken into rough pieces (see note)
 1 cup grated Parmesan cheese
 ½ cup mayonnaise
 2 tablespoons chopped fresh sage
   Salt and pepper
 1 tablespoon Dijon mustard
 1 teaspoon grated zest and 1 teaspoon juice from 1 lemon
 4 bone-in, rib-cut pork chops, ¾ to 1 inch thick

1. Adjust oven rack to middle position and heat oven to 425 degrees. Pulse Melba toast pieces, Parmesan, 2 tablespoons mayonnaise, sage, ¼ teaspoon salt, and ¾ teaspoon pepper in food processor until coarsely ground; transfer to shallow dish. Whisk remaining mayonnaise, mustard, lemon zest, and lemon juice in another shallow dish.

2. Cover pork chops with mayonnaise and mustard mixture. One at a time, dredge chops in Melba crumb mixture, pressing gently to adhere. Transfer chops to wire rack set inside rimmed baking sheet. Bake until crust is golden brown and meat registers 145 degrees, 16 to 22 minutes. Serve.

TEST KITCHEN NOTE: Don't process the Melba toast too finely: Coarsely ground crumbs are key for a super-crunchy coating.

EASY STUFFED FILLETS OF SOLE Serves 4

WHY THIS RECIPE WORKS: "Toasting" the crumbs in the microwave rather than in the oven or on the stovetop saves 10 minutes.

 4 slices hearty white sandwich bread, torn into pieces
 ½ cup mayonnaise
 3 tablespoons unsalted butter, melted
 1 tablespoon Dijon mustard
 2 garlic cloves, minced
 3 tablespoons finely chopped fresh chives
 2 teaspoons grated zest and 1 tablespoon juice from 1 lemon
   Salt and pepper
 8 skinless sole fillets (about 1½ pounds) (see note)
 ¾ cup heavy cream

1. Adjust oven rack to middle position and heat oven to 475 degrees. Grease 13- by 9-inch baking dish. Pulse bread in food processor to coarse crumbs. Transfer crumbs to large bowl and microwave, stirring occasionally, until golden and crisp, 4 to 8 minutes. Add mayonnaise, butter, mustard, garlic, 2 tablespoons chives, lemon zest, ¼ teaspoon salt, and ⅛ teaspoon pepper to bowl and stir to combine.

2. Pat fish dry with paper towels and season with salt and pepper. Arrange fillets, smooth-side down, on work surface. Place ¼ cup filling on each fillet, roll, and arrange seam-side down in prepared baking dish.

3. Combine cream, lemon juice, ¼ teaspoon salt, and ⅛ teaspoon pepper in bowl. Pour cream mixture over fish and bake until stuffing is heated through and fish flakes apart when gently pressed, 12 to 14 minutes. Sprinkle with remaining chives. Serve.

TEST KITCHEN NOTE: Look for sole fillets that weigh 3 to 4 ounces.

QUICK CHICKEN AND DUMPLING SOUP

SKILLET BBQ STEAK TIPS

SKILLET TAMALE PIE

TERIYAKI CHICKEN LO MEIN

SKILLET BBQ STEAK TIPS Serves 4

WHY THIS RECIPE WORKS: Store-bought BBQ sauce can be sticky-sweet. Here we doctor the sauce with ketchup, vinegar, and sugar for a rounded savor.

- 1½ pounds steak tips, cut into 2-inch chunks (see note)
- 2 tablespoons paprika
- ¼ teaspoon cayenne pepper
- Salt and pepper
- 2 tablespoons vegetable oil
- 1 onion, quartered and sliced thin
- ¼ cup barbecue sauce
- 3 tablespoons ketchup
- 3 tablespoons cider vinegar
- 1 tablespoon brown sugar

1. Pat steak tips dry with paper towels and sprinkle evenly with 1 teaspoon paprika, cayenne, 1 teaspoon salt, and ¼ teaspoon pepper. Heat 1 tablespoon oil in large skillet over medium-high heat until just smoking. Cook steak tips until browned all over and cooked to desired doneness, 6 to 10 minutes. Transfer to platter and tent with foil.

2. Add remaining oil, onion, and remaining paprika to empty skillet and cook until onion is softened, 3 to 5 minutes. Stir in barbecue sauce, ketchup, vinegar, and sugar and cook until thickened, about 3 minutes. Add steak tips and any accumulated juices to pan and toss to coat. Serve.

TEST KITCHEN NOTE: Steak tips may be sold as whole steaks, cubes, or strips. For this recipe, we prefer to buy strips and cut them ourselves.

QUICK CHICKEN AND DUMPLING SOUP Serves 4 to 6

WHY THIS RECIPE WORKS: The combination of rotisserie chicken and store-bought broth gives this soup a rich chicken flavor in minutes.

- 1½ cups all-purpose flour
- ⅔ cup water
- 2 large eggs, lightly beaten
- Salt and pepper
- 3 tablespoons unsalted butter
- 1 onion, chopped fine
- 2 carrots, peeled and sliced thin
- 1 celery rib, sliced thin
- 8 cups low-sodium chicken broth
- 1 rotisserie chicken, skin discarded, meat shredded into bite-sized pieces (about 3 cups)

1. Whisk flour, water, eggs, ½ teaspoon salt, and ¼ teaspoon pepper in bowl; set aside.

2. Melt butter in Dutch oven over medium-high heat. Cook onion, carrots, and celery until lightly browned, about 5 minutes. Stir in broth and bring to boil. Reduce heat to medium-low and simmer, covered, until vegetables are tender, 10 to 15 minutes.

3. Remove lid of pot. Stir in chicken and season with salt and pepper; return to simmer. Working quickly, use ½ teaspoon measuring spoon to drop pieces of dough into soup. Simmer, covered, until dumplings are set, 1 to 2 minutes. Season with salt and pepper. Serve.

TEST KITCHEN NOTE: To prevent the dumpling dough from sticking to the measuring spoon in step 3, spray the spoon with cooking spray prior to scooping the dough.

TERIYAKI CHICKEN LO MEIN Serves 4

WHY THIS RECIPE WORKS: Traditional pasta or Chinese noodles take 10 minutes or longer to cook. We use ramen noodles, which cook directly in the sauce in only 4 minutes.

- ¾ cup soy sauce
- ¼ cup rice vinegar
- 1½ tablespoons grated fresh ginger
- ⅓ cup sugar
- 1 tablespoon cornstarch
- 3½ cups water
- 4 (3-ounce) packages ramen noodles, broken into large pieces, seasoning packets discarded
- 1 (16-ounce) bag coleslaw mix (see note)
- 2 boneless, skinless chicken breasts, cut crosswise into ¼-inch-thick slices
- 1 tablespoon vegetable oil

1. Simmer soy sauce, vinegar, ginger, sugar, and cornstarch in large saucepan over medium-high heat, whisking often, until thickened, 2 to 3 minutes. Transfer half of soy sauce mixture to large bowl and reserve. Add water to saucepan with remaining soy sauce mixture and return to boil. Add ramen and cook, stirring occasionally, until tender, about 4 minutes. Off heat, stir in coleslaw mix. Cover and keep warm.

2. Pat chicken dry with paper towels. Heat oil in large skillet over medium-high heat until just smoking. Add chicken and cook until no longer pink, about 1 minute per side. Transfer chicken to bowl with reserved soy sauce mixture and toss to coat. Transfer noodles to platter and top with chicken. Serve.

TEST KITCHEN NOTE: Cole slaw mix is sold alongside the bagged lettuces in most supermarkets.

SKILLET TAMALE PIE Serves 4 to 6

WHY THIS RECIPE WORKS: The addition of shredded cheese to the topping improves flavor and texture. As the cheese melts, it binds the cornbread, producing a more cohesive, tamale-like topping.

- 10 ounces store-bought cornbread, crumbled (about 2½ cups)
- 3 cups shredded Mexican cheese blend
- Salt and pepper
- 1 tablespoon vegetable oil
- 1 onion, finely chopped
- 1 teaspoon minced canned chipotle chiles in adobo
- 1½ pounds 90 percent lean ground beef
- 2 (15-ounce) cans pinto beans, drained and rinsed
- 2 (10-ounce) cans Ro-Tel tomatoes, drained, ⅓ cup juice reserved (see note)
- ¼ cup finely chopped fresh cilantro

1. Adjust oven rack to middle position and heat oven to 450 degrees. Combine cornbread, 1½ cups cheese, ¼ teaspoon salt, and ½ teaspoon pepper in bowl.

2. Heat oil in large heatproof skillet over medium-high heat until shimmering. Cook onion and chipotle until softened, about 5 minutes. Add beef and cook until no longer pink, about 5 minutes. Stir in beans, tomatoes, and reserved tomato juice and cook until thickened, about 5 minutes. Stir in 2 tablespoons cilantro and remaining cheese. Season with salt and pepper.

3. Arrange cornbread mixture evenly over filling. Bake until cornbread is golden brown, 10 to 15 minutes. Sprinkle with remaining cilantro. Serve.

TEST KITCHEN NOTE: If you can't find Ro-Tel tomatoes, substitute 2½ cups of canned diced tomatoes and add an additional teaspoon of minced chipotle chiles in adobo.

Sock-It-to-Me Cake

For this glazed, nutty cinnamon coffee cake, could we nix the yellow cake mix but keep the ease, please? BY CALI RICH

The catchphrase "sock it to me" was first heard by most Americans—with connotations we can't mention here—when Aretha Franklin's "Respect" topped the charts in 1967. Within a year, *Rowan & Martin's Laugh-In* took up "sock it to me" in a routine that usually involved dousing an actress with water, but on one famous occasion was uttered by Richard Nixon, then running for president. (You know the rest of the story.) In the 1970s, Duncan Hines co-opted the phrase for its back-of-the-box recipe for Sock-It-to-Me Cake. That "legendary" cake, as Anne Byrn describes it in *The Cake Mix Doctor*, uses an easy dump-and-stir method—and a few extra ingredients—to transform yellow cake mix into a moist, velvety coffee cake. The recipe appears on the box to this day.

Following that recipe, I added eggs, sour cream, oil, and sugar to cake mix and then layered the resulting batter with cinnamon-pecan streusel in a baking pan (often a Bundt or tube pan). The cake had an unbelievably moist yet sturdy texture, but even the ripple of streusel couldn't mask the artificial flavor from the boxed mix. With just a little extra work, I hoped to deliver a from-scratch cake with from-scratch flavor that retained the ease of the original.

I began my search with a standard coffee cake recipe, made by beating together butter and sugar and then adding eggs, vanilla, milk, and dry ingredients (flour, baking soda and powder, and salt). The flavor was a vast improvement on the box. Unfortunately, the texture was dry and too fluffy (from the aeration in mixing). Taking a cue from the original recipe, I replaced the milk with sour cream, which yielded a moister crumb but made the texture too fragile.

Taking a step back, I considered the dump-and-stir ease of the original recipe, made possible, in part, by vegetable oil. I abandoned the mixer; at the same time, I whisked in 1 cup of oil for the same amount of butter. This produced a tighter and even more tender crumb than before, but tasters missed the flavor of butter. I reversed course, but this time I melted the butter and stirred it in. At last, a flavorful, moist cake that was a snap to make.

The original streusel recipe called for a combination of 2 tablespoons of the boxed mix, brown sugar, cinnamon, and chopped pecans, but tasters deemed it dry and shaggy. Moreover, slices fractured in two at the streusel line. Toasting the pecans improved the taste. Grinding them in the food processor with flour (instead of the mix), cinnamon, and sugar solved the structural problem and yielded neat, tidy slices. Melted butter added richness and moisture.

Since I was dirtying the food processor for the streusel anyway, I wondered if I could use it to speed up my cake batter. I processed the sugar, eggs, sour cream, and vanilla, poured the melted butter down the tube with the motor running, and then added the dry mixture. In minutes, I had a foolproof batter that was almost as easy as a mix but tasted much better. It baked up tall and golden with a pretty cinnamon-scented streusel. Later, I drizzled a vanilla-scented glaze over it. Now my cake was more than just a cute name.

SOCK-IT-TO-ME CAKE Serves 12

This cake can also be baked in a 12-cup nonstick tube pan. Using baking spray (a combination of vegetable oil and flour) is the best way to ensure a perfect release from the pan.

STREUSEL
- 2 tablespoons all-purpose flour
- 2 tablespoons unsalted butter, melted and cooled slightly
- ¼ cup packed light brown sugar
- 2 teaspoons ground cinnamon
- ¾ cup pecans, toasted

CAKE
- 2½ cups all-purpose flour
- 1 teaspoon baking powder
- ½ teaspoon baking soda
- 1 teaspoon salt
- 2 cups granulated sugar
- 4 large eggs, room temperature
- 1 cup sour cream, room temperature
- 1 teaspoon vanilla extract
- 16 tablespoons unsalted butter (2 sticks), melted and cooled

GLAZE
- 1¼ cups confectioners' sugar
- 1½ tablespoons whole or low-fat milk
- 1 teaspoon vanilla extract

Our Sock-It-to-Me Cake is chock-full of butter, sour cream, cinnamon, and toasted pecans.

1. MAKE STREUSEL Process flour, butter, brown sugar, cinnamon, and pecans in food processor until finely ground. Transfer streusel to bowl and wipe out food processor.

2. MAKE BATTER Adjust oven rack to middle position and heat oven to 325 degrees. Grease and flour 12-cup nonstick Bundt pan. Combine flour, baking powder, baking soda, and salt in bowl. In food processor, blend sugar, eggs, sour cream, and vanilla until smooth, about 1 minute. With machine running, slowly pour in butter until incorporated, then add flour mixture and pulse until just combined.

3. LAYER AND BAKE Pour half of batter into prepared pan and top with streusel mixture. Cover with remaining batter, using rubber spatula to smooth surface. Bake until golden brown and toothpick inserted in center comes out clean, 50 to 60 minutes. Cool cake in pan 20 minutes.

4. GLAZE While cake is cooling, whisk confectioners' sugar, milk, and vanilla in bowl until smooth. Turn out cake onto rack set inside rimmed baking sheet. Pour glaze over warm cake. Cool completely, at least 2 hours. Serve. (Cake can be stored at room temperature, covered in plastic wrap, for 2 days.)

Sock-It-to-Me Cake without a Food Processor

The food processor gives the cake a finer crumb, but if you don't have one, you can make the streusel and batter by hand. For the streusel, finely chop the pecans, and then combine them in a small bowl with the flour, brown sugar, and cinnamon. Stir in the melted butter until evenly incorporated. For the cake, combine the dry ingredients as directed in the recipe. Whisk the sugar, eggs, sour cream, and vanilla separately in a large bowl, and then slowly pour in the butter until the mixture is emulsified. Add the dry mixture to the wet mixture, whisking until just combined. Continue with filling the prepared pan and baking, as directed.

ON THE SIDE Glazed Butternut Squash

A sweet glaze underlines the best qualities of roasted butternut squash, but only if the squash cooks evenly and the flavors are in balance. BY KRIS WIDICAN

One-inch chunks browned nicely without taking forever.

Applying a sweet glaze to roasted butternut squash should intensify the vegetable's flavor and encourage it to caramelize and brown. But many of the recipes I tested produced sodden, sticky mashes of squash swimming in syrupy-sweet glazes, or worse, squash that barely cooked through before the glaze incinerated.

For the sweet element of the glaze, tasters preferred the complexity and depth of dark brown sugar to plain white sugar. I tried adding shallots, garlic, thyme, parsley, and chives, but my tasters were emphatic that, in this case, less was more: Salt and pepper perked up the squash without overwhelming it, and a little melted butter added nutty richness and tied the glaze together.

I knew that how I cut the squash would affect how it caramelized in the oven. I tested sizes and shapes from slender batons to hulking half-moons before settling on 1-inch cubes, which had enough surface area to brown well yet were small enough to cook to full tenderness in a reasonable 45 minutes. On impulse, after the squash came out of the oven, I reached for a bottle of cider vinegar, hoping a splash would counter the sweetness of the glaze and give the dish some zing. A mere teaspoon brought the needed brightness to this simple side dish.

BROWN SUGAR–GLAZED BUTTERNUT SQUASH
Serves 4 to 6
We like the deeper flavor of dark brown sugar in this recipe, but light brown sugar can be substituted.

- 1   butternut squash (about 2½ pounds), peeled, halved lengthwise, seeded, and cut into 1-inch chunks
- ¼   cup packed dark brown sugar (see note)
- 3   tablespoons unsalted butter, melted
- ½   teaspoon salt
- ¼   teaspoon pepper
- 1   teaspoon cider vinegar

1. PREPARE PAN Adjust oven rack to middle position and heat oven to 425 degrees. Line rimmed baking sheet with aluminum foil and coat lightly with cooking spray.

2. ROAST Toss squash, sugar, butter, salt, and pepper in large bowl until well coated. Transfer squash to prepared baking sheet. Roast, stirring every 15 minutes, until squash is well browned and completely tender, about 45 minutes. Transfer pan to wire rack, sprinkle squash with vinegar, and stir to coat. Serve.

ON THE SIDE Beer-Braised Cabbage

Sloppy, smelly cabbage is nobody's idea of good food. We were after a cooked side dish that we'd actually want to eat. BY KRIS WIDICAN

A creamy side of crisp coleslaw is an easy sell, but boiled cabbage—that's another story. Its watery, slimy texture and eye-watering stink (from hours of stewing) earn its well-deserved rap. But recently I came across a dish for beer-braised cabbage that made me think again. To make it, I simmered strips of green cabbage with ½ cup of beer in a covered skillet for just 30 minutes. I removed the lid, only to find the cabbage had expelled its liquid and was swimming in sauce. An additional 20 minutes of simmering was necessary to bubble the liquid away, and while the stink was gone and the dish had a pleasing malty flavor, the cabbage was still overcooked and soggy. I had to admit, though, I'd finally found a cooked cabbage dish that piqued my interest.

In my next attempt, I decided to pump up the flavors of the braising liquid before I added the cabbage. For beer, tasters preferred a lighter lager to ale. I tested the addition of various beer-complementing ingredients from the recipes I'd collected. We liked sautéed onion, mustard, vinegar, and thyme. Bacon was surprisingly distracting, and parsley didn't add much.

Once I'd decided on my braising ingredients, I focused on preventing the cabbage from overcooking. I again cooked the cabbage covered, this time checking it after only 10 minutes—it was already tender, so further cooking to evaporate the liquid would certainly result in overcooked cabbage. In my next test, I simmered the braising liquid until slightly thickened before adding the cabbage. Exactly eight minutes later, I lifted the lid to find crisp-tender shreds of cabbage perked up by a lively, malty, concentrated sauce.

BEER-BRAISED CABBAGE Serves 4
You can substitute ¼ teaspoon of dried thyme for the fresh. Grey Poupon Harvest Coarse Ground Mustard is our favorite whole grain mustard. This hearty side dish is a nice complement for pork.

- 2   tablespoons unsalted butter
- 1   onion, chopped fine
- ½   cup beer, preferably light-bodied lager
- 1   tablespoon whole grain mustard (see note)
- ½   teaspoon minced fresh thyme
- 1   small head green cabbage (about 1 pound), halved, cored, and sliced thin
- 2   teaspoons cider vinegar
      Salt and pepper

Melt butter in large skillet over medium-high heat. Cook onion until softened, about 5 minutes. Stir in beer, mustard, and thyme and simmer until slightly thickened, about 2 minutes. Add cabbage and vinegar and cook covered, stirring occasionally, until wilted and tender, about 8 minutes. Season with salt and pepper. Serve.

Malty and just tender with a suggestion of mustard, our Beer-Braised Cabbage makes the case for cooked cabbage.

Crispy Pan-Fried Pork Chops

In search of an easy way to build big flavor, we revisited an old-fashioned cooking method: pan-frying. Was it time to bring it back? BY MEGHAN ERWIN

Order a pan-fried pork chop at a family-style restaurant in the South and what you're served is a thing of beauty. Bone-in pork chops are dredged in highly seasoned flour and given a quick fry in lots of sizzling fat, traditionally bacon fat. At their best, the chops have a juicy, meaty interior set off by a thick, highly seasoned crust. For some reason, this no-fuss method has fallen out of favor with home cooks.

Is it because recipes can be maddeningly vague? "Season pork chop, cook in frying oil until done." Other recipes I found called for gobs of bacon fat, harkening back to a time when cooks kept coffee cans of the stuff by their stoves. Dredging a chop, then sliding it into a pan of hot fat (more fat than with searing, less than with deep-frying) seems straightforward. In fact, when I tried it, a few real challenges emerged. For one, that crispy crust kept chipping off. Also, the seasonings in many recipes proved musty, salty, or unbalanced. Finally, without the can of fat, the flavor of the chops left a lot to be desired.

Simply dredging the pork chops in flour, as most recipes instruct, produced a spotty, insubstantial crust that wouldn't stay put. I tried dipping them in buttermilk first, but the tang was a distraction, so I went back to the simple flour dredge. After several unsuccessful test batches, I noticed that the coatings on the dredged chops that sat around for a few minutes were getting a little wet and gummy. The test kitchen has had success letting floured chicken rest (just 10 minutes is enough) before re-dredging and frying. The second dredge makes for a sturdier, more substantial crust. Sure enough, my double-dipped chops emerged from the pan with a hefty, crisp, golden brown crust.

But the crust didn't taste like much. I added seasoned salt to the flour (too dusty and lacking punch), then supermarket spice mixes (musty and stale tasting). I tried making my own spice mix and went a little overboard concocting an elaborate 10-spice blend. Tasters eventually pared it down to the essentials: garlic powder, paprika, salt, pepper, and cayenne. Applying the spices directly to the meat, rather than adding them to the flour, let me season the chops more thoroughly.

I'd been frying the pork chops in ½ cup vegetable oil—just enough to come about halfway up the sides of the chops. As a nod to older recipes, a colleague suggested I render some bacon and use the fat to flavor the oil. Augmenting the oil with the fat from three slices of bacon gave the cooked chops a depth of smoky flavor that, combined with the garlicky, golden crust, had tasters licking their chops.

A shallow pan-fry yields a beautifully browned, moist pork chop and a fast weeknight supper.

PAN-FRIED PORK CHOPS Serves 4

Chops between ¾ and 1 inch thick will work in this recipe.

- 1 teaspoon garlic powder
- ½ teaspoon paprika
- ½ teaspoon salt
- ½ teaspoon pepper
- ¼ teaspoon cayenne pepper
- 1 cup all-purpose flour
- 4 bone-in rib or center cut pork chops, about ¾ inch thick
- 3 slices bacon, chopped
- ½ cup vegetable oil

1. COAT CHOPS Combine garlic powder, paprika, salt, pepper, and cayenne in bowl. Place flour in shallow dish. Pat chops dry with paper towels. Cut 2 slits about 2 inches apart through fat on edges of each chop. Season both sides of chops with spice mixture, then dredge chops lightly in flour (do not discard flour). Transfer to plate and let rest 10 minutes.

2. RENDER BACON Meanwhile, cook bacon in large nonstick skillet over medium heat until fat renders and bacon is crisp, about 8 minutes. Using slotted spoon, transfer bacon to paper towel–lined plate and reserve for another use. Do not wipe out pan.

3. FRY CHOPS Add oil to fat in pan and heat over medium-high heat until just smoking. Return chops to flour dish and turn to coat. Cook chops until well browned, 3 to 4 minutes per side. Serve.

BBQ PAN-FRIED PORK CHOPS

Prepare Pan-Fried Pork Chops, replacing first five ingredients with 3 tablespoons light brown sugar, 1 teaspoon chili powder, 1 teaspoon paprika, ½ teaspoon salt, ½ teaspoon dry mustard, ¼ teaspoon ground cumin, and ¼ teaspoon cayenne pepper.

HERBED PAN-FRIED PORK CHOPS

Prepare Pan-Fried Pork Chops, replacing first five ingredients with ½ teaspoon dried marjoram, ½ teaspoon dried thyme, ¼ teaspoon dried basil, ¼ teaspoon dried rosemary (crumbled), ¼ teaspoon dried sage, pinch ground fennel, and ½ teaspoon salt.

DON'T MAKE THIS MISTAKE Curly Chops

Pork chops—especially thin-cut chops—have a tendency to curl as they cook. When exposed to the high heat of the pan, the ring of fat and connective tissue that surrounds the exterior tightens, causing the meat to buckle and curl. To prevent it, we cut two slits about 2 inches apart through the fat and connective tissue on each chop.

BUCKLED CHOP: NO SLITS

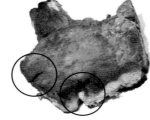

FLAT CHOP: SLITS CUT

Old-Fashioned Chicken in a Pot

Look through 19th-century American cookbooks and you will see that recipes for boiling chicken in a pot abound. The bird may be stuffed, bolstered with vegetables, or tarted up with egg sauce or oysters. However these recipes might vary, one thing was unspoken. A tough "free-range" bird (all birds were free-range before World War II) needed a lot of cooking time to become tender. Today's young, plump supermarket birds don't have to be boiled to become tender, which probably explains why this method has fallen out of favor. But chicken in a pot still has appeal. The modern, mass-produced chicken is depressingly bland, and cooking a whole bird in a pot with vegetables and aromatics seems an ideal way to infuse a 21st-century bird with flavor.

BY KELLEY BAKER

Traditional chicken in a pot is a satisfying, elegantly simple one-dish meal. Done right, the method produces a moist, velvety chicken and deeply flavored broth that doubles as a sauce. True, the skin (which so many modern recipe writers, including some in our very own test kitchen, obsess about) is neither golden nor crisp. Instead, it serves to protect the meat as it cooks and to flavor the broth. The vegetables soak up flavor from the broth and turn the dish into a complete meal.

Old recipes call for submerging the chicken in liquid and boiling it. The drawback is that all the meat cooks at the same temperature. By the time the legs are done, today's extra-lean breast meat is seriously dried out. I came across a Julia Child recipe for Casserole-Poached Chicken that noted that if the poaching liquid "comes only part way up—the dark meat of the legs and thighs simmers and the white

meat of the breast steams" for a "beautifully tender and juicy chicken" and a "perfectly flavored…chicken broth." She cooked her chicken in the oven, which made sense to me—the oven braises gently and evenly. Following her lead, I cut the water from 6 cups to 2 and baked my next chicken in a pot. As promised, all parts were "beautifully tender and juicy."

But the "perfectly flavored" chicken broth was MIA. Frankly, the chicken didn't taste like much, either. I replaced the water I'd been using with store-bought chicken broth. That helped, but tasters found it one-dimensional. I added a splash of white wine for brightness and complexity. I seared the chicken before poaching it, hoping to add another layer of flavor. Alas, the breast overcooked, a problem I thought I'd solved. In the end, browning just the back elicited enough fond (the bits left in the pan) to intensify the

broth. And flavorful broth equaled flavorful chicken.

Most recipes for chicken in a pot call for onions, carrots, and celery. Browning the vegetables was an easy way to add more flavor to the broth. The carrots held up nicely in tests, but the onions and celery had a flabby, unfit-to-serve texture so I discarded them after cooking. Cabbage, turnips, and potatoes are less common but not unheard-of additions. But my tasters found the cabbage and turnips gave the broth off-flavors, so I left them out. Quartered potatoes nicely rounded out the one-pot meal. I discovered that arranging the chicken on top of the aromatics elevated the breast further, providing extra insurance against overcooking.

I finished the broth with butter and a sprinkling of chives. It was intense and silken, good enough to sip on its own, and even better ladled over the tender, juicy chicken.

CHICKEN IN A POT Serves 4

You will need kitchen twine and a Dutch oven with a tight-fitting lid and at least a 6-quart capacity to make this recipe. Serve the chicken with Dijon mustard, pickles, and horseradish as accompaniments, if desired.

- 1 (4½- to 5-pound) whole chicken, trimmed of excess fat
  Salt and pepper
- 2 tablespoons vegetable oil
- 1 onion, peeled and halved, root end left intact
- 1 celery rib, halved crosswise
- 1 pound carrots, peeled and cut into 1-inch pieces
- 6 garlic cloves, minced
- 1 cup white wine
- 1 cup low-sodium chicken broth
- 1½ pounds small red potatoes, scrubbed and quartered
- 2 tablespoons unsalted butter
- 1 tablespoon finely chopped fresh chives

1. SEASON CHICKEN Adjust oven rack to lower-middle position and heat oven to 350 degrees. Pat chicken dry with paper towels. Using fingers, loosen skin from breasts and legs of chicken. Rub 1 teaspoon salt and ½ teaspoon pepper all over chicken and underneath skin. Tuck wings behind back and tie legs together with kitchen twine.

2. BROWN CHICKEN Heat 1 tablespoon oil in Dutch oven over medium-high heat until just smoking. Following photos, add chicken, breast-side up, and cook until back is lightly browned, 3 to 4 minutes. Transfer chicken to plate. Add remaining oil, onion, celery, and carrots to empty pot and cook until browned, about 5 minutes. Add garlic and cook until fragrant, about 30 seconds. Add wine and broth and bring to boil. Arrange chicken, breast-side up, on top of vegetables. Season potatoes with salt and pepper and arrange around chicken. Transfer pot to oven and cook, covered, until thigh meat registers 170 to 175 degrees, 50 to 70 minutes.

3. MAKE SAUCE Remove pot from oven and transfer to wire rack. Remove lid and tent pot loosely with foil; let rest 20 minutes. Carefully transfer chicken to carving board. Using slotted spoon, transfer vegetables to serving platter, discarding onion and celery. Let sit 5 minutes, then strain and skim sauce (you should have about 2 cups of sauce; if you have less, supplement with chicken broth). Whisk butter and chives into sauce and season with salt and pepper. Carve chicken and serve, passing sauce at table.

TEST KITCHEN TECHNIQUE Building Flavor Is Key
Building layers of flavor and avoiding overcooking are the keys to chicken in a pot.

1. A rich, flavorful sauce starts with searing the chicken. To avoid overcooking the breast meat, brown only the back.

2. Remove the chicken and brown the vegetables to bring out their natural sweetness and help flavor the sauce.

3. Arrange the chicken on top of the aromatics and place the potatoes around the exterior of the pot.

RATING INEXPENSIVE DUTCH OVENS

Dutch ovens are kitchen workhorses, useful for making stews, soups, and slow braises, and also handy for less obvious tasks such as deep-frying and baking crusty loaves of bread. We tested several inexpensive alternatives to our favorite 7¼-quart Dutch oven by Le Creuset ($259.95) by making stew, rice, and french fries, and liked what we found. The pots are listed in order of preference.

RECOMMENDED

TRAMONTINA 6.5-Quart Cast Iron Dutch Oven
Price: $39.97
Source: Walmart.com
Material: Enameled cast iron
Capacity: 6.5 qt. **Diameter:** 9" **Weight:** 16.5 lbs.

CRITERIA — Rice ★★★ Fries ★★★ Stew ★★★

Comments: Roomy, sturdy, and solid, this pot produced glossy, deeply flavored beef stew, fluffy white rice, and crispy french fries, all at a bargain price. It retained heat well, recovering quickly after french fries were added to hot oil.

LODGE Color Enamel 6-Quart Dutch Oven
Price: $52.35
Source: Walmart.com
Material: Enameled cast iron
Capacity: 6 qt. **Diameter:** 8" **Weight:** 16 lbs.

Rice ★★★ Fries ★★★ Stew ★★★

Comments: A solid performer, this pot had a slightly smaller cooking surface than the top-rated Tramontina, holding less meat in each batch for browning. Nonetheless, it produced excellent stew, fluffy rice, and crisp fries.

MARIO BATALI Italian Essentials Pot by Copco
Price: $109.95
Source: Amazon.com
Material: Enameled cast iron with cast stainless lid knob
Capacity: 6 qt. **Diameter:** 9¾" **Weight:** 16 lbs.

Rice ★★★ Fries ★★★ Stew ★★★

Comments: This roomy pot was slow to heat up but quickly recovered after fries were added to oil. The "self-basting" spikes inside the lid work—we never had to shake off condensation. One beef? Beef browned unevenly. Also, larger handles would have eased lifting and maneuvering the pot.

RECOMMENDED WITH RESERVATIONS

CALPHALON ONE Infused Anodized Dutch Oven
Price: $99.99
Source: Amazon.com
Material: Heavy-gauge aluminum infused with polymer; stainless steel lid
Capacity: 8½ qt. **Diameter:** 11⅞" **Weight:** 6.8 lbs.

CRITERIA — Rice ★★★ Fries ★★ Stew ★★★

Comments: This pot was very roomy and light, thus easy to handle. The low sides meant we could see inside. But the temperature of the oil plummeted when potatoes were added for fries, then fluctuated more than the other pots as the temperature slowly climbed back up.

EMERILWARE FROM ALL-CLAD Cast Iron Dutch Oven
Price: $54.95
Source: Cooking.com
Material: Preseasoned cast iron
Capacity: 6 qt. **Diameter:** 8" **Weight:** 16.9 lbs.

Rice ★★ Fries ★★ Stew ★★★

Comments: This deep, narrow pot was slow to heat up, but developed a nice fond for stew once it did. Meat for stew had to be browned in four batches rather than three. The stew's broth reduced until rich and thick, but the meat wasn't fork-tender. Boiled water appeared yellow, and fries tasted rusty, indicating that pot had lost its seasoning.

INNOVA Color Cast Porcelain Enameled Cast Iron 5-Quart Round Dutch Oven
Price: $60.27
Source: Amazon.com
Material: Enameled cast iron
Capacity: 5 qt. **Diameter:** 7⅝" **Weight:** 11.3 lbs.

Rice ★★ Fries ★★ Stew ★★

Comments: Because this pot is so narrow, we had to brown the meat for the stew in five batches rather than three. The pot runs slightly hot, yielding overcooked rice with "blown out" grains. It's slow to heat oil, and when fries were added, the temperature of the oil dropped more than we'd like.

New Mexico Pork Chili

When it comes to chili, Texans like to grab the limelight—with raucous world chili cook-offs and official state dishes (chili con carne). But cross the state line into New Mexico and you'll find a little-known chile-based dish that deserves a Texas-size reputation: carne adovada, literally "marinated meat." Like many New Mexican dishes, it's headlined by local chiles. Meltingly tender chunks of pork butt are braised in an intense, soulful red chile sauce with hints of cumin, oregano, onion, and garlic. It's at once smoky yet bright, spicy yet sweet. BY KELLEY BAKER

It's easy to find recipes for carne adovada. If you don't live in the Southwest, however, it may not be so easy to find the requisite chiles. I tested several, and the recipe that emerged as most promising required toasting, seeding, and grinding nearly two dozen dried New Mexico chiles (commonly Anaheims left to ripen until red). Tasters loved the toasty, fruity notes added by all those chiles, which also thickened the sauce nicely. But I wanted to reproduce those rich and complex flavors using ingredients available in any supermarket.

I began by reaching for a jar of chili powder, typically a combination of dried ground chiles, cumin, oregano, and garlic—the same spices used in traditional recipes for carne adovada. I browned cubed pork shoulder in oil and then set it aside (I decided upon 1½-inch chunks because they held their shape yet still qualified as bite-sized). After softening onion and garlic in the residual fat, I added ½ cup supermarket chili powder, about the same amount as carne adovada recipes usually specify for freshly roasted and ground dried New Mexico chiles. Then I stirred in chicken broth, pureed the mixture, added back the reserved meat, and put the pot in the oven (for even cooking, the test kitchen prefers the oven for stews). After two hours, the meat was tender and the sauce was an attractive rust-red, but the dish tasted utterly flat, and the meat juices had made the sauce runny.

In the test kitchen, we often use canned chipotle chiles in adobo to provide smoky depth. I tried various quantities before deciding that a tablespoon brought the right amount of complexity and heat. Wondering how to replicate the fruity quality of dried chiles, it occurred to me that I could use actual fruit. Since the flavor of chiles is sometimes described as raisin-y, I hoped raisins might supply that nuance, but tasters rejected the dots of dried fruit in the sauce. I tried soaking the raisins in hot water to soften them, then made a puree and stirred it in. Tasters liked the agreeably subtle flavor it contributed. To replicate the bitter quality of freshly ground dried chiles, I borrowed an idea from some Mexican mole sauces and stirred in both cocoa and unsweetened chocolate. In carne adovada, however, they tasted wrong—"like dirt," according to one taster. A colleague suggested I soak the raisins in coffee instead of water, and indeed, a half-cup of joe brought the flavors into robust, bittersweet balance.

To thicken the sauce, I stirred in flour with the spices, which gave it the necessary heft. I also tried a dash of cinnamon—a classic carne adovada seasoning—but just as quickly removed it; it bullied the sauce. Tasters couldn't detect the miniscule amount of oregano included in the chili powder blend. This herb is a must in carne adovada, so I added a full teaspoon. At the last minute, I stirred in lime juice, lime zest, and cilantro to brighten the otherwise earthy dish. These aren't traditional, but my tasters insisted that flavor trumps authenticity. At last, using ordinary off-the-shelf ingredients, I'd developed an easy version that rivals the original and brought carne adovada a la casa.

CARNE ADOVADA Serves 6 to 8

Pork shoulder—usually labeled pork butt or Boston butt—comes either boneless or on the bone. If using bone-in pork shoulder, buy a 6- to 6½-pound roast. When trimming excess fat, leave at least ⅛-inch thickness on the exterior. Serve the finished dish over rice or with warm corn tortillas.

- ¼ cup raisins
- ½ cup brewed coffee
- 1 (4- to 5-pound) boneless pork shoulder roast, trimmed of excess fat and cut into 1½-inch chunks
  Salt and pepper
- 1 tablespoon vegetable oil
- 2 onions, chopped
- ¼ cup all-purpose flour
- ½ cup chili powder
- 1 teaspoon dried oregano
- 1 tablespoon minced canned chipotle chiles in adobo
- 6 garlic cloves, minced
- 2½ cups low-sodium chicken broth
- 1 teaspoon grated zest and 1 tablespoon juice from 1 lime
- ¼ cup chopped fresh cilantro

1. PLUMP FRUIT Adjust oven rack to lower-middle position and heat oven to 350 degrees. Combine raisins and coffee in small bowl. Wrap tightly with plastic and microwave until liquid begins to boil, 1 to 3 minutes; let stand 5 minutes, until raisins are plump.

2. BROWN PORK Pat pork dry with paper towels and season with salt and pepper. Heat oil in Dutch oven over medium-high heat until just smoking. Brown half of pork, about 10 minutes. Transfer to plate and repeat with remaining pork.

3. MAKE SAUCE Pour off all but 1 tablespoon fat from Dutch oven. Add onions and cook until softened, about 5 minutes. Add flour, chili powder, oregano, chipotle, and garlic and cook until fragrant, about 1 minute. Add broth and raisin mixture, scraping up any browned bits, and bring to boil. Working in 2 batches, transfer mixture to blender or food processor and puree until smooth. Return sauce to pot.

4. BAKE AND FINISH Add browned pork to sauce in pot and transfer to oven. Cook, covered, until pork is fork-tender, about 2 hours. Skim sauce, then stir in lime zest, lime juice, and cilantro. Season with salt and pepper. Serve. (Pork can be refrigerated in airtight container for 3 days.)

TEST KITCHEN DISCOVERY Building Complex Chile Flavor
Our goal was to develop complexity and subtle heat in our Carne Adovada—without having to toast and grind a heap of hard-to-find dried chiles. In the end, we replicated the taste of dried chiles by enhancing supermarket chili powder with a few common ingredients.

BITTERSWEET
A surprising combination of raisins and brewed coffee mimics the bittersweet complexity of dried chiles.

HOT AND SMOKY
Just 1 tablespoon of minced chipotle chiles in adobo gives the sauce smokiness and subtle heat.

WHAT TO DO WITH LEFTOVERS Spicy Pork Empanadas

A little kitchen ingenuity and 15 minutes transform New Mexico Pork Chili. BY DIANE UNGER

If you happen to be in Latin America, empanada is just another way to say turnover. They can be savory or sweet, fried or baked. Recipes for the savory version often instruct the cook to stuff a corn, flour, or even yucca pastry crust with various ground or shredded meat fillings. With leftover carne adovada in the refrigerator, I wondered if I could shortcut the usual recipe and put an easy, inventive second meal on the table without too much effort.

Since speed was key to my plan, homemade pie dough was out of the question. I used supermarket refrigerated pie dough, cutting each round in half; big, dinner-size empanadas would be quicker to assemble than small ones. To turn the pork cubes into a more manageable filling, I chopped them up, but the chunks of meat in thick sauce made for messy eating. I was happier with the next method I tried—microwaving the leftover refrigerated meat for a few minutes until it was soft enough to shred with forks.

To ensure the filling held its own against the rich pastry crust, I bumped up its flavor with minced scallions, chopped cilantro, chopped olives, shredded sharp cheddar, and extra chipotle chiles. I found that high heat (450 degrees) turned the pastry a beautiful golden brown before the meat juices had a chance to thin and leak out (a good seal is key, too). After 30 minutes, the empanadas emerged from the oven impressive, fragrant, and crisp. Leftovers have rarely tasted this good.

SPICY PORK EMPANADAS Serves 4

Use your favorite pie dough or use one 15-ounce box of Pillsbury Just Unroll! Pie Crusts. You can make empanadas up to 12 hours in advance and keep them refrigerated until ready to bake. Serve with sour cream and lime wedges.

- 3 cups leftover carne adovada
- 4 scallions, chopped fine
- 1 cup pimento-stuffed green olives, chopped fine
- 1 cup shredded sharp cheddar cheese
- 3 tablespoons chopped fresh cilantro
- 1 tablespoon minced canned chipotle chiles in adobo
- 2 (9-inch) pie dough rounds (see note)

1. MAKE FILLING Adjust oven rack to middle position and heat oven to 450 degrees. Line rimmed baking sheet with parchment paper. Place pork in bowl and microwave until heated through, 2 to 5 minutes. Using two forks, pull into shreds. Let cool slightly, then stir in scallions, olives, cheese, cilantro, and chipotle.

2. ASSEMBLE TURNOVERS Cut each dough round in half. Arrange one-quarter of filling on one side of each half, leaving ½-inch border around edges. Brush edges of dough with water, fold over filling, and crimp edges to seal. Transfer to prepared baking sheet. Using fork, dock dough at 2-inch intervals so steam can escape. Bake until golden, about 30 minutes. Serve.

TEST KITCHEN TECHNIQUE Forming Empanadas

1. After placing the filling over half the dough crescent, fold the other side over the filling.

2. Crimp the edges of the turnover to seal; use your fingers for a decorative touch or crimp with a fork.

Our easy Spicy Pork Empanadas give leftovers a good name.

ON THE SIDE Creamy Blue Cheese Dressing

We puree the dressing to ensure a creamy texture and even distribution of the potent blue cheese.

Blue cheese can boost flavors or bully them. How do you make this ingredient your friend?

BY MARÍA DEL MAR SACASA

Fans of blue cheese love that it balances brash, pungent, funky, salty, sharp, and sweet in a single bite. But turn the cheese into a salad dressing and that balance can go dangerously out of whack, or surprisingly, the flavors can get lost altogether. I set out to make a version that would bring out the best of the blue.

In the test kitchen we often combine sour cream, mayonnaise, and buttermilk as a base for creamy dressings. I started with equal amounts of each (¾ cup) and quickly determined that the same amount of blue cheese was about right. A dressing seems a poor use of pricey, exquisite artisanal cheese, so I relied on blue cheese from the supermarket. Tasters quickly narrowed the cheese options to Gorgonzola, Roquefort, and Stilton, much preferring them to generic precrumbled blues. All three of our top choices ramped up the blue cheese flavor, but ultimately tasters settled on Stilton for its sweet nuttiness.

To make the dressing thicker and creamier, I reduced the sour cream by half and omitted the most liquid ingredient: the buttermilk. The dressing was now nice and thick, and buzzing everything in the food processor made for quick, easy incorporation. For a final touch of seasoning, a few grinds of pepper (the Stilton added all the necessary salt), a smidgen of garlic powder, and a splash of cider vinegar were just enough to complement, but not overwhelm, the assertive blue cheese.

CREAMY BLUE CHEESE DRESSING
Makes about 1½ cups
Stilton is an English blue cheese with a pungent, slightly sweet flavor. You will need 3 ounces of Stilton for this recipe.

- ¾ cup crumbled Stilton cheese
- ¾ cup mayonnaise
- 6 tablespoons sour cream
- 1½ tablespoons cider vinegar
- ¼ teaspoon pepper
- ⅛ teaspoon garlic powder

Combine all ingredients in food processor and process until smooth, scraping down sides as necessary. Serve. (Dressing can be refrigerated in airtight container for 1 week.)

PARTY FAVORITE Crispy Bacon-Cheddar Potato Skins

We wanted crunch you could hear across the room—no deep fryer required. BY MEGHAN ERWIN

With tasty hits of salt, cheese, and bacon, it's easy to understand the appeal of potato skins. But if your house isn't a restaurant or sports bar with a preheated deep-fat fryer at the ready, it can be hard to get them perfectly crisp. Most recipes I found instruct the home cook to bake the potatoes, scoop out and discard the flesh, top the shells with cheese and bacon, and then bake again. One and all, these failed to produce satisfying crunch.

Right off the bat, I opted to save time by microwaving the potatoes. Although they were a little soggy coming out of the microwave, I dutifully scooped out the flesh, filled the skins with cooked bacon and plenty of cheese, and hoped that baking them in a ripping-hot (475-degree) oven would crisp them up. It didn't. For my next test, I tried brushing the skin side of the shells with rendered bacon fat. This added flavor and dialed up the crispness, but not enough. A colleague happened to be baking crisp-crust pizza on a hot pizza stone, and following course, I preheated a baking sheet and put the filled skins directly on the hot metal. The louder crunch of these skins showed I was making progress.

Up to now, I'd been using hollowed-out potato halves. I cut the shells in quarters on the theory that increasing the surface area that made contact with the hot sheet would mean more crispy bits. It did, but I still wasn't satisfied. Then I remembered a test kitchen recipe for twice-baked potatoes that bakes the shells before they are filled. I microwaved the potatoes, scooped out the flesh, baked the skins for 15 minutes to cook out excess moisture, filled them, and returned them to the oven to melt the cheese. I held my breath while colleagues chomped. Touchdown!

BACON-CHEDDAR POTATO SKINS
Makes 16 potato skins
The potatoes can be cooked, scooped, and refrigerated in an airtight container for 2 days before proceeding with the recipe. Serve with sour cream and sliced scallions, if you like.

- 4 russet potatoes, scrubbed
- 6 slices bacon, chopped
- Salt and pepper
- 1 cup shredded sharp cheddar cheese
- 1 cup shredded Monterey Jack cheese
- 1 tablespoon cornstarch

1. MICROWAVE POTATOES Adjust oven rack to upper-middle position and heat oven to 475 degrees. Set rimmed baking sheet inside oven. Prick potatoes all over with fork, place on paper towel, and microwave until tender, 10 to 15 minutes, turning potatoes over after 5 minutes.

2. FRY BACON Cook bacon in large skillet over medium heat until crisp, about 8 minutes. Reserve 2 teaspoons bacon fat, then transfer bacon to paper towel–lined plate. Blot bacon with paper towels to remove excess grease.

3. CRISP SKINS Quarter potatoes lengthwise, let cool 5 minutes, and then scoop out most of flesh (reserve for another use), leaving ¼-inch layer of potato flesh. Brush exterior of potatoes with reserved bacon fat and season with salt and pepper. Transfer potatoes, skin-side down, to preheated baking sheet and bake until golden brown and crisp, 15 to 20 minutes.

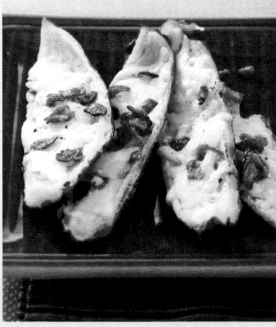

Everything you ever wanted in a snack: salt, bacon, and crunch. These really deliver.

4. FILL SKINS Combine cheeses, cornstarch, half of bacon, ½ teaspoon salt, and ¼ teaspoon pepper in bowl. Remove potato shells from oven and top with cheese mixture. Return to oven and bake until cheese melts, 2 to 4 minutes. Transfer skins to paper towel–lined plate and sprinkle with remaining bacon. Serve.

Boneless Buffalo Chicken

To capture the crunch and fire of this habit-forming bar snack, we wrestled with tough chicken, soggy crusts, and scorching burn. BY LYNN CLARK

There is plenty of crunch under the fiery, neon-orange sauce that coats this chicken.

Anyone who's been to a sports bar knows Buffalo wings, and these days deep-fried nuggets of boneless chicken breasts are likely to get the same treatment. Maybe it's because Americans don't want the hassle of prying small amounts of meat from messy bones. More likely, it's that every inch of every nugget gets a crunchy fried-chicken coating that can be habit-forming. To finish, the nuggets are tossed in a blend of hot sauce and butter. Its blaze-orange color is as hot as its burn, which only a cold beer can douse.

But with so many steps—marinating the chicken, dredging it in a flour-based coating, frying, and tossing with Buffalo sauce—there's plenty of room for error, as I found out to my dismay early in my testing. I was stymied by recipes that produced dry, tough chicken and by crusts that turned soggy and greasy the minute they hit the sauce.

I hoped I could ensure moist chicken meat by soaking it in a marinade before dredging in flour and frying. One recipe I'd seen called for marinating the meat right in the Buffalo sauce, which I assumed would add moisture and another layer of flavor. The cooked chicken was indeed moist, but the extra sauce made it too hot to eat. The oil-based marinade I turned to next was greasy. But a fried chicken–style marinade of buttermilk and salt kept the delicate white meat juicy and moist, and helped season it as well.

To prevent the fried crust from getting soggy when sauced, I knew I'd have to create a coating more substantial than

the seasoned flour in the failed recipes. I turned to a technique we use in the test kitchen for an extra-crunchy coating on fried chicken: dipping the chicken in beaten egg whites, then dredging it in a mixture of cornstarch, flour, and baking soda (for browning) that turns moist and lumpy with the addition of a little buttermilk. The idea is that this pebbly coating fries up craggy and extra-crisp, and it worked beautifully. Since the quantity of liquid is so small, swapping out the buttermilk for a little of the hot sauce mixture added flavor without too much heat.

I had been using the standard sauce of equal parts melted butter and hot sauce, but with the fried coating the dish was much too greasy. Cutting the butter way back (to just 1 tablespoon) solved that problem. Unfortunately, without butter to thicken the sauce and soften its burn, the sauce slid off the nuggets in a scorching puddle.

Attempting to solve the first problem, I went back to that box of cornstarch. Admittedly, it was an unusual approach to Buffalo sauce, but I wasn't going to be a stickler if the method worked. I was pleased to see that 2 teaspoons cornstarch yielded a thick, glazy sauce that coated the nuggets without undoing their crunch. I turned my attention to the heat level. A simple fix—cutting the hot sauce with some water—reduced the burn.

At last, I'd made boneless Buffalo chicken that hit every mark: crunchy, juicy, fiery, and tender. Best of all, I could enjoy it in the comfort of my own kitchen.

BONELESS BUFFALO CHICKEN
Serves 4 to 6

In step 3, the fried chicken pieces can be held in a 200-degree oven for 30 minutes before being tossed with the sauce. A relatively mild cayenne pepper–based hot sauce, like Frank's, is essential; avoid hotter sauces like Tabasco. If desired, serve with our Creamy Blue Cheese Dressing on page 24.

- **4** boneless, skinless chicken breasts (about 1½ pounds), cut into 1½-inch chunks
- **½** cup buttermilk
- **1** teaspoon salt
- **¾** cup hot sauce (see note)
- **¼** cup water
- **¼** teaspoon sugar
- **1** tablespoon unsalted butter
- **1½** cups cornstarch
- **4** large egg whites
- **½** cup all-purpose flour
- **½** teaspoon baking soda
- **4** cups vegetable oil

1. MARINATE Combine chicken, buttermilk, and salt in large zipper-lock bag and refrigerate 30 minutes or up to 2 hours. Combine hot sauce, water, sugar, butter, and 2 teaspoons cornstarch in saucepan. Whisk over medium heat until thickened, about 5 minutes.

2. COAT Whisk egg whites in shallow dish until foamy. Stir flour, baking soda, remaining cornstarch, and 6 tablespoons hot sauce mixture in second shallow dish until mixture resembles coarse meal. Remove chicken from marinade and pat dry with paper towels. Toss half of chicken with egg whites until well coated, then dredge chicken in cornstarch mixture, pressing to adhere. Transfer coated chicken to plate and repeat with remaining chicken.

3. FRY Heat oil in Dutch oven over medium-high heat until oil registers 350 degrees. Fry half of chicken until golden brown, about 4 minutes, turning each piece halfway through cooking. Transfer chicken to paper towel–lined plate. Return oil to 350 degrees and repeat with remaining chicken.

4. TOSS Warm remaining hot sauce mixture over medium-low heat until simmering. Combine chicken and hot sauce mixture in large bowl and toss to coat. Serve.

French Silk Chocolate Pie

Don't let the name fool you: French Silk Pie was "born" in America. Betty Cooper, who lived in Maryland, won a $1,000 prize for the recipe in 1951 in the third annual Pillsbury Bake-Off. Betty's recipe is an old-fashioned icebox pie—the exotic name reflects the international curiosity of postwar America and the Pillsbury contest. Cooper and other contestants wore corsages and dined on such swank dishes as breast of guinea hen and nectarines flambé. That's a far cry from the modern Pillsbury contests, where cooks create recipes from convenience products: Last year's winner, Double-Delight Peanut Butter Cookies, starts with refrigerated peanut butter cookie dough! In contrast, the Pillsbury product Betty Cooper used in French Silk Pie was flour (in the crust), plain and simple. BY DIANE UNGER

While some of these prize-winning recipes have gone the way of the black-and-white television, others stayed in the public eye long after the checks were cashed. To make the filling for her icebox pie, Betty whipped together butter, sugar, three squares of melted-and-cooled unsweetened chocolate, and raw eggs until the mixture was incredibly light and fluffy. She poured the filling into a homemade prebaked pie crust and chilled it until it was firm; no baking required. Served with dollops of whipped cream, French Silk Chocolate Pie was an instant hit.

Although you can find commercial versions of French Silk Pie in the freezer section of the supermarket, not many home cooks tackle it these days, possibly because the recipe calls for raw eggs. When I made Betty's original prize-winning recipe, I uncovered another reason: The pie barely tasted like chocolate. It may have pleased eaters 60 years ago, but

Americans today have become accustomed to ramped-up chocolate flavor.

In the interest of food safety, the recipe on the Pillsbury website calls for egg substitutes in place of the original raw eggs. I tested a few pies with various brands, but the fillings had an off, artificial flavor. I decided to stick with real eggs and cook the eggs and sugar on the stovetop, almost like making a custard. Once the egg and sugar mixture was light and thick (and cooked to a safe 160 degrees), I removed it from the heat and continued whipping it until it was fully cooled.

The original recipe called for 3 ounces of melted unsweetened chocolate. Wanting a more chocolaty pie, I tried doubling the amount, but the unsweetened chocolate was acidic and harsh at that volume (and adding more sugar ruined the texture). Next I made pies with semisweet and bittersweet, in combination and alone. Across the board, tasters preferred

the bold-but-balanced flavor of pies made with bittersweet chocolate. I tried different amounts and settled on 8 ounces, which I folded into the cooled egg and sugar mixture.

The filling tasted terrific, but it was much too dense when I beat in the two sticks of softened butter called for in the original recipe. Cutting the amount of butter in half got me closer to the satiny texture I wanted. But the filling wasn't quite silky or light enough.

Most recipes suggest serving the pie with whipped cream. I wondered if I could lighten the pie by incorporating whipped cream into the filling. I whipped 1 cup of cream, folded it into the chocolate mixture, and spooned the filling into the pie shell. I waited patiently for the pie to set (it took about three hours), sliced the pie, and dug in. The filling was light, but rich, thick, and chocolaty all at once. It was, finally, as smooth as French silk.

For a light, silky texture—without the raw eggs in the original recipe—we turned to a double boiler and an electric mixer.

1. Beating the eggs and sugar together in a double boiler incorporates air and gives the filling a light, ethereal texture.

2. When the egg mixture reaches 160 degrees, it will be very thick. Remove it from the heat and continue beating until it is fluffy and cool.

3. After incorporating the melted chocolate, beat in softened butter to give the pie rich flavor and silky-smooth texture.

FRENCH SILK CHOCOLATE PIE

Serves 8 to 10

You will need a fully baked pie shell for this recipe. Use your favorite pie dough or go to CooksCountry.com for our No-Fear Pie Crust recipe. Serve with lightly sweetened whipped cream.

- 1 cup heavy cream, chilled
- 3 large eggs
- ¾ cup sugar
- 2 tablespoons water
- 8 ounces bittersweet chocolate, melted and cooled
- 1 tablespoon vanilla extract
- 8 tablespoons (1 stick) unsalted butter, cut into ½-inch pieces and softened
- 1 (9-inch) pie shell, baked and cooled (see note)

1. WHIP CREAM With electric mixer on medium-high speed, whip cream to stiff peaks, 2 to 3 minutes. Transfer whipped cream to small bowl and refrigerate.

2. BEAT EGGS Combine eggs, sugar, and water in large heatproof bowl set over medium saucepan filled with ½ inch barely simmering water (don't let bowl touch water). With electric mixer on medium speed, beat until egg mixture is thickened and registers 160 degrees, 7 to 10 minutes. Remove bowl from heat and continue to beat egg mixture until fluffy and cooled to room temperature, about 8 minutes.

3. BEAT, FOLD, COOL Add chocolate and vanilla to cool egg mixture and beat until incorporated. Beat in butter, a few pieces at a time, until well combined. Using spatula, fold in whipped cream until no streaks of white remain. Scrape filling into pie shell and refrigerate until set, at least 3 hours and up to 24 hours. Serve.

The American Table

Birth of a Bake-Off

In 1949, General Mills launched what was to become the grand dame of the modern American recipe contest. Billed as the "Grand National Recipe and Baking Contest" (known today as the Pillsbury Bake-Off), it was held at the posh Waldorf-Astoria Hotel in New York. The grand-prize winner (for No-Knead Water Rising Twists) brought home $50,000; Eleanor Roosevelt was one of the luminaries on hand to present the awards. Since then, many prize-winning Pillsbury recipes have become part of our culinary heritage, among them Open Sesame Pie in 1954 (which caused a run on sesame seeds nationwide), Peanut Blossom Cookies (with the Hershey's Kiss in the middle), and Tunnel of Fudge Cake (which prodded Bundt pan factories into around-the-clock production to meet consumer demand).

Youngest contestant in the Bake-Off, 1961

DRESSING UP Rice Krispies Treats

We set out to dress up this kids' favorite for Valentine's Day. While we were at it, we put the back-of-the-box recipe under the test kitchen microscope. BY JEREMY SAUER

As irresistibly nostalgic as Rice Krispies treats are, we'd hardly hand them to a sweetheart in hopes of a kiss. To doll up this kid's classic for Valentine's Day, we first reviewed the back-of-the-cereal-box recipe and discovered that—with some minor adjustments—it held up to the test of time just fine. We found that using 5 cups of Rice Krispies cereal (as opposed to the 6 cups called for in the traditional recipe) to one 10-ounce bag of marshmallows produced creamier, richer treats, while a little vanilla extract and salt (both missing from the original recipe) added lots of flavor. Our tasters wanted thicker, more substantial squares, so we patted the mixture into an 8-inch square pan instead of the usual 13- by 9-inch pan.

We decided that the seasonal flavors of chocolate and cherries fit the bill, so I stirred 1 cup of chopped dried cherries in with the cereal (maraschino cherries were wet and messy, and fresh cherries made the treats soggy). Many recipes smother the cooled treats with a layer of melted chocolate, but we wanted flavor in, not just on, the treats. Dark chocolate gave the cereal an unattractive muddy look (though it worked nicely with Cocoa Krispies as a variation), so we melted white chocolate chips with the butter and marshmallows and saved the semisweet chocolate for a decorative drizzle on top.

Dried cherries and semisweet chocolate give these addictive treats a festive touch.

CRISPY CHOCOLATE CHERRY TREATS **Makes 16 squares**

Melt the chocolate by microwaving the chips in a small bowl until smooth, 30 to 60 seconds.

- 3 tablespoons unsalted butter
- 1 (10-ounce) bag marshmallows
- ½ cup white chocolate chips
- ½ teaspoon salt
- ¼ teaspoon vanilla extract
- 5 cups Rice Krispies cereal
- 1 cup dried cherries, chopped
- ½ cup semisweet chocolate chips, melted (see note)

1. PREPARE PAN Line 8-inch square baking pan with foil, allowing excess foil to hang over pan edges. Grease foil. Melt butter in large pot over low heat. Add marshmallows, white chocolate chips, and salt and cook, stirring constantly, until melted and smooth, about 8 minutes; stir in vanilla.

2. ASSEMBLE TREATS Off heat, stir in Rice Krispies and cherries until incorporated. Scrape mixture into prepared pan and press into bottom and corners with greased spatula. Let cool completely, about 1 hour.

3. DRIZZLE CHOCOLATE Drizzle melted semisweet chips over cooled treats. Allow chocolate to cool, about 15 minutes. Using foil overhang, lift treats from pan. Cut into squares. Serve.

DOUBLE CHOCOLATE CARAMEL TURTLE TREATS

Prepare Crispy Chocolate Cherry Treats, substituting ½ cup semisweet chocolate chips for white chocolate chips in step 1. Omit the cherries and stir in 15 soft caramel candies, quartered, and 1 cup chopped toasted pecans with Rice Krispies.

FLUFFER-NUTTER TREATS

Prepare Crispy Chocolate Cherry Treats, substituting ½ cup peanut butter chips for white chocolate chips, 1 cup dry-roasted peanuts for dried cherries, and ½ cup peanut butter chips for semisweet chocolate chips.

Equipment Review Plastic Wrap

Our tests showed that wraps either cling or keep food fresh—not both. BY MEREDITH BUTCHER

Plastic wrap is essential for storing, freezing, and keeping food fresh, but using it can drive you crazy: The roll rips and wraps around itself; the plastic clings to itself more than the dish or won't stick at all; the box falls apart, letting the roll drop out; the sharp metal teeth slice more than the plastic—or merely shred it; and most important, it doesn't keep food from spoiling quickly. Has any brand overcome these failings?

TUG OF WAR First, we measured strength by pulling foot-long pieces of wrap in a series of sharp, short tugs until they tore or lost their shape. Two brands shone, Stretch-Tite and Freeze-Tite, because they were almost impossible to destroy.

STICKY SITUATION To test the ability of the wraps to cling, we placed 8 ounces of grapes in plastic, metal, and glass bowls and covered each bowl with one sheet of wrap. With a few shakes of an inverted bowl, we instantly could see which wraps had the most cling—and which let the grapes fly out. All brands performed well on glass bowls. On metal, some brands failed in as few as three shakes, spilling grapes all over the counter. Others held their grip through all 10 shakes. Plastic bowls presented the biggest challenge, and only a few brands could hold on for even a few shakes. Just one wrap, Glad Press'n Seal, stuck through every shake on every surface, although Stretch-Tite came close.

FRESH TEST The most important test measured the ability of the wraps to keep foods fresh. We were looking for an impermeable wrap that prevented air and moisture from passing through. Since it was difficult to quantify "freshness" with a real-world food test (Check for mold? Off smells?), we took a scientific approach. We purchased a bottle of Indicating Drierite (calcium sulfate), an absorbent used in packaging, whose small purple-blue pebbles turn bright pink when exposed to moisture. We put 1 tablespoon of Drierite in small glass bowls covered tightly with a sheet of each wrap. After two days, the Drierite in bowls covered with Stretch-Tite, Freeze-Tite, and Reynolds Seal-Tight had turned bright pink, indicating that the wrap had allowed moisture in, which means food would spoil faster. The Drierite under the other wraps lasted more than three weeks without a color change, indicating that these wraps were impermeable. This shocked us: A leading

contender, Stretch-Tite, had failed. In disbelief, we repeated the test, with the same results. What had happened?

MATERIAL DIFFERENCES As it turns out, plastic wrap can be made from two distinctly different substances. The earliest plastic wrap was made of PVC (polyvinyl chloride), a highly clinging material. But plasticizers and chlorine in these wraps held a risk of food contamination, so manufacturers came up with safer substitutes. Some stuck with a new food-safe version of PVC; others switched to low-density polyethylene (LDPE). The main difference? PVC clings but is not

impermeable; LDPE is impermeable but has far less cling. Our research revealed that Stretch-Tite, Freeze-Tite, and Reynolds are all made of clingy PVC, and the rest of the lineup is less-clingy LDPE. Another style of LPDE wrap, marketed as "press'n seal" by Glad, is made with an edible dimpled adhesive. We don't like this style. While it works well initially, once the seal is broken (say, if you were taking a helping of potato salad out of a bowl), this wrap won't reattach.

GOOD DESIGN Our testers much preferred packaging with metal teeth on the top edge, inside the cover, to those

with teeth on the exposed bottom of the box, which were more apt to snag testers' clothing and skin. We liked boxes with a sticky pad on the front to hold the sheet, keeping it from rolling back on itself and getting tangled and crumpled. We've yet to find perfect packaging.

WRAPPING UP Clingy PVC wraps such as Reynolds, Stretch-Tite, and Freeze-Tite are preferable if you are transporting food or are worried about spills and leaks, but to keep foods fresh longer, select plastic wraps made from LDPE and reach for a box of our all-around winner, Glad Cling Wrap.

KEY Good ★★★ Fair ★★ Poor ★

RECOMMENDED	CRITERIA		TESTERS' NOTES
GLAD Cling Wrap Clear Plastic Price: $1.20 per 100 square feet Material: Low-Density Polyethylene (LDPE) 	Impermeability Strength and Cling Packaging	★★★ ★★ ★★	**Comments:** This wrap aced the impermeability test. Its box featured well-placed, sharp teeth that easily tore the plastic, and "Glad Grab" (a 1-inch adhesive pad to hold the cut end of the wrap). It clung slightly less well than PVC-based wraps, but it got the job done and offered good value.

RECOMMENDED WITH RESERVATIONS	CRITERIA		TESTERS' NOTES
STRETCH-TITE Plastic Food Wrap Price: $1.72 per 100 square feet Material: Polyvinyl Chloride (PVC) 	Impermeability Strength and Cling Packaging	★ ★★★ ★★	**Comments:** This wrap had the most cling and was by far the toughest of the lineup. Unfortunately, it was one of the first wraps to turn pink in the Drierite test, meaning it allowed moisture to penetrate. And without any adhesive on the box, the plastic wrap kept rolling back on itself.
SARAN Premium Wrap Price: $2.99 per 100 square feet Material: Low-Density Polyethylene (LDPE) 	Impermeability Strength and Cling Packaging	★★★ ★ ★★	**Comments:** Its easy "tear and restart" strip earned this wrap points, as did its ability to keep moisture out. However, it bombed the cling test, dropping the grapes after just three shakes of a metal bowl. Plus, it wouldn't stick to plastic bowls.
GLAD Press'n Seal Plastic Wrap Price: $4.56 per 100 square feet Material: Low-Density Polyethylene (LDPE) with Griptex 	Impermeability Strength and Cling Packaging	★★★ ★★ ★	**Comments:** This wrap will stick to anything, and it performed well in our moisture test, but its high price and inability to restick once the initial seal is broken pushed its rating down. Also, the frosted film makes it impossible to see into the bowl.
SARAN Cling Plus Wrap Price: $1 per 100 square feet Material: Low-Density Polyethylene (LDPE) 	Impermeability Strength and Cling Packaging	★★★ ★ ★	**Comments:** It passed the moisture-proof test and offered the best value of the lineup. But the box design, with sharp teeth along the bottom, sent testers running for Band-Aids. Also, while the wrap clung tightly to glass in the grape-shaking tests, the seal broke after six shakes of a metal bowl and just three in a plastic one.

NOT RECOMMENDED	CRITERIA		TESTERS' NOTES
FREEZE-TITE Freezer Wrap Price: $4.01 per 100 square feet Material: Polyvinyl Chloride (PVC) 	Impermeability Strength and Cling Packaging	★ ★★★ ★	**Comments:** This brand offered the widest sheets (14 5/8 inches versus the standard 12 inches) of the wraps we tested, but it failed our moisture-proof test. In the kitchen, that would mean freezer burn. Also, this wrap often tore as it was dispensed, and its price was among the highest per square foot.
REYNOLDS Seal-Tight Plastic Wrap Price: $2 per 100 square feet Material: Polyvinyl Chloride (PVC) 	Impermeability Strength and Cling Packaging	★ ★★ ★	**Comments:** This wrap frustrated testers within seconds. A "quick release" tab tore off, causing the wrap to stick to itself before testing even began. While its sticking performance was fine, it allowed moisture to penetrate within two days (compared to three weeks for other wraps).

Taste Test Hot Cocoa Mixes

The best cocoa mixes feature a double-dose of chocolate. BY SCOTT KATHAN

We wish that everybody had time to make homemade hot cocoa. It's not difficult—stir together cocoa, sugar, hot milk, and maybe a splash of vanilla and a pinch of salt. But we admit that instant mixes are unbeatably convenient. To find out which are best, we rounded up leading supermarket brands as well as mixes from a few upscale chocolatiers.

Following the instructions on the package, we used water to make the cocoas from Starbucks, Hershey's, and Land O'Lakes. Two of our contenders, Nestlé and Swiss Miss, can be reconstituted with either hot water or milk; we preferred them with 2 percent milk,

which we then used to make the mixes that called for milk. Across the board, tasters valued creaminess, which can come from either the added milk or from dry milk in the mix (all mixes that can be reconstituted with water contain some form of dried milk). In the end, however, what separated winners from losers was big chocolate flavor.

The cocoa mix from Godiva won in a landslide. The mix includes both Dutch-processed cocoa powder and bittersweet chocolate. Our runner-up, from Ghirardelli, also has two sources of chocolate: cocoa powder and unsweetened chocolate. Nestlé, a milder, milkier cocoa, captured third place. Tasters rated this kid-friendly cocoa the

creamiest of the lot, thanks not only to the "dairy product solids" on the ingredient list, but also to hydrogenated oils and stabilizers like guar gum. The last on our list of recommended brands, Barefoot Contessa, has notes of coffee and cinnamon, and is aimed squarely at grown-up palates.

What was wrong with the others? The mixes from Hershey's, Starbucks, and Land O'Lakes were all reconstituted with hot water, and they tasted watery. The cocoa from Swiss Miss was disgustingly sweet—on the ingredient list, sugar, corn syrup, and modified whey all precede cocoa powder. We've listed the cocoas below, with tasters' comments, in order of preference.

HIGHLY RECOMMENDED

GODIVA Chocolatier Dark Chocolate Hot Cocoa
Price: $10 for 14.5 ounces (about $0.91 per serving) at Godiva.com

TASTERS' NOTES

Comments: The "deep, rich chocolate flavor" and "nice depth" of this cocoa made it a hit: "I love everything about this one!" Tasters described it as "balanced and complex," with "intense" flavor and "a nice bitter edge" that made it "actually taste like chocolate."

RECOMMENDED

GHIRARDELLI Chocolate Premium Double Chocolate Hot Cocoa
Price: $5.19 for 16 ounces (about $0.47 per serving)

TASTERS' NOTES

Comments: The second most-chocolaty cocoa in our lineup (according to tasters), it won high marks for a "good balance of chocolate and sugar" and "good bitter chocolate taste." A few tasters complained, however, that the texture was "chalky."

NESTLÉ Rich Chocolate Flavor Hot Cocoa Mix
Price: $2.09 for 7.12 ounces (about $0.21 per serving)

Comments: This "creamy and sweet" hot chocolate transported several tasters back to the skating rinks and sledding hills of their childhoods. They described it as "frothy," "more milky than chocolaty," "bland but not unpleasant," and "just like Mom used to make."

BAREFOOT CONTESSA Sinful Hot Chocolate Mix
Price: $11.98 for 16 ounces (about $1.09 per serving) at Cooking.com

Comments: With both coffee and cinnamon supplementing the cocoa powder, this brand may not please children. But tasters found this "very dark and chocolaty" mix "rich, complex, a bit exotic." It's "not classic hot chocolate," one said, but many tasters liked it.

NOT RECOMMENDED

HERSHEY'S Goodnight Kisses Milk Chocolate Hot Cocoa Mix
Price: $2.19 for 5 ounces (about $0.55 per serving)

TASTERS' NOTES

Comments: "Tastes cheap," tasters said of this "thin, watery" mix. The ingredient list includes partially hydrogenated soybean and coconut oils as well as artificial flavors, so it's not surprising tasters detected a "weird, artificial taste."

STARBUCKS Gourmet Hot Cocoa
Price: $18.99 for 30 ounces (about $0.79 per serving)

Comments: This hot cocoa mix had "strong," "dark" chocolate flavor but was also "thin," "dull," and "watery," perhaps because the package calls for it to be stirred into hot water, not milk. Although this mix does contain nonfat dry milk, it was rated the least creamy of the lineup.

LAND O'LAKES Cocoa Classics Hot Cocoa Mix
Price: $6.46 for 15 ounces (about $0.54 per serving)

Comments: With its ingredient list full of polysyllabic items, we weren't surprised that tasters called this cocoa mix "plasticky." Tasters detected little chocolate flavor, but did note a vanilla or "white chocolate" presence. "Like a hot Yoo-hoo: thin and watery."

SWISS MISS Milk Chocolate Hot Cocoa Mix
Price: $1.99 for 10 ounces (about $0.20 per serving)

Comments: Its first two ingredients are sugar and corn syrup; tasters found this cocoa "really sweet," with "more sugar than chocolate." They rated it the sweetest of all with the second-weakest chocolate profile; one called it "super-mild and artificial."

All About Onions

There are more varieties of onions in the world than we care to count. We've listed below the ones that are commonly stocked in supermarkets. Store all onions in a cool, dry place with plenty of air circulation.

YELLOW

Yellow onions are the most common variety in the U.S. and are versatile in the kitchen. They have a robust flavor and a sturdy texture that can stand up

GO-TO VARIETY

to long cooking, and they store well. For all these reasons, yellow onions are our first choice in nearly every cooked application.

WHITE

White onions have more moisture than yellow onions, which makes them watery and bland in comparison. We're not fond of this variety's bitter aftertaste, either. In a pinch, white onions can substitute for yellow.

IF YOU MUST

RED

Red onions have a complex, peppery bite that makes them delicious raw. We like them in salads or salsas or sliced over burgers. Because cooking mellows them considerably, red onions can replace shallots in most cooked applications.

PEPPERY PUNCH

SHALLOTS

Shallots have the same papery skin as onions but are usually composed of multiple cloves. Their flavor is

SMALL AND MILD

sweeter and more complex ("peppery" and "mineral-y") than many other onion varieties, with scant sharpness or bite. We like to use raw minced shallots in vinaigrettes and cold salads or to roast shallots whole alongside roasting meats or poultry.

SWEETS

Known for their mild flavor and high moisture and sugar content, "sweets" are grown in temperate climates such as Vidalia, Ga., and Walla Walla, Wash. (places that give two regional varieties their names). We like sweet

CANDY GIRL

onions raw, grilled, or quickly cooked. Avoid caramelizing, where their high sugar level makes them saccharine. Sweet onions (others include Texas 1015s and Maui onions) spoil faster than other varieties.

Notes from the Test Kitchen

Best Wine for Cooking

What's the best type of red wine to use for cooking? To find out, we tested more than 30 bottles—from $5 jug wines to a $30 Bordeaux—using each to make a hearty tomato sauce, a quick-cooking pan sauce, and a slow-simmered beef stew. When the dust settled, we were able to divine a few general guidelines. First, save the expensive wine for drinking. Although one or two tasters perceived "greater complexity" in the pan sauces made with the $30 bottles, the differences were minimal at best; wines that cost $10 and under are usually fine for cooking. Second, stick with blends like Côtes du Rhône or generically labeled "table" wines that use a combination of grapes to yield a balanced, fruity finish. If you prefer single grape varietals, choose medium-bodied wines, such as Pinot Noir and Merlot. Steer clear of oaky wines like Cabernet Sauvignon, which turn bitter when cooked. Finally, whatever you do, avoid the "cooking wines" sold in supermarkets. These low-alcohol concoctions have little flavor, a high-pitched acidity, and enormous amounts of salt, all of which combine to produce inedible dishes.

Test Kitchen Technique
The Oven Keeps It Even

In the test kitchen, we prefer to cook stews and braises (such as pot roast) in the oven, where the heat surrounds the food evenly. On the stovetop, the heat can fluctuate, and the food on the bottom of the pot can scorch, so continual stirring is a must. This method works well for our **Chicken in a Pot** recipe (page 21), which has relatively little liquid in the pot in order to produce a concentrated sauce. In the oven, the food in the entire pot cooks at the same rate—without stirring.

For even heat, we turn to the oven rather than the stovetop.

Test Kitchen Technique **Separation Anxiety**

Separate the leaves of tender greens from their stems before you begin cooking. In some cases, the stems are tough and stringy and you'll want to discard them. Or, as with Swiss chard, since the stems take longer to cook than the leaves, the stems should start cooking sooner. Here is how we like to stem beet greens, curly-leaf spinach, and Swiss chard—not incidentally, the three greens we recommend using (alone or in combination) in **Garlicky Greens with Andouille and Onion** (page 14).

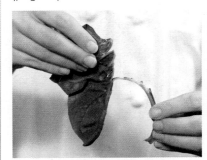 

BEET GREENS OR CURLY-LEAF SPINACH Hold each leaf with one hand and use the other hand to pull down and remove the stem.

SWISS CHARD Steady each leaf near the base of the stem, then use a sharp knife to cut the leaves from each side of the stem.

The Baking Stone Advantage

The crust on our **Make-Ahead Pizza** (page 6) was doughy and soft until we started baking the pizza on a ceramic baking stone. Baking stones (aka pizza stones) are prized for their ability to retain heat and lessen the effects of hot spots and temperature fluctuations in home ovens. The stones also absorb moisture, so the pizzas, breads, and calzones you bake on them emerge drier and crispier. To use a baking stone, place it either on the oven rack or the floor of the oven before you turn the oven on. Allow 30 to 45 minutes for it to heat through. When shopping for a pizza stone, look for large stones without lipped edges. Edges make it hard to place and remove the food. Many styles are available; our favorite is the Baker's Catalogue Pizza Baking Stone. We like its moderate weight and good size (16½ inches by 14½ inches).

Corn Tortilla Taste-Test

Fresh corn tortillas can be wrapped around fillings for soft tacos and enchiladas, fried and shaped into hard taco shells, or cut into wedges and fried to make tortilla chips. To figure out what makes a corn tortilla stand out, we tasted six brands. We tried them lightly heated, as if for soft tacos, and oven-"fried" until crisp. The flavor differences between the brands were slight, but we did find some textural differences. Thicker tortillas browned poorly in the oven and emerged chewy instead of crisp. Oven-fried thin tortillas, however, were feather-light and crisp. Remember to look at the label before you buy: We recommend tortillas made with nothing but ground corn treated with lime (an alkali that removes the germ and hull) and water. You're best sticking with brands sold in the refrigerator case of the supermarket. These have few, if any, preservatives, and our tasters found them moist and flavorful.

Easier Melted Chocolate

Put away your double boiler. When it comes to melting chocolate, we prefer the ease of the microwave. To ensure even melting, finely chop the chocolate, place it in a microwave-safe bowl, and cover it with plastic wrap. Microwave the chocolate on 50 percent power for 2 minutes, then stir the chocolate and continue heating until melted, stirring once every additional minute. If the recipe calls for melting chocolate and butter together, add the butter after the first 2 minutes.

Buying Brisket

Our recipe for **Slow Cooker BBQ Beef Brisket** (page 5) calls for a 4- to 5-pound brisket roast. Whole briskets weigh upward of 10 pounds, so they're typically butchered and sold as two separate cuts: point and flat. Point-cut brisket is fattier, irregularly shaped, and not readily available in most supermarkets. Even with access to both cuts, we prefer the flatter, leaner flat-cut brisket. Be sure to buy a brisket roast with some fat attached—the fat will render during cooking, resulting in moister meat.

Gadgets and Gear Cakes

The right tools will make preparing any cake easier than you think.

9-INCH ROUND CAKE PAN

The best cake pans are sturdy enough [to] withstand denting and have tall, straight sides to accommodate high-rising cakes.

★ **TEST KITCHEN WINNER**
CHICAGO METALLIC Professional Lifetime 9-inch Nonstick Cake Pan, $14.95

PARCHMENT PAPER

Parchment paper is paper that has bee[n] treated with sulfuric acid and coated in silicone to make it heat-resistant and impervious to grease and moisture. We use parchment paper to line cake pan[s] and baking sheets.

★ **TEST KITCHEN WINNER**
REYNOLDS Parchment Paper, $4.99

NONSTICK BAKING SPRAY

Nonstick baking sprays are a mixture of vegetable oil and flour. They are easier to apply than the traditional butter and flour coat, plus they work better, making for easier, neater releasing.

LARGE OFFSET SPATULA

The wide blade and crook shape of th[e] spatula allow for excellent control to make icing cakes easier. We also use offset spatulas to spread brownie and cake batter into large pans evenly.

★ **TEST KITCHEN WINNER**
ATECO 8½-inch Offset Spatula, $5

WIRE RACK

A good wire rack should be sturdy, be able to withstand a hot oven or broiler, and clean up without warping or damage. We prefer grid-style racks with crisscrossing bars, which leave few[er] marks on cakes and cookies. Larger racks, like our winner below, fit snugly i[n] an 18- by 13-inch sheet pan.

★ **TEST KITCHEN WINNER**
LIBERTY CROSS Wire Cooling Rack, $5.95

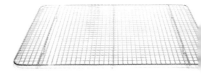

Test Kitchen Cooking Lesson Pan-Searing Steaks

Cooking steaks in a skillet is fast but hardly foolproof. Who hasn't ruined good steaks with imperfect technique? The secrets we've uncovered in the test kitchen guarantee reliable results—no extra time necessary.

1. TRIM FAT Expect splattering when searing steaks on your cooktop. To keep the mess to a minimum, trim any hard, white fat from the perimeter of the steaks. Leave no more than ⅛ inch of fat. Place a splatter screen covered with fine mesh over the skillet to reduce splattering further.

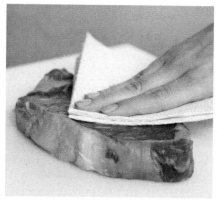

2. PAT DRY FOR BETTER FLAVOR We've found that blotting steaks dry with paper towels yields tastier steaks. The moisture that collects in shrink-wrapped packages inhibits browning; since browning equals flavor, the moisture must go.

3. SEASON LIBERALLY Before cooking, sprinkle steaks with kosher salt (we've found that the large crystals ensure even distribution) and freshly ground black pepper. Use ½ teaspoon of kosher salt per steak and as much pepper as you like. Remember to season both sides of the steak.

4. LET PAN SIZZLE Put steaks in a too-cool pan and they'll stick and fail to develop a proper crust. But how do you know the pan is hot enough? Heat 1 tablespoon of vegetable oil over medium-high heat. When the oil just begins to smoke, the pan is ready.

5. GIVE THEM ROOM Lay the steaks in the pan, making sure to leave a little room between them. If you crowd the pan, the steaks will steam rather than sear, and they won't brown. A 12-inch skillet is a must for cooking 4 small steaks.

6. LEAVE THEM BE Don't fuss with steaks as they cook. Leaving the meat in place helps build a better crust. After 3 or 4 minutes, lift the edge of a steak to check on browning. Don't use a fork to turn steaks. Skewering the meat can lead to loss of juices. Instead, grab each steak with tongs and flip onto the second side.

7. GET THE TEMPERATURE RIGHT Don't cut into steaks to gauge doneness. Use tongs to lift a steak out of the pan and then slide in an instant-read thermometer. Here are the temperatures to look for: 115 degrees (rare), 125 degrees (medium-rare), 135 (medium), 145 (medium-well), and 155 (well-done).

8. REST BEFORE SERVING Letting steaks rest on a plate loosely covered with foil gives the meat time to reabsorb juices otherwise lost when steaks are cut. Those 5 to 10 minutes also give you time to turn the flavorful browned bits in the pan into a quick pan sauce (see page 7).

Don't Make This Mistake

Buying Bone-In Steaks While bones add great flavor, they also prevent steaks from maintaining direct contact with the hot pan. Bone-in steaks are fine for grilling, but when pan-searing, stick with boneless cuts that will rest flush on the pan.

Buying Select Meat Steer clear of steaks labeled "select." They contain very little fat and will be dry and not terribly flavorful. Choice steaks, with thin white lines of fat running throughout the meat, are a much better bet.

Buying Big Steaks Extra-thick steaks are hard to cook through in a skillet (save them for grilling). When pan-searing, buy steaks that are 1 to 1¼ inches thick.

SMART SHOPPING Small Price, Big Flavor
It's hard to go wrong with a high-priced steak. (Our favorites are the strip, rib-eye, and tenderloin.) But are there any good steaks that don't cost a fortune? To find out, we tasted a dozen choices (all about half the cost of the premium cuts). Our favorite cheap steak for pan-searing is the top sirloin (also known as the boneless shell sirloin, New

TOP SIRLOIN

York sirloin, sirloin butt, or top butt). A top sirloin steak usually weighs about 1 pound and will serve two.

THE RIGHT STUFF The Pan Matters
To cook four steaks, use a heavy-bottomed 12-inch pan. We like pans with stainless steel exteriors and aluminum cores. These pans hold heat, and their shiny surface makes it easy to judge browning. You can get decent browning in a nonstick skillet, but there

ALL-CLAD
12-INCH SKILLET

won't be much fond, and you need these bits to make a tasty pan sauce. Cast iron can put a terrific crust on steaks; but acidic pan sauces can react with the pan and take on an off-flavor.

Looking for a Recipe

ARE YOU LOOKING FOR A SPECIAL RECIPE?

Cook's Country is the place where readers can help track down recipes for each other. Post your requests—and recipes that others have requested—at **CooksCountry.com** and click **Looking for a Recipe**. We'll share all your submissions on the website and print as many as we can in the magazine. You may also write to us at Looking for a Recipe, Cook's Country, P.O. Box 470739, Brookline, MA 02447.

Farina Soup
Pam Bartlett, New Britain, Conn.

I am looking for a recipe for the farina soup that my grandmother used to make when I was little. Unfortunately, I was not able to get her recipe before she passed away. I remember she would bring chicken broth to a boil and drop in balls of farina, shortening, and egg to cook. I hope someone out there can help. I would love to have it again and make it for my grandchildren.

Sauerkraut Pie
Pauline Taylor, Canisteo, N.Y.

I recently heard about a pie brought to Minnesota by Scandinavians called Sauerkraut Pie. I'm not exactly sure what it is but I love sauerkraut and am interested in trying new dishes that include it. If anyone has a recipe, I'd appreciate them sharing it. Thanks!

Tourtière
Sandra Holevas, Chanhassen, Minn.

I'm looking for a recipe for the traditional French-Canadian meat pie known as tourtière. It's a holiday specialty in my part of the country, and when done well, is a real treat. Yet every time I've attempted it, the bottom crust became soggy from excess grease. I'd love to have a recipe that actually works!

Midnight Cake
MaryAnn Salsgiver, Star, Idaho

When I was growing up, my mother's cousin made a wonderful chocolate cake called midnight cake. These relatives are now gone, and I can't find a copy of this recipe. Has anyone heard of it? I know that it called for cocoa, but that is all I can remember. I also suspect that it was published in the *New York Daily News* years and years ago, but they can't find any evidence of it. Any help would be much appreciated.

The Tavern's Coffee Cake
Pam Saletan, North Bergen, N.J.

During the 1950s, there was a restaurant in Newark called The Tavern. They made a yeasted coffee cake that was truly outstanding. I have tried many versions but none equal The Tavern's light, yeasty cake packed with cinnamon and raisins. I know that someone must have this recipe.

Christmas Bread
Linda Smith, Warsaw, Va.

About 30 years ago, I had a recipe for a bread shaped like a Christmas tree. It was not a yeasted bread and was very quick and mildly sweet. I have been looking for years for a similar recipe with no success. Can you help?

Triple-Layer Loaf
Michael J. Naydock, Hazleton, Pa.

I am looking for a special recipe for a three-layer cake baked in a loaf pan. The bottom is spice-flavored, the center is chocolate, and the top is vanilla. I remember that the spice layer had hot coffee in the batter and that the baked cake was finished with a thin icing.

Apple-Carrot Cake
Kathy Miller, via e-mail

Some years back, my husband bought me an Oster Kitchen Center. It came with a cookbook that had a recipe for an apple-carrot cake. It was wonderful and my grandson asked for it every year as his birthday cake. I lost my book when we moved and have missed the recipe ever since. My grandson's birthday is coming up and I would love to surprise him with this cake!

Chocolate Chip Cake
Lois Benvenuti, North Adams, Mass.

When I was teaching school, a student from the Webatuck, New York, school system presented me with a cake. It was a very moist and flavorful white (or maybe yellow) cake with chocolate chips and walnuts in it. I was given the recipe, but it has since been lost in a move. Does anyone have a similar recipe?

Crimp Bread
Shannon Phelan, Swampscott, Mass.

This weekend I picked up a loaf of Crimp Bread from a local farm. It was shaped like a tube and the outside was coated in cinnamon and sugar. I tried to find a recipe and a little history for this bread online but had no success. Have you heard of it?

FIND THE ROOSTER!

A tiny version of the rooster depicted on the front cover has been hidden somewhere in the pages of this issue. If you find it, write to us with its location (plus your name and address) and you will be entered into a random drawing. The first correct entry drawn will receive a Michael Graves Design Hamilton Beach 4-Slice Toaster (our top-rated toaster), and the next five will each receive a complimentary one-year subscription to *Cook's Country*. To enter the contest, visit **CooksCountry.com/emailus** or write to us at Rooster, Cook's Country, P.O. Box 470739, Brookline, MA 02447. Entries are due by January 31, 2009.

Did you find the rooster in the August/September 2008 issue? It was hidden in the Beef and Vegetable Kebabs photo on page 10. Diane Tyler of Kirby, Texas, spotted it and won an Anolon Advanced Double Burner Griddle.

Our Favorite Responses This Month

LEMON SPONGE PIE Serves 8
Ethel Carey, Warren, R.I.

"My mom used to make this pie years ago, and I remember it for its fluffy, spongelike top layer and creamy base." Use your favorite pie dough or go to CooksCountry.com for our recipe.

- 2 eggs, separated
- 1 cup sugar
- 3 tablespoons butter, softened
- 3 tablespoons flour
- 1 large lemon, zested and juiced
- 1 cup milk
- 1 (9-inch) unbaked pie shell

1. Adjust oven rack to lowest position and heat oven to 325 degrees. Whip egg whites to soft peaks. In separate bowl, beat sugar, butter, and egg yolks until creamy. Mix in flour, lemon zest, lemon juice, and milk. Fold in whipped egg whites.

2. Pour filling into crust and bake until golden brown and toothpick inserted into center comes out clean, 50 to 60 minutes. Cool and serve. (Pie can be wrapped in plastic and refrigerated for 2 days.)

ROSLYN'S BUTTERMILK COOKIES
Makes about 3½ dozen cookies
Erin Margenau, Fort Collins, Colo.

"Roslyn's Bakery has been sorely missed by my family since it closed, but luckily I have a recipe for their soft and delicate buttermilk cookies." You will need a piping bag with a large star tip for this recipe.

- 1 cup sugar
- 1⅓ cups vegetable shortening
- ½ teaspoon salt
- 1 large egg
- 1 teaspoon vanilla extract
- 2½ cups cake flour
- ½ teaspoon baking soda
- 6 tablespoons buttermilk

1. Adjust oven racks to upper-middle and lower-middle positions and heat oven to 375 degrees. Line two baking sheets with parchment paper.

2. Beat sugar, shortening, and salt until light and fluffy, about 2 minutes. Mix in egg and vanilla until combined. Add flour, baking soda, and buttermilk and mix until light and fluffy, about 2 minutes. Transfer dough to piping bag fitted with large star tip.

3. For each cookie, pipe 1 star surrounded by 6 stars onto prepared baking sheets, spacing cookies 2 inches apart. Bake until light golden, 10 to 15 minutes. Cool on baking sheets. Repeat with remaining dough. Serve. (Cookies can be stored in airtight container at room temperature for up to 3 days.)

Smith Island Cake

Smith Island, Maryland, may be a small place, but it boasts a cake with a reputation so grand, it recently became the official state dessert. With its multiple cake layers and rich, fudgy frosting, Smith Island Cake looks impressive, yet it doesn't require the precise cutting of layers that you might think.

To make this cake you will need:

- **10 ounces bittersweet chocolate, chopped**
- **1 cup heavy cream**
- **1 cup sugar**
- **¼ teaspoon salt**
- **1 teaspoon vanilla extract**
- **8 tablespoons (1 stick) unsalted butter, softened**
- **1 recipe yellow layer cake batter (enough to make two 8-inch layers; about 5⅓ cups of batter)***

For the frosting: Place chocolate in large bowl. Heat cream, sugar, and salt in saucepan over medium-low heat, stirring occasionally, until sugar dissolves and mixture begins to simmer. Pour hot cream mixture over chocolate and whisk until smooth. Whisk in vanilla and butter until glossy. Cover and refrigerate until icing is firm but still spreadable, about 1 hour.

For the cake: Adjust oven rack to middle position and heat oven to 350 degrees. Grease and flour two 8-inch cake pans and line with parchment paper. Spread one-eighth of batter (about ⅔ cup) evenly in each pan and bake until edges are golden brown and cake springs back when touched, 10 to 14 minutes. Cool on rack 5 minutes. Run a knife around pan perimeter to loosen cake, then invert onto rack to finish cooling. Cool pans to room temperature, then wipe clean and repeat process 3 more times for a total of 8 layers.

To assemble: Place 1 cooled cake layer on serving platter. Spread ¼ cup frosting over cake. (If frosting is too firm, let warm at room temperature 5 minutes, then stir to soften.) Top with second cake layer and additional ¼ cup frosting. Repeat, alternating layers of cake and frosting and finishing with cake layer. Frost top and sides with remaining frosting. Serve.

*Go to CooksCountry.com for our Yellow Layer Cake recipe or use your own.

Recipe Index

RC = Recipe Card

Cook's Country

APRIL/MAY 2009

Lemony Chicken
Crispy, Zesty, Easy

Make-Ahead Mac & Cheese
New Freezer-to-Oven Recipe

Au Gratin Potatoes
Cheesy, Creamy, Not Greasy

The Best Quiche
With Pat-in-the-Pan Crust

Lemon Pudding Cake
Fluffy Cake, Silky Sauce

Pie Plate Bake-Off!
Eight Models Rated

Beef Enchilada Casserole
Retooling a Tex-Mex Classic

Slow-Cooker Cacciatore
Foil Packet Seals in Juices

Tasting Strawberry Yogurts
Real Berry Flavor, Anyone?

Healthy Carrot Cake
Our Secret Fat Fake-Out

Chicken-Fried Steak
Crunchy, Tender, Hot, Salty!

Grill-Roasted Ham
Smoky, Crackling Crust

Watch Our New Show on Public Television!
Cook's Country from America's Test Kitchen debuted last fall on public television stations across the country. The show relies on the same practical, no-nonsense recipes that have made *Cook's Country* magazine an indispensable resource for the home cook. Watch us develop recipes, test equipment, and taste supermarket ingredients. Go to **CooksCountryTV.com** to learn more.

$4.95 U.S./$6.95 CANADA

0 5>

0 74470 05251 7

Cook's Country

Dear Country Cook,

Long before the rise of the supermarket, American settlers bought from door-to-door peddlers. By the mid-19th century, retailers had sprung up, offering staples and household goods and even importing olive oil from Italy and mushrooms from France. The first chain grocery store, the Great Atlantic and Pacific Tea Company, was founded in New York City in 1859. The A&P turned into a large chain operation (14,000 small neighborhood stores by 1925), and then Piggly Wiggly came along in Memphis in 1916 with a brand-new concept: the checkout counter, an innovation that saved labor.

I grew up in Vermont, where eggs, bread, milk, meat, and many fruits and vegetables were produced on our small farm, and everything else—mostly staples—was purchased at the Wayside Country Store. I remember some pretty odd foods, including pickled calf's tongue kept in large, green glass jars (sealed with wax paper and rubber bands), eggs that were hard-cooked in the evaporator out back by Fred Woodcock during sugaring season, and slow-cooker spaghetti sauce made from squirrel. Today, the wheel seems to have started turning in reverse as our family once again grows or raises much of what we consume, including beef, pork, eggs, potatoes, apples, honey, maple syrup, jams and jellies. But that doesn't mean that we aren't happy about the new Price Chopper opening just a few miles down the road!

All of this makes me think about what it means to be a country cook. The food can come from the garden out back or from the supermarket, but when someone mentions country cooking, I always remember the people first: Marie Briggs comes to mind before her Anadama Bread does. Maybe that's why I love country food so much. There's a real cook in every bite.

Christopher Kimball
Founder and Editor, Cook's Country Magazine

Cook's Country

Founder and Editor Christopher Kimball
Editorial Director Jack Bishop
Executive Editor Peggy Grodinsky
Deputy Editor Bridget Lancaster
Senior Editors Scott Kathan, Lisa McManus, Jeremy Sauer
Test Kitchen Director Erin McMurrer
Associate Editors Cali Rich, Diane Unger
Test Cooks Lynn Clark, Kris Widican
Assistant Editors Meredith Butcher, Peggy Chung Collier
Assistant Test Cooks Meghan Erwin, María del Mar Sacasa
Assistant Test Kitchen Director Matthew Herron
Copy Editor Amy Graves
Editorial Assistant Abbey Becker

Online Managing Editor David Tytell
Online Editor Kate Mason
Online Associate Editor Leaya Lee
Online Editorial Assistant Mari Levine
Executive Assistant Meredith Smith
Senior Kitchen Assistant Nadia Domeq
Kitchen Assistants Maria Elena Delgado, Ena Gudiel
TV Producer Melissa Baldino
Contributing Editor Eva Katz
Consulting Editor Meg Ragland
Science Editor Guy Crosby, Ph. D

Design Director Amy Klee
Art Director, Magazines Julie Bozzo
Designers, Magazines Jay Layman, Lindsey Timko
Deputy Art Director, Marketing and Web Christine Vo
Staff Photographer Daniel J. van Ackere

Director, Information Technology Rocco Lombardo
Systems Administrator S. Paddi McHugh
Web Production Coordinator Evan Davis
IT Support Technician Brandon Lynch

Production Director Guy Rochford
Traffic & Projects Manager Alice Carpenter
Production & Imaging Specialists Judy Blomquist, Lauren Pettapiece
Color & Imaging Specialist Andrew Mannone

Vice President Marketing David Mack
Circulation Director Doug Wicinski
Fulfillment & Circulation Manager Carrie Horan
Partnership Marketing Manager Pamela Putprush
Marketing Assistant Megan Cooley
Direct Mail Director Adam Perry
Marketing Database Analyst Ariel Gilbert-Knight
Products Director Steven Browall
Product Promotions Director Randi Lawrence
E-Commerce Marketing Director Hugh Buchan
E-Commerce Marketing Manager Laurel Zeidman
Marketing Copywriter David Goldberg
Customer Service Manager Jacqueline Valerio
Customer Service Representatives Jillian Nannicelli, Kate Sokol

Chief Financial Officer Sharyn Chabot
Human Resources Director Adele Shapiro
Controller Mandy Shito
Senior Accountant Aaron Goranson
Staff Accountant Connie Forbes
Accounts Payable Specialist Steven Kasha
Office Manager Tasha Bere
Receptionist Henrietta Murray

Sponsorship Sales Director Marcy McCreary
Retail Sales & Marketing Manager Emily Logan
Corporate Marketing Associate Bailey Vatalaro
Publicity Deborah Broide

COLOR FOOD PHOTOGRAPHY: Keller + Keller
STYLING: Mary Jane Sawyer
ON THE COVER: Apricots, H. Armstrong Roberts/Stringer

ILLUSTRATION: Russell Brocklehurst
Greg Stevenson (cover illustration)

Cook's Country magazine (ISSN 1552-1990), number 26, published bimonthly by Boston Common Press Limited Partnership, 17 Station Street, Brookline, MA 02445. Copyright 2009 Boston Common Press Limited Partnership. Periodicals Postage paid at Boston, Mass., and additional mailing offices. Publications Mail Agreement No. 40020778. Return undeliverable Canadian addresses to P.O. Box 875, Station A, Windsor, Ontario N9A 6P2. POSTMASTER: Send address changes to Cook's Country, P.O. Box 382, Red Oak, IA 51591-1382. **Customer Service:** It's easy to subscribe, give a gift subscription, change your address, and manage your subscription online. Visit www.americastestkitchen.com/customerservice for all of your customer service needs or write to us at Cook's Country, P.O. Box 8382, Red Oak, IA 51591-1382.
PRINTED IN THE USA

Contents

APRIL/MAY 2009

DREAM BARS, 17

WALDORF SALAD, 11

ROAST LEMON CHICKEN, 15

Features

In Every Issue

America's TEST KITCHEN

America's Test Kitchen is a 2,500-square-foot kitchen located just outside of Boston. It is the home of *Cook's Country* and *Cook's Illustrated* magazines and is the workday destination for more than three dozen test cooks, editors, and cookware specialists. Our mission is to test recipes until we understand how and why they work and arrive at the best version. We also test kitchen equipment and supermarket ingredients in search of brands that offer the best value and performance. You can watch us work by tuning in to *America's Test Kitchen* (www.americastestkitchen.com) on public television.

Kitchen Shortcuts

Egg Tray

Rebecca Fingleton
Breckenridge, Colo.

I make a lot of custards with just the yolks of eggs, leaving me with an abundance of egg whites. I like to freeze them for later use, but I learned the hard way that once they are frozen, it's impossible to separate them from each other. So I drop each egg white into an ice cube tray to freeze. Once they're frozen, I transfer them to a zipper-lock bag and then can pull one or two out, as needed.

SMART PREP
Speedy Chile Seeding

Kelly Johnson
Austin, Texas

My family likes the mild heat of jalapeños, but if I don't remove the seeds and ribs, they can be too spicy for the kids. I figured out an efficient way to remove them: I slice off both ends of the chile pepper and insert an apple corer into the center. A quick twist and the ribs and seeds come out in one fell swoop!

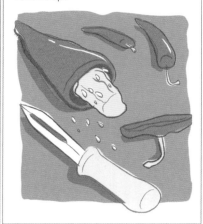

KITCHEN EFFICIENCY
Garlic Microwave Magic

Ashley Byers
Maui, Hawaii

When recipes call for whole, peeled garlic, I've found that rather than tediously peeling off the papery skin, if I zap the cloves in the microwave for 15 seconds, the skins slip right off.

HANDY TIP
Rosemary Whirlwind, Tamed

Patty Maguder
Alexandria, Va.

I always find chopping fresh or dried rosemary to be a real chore. The spindly needles go flying all over the kitchen, and I lose half of what I've chopped. But if I pour just enough oil on the needles to barely moisten them, I can chop with ease.

If you'd like to submit a tip, please e-mail us by visiting **CooksCountry.com/kitchenshortcuts** or send a letter to Kitchen Shortcuts, Cook's Country, P.O. Box 470739, Brookline, MA 02447. Include your name, address, and phone number. If we publish your tip, you will receive a free one-year subscription to *Cook's Country*.

DOUBLE DUTY
Improvised Rack

Irene Kim
Lakeside, Ariz.

I live in a small apartment, so I don't have a lot of storage space for kitchen accessories. One day I wanted to make a roast chicken, but the recipe called for a roasting rack, which I don't have. I searched around the house for a substitute and uncovered my collection of metal holiday cookie cutters. I placed the cutters in the roasting pan and put the chicken on top. They worked perfectly to lift the chicken off the bottom of the pan.

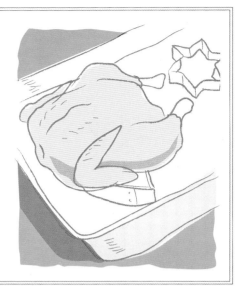

KITCHEN EFFICIENCY
Slaw Spin Cycle

Colleen Costigan
San Diego, Calif.

Many recipes for coleslaw call for salting and draining the cabbage as a way to avoid watery slaw. To make neat work of this, I use my salad spinner. I salt the cabbage in the spinner insert, let it sit, then rinse the slaw, and spin. No more watery coleslaw!

HANDY TIP
Meat Mash

Jodi Comiskey
Chehalis, Wash.

While cooking ground beef and sausage for meat sauce, I discovered that a whisk works better than a wooden spoon to break up the meat, especially leaner sausage, into evenly sized bits.

DOUBLE DUTY
French Fry Lifter

Bob Grant
Bangor, Maine

I like to cook while I'm on vacation, so we usually rent a house rather than stay in a hotel. On one recent trip, I was frying French fries for the family and realized I didn't have a spider strainer, which I use at home to scoop the fried food from the hot oil. The house did have a grid-style potato masher, however, and I found that I could use it to pull a bunch of the fries out of the hot oil at a time.

Ask Cook's Country

Can I leave my pizza stone in the oven when I'm not baking pizza?
Audrey Kurn, Hanover, N.H.

Pizza stones are finely porous, ceramic slabs that mimic the high heat of commercial pizza ovens to develop crisp crusts on pizza and bread baked at home. As the oven is preheated, the stone gradually absorbs and stores heat. Once the stone is searing hot, the dough is placed directly on it. As the dough bakes, the clay absorbs moisture, further promoting a crackly crust.

Can they be left in the oven all the time? Some sources claim that the heat-retaining stone ensures a more consistent oven temperature since the heating elements in ovens cycle up and down. We tested three configurations of this, baking sugar cookies, pie crusts, and yellow layer cakes in ovens without a stone, with a stone on the rack above the baking sweets, and with a stone on the rack below. We found that the stone consistently impeded browning on the surface closest to it (see bottom photo below), thus extending baking time.

When we tried placing baking sheets directly on the stone, the stone caused slight over-browning on the bottom of the baked goods. We recommend removing your pizza stone from the oven when you're not baking pizza or bread.

BAKED EVENLY
Baked with no pizza stone in oven.

BROWNING IMPEDED
Baked with pizza stone on rack below.

Help! I'm always throwing out rotting fresh herbs. How can I dry them?
Shelley Carlisle, Cedar Point, N.C.

Air-drying herbs can take several weeks, but we found that drying them (OK, some of them) in a microwave can be a quick, easy alternative. Lay a single layer of herbs on a paper towel–lined plate and cover with a second paper towel. Microwave on high power for 1 to 3 minutes, checking occasionally, until the herb appears slightly dehydrated. Cool at room temperature and then crumble or store whole in a plastic bag.

We used this method to test a slew of herbs. It worked with hearty herbs such as bay leaf, oregano, rosemary, sage, and thyme. But delicate, moist herbs such as basil, cilantro, dill, and parsley actually combusted and ignited the paper towel!

My buttercream frosting always turns out thin and soupy. What am I doing wrong?
Nicola Ray, Easton, Conn.

We usually frost our cakes with a quick, no-cook version of buttercream frosting made by creaming together softened butter and confectioners' sugar (sometimes called American buttercream). But traditional buttercream (European buttercream), which is intensely rich, silken, and buttery, is quite a bit more complicated, and we're guessing that's what you're asking about. It's made by heating a mixture of eggs and sugar to 160 degrees over a pan of simmering water. The mixture is taken off the heat and beaten until it's light and airy and has cooled to room temperature. Bit by bit, softened butter is whipped in.

European buttercream is quite sensitive. If it's overheated, it can easily become runny; essentially the butter melts. Fortunately, the problem is easy to fix: Simply plunge the bowl of frosting into ice water and whisk the buttercream until it has thickened. If, on the other hand, the frosting appears curdled, it is probably too cold and the butter has "seized." In this case, wrap a hot water–soaked towel around the bowl to warm it and whisk the mixture until smooth.

How do cup measurements for cheese translate into weight measurements?
Kate Chuprevich, Monmouth, Maine

Our recipes specify cup amounts of cheese instead of weights to reflect the habits of the typical home cook. But cheese is sold by weight, so it can be hard to determine how much to buy. Also, one person's measure may not precisely equal another's. To complicate matters, we classify cheese into three categories: hard, such as Parmesan and Pecorino Romano; semisoft, such as cheddar and Monterey Jack; and soft, such as feta, blue, and fresh goat cheeses. Each packs into cup measures differently.

To develop a standard weight for each cheese category, we gathered 10 test cooks and had each weigh out 1-cup samples of each type. We averaged the weights to account for the heavy and lighter hands of different individuals. We found that 1 cup of grated hard cheese equals about 2 ounces, while the same measure of soft and semisoft is about 4 ounces. And remember, when measuring cheese, lightly pack measuring cups meant for dry ingredients; don't use liquid measuring cups.

If a recipe calls for salt pork or fatback, can I use bacon instead?
Sophie Wyatt, Bozeman, Mont.

While all three of these pork products are used to add flavor to soups, stews, and braises, they cannot be used interchangeably. Bacon and salt pork are both cured meat from the hog's belly, but bacon is usually smoked and thus has a distinctive flavor. Salt pork is fattier than bacon and is usually removed from the pot before serving. Fat back, which (as you might have guessed) comes from the hog's back, is raw fat that has not been salted, smoked, or cured, making it much more perishable than the other products.

I've heard Sili Twists are handy for trussing chicken and tying roasts. Are they?
Jay Bomze, Bryn Mawr, Pa.

Silicone Zone's 16-inch Sili Twists are marketed as an easy, reusable alternative to cotton kitchen twine. Their flexible wire core is coated with food-safe silicone that can withstand temperatures up to 675 degrees. For our test, we used them to truss a roast chicken and tie a pork loin roast before searing.

The twists worked well to truss the chicken legs together, but their bulk impeded a flat sear on the roast, especially on the side where the twists were secured. So while the twists are durable and easy to clean (they are dishwasher-safe), their fixed length and bulkiness can yield imperfect results.

UNEVEN SEAR

Some salad recipes call for rubbing salad bowls with a clove of garlic. Does this do anything?
Elaine Azevedo, San Diego, Calif.

To discern if this technique adds any flavor, we first compared salad greens dressed in a wooden salad bowl rubbed with a halved garlic clove to greens dressed in an unrubbed wooden bowl.

Every last taster was able to identify the greens from the garlic-rubbed bowl. Was it the porous wood of the bowl that accounted for it? For our next test, we rubbed aluminum, plastic, glass, and sealed wooden bowls with halved garlic cloves and asked tasters to weigh in. Once again, they immediately pinpointed the garlic flavor, whatever the construction of the bowl. Conclusion: Rubbing a salad bowl with garlic is an easy, efficient way to add subtle garlic flavor to a salad.

I'm baffled by the different types of ground cinnamon for sale. Which do you recommend?
Kate True, Roxbury, Mass.

Unless specifically labeled Ceylon, most cinnamon sold in the United States is cassia, not true cinnamon. Both spices are harvested from the inner bark of a tropical evergreen tree, but cassia is more robust and less expensive than cinnamon.

The most common varieties of cassia "cinnamon" are Vietnamese (also known as Saigon) and Indonesian (or Korintji); the latter is the staple "cinnamon" in the United States. The Vietnamese variety is marketed for its robust spiciness, thanks to its high aromatic oil content. Curious to see if we could taste the difference, we tested two samples of each variety: McCormick's and Badia's ground cinnamon, and McCormick's Gourmet Collection Saigon Cinnamon and Spice Island's Saigon Cinnamon. We made seasoned applesauce and baked cinnamon streusel muffins to taste the cinnamons both raw and cooked. Applesauce eaters favored the "hot," "complex" spice of the Vietnamese cinnamon over the milder Indonesian cinnamon. However, while a few muffin-eaters noted stronger cinnamon flavor in the Vietnamese samples, they deemed all the muffins acceptable. So while we like the assertive flavor of Vietnamese varieties, at twice the price of standard (Indonesian) cinnamon, it's not essential.

BALANCED BLEND

HOT AND SPICY

If you'd like to ask a question, e-mail us by visiting **CooksCountry.com/emailus** or send a letter to Ask Cook's Country, P.O. Box 470739, Brookline, MA 02447. Include your name, address, and phone number. If we publish your tip, you will receive a free one-year subscription to *Cook's Country*.

Recipe Makeover Carrot Cake

Our slimmed-down carrot cake doesn't skimp on moisture, flavor, or frosting.

Sure, carrots are good for you. But carrot cake? At 500 calories a slice, this cake needed a trim.

BY KRIS WIDICAN

REDUCED-FAT CARROT CAKE WITH CREAM CHEESE FROSTING
Serves 15

Any cream cheese with ⅓ less fat will work here. To ensure thick frosting, use marshmallow creme (such as Fluff or Kraft Jet-Puffed), not marshmallow sauce. Shred carrots on large holes of a box grater or with the shredding disk of a food processor.

CAKE
- 2½ cups all-purpose flour
- 2 teaspoons baking powder
- 1 teaspoon baking soda
- 1½ teaspoons ground cinnamon
- ½ teaspoon ground nutmeg
- ⅛ teaspoon ground cloves
- ½ teaspoon salt
- 2 large eggs
- 1 (4-ounce) jar carrot baby food
- 1 cup packed dark brown sugar
- ½ cup vegetable oil
- 1 pound carrots, peeled and shredded

FROSTING
- 1 (8-ounce) package Neufchâtel cream cheese, softened
- 1 cup marshmallow creme (see note)
- 1½ teaspoons vanilla extract
- ¼ cup confectioners' sugar

1. HEAT OVEN Adjust oven rack to middle position and heat oven to 350 degrees. Lightly grease 13- by 9-inch baking pan with cooking spray and line bottom of pan with parchment paper.

2. MAKE BATTER Whisk flour, baking powder, baking soda, cinnamon, nutmeg, cloves, and salt in large bowl. With electric mixer on medium speed, beat eggs, baby food, and sugar until smooth and creamy, 1 to 2 minutes. With mixer still running, slowly add oil and mix until thoroughly incorporated, about 1 minute. Reduce speed to low. Add flour mixture in two additions, scraping down sides of bowl as necessary, and mix until batter is nearly smooth. Fold in carrots.

3. BAKE CAKE Spread batter in prepared pan and bake until toothpick inserted in center comes out with few moist crumbs attached, 24 to 28 minutes, rotating pan halfway through baking. Cool cake in pan 10 minutes, then invert onto wire rack. Remove parchment and flip cake right-side up to cool completely, about 1½ hours.

4. MAKE FROSTING With mixer on medium-high speed, beat together cream cheese, marshmallow creme, and vanilla. Sift confectioners' sugar over cream cheese mixture and beat on low speed until mixture is smooth, about 1 minute. Frost cooled cake. Serve.

The Numbers
All nutritional information is for one serving.

Traditional Carrot Cake with Cream Cheese Frosting
CALORIES **530**
FAT **33g** • SATURATED FAT **8g**

Cook's Country Reduced-Fat Carrot Cake with Cream Cheese Frosting
CALORIES **280**
FAT **11g** • SATURATED FAT **3g**

Many people are under the delusion that because its principal ingredient is carrots and it uses oil instead of butter, carrot cake must be a healthy dessert. What they forget is that a single serving can tip the scales at more than 500 calories and 30 grams of fat.

I gathered half a dozen so-called healthy recipes and headed into the test kitchen. The worst contained a grab bag of health food clichés—soy flour, flax seed meal, tofu—and produced a sodden cake with wobbly tofu icing. Recipes that incorporated fat-free dairy ingredients (sour cream, cream cheese, and even mayonnaise!) tasted artificial, while those that used fruit purees in place of fat made for cakes with the texture of damp sponges.

Maybe I'd do better to start with a winning high-fat carrot cake and put it on a diet. Right off the bat, I nixed the nuts and raisins—tasty, yes, but they add fat and calories. I halved the eggs in the test kitchen's favorite carrot cake recipe from four to two, and cut the oil to just ½ cup. Unsurprisingly, the cake was dry and chalky. Since carrots contribute much of the moisture, I gradually increased their quantity. In cake after cake, the extra carrots made the batter difficult to spread and the cakes heavy. Ultimately, I realized that the 1 pound of shredded carrots in the original recipe was all the batter could handle.

A recipe I'd tested early on used strained prunes in place of all the oil. It had made the cake unpleasantly bouncy but exceptionally moist. Maybe the prunes working in tandem with ½ cup of oil could produce a moist, tender cake. They did. Unfortunately, its dark color was all wrong, plus it tasted like a cross between spice cake and fruitcake. Tests that combined oil with apple and pear purees didn't taste like carrot cake, either. But pureed carrots—a.k.a. baby food—contributed moisture and just the right flavor.

The cake was now good enough to eat on its own, but no way would my tasters and I pass up the frosting. Most icing recipes beat cream cheese, butter, and confectioners' sugar together. Tasters rejected the batch I made with fat-free cream cheese as "unnatural" and gummy. The flavor of light cream cheese (less than half the fat of full-fat cream cheese) was better, but the frosting was runny. Neufchâtel (⅓ less fat) contributed the right amount of heft and tang.

Replacing the butter was trickier. I needed something light and fluffy, like creamed butter. I rejected making my own meringue (too fussy) but figured marshmallow creme—which is made with egg whites, corn syrup, and sugar and is fat free—might work. Sure enough, the creme blended easily with the Neufchâtel, giving me a much healthier carrot cake that still tasted like the real deal.

Test Kitchen Discovery Fat Fake-Out
To give our reduced-fat and -calorie carrot cake the flavor and texture of a full-fat cake, we had to get a little creative.

MARSHMALLOW CREME
Using marshmallow creme in place of some of the butter and sugar yielded thick, rich frosting with no additional fat.

CARROT BABY FOOD
Just one tub of carrot baby food added moisture and a mild carroty sweetness. Look for brands that contain only carrots and water.

Make Ahead Creamy Macaroni and Cheese

We sought convenience, creaminess, and comfort in a straight-from-the-freezer casserole. Was that too much to ask? BY MEGHAN ERWIN

Homemade macaroni and cheese is an easy dish with unbeatable payoff in creamy goodness. But just try freezing it. Or rather, don't. I did, and it was a disaster: The noodles bloated, the sauce curdled, the entire dish dried out. I wanted to be able to pull macaroni and cheese from the freezer on busy weeknights for an easy, familiar supper. But it's not convenient if it's not edible.

To make mac 'n' cheese from scratch, you boil macaroni until al dente; make a white sauce by whisking flour into melted butter and stirring in milk and shredded cheese; combine the two; dot with seasoned, buttered bread crumbs; and bake. Fortunately, I found one from-the-freezer recipe that curdled slightly and was a little dry, but wasn't gruesome. I used it as my jumping-off point. I noticed that it used a higher ratio of sauce to macaroni than typical— about 5½ cups sauce to 1 pound pasta. (Typically, recipes use as little as 2½ cups sauce.) I figured the extra sauce was intended to keep the pasta from drying out. Since it wasn't quite accomplishing that, I increased the volume of milk. An additional ¼ cup did little, so I tried an extra ½ cup. I stirred in the cheese (a blend of mild colby that melts nicely and extra-sharp cheddar for flavor), mixed sauce and noodles together, and poured it all into a 13- by 9-inch casserole. The loose mix looked like soup but, amazingly, when I baked it after freezing, it was thick and moist.

It was still curdling, though. I knew from test kitchen experience that heavy cream might be my answer. I consulted our science editor, who explained that cream has more fat and therefore less protein (casein) than milk, and it's the protein that's prone to curdling as dairy products freeze and thaw. When I tried the sauce with heavy cream, the problem disappeared, as predicted. But it was far too rich for a weeknight meal. I reached for chicken broth, the test kitchen's usual cream sauce lightener. Many casseroles later, my tasters settled on a ratio of 1½ cups heavy cream combined with 4½ cups chicken broth. For added insurance, I cooled the boiled noodles on a baking sheet instead of rinsing them in a colander. I knew the starch that clings to cooked noodles would do its bit to keep the sauce nice and thick.

The flavor was getting there, but the noodles remained bloated and mushy. They seemed to be drinking up the cream sauce. A colleague suggested I try undercooking them. Instead of boiling them until al dente (6 to 10 minutes, according to the box), I pulled them out of the boiling water after just 3 minutes. I made, froze, and baked a casserole with the undercooked noodles. Problem solved. But the final product took an eternity to bake, and I began to doubt that the frozen lump in its center would ever thaw. This was hardly the convenient, from-the-freezer weeknight dinner I'd pictured. The solution? I divided the mixture between two 8-inch square baking dishes. I took one out of the freezer and microwaved it for about 10 minutes to speed the thawing process. Portioning let me reduce the oven time from an hour and 15 minutes to just 40 minutes.

One small problem remained. My mixture was soupy before I froze it, and I was stirring it periodically in the microwave to help it thaw evenly. As a result, I had to figure out when to spread the crumb topping over the casseroles. I froze the crumbs separately, strewing them over the macaroni and cheese after it baked for 20 minutes and had a chance to firm up a bit. In the remaining 20 minutes, the topping crisped and browned, and the inviting smell called everyone to dinner.

MAKE-AHEAD CREAMY MACARONI AND CHEESE
Serves 8 to 10
You will need 2 microwave-safe 8-inch square baking dishes for this recipe.

- 4 slices hearty white sandwich bread, torn into pieces
- ¼ cup grated Parmesan cheese
- 1 garlic clove, minced
- 8 tablespoons (1 stick) unsalted butter, melted
- Salt and pepper
- 1 pound elbow macaroni
- 6 tablespoons all-purpose flour
- 1 teaspoon dry mustard
- ⅛ teaspoon cayenne pepper
- 4½ cups low-sodium chicken broth
- 1½ cups heavy cream
- 4 cups shredded colby cheese
- 2 cups shredded extra-sharp cheddar cheese

1. PROCESS TOPPING Pulse bread, Parmesan, garlic, and 2 tablespoons butter in food processor until coarsely ground. Divide crumb mixture between 2 zipper-lock freezer bags and freeze.

2. COOK PASTA Bring 4 quarts water to boil in Dutch oven over high heat. Add 1 tablespoon salt and macaroni and cook until barely softened, about 3 minutes. Drain pasta, then spread out on rimmed baking sheet and let cool.

3. MAKE SAUCE Heat remaining butter, flour, mustard, and cayenne in

Creamy mac and cheese gets a crunchy, buttery, garlicky topping.

empty pot over medium-high heat, stirring constantly, until golden and fragrant, 1 to 2 minutes. Slowly whisk in broth and cream and bring to boil. Reduce heat to medium and simmer until slightly thickened, about 15 minutes. Off heat, whisk in colby, cheddar, 1 teaspoon salt, and ½ teaspoon pepper until smooth.

4. FREEZE Stir cooled pasta into sauce, breaking up any clumps, until well combined. Divide pasta mixture between two 8-inch square baking dishes. Cool to room temperature, about 2 hours. Wrap dishes tightly with plastic, cover with foil, and freeze for up to 2 months.

5. BAKE Adjust oven rack to middle position and heat oven to 375 degrees. Remove foil from casserole and reserve. Microwave casserole until mixture is thawed and beginning to bubble around edges, 7 to 12 minutes, stirring and replacing plastic halfway through cooking. (If preparing both dishes, microwave one at a time.) Discard plastic and cover pan with reserved foil. Bake 20 minutes, then remove foil and sprinkle with 1 bag frozen bread crumbs. (If preparing both dishes, sprinkle second bag of crumbs over second dish.) Continue to bake until crumbs are golden brown and crisp, about 20 minutes longer. Let cool 10 minutes. Serve.

FREEZE WITH EASE Keys to Make-Ahead Mac and Cheese
The freezer wreaks havoc with foods, robbing them of moisture and causing other problems. We had to figure out how to safeguard our make-ahead macaroni and cheese.

1. To avoid mushy, blown-out macaroni, undercook the pasta, boiling it for just 3 minutes; it will finish cooking in the oven.

2. To cool the pasta quickly yet retain its starches (which help stabilize the sauce), spread it on a baking sheet instead of rinsing.

3. The freezer can dry out any dish. To keep macaroni and cheese creamy, compensate by making a soupy sauce.

Slow Cooker Chicken Cacciatore

Tender chicken and robust tomato sauce are the heart and soul of chicken cacciatore. The slow cooker just didn't understand. BY LYNN CLARK

A combination of dark and white meat gives this cacciatore broad appeal.

Nestle bone-in chicken pieces into garlicky tomato sauce. Stud the sauce with onions and woodsy mushrooms, enliven it with a splash of red wine, and season liberally with gutsy herbs. Simmer the stew on the stovetop until the sauce is hearty and luscious and the chicken is falling off the bone. That's chicken cacciatore, "hunter's chicken" in Italian. I love the dish and hoped to adapt it for the slow cooker.

But my first round of testing was a washout, literally. Most of the recipes I'd gathered suggested I dump all the ingredients into the slow cooker at once, turn it on, and wait. Predictably, the sauce was weak and watery, the long-cooked chicken dry and stringy. On the stovetop, the liquids would have evaporated as the sauce bubbled away, reducing and concentrating in flavor—but that's not possible in a steamy, covered slow cooker. The best of these imperfect recipes wasn't bad, but it thickened the cacciatore with flour, which muted the vibrant sauce and turned it pasty. When I omitted the flour, the sauce became too watery—but at least I had a better place to start.

This recipe called for 2 cups of chicken broth and ½ cup red wine, plus canned tomatoes. In a series of tests, I decreased the broth little by little, ultimately jettisoning it entirely. Amazingly, the sauce was still too loose. I'd been using diced tomatoes, and draining them helped;

sautéing the drained tomatoes dried them further and deepened their flavor. But now I'd gone too far and ended up with chunks of tomato instead of sauce. Pureeing the drained, sautéed tomatoes in the food processor fixed the problem, producing a sauce that was full-bodied and thick.

Turning to the flavorings, mushrooms are essential to cacciatore. In a taste test, cremini beat out button mushrooms. They were even better in combination with dried porcini mushrooms, which added complexity and depth (I pureed the porcini with the tomatoes for added body). I tested various dried herbs (dried hold up better than fresh in long cooking) before settling on oregano and red pepper flakes, which paired well with the garlic and mushrooms.

The test kitchen is divided on the question of white versus dark meat, and so I tried to please everyone by including both chicken thighs and chicken breasts. I began by browning the chicken parts; the skin provided some flavorful fat in which to sauté the mushrooms and onions. Then everything went into the slow cooker. Four hours later, the thighs emerged moist and tender, but the delicate breasts had dried out. This is familiar territory for the test kitchen, so I knew what to do: I wrapped the raw breasts in foil to insulate them from the heat and slow their cooking—I didn't sear them first, as they were already overcooking. When we've used this technique before, we've subsequently shredded or cubed the breasts to stir into soups or stews. Unfortunately, with chicken cacciatore, the breasts are served whole, so there was no disguising their utter lack of flavor. On a hunch, I dribbled some sauce into the foil packet before cooking the breasts, hoping the herb, mushroom, and tomato flavors would seep in. This did the trick.

My slow-cooker cacciatore finally tasted pretty good, but after 4 hours of cooking, the sauce had dulled, and tasters missed the fresh, lively punch of uncooked tomatoes. I tried again. This time, I reserved half of the diced canned tomatoes at the outset, neither browning nor pureeing them. In the final minute of cooking, I stirred them into the cacciatore, along with ¼ cup chopped fresh basil and 1 tablespoon of vinegar. It made all the difference.

SLOW-COOKER CHICKEN CACCIATORE Serves 6

See page 31 for information about cleaning mushrooms.

- 4 bone-in, skin-on chicken thighs (about 2 pounds), excess fat trimmed Salt and pepper
- 1 tablespoon vegetable oil
- 1 pound cremini mushrooms, quartered
- 1 onion, chopped fine
- 4 garlic cloves, minced
- 2 teaspoons dried oregano
- ½ teaspoon red pepper flakes
- ¼ cup tomato paste
- 1 (28-ounce) can diced tomatoes, drained
- ½ cup red wine
- ¼ ounce dried porcini mushrooms, rinsed and patted dry
- 4 bone-in, split chicken breasts (about 3 pounds), skin discarded
- ¼ cup finely chopped fresh basil
- 1 tablespoon red wine vinegar

1. BROWN THIGHS Pat chicken thighs dry with paper towels and season with salt and pepper. Heat oil in large skillet over medium-high heat until just smoking. Brown thighs, about 5 minutes per side, then transfer to plate. Let cool 5 minutes, then discard skin and transfer thighs to slow cooker.

2. COOK AROMATICS Pour off and discard all but 1 tablespoon fat from skillet. Cook cremini mushrooms, onion, and ¼ teaspoon salt over medium heat until golden brown, about 10 minutes. Stir in garlic, oregano, and pepper flakes and cook until fragrant, about 30 seconds. Transfer to slow cooker.

3. PROCESS TOMATOES Add tomato paste and half of diced tomatoes to empty pan and cook until deep red and dry, about 3 minutes. Stir in wine and porcini and simmer until liquid is thickened and porcini are softened, about 2 minutes. Transfer tomato mixture to food processor and pulse until nearly smooth. Transfer ⅓ cup tomato mixture to slow cooker.

4. PREPARE BREASTS Place chicken breasts on one side of large piece of heavy-duty aluminum foil. Spoon remaining tomato mixture over chicken, then fold foil over chicken to form packet that will fit in slow cooker; crimp edges to seal. Place packet in slow cooker. Cover and cook on low until chicken is tender and cooked through, about 4 hours.

5. FINISH Carefully remove packet from slow cooker. Transfer breasts and thighs to serving platter and pour any accumulated juices from packet back into slow cooker. Stir remaining tomatoes, basil, and vinegar into sauce. Spoon sauce over chicken and serve.

STEP-BY-STEP **Puree Power**

Watery sauce and bland, overcooked chicken plague most slow-cooker cacciatore recipes. Here's how we solved these problems:

1. Pureeing the sautéed tomatoes with wine and porcini mushrooms helps thicken the sauce before it goes into the cooker insert.

2. Wrapping the chicken breasts in an insulating foil packet ensures moist chicken. A bit of the tomato mixture flavors the chicken as it cooks.

VISIT US ONLINE!

What separates a good slow cooker from a bad one? Visit **CooksCountry.com** and click on **Equipment Ratings** to read our latest testing of slow cookers. We tell you what features to look for—and which to avoid—when buying a slow cooker.

Simmer down! Gentle treatment guarantees tender deviled eggs. BY JEREMY SAUER

In theory, the recipe is simple: Boil, peel, and halve eggs. Remove yolks and mash with mayonnaise and mustard. Fill white "boats" with mashed yolk mixture. In fact, many cooks find making deviled eggs bedeviling. Over the years, the test kitchen has developed a handful of tips and techniques that guarantee perfect, no-fuss deviled eggs every time.

They're called hard-cooked eggs, but be gentle with them: Overcook the eggs, either by boiling them for several minutes or dropping them into boiling water, and the whites will turn rubbery, the yolks chalky and tinged with green. Moreover, the eggs will smell sulphurous.

To avoid these problems, place the eggs in a saucepan, cover them with cold water by an inch, and bring them to a hard boil. Immediately remove the pan from the heat, cover it, and let the residual heat of the water finish cooking the eggs for exactly 10 minutes, which is just long enough for large eggs to cook through.

Pour off water from the pan and gently shake the pan so that the shells crack all over. Immediately plunge the eggs into ice water to stop them from cooking further. The water will also seep under the cracked shells, which will loosen them for easier peeling. Begin peeling from the large, more-rounded end of each egg; this end has an air pocket that lets you grasp the shell for easy removal without marring the white.

Most recipes call for mashing the cooked yolks with a fork to make the filling, but we've never cared for the lumps in what should be a creamy mix. To make it smooth, we press the cooked yolks through a fine-mesh strainer. Mayonnaise is key, but augmenting it with a little sour cream adds flavor and silkiness. Mustard provides spice, vinegar offers tang, and the merest speck of sugar lends the merest speck of sweetness.

Deviled eggs are easy to dress up. The yolks take especially well to assertive ingredients like pickles, olives, and cheese. But nothing says winter's gone and spring has sprung like delicate fresh herbs, hence our variation for eggs with tarragon, parsley, chives, and chervil.

BASIC DEVILED EGGS Makes 1 dozen

You can use reduced-fat mayonnaise and sour cream in this recipe. To fill the eggs, a spoon works just fine, but for eggs that look their Sunday best, use a pastry bag fitted with a fluted (star) tip or make your own pastry bag (see below).

- 6 large eggs
- 2 tablespoons mayonnaise (see note)
- 1 tablespoon sour cream (see note)
- ½ teaspoon white vinegar
- ½ teaspoon spicy brown mustard (such as Gulden's)
- ¼ teaspoon sugar
- ⅛ teaspoon salt
- ⅛ teaspoon pepper

1. COOK EGGS Combine 4 cups water and 4 cups ice cubes in large bowl; set aside. Place eggs in saucepan, cover with 1 inch water, and bring to boil over high heat. Remove pan from heat, cover, and let stand 10 minutes. Pour off water from saucepan and gently shake pan back and forth to crack egg shells. Transfer eggs to ice water and cool 5 minutes.

2. MAKE FILLING Peel eggs and halve lengthwise. Transfer yolks to fine-mesh sieve set over medium bowl. Using spatula, press yolks through sieve into bowl. Stir in remaining ingredients until smooth.

3. FILL Arrange whites on serving platter. Divide yolk mixture among whites. Serve. (Egg white halves and filling mixture can be refrigerated separately for 2 days. Wrap egg whites in double layer of plastic wrap. Transfer filling mixture to zipper-lock bag, squeeze out air, and seal.)

HERBED DEVILED EGGS

You can substitute an equal amount of finely chopped watercress for the chervil.

Prepare Basic Deviled Eggs, replacing white vinegar with ½ teaspoon white wine vinegar and brown mustard with ½ teaspoon Dijon mustard. Stir 2 teaspoons each finely chopped fresh tarragon, fresh parsley, fresh chives, and fresh chervil into remaining ingredients.

SPANISH-STYLE DEVILED EGGS

For a smoky, spicy kick, use smoked rather than plain paprika.

Prepare Basic Deviled Eggs, replacing white vinegar with ½ teaspoon sherry vinegar. Stir ¼ cup finely chopped green olives with pimento, ¼ cup shredded cheddar cheese, and 1 teaspoon paprika into remaining ingredients.

DILL-PICKLED DEVILED EGGS

Avoid dried dill here. Used in this quantity, it will taste dusty and stale.

Prepare Basic Deviled Eggs, replacing white vinegar with ½ teaspoon dill pickle juice and brown mustard with ½ teaspoon yellow mustard. Stir in 1 tablespoon finely chopped dill pickles and 1 tablespoon finely chopped fresh dill with remaining ingredients.

BLUE CHEESE DEVILED EGGS

A relatively mild blue cheese like Stella Blue works best here.

Prepare Basic Deviled Eggs, replacing white vinegar with ½ teaspoon cider vinegar and brown mustard with ½ teaspoon Dijon mustard. Increase pepper to ¼ teaspoon and stir ¼ cup crumbled blue cheese into remaining ingredients.

We push yolks through a fine-mesh sieve for an extra-creamy filling.

STEP-BY-STEP Filling Deviled Eggs without a Pastry Bag

A little ingenuity can turn an ordinary plastic bag into a homemade pastry bag.

1. Set a plastic bag inside a measuring cup and fold the bag over the lip; this makes it easy to spoon the filling into the bag.

2. Once you've filled the bag with the yolk mixture, use scissors to snip about ½ inch off of one corner of the bag.

3. Twist the top of bag and squeeze to force filling to the snipped corner. Fill egg whites by squeezing filling through the hole.

Au Gratin Potatoes

Few foods seem as all-American as potatoes. In fact, it was Thomas Jefferson who helped bring them into vogue in the new nation. But while historians link him to French food, and Jefferson's own notes contain the earliest American recipe for French fries, if he dined on au gratin potatoes at Monticello, he left no record of it. Plenty of other Americans have eaten them, however, and today, despite the (partly) French name and famous French pedigree, au gratin potatoes are at home at countless church suppers and family dinners in America. Oddly, practice seemed to lead to imperfection. Homemade versions can be slipshod. We were determined to get this crispy, creamy, golden dish just right. BY LYNN CLARK

Well-made au gratin potatoes transform humble ingredients into something almost ethereal. To my mind, perfection would be layers of paper-thin, tender potatoes; a crunchy, browned crust; lots of cheese; and the cohesiveness to be sliced into neat, elegant squares. What you actually get can range from curdled cream and unevenly cooked potatoes to cheese that's barely there and slices that fall into sloppy heaps. We tested and tasted half a dozen recipes, picked the version that came closest to my ideal, and continued testing.

The choice of potato was critical. Yukon golds and red potatoes produced loose, wobbly gratins, so I decided on starchy russets. Test kitchen experience had taught me that the starch would help the casserole firm up. I came across many recipes that warned cooks not to rinse the potato slices: Rinse them and you rinse away the starch. Thick potato slices took forever to cook and never fused. But short of hiring a surgeon, how could I cut the potatoes to an even thinness? Happily, an inexpensive mandoline made short work of slicing 3 pounds of potatoes to an even, near-translucent thinness. I tested one more technique to help the gratin bind (which by happy coincidence, intensified the cheese flavor): Rather than sprinkling all the cheese on top, I used half of it in the center. This

gratin sliced into attractive, cohesive squares.

My working recipe called for milk and cream, but the dairy kept curdling in the oven. I'd seen a recipe that suggested baking the gratin at a low temperature (300 degrees), then cranking up the heat at the finish to brown the top. Alas, the gentle temperature meant a longer cooking time without any payoff—the dairy curdled regardless. Next, I made the gratin with all heavy cream; with less protein than milk, cream is less apt to curdle. This time it didn't curdle, but tasters found it one-dimensional and excessively rich. I tried cutting the cream with chicken broth. As I'd expected, it lightened the dish and let the potatoes be the star.

With flavor still on my mind, I tried a simple trick I'd read about: rubbing an empty gratin dish with a crushed clove of garlic. In a side-by-side test of two finished dishes, not a single taster could tell the gratins apart. So much for that! I'd been using 1 cup of grated sharp cheddar cheese, standard in American versions

of the dish. From the start, tasters demanded, "More cheese!" I tripled the amount before they were satisfied. Unfortunately, like most aged cheeses, sharp cheddar separates and becomes greasy when melted. Looking for better melting, I replaced some of the cheddar with an unconventional choice: Monterey Jack, which melts well. Unfortunately, it was so mild that we could barely taste it. By replacing some of the Monterey Jack with ½ cup Parmesan, I achieved an acceptable balance of good melting and flavor. For extra insurance, I tossed the shredded cheeses with 2 teaspoons cornstarch, which helps prevent the cheeses from clumping when melted.

Delicious as it finally was, my gratin dawdled in the oven. Some recipes call for warming the liquids before pouring them over the potatoes—might that trim the oven time? Sad to say, it shaved just two minutes—minus the minute and a half needed to heat the liquid in the first place. I'd just have to accept that good things come to those who wait.

SLOPPY AND UNDERCOOKED

NEAT AND COOKED JUST RIGHT

CHEESY AU GRATIN POTATOES
Serves 6

You do not need to grease the baking dish. You will need a 2- to 3-quart gratin dish; see page 31 for more information.

- 1¼ cups shredded sharp cheddar cheese
- 1¼ cups shredded Monterey Jack cheese
- ½ cup grated Parmesan cheese
- 2 teaspoons cornstarch
- 3 pounds russet potatoes, peeled and sliced ⅛ inch thick
  Salt and pepper
- ¾ cup heavy cream
- ½ cup low-sodium chicken broth

1. COMBINE CHEESES Adjust oven rack to middle position and heat oven to 350 degrees. Toss cheeses and cornstarch in large bowl until evenly coated.

2. ASSEMBLE GRATIN Shingle half of potatoes in large gratin dish, sprinkle evenly with 1 cup cheese mixture, ¾ teaspoon salt, and ¼ teaspoon pepper. Top with remaining potatoes, additional ¾ teaspoon salt, and additional ¼ teaspoon pepper.

3. BAKE Combine cream and broth in large measuring cup and pour over potatoes. Top with remaining cheese mixture and bake until golden brown and fork inserted into center meets little resistance, 75 to 90 minutes. Let cool 10 minutes. Serve.

Troubleshooting Cheesy au Gratin Potatoes

Given its short list of ingredients and uncomplicated techniques, you might think making Cheesy au Gratin Potatoes would be child's play, but we found the devil lurking in the details. A few test kitchen techniques prevented trouble:

PROBLEM: Unevenly Cooked Potatoes
SOLUTION: Use a Mandoline
Thick, uneven hand-sliced potatoes won't lie flat in the dish or cook evenly. To get perfectly sliced potatoes easily and efficiently, use a mandoline slicer. A mandoline makes quick work of the 3 pounds of potatoes called for in this recipe.

PROBLEM: Disappearing Cheese Flavor
SOLUTION: Layer a Combo
Most recipes call for sprinkling a little cheese over the top of the casserole. For a cheesier gratin, we used a combination of sharp cheddar, tangy Parmesan, and easy-melting Monterey Jack not only on top of the spuds, but also in between. This boosted the flavor and helped the casserole coalesce.

PROBLEM: Rich and Boring
SOLUTION: Combine Chicken Broth and Cream
Heavy cream won't separate when it's cooked. But too much makes the gratin heavy and overwhelms the potatoes. We cut the cream with chicken broth.

ON THE SIDE
Broiled Asparagus with Mustard Vinaigrette

Can a delicate vegetable meet a bold dressing head-on? BY JEREMY SAUER

THE TEST KITCHEN'S method for broiling asparagus is simple: Toss thin spears with olive oil, season with salt and pepper, and run under the broiler until flecked with brown. To complement the asparagus, we wanted a bold mustard vinaigrette. Dijon mustard, white wine vinegar, and olive oil gave us a bright base to work with. Garlic was a must; "roasting" it in the microwave (with a little sugar and oil) helped take its edge off. Tarragon added an herbal note. For even more garlicky flavor, we reserved the garlic-flavored oil and tossed it with the asparagus before placing the spears under the broiler.

BROILED ASPARAGUS WITH MUSTARD VINAIGRETTE
Serves 6 to 8

The asparagus should be no more than ½ inch thick.

- 3 garlic cloves, peeled and halved lengthwise
- ¼ cup extra-virgin olive oil
- ¼ teaspoon sugar
- 1 tablespoon white wine vinegar
- 1 tablespoon Dijon mustard
- 1 teaspoon finely chopped fresh tarragon
  Salt and pepper
- 2 pounds thin asparagus spears, trimmed (see note)

1. MICROWAVE GARLIC Adjust oven rack to upper position and heat broiler. Combine garlic, 1 tablespoon oil, and sugar in small bowl and microwave, uncovered, until garlic is softened and fragrant, about 1 minute. Carefully transfer softened garlic to cutting board, reserving garlic-cooking oil. Using side of chef's knife, mash garlic to fine paste.

2. MAKE DRESSING Combine vinegar, mustard, tarragon, and garlic paste in medium bowl. Gradually whisk in remaining oil until incorporated. Season with salt and pepper. (Dressing can be refrigerated in airtight container for 2 days. Refrigerate garlic oil separately, also in airtight container.)

3. BROIL ASPARAGUS Place asparagus in single layer on rimmed baking sheet. Drizzle with reserved garlic oil and season with salt and pepper, tossing gently to coat. Broil until asparagus is lightly browned and tender, 8 to 10 minutes, shaking pan to redistribute spears halfway through cooking time. Transfer to platter and drizzle with dressing. Serve.

"Roasted" garlic is key to this easy dish.

Grill-Roasted Ham

We thought we knew everything there was to know about ham—until we tried grilling one for Easter.

BY LYNN CLARK

Spending time on the grill reinforces the smoky flavor of ham—and builds a delicious crust.

Over the years in the test kitchen, we've baked wet-cured hams in oven bags and in foil, brushed them with glazes, and rubbed them with sugar and spice. We thought we'd cooked ham every which way, so when a colleague talked about grilling ham for Easter, I was intrigued. I'd never heard of grilled ham before. Apparently, with unexpected guests on the way and a turkey hogging the oven, she'd thought fast and stuck a spiral-sliced ham on the grill. A couple hours later, guests sat down to an intensely smoky ham with a crisp, charred crust unmatched by any oven-roasted ham. She admitted it was far from perfect. The meat had dried out and there were random charred bits, but these were problems I was confident I could solve.

I tested recipes that called for an array of techniques—direct heat, indirect heat, disposable aluminum pans—but the results were disappointing. Hams cooked over direct heat developed a crusty exterior but either burned or dried out. Those cooked in disposable pans or over indirect heat were moist, but without any contact with the grill, they developed no crust and simply tasted baked. The most promising recipe combined the two methods. It called for grilling the ham in a disposable pan over indirect heat to warm it through, then "de-panning" it and moving it over direct heat to obtain a tasty char.

The first thing I realized was that a spiral-sliced ham was never going to work on the grill. Moisture evaporated from the interior, drying out the meat and turning the crust into a tough, unappetizing facsimile of jerky. By contrast, an uncut ham, with a protective layer of fat on the outside and scant exposed meat, stayed relatively moist.

I was cooking uncut ham over indirect heat and finishing it over direct heat when a new problem emerged: The fat kept dripping onto the grill, setting fire to grill and meat. In previous test kitchen recipes, we have used a roasting V-rack to keep grill-roasted chickens a safe distance from the flames. I loaded the ham on a rack, set it over indirect heat, and cooked it through. When the ham reached 100 degrees (our test kitchen standard temperature for ham), I switched to direct heat. The extra inches of protection that the rack afforded kept the ham safe from the flare-ups, and the exterior fat transformed into a crisp, pleasingly charred, flavorful crust. Unfortunately, only the side of the ham facing the fire developed that crust.

For a well-rounded crust, I'd obviously have to turn the ham. But with a hot, open flame, how the heck could I rotate a bulky 10-pound ham safely? I was stymied—until it occurred to me to use metal skewers to simulate a rotisserie. I skewered the meat on either side of the bone, creating handles. Once the ham had cooked through, I began to turn it every five or so minutes on my makeshift rotisserie. The fat rendered off, creating a tantalizing, smoky charred exterior all around.

The ham now had unrivaled grilled flavor, but to me it didn't qualify as holiday ham without a sweet, syrupy glaze. I tried basting it with a glaze near the end of cooking, but even with protection from the V-rack, the sugary glaze burned. Next, I coated the ham with a traditional dry barbecue rub (which seemed apt) of dark brown sugar, paprika, black pepper, and cayenne

before grilling. The rub had sugar too, but far less, and as it was dry, it stayed put, caramelizing nicely on the ham into a tasty, crunchy coating. The indirect cooking ensured moist, tender meat. The direct grill contact accentuated the ham's smoky flavor. Taken together, this grilled ham was a thing of beauty.

GRILL-ROASTED HAM
Serves 16 to 20

Do not use a spiral sliced ham; it will dry out on the grill. You will need two 12-inch metal skewers for this recipe.

- 1 (7- to 10-pound) cured bone-in ham (see note), preferably shank end, skin removed and fat trimmed to ¼ inch thick
- ¼ cup packed dark brown sugar
- 2 tablespoons paprika
- 1 teaspoon pepper
- ¼ teaspoon cayenne pepper

1. SCORE AND SEASON Score ham at 1-inch intervals in crosshatch pattern. Combine sugar, paprika, pepper, and cayenne in small bowl. Rub spice mixture all over ham. Transfer to V-rack and let stand at room temperature 1½ hours. Thread ham with metal skewers on both sides of the bone.

2. ROAST HAM Heat all burners on high for 15 minutes, then leave primary burner on high and turn other burner(s) off. (For charcoal grill, open bottom vent on grill. Light 100 coals; when covered with fine gray ash, spread over half of grill. Set cooking grate in place and heat covered, with lid vent open halfway, for 5 minutes.) Scrape cooking grate. Arrange V-rack over cooler side of grill. Cook ham, covered, until meat registers 100 degrees, about 1½ hours.

3. CRISP HAM Turn all burners to low. (For charcoal grill, light about 25 coals. When coals are covered with fine gray ash, remove grill grate and scatter over top of spent coals. Replace grill grate and position V-rack directly over coals.) Grill ham until lightly charred on all sides, about 30 minutes, turning ham every 5 minutes. Transfer to cutting board, tent with foil, and let rest 15 minutes. Carve and serve.

TEST KITCHEN TECHNIQUE
Ham on the Move

To develop the smoky char of the grill on all sides, we needed a way to manipulate the unwieldy ham as it sat in a V-shaped roasting rack. We used metal skewers as a makeshift rotisserie. They let us turn the bulky ham with ease. Don't forget oven mitts—the skewers get hot as the ham heats.

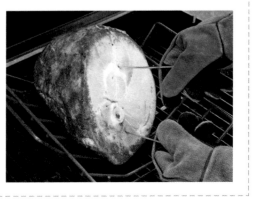

Waldorf Salad

We set out to enliven a classic salad—without forgetting what it's all about. BY DIANE UNGER

Nostalgia is nice, but revving up the flavors of this classic salad is even nicer.

Waldorf Salad was created in 1893 at New York's posh Waldorf Hotel by maître d'hôtel Oscar Tschirky for a charity fund-raiser hosted by the equally posh Mrs. William Vanderbilt. The recipe, which appeared in the *Oscar of the Waldorf* cookbook three years later, was little more than peeled apples, celery, and mayonnaise. To this day, it remains the single most requested recipe at the hotel's restaurant.

In the 1970s, many Americans dressed up the salad with raisins, walnuts, and sometimes even mandarin orange segments. While we love the underlying combination of the original, today, it is one of those throwback dishes that make us nostalgic even when the reality falls short.

We wanted to wake up the flavors of the early version and develop new variations, but certainly not get as fancy as the executive chef, John Doherty. His recipe in the 2006 *Waldorf-Astoria Cookbook* calls for homemade mayonnaise, crème fraîche (a rich, thickened cream from France), apples cut in perfect matchstick slices (only a chef with a large staff and sharp knives could bother), homemade candied walnuts, microgreens, and black truffles.

Many of the recipes I tried call for diced Granny Smith apples, but my tasters preferred the salad when I balanced the tart Grannies with sweet Braeburn or Gala apples; I left the peel on for color. Tasters preferred diced celery to larger slices, as the latter made the salad cumbersome to eat. I toasted the walnuts—usually tossed

TEST KITCHEN TIP
Keeping Apples Fresh
If you are dicing the apples ahead of time, toss them with 1 teaspoon of the cider vinegar to prevent them from browning and reserve the rest of the vinegar for the dressing.

in raw—to enhance their flavor. We also liked golden raisins, plumped in a little water, for sweetness.

Dressed with mayonnaise alone, the salad was gloppy and greasy. Adding lemon juice helped, but tasters preferred cider vinegar, which subtly reinforced the taste of apple. A spoonful of honey and a healthy shake of salt and pepper helped unite the flavors. Among several variations I developed, tasters liked best one that paired red grapes with toasted almonds, another that featured dried cherries and pecans, and a third that went out on more of a limb, using peanut butter, curry powder, and grapes. These Waldorf salads were more than good memories—they were good eating.

WALDORF SALAD Serves 4 to 6

Toast the walnuts in a dry skillet over medium heat, stirring frequently, until lightly browned and fragrant, about 5 minutes. You can use reduced-fat mayonnaise here, and regular raisins will work in place of the golden raisins.

- ¾ cup golden raisins
- ¼ cup water
- ⅓ cup mayonnaise (see note)
- 3 tablespoons cider vinegar
- 1 tablespoon honey
- 3 Granny Smith apples, cored and cut into ½-inch pieces
- 3 Gala or Braeburn apples, cored and cut into ½-inch pieces
- 3 celery ribs, chopped fine
- ¾ cup toasted walnuts, chopped (see note)
  Salt and pepper

1. PLUMP RAISINS Combine raisins and water in bowl. Wrap tightly with plastic and microwave until water begins to boil, about 1 minute. Let stand until raisins are soft and liquid has been absorbed, about 5 minutes.

2. TOSS SALAD Whisk mayonnaise, vinegar, and honey in large bowl. Add apples, celery, walnuts, and plumped raisins to bowl and toss until well coated. Refrigerate, covered, for 30 minutes. Season with salt and pepper. Serve. (Salad can be stored in airtight container for 2 days.)

WALDORF SALAD WITH DRIED CHERRIES AND PECANS

Prepare Waldorf Salad, substituting ¾ cup dried cherries for raisins and ¾ cup toasted, chopped pecans for walnuts.

WALDORF SALAD WITH RED GRAPES AND ALMONDS

Prepare Waldorf Salad, omitting step 1. In step 2, substitute 1 cup seedless red grapes, halved, for plumped raisins and ¾ cup toasted sliced almonds for walnuts.

CURRIED WALDORF SALAD WITH GREEN GRAPES AND PEANUTS

Prepare Waldorf Salad, omitting step 1. In step 2, whisk 2 tablespoons peanut butter and 1 teaspoon curry powder into mayonnaise mixture and substitute 1 cup seedless green grapes, halved, for plumped raisins and ¾ cup dry-roasted peanuts for walnuts.

TEST KITCHEN TECHNIQUE **Chopping an Apple**
Chopping six apples doesn't have to be a chore: If you follow our simple method, the work goes quickly and the apples dice neatly.

1. Slice four planks away from each apple's core.

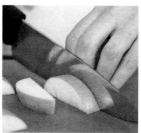

2. Slice each plank into ½-inch-wide strips.

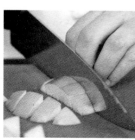

3. Cut each strip crosswise into ½-inch pieces.

Yes, Quiche Is Back!

Quiche may have originated in 16th-century Europe, but we'd argue that in the past 50 years it's practically become an American citizen. Julia Child introduced many of us to quiche in the 1960s. Within a decade, fashionable restaurants and hostesses were measured by their interpretations. Wild popularity was followed by disdain. "I wouldn't be caught dead serving it," proclaimed then–New York Times food editor Craig Claiborne, a onetime quiche lover. Perhaps it was the overly inventive combinations, like the cranberry-carrot quiche that appeared in the pages of Gourmet magazine in 1971. Or maybe it was the fact that, like many of the dishes Child made popular, it wasn't easy to make. We were determined to make it accessible.

BY CALI RICH

Any American who has eaten brunch in the last 40 years has encountered quiche Lorraine—and probably been smitten by the combination of creamy custard, salty bacon, and nutty Gruyère cheese. But making it from scratch—yes, including the crust—can be intimidating. Julia may have reassured nervous cooks that it was "just a custard in a fancy dress." With all due respect to her, few worthwhile quiche recipes are a walk in the park. To begin with, the pie dough requires a meticulous mixing technique, long chilling, gentle rolling, careful shaping, and parbaking. Even if you manage that, achieving the custard's beautifully silken texture, and keeping it from breaking, let alone under- or overcooking, requires lots of hands-on attention. I sought a recipe that would take the fear out of making quiche. And if I couldn't find one (I tested five; none was idiot-proof), I'd have to come up with my own.

Sure, you can buy pie crust, but even the best can't touch homemade for flavor and flakiness. Standard doughs require cutting cold fat (butter, shortening, or lard) into flour, then adding ice water by spoonfuls until the dough just comes together. Trust me, this is fussier than it sounds. If you overwork the dough, the crust will be tough and unpleasant.

In the test kitchen, we've had success with a pat-in-the-pan, sweet pie crust that resembles basic shortbread cookie dough. I attempted a savory version, beating softened butter and cream cheese (the acidic cheese acts as a tenderizer) in a mixer, adding flour and salt, and beating for another minute. Traditional pie dough demands hours of chilling before rolling; I simply pressed my dough onto the bottom and up the sides of a pie plate. I rolled a bit that I'd reserved into coils, which I laid around the rim of the pie plate and

crimped for a decorative edge. After the crust chilled for 30 minutes, I baked it empty (called blind- or parbaking). It emerged as light and flaky as traditional crust, but with far less anxiety and effort.

I tested several custard recipes and got results that ranged from soupy to extra-firm. I decided to work from an old test kitchen recipe that called for 2 cups half-and-half, two whole eggs, plus two yolks; we liked this custard, but found it "a little loosey-goosey," as one taster said. After testing a series of ratios, I ultimately eliminated ½ cup of the half-and-half as well as one of the yolks. Now the quiche was setting up nicely, but it tasted a tad lean. I baked quiches with heavy cream, and with a combination of heavy cream and half-and-half. I baked one with a mixture of sour cream and half-and-half, an idea that isn't as far-fetched as it sounds; French cooks often use crème fraîche, their version of sour cream, in quiche. As soon as I tasted the quiche made with sour cream, I knew I'd turned the corner. The custard had a faint but appealing tang. It set firmly, yet had an astoundingly silken texture.

Classic quiche Lorraine recipes in Alsace-Lorraine (the region in northeast France where the dish originated) omit cheese. Try explaining that to an American quiche fan! Here recipes typically instruct the cook to sprinkle 1 cup Gruyère over the parbaked crust before gently pouring in the custard and baking. Each time I tried this, the custard set before the cheese fully melted. I tried a more complicated technique—stirring the cheese into a custard I'd warmed on the stovetop—to no avail. The mixture separated in the oven.

In the end, I achieved success by combining several techniques: I cut the amount of cheese in the recipe in half, shredded it quite fine, and stirred it into room-temperature custard. I poured the mixture into a warm pie shell to give it a small head-start heating up. After about 30 minutes in the oven, the custard had melded into a harmonious whole. Unfortunately, my solution came at a price: meager cheese flavor.

It occurred to me that I might be able to incorporate extra cheese into the crust—after all, New Englanders sometimes add cheddar to the crust when making apple pie. I whisked ½ cup Gruyère in with the flour. It barely registered. I upped the amount, but the crust turned greasy. When I tried the same idea with ½ cup Parmesan, that version got the thumbs-up for its more intense cheese flavor.

The quiche was nearly perfect and was as easy as I'd hoped, but I couldn't help noticing that the chopped bacon (which I'd been stirring into the custard) kept sinking to the bottom of my pie. The next time I baked the quiche, I set some of the bacon aside. After the quiche had baked about 25 minutes and the custard was beginning to firm at the edges, I sprinkled the bacon over the quiche. Bon appétit!

STEP-BY-STEP No Fuss Crust

The savory pat-in-the-pan pie dough for our quiche provides a flaky, tender, flavorful crust without the headache of rolling out dough or waiting hours for it to chill. It really *is* easy.

1. Working from center out, evenly press disk over bottom and up sides of pie plate.

2. Roll reserved dough into 3 8-inch coils and lay around lip of pie plate.

3. Squeeze coil ends together and to sides of pie dough to make pie crust's cuff.

4. Crimp dough, using knuckle of one hand and thumb and forefinger of other hand.

QUICHE LORRAINE Serves 8

Once the dough is pressed into the pie plate, it can be refrigerated for 2 days or double-wrapped in plastic and frozen for 1 month. After it has baked and cooled, the shell can be wrapped in plastic and held at room temperature for 1 day. If making ahead, heat the pie shell in a 350-degree oven for 5 minutes before adding the custard in step 4. Grate the Gruyère on the small holes of a box grater for the best texture.

CRUST
- 1 cup all-purpose flour
- ½ cup finely grated Parmesan cheese
- ¼ teaspoon salt
- 6 tablespoons unsalted butter, softened
- 2 ounces cream cheese, softened

CUSTARD AND TOPPING
- 5 slices bacon, chopped fine
- ¾ cup half-and-half
- ¾ cup sour cream
- 2 large eggs plus 1 yolk
- ¼ teaspoon salt
- ¼ teaspoon pepper
- Pinch nutmeg
- ½ cup finely shredded Gruyère cheese

1. MAKE DOUGH Adjust oven rack to lower-middle position and heat oven to 375 degrees. Whisk flour, Parmesan, and salt in bowl. With electric mixer on medium-high speed, beat butter and cream cheese until smooth and creamy, about 1 minute. Reduce speed to low, add flour mixture, and mix until dough forms large clumps, about 1 minute. Reserve 3 tablespoons dough. Flatten remaining dough into 6-inch disk and transfer to center of 9-inch pie plate.

2. BLIND-BAKE Following photos 1 to 4, press dough evenly into bottom and sides of pie plate and use reserved dough to form crimped rim. Refrigerate dough for 20 minutes, then transfer to freezer until firm, about 10 minutes. Spray two 12-inch-square pieces of foil lightly with cooking spray and arrange greased-side down in chilled pie shell. Top with pie weights and fold excess foil over edges of dough. Bake until surface of dough no longer looks wet, 15 to 20 minutes. Carefully remove foil and weights and continue to bake until crust just begins to brown, about 5 minutes. Transfer to wire rack and cool until just warm, about 15 minutes. Reduce oven temperature to 350 degrees.

3. MIX CUSTARD While crust cools, cook bacon in large skillet over medium heat until crisp, about 8 minutes; transfer to paper towel–lined plate. Whisk half-and-half, sour cream, eggs, yolk, salt, pepper, nutmeg, Gruyère, and ¾ of bacon in large bowl.

4. BAKE Pour custard mixture into warm pie shell and bake until crust is golden and custard is set around edges, about 25 minutes. Sprinkle remaining bacon over surface of quiche and continue to bake until center of quiche is barely set, 5 to 10 minutes. Cool on wire rack for 15 minutes. Serve. (Quiche can be refrigerated in airtight container or wrapped in plastic for 3 days.)

QUICHE WITH SCALLIONS AND CHEDDAR CHEESE

Prepare recipe for Quiche Lorraine, substituting ½ cup sharp cheddar for Gruyère. Add 1 minced scallion to custard with bacon. Sprinkle 1 thinly sliced scallion over quiche after it has baked for 25 minutes.

SECRET INGREDIENTS Thinking outside the Crust

The list of ingredients for quiche Lorraine is remarkably consistent in most recipes: eggs, heavy cream, bacon, and—in the American version—cheese. We reached into our larder for a few unexpected items that simplified our quiche and improved its texture and taste.

SOUR CREAM
Tangy, silky custard

PARMESAN
Nutty richness in crust

CREAM CHEESE
Flaky, tender crust

ON THE SIDE Skillet Rosemary Carrots

First, brash rosemary stole the show. Next, it vanished. Getting it right was harder than we'd thought. BY CALI RICH

Slicing the carrots on the diagonal lets more surface area brown, which helps develop flavor.

SKILLET-ROASTING CARROTS is a nice way to draw out their sweet flavor, which I planned to counterpoint with woodsy rosemary. First, I browned the carrots in a little oil over medium-high heat. Then I gently simmered them, covered, with a small amount of chicken broth (for richness and flavor) until tender. I figured I'd simply throw a handful of chopped rosemary in at the end, but when I did that, the carrots tasted medicinal, and the rosemary speckled them like grass clippings. While the test kitchen has had luck finishing vegetable dishes with delicate fresh herbs such as chives or basil, I quickly discovered that domineering rosemary was going to require some taming.

To avoid the distracting look of chopped rosemary, I started using a sprig, intending to discard it once its flavor had permeated the dish. I was already heating 2 tablespoons of oil to brown the carrots, so I decided to try infusing the oil with the rosemary. Once the oil was strongly perfumed, I discarded the sprig and this time browned the carrots in the aromatic oil. But by the time I'd added the broth and let the carrots cook through, the rosemary flavor had pretty much disappeared. I phoned our food scientist to ask why its flavor was so fleeting. He explained that because most of the aromatic compounds in rosemary are fat soluble, when rosemary is heated in oil, these compounds quickly leach out and evaporate.

After mulling this over, I tried adding the sprig to the carrots with the broth instead of the oil. The water-rich environment gently coaxed flavor out of the herb, giving the sweet, toasty carrots a marked but mellow rosemary taste.

ROSEMARY CARROTS Serves 4 to 6

When stirring the carrots in step 2, be sure to do so gently to prevent the rosemary leaves from falling off the stem.

- 2 tablespoons vegetable oil
- 2 pounds carrots, peeled and cut diagonally into ½-inch-thick pieces
- ½ cup low-sodium chicken broth
- 2 teaspoons brown sugar
- ½ teaspoon salt
- ¼ teaspoon pepper
- 1 sprig fresh rosemary

1. BROWN CARROTS Heat oil in large skillet over medium-high heat until shimmering. Cook carrots until golden brown, 10 to 14 minutes, stirring occasionally.

2. SIMMER Stir in broth, sugar, salt, and pepper. Add rosemary and simmer, covered, stirring occasionally, over medium-low heat until carrots are tender and liquid is nearly evaporated, 8 to 12 minutes. Remove lid and discard rosemary. Continue to cook until all liquid has evaporated, about 1 minute. Serve.

ON THE SIDE Creamy Italian Dressing

Although the right herbs and dairy products were key, an unconventional technique ultimately made the difference. BY MEGHAN ERWIN

BEGIN WITH AN OIL and vinegar dressing. Sprinkle in grated cheese, minced garlic, and Italian herbs like oregano and basil. Add some dairy. Whisk vigorously. What do you get? Creamy Italian dressing. Agreed, Italians might not recognize the stuff, but any American who has ever dipped into a salad bar would. I love creamy Italian dressing, but I'm sad to say that it's often a disappointment: Bottled versions are too sweet and taste a little tired.

The recipes I gathered called for adding heavy cream, buttermilk, sour cream, or mayonnaise to a base of olive oil and red wine vinegar. I tried each alone and in combination and found that my tasters liked mayonnaise (for body) with sour cream (for tang, lightness, and silkiness). I embarked on a similar round of testing for the flavors, experimenting with a range of dried Italian herbs and spices. Oregano and red pepper flakes made the cut, but tasters dismissed dehydrated onion and powdered garlic as "artificial-tasting." They insisted on fresh for those ingredients and for basil, too.

I whisked up a new batch of dressing. The fresh minced onion tasted harsh and the dried herbs seemed slightly dusty. Replacing the onion with milder shallots was an easy fix. Then I turned to a technique we often use in the test kitchen: "blooming" herbs and spices in warm liquid to draw out their flavors. I combined dried oregano, pepper flakes, and vinegar and warmed the mixture in the microwave. Happily, I got the rounder, fuller flavors I wanted.

The use of Parmesan in creamy Italian dressing is pretty standard, but no matter what I did—whether I blended the ingredients in the food processor or grated the cheese into a powdery dust—it made the dressing gritty. Yet tasters demanded its nutty flavor, leaving me to solve the textural issues. It occurred to me that the Parmesan might melt if I warmed it in the microwave along with the vinegar and herbs—and while I was at it, I tossed in the minced shallot and garlic to mellow them. The mixture bloomed, the cheese melted, and the flavors melded. I stayed with the food processor because it made my dressing as creamy as its name and drizzled in the oil so that the dressing emulsified. Finally, a creamy Italian dressing that lived up to its potential.

CREAMY ITALIAN DRESSING Makes about 1½ cups

This creamy vinaigrette pairs best with a crisp lettuce such as iceberg or romaine.

- 3 tablespoons red wine vinegar
- 3 tablespoons grated Parmesan cheese
- 1 shallot, minced
- 1 garlic clove, minced
- 2 teaspoons dried oregano
- ¼ teaspoon red pepper flakes
- ½ cup mayonnaise
- ¼ cup sour cream
- 1 tablespoon chopped fresh basil
- ½ cup olive oil
- Salt and pepper

Fresh basil, garlic, and shallot give this dressing brighter flavor than the supermarket stuff.

1. BLOOM Whisk vinegar, Parmesan, shallot, garlic, oregano, and pepper flakes in small bowl. Microwave until cheese is melted (vinegar will look cloudy) and mixture is fragrant, about 30 seconds. Let cool.

2. ASSEMBLE DRESSING Process mayonnaise, sour cream, basil, and vinegar mixture in food processor until smooth. With motor running, slowly add oil until incorporated, about 1 minute. Season with salt and pepper. Serve. (Dressing can be refrigerated in airtight container for 4 days.)

Roast Lemon Chicken

To get lemon flavor that's more than skin deep, we squeezed, buttered, and brined. Then we got a better idea. BY DIANE UNGER

This lemony sauce is finished with butter to give it sheen, body, and richness.

Flavoring a roast chicken with lemon seems simple and ought to be out-and-out delicious. But after trying several recipes, I realized it wasn't so straightforward. The flavors can be bitter or bland. Add sauce and the problems multiply. Some sauces taste lemon-less, others pucker-up harsh. I wanted a recipe quick enough for a weeknight meal, one that wouldn't require me to squeeze a bushel of lemons yet would infuse the meat with lemon flavor that actually appealed.

Putting lemon halves in the cavity of a chicken is a common technique, but it did little to flavor the meat. Next, I brined a chicken in a lemon-saltwater solution. It made for a moist chicken, but with diluted lemon flavor. After that, I slid lemon butter under the skin of a bird; the flavor melted away. I roasted a fourth chicken, this time tucking strips of peel under its skin. The pigment from the lemon strips turned the chicken meat Big Bird yellow, but the lemon flavor seemed worth pursuing—maybe in a more user-friendly form? I started my next round of testing there.

Instead of strips of peel, I tried grating lemon zest and mixing it with a little sugar. I figured grating the zest would strengthen the lemon flavor and the sugar would tame its tang. Grated zest was also easier to distribute under the skin of the chicken and eliminated the unwieldy strips of sour peel. I roasted the chicken according to the test kitchen's preferred method: breast-side down at 375 degrees for about

35 minutes, raise the heat to 450, and flip breast-side up to crisp the skin. The lemon flavor was stronger but not sour. For my next test, I added salt to the mixture of zest and sugar; this seasoned the meat nicely and brought the bird into sweet, sour, and salty balance. I was getting closer, but tasters still felt the lemon flavor wasn't permeating the chicken.

One of the first recipes I'd tried had called for carving the bird after roasting, then arranging the pieces in a lemony sauce and broiling the chicken to crisp the skin. Tedious, yes, but the meat that came in contact with the sauce as the chicken broiled tasted fantastic.

What if I split the chicken open and roasted it, start to finish, right in a lemony sauce? I removed the backbone with a pair of kitchen shears, rubbed my lemon-sugar-salt mixture under the skin (easier now that the bird was butterflied), and set the chicken in a roasting pan. I added ⅓ cup fresh lemon juice mixed with water and chicken broth (to tame the acidity and guard against burning) so that the meat of the chicken was resting in the flavorful liquid, with the skin safely above the juice to let it get crisp. After roasting one chicken, I realized that a higher temperature of 475 degrees for the entire time made it crispier. This chicken had golden, incredibly crisp skin with a salty-sweet hit, plus meat with bright, balanced lemon flavor in every bite.

The juices were almost perfect straight

from the roasting pan. But with just a little work, I could take them over the top. While the chicken was resting, I skimmed the fat, reduced the liquid to concentrate its flavor, and thickened it slightly with butter and cornstarch.

ROAST LEMON CHICKEN Serves 3 to 4

Avoid using nonstick or aluminum roasting pans in this recipe. The former can cause the chicken to brown too quickly, while the latter may react with the lemon juice, producing off-flavors.

- 1 (3½- to 4-pound) whole chicken, backbone removed and butterflied (see photo 1 at left)
- 3 tablespoons grated zest plus ⅓ cup juice from 3 lemons
- 1 teaspoon sugar
  Salt and pepper
- 2 cups low-sodium chicken broth
- 1 cup plus 1 tablespoon water
- 1 teaspoon cornstarch
- 3 tablespoons unsalted butter
- 1 tablespoon finely chopped fresh parsley

1. SEASON Adjust oven rack to middle position and heat oven to 475 degrees. Pat chicken dry with paper towels. Combine lemon zest, sugar, and 1 teaspoon salt in small bowl. Following photo 2, rub 2 table-spoons zest mixture under skin of chicken. Season chicken with salt and pepper and transfer to roasting pan. (Seasoned chicken can be refrigerated for 2 hours.)

2. ROAST Whisk broth, 1 cup water, lemon juice, and remaining zest mixture in 4-cup liquid measuring cup, then pour into roasting pan. (Liquid should just reach skin of thighs. If it does not, add enough water to reach skin of thighs.) Roast until skin is golden brown and thigh meat registers 170 to 175 degrees, 40 to 45 minutes. Transfer to cutting board and let rest 20 minutes.

3. MAKE SAUCE Pour liquid from pan, along with any accumulated chicken juices, into saucepan (you should have about 1½ cups). Skim fat, then cook over medium-high until reduced to 1 cup, about 5 minutes. Whisk cornstarch with remaining water in small bowl until no lumps remain, then whisk into saucepan. Simmer until sauce is slightly thickened, about 2 minutes. Off heat, whisk in butter and parsley and season with salt and pepper. Carve chicken and serve, passing sauce at table.

STEP-BY-STEP **More Lemon Flavor in Less Time**
Butterflying the chicken may be unfamiliar, but this surprisingly simple process makes it easier to flavor the chicken with lemon—and it speeds roasting, too.

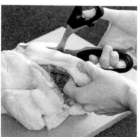

1. Use kitchen shears to cut out the backbone. Flip the bird over and press to flatten the breastbone.

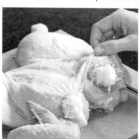

2. Carefully loosen the skin, then rub zest mixture into the breast, thigh, and leg meat.

3. Roast the flattened chicken in the lemony sauce so that its flavor can permeate the meat.

Getting to Know Carrots

Before Dutch farmers bred orange carrots to honor the House of Orange in the 17th century, these root vegetables were white, yellow, green, red, and even black. Recently, carrots of many colors have come back into favor. Here are 12 varieties, along with our tasting notes.

Dragon
FAR-EAST CHARMER

This medium-sized bicolor variety from China sports a magenta skin and a brilliant yellow-orange core. Although the dragon carrot's "slightly spicy," "nutty" flavor and "juicy-crisp" texture make it suitable for eating raw or cooked, some tasters found it "noticeably more bitter" when cooked.

Yellow
MELLOW YELLOW

This pale yellow variety has an unusual, near-cylindrical shape. Eaten raw, the yellow carrot has a "light crunch" and "fruity aftertaste" that is "devoid of bitterness." Cooked, this carrot turns "fluffy," its color deepens to lemon yellow, and it tastes "earthy-sweet," like a "sweet potato."

White
PARSNIP STUNT-DOUBLE

You might mistake this pale carrot for a parsnip—until you taste it. It has a "spicy, cedar-y bite" and a "super-crisp" texture, both of which fade with cooking; we recommend enjoying white carrots raw.

Cobalt
TWO-TONED ROOTS

The striking eggplant hue of the cobalt carrot's exterior is even more impressive juxtaposed with its yellow core. Raw, it has a "sweet, winy complexity" and a "hearty crunch." Cooked, it turns brownish-purple and assumes a "mild, grassy" taste and a "dense" texture.

Pink
COLOR ME BEAUTIFUL

Tasters described the flavor of this pink carrot as "bright," "spicy-soapy," "herbal," and "similar to cilantro." When cooked, it turns a deep coral color and develops "yeasty" and "wheaty, earthy" flavors.

Baby
SMALL WONDER

Picked early in its growth cycle, this immature carrot is small—usually no more than 3 or 4 inches—and has a delicate skin that needs no peeling. It's "sweet and tender" with "none of the bitterness" of more mature carrots, but its delicate taste doesn't hold up to cooking. It is often eaten as a crudité.

Orange Long
SUPERMARKET STAPLE

The most common supermarket variety, it has the prototypical carrot shape and color that its name implies: long, tapered, and orange. The orange long is "earthy" and "slightly bitter," with a "sweet, mineral-y background." It is excellent for cooking or eating raw.

Round
CROWD PLEASER

The dense flesh of this stubby variety is extraordinarily crunchy. With "intense, straightforward carrot flavor" and a "faintly bitter" aftertaste, it was a nearly unanimous favorite in our testing. When raw, it is "crisp and juicy"; when cooked, "firm and sweet." Peel carefully, as its thick skin is bitter.

Parsley Root
CARROT COUSIN

Also known as "Hamburg parsley," this variety of parsley (a close cousin of the carrot) is grown for its plump, cream-colored root. Parsley root looks like a parsnip but tastes "more pungent and sharp," like a combination of "parsnip and really strong celery." Because parsley root is so starchy, it's best cooked. We like it roasted, boiled, or mashed.

Purple Carrot
DRAMA QUEEN

This thick, deep purple carrot originated in the Middle East. Its flavor is "complex and tannic" and "less sweet" than orange carrots. Restaurants favor purple carrots because they make for a dramatic presentation. Much like beets, the vibrant exterior of this carrot may stain hands, clothing, and work surfaces.

Parsnip
WINTER WARMER

A relative of the carrot and a winter root staple, its "sugary and floral" taste is like a carrot "doused in perfume." Older, larger parsnips can be tough and fibrous, so avoid any that are more than 1 inch in diameter. Eaten raw, it can be tough and starchy, but steamed, boiled, sautéed, or roasted, it develops a winning creaminess and a mellow sweetness.

Baby-Cut
SWEET CONVENIENCE

Baby-cut carrots are actually whittled from large, mature, misshapen carrots otherwise unfit for commercial sale. Tasters appreciated their convenience (they are sold peeled) and "intense sweetness" but found them "chalky and dry." Glazing or roasting improves their texture and flavor.

CHICKEN AND CHEESE QUESADILLA PIE

INDOOR BARBECUED PULLED PORK

TUSCAN GARLIC CHICKEN PASTA

HOT AND SPICY SHRIMP

INDOOR BARBECUED PULLED PORK Serves 4

WHY THIS RECIPE WORKS: Because we used pork tenderloin instead of the traditional pork shoulder, we were able to approximate the tender, shredded texture of pulled pork in a fraction of the time.

- 1 teaspoon chili powder
- 1 teaspoon paprika
- 1 teaspoon garlic powder
  Salt and pepper
- 2 pork tenderloins (1½ to 2 pounds total), cut into 1-inch-thick slices (see note below)
- 1 tablespoon vegetable oil
- ½ cup low-sodium chicken broth
- ½ cup barbecue sauce
- 3 tablespoons cider vinegar

1. Combine chili powder, paprika, garlic powder, ¼ teaspoon salt, and ½ teaspoon pepper in small bowl. Pat pork dry with paper towels and sprinkle all over with spice mixture.
2. Heat oil in large skillet over medium-high heat until just smoking. Add pork and cook until well browned, 4 to 5 minutes per side. Transfer pork to large bowl, tent with foil, and let rest 5 minutes. Using 2 forks, shred meat into bite-sized pieces.
3. Meanwhile, add broth, barbecue sauce, and vinegar to empty skillet, scraping up any browned bits. Simmer over medium-low heat until sauce has thickened, about 3 minutes. Stir in shredded pork and cook until heated through, about 2 minutes. Season with salt and pepper. Serve.

TEST KITCHEN NOTE: To make shredding the meat easier, trim the tenderloins well before cooking. Serve on hamburger buns with pickles.

CHICKEN AND CHEESE QUESADILLA PIE Serves 4

WHY THIS RECIPE WORKS: By adding a batter of eggs, milk, flour, and baking powder, we turned a simple quesadilla filling into a quick Southwestern-inspired quiche. The "crust" is simply a greased flour tortilla.

- 1 (10-inch) flour tortilla (see note below)
- 1 rotisserie chicken, skin discarded, meat shredded into bite-sized pieces (about 3 cups)
- ½ cup finely chopped fresh cilantro
- ⅓ cup drained jarred pickled jalapeños, chopped
- 2 cups shredded sharp cheddar cheese
  Salt and pepper
- 2 large eggs
- 1 cup whole milk
- 1 cup all-purpose flour
- 1 teaspoon baking powder

1. Adjust oven rack to middle position and heat oven to 450 degrees. Grease 9-inch pie plate. Press tortilla into prepared pie plate and spray lightly with cooking spray. Toss chicken, cilantro, jalapeños, 1 cup cheese, ½ teaspoon salt, and ½ teaspoon pepper in large bowl until combined. Spread filling over tortilla.
2. Whisk eggs, milk, flour, baking powder, and ½ teaspoon salt in bowl until smooth. Slowly pour over filling, then sprinkle with remaining cheese. Bake until surface is golden brown, about 20 minutes. Let cool 5 minutes. Cut into wedges and serve.

TEST KITCHEN NOTE: You will need one 10-inch flour tortilla (sometimes labeled "burrito size") for this recipe. Serve with sour cream and salsa.

HOT AND SPICY SHRIMP Serves 4

WHY THIS RECIPE WORKS: Searing develops color and flavor on the shrimp, which finish cooking right in the spicy sauce.

- 2 pounds extra-large shrimp, peeled and deveined
  Salt and pepper
- 2 tablespoons vegetable oil
- 4 tablespoons unsalted butter
- 3 garlic cloves, minced
- ½ cup beer
- ½ cup clam juice
- ¼ cup chopped fresh cilantro
- 3 scallions, sliced thin
- 2 tablespoons hot sauce (see note below)

1. Pat shrimp dry with paper towels and season with salt and pepper. Heat 1 tablespoon oil in large skillet over medium-high heat until just smoking. Cook half of shrimp without moving until spotty brown on one side, about 1 minute; transfer to plate. Repeat with remaining oil and shrimp.
2. Melt 1 tablespoon butter in empty skillet over medium heat. Add garlic and cook until fragrant, about 30 seconds. Stir in beer, clam juice, and any accumulated shrimp juices, scraping up any browned bits. Bring to boil and cook until sauce is reduced to ⅓ cup, 3 to 5 minutes.
3. Return shrimp to skillet and cook, covered, over medium-low heat until shrimp are cooked through, about 2 minutes. Off heat, stir in cilantro, scallions, hot sauce, and remaining butter. Serve.

TEST KITCHEN NOTE: Frank's RedHot is the test kitchen's favorite brand of hot sauce. If using a spicier sauce such as Tabasco, reduce the amount to 1 tablespoon.

TUSCAN GARLIC CHICKEN PASTA Serves 4 to 6

WHY THIS RECIPE WORKS: Microwaving the garlic, pepper flakes, and olive oil until fragrant blooms the flavors and infuses the oil.

- 6 garlic cloves, minced
- ¼ teaspoon red pepper flakes
- 6 tablespoons extra-virgin olive oil
- 4 boneless, skinless chicken breasts (about 1½ pounds)
  Salt and pepper
- 1 pound penne pasta
- 1 (5-ounce) bag baby arugula (see note below)
- ½ cup chopped fresh basil
- 6 tablespoons juice from 2 lemons
- 1 cup grated Parmesan cheese

1. Bring 4 quarts water to boil in large pot. Meanwhile, combine garlic, pepper flakes, and oil in bowl and microwave until garlic is golden and fragrant, about 1 minute.
2. Pat chicken dry with paper towels and season with salt and pepper. Transfer 1 tablespoon oil from bowl with garlic mixture to large skillet and heat over medium-high heat until just smoking. Add chicken and cook until well browned and cooked through, about 5 minutes per side. Transfer to cutting board and tent with foil. Let rest 5 minutes, then slice thin and set aside.
3. Add 1 tablespoon salt and pasta to boiling water and cook until al dente. Reserve ½ cup cooking water. Drain pasta and return to pot. Stir in sliced chicken, arugula, basil, lemon juice, Parmesan, and remaining garlic mixture, adding reserved pasta water as needed. Season with salt and pepper. Serve.

TEST KITCHEN NOTE: An equal amount of baby spinach can be substituted for the arugula.

SESAME NOODLES WITH CHICKEN AND ASPARAGUS

CRISPY BREADED PORK CHOPS
WITH PARSLEY-CAPER SAUCE

STEAK TIPS AU POIVRE

PENNSYLVANIA DUTCH CORN AND CHICKEN SOUP

CRISPY BREADED PORK CHOPS WITH PARSLEY-CAPER SAUCE Serves 4

WHY THIS RECIPE WORKS: A briny, lemony sauce is a good foil for the richness of pan-fried pork cutlets.

- 1 cup chopped fresh parsley
- ¼ cup drained capers
- 3 tablespoons lemon juice
- 1½ cups olive oil
  Salt and pepper
- ½ cup all-purpose flour
- 2 large eggs
- 2 cups panko bread crumbs (see note below)
- 8 boneless pork chops (3 to 4 ounces each), about ¼ inch thick

1. Adjust oven rack to middle position and heat oven to 200 degrees. Place parsley, capers, and lemon juice in blender. With blender running, slowly drizzle in ½ cup oil and blend until smooth and emulsified, about 1 minute. Transfer to serving bowl and season with salt and pepper.
2. Place flour in shallow dish. Beat eggs in second shallow dish. Place bread crumbs in third shallow dish. Pat chops dry with paper towels and season with salt and pepper. One at a time, coat chops lightly with flour, dip them in egg, and dredge in crumbs, pressing to adhere. Transfer cutlets to large plate and let dry 5 minutes.
3. Heat ½ cup oil in large nonstick skillet over medium heat until just smoking. Add half of pork and cook until golden brown and crisp, about 2 minutes per side. Transfer to wire rack set inside rimmed baking sheet and keep warm in oven. Wipe out skillet with paper towels and repeat with remaining oil and pork. Serve, passing sauce at table.

TEST KITCHEN NOTE: Panko, Japanese-style bread crumbs, are extra crunchy.

SESAME NOODLES WITH CHICKEN AND ASPARAGUS Serves 4

WHY THIS RECIPE WORKS: Thinning the peanut butter with some of the reserved pasta water ensures a creamy sauce.

- 2 boneless, skinless chicken breasts (about 12 ounces), cut crosswise into ¼-inch pieces
- 1 tablespoon vegetable oil
- 1 pound linguine (see note below)
- 1 pound asparagus, trimmed and cut into 1-inch pieces
- ⅓ cup peanut butter
- 5 tablespoons rice vinegar
- ¼ cup oyster sauce
- 2 teaspoons chili-garlic sauce
- 1½ teaspoons grated fresh ginger
- 1½ tablespoons toasted sesame oil

1. Bring 4 quarts water to boil in large pot. Pat chicken dry with paper towels. Heat oil in large skillet over medium-high heat until just smoking. Cook chicken until no longer pink, 1 to 2 minutes per side. Transfer to plate.
2. Add pasta to boiling water and cook until just beginning to soften, about 8 minutes. Add asparagus to pot and cook until bright green and pasta is al dente, about 4 minutes. Reserve 1 cup cooking water, drain pasta and asparagus, and return to pot.
3. Whisk peanut butter, vinegar, oyster sauce, chili-garlic sauce, ginger, sesame oil, and ½ cup pasta cooking water in bowl until smooth. Add peanut butter mixture and chicken to pot and toss to combine, adding reserved pasta water as needed. Serve.

TEST KITCHEN NOTE: Any long-strand pasta, such as spaghetti or fettuccine, can also be used here.

PENNSYLVANIA DUTCH CORN AND CHICKEN SOUP
Serves 4 to 6

WHY THIS RECIPE WORKS: Gently poaching the chicken breasts in the simmering soup improves their flavor and keeps them tender.

- 1 (16-ounce) bag frozen corn, thawed
- 8 cups low-sodium chicken broth
- 1 tablespoon unsalted butter
- 1 onion, chopped
- 1 celery rib, sliced thin
  Salt and pepper
- 2 boneless, skinless chicken breasts (about 12 ounces), cut into ½-inch chunks
- 3 cups egg noodles (see note below)

1. Combine 2 cups corn and 2 cups broth in blender and puree until smooth. Melt butter in Dutch oven over medium-high heat. Cook onion, celery, remaining corn, and ½ teaspoon salt until softened, 5 to 7 minutes.
2. Stir in remaining broth, chicken, noodles, and pureed corn mixture. Bring to boil, then reduce heat to medium and simmer until noodles are tender and chicken is cooked through, 6 to 8 minutes. Season with salt and pepper. Serve.

TEST KITCHEN NOTE: Light 'n Fluffy Wide Egg Noodles is the test kitchen's top-rated brand.

STEAK TIPS AU POIVRE Serves 4

WHY THIS RECIPE WORKS: The browned bits left in the pan after cooking the steak tips are essential for this recipe. To release them, deglaze the pan with a combination of wine and broth.

- 1½ pounds steak tips, cut into 2-inch chunks (see note below)
- 1 tablespoon coarsely ground pepper
  Salt
- 1 tablespoon vegetable oil
- 4 tablespoons unsalted butter
- 1 shallot, minced
- ½ cup red wine
- ½ cup low-sodium beef broth
- ½ teaspoon minced fresh thyme

1. Pat steak tips dry with paper towels. Rub all over with pepper and season with salt. Heat oil in large skillet over medium-high heat until just smoking. Cook steak tips until browned all over and cooked to desired doneness, 6 to 10 minutes. Transfer to platter and tent with foil.
2. Add 1 tablespoon butter and shallot to empty skillet and cook until softened, about 1 minute. Add wine, broth, and thyme to skillet. Simmer, scraping up any browned bits, until slightly thickened, 5 to 7 minutes. Off heat, whisk in any accumulated steak juices and remaining butter and season with salt. Spoon sauce over steaks. Serve.

TEST KITCHEN NOTE: Steak tips can be sold as whole steaks, cubes, or strips. For this recipe, we prefer to buy strips or whole steaks and cut them ourselves.

Dream Bars

We wanted chewy, toffee-flavored layer bars that shouted coconut and pecans. Getting back to the original recipe was a good first step. BY MARÍA DEL MAR SACASA

Soaking the shredded coconut in cream of coconut makes for a rich, moist topping that browns beautifully.

In the depths of the Depression, Americans badly needed sweet dreams. And that's exactly when recipes for this rich, nutty coconut bar first made the rounds in newspapers. Within 20 years, dream bars were so popular that manufacturers had taken to using them to promote a wide range of ingredients. A Domino sugar advertisement went so far as to promise that the housewife who used its brown sugar to make her dream bars would become known as "a cook with a touch of genius."

Early recipes called for a simple brown-sugar pat-in-the-pan shortbread crust topped by a sticky, uncluttered filling (eggs, more brown sugar, shredded "cocoanut," and "nut meats"). By the 1940s and '50s, dream bars might include chocolate chips, cornflakes, graham cracker crumbs, dried apricots, or even rolled oats. A number of these fully loaded versions originated as back-of-the-box recipes (most famously for bars that incorporate sweetened condensed milk). As the ingredient list swelled, the recipes were rechristened several times over. But Hello Dolly bars, seven-layer bars, and magic bars all are a far cry from the pared-down, toffee-flavored original that I was determined to re-create.

Even the simplest versions I tested were too sweet for modern tastes, and the coconut and pecans all but disappeared because the sugar was so

forward. To bring out their flavor, I tried toasting them. Now the pecans tasted crunchy and rich. The shredded coconut, alas, dried out. Perhaps a structural change was in order: If I separated the filling into two layers, I figured the coconut had a fighting chance to hold its own. Wrong.

I was stumped—until a colleague came up with an interesting idea. She suggested I intensify the flavor of the shredded coconut by soaking it in coconut milk. Nobody liked the white, cottony topping that resulted, but the test wasn't a total failure: It led me to cream of coconut, which has almost 10 times as much sugar as coconut milk. That sugar helped the coconut topping caramelize.

Unfortunately, my initial problem resurfaced with a vengeance—the bars were cloyingly sweet. Up to now, I'd been using a standard shortbread crust. Reducing the amount of brown sugar in the crust was a good first step. Making the crust thicker and adding pecans to it created a nutty density that helped counterbalance the sweet topping.

To create an even crust, I scattered the crust mixture into the prepared baking pan and then used the bottom of a metal measuring cup to firmly compact it into a uniform layer before baking. These chewy, butterscotch-y Dream Bars were their own advertisement.

DREAM BARS Makes 24 bars

Spread the coconut mixture as evenly as possible over the pecan layer, but don't worry if it looks patchy. Cream of coconut is available in the baking aisle alongside other coconut products.

CRUST

- 2 cups all-purpose flour
- ¾ cup packed dark brown sugar
- ½ cup pecans
- ¼ teaspoon salt
- 10 tablespoons (1¼ sticks) unsalted butter, cut into ½-inch pieces and chilled

TOPPING

- 1½ cups sweetened shredded coconut
- 1 cup cream of coconut (see note)
- 2 large eggs
- ¾ cup packed dark brown sugar
- 2 tablespoons all-purpose flour
- 1½ teaspoons baking powder
- 1 teaspoon vanilla extract
- ½ teaspoon salt
- 1 cup pecans, toasted and chopped rough

1. PREPARE PAN Adjust oven rack to middle position and heat oven to 350 degrees. Line 13- by 9-inch baking pan with foil, allowing excess foil to hang over pan edges. Coat foil lightly with cooking spray.

2. MAKE CRUST Process flour, sugar, pecans, and salt in food processor until pecans are coarsely ground. Add butter and pulse until mixture resembles coarse meal. Press mixture firmly into prepared baking pan. Bake until golden brown, about 20 minutes. Cool on wire rack 20 minutes.

3. MAKE TOPPING Combine coconut and cream of coconut in bowl. In another bowl, whisk eggs, sugar, flour, baking powder, vanilla, and salt until smooth. Stir in pecans, then spread filling over cooled crust. Dollop heaping tablespoons of coconut mixture over filling, then spread into even layer.

4. BAKE AND COOL Bake until topping is deep golden brown, 35 to 40 minutes. Cool on wire rack, about 2 hours. Using foil overhang, lift bars from pan and cut into 24 pieces. Serve. (Bars can be refrigerated in airtight container for 5 days.)

ON THE SIDE Guacamole Salad

We wanted a salad with the bright flavors of the popular dip, but the tomatoes threw a wrench into our plans. BY KRIS WIDICAN

More substantial than its namesake dip, this chunky salad pairs well with grilled meats or fish.

FLIPPING CHANNELS ONE NIGHT, I came across a TV chef slicing avocados, mincing chiles, and squeezing limes to make an intriguing, lively-looking dish he called guacamole salad. I'd never heard of it, but a little Internet research uncovered lots of recipes. Those I tried, however, were complicated by ingredients that did little for the salad or for me. Even the best recipe I tested—a straightforward combination of tomato, avocado, cilantro, red onion, garlic, and jalapeño with a lime vinaigrette—needed fine-tuning.

Tasters liked the consistently sweet taste of grape tomatoes compared to other varieties. They preferred scallions and garlic (which I mellowed first by steeping them in lime juice) to harsher raw onion. I wanted plenty of peppers for crunch and bulk, but a large quantity of jalapeños made the salad too hot to eat. Poblanos, with just a hint of heat, were a better choice.

Tasters liked my combination of flavors and textures, but after five minutes, liquid pooled in the salad bowl and the flavors became diluted. The tomatoes were at fault: They were giving off a lot of moisture. The next time I made the salad, I tossed the tomatoes with a little salt and let them drain on paper towels for 15 minutes. Meanwhile, I prepped the rest of the ingredients. When I assembled the dish, I was happy to find that the flavors were assertive and the salad was lightly coated in dressing, not drowning in juice.

GUACAMOLE SALAD Serves 4 to 6

If you can't find poblano peppers, substitute an equal number of Anaheim chiles, or a large green bell pepper mixed with up to 2 tablespoons of minced jalapeño chile.

- 1 pint grape tomatoes, halved
  Salt and pepper
- 4 scallions, sliced thin
- 1 garlic clove, minced
- 1 tablespoon grated zest and ⅓ cup juice from 3 limes
- ¼ cup olive oil
- 2 poblano chiles, seeded and sliced into 2-inch matchsticks (see note)
- 2 ripe avocados, pitted, skinned, and cut into ½-inch pieces (as shown on page 31)
- ¼ cup finely chopped fresh cilantro

1. SALT TOMATOES Toss tomatoes and ½ teaspoon salt in medium bowl. Transfer to paper towel–lined baking sheet and let drain 15 minutes.

2. MAKE DRESSING Combine scallions, garlic, lime zest, lime juice, ½ teaspoon salt, and ½ teaspoon pepper in large bowl. Let sit 5 minutes, then slowly whisk in oil.

3. TOSS SALAD Add chiles, avocados, cilantro, and drained tomatoes to bowl with dressing and toss to combine. Season with salt and pepper. Serve.

ON THE SIDE Roasted Salsa

A good tomato is hard to find. Could we make great salsa regardless? BY LYNN CLARK

TOP-NOTCH SALSA depends on top-notch tomatoes, but most tomatoes aren't up to the task. Grilling over a smoky fire neatly solves the problem. As the tomatoes sizzle alongside onions, chiles, and garlic, they sweeten and develop a smoky char.

I didn't want to bother with the grill, however, so I consulted a few recipes that attempted to capture that char through other methods. I tried roasting the vegetables in the oven; the tomatoes tasted stewed. I ran a batch under the broiler; these vegetables developed a nice outside char, but the insides never fully roasted. Tasters liked the third batch best, cooked in a skillet on the stovetop. The vegetables charred on the outside (thanks to direct contact with the heat) and grew sweet within. Cutting the tomatoes in half allowed more surface area to caramelize.

In a side-by-side test, tasters favored plum tomatoes over beefsteaks. To mimic ripeness, I sprinkled the cut sides lightly with sugar before I put them in the skillet—after all, what is ripeness but sweetness by another name?

I pulsed the skillet-roasted vegetables in the food processor, stopping while they were still a bit chunky, and combined them with lime and cilantro. The salsa was a little dull—high treason, in my book. The next time, I held one clove of garlic and half a jalapeño pepper back from the skillet. I minced these and stirred them in at the end, which supplied the missing fire and spice.

ROASTED TOMATO SALSA Serves 4 to 6

For spicier salsa, don't seed the jalapeños. Add a little water to the salsa if it seems too thick.

- 2 teaspoons vegetable oil
- 1¼ pounds plum tomatoes (about 5 medium), cored and halved lengthwise
- 1 teaspoon sugar
- 2 jalapeño chiles, halved, stemmed, and seeded (see note)
- 1 small onion, cut into wedges
- 4 garlic cloves, peeled, 3 cloves left whole, and 1 clove minced
- ¼ cup finely chopped fresh cilantro
- 1 tablespoon lime juice
  Salt

1. SUGAR TOMATOES Heat 1 teaspoon oil in large nonstick skillet over medium-high heat until shimmering. Sprinkle cut side of tomatoes with sugar. Cook tomatoes, cut-side down, until browned, about 5 minutes. Flip tomatoes and cook until browned on skin side, about 5 minutes. Transfer to plate.

2. BROWN VEGETABLES Add remaining oil to empty skillet and heat until shimmering. Cook 3 jalapeño halves, onion wedges, and whole garlic cloves, turning once, until well browned, about 5 minutes per side. Transfer to plate.

3. PROCESS VEGETABLES Using fingers, remove skin

The two secrets to making great salsa from mediocre (or worse) tomatoes? A skillet and some sugar.

from tomatoes and discard. Pulse browned vegetables in food processor until finely chopped; transfer to large bowl. Pulse tomatoes in empty processor until coarsely chopped; transfer to bowl with other vegetables.

4. MIX SALSA Mince remaining jalapeño half and add to bowl with tomatoes. Stir in cilantro, lime juice, and minced garlic clove. Season with salt. Let sit at room temperature 15 minutes. Serve. (Salsa can be refrigerated in airtight container for 3 days.)

Southwest Enchilada Casserole

Our layered Tex-Mex classic depended on corn tortillas for taste, texture, and structure. So how did they keep getting in the way? BY DIANE UNGER

A topping of melted cheese studded with minced jalapeños crowns this hearty casserole.

You can make casseroles ahead of time, transport them to potlucks with minimal trouble, and feed a crowd, all of which makes them very practical. But many casserole-makers take unfortunate shortcuts, tossing the contents of the larders into their casseroles. Case in point: beef enchilada casserole, a Tex-Mex lasagna of sorts.

The model (beef enchiladas) is made with seared, braised, shredded steak. The meat is wrapped in corn tortillas that have been dipped in a rich, spicy, homemade chile sauce; the stuffed tortillas are lined up in a baking dish; and the whole thing is sprinkled with cheese. At some point, time-pressed cooks reached for the ground beef and decided to layer rather than roll, and a Tex-Mex standard was born. Judging by the recipes I tested, cooks also reached for canned enchilada sauce, canned olives, ersatz cheese, frozen corn, and condensed tomato soup. I tested those recipes, and no surprise, they produced greasy, busy, bland casseroles. I wanted to mimic the straightforward quality of enchiladas, but keep the casserole's hearty, satisfying ease.

My tasters nixed canned enchilada sauce as one-dimensional, so I started by adapting a beef enchilada sauce the test kitchen has made in the past. I sautéed onion and lots of garlic in oil, then stirred in chili powder and ground cumin. I

poured in canned tomato sauce followed by beef broth, to give the ground beef all the reinforcement I could. After the sauce had simmered for a few minutes to thicken and concentrate, I mixed half of it with beef I'd browned (my tasters preferred the flavor of 85 percent lean ground beef over anything leaner), and I turned up the heat by stirring in minced jalapeño and hot sauce.

Everybody agreed that deep corn flavor was key to a successful beef enchilada casserole, but used straight from the plastic bag, the corn tortillas turned slimy in the casserole; baking rendered them tough, chewy, and flavorless. I tried toasting them in a dry skillet. As the tortillas blistered and charred, they filled the test kitchen with an enticing aroma reminiscent of popcorn. Once again, I started building: three layers of toasted tortillas sandwiching two of beef filling, sauce poured and cheese sprinkled over all. The casserole smelled fantastic in the oven, but that middle layer of tortillas tasted papery and unpleasant. When I tried eliminating it, the simplest fix, tasters missed both its corn presence and the cohesiveness it had given the casserole.

One test kitchen recipe for chili uses corn tortillas as a thickener. I decided to borrow the technique. I put eight of the toasted tortillas in the food processor with a can of green chili–dotted Ro-Tel tomatoes and ¾ cup beef broth (cutting an equivalent amount of broth from the sauce). I processed the mix until it had the consistency of creamy mashed potatoes, then folded it into the browned beef. This time I sandwiched the filling between just two tortilla layers. I poured the remaining enchilada sauce over everything. After the casserole had baked for 30 minutes, I sprinkled it with colby-Jack cheese and more minced jalapeño. I returned the dish to the oven until the casserole was golden brown and bubbling. I sat on my hands for 20 minutes, giving it time to set up, then cut myself a hefty square. Finally, a big casserole with a big payoff.

TEST KITCHEN TECHNIQUE
Toasting Tortillas

To heighten the corn tortilla flavor in our casserole, we first toasted the tortillas in a dry skillet.

BEEF ENCHILADA CASSEROLE
Serves 8 to 10
If you can't find Ro-Tel tomatoes, substitute 1¼ cups of diced tomatoes plus an additional jalapeño. Monterey Jack cheese may be substituted for the colby-Jack. Serve with sour cream, chopped scallions, and lime wedges.

- 20 (6-inch) corn tortillas
- 1½ cups low-sodium beef broth
- 1 (10-ounce) can Ro-Tel tomatoes (see note)
- 2 pounds 85 percent lean ground beef
- 2 tablespoons vegetable oil
- 2 onions, chopped fine
- 8 garlic cloves, minced
- 2 tablespoons chili powder
- 1 teaspoon ground cumin
- 3 (15-ounce) cans tomato sauce
- 4 cups shredded colby-Jack cheese (see note)
- 3 jalapeño chiles, seeded and minced
- ½ cup chopped fresh cilantro
- 1 tablespoon hot sauce
  Salt and pepper

1. TOAST TORTILLAS Adjust oven rack to middle position and heat oven to 450 degrees. Grease 13- by 9-inch baking dish. Toast 3 tortillas in large nonstick skillet over medium-high heat until they bubble and turn spotty brown, 1 to 2 minutes per side. Transfer to plate and

repeat with remaining tortillas.

2. PROCESS TORTILLAS Tear 8 toasted tortillas into rough pieces and transfer to food processor. Add ¾ cup broth and Ro-Tel tomatoes (with juice) and process until smooth; transfer to large bowl. Add beef to empty skillet and cook over medium-high heat until no longer pink, about 5 minutes. Drain beef in colander, then transfer to bowl with tortilla mixture.

3. MAKE FILLING Add oil and onion to empty skillet and cook until softened, about 5 minutes. Stir in garlic, chili powder, and cumin and cook until fragrant, about 30 seconds. Add tomato sauce and remaining broth to skillet and simmer until slightly thickened, 5 to 7 minutes. Stir half of tomato sauce mixture, 1½ cups cheese, 1 minced jalapeño, cilantro, and hot sauce into bowl with tortilla mixture. Season with salt and pepper.

4. ASSEMBLE AND BAKE Arrange 6 toasted tortillas in bottom of baking dish. Spread filling evenly over tortillas. Arrange remaining tortillas over filling and top with remaining tomato sauce mixture. Bake until filling is bubbling around edges, about 30 minutes. Sprinkle remaining cheese and remaining minced jalapeño evenly over casserole. Bake until cheese is browned, 15 to 20 minutes. Let cool 20 minutes. Serve.

Chicken-Fried Steak

Like New Yorkers and their bagels, Texans are passionate, partisan, some might say a little nuts about chicken-fried steak. The dish—a cheap steak pounded to tenderness, coated, fried, and served (always!) with a peppery cream gravy and mashed potatoes—was once described by the Dallas newspaper columnist Jerry Flammons as the food that best "defines the Texas character." The earliest printed recipe dates back only to 1949, but the dish itself, sometimes called country-fried steak, is much older. Most culinary historians trace its origins to Wiener schnitzel, brought by German immigrants to Texas in the mid-19th century. According to this theory, the coating and the cooking method were adapted for local beef. (No tender veal on the range.) BY DIANE UNGER

CFS (its nickname in many diners) has moved beyond the borders of Texas and morphed with time and geography. You can find versions all over the South and Midwest. The technique—pound, coat, and fry a tough cut of beef to make it palatable—is the same, but the details vary. One camp (mostly in Texas) demands adherence to the "original" concept: Only a simple flour dredge and a skillet will do. Others (including some renegades in Texas) coat the steaks in batter and cook them in a bubbling deep-fat fryer. As someone who was only casually familiar with chicken fried steak, I was uncommitted. As long as the steaks lived up to the advance billing—crunchy on the outside, tender within, hot, salty, and big enough to hang over the edge of a dinner plate—I was willing to throw my lot in with either camp. I headed for the kitchen.

All the recipes in my initial testing used cube steak—steaks cut from the round and put through a tenderizing machine that makes small, cubelike indentations. Breaded and fried, it makes serviceable steak. Unfortunately, overzealous supermarket butchers often mangle the job, turning out cube steak the texture of coarse hamburger. I attempted to pound out round steaks myself instead. Big mistake—those tough steaks were a bear to beat down.

I turned to other cheap beef options. Blade steaks had an obstructive line of gristle, so I ruled them out, but tasters loved the flavor of sirloin tips. Even pounded, coated, and fried, however, the tips were a little tough. I borrowed an idea from the cubing process and tried scoring the meat at ¼-inch intervals on both sides (scoring shortens the meat fibers, making the beef easier to pound), then bashed the tips with a meat mallet until they were thin and would fry up nice and tender. Then I turned my attention to the coating.

Some recipes called for the steaks to be dredged in flour. The result was too bare. Other recipes used a tempuralike batter, which gave me puffy, pasty coatings. Since the very name CFS suggests fried chicken, I wondered how a favorite test kitchen recipe for fried chicken would fare with steak tips. I pulled out the recipe, then dredged the steaks in seasoned flour (plus baking powder to lighten and cornstarch for extra crispness), dipped them in egg, and then coated them in a pebbly mixture of more seasoned flour, to which I'd added a little milk. These steaks were light and crisp right out of the oil. But victory was fleeting: Within moments, the crust became soggy and peeled off the meat.

I looked through my recipes and found unexpected guidance from the *Household Searchlight Recipe Book*, *Topeka, Kan.* (1949), which included the oldest published recipe for chicken-fried steak I'd been able to find: "One round steak, cut ¾ inch thick. Rub with salt and pepper. Pound all the flour possible into the steak. Sear on both sides in hot cooking fat. Cook until browned." I'd been lightly coating the steaks in flour, not pounding it in. What would that do? So, after scoring the sirloin tips on both sides, I pounded in flour until it disappeared, dipped the steaks in egg, and again applied my fried chicken coating. Now the crust held on, the flour essentially "gluing" the coating to the meat. Alas, the crust was as soggy as ever.

I discussed the challenge with our science editor. Pound more, he suggested. Pounding damages the cell structure of meat, releasing moisture to the surface. Second, ditch the deep-fry method I'd been using in favor of a shallower fry. Submerging the coated meat in deep fat traps the moisture, he explained, and prevents it from evaporating. I returned to the kitchen, where I pounded the steaks to ⅛ inch thick and added just enough oil to the skillet, about 1½ cups, for my steaks to float. The difference was dramatic. Visible steam wisped upward, and as I flipped the steaks, the juices sputtered away. I knew I'd hit the mark. Sure enough, a tuck-in with a fork and knife rewarded me with heat, salt, beefy flavor, and serious crunch.

The traditional recipe for cream gravy starts by cooking flour in the pan drippings, then whisking in milk, salt, and pepper. I took the opportunity to buck tradition and amp up the flavors with the addition of chicken broth and garlic powder. This was tasty, but the real problem with the gravy was that by the time it was ready, my steaks were almost cold. I decided a preemptive strike was in order and made the gravy before frying the steaks, using butter in place of any pan drippings. By the time the steaks were golden brown and crispy, the cream gravy was good to go.

CHICKEN-FRIED STEAK Serves 4

Flap meat is also sold as steak tips or sirloin tips and can be packaged variously as whole steaks, cubes, or strips. For this recipe, buy a whole 1-pound steak and cut it yourself. Serve with mashed potatoes and Cream Gravy.

- 3½ cups all-purpose flour
- ½ cup cornstarch
- 1 tablespoon garlic powder
- 1 tablespoon onion powder
- ½ teaspoon cayenne pepper
- 2 teaspoons baking powder
  Salt and pepper
- 4 large eggs
- ¼ cup whole milk
- 1 pound beef flap meat, cut into four 4-ounce pieces (see note)
- 1½ cups peanut or vegetable oil

1. MAKE COATING Whisk flour, cornstarch, garlic powder, onion powder, cayenne, baking powder, 1 teaspoon salt, and 2 teaspoons pepper in large bowl. Transfer 1 cup seasoned flour mixture to shallow dish. Beat eggs in second shallow dish. Add milk to bowl with remaining flour mixture and rub with fingers until mixture resembles coarse meal.

2. PREPARE STEAKS Pat steaks dry with paper towels and season with salt and pepper. Following photos 1 and 2, score meat lightly and then dredge meat in seasoned flour. Using a meat pounder, pound steaks to between ⅛ and ¼ inch thick. One at a time, coat steaks lightly with seasoned flour again, dip in egg mixture, and then transfer to bowl with milk and flour mixture, pressing to adhere. Arrange steaks on wire rack set inside rimmed baking sheet and refrigerate 15 minutes (or up to 4 hours); do not discard milk and flour mixture.

3. FRY AND SERVE Adjust oven rack to middle position and heat oven to 200 degrees. Heat oil in large Dutch oven over medium-high heat until just smoking. Return 2 steaks to bowl with milk and flour mixture and turn to coat. Fry 2 steaks until deep golden brown and crisp, 2 to 3 minutes per side. Transfer to clean wire rack set inside rimmed baking sheet and keep warm in oven. Repeat with remaining steaks. Serve.

STEP-BY-STEP Keys to Chicken-Fried Steak

Pounding seasoned flour into the scored steaks is the first step to an ultra-crunchy coating. To finish the process, the steaks go back in the flour, into beaten egg, and finally into a flour-and-milk mixture. Resting the steaks gives the coating time to adhere.

1. Tenderize the meat by scoring it at ¼-inch intervals in a crosshatch pattern. Repeat on the other side.

2. Dredge each steak in seasoned flour, then use a meat pounder to flatten. The flour helps the subsequent coating stick.

3. After the final dredge, fry two steaks at a time in a heavy-bottomed Dutch oven to minimize splatter and mess.

CREAM GRAVY Makes about 3 cups

Avoid low-fat or skim milk in this recipe.

- 3 tablespoons unsalted butter
- 3 tablespoons all-purpose flour
- ½ teaspoon garlic powder
- 1½ cups low-sodium chicken broth
- 1½ cups whole milk (see note)
- ¾ teaspoon salt
- ½ teaspoon pepper

Melt butter in large skillet over medium heat. Stir in flour and garlic powder and cook until golden, about 2 minutes. Slowly whisk in broth, milk, salt, and pepper and simmer until thickened, about 5 minutes. Serve. (Gravy can be refrigerated for 2 days.)

RATING FROZEN DINNER ROLLS

A warm, golden homemade roll is ideal for mopping up cream gravy. But get real. How often do you have time to bake a yeast roll from scratch? We wondered: Can any supermarket frozen dinner rolls pass for homemade? Sad to say, after tasting five styles from three brands, our answer is a resounding "No!" But we did find a few that will do in a pinch. Our tasters preferred rolls that are neither overly sweet nor overly salty. The Pillsbury Oven Baked Dinner Rolls in the Crusty French variety came out on top for their light, fluffy crumb and substantial crust. The rolls are listed in order of preference. BY MEREDITH BUTCHER

RECOMMENDED WITH RESERVATIONS

PILLSBURY Oven Baked Dinner Rolls/Crusty French
Sodium: 200mg
Sugar: 2g
Price: $3.69 for 12.4-ounce bag (10 rolls)

Comments: Tasters liked these for their fluffy insides and crispy crust. The flavor was less pleasingly yeasty than that of some competitors, but the texture was the best in our tasting—and closest to homemade.

RHODES Frozen White Dinner Rolls
Sodium: 130mg
Sugar: 2g
Price: $3.99 for 48-ounce bag (36 rolls)

Comments: Their "sweet," "yeasty," "fresh" flavor earned praise; their doughy, "squishy" texture did not. Tasters demanded: Where's the crust? Plus, a proofing time of more than an hour turned this "convenience" item into an inconvenience.

PILLSBURY Oven Baked Dinner Rolls/Soft White
Sodium: 190mg
Sugar: 4g
Price: $3.99 for 12.4-ounce bag (10 rolls)

Comments: Looks aren't everything. These rolls have an appealing, even "adorable," shape, but—beyond a slightly sweet aftertaste—not much flavor. Tasters were satisfied with the texture.

NOT RECOMMENDED

SISTER SCHUBERT'S Dinner Yeast Rolls
Sodium: 240mg
Sugar: 4g
Price: $9.95 for two 15-ounce bags (10 rolls)

Comments: These unusually sweet rolls were wannabe pastries, tasters said, not proper dinner rolls. Worse, they were squat, dense, and leaden.

PILLSBURY Oven Baked Dinner Rolls/Butterflake
Sodium: 370mg
Sugar: 7g
Price: $3.49 for 20.3-ounce bag (12 rolls)

Comments: Tasters downgraded these for an artificially sweet, "fake movie popcorn" flavor. Also, the flaky crescent-roll style seemed more like puff pastry than American dinner rolls, according to tasters.

ON THE SIDE Sweet and Sour Broccoli Rabe

Could an Italian sauce that balances sweet with sour tame a headstrong green? BY JEREMY SAUER

AN ITALIAN GREEN with potent broccoli flavor and a bitter, peppery edge, broccoli rabe makes its presence known. Traditionally, the vegetable is trimmed of its thicker, woodier stems, chopped in bite-sized pieces, and then sautéed in olive oil. In the test kitchen, however, we've found that a sauté alone won't suffice. Instead, we first blanch the broccoli rabe, which simultaneously softens its crunch and its mustardy bite.

In southern Italy, broccoli rabe is often flavored with a sauce called *agrodolce* (which roughly translates as "sweet and sour"). Italians make it by simmering vinegar with sugar and sometimes aromatics until the mixture is syrupy.

In the empty pot that we'd used to blanch the rabe, we sautéed onions and garlic. We reached for red wine vinegar in preference to balsamic because the latter became unpleasantly heavy when reduced. Most recipes call for white sugar, but we found that brown sugar added warmth along with sweetness. Simmered alone, the mixture needed more complexity. Happily, raisins and orange juice (both called for in some authentic *agrodolce* recipes) rounded out our sauce. When this mixture became syrupy, we tossed in the blanched rabe, and in minutes turned an aggressive vegetable into a gentleman.

ITALIAN SWEET AND SOUR BROCCOLI RABE
Serves 4
Sweet golden raisins balance the somewhat bitter broccoli rabe. If using black raisins, increase the brown sugar by 1 teaspoon.

- 1 large bunch broccoli rabe (about 1 pound), ends trimmed, and cut into 1-inch pieces
  Salt and pepper
- 2 tablespoons extra-virgin olive oil
- 1 onion, chopped fine
- 2 garlic cloves, minced
- ¼ cup golden raisins (see note)
- 3 tablespoons red wine vinegar
- 1 tablespoon orange juice
- 1 tablespoon brown sugar

1. **BLANCH** Bring 4 quarts water to boil in a large pot. Add broccoli rabe and 1 tablespoon salt and cook until just tender, about 2 minutes. Drain thoroughly.

2. **MAKE SAUCE** Heat oil in empty pot over medium heat until shimmering. Cook onion until softened, about 5 minutes. Stir in garlic and cook until fragrant, about 30 seconds. Add raisins, vinegar, orange juice, and sugar and cook until syrupy, 3 to 5 minutes. Add drained broccoli rabe to pot and cook, stirring occasionally, until well coated and just beginning to brown, about 2 minutes. Season with salt and pepper. Serve.

Blanching the broccoli rabe before sautéing softens it.

ON THE SIDE Orzo "Pilaf"

Like all pastas, orzo is typically boiled. If we changed the technique, could we change its profile? BY MEGHAN ERWIN

MAYBE BECAUSE IT looks so much like rice, recipe writers can't resist trying orzo—a small rice-shaped pasta—in pilaf, for which rice is sautéed in fat as a way to give the grain flavor. I was tired of the same old side dishes and looking for something to give my weeknight cooking a little pizzazz, so I made a few of those recipes.

I sautéed onions and garlic in butter and then added the orzo, stirring often to coat it with the butter as it toasted. But despite my diligent stirring, the pasta browned unevenly. Some burned, some didn't color at all. I scolded myself for sloppy thinking: True, orzo looks like rice, but cinnamon looks like ground cumin seed, and you wouldn't try using them the same way.

How, then, could I get that toasty flavor I desired? It occurred to me to try toasting the orzo in a dry skillet. The test kitchen uses the method to toast nuts and spices. Maybe it'd work for pasta. After about eight minutes over medium heat, the orzo turned an even golden brown.

Again thinking about pilaf, as well as ways to build more flavor, I decided I'd cook the toasted orzo in chicken broth instead of the water it's usually boiled in. Once again I sautéed onions and garlic in butter, but this time I added the orzo after it had been toasted. I poured in the broth, brought it to a boil, then covered the pot and turned the heat down to a simmer. Twenty minutes later, I found an inedible mess. The orzo was bloated, overcooked, and clumpy.

I tried again, this time leaving the lid off and stirring regularly to prevent the pasta from clumping. This orzo tasted OK, but the texture was sticky and heavy because the stirring was releasing the starch in the orzo. That's great for risotto, where creaminess is the object. Here, though, it was producing a stodgy mess. When I made the orzo next, I stirred with restraint, just three times during 15 minutes. Now each piece of orzo was separate and distinct.

In celebration of spring, I reached for classic culinary heralds of the season to flavor my dish: peas and mint. In a final few tests, I fine-tuned the flavors—exchanging some of the chicken broth for wine to add complexity and stirring in lemon juice to brighten.

ORZO WITH PEAS AND MINT Serves 6
In step 1, watch the orzo closely toward the end of the toasting time—it can quickly go from browned to burnt. Be sure to use low-sodium chicken broth or the dish will be too salty.

- 1 pound orzo
- 2 tablespoons unsalted butter
- 1 onion, chopped fine
- 2 garlic cloves, minced
- 3½ cups low-sodium chicken broth (see note)
- ½ cup white wine
  Salt and pepper
- 1½ cups frozen peas
- 2 tablespoons finely chopped fresh mint
- 2 teaspoons grated zest plus 2 teaspoons juice from 1 lemon

1. **PREPARE ORZO** Toast orzo in large skillet over medium heat, stirring frequently, until golden brown, about 8 minutes; transfer to bowl. Melt butter in empty skillet. Cook onion until softened, about 5 minutes. Add garlic and cook until fragrant, about 30 seconds.

2. **SIMMER** Add broth, wine, toasted orzo, and ¾ teaspoon salt to pan and bring to boil. Reduce heat to medium-low and simmer, stirring every 5 minutes until liquid has been absorbed and orzo is tender, about 15 minutes. Stir in peas, mint, lemon zest, and lemon juice and cook until heated through, about 1 minute. Season with salt and pepper. Serve.

A combination of technique and ingredients draws big flavors from a small pasta.

Chicken Florentine

We wanted a simplified recipe with clearer, brighter flavors. To go forward, we looked back. BY MEGHAN ERWIN

Our fresher, layered version of this classic dish features fresh spinach—and no creamy condensed soup.

The idea of chicken Florentine as a dish made from chicken, spinach, and a cheesy cream sauce appeared in print as early as 1931, when the *Lowell Sun* (of Massachusetts) breathlessly described Chicken Mornay Florentine as served at a Manhattan restaurant: "They make magic passes over spinach, then cover it with breasts of chicken and a Mornay sauce."

Sounds charming, but we haven't a clue what magic passes are. As far as we can tell, neither does anybody else. That might explain why over the years the recipe has been so darn muddled: Chicken Florentine morphed from a 1960s casserole (made with frozen spinach, margarine, packaged bread crumbs, and condensed soups) to wedding banquet fare in the 1970s and '80s (breasts stuffed with spinach, rolled, fried, and served with a cheesy sauce). I wanted to deconstruct the casserole, unroll the spirals, and return chicken Florentine to its earliest version: a bright, elegant, streamlined sauté with a pan sauce. No magic passes involved.

Many modern recipes call for frozen spinach. I tried fresh baby spinach instead, and it tasted much better. To ensure that my sauce wouldn't be watery, I pressed on the greens after I'd cooked them, discarding the liquid. Then I tackled the sauce, which would have to tie the dish together. I made Mornay sauce,

in homage to that early Manhattan restaurant version, melting butter in a pan, then whisking in flour, heavy cream (for silkiness), and Parmesan cheese (for its nutty, salty punch). The results were ho-hum. I tried again, this time building flavor by first sautéing shallots and garlic in butter. The sauce was tasty but pasty. In my next test, I eliminated the flour, which improved the consistency considerably. I had the sauce under control (or so I thought), so I turned to the third main component—the chicken; to keep things uncomplicated I used boneless, skinless breasts.

Some recipes call for sautéing the chicken until done and then setting it aside while the sauce is made. It's standard and I expected it to work, but the chicken developed no flavor. A colleague suggested searing the chicken breasts, and then poaching them in simmering sauce to intensify the flavor of both. Back at the stove, I wilted the spinach and set it aside. I used the hot skillet to sear the chicken breasts. When they were nice and brown on the outside and pink in the middle, I was ready to build my sauce.

I made the sauce as I had before, scraping up the fond (the flavorful browned bits left in the pan) for added flavor, then letting the chicken cook in the liquid. I could see immediately that my pan didn't have nearly enough sauce in which to poach the chicken. Adding chicken broth was an easy way to build volume, but as the broth reduced, the sauce grew unpleasantly salty. I cut the chicken broth with an equal amount of water (1¼ cups of each). Now I had enough sauce, but it tasted flat. I made two more versions, one with a slug of wine, the second with a squeeze of lemon juice and a hit of zest. The lemon edged out the wine for its bright zing. For simplicity's sake, I omitted the butter in the sauce; the vegetable oil I was using to wilt the spinach and sear the chicken was enough.

I layered all the components on a platter, sprinkled them with an additional 2 tablespoons of cheese, and gave the dish a quick run under the broiler—an idea I borrowed from casserole versions. The elegant, burnished look of my Chicken Florentine matched its streamlined formulation.

Draining Spinach

As it cooks, spinach releases a lot of moisture, which can make dishes like our Chicken Florentine watery. To prevent that, we transferred the spinach to a colander and pressed the leaves with a spoon to force the liquid out. We drained nearly ¼ cup of liquid from the 12 ounces of spinach used in this recipe.

LOSE THE LIQUID

CHICKEN FLORENTINE Serves 4 to 6
We like tender, quick-cooking bagged baby spinach here; if using curly-leaf spinach, chop it before cooking.

- 2 tablespoons vegetable oil
- 2 (6-ounce) bags (about 8 cups) baby spinach (see note)
- 4 boneless, skinless chicken breasts (about 1½ pounds)
  Salt and pepper
- 1 shallot, minced
- 2 garlic cloves, minced
- 1¼ cups low-sodium chicken broth
- 1¼ cups water
- 1 cup heavy cream
- 6 tablespoons grated Parmesan cheese
- 1 teaspoon grated zest and 1 teaspoon juice from 1 lemon

1. COOK SPINACH Adjust oven rack to upper-middle position and heat broiler. Heat 1 tablespoon oil in large skillet over medium-high heat until shimmering. Add spinach and cook, stirring occasionally until wilted, 1 to 2 minutes. Transfer spinach to colander set over bowl and press with spoon to release excess liquid. Discard liquid.

2. BROWN CHICKEN Pat chicken dry with paper towels and season with salt and pepper. Wipe out pan and heat remaining oil over medium-high heat until just smoking. Cook chicken until golden, 2 to 3 minutes per side. Add shallot and garlic to skillet and cook until fragrant, about 30 seconds. Stir in broth, water, and cream and bring to boil.

3. MAKE SAUCE Reduce heat to medium-low and simmer until chicken is cooked through, about 10 minutes; transfer chicken to plate and tent with foil. Continue to simmer sauce until reduced to 1 cup, about 10 minutes. Off heat, stir in 4 tablespoons Parmesan, lemon zest, and lemon juice.

4. BROIL Cut chicken crosswise into ½-inch-thick slices and arrange on broiler-safe platter. Scatter spinach over chicken and pour sauce over spinach. Sprinkle with remaining Parmesan and broil until golden brown, 3 to 5 minutes. Serve.

Kentucky Burgoo

My nose led me straight into the Moonlite Bar-B-Q Inn—past the framed black-and-white family photographs, past the pictures of rural Kentucky, past the neatly stacked jars of jam and relish. It was drawn by the powerful scent of hickory smoke and barbecuing meat that curled through the dimly lit restaurant. At barely noon, lines of local businessmen, families, lunching regulars, and tourists had already formed at the buffet and carryout. I scanned the room for Pat Bosley, an owner of the inn. I had traveled almost a thousand miles to Owensboro, Kentucky, to meet Pat and learn about Kentucky's best-kept secret: burgoo. BY KRIS WIDICAN

Today, burgoo is a chunky stew of tomatoes, corn, potatoes, chicken, and mutton (mature lamb), but I'd heard that it began as a way to make use of whatever was hunted or ready to harvest: cabbage, lima beans, squirrel, opossum, deer... It goes without saying that I was curious. Pat wanted me to meet a bunch of "old-timers." He led me to a table where a group of men relished the last of their lunch. These were the real burgoo cooks, men who had grown up stirring the burgoo pot at the fund-raising picnics of their neighborhood parishes. They were a friendly bunch, but guarded, unwilling to tell a stranger the secrets of the stew. Finally, after a steady drum of banter, one man stopped the conversation cold. "You really want to know what goes into burgoo? I'll tell ya: anything that's free!"

Pat returned with a waitress, who set a brimming bowl of burgoo before me. Reddish orange and nearly as thick as oatmeal, it was too murky for me to discern individual ingredients. I nudged my spoon in, doubtful. Before I knew it, I'd polished it off. Heady and meaty, this burgoo had a warming, slow heat, a strangely compelling, tangy quality, and a familiar taste I liked but couldn't quite place. I was a convert.

Back in the test kitchen, my work was cut out for me. I had tasted burgoo at all the barbecue restaurants

in Owensboro and gathered a half-dozen recipes, but how would I ever squeeze the long list of ingredients into even my largest pot? Burgoo is traditionally cooked in a humongous cauldron over an open flame. It's stirred with something that looks like an oar. The cook boils whole chickens (and sometimes beef or pork stewing meat) to make broth; uses a second pot to boil mutton until tender (to tame the funky smell and taste); removes the meat from both pots; shreds it; chops vegetables; then cooks everything together until the flavors meld and the broth concentrates.

I peeled, chopped, shredded, and reduced, hoping to re-create a reasonable approximation. Many hours later, I had many gallons of burgoo. Some tasted pretty good, too, but it had been a project and a half to make. For this recipe to work at home, I needed to streamline the ingredients, cut back the cooking time, and find new ways to build flavor.

The test kitchen has a few "rules" for making stew: Brown the meat first. Add aromatic vegetables. Sprinkle in flour as a thickener. Deglaze the pan and simmer everything with broth, herbs, and spices until tender. If you're adding more vegetables, do it in stages so that the delicate ones don't overcook. I thought if I followed these rules, I might get away with using store-bought broth, precut frozen or canned for some of the vegetables, and small pieces of chicken and mutton for a tasty, reasonably quick burgoo.

I hit my first stumbling block while shopping. The supermarket didn't carry mutton—ever. My butcher suggested substituting a more common cut of stewing meat from lamb. Shank made the burgoo greasy. Leg of lamb was labor-intensive, requiring that I bone, then cube it. Lamb shoulder chops, however, became tender in less than 1½ hours and tasted wonderful. The bones added flavor and body. Tasters preferred chicken thigh meat to breasts, which dried out and got lost in the busy stew. As for vegetables, the ease of using canned tomatoes, frozen corn, and frozen lima beans made up for the onions, garlic, and potatoes I had to chop by hand.

The burgoo was now thick and tasted pretty good, but it lacked the rich meatiness and heat I remembered. Adding more meat to my already full pot was not an option. I thought long and hard and realized that the flavor that had eluded me in the burgoos I'd tasted must be my missing ingredient. I went back to the recipes I'd collected, and a light went on—Worcestershire sauce! Astonishingly, it took a full ¼ cup to give the stew the richness it lacked. Adding ¾ teaspoon of black pepper at the end of cooking rather than at the beginning restored a pleasant, spicy heat. To brighten the burgoo, I tried both vinegar and lemon juice. Lemon won hands-down.

"Insulting a man's burgoo is on par with insulting his mama," a colleague from that part of the country had told me. No worries, this version guarantees compliments.

KENTUCKY BURGOO Serves 6 to 8

If you can't find lamb shoulder chops (see page 31), substitute 1½ pounds of lamb stew meat or beef chuck stew meat.

- 4 bone-in, skin-on chicken thighs (about 2 pounds)
- 6 lamb shoulder blade chops (6 to 8 ounces each), about ½ inch thick (see note)
  Salt and pepper
- 1 tablespoon vegetable oil
- 2 onions, chopped
- 2 garlic cloves, minced
- 2 tablespoons all-purpose flour
- 6 cups low-sodium chicken broth
- 1 (14.5-ounce) can diced tomatoes
- ¼ cup Worcestershire sauce
- 2 Yukon gold potatoes, peeled and cut into ½-inch chunks
- 1½ cups frozen corn
- 1½ cups frozen baby lima beans
- ¼ cup juice from 2 lemons

1. BROWN MEATS Pat chicken and lamb dry with paper towels and season with salt and pepper. Heat oil in Dutch oven over medium-high heat until just smoking. Brown chicken, about 5 minutes per side; transfer to plate. Pour off fat from pan and reserve. (You should have about 3 tablespoons fat; if you have less, supplement with vegetable oil.) Add 1 tablespoon reserved fat to Dutch oven and heat until just smoking. Brown half of chops, about 5 minutes per side; transfer to plate. Repeat with additional 1 tablespoon fat and remaining chops.

2. COOK AROMATICS Add remaining fat and onions to now-empty pot and cook until softened, about 5 minutes. Add garlic and flour and cook until fragrant, about 1 minute. Stir in broth, tomatoes, and Worcestershire, scraping up any browned bits with wooden spoon. Return chicken and lamb to pot and bring to boil.

3. SIMMER MEATS Reduce heat to medium-low and simmer, covered, until chicken is tender, about 30 minutes. Transfer chicken to plate. When cool enough to handle, pull chicken into bite-sized pieces and reserve in refrigerator; discard bones and skin. Continue to simmer stew until lamb is tender, about 40 minutes longer. Transfer lamb to plate. When cool enough to handle, pull lamb into bite-sized pieces and reserve in refrigerator; discard bones.

4. ADD VEGETABLES Add potatoes to pot and simmer until tender, about 15 minutes. Add corn, lima beans, reserved chicken, and reserved lamb and simmer until heated through, about 5 minutes. Stir in lemon juice and ¾ teaspoon pepper. Season with salt. Skim fat, if necessary. Serve.

KEY INGREDIENTS **Secrets to Layers of Flavor**
Authentic burgoo is usually an all-day affair. To achieve the same depth of flavor in a shorter time, we use bold ingredients.

BLACK PEPPER   **LEMON**   **WORCESTERSHIRE SAUCE**

WHAT TO DO WITH LEFTOVERS Burgoo Shepherd's Pie

Top burgoo with mashed potatoes for a stellar Day 2 dish. BY JEREMY SAUER

THE IDEA OF USING leftover burgoo—chock-full of vegetables and tender lamb—as the foundation for a great shepherd's pie wasn't much of a stretch. To give the mashed potatoes the force to stand up to the burgoo, we mixed them with tangy buttermilk—half the amount we ordinarily would use so they would stay afloat when baked in the oven. For the same reason, before topping the burgoo, we thickened it with a roux of butter and flour. A little tomato paste brightened the dish.

EASY SHEPHERD'S PIE Serves 6

You will need six 6-ounce oven-safe ramekins for this recipe.

- 1½ pounds Yukon gold potatoes, peeled and cut into 1-inch chunks
- ¼ cup buttermilk
- 5 tablespoons unsalted butter
  Salt and pepper
- 3 tablespoons all-purpose flour
- 1 tablespoon tomato paste
- 4 cups leftover Kentucky Burgoo
- 1 large egg, lightly beaten

1. MASH POTATOES Adjust oven rack to upper-middle position and heat oven to 450 degrees. Bring potatoes and enough water to cover by 1 inch to boil in large pot over high heat. Reduce heat to medium and simmer until potatoes are tender, about 15 minutes. Drain potatoes, then return to pot and mash until smooth. Add buttermilk and 3 tablespoons butter and stir gently until butter is melted and liquid has been absorbed. Season with salt and pepper.

2. MAKE FILLING Melt remaining butter in large saucepan over medium heat. Stir in flour and tomato paste and cook until dark red and fragrant, about 2 minutes. Slowly stir in burgoo and bring to boil. Reduce heat to medium-low and simmer until thickened slightly, about 3 minutes. Divide filling evenly among six 6-ounce ramekins.

3. TOP AND BAKE Spread mashed potatoes over filling, using spatula to smooth. Brush with egg and drag fork over potatoes to make ridges. Bake on rimmed baking sheet until filling is bubbling and potatoes are golden, about 10 minutes. Let cool 5 minutes. Serve.

Chock-full of tender lamb and vegetables, our hearty burgoo makes a rich, substantial base for shepherd's pie.

Lemon Pudding Cake

Like magic, pudding cakes separate into two layers during baking: airy and soufflélike on top, dense and custardy below. Somewhere between a cake and custard, pudding cakes have very little flour, quite a bit of egg, and a lot more liquid than you might expect. In fact, it's the water in that liquid that sinks to the bottom, taking the batter with it; the egg whites float to the top. This bit of culinary wizardry is possible because the pudding cake bakes in a water bath, and it's that steady, low heat that prevents the mixture from scrambling and gives it enough oven time to split in two. The science is amazing. The taste of lemon pudding cake—almost forgotten today in a nation of brownie and ice cream eaters—will impress you, too.

BY KRIS WIDICAN

Pudding cake is thought to have roots in "flour pudding," so I baked Amelia Simmons' 1796 recipe for that from *American Cookery* (see box on page 27). It calls for nutmeg, cinnamon, and whole eggs, and—um—the recipe doesn't hold up. The pudding was dense, slightly curdled, and rubbery. "Maybe something was lost over the generations," I wrote in my test kitchen notes, "but I wouldn't waste my time with it today." By the 1850s, lemon had replaced the spices, and stiffly beaten egg whites had become a favored technique. The late 19th-century version, "sponge pudding," added a water bath, and lemon pudding cake as we know it was born.

I found a handful of recipes spanning the decades. Old and new included the same basic ingredients (butter, sugar, milk, eggs, flour, and lemon juice) and

used the same water bath technique, but the puddings that emerged varied remarkably. Some older recipes produced short, squat specimens with barely perceptible layers. Newer recipes had more height, though the bottom layers in some were more sauce than pudding. Many were merely sweet, a few hinted at lemon, and one tasted of sour egg—"like breakfast gone bad," as a taster put it. I wanted a pudding cake with rich, creamy pudding; delicate, tender cake; and bright, balanced lemon flavor.

The best recipe of the bunch creamed butter with sugar, added yolks and flour, poured in milk and lemon juice, then folded in stiffly beaten egg whites. It had good height and clear separation between the pudding and cake layers, but it didn't taste especially lemony. I gradually increased the lemon juice from

¼ cup to ½ cup. The flavor was bracing but not off-putting with a full 1¼ cups of sugar. To coax even more flavor from the lemons, I creamed varying amounts of grated zest (which has a high concentration of flavorful lemon oil) with the butter and sugar. Ultimately, I used two tablespoons of zest.

The cake now tasted good, but the extra lemon juice made the bottom layer soupy. Thinking that the ratio of liquid ingredients to dry was off, I increased the flour. The bottom layer thickened from the added starch, but the lemon flavor dulled appreciably and the top layer became gummy. Our science editor reminded me that in addition to starch, flour contains protein and fat, which can affect taste. He suggested substituting cornstarch (which is virtually tasteless) for some of the extra flour. Two teaspoons

Below are the Spelling words from Unit #3. The highlighted words are those that your child was unable to recognize during their assessment. Please continue to help them practice these words. Thank you for supporting their learning at home.

Carson was able to recognize all his words. ☺

came	spike	cube
game	age	cute
gate	page	book
late	nice	cook
make	rice	look
take	ledge	took
like	wedge	hood
bike	note	wood
ride	hope	
hide	nose	
mine	rope	

gently firmed the pudding layer without muddying the lemon flavor.

I noticed that when the cake was in the oven, the top layer first puffed and swelled, and then—about halfway through baking—deflated. I immediately suspected the egg whites. My first instinct was to add lemon juice to the whites as they were whipping, because the acid helps stabilize them. This had no effect on my pudding cake. Reading up on the science, I learned that merely by folding the whites into the acidic batter, they stabilized, which meant that adding acid to the whites alone wasn't contributing much. At the same time, my reading reminded me that beating sugar into egg whites as they whip helps stabilizes them. For my next test, I split the sugar in the recipe between the batter and the egg whites. This cake was high, golden, and fluffy, and its neat, layered effect pleased me as much in 2009 as I bet it delighted cooks more than a century ago.

LEMON PUDDING CAKE Serves 8

This dessert is best served warm or at room temperature the same day it is made. Scoop it out and serve in a bowl.

- ¼ cup all-purpose flour
- 2 teaspoons cornstarch
- 1¼ cups sugar
- 5 tablespoons unsalted butter, softened
- 2 tablespoons grated zest and ½ cup juice from 4 lemons
- 5 large eggs, separated
- 1¼ cups whole milk, room temperature
- 2 quarts boiling water

1. MIX BATTER Adjust oven rack to lowest position and heat oven to 325 degrees. Grease 8-inch square baking dish. Whisk flour and cornstarch in bowl. With electric mixer on medium-high speed, beat ½ cup sugar, butter, and lemon zest until light and fluffy, about 2 minutes. Beat in yolks, one at a time, until incorporated. Reduce speed to medium-low. Add flour mixture and mix until incorporated. Slowly add milk and lemon juice, mixing until just combined.

2. BEAT EGG WHITES Using clean bowl and whisk attachment, beat egg whites on medium-high speed until soft peaks form, about 2 minutes. With mixer running, slowly add remaining sugar until whites are firm and glossy, about 1 minute. Whisk one-third of whites into batter, then gently fold in remaining whites, one scoop at a time, until well combined.

3. BAKE Place kitchen towel in bottom of roasting pan and arrange prepared baking dish on towel. Spoon batter into prepared dish. Carefully place pan on oven rack and pour boiling water into pan until water comes halfway up sides of baking dish. Bake until surface is golden brown and edges are set (center should jiggle slightly when gently shaken), about 60 minutes. Transfer to wire rack and let cool at least 1 hour. Serve.

STEP-BY-STEP Using a Water Bath

The water lowers the temperature surrounding the baking dish for gentle, even cooking.

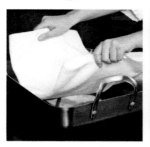

1. To prevent the baking dish from sliding, line the bottom of the roasting pan with a kitchen towel.

2. Set the roasting pan on the oven rack and carefully pour boiling water into the pan, partway up the sides of the baking dish.

3. After baking, promptly remove the baking dish from the water. Let the water cool before moving the water bath.

RATING INEXPENSIVE JUICERS

A good juicer should extract maximum juice from a lemon with minimum mess—and minimum expense. We bought a bushel of lemons and compared several styles of inexpensive lemon juicing tools. BY LISA McMANUS

Key Good ★★★ Fair ★★ Poor ★

HIGHLY RECOMMENDED		CRITERIA		TESTERS' NOTES
BLACK AND DECKER CitrusMate Plus Model CJ525 **Price:** $19.95		Effectiveness Ease of Use Design/Construction	★★★ ★★★ ★★★	**Comments:** With no effort, lemons were squeezed of all their juice. As you pressed gently, the reamer rotated to clean out the fruit half, and an adjustable pulp screen kept out seeds and let you adjust the pulp level of the juice. Simple to assemble and clean.

RECOMMENDED		CRITERIA		TESTERS' NOTES
AMCO Houseworks Enameled Lemon Squeezer Model 06-0354 **Price:** $11.95		Effectiveness Ease of Use Design/Construction	★★★ ★★★ ★★	**Comments:** Surprisingly easy to use—juice gushes out. Of the squeeze-style juice presses we tested, this was the most comfortable and effective, with curved handles and a well-shaped plunger. Plus seeds were contained. Hand-washing is best if you want to keep the paint from chipping.
OXO Good Grips Citrus Juicer Model 34781 **Price:** $12.99		Effectiveness Ease of Use Design/Construction	★★★ ★★★ ★★	**Comments:** This juicer removed all trace of juice in each lemon half with its sharp-edged, open-sided reamer. Seeds stayed out of the juice in the collection cup, which was easy to pour. It is sturdily constructed, but its many parts make it harder to clean than other manual juicers.

RECOMMENDED WITH RESERVATIONS		CRITERIA		TESTERS' NOTES
CHEF'N JUICESTER Citrus Juicer and Reamer Model JUC-380CI **Price:** $14.99		Effectiveness Ease of Use Design/Construction	★★ ★★ ★★	**Comments:** While it did a fair job of juicing lemons, this juicer was fussy to assemble and to disassemble for cleaning. Its beaker-shaped jar and narrow neck force you to tip the container far over to pour, letting seeds fall over the strainer and into the juice being poured (unless you remove it first, empty seeds and pulp, then replace before pouring).

NOT RECOMMENDED		CRITERIA		TESTERS' NOTES
NORPRO Stainless-Steel Citrus Juice Press Model 523 **Price:** $28.40		Effectiveness Ease of Use Design/Construction	★ ★ ★	**Comments:** Two models of this juicer—the priciest in our lineup—actually broke in our hands as we used them, shearing off the connecting bolt as we squeezed. This happened after juicing just a few lemons. It was bulky and difficult to squeeze, and yielded little juice.

Tried and true versus newfangled: Have manufacturers improved on your grandma's pie plate? BY PEGGY CHUNG COLLIER

When we rated pie plates a decade ago, the Pyrex 9" Pie Plate won because it browned and crisped crusts better than the other contenders. We also liked its wide rim for easy fluting, see-through bottom that allowed pie-makers to monitor bottom crusts, and low price. But while it produced the best-baked crusts, they could have been a tad crisper. Since that time, manufacturers have designed pie plates with fancy new features (mesh bottoms, scalloped edges, crust protectors) purported to produce perfect pies. We tested seven new models against our old Pyrex favorite.

ALL-PURPOSE PLATE: In search of a versatile, all-around pie plate, we tested each by baking an unfilled pie shell (known as a parbaked or blind-baked crust), a quiche, an apple pie, and a pat-in-the-pan graham cracker crust. Except for the graham cracker crust, we used Pillsbury Just Unroll premade crusts to ensure consistency. The best pans produced blind-baked shells that were golden brown on both sides and bottoms, apple pies with evenly cooked fillings, and graham cracker crusts that didn't slump, crack, or crumble. But the real litmus test turned out to be quiche. Our winning pie plates conducted enough heat to set the egg custard to a creamy texture without overbaking the crust.

MORE IS LESS: Several plates touted special features, but in the end they proved unhelpful, even inhibiting. The decorative ruffles on Rose's Perfect Pie Plate (designed to flute the crust) created wide edges that browned too quickly. Ridges inside the rim of the Pyrex Advantage plate are meant for easy, press-in fluting, but instead made for messy-looking pies. Cosmetic damage was also wrought by plates with crust protectors designed to shield the edge of the crust from overbrowning; the same went for shields, which look like smaller pie plates with holes and are intended to replace pie weights. Two plates—the Chicago Metallic Perforated Pie Pan and the Crispy Crust Pie Pan—were designed to let steam escape so that the bottom would crisp better. But these plates produced the soggiest crusts of all because the evaporating moisture prevented the bottom surface from ever getting hotter than the boiling point of 212 degrees, a process called

"evaporative cooling." The escaping steam further cooled the dead spot (see "Clear Choice for Better Baking" on page 31) by pushing hot oven air away, exacerbating the problem.

METAL MALADIES: The dark metal Norpro Nonstick Pie Crust Pan with Shield absorbed heat too quickly and overbrowned the outside bottom and sides of pies before the filling was cooked or the center of the bottom browned. It yielded quiche custard that was overcooked near the edges, but still runny in the middle. We had somewhat better results with the Doughmakers Pie Pan, a pale metal plate whose shiny, reflective surface heated up more slowly: Pies needed to be baked longer than called for, but the filling cooked more evenly than in dark metal plates.

CLEAR WINNER: Because glass and ceramic conduct heat slowly, heat gradually builds and spreads throughout the plate, thus custard cooks evenly, and the center of the bottom (the "dead spot") has time to brown. Two glass plates, the Pyrex Bakeware 9" Pie Plate and Pyrex 9½" Advantage Pie Plate, and a ceramic one, Rose's Perfect Pie Plate, produced perfectly cooked apple and quiche fillings, golden top crusts, and satisfactory bottoms. The glass laminate plate from Corningware produced the crispest bottom crust of all but was downgraded because it steep, slippery walls caused the graham cracker crust to slump.

SUMMING UP: Our favorite all-purpose pie plate remains the glass Pyrex plate which provides slow, steady, insulating heat for even baking. Its shallow, angled sides prevent crusts from slumping, and it's just 1⅛ inches deep, which neatly fit a store-bought crust when we don't have the time or energy to make our own. Its basic, functional design, flawless performance, and low price—just $3.99—made it the clear winner.

KEY **Good ★★★** **Fair ★★** **Poor ★**

HIGHLY RECOMMENDED

		CRITERIA	TESTERS' NOTES
PYREX Bakeware 9" Pie Plate Model 6001003 **Price:** $3.99 at Shopworldkitchen.com **Material:** Ovenproof tempered glass		Blind-Baked Shell ★★★ Quiche ★★★ Apple Pie ★★★ Design ★★★	**Comments:** Good crisping and browning; a see-through bottom to monitor the bottom crust; a half-inch rim; shallow, angled sides; and a low price made this our winner—again

RECOMMENDED

		CRITERIA	TESTERS' NOTES
ROSE'S Perfect Pie Plate by Rose Levy Beranbaum Model RL3 **Price:** $19.99 at Laprimashops.com **Material:** Glazed ceramic		Blind-Baked Shell ★★★ Quiche ★★★ Apple Pie ★★★ Design ★★	**Comments:** Rose Levy Beranbaum, author of *The Pie and Pastry Bible*, designed this scalloped-edge ceramic plate to help create attractive pies. It made perfect filling, but browned edges a bit too quickly.

RECOMMENDED WITH RESERVATIONS

		CRITERIA	TESTERS' NOTES
PYREX 9½" Advantage Pie Plate Model 1073356 **Price:** $5.99 at Shopworldkitchen.com **Material:** Ovenproof tempered glass		Blind-Baked Shell ★★★ Quiche ★★★ Apple Pie ★★★ Design ★	**Comments:** Good browning and crisping, evenly cooked fillings, and large handles made this plate appealing. But scallop-shaped depressions around the edges for press-in fluting actually made pies look messy
CORNINGWARE SimplyLite 9" Pie Plate Model 1080843 **Price:** $9.99 at Target.com **Material:** Glass laminate		Blind-Baked Shell ★★ Quiche ★★★ Apple Pie ★★★ Design ★	**Comments:** This plate made impressively crisp bottom crusts, but was too deep for ready-made pie dough and produced a graham cracker crust that slumped.
DOUGHMAKERS Pie Pan with Crust Protector Model 10595825 **Price:** $19.99 at Target.com **Material:** Aluminum		Blind-Baked Shell ★★ Quiche ★★ Apple Pie ★★ Design ★	**Comments:** Pies baked in this plate required 25 percent more oven time than recipes called for—and still had pockets of unevenly cooked filling. The so-called crust "protector" crushed the fluted pastry as it baked.

NOT RECOMMENDED

		CRITERIA	TESTERS' NOTES
NORPRO Nonstick Pie Crust Pan with Shield Model 3913 **Price:** $9.99 at Amazon.com **Material:** Steel with nonstick coating		Blind-Baked Shell ★ Quiche ★ Apple Pie ★★ Design ★	**Comments:** The perforated shield/pie weight conducted heat too well and overbrowned the blind-baked crust. The nonstick coating scratched deeply at the first cut.
CHICAGO Metallic Perforated Pie Pans Model 10517934 **Price:** $8.99 for 2 at Target.com **Material:** Aluminum alloy		Blind-Baked Shell ★ Quiche ★ Apple Pie ★ Design ★	**Comments:** A perforated bottom let moisture escape and evaporate from the bottom of the pie plate, which cooled the bottom and made the crust soggy.
CRISPY Crust Pie Pan Model 1543-79271-1334 **Price:** $14.99 at Brylanehome.com **Material:** Aluminum with stainless steel mesh bottom		Blind-Baked Shell ★ Quiche ★ Apple Pie ★ Design ★	**Comments:** The mesh bottom let steam and heat escape, so the bottom crust never baked through. Fillings leaked through the mesh. The crust fused to the leaking fillings and created a sticky mess.

aste Test Low-Fat Strawberry Yogurt

What's the key to great strawberry yogurt? Surprise—strawberries! BY SCOTT KATHAN

Low-fat yogurt far outsells full-fat and nonfat versions in American supermarkets. In the last year, more strawberry yogurts have been introduced to the market than any other flavor, according to the market research firm Mintel. To see which low-fat strawberry yogurt was best, we rounded up eight national brands and called our tasters to the table.

Many in the test kitchen had high hopes for the popular (and relatively expensive) Greek-style yogurt Fage Total 2%. Greek-style yogurt is strained to remove the whey, making it thicker and tangier than American-style yogurts. (The whey contains a lot of lactose, the natural sugar in dairy products.) Our tasters either loved Fage's denser texture and stronger flavor or hated them.

Our winning low-fat strawberry yogurt comes from an industry giant, Dannon. While it didn't elicit the high scores of the Fage, it didn't receive any low scores either, and it scored at or near the top for tang, texture, and, notably, its "solid" and "real" strawberry flavor. This was the key to our tasting, as our tasters' preferences tracked closely to berry flavor (ahead of tang or texture). Along with our two other recommended yogurts, Dannon puts strawberries second (after milk) on its ingredient list; by law, ingredients are listed on labels in order of amounts. By comparison, the yogurts that list sugar second (ahead of berries) had lackluster berry flavor. And our lowest-rated brand contains no strawberries at all—just artificial strawberry flavor.

Every brand we tested, save one, contains at least two of the following stabilizers: cornstarch, pectin, tapioca, kosher gelatin, xanthan gum, or bean gums. While the type of stabilizers used didn't fully correlate with our textural preferences, none of our three recommended brands contains kosher gelatin; Yoplait, Breyers, and Colombo do. Stonyfield was the only brand to use just a single stabilizer (pectin). Stonyfield Farm does list strawberries second on the ingredient list; nonetheless, it finished second to last in our rankings in part because tasters disliked its "loose," "watery" texture.

IN SUM: When shopping for strawberry yogurt, look for brands that list strawberries ahead of sugar—the more strawberries, the more strawberry flavor. If you like its strong tang and thick texture, Greek-style Fage 2% is an excellent choice; otherwise we recommend the yogurts from Dannon and Wallaby.

RECOMMENDED | | TASTERS' NOTES

DANNON Fruit on the Bottom Strawberry Yogurt
Price: $.75 for 6 ounces
Milk Fat Content: 1%

Comments: This brand scored either first or second in all three criteria we rated: tang, texture, and strawberry flavor. Tasters liked that it "wasn't too sweet," and had "good strawberry flavor" and a "creamy" texture. The tang and berry flavor were "balanced." "Actually tastes like it has strawberries in it," one pleased taster said.

WALLABY Organic Creamy Australian Style Lowfat Strawberry Yogurt
Price: $1.19 for 6 ounces
Milk Fat Content: 1½%

Comments: This "sweet and milky" yogurt has a "strong, fresh dairy flavor." Tasters liked the flavor more than the texture, however, noting, "a bit thin, but tastes nice and bright." "Good-sized strawberry bits" contributed to its "bright berry flavor."

FAGE 2% All Natural Greek Strained Yogurt with Strawberry
Price: $1.99 for 5.3 ounces
Milk Fat Content: 2%

Comments: Tasters compared this polarizing sample to "sour cream," "brie," "mascarpone," and "crème fraîche." The pros: "What yogurt should taste like"; "creamy and super thick"; "The mother ship has arrived!" The cons: "chalky," "too thick," and "funky." Everybody agreed that this was "not your average yogurt."

RECOMMENDED WITH RESERVATIONS | | TASTERS' NOTES

YOPLAIT Original Strawberry Lowfat Yogurt
Price: $.75 for 6 ounces
Milk Fat Content: 1%

Comments: Several panelists faulted Yoplait's "very sweet," "generic berry flavor" as "fake-tasting." One compared it (unfavorably, of course) to Pop Rocks candy.

BREYERS Fruit on the Bottom Smart Strawberry Lowfat Yogurt
Price: $.79 for 6 ounces
Milk Fat Content: 1%

Comments: Tasters found this "very sweet" yogurt "artificial," "plasticky," and "not memorable." "Not really any yogurt or strawberry flavor," an unimpressed taster said.

BROWN COW Strawberry Low Fat Yogurt
Price: $.99 for 6 ounces
Milk Fat Content: 1%

Comments: The "thick, smooth" texture was fine; the flavor was not. "Strange perfume taste," one taster said. "Very strong floral-fruity flavor," another seconded. "Why," asked a third, "does this taste like banana?"

STONYFIELD FARM Organic Lowfat Strawberry Yogurt
Price: $.99 for 6 ounces
Milk Fat Content: 1%

Comments: Tasters disliked Stonyfield's "loose," "watery" texture. "Why is it separated?" asked one. The yogurt won points for its "milky," "natural-tasting" tang, but lost them for "bland," "too mild" strawberry flavor.

NOT RECOMMENDED | | TASTERS' NOTES

COLOMBO Lowfat Strawberry Flavored Yogurt
Price: $1.69 for 32 ounces
Milk Fat Content: ½%

Comments: This "overly sweet," "fake-tasting" yogurt (which does not contain strawberries) ranked last in every category—tang, strawberry flavor, and texture. Tasters compared it to "Jell-O mixed with cornstarch," "strawberry Quik," and "strawberry shampoo."

Test Kitchen Cooking Class How to Frost a Layer Cake

With a domed top, slumping posture, and patchy, uneven icing, a poorly frosted cake stands out a mile away. Luckily, a flat, smooth cake that looks like it came from a bakery is easy to produce at home and offers a good base for more advanced decorating. Here's everything you need to know—from keeping cake layers level to smoothing edges for a polished look.

The Right Stuff Frost, Turn, Slice

When it comes to frosting a cake, we rely on a large offset spatula. Its wide blade and crook shape allow for excellent control, and the offset handle keeps hands at a safe distance. A revolving cake stand allows us to rotate the cake with one hand while simultaneously smoothing it with a spatula. (A Lazy Susan can be used in a pinch to the same effect.) Finally, a large serrated knife ensures picture-perfect slices. Use a gentle sawing motion and wipe the blade clean between slices.

OFFSET SPATULA
The Ateco 8½-inch Offset Spatula ($5) offers excellent control for applying and smoothing any frosting.

CAN'T LIVE WITHOUT THIS

CAKE STAND
The Ateco Revolving Cake Stand ($19.95) is made of plastic but gets the job done for a fraction of the cost of professional metal stands.

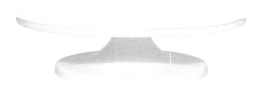

WORTH IT IF YOU MAKE LOTS OF CAKES

SERRATED KNIFE
The Victorinox Forschner 10¼-Inch Bread Knife ($24.95) has moderately sized serrations that cut without tearing or shredding.

A CUT ABOVE

Does This Look Familiar? Four Ways a Good Cake Can Go Bad

SOUPY FROSTING

"CRUMB-Y" CAKE

UNEVEN FROSTING

SMEARED CAKE

Hot Cake It might be tempting to start frosting soon after the cake has come out of the oven. But even a slightly warm cake can cause the frosting to melt and slide off. It pays to wait until the cake is completely cooled.

Cold Frosting Most frostings can be made ahead and refrigerated until they are ready to use. But if they're not left to soften at room temperature, the frosting will be stiff and difficult to spread, and their application may gouge a chunk out of a tender cake.

Domed Cake Cake layers can dome in the oven, making them hard to stack. If you don't trim the dome, you'll need extra frosting to fill the space between the layers—meaning you won't have enough for the top and sides. Even if you make extra frosting, the finished cake will be overly rich.

Reckless Slicing Even a beautifully frosted cake can turn ugly after the first slice. That's because the slicing knife drags frosting and crumbs as it cuts. For a prettier presentation, clean the knife after each cut by dipping it in hot water, then drying it off between slices.

Six Steps to Success How to Frost a Layer Cake on a Serving Platter

1. REMOVE THE DOME Cake layers with a domed top are difficult to stack and frost. If your cake layers crack and dome, you can simply slice the domed section off using a serrated knife. Gently slice back and forth using a sawing motion.

2. LINE THE PLATTER Frosting the cake right on the serving platter can be a messy enterprise. To keep the platter tidy, use strips of parchment paper to cover its edges; remove the parchment before serving the cake.

3. HOLD IT DOWN No one wants to frost a moving target. To keep the cake from sliding around, spoon a dollop of frosting in the center of the platter as "glue" and place one cake layer on top.

4. FROST THE BOTTOM Spoon some of the frosting onto the center of the first layer and, using an icing spatula, push the frosting up to, but not over, the edge of the cake. Then stack the top layer carefully to make sure that the sides are aligned.

5. TOP, THEN SIDES Spread more frosting over the surface of the top layer, up to the sides of the cake. Then, using a small amount of frosting on the tip of an icing spatula, gently smear and press the frosting onto the sides of the cake.

6. MAKE IT SMOOTH Holding the icing spatula at a slight angle, run the spatula around the cake to smooth the frosting. Where the sides and top of the frosting meet, pull the excess frosting toward the center of the cake.

Notes from the Test Kitchen

Grate Idea
After grating many pounds of cheese for our **Make-Ahead Creamy Macaroni and Cheese** (page 5), we understood just what a nuisance it is to clean a clogged box grater or food processor shredding disk. To reduce clumping as well as cleanup time, spray the grater or shredding disk lightly with cooking spray before grating.

Clear Choice for Better Baking
When we tested pie plates (page 28), we discovered that the air-flow patterns in ovens have a powerful effect on what you're baking. In standard gas and electric ovens, hot air rises from the bottom, curls out and around the edges of a pie plate, and then moves over its top. This movement of air creates a "dead spot" under the bottom center of the pie plate where the heat splits and curls. Because of the air flow, the outside bottom edge and sides of a pie heat up first, the top next, and the bottom last. Low-conducting materials, like glass, heat slowly and retain heat well, so pies baked in glass dishes heat relatively evenly, despite the air pattern; our winning pie plate, Pyrex, is made of glass. In contrast, metal pie plates conduct heat quickly where the hot air passes, so the edges of the crusts tend to darken before the pie or quiche is cooked through.

Poblanos, the Relleno Chiles
Our recipe for **Guacamole Salad** (page 18) calls for poblano chiles, a tapered, deep-green, medium-sized Mexican chile. Poblanos taste slightly bitter, similar to green bell peppers but with a spicier finish. Sold both fresh and dried (the dried are called anchos), they are used in many Mexican dishes, most famously in the United States in deep-fried, cheese-stuffed chiles rellenos. If you can't find poblanos, substitute one medium green bell pepper and 1 to 2 tablespoons of minced jalapeño (about ½ chile) per poblano.

Mushrooms—Wash or Brush?
Culinary wisdom holds that raw mushrooms must never touch water, lest they soak up the liquid and become soggy. Instead, many sources call for cooks to clean dirty mushrooms with a soft-bristled brush or a damp cloth. While these fussy techniques may be worth the effort if you plan to eat the mushrooms raw, we wondered whether mushrooms destined for the sauté pan could be simply rinsed and patted dry. To test this, we submerged 6 ounces of white mushrooms in a bowl of water for 5 minutes. After draining the water, we weighed the mushrooms and found that they had soaked up only ¼ ounce (about 1½ teaspoons) of water, not nearly enough to affect their texture. Henceforth, when we plan to cook mushrooms we won't bother with the brush. Instead, we'll place the mushrooms in a salad spinner, rinse the dirt and grit away with cold water, and spin to remove excess moisture.

Meat Pounders
Our recipe for **Chicken-Fried Steak** (page 21) forgoes cube steak in favor of flap meat pounded out at home. While our favorite pounding tool, the Norpro meat pounder ($24.95), is a kitchen workhorse, can you make our Chicken-Fried Steak without a meat pounder? Yes—if you own a relatively heavy small skillet or rolling pin to pound the meat with. For the neatest pounding, first place the steak between sheets of plastic wrap.

Homemade Panko
Our **Crispy Breaded Pork Chops with Parsley-Caper Sauce** recipe card calls for 2 cups of panko bread crumbs. To make panko at home, remove the crusts from 10 slices of white sandwich bread and process the bread through the shredding disk of a food processor. Bake in a 300-degree oven until dry but not toasted, about 6 minutes.

Gratin Dishes
Round or oval gratin dishes are designed to maximize surface area so that each serving of **Cheesy au Gratin Potatoes** (page 9) gets the utmost ratio of crisp topping to creamy potatoes. Our recipe will work in either a 2- or 3-quart baking dish; a 13- by 9-inch glass Pyrex casserole dish will do in a pinch. Our favorite gratin dish is the Emile Henry 3-quart Gratin Dish ($54.95). The large surface area and shallow sides of this ceramic casserole dish guarantee a crispy crust and evenly cooked interior. Do not use a disposable baking pan or an 8- by 8-inch baking dish—the gratin will neither brown nor cook through properly.

Butcher Shop Lamb Chops
Our recipe for **Kentucky Burgoo** (page 25) relies on inexpensive lamb shoulder blade chops for deep, meaty flavor. If you think all lamb chops are expensive, think again. Lamb rib chops and loin chops are indeed pricey (about $13 and $10 per pound, respectively); they're also relatively lean and best cooked to medium-rare. But inexpensive shoulder blade chops (about $5 per pound) are excellent value. Cooked slow and low in order to break down their connective tissue, the chops become moist, flavorful, and tender. We used the silky shredded meat from shoulder blade chops in our burgoo. The stew also benefited from the bones, which added both body and deep meaty savor.

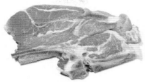

CHEAP CHOPS
Lamb shoulder blade chop

Test Kitchen Technique Dicing Avocado
Because the soft, buttery flesh of ripe avocados bruises easily, cutting neat, even dice requires delicate handling. We have a few tricks that come in handy in recipes that call for dice, such as our **Guacamole Salad** on page 18.

1. Halve the avocado. Strike the pit sharply with a chef's knife. Twist the blade to remove the pit, then use a towel to pull the pit off the blade.

2. Place the avocado half on a dish towel to secure it and make ½-inch crosshatch slices into the flesh without cutting through the skin.

3. Insert a spoon between the skin and flesh to separate the two. Gently scoop out the avocado cubes.

Gadgets & Gear Vegetable Prep
With these five essential tools—which no well-stocked kitchen should be without—you can prepare any vegetable.

CHEF'S KNIFE
The test kitchen likes chef's knives that are light enough to maneuver easily, yet sturdy enough to cut through squash or chicken bones. We've found sharp, 8-inch blades with a slight curve work best for a range of tasks, from mincing herbs and dicing onions to hacking through tough winter squashes.
•**TEST KITCHEN WINNER**
VICTORINOX FIBROX 8-inch Chef's Knife, $24.95

PARING KNIFE
Paring knives are best for small jobs—such as coring tomatoes or trimming artichokes—where larger knives would be too bulky. We like paring knives with flexible, razor-sharp blades and nonslip handles.
•**TEST KITCHEN WINNER**
FORSCHNER FIBROX 4-inch Paring Knife, $5.95

MANDOLINE
When we need large quantities of uniformly sliced fruits or vegetables, we reach for a mandoline. A sharp, adjustable blade is essential, as is the safety hand guard, which should have a comfortable grip and be at least as wide as the blade. We like mandolines with sturdy, nonslip feet and additional blades for matchsticks and waffle cuts.
•**TEST KITCHEN WINNER**
OXO Good Grips V-Blade Mandoline Slicer, $49.99

VEGETABLE PEELER
The best peelers are sharp (and stay that way), with grips that remain comfortable even with long use and blades that pivot for superior performance. We use them to peel carrots, parsnips, squash, potatoes, even tomatoes.
•**TEST KITCHEN WINNER**
MESSERMEISTER Pro-Touch Swivel Peeler, $5.95

BOX GRATER
Whether we're shredding potatoes or grating carrots, we put our box graters to work every day in the test kitchen. That's why it's so important that they be sharp, sturdy, durable, and comfortable to use. We use the fine holes to grate garlic and ginger.
•**TEST KITCHEN WINNER**
OXO Good Grips Box Grater, $14.99

Looking for a Recipe

ARE YOU LOOKING FOR A SPECIAL RECIPE?

Did you misplace a favorite recipe? Can you almost taste a chocolate cake from childhood but the bakery—and the recipe—are long gone? Ask a reader. While you're at it, answer a reader. Go to **Cooks Country.com** and click on **Looking for a Recipe.** We'll share all your submissions on the website and print as many as we can in the magazine. You may also write to us at Looking for a Recipe, Cook's Country, P.O. Box 470739, Brookline, MA 02447.

Brer Rabbit Molasses Gingersnap Cookies
Nancy Foster, Via e-mail

Way, way back in the late 1950s, I enjoyed making a gingersnap cookie from a recipe on the back of the Brer Rabbit Molasses bottle. I haven't seen my copy in several years, and I haven't been able to locate it elsewhere either. The one thing I remember is that the butter and molasses were heated to a boil before being mixed with the other ingredients. Would you have this anywhere?

Corn O'Brian
Becky Scherer, Oswego, Ill.

I am looking for a recipe called Corn O'Brian. My grandfather owned a restaurant in Illinois in the 1960s and served this dish. I recall that it contained whole kernel corn, hard-boiled egg whites, and pimento pieces. Unfortunately, the recipe has not survived. I hope someone has heard of this dish.

Liver Casserole
Alice Derry, Watertown, Minn.

Can you locate an old recipe for liver casserole made with crumbled bacon, onions, and a white sauce that is baked in a buttery crust? I would appreciate any help.

Creamed Spinach Pie
April Neihsl, West Bloomfield, Mich.

I was happy to see the lost recipe column in your magazine because I am looking for a recipe for spinach pie. My mom used to make it, and I think the recipe may have come from a box of frozen spinach. It was made by filling a pie crust with chicken, raisins, pine nuts, and creamed spinach. Any help would be appreciated.

Honey Cakes
Debbie Linde, Huntsville, Ala.

My Grandma Sophie came over from Germany in 1903 and settled in Independence, Kan. She is remembered for her fried chicken dinners and honey "cakes." They were actually very thin, melt-in-your-mouth cookies with an almond on top. As the last of 25 grandchildren, I did not know this hard-working lady well, but I would love to bake and taste a honey cake in her memory.

Goody Goody Bars
Phyllis Nichols, Sebastopol, Miss.

I am looking for a recipe called Goody Goody Bars. I know that they are made with peanut butter, cornflakes, Karo corn syrup, and sugar, but I don't have the amounts of these ingredients. Also, the mixture isn't baked; it's just pressed into a jelly roll pan.

Horn & Hardart Macaroni and Cheese
Claire Schneider, West Palm Beach, Fla.

We are born-and-bred New Yorkers, so the Horn & Hardart Automat is a big part of our heritage. Can you find the recipe for their baked macaroni and cheese? I have tried to make it a number of times, and though I've come quite close, I've never gotten it exactly right.

Brown Sugar Spice Cake
Sara Brown, Via e-mail

When I was a child, I baked a spice cake using a recipe from the back of a box of brown sugar. It was the best spice cake I'd ever tasted, but I haven't been able to find the recipe since. I do remember specific instructions for folding whipped egg whites into the cake batter. This sticks in my mind because one time I overwhipped the whites and the cake turned out flat. Does anyone remember or have this recipe from about 45 years ago?

Tomato Butter
Sandy Schofield, Fort Myers, Fla.

In the early 1950s in central Ohio, my mother used to make a tomato butter that we used like a jam. Growing up, I didn't like it, so I didn't copy the recipe for my hope chest. Now, as a senior citizen, I remember this condiment and can't find a recipe. Can you help?

Eggs à la Hitchcock
David Moulton, San Francisco, Calif.

My mother recently wanted to reproduce a recipe from her pre–World War I childhood in Pennsylvania called Eggs à la Hitchcock. Apparently the dish included a walnut ketchup made from green walnuts. Any suggestions?

FIND THE ROOSTER!

A tiny version of the rooster depicted on the front cover has been hidden somewhere in the pages of this issue. If you find it, write to us with its location (plus your name and address) and you will be entered into a random drawing. The first correct entry drawn will receive a Michael Graves Design Hamilton Beach 4-Slice Toaster (our top-rated toaster), and the next five will each receive a complimentary one-year subscription to *Cook's Country*. To enter the contest, visit CooksCountry.com/emailus or write to us at Rooster, Cook's Country, P.O. Box 470739, Brookline, MA 02447. Entries are due by May 31, 2009.

Did you find the rooster in the December/January 2009 issue? It was hidden in the Kitchen Creations photo on page 30. Pat Bell of Corona, Calif., spotted it and won a Michael Graves Design Hamilton Beach 4-Slice toaster.

Our Favorite Recent Responses

BUTTERSCOTCH MERINGUE BARS
Emily Zinos, St. Paul, Minn.

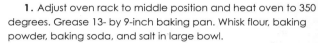

Makes 24 bars
"These bars are a family favorite. We also know them as Sunshine and Shadow Bars because of their contrasting layered appearance."

- 2 cups all-purpose flour
- 1 teaspoon baking powder
- ½ teaspoon baking soda
- ½ teaspoon salt
- 16 tablespoons (2 sticks) unsalted butter, softened
- 2 cups packed brown sugar
- ½ cup granulated sugar
- 2 large eggs, separated
- 1 teaspoon vanilla extract
- 1 tablespoon water
- 2 cups semisweet chocolate chips

1. Adjust oven rack to middle position and heat oven to 350 degrees. Grease 13- by 9-inch baking pan. Whisk flour, baking powder, baking soda, and salt in large bowl.

2. With electric mixer on medium speed, beat butter, 1 cup brown sugar, and granulated sugar until fluffy. Beat in egg yolks, vanilla, and water. Reduce speed to low and add flour mixture, mixing until combined. Spread dough evenly in prepared pan. Press chocolate chips lightly into dough.

3. In clean bowl, whip egg whites to stiff peaks and slowly mix in remaining brown sugar. Spread egg white mixture over dough and bake until golden brown, about 30 minutes. Cool in pan 1 hour. (Bars can be stored in airtight container for 3 days.)

LEMON SOUR CREAM COOKIES
Merilee Kuchon, Austin, Texas

Makes about 3½ dozen cookies
"These soft, cakelike cookies are my family's most-loved tradition." A simple confectioners' sugar glaze makes them even better.

- 3 cups all-purpose flour
- 1 teaspoon baking powder
- ½ teaspoon baking soda
- ½ teaspoon salt
- 16 tablespoons (2 sticks) unsalted butter, softened
- 1½ cups sugar
- 2 large eggs
- 1 cup sour cream
- 2 teaspoons grated lemon zest

1. Adjust oven racks to upper-middle and lower-middle positions and heat oven to 375 degrees. Line 2 baking sheets with parchment paper. Whisk flour, baking powder, baking soda, and salt in large bowl.

2. With electric mixer on medium speed, beat butter and sugar until fluffy. Add eggs, one at a time, and beat until incorporated. Reduce speed to low and beat in sour cream and lemon zest. Add flour mixture and mix until combined.

3. Refrigerate dough until slightly firm, about 1 hour. Drop rounded tablespoons of batter onto prepared baking sheets, spacing cookies 2 inches apart. Bake until just golden around edges, about 15 minutes, switching and rotating sheets halfway through baking. Cool on baking sheets. Repeat with remaining dough. (Cookies can be stored in airtight container for 3 days.)

Pink Azalea Cake

Similar to Lady Baltimore Cake, Pink Azalea Cake is a three-layer white cake swathed
in billowy seven-minute icing. It's the pretty pink hue—of the middle cake layer, the frosting,
and the fruit-nut filling—that gives the cake its name and makes it perfect for springtime.
Pink Azalea Cake is a cousin to other fanciful flower-named cakes that were popular
mid-century, such as the Brown-Eyed Susan and the Daffodil Cake.

To make this cake you will need:

- 1 **recipe white layer cake
  (enough to make three 8-inch layers)***
  Red food coloring
- 6 **cups seven-minute icing***
- 1 **cup chopped strawberries, raspberries,
  or maraschino cherries**
- ½ **cup chopped toasted almonds, walnuts,
  or pecans**
- 1 **tablespoon Kirsch (optional)**

*Go to **CooksCountry.com** for our white layer
cake and seven-minute icing recipes.

For the cake: Adjust oven rack to middle position and heat oven to 350 degrees. Grease
and flour three 8-inch cake pans and line with
parchment paper. Scrape one-third of batter
into each of 2 prepared pans. Stir ⅛ teaspoon
food coloring into remaining batter, then scrape
into third prepared pan. Bake cakes until toothpick inserted in center comes out clean, 20 to
25 minutes. Cool in pans 10 minutes, then turn
out onto wire rack, remove parchment, and
cool completely.

For the filling and frosting: Whisk ⅛ teaspoon
food coloring into icing. To make filling, transfer
2 cups icing to large bowl. Gently fold in fruit,
nuts, and Kirsch (if using) until combined.

To assemble: Place white cake layer on serving
platter. Spread half of filling over cake. Top with
pink cake layer and remaining filling. Top with
remaining white cake layer. Spread icing over
top and sides of cake, using back of spoon to
create decorative swirls and peaks.

Recipe Index

RC = Recipe Card

Cook's Country

JUNE/JULY 2009

Texas BBQ Ribs
"Bark," Smoke, and Spice

Green Chile Cheeseburgers
Best Burger You Never Heard Of

Ultimate Corn Chowder
Double the Corn,
Twice the Flavor

Rating Paper Plates
Winner Made of Rocks!

Grilled Rosemary Pork Loin
Herb Flavor in Every Bite

Huli Huli Chicken
Sweet, Smoky Hawaiian BBQ

Magic Chocolate Ice Cream
No Ice Cream Machine
Required!

Flaky Buttermilk Biscuits
Freeze the Fat, Lose the Calories

Baked Beans Rated
Winners Use Molasses

German Potato Salad
Warm Bacon Dressing

Fried Onion Rings
Shatteringly Crisp

Strawberry Pie
Real Berries, No Jell-O

Get With the Program!
Our popular television show, *Cook's Country from America's Test Kitchen*, is on summer vacation. Lucky for you, our best recipes for summer are just a click away. Visit **CooksCountryTV.com** to hone your skills on the grill and to watch segments of the show. Stay tuned—season two begins airing in September.

$4.95 U.S./$6.95 CANADA

0 74470 05251 7

07>

Cook's Country

Dear Country Cook,

For the last two summers, our son Charlie, now 14, has been running a fresh corn stand just across the road from our farm. We grow Silver Queen (still my favorite) along with Silver King, Bodacious, Butter and Sugar, and a couple of others, whatever catches our fancy in May. Our oldest daughter, Whitney, the artist in the family, spray-painted two large plywood signs you can see from the road, the gold and forest-green ears of corn bleeding into the cheap, splintered wood. We use the honor system for payment: a glass jar left in the bushel baskets. We got snookered just once last summer—Charlie estimated a $10 loss of income—but then I put a game camera on a maple tree overlooking the corn stand and that seemed to settle things down.

Just up the road, two kids still run a lemonade stand in summers much like the one in this picture. They charge 25 cents per glass, and it's still a country bargain. I looked out the window one cool, sunny morning in late September and saw one of the kids walking down the side of the road, skipping and swinging his arms, kicking a small rock this way and that. He didn't see me or anything else. He was dreaming, I suppose, of leaving town someday on a merchant ship or driving an old pickup out West. But few people have left our town and the ones who do almost always come back.

The past brings something back to us. We smile at old photos that appear outdated and congratulate ourselves on being new and improved. Then we come home again, have kids, and, as they grow older, knock together a stand by the side of the road, paint a sign, and put the glass bottle in the bushel basket. Pennies count for something again, the lemonade is cold and homemade, and we enjoy the luxury of spending hours walking down the side of the road, aimless and happy.

Christopher Kimball
Founder and Editor, Cook's Country Magazine

Cook's Country

Founder and Editor Christopher Kimball
Editorial Director Jack Bishop
Executive Editor Peggy Grodinsky
Deputy Editor Bridget Lancaster
Senior Editors Scott Kathan,
Lisa McManus, Jeremy Sauer
Test Kitchen Director Erin McMurrer
Associate Editors Cali Rich, Diane Unger
Test Cooks Lynn Clark, Kris Widican
Assistant Editors Meredith Butcher, Peggy Chung Collier
Assistant Test Cooks Meghan Erwin
Maria del Mar Sacasa
Assistant Test Kitchen Director Matthew Herron
Copy Editor Amy Graves
Editorial Assistant Abbey Becker

Online Managing Editor David Tytell
Online Editor Kate Mason
Online Associate Editor Leaya Lee
Online Editorial Assistant Mari Levine
Executive Assistant Meredith Smith
Senior Kitchen Assistant Nadia Domeq
Kitchen Assistants Maria Elena Delgado, Ena Gudiel
TV Producer Melissa Baldino
Contributing Editor Eva Katz
Consulting Editor Meg Ragland
Science Editor Guy Crosby, Ph.D

Design Director Amy Klee
Art Director, Magazines Julie Bozzo
Designers, Magazines Jay Layman, Lindsey Timko
Deputy Art Director, Marketing and Web Christine Vo
Staff Photographer Daniel J. van Ackere

Director, Information Technology Rocco Lombardo
Systems Administrator S. Paddi McHugh
Web Production Coordinator Evan Davis
IT Support Technician Brandon Lynch

Production Director Guy Rochford
Traffic & Projects Manager Alice Carpenter
Production & Imaging Specialists
Judy Blomquist, Lauren Pettapiece
Color & Imaging Specialist Andrew Mannone

Vice President Marketing David Mack
Circulation Director Doug Wicinski
Fulfillment & Circulation Manager Carrie Horan
Partnership Marketing Manager Pamela Putprush
Marketing Assistant Megan Cooley
Direct Mail Director Adam Perry
Sr. Database Analyst Marina Sakharova
Products Director Steven Browall
Product Promotions Director Randi Lawrence
E-Commerce Marketing Director Hugh Buchan
E-Commerce Marketing Manager Laurel Zeidman
Marketing Copywriter David Goldberg
Customer Service Manager Jacqueline Valerio
Customer Service Representatives
Jillian Nannicelli, Kate Sokol

Chief Financial Officer Sharyn Chabot
Human Resources Director Adele Shapiro
Controller Mandy Shito
Senior Accountant Aaron Goranson
Staff Accountant Connie Forbes
Accounts Payable Specialist Steven Kasha
Office Manager Tasha Bere
Receptionist Henrietta Murray

Sponsorship Sales Director Marcy McCreary
Retail Sales & Marketing Manager Emily Logan
Corporate Marketing Associate Bailey Vatalaro
Publicity Deborah Broide

COLOR FOOD PHOTOGRAPHY: Keller + Keller
STYLING: Mary Jane Sawyer
ON THE COVER: Plums, Keller + Keller

ILLUSTRATION: Russell Brocklehurst
Greg Stevenson (cover illustration)

Cook's Country magazine (ISSN 1552-1990), number 27,
is published bimonthly by Boston Common Press Limited
Partnership, 17 Station Street, Brookline, MA 02445.
Copyright 2009 Boston Common Press Limited Partnership.
Periodicals Postage paid at Boston, Mass., and additional
mailing offices. Publications Mail Agreement No.
40020778. Return undeliverable Canadian addresses
to P.O. Box 875, Station A, Windsor, Ontario N9A 6P2.
POSTMASTER: Send address changes to Cook's Country,
P.O. Box 8382, Red Oak, IA 51591-1382. Customer Service:
It's easy to subscribe, give a gift subscription, change your
address, and manage your subscription online. Visit www.
americastestkitchen.com/customerservice for all of your
customer service needs or write to us at Cook's Country,
P.O. Box 8382, Red Oak, IA 51591-1382.
PRINTED IN THE USA

Contents

JUNE/JULY 2009

LEMON POTATOES, 19   STRAWBERRY PIE, 24    GREEN CHILE CHEESEBURGERS, 23

Features

In Every Issue

Get a free subscription! Become a tipster!

Have you figured out how to make an ordinary kitchen chore easier, quicker, or neater? Do you have a clever make-ahead trick that helps you put weeknight dinners on the table fast? Do you use an ordinary kitchen tool (like an apple corer) in a surprising way (to remove the seeds and ribs from hot chiles)? We'd love to share your best ideas with all our readers. If we publish your shortcut, we'll send you a free one-year subscription to *Cook's Country*. E-mail us your tip by visiting **CooksCountry. com/kitchenshortcuts** or send a letter to Kitchen Shortcuts, Cook's Country, P.O. Box 470739, Brookline, MA 02447. Remember to include your name, address, and phone number.

 America's TEST KITCHEN is a 2,500-square-foot kitchen located just outside of Boston. It is the home of *Cook's Country* and *Cook's Illustrated* magazines and is the workday destination for more than three dozen test cooks, editors, and cookware specialists. Our mission is to test recipes until we understand how and why they work and arrive at the best version. We also test kitchen equipment and supermarket ingredients in search of brands that offer the best value and performance. You can watch us work by tuning in to *Cook's Country from America's Test Kitchen* (CooksCountryTV.com) and *America's Test Kitchen* (AmericasTestKitchen.com) on public television.

Kitchen Shortcuts

RECYCLE IT
Salad Solutions
Michelle Elsten, Piedmont, Okla.

I often take a salad to work for lunch but have trouble finding the right container for the dressing—most plastic containers are leaky and messy. I solved this problem by reusing empty glass spice jars. They're narrow, easy to pour from, reusable, and hold the right amount of salad dressing. Also, they absorb no odors and store easily (without leaking) in my lunch bag.

DOUBLE DUTY
Stove Storage
Amy Kennedy, Whitefish, Mont.

My oven goes largely unused during the hot summer months, when I barely bake at all. I discovered, however, that I could use that valuable kitchen real estate to house breads, buns, and other baked goods that suffer in the summertime humidity. I keep pieces of masking tape over the controls so that no one accidentally preheats the oven.

HANDY TIP
Set It and Forget It
Jeff Bush, Los Angeles, Calif.

When I make pasta sauce, I like to leave it on the stove all day to concentrate the flavor. But my gas stove's lowest setting is still too high, and my sauce boils and reduces too much. I found that placing my pot on a grill pan set over low heat allows the sauce to simmer gently. The ridges on the grill pan elevate the pot, providing a buffer between the sauce and the direct heat.

HANDY TIP
Corn for a Crowd
James Montgomery, Chicago, Ill.

When I need to butter corn on the cob for a crowd, I melt butter in the empty pot that I used for boiling the corn. Then I return the corn to the pot and toss the ears with melted butter. The residual heat of the pot also keeps the corn warm while I finish cooking the rest of the meal.

GRILL TRICK
Pop Magic
Katie Jones, Portland, Ore.

Campfire popcorn is the best, and my family enjoys popping corn on the grill at home, too. You can buy a grill popcorn popper, but rather than investing in another piece of specialty equipment, we pour a teaspoon of oil and ¼ cup of kernels into a double layer of disposable pie plates. We cover them with a large piece of aluminum foil (to make room for popped corn), poke a few holes in the top, and grill directly over medium-low heat, shaking the pan with long-handled tongs. After the last kernels pop, we eat the hot popcorn right off the grill.

SMART PREP
Bacon Freeze
Betty Pearce, Jacksonville, Fla.

I always keep a few packages of bacon in the freezer. Sometimes I want just a single slice to crumble on a salad or flavor a soup, but the frozen slices are all stuck together. Now, when I buy a package of bacon, I separate the slices and place them on a baking sheet in the freezer for 30 minutes. Once they are frozen, I transfer the bacon to a zipper-lock bag. This makes it easy to pull out one or two slices at a time.

KITCHEN EFFICIENCY
No-Spill Squeeze
Patty Bonsignore, Newton, Mass.

I buy olive oil in big jugs, but when recipes call for measuring out just a teaspoon or tablespoon, I find the wide mouth makes for messy pouring. Instead, I transfer some oil to an old ketchup or mustard bottle (cleaned, of course!). The small neck makes it easy to pour into a measuring spoon and eliminates spills.

PARTY TIP
Slip-Free Serving
Nancy Moran, East Falmouth, Mass.

When I serve veggies and dip at my summer barbecues, I put the dip in a small bowl in the center of a platter and set the veggies around the bowl. But unless I'm careful, the dip bowl slips around the platter, resulting in broken dishes or fresh-cut veggies gone astray. A party guest suggested I wrap the bottom of the bowl with plastic before placing it on the platter. No one can see the plastic and it keeps the bowl from slipping.

Ask Cook's Country

Can I use button and cremini mushrooms interchangeably?
Vlad Dorjets, Washington, D.C.

These varieties are slightly different strains of the same species of immature mushrooms harvested before their caps open; cremini (sometimes marketed as "baby bellas") mature into portobellos. In a recent recipe for long-cooking chicken cacciatore, we specified cremini for their richer flavor. A skeptical editor scoffed that no one could tell them apart after long cooking. We set out to prove him wrong.

To be scrupulously fair, we blindfolded our tasters so that color (cremini are brown) wouldn't skew our results. We expected tasters to pick up on the "meatier" flavor of the cremini in a quick sauté. We were pleased that they also discerned cremini's "stronger" flavor and firmer texture in a slow-cooked beef stew. The button mushrooms were a little "spongy" in the stew, according to tasters. Despite their slightly higher price, we prefer cremini mushrooms.

MILD
Button mushrooms

MEATY
Cremini mushrooms

When following your recipes, what temperature range should I use to grill over high, medium, or low heat?
Jen Fournier, Malden, Mass.

For optimum performance, we preheat gas grills on high heat with the lid down for 15 minutes. Once preheated, the burners should be adjusted to the desired intensity. The ambient temperature inside a grill set on high should be about 500 degrees, for medium between 300 and 400, and for low 250 to 300. Most gas grills come with a temperature display, but over the years we've found them inconsistent and unreliable. For a quick, simple, and surprisingly effective way to gauge the temperature, we rely on the "hand test." Place your hand 5 inches above the preheated grill grate. If you can comfortably leave it there for two seconds, the fire is hot (high), five to six seconds for medium, and eight seconds for low. This low-tech method works for charcoal grills, too.

Are cream of coconut and coconut cream the same?
Ashley Gordon, Charlotte, N.C.

These products are not the same and don't even think about using them interchangeably! Both products start with some iteration of coconut milk, which is made by steeping shredded coconut in an equal amount of milk or water, then straining out the solids. Coconut cream is a concentrated version of coconut milk—4 parts of shredded coconut to 1 part liquid. Cream of coconut is coconut milk that is emulsified and sweetened. Thick, syrupy, and intensely sweet, it is often used in baking.

Greek yogurt costs so much. Is it worth the extra money?
Katie Zezima, Brighton, Mass.

Greek-style yogurt is thicker and creamier than standard yogurt because most of its whey, the watery liquid found in yogurt, is strained out during production. Additionally, it's tangier and has more than twice the fat of ordinary yogurt; one-cup servings of whole milk Greek yogurt have as much as 23 grams of fat. No wonder it tastes so good.

To compare whole milk Greek and ordinary yogurt in recipes, we made muffins and coffee cake using each. A few tasters noticed that the muffins and cakes made with Greek yogurt had a slightly richer crumb; most couldn't tell them apart. Yet in uncooked recipes, such as smoothies and a creamy herb dip, the difference was obvious, with the Greek yogurt—"silky and substantial"—the clear favorite. We recommend it for rich, extra-creamy dips and shakes.

If you don't want to spend the extra money, it is possible to "fake" Greek-style yogurt. Line a fine-mesh strainer with several layers of cheesecloth, rest the strainer in a bowl, fill it with ordinary yogurt, cover, and refrigerate for 24 hours. The whey will drip out, leaving behind a thicker, creamier yogurt that is also known as yogurt cheese.

GREEK YOGURT STAND-IN
Comparably thick and creamy, for less money.

Can I make muffin batter the night before and bake the muffins the next morning? I want to sleep in!
Wendy Bruck, Rydal, Pa.

Although muffin batter comes together quickly, we love the idea of waking up in the morning with nothing to do but heat the oven, position the muffin tin, and make coffee. To find out if this would work, we made the test kitchen's recipes for corn and blueberry muffins, portioned the batter in muffin tins, sealed them with plastic wrap, and refrigerated them overnight. The next morning, when we unwrapped and baked them as usual, we were shocked (and delighted) that the muffins were as light and fluffy as if the batter had been mixed that morning.

After carefully reviewing the recipes, we noticed that the batters included both baking powder and baking soda for leavening. Baking powder is double acting, meaning it reacts twice—once when it gets wet and a second time when it gets hot. Baking soda, by contrast, reacts just once—when mixed with liquid. To determine if the baking soda was, in fact, spent after the overnight refrigeration, leaving the powder to do the heavy lifting, we made a bran muffin batter leavened with only soda. The next morning, we stuck the pan in the oven, and guess what? The muffins were tall and tender. What's going on? Our resident food scientist explained that refrigeration slows the reaction rate of both leaveners, leaving them plenty of lift power if they are held overnight. Don't refrigerate muffin batter too long (for more than 24 hours), as the strength of the leaveners will eventually diminish over time.

A friend of mine always adds lemon juice to pasta water. He says it keeps the pasta from sticking. Does it?
Jesse Womack, Charlestown, Mass.

We've heard of adding oil to pasta water to prevent the noodles from sticking together (don't try it; the sauce will slide right off the oiled pasta), but using lemon juice for the job was news to us. When we want clump-free noodles in the test kitchen, we cook them in plenty of rapidly boiling water (4 quarts for 1 pound of pasta) and stir the pasta for the first few minutes of cooking. Curious if adding lemon juice to the water would work equally well, we boiled two pots of noodles: one using our standard method, and one made by adding 2 tablespoons of lemon juice to the water (which we did not stir). While the pasta cooked using our standard method was better (absolutely no sticking), the batch made with lemon juice—and no stirring—had only a few clumps of pasta stuck together. After consulting our science editor, we learned that clumping pasta may be caused by the water. "Hard" water, typically found in cities, has higher levels of calcium and magnesium and has often been made alkaline to reduce pipe corrosion. This combination of factors produces stickier pasta. In contrast, pasta boiled in softer water is less likely to clump. If you have a sticky pasta problem, add an acid, such as lemon juice or white vinegar, to the water. It helps correct the imbalance and does reduce sticking. We used as much as ¼ cup of lemon juice without noticing any difference in the noodles' flavor. Incidentally, we tried saucing the pasta that had been boiled with lemon juice. The sauce stayed put.

Is Mom right that her cookies are better when she uses the convection setting on her oven?
Andrew Kim, Washington, D.C.

Most ovens heat from the bottom when set to "Bake." Cookies bake according to their orientation to the heat source, so if you are baking two sheets of cookies at a time (which is standard), they will brown unevenly. To prevent that, recipes often suggest switching and rotating the sheets halfway through. That's unnecessary when you bake on a convection setting; a fan (or fans) in the back of the oven circulates the hot air, and this air distribution promotes even cooking in all parts of the oven.

But while many modern ovens are equipped with a convection feature, most recipes have been developed for the standard baking cycle. We tried baking ordinary recipes in a convection oven. We baked shortbread rounds at 400 degrees and sugar cookies at 375 degrees. Even with two trays in the oven at once, all the cookies browned evenly, but they overbrowned long before the recipes' suggested baking times. We found that if we reduced the time slightly and the temperature by 25 degrees, the convection oven produced two sheets of evenly baked cookies without our needing to rotate the sheets.

UNEVENLY BAKED
Rotate the sheets in an ordinary oven or your cookies will brown irregularly.

EVEN, HANDS-OFF BROWNING
Convection ovens require no babysitting.

To ask us a cooking question, visit **CooksCountry.com/emailus.** You can also write to Ask Cook's Country, P.O. Box 470739, Brookline, MA 02447. Just try to stump us!

Recipe Makeover Buttermilk Biscuits

The Numbers
All nutritional information is for one biscuit.

TRADITIONAL BUTTERMILK BISCUIT
CALORIES **220** • FAT **12g** • SATURATED FAT **7g**

COOK'S COUNTRY REDUCED-FAT BUTTERMILK BISCUIT
CALORIES **160** • FAT **4.5g** • SATURATED FAT **3g**

Is cutting fat and calories even possible in something that relies so heavily on butter and shortening? Are we crazy to even try? BY KRIS WIDICAN

Admit it: Looking at this photo, you have no idea these are low in fat. They taste as good as they look.

TENDER, GOLDEN, and fragrant, a buttermilk biscuit fresh from the oven is its own advertisement. Unfortunately, just one average-sized biscuit can have upward of 200 calories, and worse, 12 grams of fat—and that's without so much as a smidgen of butter or jam. I wanted to make a lower-calorie version with substantially less fat, but I worried that the straightforward ingredient list gave me little room for play.

TEST KITCHEN TECHNIQUE
Cold Fat Makes Fluffy Biscuits
Freezing the cream cheese and butter for at least one hour before pulsing them with the dry ingredients practically guarantees flaky biscuits. Instead of smearing, the frozen fat forms uneven clumps slightly smaller than peas. Those clumps melt in the oven, creating pockets of steam, which in turn yield flaky, tender biscuits.

A favorite test kitchen recipe for full-fat buttermilk biscuits calls for vegetable shortening (for tenderness) and butter (for flavor) to be pulsed together in a food processor with flour, salt, sugar, and leaveners until the fat is evenly dispersed. The mixture is transferred to a bowl and the buttermilk is gently stirred in; the dough is briefly kneaded, patted into a circle, cut into rounds, and baked.

I wondered how this full-fat recipe would compare with a handful of low-fat buttermilk biscuits from "healthy" cookbooks and the Web, and was pleasantly surprised that a few of the lean recipes produced biscuits with decent buttermilk flavor. Their texture was another story: Some were crumbly and dry, one was oddly springy, and others were crusty like hard dinner rolls, which have little (if any) fat. Biscuits that used substitutes such as fat-free mayonnaise and cream cheese or low-fat margarine "tasted like chemicals," and tasters also found them gummy and unnaturally pale. Since I was resolved to (somehow) keep the texture and flavor of the full-fat biscuit, I decided to work backward, slimming the full-fat biscuit recipe where I could.

Almost 75 percent of the recipe's calories came from only 4 tablespoons of shortening and 8 tablespoons of butter. Startling, yes, but not surprising: Fat has more than twice the calories of carbohydrates (sugar and starch) and protein. I needed to reduce a substantial portion of the fat, but there was a danger in doing so: Fat adds flavor and often improves the texture of baked goods.

Removing the shortening from the recipe seemed like a logical starting point because while it improves the tenderness of baked goods, it contributes little flavor and is more caloric than butter. My tasters didn't seem to mind the texture of a batch I baked without shortening, but when I looked at the numbers, I saw I had trimmed the calories by the merest fraction. Some of the butter would have to come out, too.

The test kitchen knows from experience that how fat is incorporated can influence texture just as much as the amount. Perhaps I could get away with using less butter if I found a clever way to combine it with the other ingredients. In

the library, I studied recipes that variously folded, massaged, or layered butter into the dough in order to achieve flaky layers. In the kitchen, though, I found that no matter what technique I tried, less than eight or so tablespoons of butter made for tough, unpleasantly lean biscuits. I returned to the laundry list of fat substitutes I had already tested, and one by one replaced some of the butter with each. Ultimately, a combination of 4 tablespoons butter and 3 tablespoons Neufchatel (cream cheese with ⅓ less fat than the regular stuff) provided enough buttery flavor and tenderness to distinguish the biscuits from rolls while reducing the fat of each biscuit by almost two-thirds.

The biscuits now tasted similar to a full-fat version, but the texture had gone from appealingly fluffy to gluey and tacky. Chilled butter breaks into pieces resembling coarse meal after a few pulses with flour in the food processor. In the oven, the bits of fat melt, creating pockets of steam that contribute to the biscuits' fluffy, flaky charm. Chilled cream cheese, I learned to my dismay, smears and clumps, making the biscuits seem heavy. If I froze it, might it hold together like butter? I gave it a try, at the same time putting the butter in the freezer for good measure. One hour later, the cream cheese was hard enough to pulse into small pieces along with the butter, mimicking the texture of an all-butter biscuit.

Finding other places to whittle down calories and fat was the next challenge. I eliminated the sugar, but the biscuits refused to brown, so I added it back.

SECRET INGREDIENT Neufchatel
We used Neufchatel, which is one-third fat reduced cream cheese, in place of some of the butter, saving 25 calories and 3 grams of fat (per biscuit) without sacrificing flavor or texture. You'll find Neufchatel at the supermarket next to the regular cream cheese; sometimes it's just labeled "⅓ reduced fat" cream cheese.

NEUFCHATEL Adds flavor and promotes flaky texture.

The 2% buttermilk in the original recipe added a welcome touch of richness, yet when I secretly used fat-free buttermilk in its place, tasters barely noticed. My final recipe relies on neither difficult techniques nor surprising ingredients. Rather, little changes here and there substantially eliminated fat, shaving calories along the way. Happily, the fluffy, buttery appeal of the original biscuit stayed intact.

REDUCED-FAT BUTTERMILK BISCUITS Makes 12
Underbaked, these biscuits are gummy. Check under a biscuit after 17 minutes. If the underside is still pale, bake up to 3 minutes more until golden brown on top and bottom.

- 3   cups all-purpose flour
- 1   tablespoon sugar
- 1   tablespoon baking powder
- ½   teaspoon baking soda
- ¾   teaspoon salt
- 4   tablespoons unsalted butter, cut into ½-inch pieces and frozen for 1 hour
- 3   tablespoons Neufchatel (⅓ less fat) cream cheese, cut into ½-inch pieces and frozen for 1 hour
- 1¼   cups fat-free buttermilk

1. MIX DOUGH Adjust oven rack to middle position and heat oven to 450 degrees. Line baking sheet with parchment paper. Pulse flour, sugar, baking powder, baking soda, salt, butter, and cream cheese in food processor until mixture resembles coarse meal; transfer to large bowl. Stir in buttermilk until combined.

2. CUT BISCUITS On a lightly floured surface, knead dough until smooth, 8 to 10 times. Pat dough into 9-inch circle, about ¾ inch thick. Using 2½-inch biscuit cutter dipped in flour, cut out rounds of dough and arrange on prepared baking sheet. Pat remaining dough into ¾-inch-thick circle and cut out remaining biscuits.

3. BAKE BISCUITS Bake until biscuits begin to rise, about 5 minutes, then rotate pan and reduce oven temperature to 400 degrees. Bake until golden brown, 12 to 15 minutes more, then transfer to wire rack. Serve warm.

Make Ahead French Toast

Our goal? Crisp, custardy French toast straight from the freezer—fast enough to give cereal a run for its money. BY CALI RICH

WALK DOWN THE AISLES of any grocery store and you'll see that when it comes to breakfast, convenience is king. While I can live without Milk 'n Cereal Bars and Pop-Tarts, toaster-ready frozen French toast is a real temptation. Making French toast isn't difficult, but it's not convenient in a household where people eat breakfast at different times. So I occasionally give in and buy frozen French toast. It's a far cry from the real deal, however; it's dry, and it lacks the eggy custard flavor of homemade.

Curious how the test kitchen's standard French toast recipe would fare if simply frozen and reheated in a toaster, I decided to find out. As instructed, I dried eight slices of bread in the oven to create a dry crumb that could withstand a custard soak. I briefly soaked the bread on both sides in custard made from half-and-half, eggs, sugar, cinnamon, vanilla extract, and a couple tablespoons of flour (for a crisp crust). I fried the slices in butter and then cooled, wrapped, and froze them. A few days later, I popped a slice into the toaster. What a dud: It was desiccated and dull (both typical freezer problems) and scarcely better than the commercial product.

Ideally, I wanted to eliminate that skillet fry anyway and let the toaster do all the work. So I dried, soaked, and froze a new batch of bread, this time without frying. A few days later, I again put a slice in the toaster. It emerged soggy and pale. More important, it never reached 145 degrees, the temperature at which custard (specifically the egg in custard) is considered safe to eat. For my next test, I dried and soaked the slices, then baked them until they reached 160 degrees (I took their temperature with a digital thermometer). A few days later, the slices emerged from the toaster unattractively light in color, even when I turned the dial to "dark." If I toasted the bread a second time, it dried out. This wouldn't do.

I tried broiling the bread until golden (instead of merely drying it in the oven) and then continued with the recipe. Two days later, I was rewarded with a nicely browned slice of French toast from my toaster. Alas, looks were deceiving: It was dry. The test kitchen recipe I'd

been following warns the cook to cool the oven-dried bread before soaking it—otherwise, it says, the bread will soak up too much custard and turn to mush. For my make-ahead French toast, sogginess on the front end might be exactly what I needed to combat the dehydrating effects of the freezer. Next time around, I soaked the bread in the custard while the slices were warm. A couple mornings later, I was thrilled to bite into a golden slice of French toast that was creamy on the inside and crisp on the outside.

Now I'd just need to bolster the flavor, which had been dulled by freezing. Roughly doubling the vanilla and cinnamon in the custard helped, as did using brown sugar rather than white. But something was still missing. Suddenly it came to me: butter. Normally, you fry French toast in butter, but I was skipping that step. To mimic it, I whisked melted butter into my custard. Not bad. Then I went one better: I browned the butter in a saucepan to intensify and deepen its flavor, being careful to keep it from burning. A few days later, I tasted the fruits of my labor: The browned butter added a nutty richness that took my freezer-to-toaster French toast to a whole new level.

MAKE-AHEAD FRENCH TOAST
Makes 8 slices

Firm, high-quality white sandwich bread, such as Arnold Country White or Pepperidge Farm Hearty White, works best here.

- 4 tablespoons unsalted butter
- 2 cups half-and-half
- 2 large eggs
- ¼ cup packed light brown sugar
- 2 tablespoons all-purpose flour
- 2 tablespoons vanilla extract
- 2 teaspoons ground cinnamon
- ½ teaspoon salt
- 8 slices hearty white sandwich bread (see note)

1. MAKE CUSTARD Heat butter in large saucepan over medium-low heat until golden brown and fragrant, about 5 minutes. Off heat, whisk in half-and-half, eggs, sugar, flour, vanilla, cinnamon, and salt; transfer to 13- by 9-inch baking dish.

Once you've done the advance work, our Make-Ahead French Toast will go from freezer to toaster to table in about two minutes. So relax, sleep in, and let the kids make their own breakfast.

2. PREPARE BREAD Adjust oven rack to middle position and heat broiler. Set wire rack inside rimmed baking sheet. Arrange bread on rack and broil until golden brown, about 2 minutes per side. Decrease oven temperature to 350 degrees. Soak half of toast slices in custard mixture until just saturated, about 30 seconds per side. Return soaked bread to rack and repeat with remaining toast.

Bake until center of bread registers 160 degrees on an instant-read thermometer, about 8 minutes.

3. FREEZE Let toast cool on rack 10 minutes and then freeze until firm, about 30 minutes. Transfer slices to zipper-lock freezer bag and freeze for up to 1 month. When ready to eat, toast in toaster on medium power until heated through. Serve.

STEP-BY-STEP Preparing "Instant" French Toast for the Freezer

Sure it's convenient, but store-bought, frozen French toast is dry and tastes more like cardboard than custard. Our toaster-ready frozen French toast tastes as good as fresh.

1. Start by browning the bread slices in the oven. Besides giving them color, this step dries out the bread so it can soak up the flavorful custard.

2. For maximum absorption, transfer the warm slices of toasted bread to a baking dish filled with the custard.

3. Bake the custard-soaked bread to 160 degrees to cook the eggs, then freeze the slices and pop them into the toaster when the craving hits.

Slow Cooker Red Beans and Rice

New Orleans is justly famous for its spicy, long-stewed red beans ladled over white rice. Clearly, our slow cooker had never been there. BY MEGHAN ERWIN

Pureeing some of the beans makes for the thick, creamy texture that's a hallmark of this dish.

THE BEST RED BEANS around are simmered for the better part of a day in a rich broth of ham bone and water studded with the "holy trinity" of Louisiana cuisine: onion, green pepper, and celery. When the beans are so tender that they're starting to fall apart, they are ladled over white rice and served with spicy, smoky andouille sausage.

The test kitchen has a knockout recipe for stovetop red beans and rice. We cook the andouille with the beans to infuse them with deep, smoky flavor (no ham bone required). But something was getting lost in translation when I adapted this recipe to the slow cooker: Nothing can evaporate in a slow cooker, which meant the bean "stew" couldn't concentrate, and it was hard to produce tender beans. The liquid never reaches the vigorous simmer needed to thoroughly cook them.

To build a base so rich it wouldn't require that reduction, I browned the andouille and then refrigerated it. I used the flavorful rendered fat to sauté the aromatics and herbs, to which I added chicken broth. Now I had an intensely flavored liquid in which to cook the beans. To help them cook faster, I brought 1 pound of dried kidney beans and my stock to a boil, then simmered them for 20 minutes before adding them to the slow cooker.

To account for the lack of evaporation in a slow cooker, I cut the 14 cups of liquid down, cup by cup, until landing on 5 cups of chicken broth, just enough to cover the beans. The beans were now tender, but they weren't breaking down to make the signature velvety sauce. I removed 1 cup of the cooked beans, pureed them, and then stirred them back into the slow cooker with the andouille. The method worked nicely.

Most slow-cooker recipes for this dish slow-cook the beans and then make rice on the stovetop—the rice and beans should never be stirred together. But could I somehow isolate the rice in the cooker so they could both cook under one lid? After days of failed experiments, I came up with an idea just crazy enough that it might work: creating an impromptu rice cooker inside the slow cooker using a loaf pan. I filled a loaf pan with rice and water, covered it tightly with foil, and nestled it in with the beans. With a bit of tweaking, I was able to scoop fluffy rice out of the slow cooker at the same time the beans were done. Sweet success!

SLOW-COOKER RED BEANS AND RICE Serves 6 to 8

If you can't find andouille, use an equal amount of kielbasa sausage and add ¼ teaspoon of cayenne pepper with the other seasonings in step 1.

- ½ pound andouille sausage (see note), halved lengthwise and sliced into thin half-moons
- 1 onion, chopped fine
- 1 green bell pepper, seeded and chopped fine
- 1 celery rib, chopped fine
- 4 garlic cloves, minced
- 1 teaspoon dried oregano
- ½ teaspoon dried thyme
  Salt and pepper
- 5 cups low-sodium chicken broth
- 1 pound dried red kidney beans, rinsed and picked over
- 1 bay leaf
- 1½ cups long-grain rice
- 2 cups water

1. BROWN SAUSAGE Heat sausage in Dutch oven over medium heat until fat renders and sausage is browned, about 8 minutes. Using slotted spoon, transfer to paper towel–lined plate, cover, and reserve in refrigerator. Cook onion, bell pepper, and celery in sausage fat until softened, about 5 minutes. Stir in garlic, oregano, thyme, 1 teaspoon salt, and ½ teaspoon pepper and cook until fragrant, about 30 seconds. Add broth, beans, and bay leaf, bring to a low boil, then reduce heat and simmer, covered, until beans are just beginning to soften, about 20 minutes; transfer to slow cooker.

2. PREPARE RICE Following photos 1 to 3, place rice and water in loaf pan, cover tightly with foil, and nestle into bean mixture in slow cooker. Cover and cook on low until beans are completely tender, 4 to 5 hours (or cook on high 3 to 4 hours).

3. PROCESS BEANS Carefully remove loaf pan from slow cooker; set aside. Transfer 1 cup bean mixture to food processor and process until very smooth, about 1 minute. Stir pureed beans and reserved sausage into slow cooker, cover, and cook on high until heated through, about 10 minutes. Season with salt and pepper. Remove foil from loaf pan and fluff rice with fork. Serve.

STEP-BY-STEP Two Machines in One

Admittedly, it's a weird idea—the foil-covered loaf pan sits inside the slow cooker and acts as a miniature rice cooker, protecting the rice while trapping heat and moisture. The benefit is rice ready at the same time as the beans.

1. Combine the rice and water in a loaf pan.

2. Wrap the loaf pan tightly with foil.

3. Nestle the foil-wrapped loaf pan into the slow cooker along with bean mixture, and...

4. ...when the beans are done, you've got perfectly cooked, fluffy rice.

5 Easy Recipes Creamy Coleslaw

For great coleslaw, we take our cabbage with many grains of salt. BY JEREMY SAUER

THERE IS THE PROMISE of coleslaw: crisp and creamy. And then there is the sad reality: watery and washed out. This seemingly simple dish—shredded cabbage tossed with a mayonnaise-based dressing—is fraught with problems, most of which start with the cabbage. Fortunately, we've established a foolproof method for getting the best out of slaw.

Coring out the hard center from a round head of cabbage can be a perilous enterprise. The safest way is to cut the cabbage into quarters, right through the core. Lay each on one flat side and remove the core with a sharp knife. Now, pull apart a few leaves at a time and press on them until they lie flat. Cut ¼-inch strands lengthwise, and repeat with the remaining cabbage leaves. Alternatively, a food processor fitted with the slicing disk makes quick work of cabbage cutting.

If you dress the cabbage now, the seasoning in the dressing will draw out the cabbage's water. The leaves will soften slightly, which is good, but the dressing will become thin and watery—not so good. For surefire slaw success, we salt the cabbage first. Toss the cabbage (and any other vegetables, such as carrot and onion) with 2 teaspoons of salt in a colander that's placed over a similarly sized bowl. At the end of an hour, the salt will have drawn as much as ¼ cup water from the leaves. Throw it out, rinse the cabbage under cool running water to wash away the surface salt, and then dry it well with a kitchen towel before you dress it.

Most recipes use all mayonnaise, but we've found that cutting it with a little sour cream improves the texture of the dressing and gives it richness and a pleasant tang. Plain white vinegar plays a supportive yet not overreaching role. We balance it with 2 teaspoons of sugar. After you've tossed the dressing and cabbage together, chill the slaw for at least 30 minutes and up to two days. Resting allows the flavors to meld.

Finally, while simple, creamy coleslaw is the picnic standard, variations abound. Crunchy bell peppers and spicy chiles are excellent add-ins, and cider vinegar can be used in place of distilled. Potent spices, seeds, dried fruit, and nuts add heat, sweetness, and crunch, and chopped pickles add a briny flavor that's straight from the deli.

BASIC CREAMY COLESLAW
Serves 8 to 10
After step 1, the salted, rinsed, and dried cabbage mixture can be refrigerated in a zipper-lock bag for 24 hours.

- 1 medium head green cabbage, quartered, cored, and shredded (see photos below)
- 1 carrot, peeled and shredded on box grater
- ½ small onion, shredded on box grater
- 2 teaspoons salt
- ½ cup mayonnaise (see box)
- ¼ cup sour cream
- 1 tablespoon white vinegar
- 2 teaspoons sugar
- ¼ teaspoon pepper

1. SALT CABBAGE Toss cabbage, carrot, onion, and salt in colander set over bowl. Let stand until wilted, about 1 hour. Rinse cabbage mixture under cold water, drain, and dry well with kitchen towel.

2. DRESS SLAW Whisk mayonnaise, sour cream, vinegar, sugar, and pepper in large bowl. Stir in cabbage mixture and refrigerate until chilled, at least 30 minutes. Serve. (Coleslaw can be refrigerated in airtight container for 2 days.)

CAJUN COLESLAW
Prepare Basic Creamy Coleslaw, replacing carrot with 1 green bell pepper, seeded and sliced thin, and 1 celery rib, sliced thin. In step 2, replace white vinegar with cider vinegar and pepper with ⅛ teaspoon cayenne pepper and add 1 minced garlic clove.

COLESLAW WITH APPLES AND BLUE CHEESE
Prepare Basic Creamy Coleslaw, omitting carrot. In step 2, replace white vinegar with cider vinegar and add 1 Granny Smith apple, cored and cut into ¼-inch matchsticks; ¼ cup crumbled blue cheese; and ¼ cup chopped toasted walnuts.

CURRIED COLESLAW
Prepare Basic Creamy Coleslaw, adding an additional carrot and 1 jalapeño chile, seeded and minced, in step 1. In step 2, replace white vinegar with cider vinegar and add 1 tablespoon curry powder, ½ teaspoon cumin, ½ cup dried currants or raisins, and ¼ cup toasted slivered almonds.

DELI-STYLE COLESLAW
Prepare Basic Creamy Coleslaw, omitting carrot. In step 2, add ½ cup finely chopped kosher dill pickles, 2 teaspoons Dijon mustard, and ½ teaspoon caraway seeds.

The secret to first-rate coleslaw? Before you so much as reach for the mayonnaise, salt and drain the cabbage.

STEP-BY-STEP **Best Way to Shred Cabbage**
A safe, neat way to core and shred cabbage is easier than you think.

1. Cut the cabbage into quarters, then trim away and discard the solid core.

2. Separate the cabbage into small stacks of leaves that flatten when pressed.

3. Cut each stack of cabbage leaves into ¼-inch strips.

Corn Chowder

Thick, chunky chowder has always been a humble food made with whatever is around. In its early years in North America, that meant seafood, such as cod or haddock, added to a base of salt pork and onions. By the mid-19th century, the homey soup had moved steadily inland, where cooks eliminated the fish and added ingredients straight from the farm: milk, cream, potatoes, and butter. It was probably only a matter of time before another ordinary ingredient, an American original, found its way into the chowder pot: corn. In short order, creamy corn chowder, born in New England, was a classic from the redwood forest to the Gulf Stream waters. BY MARÍA DEL MAR SACASA

Poring over corn chowder recipes, I saw that the list of ingredients had made its way through history almost unchanged: corn, salt pork or bacon, chopped onions, broth, cubed potatoes, and milk or cream. The cooking method—which I followed myself—hadn't changed either: Chopped onions are (and were) sautéed in salt pork or bacon fat. Everything else is (and was) added and simmers together until the vegetables are tender. So I was surprised when five recipes I tried (including one of the first ever to appear in print, from *Mrs. Lincoln's Boston Cook Book* of 1884) produced noticeably different chowders. Not one delivered everything we sought in ours, namely: velvety texture; unambiguous corn flavor; plentiful, plump kernels; and, since it was summer, delicacy.

I combined the best features from the two recipes we liked most and was about to start my testing when I happened to find a *Good Housekeeping* recipe from

1888 that used a dozen ears of corn (most recipes called for three to six ears). Aha! Use more corn, get more corn flavor. Hopeful, I made the recipe, scraping 12 ears into my soup. The chowder was packed with kernels. Unfortunately, it lacked the silken, full-flavored base I sought.

To start building that base, I returned to my combined working recipe and tested salt pork versus bacon. Tasters preferred the sweet smokiness of the bacon. Next, to add depth, I sautéed the fresh kernels (with the chopped onions) in the bacon fat. Test kitchen experience taught me the technique should add toasty, slightly caramelized flavors to the corn, and by extension the chowder, and it did. As long as I had tasters at the table, I had them taste chowders made with different types of potatoes. They preferred red potatoes, which retained their shape in the chowder and added a pretty gleam of pink.

To thicken the chowder, I tried the standard roux, a paste of cooked flour and butter. It was a little heavy for summer, but it worked, as did cornstarch. I thickened a third pot of chowder with pureed potatoes. That was also acceptable, though my chowder was veering into potato soup territory. I couldn't resist trying Common Crackers, called for in several old recipes. These dense New England crackers resemble the hardtack sailors ate on long ocean voyages and probably used to thicken fish chowder. I crushed saltines, the closest match I could find. My curiosity was satisfied, if not my palate: The broth had the texture of soggy paper napkins.

Amid all these possibilities, I couldn't let go of an idea I had to use the corn to both thicken the chowder and intensify its flavor. I blended a few cups of fresh kernels with some chicken broth (the base of my soup). Even when I let the blender run for almost

10 minutes, the tough outer hulls never completely broke down. I tried the same thing with cooked kernels and broth, stirring them back into the chowder. Better—the soup was thick and robustly flavored, but it was still far from silky.

I drew up a list of ingredients that might thicken my chowder and ticked them off one by one. Frozen corn pureed with chicken broth was as raggedy as fresh. Cornmeal and polenta were grainy. Corn muffin mix produced chowder with a nasty, artificial aftertaste. Hominy (dried corn kernels that have been soaked in lye to remove the hulls) yielded the smoothest puree of all and an excellent soup to boot, but its distinctive savory flavor was all wrong for sweet, creamy chowder.

I'd saved canned corn for last. Truthfully, I wasn't all that keen on using it, certain it would taste tinny. A Fannie Merritt Farmer recipe from 1896 made me reconsider. Though the process of canning was far from new at the turn of the century, canned foods still had a certain cachet; also, fresh corn was unavailable for most of the year. I pureed some chicken broth with two 15-ounce cans and was delighted to discover that the corn broke down beautifully, yielding a golden, satiny chowder base with a vibrant, fresh corn taste. The cream I was using (some recipes use milk) underlined its velvety texture.

Reading through my file of recipes one last time, I was reminded that *Mrs. Lincoln's Boston Cook Book* based its version on a corn stock made with the shucked cobs. I streamlined that, simply tossing the cobs into my simmering chowder and then fishing them out before I served it. It was a subtle but significant difference that pushed my chowder from excellent to exceptional.

CORN CHOWDER Serves 6 to 8
Be sure to save the cobs for the chowder.

- 6 ears corn
- 2 (15-ounce) cans whole kernel corn, drained
- 5 cups low-sodium chicken broth
- 3 slices bacon, chopped fine
- 1 onion, chopped
  Salt and pepper
- 1 pound red potatoes, scrubbed and cut into ½-inch dice
- 1 cup heavy cream
- 4 scallions, sliced thin

1. PREP CORN Following photo at left, cut kernels from ears of corn; reserve kernels and cobs separately. Puree canned corn and 2 cups broth in blender until smooth.

2. SAUTÉ VEGETABLES Cook bacon in Dutch oven over medium heat until crisp, about 8 minutes. Using slotted spoon, transfer bacon to paper towel–lined plate and reserve. Cook onion, corn kernels, ½ teaspoon salt, and ¼ teaspoon pepper in bacon fat until vegetables are softened and golden brown, 6 to 8 minutes.

3. FINISH SOUP Add potatoes, corn puree, remaining broth, and reserved corn cobs to Dutch oven and bring to boil. Reduce heat to medium-low and simmer until potatoes are tender, about 15 minutes. Discard cobs and stir in cream, scallions, and reserved bacon. Season with salt and pepper. Serve. (Soup can be refrigerated in airtight container for 3 days.)

NEW ORLEANS–STYLE CORN CHOWDER
Prepare Corn Chowder, replacing bacon with 4 ounces finely chopped andouille sausage and adding 1 celery rib, chopped fine, and 1 red bell pepper, seeded and chopped fine, along with onion in step 2.

CORN CHOWDER WITH CHORIZO AND CHILES
Prepare Corn Chowder, replacing bacon with 4 ounces finely chopped chorizo sausage and replacing scallions with ¼ cup chopped fresh cilantro. In step 2, add 1–2 jalapeño chiles, seeded and minced, and ½ teaspoon ground cumin along with onion.

CORN CHOWDER WITH SWEET POTATOES AND CAYENNE
Prepare Corn Chowder, replacing red potatoes with 1 pound sweet potatoes, peeled and cut into ½-inch pieces. In step 3, stir in 1 tablespoon maple syrup and ¼ teaspoon cayenne pepper along with cream.

CORN CHOWDER WITH PROSCIUTTO AND SAGE
Prepare Corn Chowder, replacing bacon with 4 ounces finely chopped deli prosciutto and replacing scallions with 2 tablespoons finely chopped fresh sage.

Block Party Beans

Boston Baked Beans meet Sloppy Joe in this easy, crowd-pleasing dish. Could we take it from decent to delicious? BY DIANE UNGER

Ground meat makes this hearty dish different from the usual baked beans.

BLOCK PARTY BEANS, sometimes called calico beans or seven-bean casserole, are a perennial potluck and backyard barbecue favorite. They're a snap to make; they make enough to feed multitudes (hence the name); and they have definite crowd appeal. The recipe—a fixture in Junior League, community, and church cookbooks—is pretty basic: You brown lots of ground beef, stir in a pantry full of canned beans and condiments (mustard, sugar, vinegar, ketchup, or barbecue sauce), and bake.

Judging by the recipes I found, the dish seemed more like opening cans than actual cooking, but in fact the first few I tested won over even the skeptics. The best among them were meaty, very gently spiced, sweet yet tangy, and with a comforting Sloppy Joe–like texture. Having said that, both texture and taste were one dimensional, plus the sheer variety of beans made for a muddle. I wanted to freshen up and pare down the ingredient list.

First, I had to decide which beans to invite to my party, and which to show the door. Almost every recipe I found started with canned baked beans (or pork and beans), as well as canned green beans and canned lima beans. Other typical additions were canned navy, great Northern, pinto, kidney, or butter beans.

Practically on automatic pilot, I set aside the can opener and reached for the dried beans. True, I'd have to soak them overnight, but the payoff—firmer, more flavorful beans—seemed worth the slight trouble of planning ahead. I tested several varieties, but in the end, tasters overruled me. They found the difference between canned and dried minimal at best in this particular recipe, certainly not worth the additional time and bother it took to soak and precook them.

Most of the recipes I tested relied on sweet sauces from the canned baked beans combined with ketchup. Those sauces weren't bringing much to the party (they were uninteresting and tinny), so I decided to make my own sauce, but—in the spirit of the dish—I wanted to keep it simple. I mixed tomato sauce with brown sugar (for its pleasing hint of molasses), bottled barbecue sauce (which added a smoky note), and red pepper flakes and cider vinegar for a bright finish.

Next I turned to the meat. Ground meat is standard in party beans, but I hoped to improve things. I confidently tested combinations of ground beef, bacon, and Italian and breakfast sausage—and failed to win over a single taster. They nixed the sausage (it clashed with the sauce, they said) and the bacon (getting lost in the crowd, they said). The traditional choice was right here: straight-up ground beef it would be.

I browned the meat, seasoned it with onion and garlic, and stirred in my tomato-based sauce and the canned beans. I baked everything in a Dutch oven for about an hour, and I was pleased with the result. The flavors were excellent—beefy, sweet, tangy—and a big improvement over my initial tests. But party-worthy? I wasn't so sure.

Most recipes for party beans stir in canned green beans and canned lima beans as a final addition. I'd been stirring them in, but on reflection, I drew the line at these. Instead, I cut fresh green beans into ½-inch pieces and then stirred them in partway through the cooking. At the same time, I tossed in a box of frozen lima beans, which—unlike canned—retain their creamy texture. Together, the two added crunch, freshness, creaminess, and visual pleasure.

BLOCK PARTY BEANS Serves 10 to 12

For a festive presentation worthy of its name, we recommend using beans of varying shapes and colors, such as kidney beans, navy beans, black beans, and pinto beans. Serve with hot sauce.

- 2½ pounds 85 percent lean ground beef
- 1 onion, chopped fine
- 4 garlic cloves, minced
- 4 (15-ounce) cans beans, drained and rinsed (see note)
- 2 (28-ounce) cans tomato sauce
- ½ cup barbecue sauce
- ⅓ cup packed dark brown sugar
- ¼ cup cider vinegar
- ½ teaspoon red pepper flakes
  Salt and pepper
- 12 ounces green beans, trimmed and cut into ½-inch pieces
- 1 (10-ounce) package frozen lima beans

1. MAKE SAUCE Adjust oven rack to lower-middle position and heat oven to 350 degrees. Cook beef in Dutch oven over medium-high heat until no longer pink, about 8 minutes. Drain beef in colander, then return to pot. Stir in onion and cook until softened, about 3 minutes. Add garlic and cook until fragrant, about 30 seconds. Stir in beans, tomato sauce, barbecue sauce, sugar, vinegar, pepper flakes, ½ teaspoon salt, and ½ teaspoon pepper and bring to boil.

2. BAKE Transfer pot to oven and cook, covered, until sauce is slightly thickened, about 30 minutes. Stir in green beans and lima beans and continue to cook, covered, until green beans are tender, about 30 minutes. Season with additional salt and pepper, if necessary. Serve. (Beans can be refrigerated in airtight container for 3 days or frozen for 1 month.)

TEXTURE TIP **Full of Beans**

Block Party casseroles typically contain a hodgepodge of canned beans swimming in an ersatz Sloppy Joe mix. While canned beans were a good start, we found that the addition of meaty frozen lima beans and crunchy fresh green beans gave the casserole much needed textural contrast, plus some spark.

Fresh beans, frozen beans, and canned beans each brought something to the party.

German Potato Salad

It's easy to understand why Americans claimed this lively German classic as our own. With strong flavors like mustard and vinegar, the trick is getting the balance just right. BY DIANE UNGER

SLICED NEW POTATOES and sautéed onions tossed in a pungent, mustardy, bacon-based dressing and served warm is nothing new to most Americans. German Potato Salad hitched a ride with immigrants, acquiring new fans along with the "German" in its name. The felicitous combination of flavors gives it popularity, but it suffers in many translations. Recipes variously produced waterlogged or unevenly cooked potatoes with stodgy dressings lacking the necessary tart-sweet balance. Surely I could fix that.

I started with the potatoes. Mild, waxy red potatoes tasted good and held up best when boiled, which is how most recipes suggest cooking them. Never one to take somebody else's recipe as gospel truth, I tried steaming them nonetheless, thinking it would lock in more potato flavor. But steaming produced unevenly cooked slices, alternately crunchy or mushy depending on where the potatoes had landed in the steamer basket. I went back to boiling. Still, even with careful attention, it was hard not to overcook the thin slices; I was cooking the potatoes thus to avoid the awkward task of having to slice them hot. Resigned to watching the clock, I moved on to consider flavor.

In hopes of getting a jump-start on seasoning the potatoes, I added vinegar to the potato cooking water. It worked, and along the way I made a puzzling (and ultimately serendipitous) discovery. The vinegar had mysteriously extended the cooking time, yet the potatoes emerged both tender and structurally sound (now I could relax a little!). A call to our science editor helped me figure out what was going on. It turns out that cells in vegetables are held together by pectin, which acts like glue. When vegetables are heated in water, the pectin slowly dissolves, cell walls break down, and starch is released. Acidic vinegar slows pectin's dissolving, letting the potatoes stay firmer longer and simplifying the timing.

I turned to the dressing, starting by frying four slices of chopped bacon. Tasters demanded more, and more again. I kept going—all the way up to eight slices—before they were happy. I transferred the cooked bacon to a plate, leaving 2 tablespoons of rendered fat in my skillet, just enough to flavor the dressing but not so much that the fat would turn waxy as it cooled. To that I added olive oil; untraditional, but I found it cut the heaviness of the bacon fat. Next I added onion, which is traditional, sautéing it until softened and lightly browned.

For the acid component—key to German potato salad—I tested cider, distilled white, and both red and white wine vinegars. Tasters liked white vinegar best for its clean, sharp flavor. They also preferred whole-grain mustard to creamy. I stirred in a little sugar to get the salad's characteristic sweet-sour flavor. Finally, I coated the warm potatoes in warm dressing, folded in the cooked bacon and chopped parsley, and tasted. Not bad. The bacon flavor had permeated the potatoes, and the dressing was nicely balanced.

But it definitely lacked excitement. I dusted off some old German cookbooks and found some interesting additions to this recipe, among them chopped pickles, sauerkraut, and sliced cucumber. The cucumber added crunch and freshness; the pickles and sauerkraut, welcome brininess. It occurred to me to streamline their attractions by making a quick pickle of my own. I sliced and marinated a cucumber in a mixture of vinegar, sugar, salt, and dried dill. Twenty minutes later, I had a fresh "pickle" whose tang, crunch, and vibrancy beautifully offset the tender potato slices. At the same time, I revisited my dressing, ultimately eliminating the vinegar and sugar and replacing them with the cucumber marinade. Now the dressing had a fresher, brighter flavor, as did the entire dish.

For this warm, potent potato salad, mayonnaise need not apply.

GERMAN POTATO SALAD Serves 8

Grey Poupon Country Dijon and Grey Poupon Harvest Coarse Ground are our favorite mustards to use here. Farmland Hickory Smoked Bacon is our winner for its balanced, smoky flavor.

- 2 tablespoons sugar
- 1 cucumber, peeled, quartered, seeded, and cut into ¼-inch slices
- 1 cup white vinegar
- ½ teaspoon dried dill
  Salt and pepper
- 3 pounds small red potatoes, scrubbed and sliced ¼ inch thick
- 8 slices bacon, chopped (see note)
- 1 onion, minced
- ¼ cup olive oil
- ¼ cup coarse-grain mustard (see note)
- ¼ cup chopped fresh parsley

1. PREP CUCUMBER Stir sugar, cucumber, ½ cup vinegar, dill, and ½ teaspoon salt together in bowl; set aside while preparing potatoes.

2. COOK POTATOES Bring potatoes, remaining vinegar, 1 tablespoon salt, and 8 cups water to boil in large pot. Reduce heat to medium and simmer until potatoes are just tender, 10 to 15 minutes. Drain potatoes and return to pot.

3. MAKE DRESSING Meanwhile, fry bacon in large skillet over medium heat, stirring occasionally, until brown and crisp, 8 minutes. With slotted spoon, transfer bacon to paper towel–lined plate; pour off and discard all but 2 tablespoons bacon grease. Add onion and oil to skillet and cook, stirring occasionally, over medium heat until onion is softened and beginning to brown, about 4 minutes. Drain cucumbers and reserve juice. Whisk cucumber juice, mustard, and 1 teaspoon pepper into skillet; bring to simmer. Pour dressing over warm potatoes, stir to combine, and let sit until slightly cooled and potatoes have absorbed dressing, about 10 minutes.

4. ASSEMBLE SALAD Stir parsley, drained cucumbers, and bacon into potatoes to combine. Season with salt and pepper. Transfer to serving bowl and serve. (Salad can be refrigerated in airtight container for 1 day. Bring to room temperature before serving.)

Texas Barbecued Beef Ribs

Pork ribs may reign supreme across most of this country, but in Texas, where cowboys and cattle rule, ribs mean beef ribs. They differ from barbecued pork ribs in nearly every way, from the Flintstonian size to an unapologetically meaty flavor. You don't have to wear pointy boots to eat them, but your expectations may need some corralling. While pork ribs often cook until the meat slips off the bone, beef ribs retain some chew. Bite into a good beef rib and it'll fight back—just a little. Don't expect a sticky coat of sauce on beef ribs, either. While a thin sauce is sometimes served on the side, beef ribs need no distractions. BY KRIS WIDICAN

The challenge of replicating these ribs at home is two-fold: lack of specialized equipment and lack of patience. I've seen industrial smoke pits 20 feet long, the interior grates lined head to toe with beef ribs. A smoke box at one end is fed around the clock on a steady diet of seasoned hickory, post oak, or mesquite logs. As the wood burns, the low heat and smoke permeate the meat, melting away the fat, building flavor, and creating unforgettable crust—known to barbecue fans as bark. The process can take six, eight, or even 10 hours, plus a lot of dedication. Could I streamline it to work on my kettle grill without shortchanging the ribs?

I tried smoking the ribs indirectly (all the coals banked to one side of the grill, and the ribs placed over the empty side) and used wood chips to try to duplicate the smoke of a pit. The ribs required seven long hours. The beef itself is the toughest problem—literally. Beef

ribs contain a lot of connective tissue, which is also known as collagen. Collagen needs a slow, steady supply of low heat to break down and tenderize. I'd found plenty of recipes that parboiled the ribs before placing them on a smoker. It made sense, as boiling, braising, and steaming are all efficient ways to break down collagen. But in the test kitchen, we've found that any tenderness gained by boiling meat is canceled out by its washed-out flavor. Might one of those other techniques help render the nastier, fattier bits and speed things along?

Next I smoked the ribs for just an hour and a half. I brought them inside, placed them on a baking rack set over a pan of water, wrapped both ribs and pan tightly with foil, and cooked them in a 300-degree oven for two hours. The smoky flavor was strong, and the ribs were tender with just a tug of resistance. The low, moist heat had done the trick. Unfortunately, the

crusty bark had turned soggy in the oven.

I thought a hotter oven might speed the cooking time (making for a drier exterior) but succeeded only in making the meat overcook and shred. I next eliminated the water from the pan and instead clustered the ribs in a heavy sheet of foil, figuring their natural juices would finish steaming them. The bark was as soggy as before, and the ribs were far from tender. Finally, it dawned on me that I should try reversing the order of cooking: Steam the ribs first, then finish by smoking them on the grill. I tried my reverse two-step cooking process: The meat was tender with just the right amount of chew and was surrounded by a crusty layer of spice and smoke. With input from tasters, I gave the rub balance by adding 3 tablespoons of sugar and went out to the grill one last time. I now had the flavors of Texas in my own backyard.

TEXAS BARBECUED BEEF RIBS

Serves 4

Beef ribs are sold in slabs with up to 7 bones, but slabs with 3 to 4 bones are easier to manage on the grill. If you cannot find ribs with a substantial amount of meat on the bones, don't bother making this recipe.

- 3 tablespoons brown sugar
- 4 teaspoons chili powder
- ½ teaspoon cayenne pepper
- 1 tablespoon salt
- 2 teaspoons pepper
- 3–4 beef rib slabs (3 to 4 ribs per slab, about 5 pounds total) (see note)
- 1 cup wood chips, soaked for 15 minutes

1. MAKE RUB Combine sugar, chili powder, cayenne, salt, and pepper in bowl. Pat ribs dry with paper towels and rub sugar mixture all over ribs. (Ribs can be wrapped in plastic and refrigerated for 24 hours.)

2. STEAM RIBS Adjust oven rack to middle position and heat oven to 300 degrees. Arrange ribs on wire rack set inside rimmed baking sheet. Add just enough water to cover pan bottom, then cover pan tightly with aluminum foil and bake until fat has rendered and meat begins to pull away from bones, about 2 hours.

SHOPPING WITH THE TEST KITCHEN
Rib Wrangling

Texas-style barbecued beef ribs are all about the meat. Because beef ribs are located on the cow next to expensive cuts such as rib-eye and prime rib, butchers often overtrim the ribs so they can maximize the bulk (and their profits) on the pricier cuts. Be sure to buy slabs with a thick layer of meat that covers the bones. Also, steer clear of the gargantuan seven-rib slabs, which won't fit on the kettle grill. A three- or four-rib slab works best.

WHERE'S THE BEEF?
These bony ribs are better suited for the stockpot than the smoke pit.

HERE'S THE BEEF!
These meaty-but-manageable ribs are worth the time and effort.

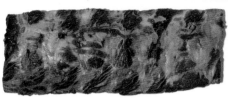

WON'T FIT
These mammoth ribs are hard to squeeze onto a kettle grill.

3. SMOKE RIBS Tightly seal wood chips in foil packet and cut vent holes in top of packet. Open bottom vent on grill. Light about 100 coals; when covered with fine gray ash, carefully pile on one side of grill. Arrange foil packet directly on coals. Set cooking grate in place and heat, covered, with lid vent open halfway, until wood chips begin to smoke heavily, about 5 minutes. (For gas grill, place foil packet directly on primary burner. Heat all burners on high, covered, until wood chips begin to smoke heavily, about 15 minutes. Leave primary burner on high, shut other burner[s] off.) Scrape cooking grate clean. Arrange ribs on cool side of grill and barbecue, covered, flipping and rotating slabs once, until ribs are lightly charred and smoky, about 1½ hours. Transfer to cutting board, tent with foil, and let rest 10 minutes. Serve.

TEXAS BARBECUE SAUCE

Makes about 2 cups

This peppery, tangy barbecue sauce works well with beef, chicken, and pork. In Texas, barbecue sauce is usually served on the side.

- 2 tablespoons unsalted butter
- ½ small onion, chopped fine
- 2 garlic cloves, minced
- 1½ teaspoons chili powder
- 1½ teaspoons pepper
- ½ teaspoon dry mustard
- 2 cups tomato juice
- 6 tablespoons white vinegar
- 2 tablespoons Worcestershire sauce
- 2 tablespoons brown sugar
- 2 tablespoons molasses
  Salt

1. COOK AROMATICS Melt butter over medium heat in saucepan. Cook onion until softened, about 5 minutes. Stir in garlic, chili powder, pepper, and mustard and cook until fragrant, about 30 seconds.

2. SIMMER SAUCE Stir in tomato juice, vinegar, Worcestershire, sugar, and molasses and simmer until sauce is reduced to 2 cups, about 20 minutes. Season with salt. Serve at room temperature. (Sauce can be refrigerated in airtight container for 1 week.)

TEST KITCHEN TECHNIQUE
Steam and Smoke Two-Step

We ask for a lot from our beef ribs: smoky flavor, formidable crust, just the right amount of chew, and speed. Here's how.

1. Before we heat up the grill, we steam the ribs over a tray of water in the oven to tenderize the tough connective tissue.

2. After searing, the ribs are ready to be smoked on the grill, where the surface will dry and a beautiful bark will form. The foil packet contains wood chips.

RATING CHIMNEY STARTERS

We wouldn't dream of starting a charcoal fire without a chimney starter. These cylindrical canisters, shaped like giant metal coffee mugs, quickly ignite quarts of briquettes without lighter fluid (which can leave residual flavor on food). You put briquettes in the large top chamber, place a crumpled sheet of newspaper in the smaller chamber under the coals, and light it. In about 20 minutes, the coals are red-hot, covered with fine gray ash, and ready to pour into your grill. BY MEREDITH BUTCHER

HIGHLY RECOMMENDED

WEBER Rapid Fire Chimney Starter, model 7416
Price: $12.99
Source: www.cookware.com
Briquette Capacity: 6 quarts

CRITERIA
Design/Construction ★★★
Handle Stays Cool ★★★
Coals Ready: 21 minutes

TESTERS' NOTES
Comments: Our test kitchen winner from 2006 once again beat the competition—at about half the price of other models. We loved its sturdy construction, generous capacity, heat-resistant handle, and second handle for pouring control. With the most ventilation holes in its canister, coals ignited quickly.

RECOMMENDED WITH RESERVATIONS

LODGE Camp Dutch Oven Charcoal Chimney Starter, model A5-1
Price: $25.46
Source: www.cooking.com
Briquette Capacity: 5 quarts

CRITERIA
Design/Construction ★★
Handle Stays Cool ★★★
Coals Ready: 25 minutes

TESTERS' NOTES
Comments: Construction was sturdy and the handle remained cool to the touch. Unfortunately, the smaller capacity meant fewer coals and less heat output. And with fewer air-circulation holes than the top performer, heating the coals took four minutes longer.

NOT RECOMMENDED

OUTSET Stainless Steel Chimney Grill Starter, model QS10
Price: $22.46
Source: www.cheftools.com
Briquette Capacity: 4 quarts

CRITERIA
Design/Construction ★
Handle Stays Cool ★★★
Coals Ready: 26 minutes

TESTERS' NOTES
Comments: Although the handle remained cool, its flimsy construction made us worry that it might pop off at any time. With no holes for air circulation, heating took more time, even with only 4 quarts of briquettes.

GRILLPRO Charcoal Starter, model 39470
Price: $19
Source: www.cooking.com
Briquette Capacity: 4 quarts

CRITERIA
Design/Construction ★
Handle Stays Cool ★
Coals Ready: 27 minutes

TESTERS' NOTES
Comments: Problems started with the cryptic assembly instructions. The bolts never tightened completely, so the handle felt loose. Heat from the lit coals melted the finish, and this was the only model where the metal around the handle became hot. The coals took 27 (very long) minutes to heat.

Chicken Spiedies

These grilled sandwiches are upstate New York's best-kept secret. The key to their flavor is a very long marinade. Or is it? BY KRIS WIDICAN

Spiedies are no ordinary chicken sandwich. Marinated chicken cubes are skewered, grilled, then slid directly onto soft white bread or buns.

HOW CAN A SANDWICH that's marinated for nearly a week be called a speedy? It turns out the sandwich, spelled s-p-i-e-d-i-e (pronounced "speedy"), gets its name not from haste but from *spiedo*, Italian for spit. Cubed meat—anything from chicken to venison—sits in an acidic, highly seasoned marinade for up to a week before it is skewered and grilled. Its origins in the Binghamton region of New York can be traced to a pair of local businessmen, Agostino Iacovelli and Peter Sharak, who each claim to have invented it at restaurants they operated in the 1930s and '40s, though variations of the spiedie were popular with Italian immigrants who came to the region starting in the early 1920s. Spiedies remain so popular there that every summer over 100,000 people attend Spiedie Fest, a weekend festival devoted to the sandwich.

Spiedies were originally made with lamb, which may account for the historically long marinade time and the strong seasoning, techniques that would mitigate gaminess and break down tough cuts of meat. Although tender chicken is now the most popular choice, the tradition of the long marinade continues. Not one recipe

I found called for a marinade time shorter than 24 hours, so I wasn't surprised that my first batch of spiedies tasted pickled. Worse, the chicken was grainy and chalky, as if it had been overcooked. My goals were simple: keep the chicken moist, develop a flavorful but not overwhelming seasoning combination, and reduce the time from prep counter to the table.

I began with a variation of the marinade recipe tasters preferred from my

first round of testing—lemon juice, red wine vinegar, olive oil, garlic, dried oregano, red pepper flakes, and fresh basil. I hoped that simply reducing the marinade time from 24 hours to a few would improve the texture of the chicken, but exactly how long was needed for the optimum flavor and texture? Even when I reduced the marinade time to just two hours, tasters complained the chicken was dry. A consultation with our science editor confirmed my suspicion that the acid in the marinade was to blame: It chemically "cooked" the chicken before it even hit the grill.

The logical next step was to remove the acid. This chicken was moister and well seasoned, but the tangy, bright flavor—the essence of a spiedie—was missing. A colleague reminded me that the test kitchen often brushes or rolls grilled meat in a fresh batch of marinade after it comes off the grill. I split the oil-based marinade into two bowls, adding the chicken to one and the vinegar and lemon juice to the other, making a "dressing" to dribble on the cooked meat. Only two hours in the marinade, a quick spin on the grill, and a drizzle of the dressing yielded a great-tasting spiedie. The oil, salt, spices, and garlic in the marinade flavored the meat and improved its texture by acting as a brine, while the dressing "refreshed" the marinade flavors. Adding lemon zest to the marinade boosted flavor and, although unconventional, whisking 3 tablespoons of mayonnaise into the

dressing gave it body and helped it cling to the chicken.

I was almost done but still hoped to further reduce the marinating time. Borrowing a test kitchen technique, I pricked the raw chicken all over with a fork before marinating to help the flavors penetrate. In just half an hour, the chicken cubes were well seasoned and ready to grill. This was a speedy chicken sandwich, indeed.

CHICKEN SPIEDIES Serves 6

You will need six 12-inch metal skewers here. To prevent sticking, preheat the grill, covered, for 15 minutes (5 minutes if using charcoal) and scrape and oil the cooking grates before grilling.

- ½ cup olive oil
- 2 garlic cloves, minced
- 2 tablespoons finely chopped fresh basil
- ½ teaspoon dried oregano
- 2 teaspoons grated zest plus 1 tablespoon juice from 1 lemon
- 1 teaspoon salt
- ½ teaspoon pepper
- ¼ teaspoon red pepper flakes
- 3 tablespoons mayonnaise
- 1 tablespoon red wine vinegar
- 4 boneless, skinless chicken breasts (about 1½ pounds)
- 6 (6-inch) sub rolls, slit partially open lengthwise

1. MAKE SAUCES Combine oil, garlic, basil, oregano, lemon zest, salt, pepper, and pepper flakes in large bowl. Transfer 2 tablespoons oil mixture to separate bowl and whisk in mayonnaise, vinegar, and lemon juice; refrigerate. (Sauces can be refrigerated, covered, for 2 days.)

2. PREP CHICKEN Following photos 1 to 3, prick chicken breasts all over with fork, cut into 1¼-inch chunks, and transfer to bowl with remaining oil mixture. Refrigerate, covered, for 30 minutes or up to 3 hours.

3. GRILL CHICKEN Remove chicken from marinade and thread onto six 12-inch metal skewers. Grill chicken over hot fire, covered and turning frequently, until lightly charred and cooked through, 10 to 15 minutes. Transfer chicken to sub rolls or bread, remove skewers, and drizzle with mayonnaise mixture. Serve.

STEP-BY-STEP **Speedy Spiedie Prep**
For the most flavor in the least time, follow these quick steps.

1. To help the marinade penetrate the meat, prick the chicken breasts all over with a fork.

2. To expose more surface area to the marinade, cut the chicken into 1¼-inch cubes.

3. The highly seasoned marinade builds a lot of flavor in only 30 minutes.

ON THE SIDE One-Hour Dilly Beans

Canning takes time, effort, and special equipment. Could we make these crisp pickled beans in one hour with one pot? BY MEGHAN ERWIN

DILLY BEANS ARE CRUNCHY, sweet-sour pickled green beans flavored—as the name implies—with dill, plus the classic pickling spices of garlic, mustard seeds, and peppercorns. Traditionally, it takes hours to make them and days before they're ready to eat. I set out to speed up the process without sacrificing flavor or texture.

The usual canning method begins with pouring hot pickling liquid (vinegar, sugar, spices) over raw beans, so that's where I started, too. But instead of tediously portioning the beans into sterilized jars and vacuum-sealing them in a boiling water bath, I simply marinated them in the liquid and then refrigerated them for one hour. Tasters found them tough, as the accelerated pickling time meant the beans didn't soften. I tried blanching them, hoping the technique would soften the beans so that the hot pickling liquid could penetrate. Three minutes in boiling water (followed by a shock in ice water to prevent overcooking) produced crisp-tender beans that were ready for their vinegar soak.

Dill comes in three forms: seed, dried (or weed), and fresh. After testing each, I determined that dill seed was the most pungent and aromatic—exactly what was needed to boost flavor in the shortened pickling time. I stirred dill seeds, mustard seeds, peppercorns, and garlic into a hot vinegar–sugar mixture, but the liquid (and beans) tasted a little flat. Dry-toasting the spices first boosted their flavor considerably. After just five minutes on the stovetop, the liquid was infused with the spices, so I strained them out—

that way, we wouldn't crunch on them while munching the beans. For a fresh-from-the-garden touch that reinforced the dill flavor, I added chopped fresh dill at the end.

DILLY BEANS Makes 1 quart
For the best dill flavor, use dill seeds—not dill weed—in the pickling brine.

- 1 pound green beans, stem ends trimmed
  Salt
- 2 tablespoons dill seeds (see note)
- 1 tablespoon mustard seeds
- 1 tablespoon black peppercorns
- 1½ cups white vinegar
- ½ cup water
- ¾ cup sugar
- 6 garlic cloves, peeled and crushed
- 2 tablespoons finely chopped fresh dill

1. BLANCH BEANS Fill large bowl with ice water. Bring 4 quarts water to boil in large pot over high heat. Add beans and 1 tablespoon salt and cook until just tender, about 3 minutes. Drain beans in colander and immediately transfer to ice water. Once cool, drain again and dry thoroughly with paper towels. (Beans can be refrigerated in zipper-lock bag for 24 hours.)

2. MAKE BRINE Heat dill seeds, mustard seeds, and peppercorns in empty pot over medium heat until fragrant and seeds begin to pop, about 2 minutes. Add vinegar, water, sugar, garlic, and 1 teaspoon salt and bring to boil. Reduce heat to low and simmer until mixture darkens, about 5 minutes.

3. PICKLE Pour vinegar mixture through fine-mesh strainer into large bowl; discard solids. Add cooled beans and fresh dill, cover tightly with plastic wrap, and refrigerate at least 1 hour or up to 2 weeks. Serve.

A sprinkling of fresh dill reinforces the dill seed in the pickling mixture.

ON THE SIDE Greek Rice Salad

When two become one, the problems can multiply. Could we translate the vibrancy of a Greek salad into a rice salad? BY JEREMY SAUER

ONE STIFLING SUMMER DAY when everything seemed too taxing to eat, we got the idea of taking the ingredients of a classic Greek salad (cucumbers, tomatoes, feta, olives) and incorporating them into a chilled rice salad. It sounded cool and fresh, and we figured there'd be nothing to it: Add cooked and cooled rice to Greek salad, toss with extra-virgin olive oil and vinegar. Not so. Recipes produced flavors that never really melded, to say nothing of oily grains.

Most recipes cook rice in the traditional way—bringing rice and water to a boil, covering the pot, and simmering until the rice is tender. We've found when making rice salad, it's better to treat the rice like pasta, boiling it in plenty of salted water until al dente. At that point we drain the rice in a sieve and then spread it out on a baking sheet to cool rapidly. Cooked and cooled this way, the starch is washed away and the rice doesn't stick together.

To eliminate the slipperiness we disliked in other rice salads we tested, we processed the dressing ingredients (extra-virgin olive oil, red wine vinegar, and dried oregano) with some honey and a little feta cheese. The last two helped the mixture emulsify. To ensure flavorful vegetables, we tossed them in the dressing and let them sit while we cooked the rice. After we'd combined the rice with the vegetables and dressing, we scattered in a handful more of crumbled feta. Now the salad was bright, light, and refreshing, and our wearied appetites revived.

GREEK RICE SALAD Serves 6 to 8
In step 1, do not marinate the vegetables for more than 1 hour or the salad will become soggy. Feta sold already crumbled is prone to drying out.

- ½ cup crumbled feta cheese
- 3 tablespoons extra-virgin olive oil
- 3 tablespoons red wine vinegar
- 2 teaspoons honey
- ½ teaspoon dried oregano
- 1 cucumber, peeled, halved lengthwise, seeded, and chopped
- 1 cup cherry tomatoes, halved (quartered if large)
- ¼ cup pitted kalamata olives, chopped
- 3 scallions, sliced thin
- 1½ cups long-grain rice
  Salt and pepper

1. MAKE DRESSING Process ¼ cup feta, oil, vinegar, honey, and oregano in food processor until smooth. Transfer to large bowl and stir in cucumbers, tomatoes, olives, and scallions.

2. BOIL RICE Bring 4 quarts water to boil in large pot. Add rice and 1 tablespoon salt to boiling water and cook until just tender, 12 to 14 minutes. Drain rice, spread on rimmed baking sheet, and cool completely, at least 20 minutes.

We puree half the feta and add a touch of honey to thicken the dressing of this Greek salad.

3. COMBINE SALAD Add cooled rice and remaining feta to bowl with vegetable mixture and toss to combine. Season with salt and pepper. Serve. (Salad can be refrigerated for 1 day. Bring to room temperature before serving.)

Getting to Know Summer Squash

Unlike winter squash, summer squash have thin, edible skin and tender flesh. Supermarkets usually carry just one or two varieties, but summer squash can be large or small, round or scalloped, pastel or bright.

One Ball
A FIRM BET

A spherical squash, the one ball gets its name from the billiard ball it resembles. (Its dark green cousin is known as the "eight ball.") The one ball's flesh is "firm and crisp," its flavor "mildly smoky" with a "hint of acidity." It's best to scoop out and discard the many seeds, then stuff and roast the shell.

Zucchini
SUPERMARKET CELEB

Infinitely adaptable—tasty shredded or sliced, raw or cooked, savory or sweet—zucchini has cornered the (super)market. It multiplies fruitfully and can grow to be enormous. Stick with specimens 8 inches and under, which taste "subtle," "savory," and "wheat-y" (as opposed to seedy, spongy, and watery large zucchini). In the test kitchen, we often salt sliced (or grated) zucchini to draw out the water.

Yellow Squash
SEMISWEET SOFTIE

Yellow squash has thin skin, a slightly crooked neck, cream-colored "soft and very wet" flesh, and a "mildly vegetal," "slightly sweet" flavor. Avoid disagreeably seedy specimens by choosing squash that are relatively cylindrical from blossom to stem end and thinner than 2 inches around.

Gold Zucchini
WORTH ITS WEIGHT

This golden-skinned zucchini has a straight, cylindrical shape and a green stem. Tasters compared its flavor—"nuttier" than that of green zucchini—to "fresh corn." "Dense" and "crisp," it's tasty raw in salads, but can also be roasted, sautéed, or grilled.

Baby Zucchini
TENDER TOT

Adorable baby zucchini, picked before it reaches maturity, is prized by restaurant chefs. It is "mild but quite sweet" and "exquisitely tender" with "hardly a speck of seeds." Unfortunately, it usually costs a lot and is hard to find. Serve raw as crudité or split lengthwise and roast or sauté.

Zephyr
PEOPLE'S CHOICE

Its two-toned color—pale yellow at the neck and green at the blossom end—distinguishes the zephyr. It has a "brassy and vegetal" start and an appealing "honeylike" finish, and its firm, "almost crunchy" texture made it a near-unanimous favorite. Slice thinly to eat raw or chop to roast or sauté.

Squash Blossom
STUFF IT

The blossoms from nearly any variety of squash are edible. Chop and add to pasta and omelets or stuff, batter, and fry the blossoms, which taste "mildly squashy" and "floral" when cooked. However you prepare them, do it quickly—they are extremely perishable and should be eaten within a day or two of being picked.

Pattypan
STAR QUALITY

A small, squat, brilliant-yellow squash with fluted, star-shaped edges, the pattypan has a "very firm and meaty" texture and "earthy and pumpkin-y" flavor. Choose ones no bigger than 2 or 3 inches in diameter; the larger squash are usually seedy. Stuffed and roasted, pattypan makes an elegant canapé but is also delicious roasted plain or sautéed.

Sunshine
SMALL IS BEAUTIFUL

This disk-shaped summer squash has deeply scalloped edges, few seeds, and a mottled green and yellow skin. Tasters described it as "sweet and buttery" and "creamy and smooth" with a "nutty" finish. Large squash tend to have mealy flesh and tough, thick skin, so look for ones that are no more than 3 or 4 inches across. Roast or sauté.

Scallopini
GREEN COOKER

The scallopini squash looks like a pattypan squash with green skin. Tasters liked its "buttery-sweet," "popcorn-y" flavor but not its "waxy," "squeaky" texture. We don't recommend eating it raw, but it's acceptable roasted or stuffed.

Cousa
PLUMP PLEASER

This Middle Eastern squash is thick, stubby, and pastel-green. Its flesh is "dense" and "crisp like a cucumber," its flavor "slightly herbal," "grassy," and mildly sweet. Its girth makes it a good candidate for stuffing, but it is also excellent raw. Sliced thin and dressed with olive oil and lemon juice, cousa makes a refreshing salad.

Chayote
SNUBBED IN THE STATES

Sadly neglected in American cooking (except in Louisiana, where it is revered as "mirliton"), this pear-shaped squash is popular around the world. Raw, chayote is "crisp and juicy" with an "apple-potato" flavor tasters compared to jicama. Cooked, it develops a "squashy," "earthy" savor. Peel it before eating, then boil and mash it or shred raw for salad.

TERIYAKI FLANK STEAK WITH SCALLIONS

ITALIAN GRILLED CHEESE SANDWICH

PORTUGUESE-STYLE GRILLED PORK CUTLETS

SEARED SALMON WITH MANGO-MINT SALSA

ITALIAN GRILLED CHEESE SANDWICH Serves 4

WHY THIS RECIPE WORKS: This Italian-inspired take on the classic American grilled cheese with tomato soup benefits from rustic bread, spicy pepperoni, and lots of fresh basil.

- 2 tablespoons extra-virgin olive oil
- 4 garlic cloves, minced
- 1 (14.5-ounce) can diced tomatoes
- ⅓ cup chopped fresh basil
  Salt and pepper
- 4 ounces thinly sliced deli pepperoni
- 8 ounces thinly sliced deli provolone cheese
- 8 slices thick-cut crusty bread (see note below)
- 8 ounces thinly sliced deli mozzarella cheese

1. Heat oil in saucepan over medium-high heat until shimmering. Add garlic and cook until fragrant, about 30 seconds. Stir in tomatoes and cook until slightly thickened, about 5 minutes. Mash mixture with potato masher until only small chunks of tomato remain. Stir in 1 tablespoon basil and season with salt and pepper. Cover and keep warm.

2. Arrange pepperoni in single layer on paper towel–lined plate. Cover with paper towels and microwave until fat has rendered, about 30 seconds.

3. Layer provolone on 4 slices bread, then top with pepperoni, remaining basil, and mozzarella. Top with remaining bread. Heat grill pan or large nonstick skillet over medium heat for 1 minute. Place 2 sandwiches in pan and weight with Dutch oven. Cook sandwiches until golden brown and cheese is melted, about 5 minutes per side. Repeat with remaining sandwiches. Serve with tomato sauce.

TEST KITCHEN NOTE: For the best results, buy a rustic 8-inch loaf (often called a boule) with a crusty exterior and substantial, slightly chewy crumb and cut into ½-inch slices yourself.

TERIYAKI FLANK STEAK WITH SCALLIONS Serves 4

WHY THIS RECIPE WORKS: Here we treat the scallions more like a green vegetable than an herb, cutting them into 1-inch lengths and sautéing them until lightly browned and tender.

- ½ cup soy sauce
- ⅓ cup sugar
- 2 tablespoons rice vinegar
- 1 tablespoon grated fresh ginger
- ¼ teaspoon red pepper flakes
- 1 teaspoon cornstarch
- 1 flank steak (about 1½ pounds)
- 2 tablespoons vegetable oil
- 12 scallions, cut into 1-inch lengths
- 2 teaspoons toasted sesame seeds (see note below)

1. Whisk soy sauce, sugar, vinegar, ginger, pepper flakes, and cornstarch in medium bowl.

2. Pat steak dry with paper towels. Heat 1 tablespoon oil in large nonstick skillet over medium-high heat until just smoking. Cook steak until well browned and cooked to desired doneness, 4 to 6 minutes per side. Transfer to cutting board and tent with foil.

3. Add remaining oil and scallions to empty skillet and cook until lightly browned, 2 to 3 minutes; transfer to bowl. Stir soy sauce mixture and any accumulated beef juices into skillet and simmer, scraping up any browned bits, until thickened, 2 to 3 minutes. Slice beef thin on bias against grain. Transfer to platter and top with sauce, scallions, and sesame seeds. Serve with rice.

TEST KITCHEN NOTE: To toast the sesame seeds, cook them in a dry skillet over medium heat, stirring often, until golden and fragrant, about 5 minutes.

SEARED SALMON WITH MANGO-MINT SALSA Serves 4

WHY THIS RECIPE WORKS: The combination of sweet mangos, tart lime, and cool mint balances the richness of the seared salmon.

- 2 mangos, peeled, pitted, and cut into ½-inch pieces
- 1 jalapeño chile, stemmed, seeded, and minced
- 2 tablespoons chopped fresh mint
- 3 tablespoons juice from 2 limes
  Salt and pepper
- ¼ cup olive oil
- 4 salmon fillets (each 6 to 8 ounces and 1¼ inches thick), skin removed (see note below)

1. Toss mangos, jalapeño, mint, lime juice, ½ teaspoon salt, ½ teaspoon pepper, and 3 tablespoons oil in large bowl. Let sit at room temperature 15 minutes.

2. Pat salmon dry with paper towels and season with salt and pepper. Heat remaining oil in large nonstick skillet over medium-high heat until just smoking. Cook salmon until well browned and cooked to desired doneness, 3 to 5 minutes per side. Top with mango mixture. Serve.

TEST KITCHEN NOTE: Most fishmongers will skin salmon fillets on request. Or you can remove salmon skin by gently sliding a thin, wide spatula between the flesh and the skin (after the fish is cooked), using your fingers to separate them.

PORTUGUESE-STYLE GRILLED PORK CUTLETS Serves 4

WHY THIS RECIPE WORKS: For the best flavor and texture, we make our own cutlets with pork tenderloin rather than relying on packaged pork loin cutlets.

- ¼ cup extra-virgin olive oil
- 2 teaspoons paprika (see note below)
- 1 teaspoon sugar
- ¼ teaspoon red pepper flakes
- 6 garlic cloves, sliced thin
- 3 tablespoons juice from 1 lemon
- 2 tablespoons finely chopped fresh parsley
  Salt and pepper
- 2 pork tenderloins (1½ to 2 pounds total), each cut into 4 equal pieces and pounded ¼ inch thick (see note above)

1. Combine oil, paprika, sugar, pepper flakes, and garlic in bowl. Microwave until garlic is softened and fragrant, about 1 minute. Reserve 2 tablespoons infused oil, then whisk lemon juice and parsley into remaining oil mixture and season with salt and pepper.

2. Pat cutlets dry with paper towels and season with salt and pepper. Rub cutlets all over with reserved infused oil. Grill pork over hot fire until lightly charred on first side, about 2 minutes. Flip cutlets and grill until just cooked through, about 1 minute longer. Transfer to platter, tent with foil, and let rest 5 minutes. Drizzle with sauce. Serve.

TEST KITCHEN NOTE: Penzeys paprika is the test kitchen's top-rated brand. Avoid using hot or smoked paprika, as they will overwhelm the cutlets.

FRENCH COUNTRY CHICKEN WITH HERBS AND HONEY

PASTA WITH CHICKEN, TOMATOES, AND FETA

BBQ CHICKEN PIZZA

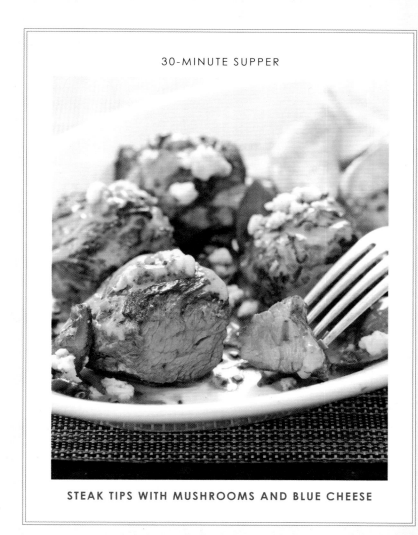

STEAK TIPS WITH MUSHROOMS AND BLUE CHEESE

PASTA WITH CHICKEN, TOMATOES, AND FETA Serves 4

WHY THIS RECIPE WORKS: Adding 1 cup of the hot pasta cooking water to the pot in step 2 melts the feta and coats the pasta with a light, creamy sauce.

2   boneless, skinless chicken breasts (about 12 ounces)
    Salt and pepper
2   tablespoons extra-virgin olive oil
1   pound rotini pasta (see note below)
2   cups (1 pint) cherry tomatoes, halved
1½ cups crumbled feta cheese (about 6 ounces)
½   cup pitted kalamata olives, halved
¼   cup chopped fresh parsley

1. Bring 4 quarts water to boil in large pot. Pat chicken dry with paper towels and season with salt and pepper. Heat 1 tablespoon oil in skillet over medium-high heat until just smoking. Cook chicken until well browned and cooked through, about 5 minutes per side. Transfer to cutting board and tent with foil. Let rest 5 minutes, then slice thin crosswise and reserve.

2. Add 1 tablespoon salt and pasta to boiling water and cook until al dente. Reserve 1½ cups cooking water. Drain pasta and return to pot. Stir in sliced chicken, tomatoes, feta, olives, parsley, and 1 cup reserved pasta water (adding additional water as needed). Season with salt and pepper. Serve.

TEST KITCHEN NOTE: Other short pastas, such as penne, gemelli, or campanelle, will also work well in this dish.

FRENCH COUNTRY CHICKEN WITH HERBS AND HONEY
Serves 4

WHY THIS RECIPE WORKS: Cooking the chicken skin-side down ensures that the skin will be crisp.

4   bone-in, skin-on split chicken breasts (about 3 pounds), halved crosswise
    Salt and pepper
1   tablespoon vegetable oil
1   (9-ounce) box frozen artichoke hearts, thawed
½   cup low-sodium chicken broth
2   tablespoons honey
2   teaspoons herbes de Provence (see note below)
4   tablespoons unsalted butter, cut into 4 pieces
2   teaspoons white wine vinegar (see note below)

1. Pat chicken dry with paper towels and season with salt and pepper. Heat oil in large skillet over medium-high heat until just smoking. Cook chicken skin-side down until well browned, about 5 minutes. Reduce heat to medium, cover, and cook until meat registers 160 degrees, about 15 minutes. Transfer chicken to platter and tent with foil.

2. Pour off all but 1 tablespoon fat from skillet. Add artichokes and cook until lightly browned, about 3 minutes; transfer to platter with chicken. Add broth, honey, herbs, and any accumulated chicken juices to skillet and simmer, scraping up any browned bits, until reduced to ¼ cup, about 3 minutes. Off heat, whisk in butter and vinegar. Pour sauce over chicken and artichokes. Serve.

TEST KITCHEN NOTE: Herbes de Provence, a dried herb blend, can be found in the jarred herb section of the supermarket. Cider or white vinegar can be substituted for the white wine vinegar.

STEAK TIPS WITH MUSHROOMS AND BLUE CHEESE Serves 4

WHY THIS RECIPE WORKS: Whisking half of the blue cheese into the sauce adds richness and ensures that each bite is packed with blue cheese flavor.

1½ pounds sirloin steak tips, cut into 2-inch pieces (see note below)
    Salt and pepper
3   tablespoons vegetable oil
4   portobello mushroom caps, halved and sliced thin
2   shallots, halved and sliced thin
½   cup low-sodium chicken broth
½   cup heavy cream
½   cup crumbled blue cheese
2   tablespoons minced fresh chives

1. Pat steak tips dry with paper towels and season with salt and pepper. Heat 1 tablespoon oil in large skillet over medium-high heat until just smoking. Add steak tips and cook until well browned all over, 6 to 8 minutes. Transfer to serving platter and tent with foil.

2. Add remaining oil, mushrooms, and ½ teaspoon salt to empty skillet. Cover and cook over medium heat until softened, 3 to 4 minutes. Add shallots and cook until softened, about 1 minute. Stir in broth, cream, and any accumulated beef juices and simmer, scraping up any browned bits, until slightly thickened, about 5 minutes. Off heat, whisk in ¼ cup cheese. Pour sauce over meat and sprinkle with remaining cheese and chives. Serve.

TEST KITCHEN NOTE: Steak tips, also known as flap meat, are sold as whole steaks, cubes, and strips. To ensure evenly sized pieces, we prefer to buy whole steaks and cut them ourselves.

BBQ CHICKEN PIZZA Serves 4

WHY THIS RECIPE WORKS: The combination of store-bought dough, a rotisserie chicken, and a very hot oven gets this pizza to the table quickly.

1   rotisserie chicken, skin discarded, meat shredded into bite-sized pieces (about 3 cups)
½   cup barbecue sauce
¼   cup finely chopped fresh cilantro
½   red onion, sliced thin
5   tablespoons extra-virgin olive oil
    Salt and pepper
1   (1-pound) ball ready-made pizza dough (see note below)
1   cup shredded Mexican cheese blend
½   cup sour cream
2   tablespoons juice from 2 limes

1. Adjust oven rack to upper-middle position and heat oven to 500 degrees. Combine chicken, barbecue sauce, and 2 tablespoons cilantro in medium bowl. Toss onion, 1 tablespoon oil, ¼ teaspoon salt, and ¼ teaspoon pepper in small bowl.

2. Brush additional 2 tablespoons oil all over rimmed baking sheet. On lightly floured surface, roll dough into 16- by 9-inch oval (about ¼ inch thick) and transfer to prepared baking sheet. Brush dough with remaining oil and bake until dough begins to brown and bubble, about 6 minutes.

3. Scatter chicken mixture over dough and top with onion mixture. Bake until onion begins to brown, about 10 minutes. Sprinkle cheese over pizza and bake until melted, about 5 minutes. Transfer to cutting board. Whisk sour cream, lime juice, and remaining cilantro in small bowl, then drizzle over pizza. Slice and serve, passing sauce at table.

TEST KITCHEN NOTE: Fresh pizza dough can be found in the refrigerator section of most supermarkets or purchased from a pizzeria.

Magic Chocolate Ice Cream

With just 10 minutes of work, we made creamy chocolate ice cream without an ice cream machine. Yes, we're serious. BY LYNN CLARK

AN ICE CREAM MAKER turns up in just about every wedding registry. The young couples envision themselves churning out batches of creamy homemade ice cream. But once the honeymoon is over, most machines wind up in the back of a closet. It's easy to see why. Few people can remember to freeze the insert ahead of time. If your freezer doesn't get cold enough, neither will the insert, and the ice cream machine won't work. Many recipes use a fussy French egg custard that must be cooked, strained, cooled, and chilled before churning. Could we make really good ice cream—with intense chocolate flavor and lush texture—without the machine or the hassle?

Ice cream makers work by incorporating air, which reduces ice crystals and helps ensure a smooth, creamy texture. Recipes I tried that called for simply freezing a mixture of melted chocolate, cream, and sugar were more like frozen truffles than ice cream. Other recipes incorporated air by freezing the mixture and then stirring it every 30 minutes for hours; this was tedious, to say the least. I found one recipe based on semifreddo (an Italian dessert) that called for folding whipped egg whites or whipped cream into an egg yolk base, but it tasted too light and icy. I also considered the old summer camp method in which a small coffee can is filled with cream, sugar, and chocolate syrup and set inside a larger coffee can filled with rock salt and ice; the entire contraption is then shaken vigorously for 30 minutes. This requires cans, rock salt, and a crew of campers willing to shake, rattle, and roll. Puh-leeze!

Things began looking up when I found a recipe that used sweetened condensed milk in place of cream. I added chopped semisweet chocolate to the condensed milk, melted the mixture in the microwave, and then froze it. In the freezer, the condensed milk maintained its velvety texture. Unfortunately, its cloying sweetness overpowered the chocolate. Thinking about the semifreddo, I tried folding in whipped cream to lighten the mixture. After several hours, I pulled my container from the freezer and found dense, creamy chocolate ice cream with a luscious texture that rivaled any I'd ever made in a machine. But while the texture hit the mark, the flavor was sickly sweet and barely tasted of chocolate.

I tried replacing semisweet chocolate with unsweetened. That cut the sweetness but—alas—spoiled the texture. Because unsweetened chocolate (and cocoa powder, which I also tried) have more cocoa solids than semisweet chocolate, they made the ice cream chalky. Next, I tried using equal parts of unsweetened and white chocolate (which has no cocoa solids). Although this did lighten the ice cream, the white chocolate masked the dark chocolate flavor. Bittersweet chocolate, which has slightly less sugar than semisweet, worked best in maintaining the texture, but tasters continued to find the ice cream too sweet and the chocolate flavor lacking.

In the test kitchen, we often add instant coffee granules to heighten chocolate flavor. The note of bitterness intensifies the chocolate without making it taste like a cup of coffee. Not only did the coffee enhance the chocolate, the ice cream—balanced by the coffee—tasted less sweet. A pinch of salt and a little vanilla extract rounded out the flavor of this mousselike, ultra-rich, full-on chocolate dessert. As a final test, we tasted our ice cream against some premium commercial brands: Ours won hands down.

EASY CHOCOLATE ICE CREAM
Makes 1 quart
If you plan to store the ice cream for more than a few days, place plastic wrap directly on its surface before freezing.

- 1 teaspoon instant coffee or espresso powder
- 1 tablespoon hot water
- 4 ounces bittersweet chocolate, chopped fine
- ½ cup sweetened condensed milk
- ½ teaspoon vanilla extract
  Pinch salt
- 1¼ cups cold heavy cream

This homemade ice cream is so rich, creamy, and easy to make that you may never buy the supermarket stuff again.

1. MELT CHOCOLATE BASE Combine coffee (or espresso) powder and hot water in small bowl. Let stand until coffee dissolves, about 5 minutes. Microwave chocolate, sweetened condensed milk, and coffee mixture in bowl, stirring every 10 seconds, until chocolate is melted, about 1 minute. Stir in vanilla and salt. Let cool.

2. MIX AND FREEZE With electric mixer on medium-high speed, whip cream to soft peaks, about 2 minutes. Whisk one-third of whipped cream into chocolate mixture. Fold remaining whipped cream into chocolate mixture until incorporated. Freeze in airtight container until firm, at least 6 hours or up to 2 weeks. Serve.

STEP-BY-STEP No Machine, No Churning, No Fuss
Follow these steps for chocolate ice cream that's incredibly easy—and delicious.

1. Skip the double boiler. Start by microwaving the chocolate, coffee, and condensed milk until the chocolate is melted.

2. Skip the ice cream machine. For fluffy texture that mimics churned ice cream, gently fold in whipped cream.

3. Skip the stirring. Simply pour the mixture into a container and freeze for at least six hours.

It takes just a spiral of rosemary and garlic to turn a backyard pork roast into something special.

Grilled Rosemary Garlic Pork Roast

In theory, rosemary, garlic, and pork make a perfect trio. Turning theory into dinner is another matter. BY ADAM RIED

WHAT MAKES BONELESS pork loin so appealing—its lean nature and lack of sinew or gristle—also makes it a challenge to cook: Little fat translates to little flavor and meat that easily dries out. Rosemary and garlic can team up to address the flavor issue, but neither does anything to solve the basic cooking problem. That requires careful grilling technique.

In the test kitchen, we've found it better to score, rather than trim, the thin layer of fat on the top of a pork loin; scoring encourages the fat to melt and baste the meat during cooking. After scoring, we use kitchen twine to tie the roast into an even, cylindrical shape, brown it directly over high heat, and finish cooking it on a cooler section of the grill until the meat reaches an internal temperature of 140 degrees. Yes, the roast will be a bit pink in the middle, but after a 15-minute rest on a carving board, the temperature will rise to a perfectly safe (and still juicy) 150 degrees. Cooking lean pork any further is a recipe for shoe leather.

Potent garlic and rosemary are a natural pairing with pork, but how you add those flavors matters. Studding the roast with garlic slivers and rosemary leaves perfumed the air as I cooked, but the meat itself was disappointingly bland. I ran across recipes that recommended using kitchen twine to lash long branches of rosemary to the outside of the roast. The dramatic appearance was a thrill. Unfortunately, the branches turned to bitter rosemary ash over the heat of the fire. Next, I tried rubbing the outside of the roast with minced rosemary and garlic—about half the mixture immediately fell into the flames. I smeared the roast with a potent rosemary, garlic, and oil paste—it burned over the direct hot fire. I was running out of ideas when it occurred to me that maybe the paste would fare better inside the pork, where it could flavor every bite of the meat and at the same time be shielded from the incinerating heat.

I cut open the next roast, a method called butterflying, unfolded it like a book, spread the exposed surface with the rosemary paste, and then tightly rolled it back up and tied it shut. I brushed the roast's surface with olive oil to help it brown and to reduce sticking on the grill.

Not quite an hour later, my tasters dug in. This pork sure had flavor, but now it had too much of a good thing. The rosemary was so overpowering, it was downright medicinal. The next time I made the pork, I replaced some of the assertive rosemary with gentler fresh parsley. My reward was a browned, juicy pork loin with a robust yet balanced hit of garlic and herbs.

GRILLED ROSEMARY PORK LOIN
Serves 6 to 8

Freezing the pork for 30 minutes will make butterflying it much easier. Mincing the parsley, rosemary, and garlic makes for a homogenous filling.

- ⅓ cup minced fresh parsley
- 1½ tablespoons minced fresh rosemary
- 2 garlic cloves, minced
  Salt and pepper
- 3 tablespoons extra-virgin olive oil
- 1 boneless pork loin roast (2½ to 3 pounds), fat on top scored lightly

1. BUTTERFLY ROAST Combine parsley, rosemary, garlic, ¾ teaspoon salt, ¾ teaspoon pepper, and 2 tablespoons oil in bowl. Following photos 1 to 3, butterfly pork roast and spread with herb mixture, leaving ½-inch border on all sides. Roll tightly, then tie roast at 1-inch intervals with kitchen twine. (Roast can be wrapped tightly with plastic and refrigerated for 24 hours.)

2. HEAT GRILL Heat all burners on high, covered, for 15 minutes. (For charcoal grill, light 100 coals; when covered with fine gray ash, spread over half of grill. Set cooking grate in place and heat covered, with lid vent open completely, for 5 minutes.) Scrape and oil cooking grate.

3. GRILL AND SLICE Rub prepared roast all over with remaining oil and season with salt and pepper. Place roast opposite primary burner (for charcoal grill, place roast directly over coals) and grill until well browned all over, about 12 minutes. Arrange roast fat-side up, leave primary burner on high, and shut off other burner(s). (For charcoal grill, position roast fat-side up on cooler side of grill.) Cook, covered, until meat registers 140 degrees, 35 to 45 minutes. Transfer pork to cutting board, tent with foil, and let rest 15 minutes. The temperature will continue to rise. Remove twine, slice, and serve.

STEP-BY-STEP **Herb Flavor in Every Bite**
To flavor the pork roast from the inside out, we butterflied the loin and then spread the interior with a heady herb paste. The technique is easier with a relatively short, wide roast (about 7 to 8 inches long and 4 to 5 inches wide). Here's how we did it.

1. Place roast fat-side up on cutting board. Starting about 1 inch up from cutting board, cut horizontally, stopping about ½ inch before edge.

2. Now cut into thicker half of roast again, starting about 1 inch from cutting board and stopping about ½ inch before edge.

3. Spread herb mixture evenly over surface of butterflied roast, leaving ½-inch border on all sides. Roll tightly and tie with kitchen twine.

ON THE SIDE Lemon Potatoes

Creamy and bright, these Greek-inspired potatoes deserve wider play in American kitchens. BY LYNN CLARK

AT MODEST GREEK RESTAURANTS in American cities, we've often enjoyed lemony, garlicky, golden potatoes—a tasty cross between home fries and roasted potatoes. Many recipes call for covering potato wedges with a mixture of olive oil and equal parts water and lemon juice, baking them in a slow oven for up to 1½ hours, then crisping the wedges on a hot griddle. The method makes sense at a restaurant where the potatoes are finished to order, but was time-consuming and somewhat laborious at home. Could I streamline it?

I tried skipping the crisping step, baking the potatoes until the liquid evaporated. High marks for ease, low marks for soggy texture. Next, I sautéed the potatoes in a skillet, then dressed them with lemon juice. Great color, scant lemon flavor. To combine the best facets of each, I skillet-simmered the potatoes in the liquid, covered, until tender, and then uncovered the pan to let the liquid evaporate. Once the pan was dry, I added a little oil to brown the potatoes. The potatoes fell apart.

I'd been using medium-starch Yukon gold potatoes. To eliminate the mushy potato problem, I tried waxy red potatoes. To eliminate the crumbling problem, I cut them in half instead of in wedges. The potatoes stayed intact, but the starch still burned slightly. A classic French fry prep technique—rinsing the raw potatoes to wash off the starch—solved the problem.

For the simmering liquid, a 1:1 ratio of water to lemon juice proved too puckery. After several tests, I went with 1 cup of water to just 2 tablespoons of lemon juice, plus a little grated zest. For added richness, I replaced the water with chicken broth and tossed in two cloves of garlic.

LEMON POTATOES Serves 4

- 2 pounds baby red potatoes, scrubbed and halved (quartered if large)
- 2 garlic cloves, peeled and smashed, plus 2 cloves, minced
- 1½ teaspoons grated zest and 2 tablespoons juice from 1 lemon
- 1 cup low-sodium chicken broth
  Salt and pepper
- 2 tablespoons extra-virgin olive oil
- 2 tablespoons finely chopped fresh parsley

1. RINSE POTATOES Place potatoes in colander set over large bowl. Rinse under running water, tossing with hands until water runs clear. Drain potatoes well.

2. COOK POTATOES Bring potatoes, smashed garlic, lemon juice, chicken broth, and ½ teaspoon salt to boil in large nonstick skillet. Reduce heat to medium-low and cook, covered, until potatoes are just tender, 12 to 15 minutes. Remove lid and increase heat to medium. Cook, stirring occasionally, until liquid evaporates, about 5 minutes.

3. CRISP POTATOES Discard garlic cloves and add oil to pan. Turn all potatoes cut-side down and continue to cook until deep golden brown, about 6 minutes. Off heat, stir in parsley, lemon zest, and minced garlic. Season with salt and pepper. Serve.

We finished the potatoes with garlic, parsley, and lemon zest.

ON THE SIDE Minty Sugar Snap Pea Salad

Good technique and a few surprise ingredients transform mint and peas into a sophisticated salad. BY MARÍA DEL MAR SACASA

WARM ENGLISH PEAS with mint is a winning springtime classic, so we were intrigued when we came across recipes for a contemporary variation: sugar snap peas with mint in a room-temperature salad. Unfortunately, the recipes we tested disappointed us. The sugar snaps were either raw or overcooked, and several were slicked with vinaigrette that tasted more like mouthwash than bright, fresh mint.

Before even considering how we might improve the salad, we snapped off the stems from each pod and removed their fibrous strings. Then, we turned to the test kitchen's standard method for achieving emerald green, crisp-tender snap peas: We blanch them in well-seasoned boiling water, then plunge them into ice water to stop the pods from cooking further and lock in their texture, flavor, and color.

To make the vinaigrette, we gently heated the mint leaves in oil in the hopes they would impart their flavor. It didn't go as planned. We intended infusion; we got mouthwash, and began to understand where the other recipes had gone wrong. We changed track, now reaching for a lemon, with the idea that the acidity (from both the zest and juice) would help draw out the herb's flavor. To offset sharp mint and sour lemon, we added minced shallot and a teaspoon each of Dijon mustard and honey.

We thought we were done, but our salad still tasted like a work in progress. We wandered the test kitchen for ideas, opening cabinets and investigating the contents of refrigerators. After a few unsuccessful additions, we tried goat cheese. A restrained ¼ cup was enough to pull the salad together, providing tangy, creamy richness without weighing it down. Finally, to make for easier eating and to help the peas hold more dressing, we sliced the pods in half crosswise.

MINTY SUGAR SNAP PEA SALAD Serves 4 to 6

- 1½ pounds sugar snap peas, stems snapped off and strings removed
  Salt and pepper
- ¼ cup finely chopped fresh mint
- 1 small shallot, minced
- 1 teaspoon grated zest plus 1 tablespoon juice from 1 lemon
- 1 teaspoon Dijon mustard
- 1 teaspoon honey
- 3 tablespoons extra-virgin olive oil
- ¼ cup crumbled goat cheese

1. PREP PEAS Combine 4 cups water and 4 cups ice cubes in large bowl; set aside. Bring 4 quarts water to boil in large pot over high heat. Add peas and 1 tablespoon salt and cook until crisp-tender, about 2 minutes. Drain peas, then transfer to ice bath to cool completely. Remove peas from water, pat dry with kitchen towel, and cut in half crosswise. (Halved peas can be refrigerated in zipper-lock bag for 2 days.)

2. DRESS SALAD Whisk mint, shallot, lemon zest, lemon juice, mustard, honey, and oil in large bowl. Add peas and cheese to bowl and toss to combine. Season with salt and pepper. Serve chilled or at room temperature. (Salad can be refrigerated in airtight container for 1 day.)

To the classic combination of mint, peas, and lemon, we added outliers: goat cheese and honey. They fit right in.

Huli Huli Chicken

"Huli! Huli!" workers shout to one another as they man the 10-foot-long portable grills that dot the roads and parking lots of Hawaii, each cooking more than 30 split chickens at a time. The birds are continually basted with a sticky-sweet sauce and "huli"-ed (turned, in Hawaiian) to keep from burning. "You can stand on my deck above the city and watch for smoke on a weekend," says Wanda Adams, cookbook author and food editor at the Honolulu Advertiser. "Head in that direction and you're sure to find a parking lot huli huli sale." True huli huli chicken is something home cooks buy instead of make, she adds, as the grill apparatus and incessant flipping discourage even the most adventurous grillers. BY DIANE UNGER

Since I didn't have the rig, the Hawaiian *kiawe* wood used for grilling, or the good fortune to live in Hawaii, I'd have to figure out how to make this sweet, smoky, burnished bird at home. Between cookbooks and the Internet, I found adaptations of the teriyaki-like sauce to which sweet ingredients are added.

I made, remade, adapted, developed, and tweaked. Ultimately, tasters picked a version with soy sauce, rice vinegar, ginger, garlic, chili sauce, ketchup, brown sugar, and lots and lots of pineapple juice. I boiled the sauce down until it was thick, glossy, and sweet. Then I marinated the chicken in the sauce, as most recipes instruct. But on the grill, by the time the chicken was cooked through, its skin had incinerated. Also, the meat was dry, and the marinade didn't add much flavor. (Maybe if I'd left it in the sauce overnight, it would have worked, but I was hungry now.)

Could I get my grill to mimic a Hawaiian rotisserie? Huli huli rotisseries strap chicken halves to parallel poles, suspended a ways above the coals and continually turned (think foosball). For me, high, direct heat proved a direct path to scorched chicken. Indirect heat resulted in flabby chicken skin. My best bet was a moderate number of coals (about 75) spread in a single layer over the entire grill. The direct heat rendered the fat and crisped the skin, but the chicken was far enough from the coals to avoid burning—or so I hoped.

We often brine chicken to keep it moist and flavorful. For my next test, instead of soaking the chicken in sauce, I brined it in salted water, planning to paint on the sauce on the grill. This chicken was moist, but once I started to baste, it burned yet again—not as badly as before, but still... Despite my careful grill setup, with so much sugar in the sauce the chicken didn't stand a

chance. Also, the flavor was only skin-deep. What if I used some of my sauce ingredients as a brine? I mixed together soy sauce, water, garlic, and ginger (I sautéed the last two to bring out their flavors). In another bid for flavor, I added soaked mesquite chips to the grill—kiawe is a species of mesquite. This chicken had a deep, seasoned-to-the-bone flavor.

If only I could fix that smoldering problem. Since the glaze was to blame, why not save it until the chicken came off the grill? After all, the chicken was already highly seasoned from the brine and well smoked from the wood. I grilled the chicken skin-side up to render the fat, and then turned it skin-side down to finish cooking and crisp the skin (just one turn sufficed). As soon as the chicken came off the grill, I painted on the glaze. This chicken was bronzed and beautiful, smoky, moist, sweet, and flavorful throughout.

HULI HULI CHICKEN Serves 4 to 6

Split chicken halves are whole chickens that have been split in two through the breastbone. Buy them at the market or see page 31 for instructions on how to prepare them yourself. Lee Kum Kee Tabletop Soy Sauce is our favorite supermarket brand.

CHICKEN
- 2 quarts water
- 2 cups soy sauce
- 1 tablespoon vegetable oil
- 6 garlic cloves, minced
- 1 tablespoon grated fresh ginger
- 4 split chicken halves (about 8 pounds total) (see note)

GLAZE
- 3 (6-ounce) cans pineapple juice
- ¼ cup packed light brown sugar
- ¼ cup soy sauce
- ¼ cup ketchup
- ¼ cup rice vinegar
- 4 garlic cloves, minced
- 2 tablespoons grated fresh ginger
- 2 teaspoons Asian chili-garlic sauce
- 2 cups wood chips (see box at right), soaked for 15 minutes

1. BRINE CHICKEN Combine water and soy sauce in large bowl. Heat oil in large saucepan over medium-high heat until shimmering. Add garlic and ginger and cook until fragrant, about 30 seconds. Stir into soy sauce mixture. Add chicken and refrigerate, covered, for at least 1 hour or up to 8 hours.

2. MAKE GLAZE Combine pineapple juice, sugar, soy sauce, ketchup, vinegar, garlic, ginger, and chili-garlic sauce in empty saucepan and bring to boil. Reduce heat to medium and simmer until thick and syrupy (you should have about 1 cup), 20 to 25 minutes.

3. PREP GRILL Seal wood chips in foil packet and cut vent holes in top. Open bottom vents on grill. Light about 75 coals. When coals are covered with fine gray ash, spread evenly over bottom of grill. Arrange foil packet directly on coals. Set cooking grate in place and heat, covered with lid vent open halfway, until wood chips begin to smoke heavily, about 5 minutes. (For gas grill, place foil packet directly on primary burner. Heat all burners on high, covered, until wood chips begin to smoke heavily, about 15 minutes. Turn all burners to medium-low.) Scrape and oil cooking grate.

4. GRILL CHICKEN Remove chicken from brine and pat dry with paper towels. Arrange chicken skin-side up on grill (do not place chicken directly above foil packet). Grill, covered, until chicken is well browned on bottom and meat registers 120 degrees, 25 to 30 minutes. Flip chicken skin-side down and continue to grill, covered, until skin is well browned and crisp and thigh meat registers 170 to 175 degrees, 20 to 25 minutes longer. Transfer chicken to platter, brush with half of glaze, and let rest 5 minutes. Serve, passing remaining glaze at table.

MAKE AHEAD: Both the brine and the glaze can be made ahead and refrigerated for up to 3 days. Do not brine the chicken for longer than 8 hours or it will become too salty.

KEY TO BOLD FLAVOR Mesquite
Authentic huli huli chicken is grilled over kiawe wood, from a hardwood tree that is a species of mesquite. The test kitchen finds mesquite wood chips too assertive for long-cooked chicken and pork dishes; after an hour or two, the smoke turns the meat bitter. But we liked them in this comparatively quick recipe. Our Huli Huli Chicken recipe will work with any variety of wood chips, but if you care about authenticity, mesquite is the chip of choice.

WHEN THE CHIPS ARE DOWN Assertive mesquite doesn't always work, but we like it here.

ON THE SIDE Hawaiian-Style Macaroni Salad

Hawaiians cook their macaroni until it's "fat." Turns out they know what they're doing. BY DIANE UNGER

We dress this macaroni salad twice: first with vinegar and then with creamy mayonnaise.

MACARONI SALAD IS an integral part of what's known as a "plate lunch," Hawaii's version of diner food: one big scoop macaroni, two big scoops sticky white rice, plus a big portion of a satisfying protein like huli huli chicken. Plate lunches can be found at fund-raisers, church picnics, and beach parking lot trucks throughout the Islands.

My research turned up quite a few variations on Hawaiian macaroni salad. But the key ingredients were consistent: elbow macaroni cooked until very soft, a creamy dressing of mayonnaise thinned with milk, grated carrot, and plenty of salt and pepper. With a few tweaks, I hoped to make this dish ready for the mainland.

Overcooking the pasta, while it seems a bad idea, actually enables it to absorb more dressing (and flavor), so the dressing has to be thin enough to soak in. It took 2 cups each of mayonnaise and milk to get the right texture. I added cider vinegar to boost flavor, but it curdled the milk—not pretty. Instead I poured the vinegar directly over the hot macaroni. After the vinegar soaked in, I poured on about half the dressing, gave the mixture a stir, and let it cool. Then I stirred in the remaining dressing and added grated carrot, chopped celery (for crunch), scallion, a tablespoon of brown sugar, and some vigorous shakes of salt and black pepper.

HAWAIIAN MACARONI SALAD Serves 8 to 10
Low-fat milk or mayonnaise will make the dressing too thin.

- 2 cups whole milk (see note)
- 2 cups mayonnaise (see note)
- 1 tablespoon brown sugar
- Salt and pepper
- 1 pound elbow macaroni
- ½ cup cider vinegar
- 4 scallions, sliced thin
- 1 large carrot, peeled and grated
- 1 celery rib, chopped fine

1. MAKE DRESSING Whisk 1½ cups milk, 1 cup mayonnaise, sugar, ½ teaspoon salt, and 2 teaspoons pepper in bowl.

2. COOK PASTA Bring 4 quarts water to boil in large pot. Add 1 tablespoon salt and pasta and cook until very soft, about 15 minutes. Drain pasta and return to pot. Add vinegar and toss until absorbed. Transfer to bowl. Cool pasta 10 minutes, then stir in dressing until pasta is well coated. Cool completely.

3. MAKE SALAD Add scallions, carrot, celery, remaining milk, and remaining mayonnaise to pot with pasta mixture and stir to combine. Season with salt and pepper. Transfer to serving bowl and refrigerate, covered, for at least 1 hour or up to 2 days. Serve.

Beer-Battered Onion Rings

The soggy, doughy reality is that onion rings fried in beer batter are rarely good. We hoped to improve the odds. BY LYNN CLARK

Use bolder beers, such as Bass or Samuel Adams, to give the coating toasty, malty flavors.

ON A RECENT NIGHT out with friends, I ordered beer-battered onion rings and hoped that for once I'd avoid disappointment. (In my experience, good onion rings are rare.) Several minutes later, eight fat, golden onion rings arrived at the table to "oohs" and "ahhs." To my surprise, these tasted as good as they looked. The coating had maximum crunch with the barest trace of bitterness; the onions were tender and sweet. I was inspired to head into the test kitchen to make some myself.

What a disaster! Not a single recipe produced rings nearly as good as those I'd eaten with my friends, despite the (beer) battering the kitchen took. They offered up a litany of frying flaws: soggy, doughy, heavy, raw—and where had that distinctively yeasty, malty undertone gone?

I started by stirring together a basic batter of flour, beer, and salt. I'd finesse it later; first I wanted to figure out which onion to use. I coated the onions in batter and fried them in 350-degree peanut oil. Sweet onions creamed the competition; tasters preferred their gentle flavor. I turned my attention back to the batter.

Beer gives the coating flavor. Also, the carbonation in beer provides lift to the batter. But with just beer, my rings were doughy. Clearly, I'd need a second leavener. Recipes are split on whether to use eggs or baking powder. Eggs (either whole or separated) did little, but baking powder yielded a coating that was thick and substantial, yet light. To add crunch to the coating, I used cornstarch, a technique I knew worked from test kitchen experience. I gradually substituted cornstarch for flour until I had a 1:1 ratio. Now my rings shattered when I bit into them.

Unfortunately, part of that crunch came from the onions, and while a crunchy coating appealed, crunchy onions definitely did not. Some recipes call for soaking the onions in water, milk, or buttermilk to soften them. They all worked, but I wondered if I could use the soak to build flavor, too. Since these were beer-battered onion rings, I soaked them in beer for an hour before proceeding with my recipe. At last, I had nicely flavored rings with crisp coating encasing tender slices of onion.

But did I really have to wait an hour?

To shorten the soaking time, a colleague suggested adding salt, which works by breaking down, thus softening, the exterior cell walls of the onion. To build flavor, I added 2 teaspoons of white vinegar to the soak. In one final test, I tried malt vinegar, which subtly echoed the caramel beer notes of the batter. These rings ran circles around the competition.

BEER-BATTERED ONION RINGS
Serves 4 to 6

In step 1, do not soak the onion rounds longer than 2 hours or they will turn soft and become too saturated to crisp properly. Cider vinegar can be used in place of malt vinegar. Use a candy thermometer to make sure the oil gets to 350 degrees. Ordinary yellow onions will produce acceptable rings here.

- 2 sweet onions, peeled and sliced into ½-inch-thick rounds
- 3 cups beer
- 2 teaspoons malt vinegar (see note)
  Salt and pepper
- 2 quarts peanut or vegetable oil
- ¾ cup all-purpose flour
- ¾ cup cornstarch
- 1 teaspoon baking powder

1. SOAK ONIONS Place onion rounds, 2 cups beer, vinegar, ½ teaspoon salt, and ½ teaspoon pepper in zipper-lock bag; refrigerate 30 minutes or up to 2 hours.

2. MAKE BATTER Heat oil in large Dutch oven over medium-high heat to 350 degrees. While oil is heating, combine flour, cornstarch, baking powder, ½ teaspoon salt, and ¼ teaspoon pepper in large bowl. Slowly whisk in ¾ cup beer until just combined (some lumps will remain). Whisk in remaining beer as needed, 1 tablespoon at a time, until batter falls from whisk in steady stream and leaves faint trail across surface of batter.

3. FRY RINGS Adjust oven rack to middle position and heat oven to 200 degrees. Remove onions from refrigerator and pour off liquid. Pat onion rounds dry with paper towels and separate into rings. Transfer one-third portion of rings to batter. One at a time, carefully transfer battered rings to oil. Fry until rings are golden brown and crisp, about 5 minutes, flipping halfway through frying. Drain rings on paper towel–lined baking sheet, season with salt and pepper, and transfer to oven. Return oil to 350 degrees and repeat with remaining onion rings and batter. Serve.

Troubleshooting
Beer-Battered Onion Rings

PROBLEM: **Crunchy Onions**
SOLUTION: **Soak in Beer**
Soaking the rings in a combination of beer, vinegar, and salt softens and flavors the raw onion.

PROBLEM: **Bad Battering**
SOLUTION: **Add Beer Gradually**
If the batter is too thick, the rings will be doughy; too thin and it will run off. Add the beer gradually until the batter falls from a whisk to form a ribbon trail.

PROBLEM: **Fused Onion Rings**
SOLUTION: **Don't Crowd the Pot**
Fry the battered onion rings in small batches and transfer them one at a time to the hot oil so they don't stick together.

Green Chile Cheeseburgers

This New Mexican classic may just be the best burger you've never had. BY LYNN CLARK

Authentic fire-roasted Hatch chiles may be several states away, but a good substitute is as near as your local grocery store.

GREEN CHILES SHOW up on menus everywhere in New Mexico—even at McDonald's. Farmers harvest the chiles in late summer, when they are bought by the bushel to be roasted and frozen for year-round use. The chiles make their way into all kinds of dishes, even apple pie and chocolate ice cream! One especially beloved tradition is the green chile burger. At roadside restaurants all over New Mexico, ground beef patties are grilled to a crusty brown and topped with fire-roasted, chopped chiles and a slice of cheese.

I mail-ordered a big bag of fire-roasted, hot green chiles from Hatch, New Mexico, the self-proclaimed green chile capital of the country. Almost as soon as they arrived, I headed out to grill some burgers. As advertised, the chiles had intense heat and a captivating sweet and smoky flavor. Nonetheless, waiting for chiles to arrive in the mail so I could make a burger was out of the question. To bring this regional favorite out of the Southwest, I'd need to use ordinary supermarket ingredients.

Most recipes suggest canned chiles as a substitute. We found them tinny, and they were so mild you could eat them with a spoon. Casting about for an alternative, I spied Anaheim chiles at the supermarket. In fact, these do grow in New Mexico, but experts say that the state's hot, arid climate produces hotter Anaheims than those grown in California or Florida, the states that supply most supermarkets around the country. I roasted the supermarket Anaheims and found them far milder than the Hatch I'd mail-ordered. To fix that, I tried combining them with poblano peppers, which have a spicy, smoky edge. The mix tasted unpleasantly vegetal and the heat barely registered. Moving up the heat scale, I combined the Anaheims with jalapeños. Much better! These came close to the mail-order chiles. To round out the flavor, I borrowed from recipes I'd seen that added sautéed onions and garlic to the chiles. Rather than dirtying a pan, I simply grilled the onions with the chiles, then chopped them with fresh garlic in the food processor.

Now that the topping was in order, I turned to the burger. Tasters preferred the flavor and fat of 85 percent lean ground beef. After a few trial runs, I settled on 6-ounce patties, which could accommodate a generous chile topping. To shape the burgers, I used a proven test kitchen technique—making a small indentation in each patty to keep them from buckling and dislodging the topping. I grilled the burgers to medium doneness over high heat. They were juicy and meaty, but tasters complained the chile was being upstaged. The obvious solution was extra topping, but if I heaped on any more, it'd just fall into the grill. Wait a sec—what if I put chile *into* the burgers? This time, I set aside some of my chile mixture for the topping and pureed the rest into a smooth paste, which I then mixed into the ground raw meat. These burgers packed a pleasurable, hot punch through and through. For my last test, I tried topping the burgers alternately with cheddar, Monterey Jack, and American. Tasters preferred mild American cheese, which melts well and is traditional on these burgers.

I flipped a final batch of burgers over and topped them with spoonfuls of chile mixture and a slice of cheese; the cheese melted as the burger finished cooking, which helped the topping stay put. The burger, by contrast, was ready to travel—straight into your kitchen.

GREEN CHILE CHEESEBURGERS
Serves 4

In step 2, you may need to add a teaspoon or two of water to the food processor to help the chile mixture puree. Pressing a shallow divot in the center of each burger patty keeps the burgers flat during grilling.

- 3   Anaheim chiles, stemmed, halved lengthwise, and seeded
- 3   jalapeño chiles, stemmed, halved lengthwise, and seeded
- 1   onion, peeled and sliced into ½-inch-thick rounds
- 1   garlic clove, minced
      Salt and pepper
- 1½ pounds 85 percent lean ground beef
- 4   slices deli American cheese

1. CHAR VEGETABLES Grill chiles and onion, covered, over hot fire until vegetables are lightly charred and tender, 2 to 4 minutes per side. Transfer vegetables to bowl, cover, and let cool 5 minutes. Remove skins from chiles and discard; separate onion rounds into rings.

2. PROCESS CHILE MIXTURE Transfer chiles, onion, and garlic to food processor and pulse until coarsely chopped. Transfer all but ¼ cup chopped chile mixture to empty bowl and season with salt and pepper; set aside. Process remaining mixture until smooth.

3. FORM BURGERS Combine beef, pureed chile mixture, ½ teaspoon salt, and ¼ teaspoon pepper in large bowl and knead gently until well incorporated. Shape into four ¾-inch-thick patties and press shallow divot in center of each.

4. GRILL AND TOP Grill burgers, covered, over hot fire until well browned on first side, 3 to 5 minutes. Flip burgers, top with chopped chile mixture and cheese, and continue to grill, covered, until cheese is melted and burgers are cooked to desired doneness, 3 to 5 minutes. Serve.

TEST KITCHEN DISCOVERY **Chile Pinch Hitter**
For complex green chile flavor outside of New Mexico, we found that a combination of mild Anaheims and spicy jalapeños has a nice peppery balance.

MILD HEAT
Anaheim chiles add a mildly sweet, grassy flavor.

SPICE IS NICE
Jalapeño chiles have just enough heat to stand up to the beefiness of the burger.

Diner-Style Strawberry Pie

The pie case is the first thing I size up when I step into a diner. The mile-high lemon meringue and banana cream pies tempt me mightily, but it's the strawberry pie that gets me every time: a red so bright it hurts, berries so big they could be plums, whipped cream so pouffy it looks like a drift of fresh snow. Inevitably, I order a humongous slice and eagerly dive in when the waitress sets it down. But diner strawberry pies rarely deliver, tasting more of plastic than pie. The "baker" (I use the word loosely) seems to toss a few underripe berries with a can of dyed, gelatinous, tooth-achingly sweet strawberry pie filling (a.k.a. red goo) and then calls it a day. Could better ingredients and techniques deliver a pie that lives up to its looks? BY CALI RICH

Unlike strawberry-rhubarb pie, diner-style strawberry pie isn't baked. The filling is cooked on the stove, poured into a prebaked pie crust, and chilled. Perhaps the most famous version is the one served at Shoney's, a restaurant chain based in Nashville, Tennessee. I trolled their website for a recipe. No luck. A call to their test kitchen also came up short, with a tight-lipped employee offering only that the strawberry filling is a secret recipe made for and distributed to each Shoney's, where the pies are assembled fresh every day.

Most of the recipes I was able to find were virtually identical. You combine 1 cup each of water and sugar with a small amount of cornstarch until thickened. Once the mixture is cool, you stir in a pound of fresh whole berries and a few drops of red food coloring, and then pour the mixture into the shell. Some versions had one significant variation—namely, adding as much as a box of strawberry Jell-O to the filling. The cornstarch-only version thickened nicely, but in the refrigerator, the filling began to weep; the chill apparently loosened the starch's hold. At the other extreme, pie made with Jell-O was disagreeably bouncy (and, worse, had a fake strawberry taste). But getting the texture right was the least of my problems. All of the recipes called for just 1 pound of berries and provided modest berry flavor at best. Meant to tempt the eye, these pies did little for the palate. I would start my testing from square one.

Right off the bat, I decided the red dye would have to go. That settled, I began to wonder about the generous measure of water (1 cup) added to the filling. Like most soft fruits, strawberries are naturally moist, so shouldn't you concentrate their juices? Instead, these recipes made a watery filling and then thickened it. That seemed crazy, so I struck out in a new direction, beginning my testing by simmering 3 pounds of sliced fresh berries (what's strawberry pie if not a lot of strawberries?) in a dry saucepan. The berries released their juices, and after 20 minutes my mixture was thick, concentrated, and flavorful. All good, except for one thing: Tasters missed the freshness of uncooked berries.

The next time I made the pie, I divided the fruit, cooking down 2 pounds of frozen berries—they worked equally well for cooking and cost less—and then stirring in 1 pound fresh berries off the heat (I sliced the fresh berries first to make the pie easier to cut). I poured this mixture into the shell and chilled the pie. This pie had all the berry flavor I could want. As it chilled, however, the uncooked berries softened, making the filling watery.

Strawberries are low in pectin, a natural thickener found in citrus fruits and many other plants. To make up for the lack of pectin in strawberries, I added 2 tablespoons of lemon juice, which also encourages thickening. It tightened the texture of the filling (and perked up the flavor), but not enough—the pie still wouldn't hold its shape when sliced. Many jams rely on powdered pectin, such as Sure-Jell, to thicken. After using an entire box without getting a sliceable pie, I nixed this ingredient. Next, I tried Minute Tapioca, which the test kitchen often uses to thicken crisps and puddings—but it made my strawberry filling unpleasantly slippery. Then it dawned on me that I might replace the strawberry Jell-O in some of the original recipes with unflavored gelatin. I tested various quantities and found that 1 tablespoon (a smidgen over one packet of Knox gelatin) produced a clean-slicing yet not bouncy pie. I tasted a spoonful of the filling, then stirred in a pinch of salt. As I'd anticipated, it sharpened the flavors.

Diner strawberry pies typically get a squirt of Reddi-wip. I hadn't gone to the trouble of making my own filling to reach for the can now. Instead, I whipped cream cheese into real whipped cream (along with vanilla and sugar) for a slightly tangy topping that balanced the sweetness of the berries and, thanks to the cream cheese,

gave the topping some pleasing heft. Then I sat down to enjoy my bright, fresh, very red, and very berry pie.

ICEBOX STRAWBERRY PIE Serves 8

In step 1, it is imperative that the cooked strawberry mixture measures 2 cups; any more and the filling will be loose. If your fresh berries aren't fully ripe, you may want to add extra sugar to taste in step 2. Use your favorite pie dough or go to CooksCountry.com for our recipe. Chill the heavy cream in step 4 to help it whip more quickly.

FILLING
- **2 pounds frozen strawberries (see box below)**
- **2 tablespoons lemon juice**
- **2 tablespoons water**
- **1 tablespoon unflavored gelatin**
- **1 cup sugar**
- **Pinch salt**
- **1 pound fresh strawberries, hulled and sliced thin**
- **1 (9-inch) pie shell, baked and cooled (see note)**

TOPPING
- **4 ounces cream cheese, softened**
- **3 tablespoons sugar**
- **½ teaspoon vanilla extract**
- **1 cup heavy cream**

1. COOK FROZEN BERRIES Cook frozen berries in large saucepan over medium-low heat until berries begin to release juice, about 3 minutes. Increase heat to medium-high and cook, stirring frequently, until thick and jamlike, about 25 minutes (mixture should measure 2 cups).

2. ADD GELATIN Combine lemon juice, water, and gelatin in small bowl. Let stand until gelatin is softened and mixture has thickened, about 5 minutes. Stir gelatin mixture, sugar, and salt into cooked berry mixture and return to simmer, about 2 minutes. Transfer to bowl and cool to room temperature, about 30 minutes.

3. ADD FRESH BERRIES Fold fresh berries into filling. Spread evenly in pie shell and refrigerate until set, about 4 hours. (Filled pie can be refrigerated for 24 hours.)

4. MAKE TOPPING With electric mixer on medium speed, beat cream cheese, sugar, and vanilla until smooth, about 30 seconds. With mixer running, add cream and whip until stiff peaks form, about 2 minutes. Serve pie with whipped cream topping.

Don't Make This Mistake
In step 1, be sure to accurately measure the reduced strawberry mixture: You'll need exactly 2 cups. Scrape the strawberry mixture into a large liquid measuring cup. If it measures more than 2 cups, return it to the pan to cook down. It may seem fussy to stop to measure, but the pie will not set or slice properly if you have more than 2 cups of the strawberry mixture.

MEASURE METICULOUSLY

Troubleshooting Blind-Baked Crusts

Even if the pie you're making requires little or no baking, chances are good the crust needs oven time. In those cases, bakers "blind" bake, or prebake, the crust, a step that presents a number of challenges. Here's how to avoid trouble.

PROBLEM: **Tough and Shrunken**
SOLUTION: **Cool the Crust**
After the dough is rolled out and shaped, but before it is baked, chill it for at least 20 minutes in the refrigerator. This allows the gluten in the flour to "relax" and the butter to chill. Then freeze for 10 minutes to set its shape. Skip these steps at your peril: The crust will be misshapen and tough.

PROBLEM: **Bubbled and Irregular**
SOLUTION: **Weigh It Down**
Left to their own devices, pie crusts will puff, crater, and bake unevenly. To avoid those problems, line the shells with foil and fill them with pie weights before baking. Spray two 12-inch squares of foil and overlap over the dough, greased-side down, making sure to cover the crimped crust. Then fill them with 2 cups of ceramic pie weights, pennies, or dried beans.

PROBLEM: **Pale Bottom**
SOLUTION: **Rearrange the Rack**
Prevent a doughy crust by baking the (weight-filled) pie shell on the lower-middle oven rack at 375 degrees. Bake until the dough no longer looks wet under the foil, about 20 minutes. Carefully remove the hot foil and weights and—for an icebox pie—continue to bake the crust until firm and light brown, another 10 to 15 minutes.

RATING FROZEN STRAWBERRIES

Our Icebox Strawberry Pie recipe calls for 2 pounds of frozen strawberries. Would the brand of berry matter? We thawed and sampled three national brands, both plain and cooked in pie. Tasted plain, each brand had a surprisingly different flavor (one even tasted "pickled"), while textures ranged from mushy to firm and sizes from small to exceptionally large. The flavor variations were less pronounced but didn't disappear when the berries were used in pie.

What made them different? All three brands were Individually Quick Frozen (a system of rapidly freezing individual items to retain flavor, shape, and nutritional value), and none added sugar. While IQF increases the shelf life of the fruit, freezing can also damage it. As the berry thaws, sulfide ions are released, increasing the possibility of off-flavors. Two brands had these off-flavors, which tasters noticed in both raw and cooked berries. To be certain that this wasn't the result of supermarket handling or other outside factors, we tested multiple bags over time; our results were the same. Tasters preferred the only brand with no off-flavors: Cascadian Farm Frozen Premium Organic Strawberries. They were also the plumpest, juiciest berries, with good strawberry flavor and "balanced sweetness." –MEREDITH BUTCHER

RECOMMENDED		TASTERS' NOTES
CASCADIAN FARM Frozen Premium Organic Strawberries **Price:** $3.50 for 10 ounces		**Comments:** Tasted on their own, these strawberries had the "strongest berry flavor, deepest red color, and plumpest texture." They had the right balance of tartness and the "sweetness didn't override the berry taste." The berries were the largest and firmest of the three brands we tasted. And the pie made with this brand had the truest, brightest strawberry flavor.

NOT RECOMMENDED		TASTERS' NOTES
WYMAN'S Stand-Up Bag Quick-Frozen Strawberries **Price:** $3.99 for 15 ounces		**Comments:** Tasters described these berries as "woody" and "moldy," with a "bitter, grassy aftertaste." Their tartness overpowered any strawberry flavor, and the puckery, acidic punch left tasters wishing for a spoonful of sugar. Even in the pie, these berries were too tart, and some found their flavor plasticky.
DOLE Whole Frozen Strawberries **Price:** $2.99 for 16 ounces		**Comments:** Tasters disliked this brand's "metallic," "tinny," and even "pickled" taste and found these berries the tartest of the bunch. The sugar muted most of the sour flavors when we baked the berries in the pie.

7UP Pound Cake

In the early 1950s, soda companies began marketing their products as more than mere drink, urging consumers to think of soda as a pantry staple. For one such effort, an advertising campaign to "get some extra 7UP for cooking," the company distributed free promotional recipe booklets that touted dishes like 7UP Salad (blend lime Jell-O, applesauce, and soda) and 7UP Parfait Pie (add the soda to both ice cream filling and crust). Over the years, most of these recipes have (mercifully) been forgotten. But 7UP Pound Cake remains a treasured favorite. The effervescent, slightly acidic soda gives this cake its flavor, lift, and uniquely tender texture. BY CALI RICH

Except for the 7UP, the recipes I found for 7UP Pound Cake mirror traditional pound cake in both method and ingredients: Sugar and softened butter (or shortening) are beaten together until light and fluffy. Eggs are added, followed by 7UP and lemon extract or zest. The flour is mixed in until just combined, the batter poured into a tube pan and baked at a moderate temperature (to prevent overbrowning) for a little over an hour. While traditional pound cakes can be dense, the 7UP version emerged with a tight yet light crumb, thanks to the soda's citric acid (which tenderizes) and carbonated water (which lifts).

Unfortunately, the flavor didn't wow me as much as the texture. The cake made with extract tasted like I'd dusted it with furniture polish, while the sugar (a generous 3 cups) overwhelmed the citrus flavor of those made with zest. Also, every last recipe omitted lime altogether—surprising, given 7UP's hallmark lemon-lime combination.

Working from a recipe that fortified the 7UP cake with zest, I began scaling back the sugar to bring out some citrus zing. Eventually, I achieved balanced sweetness by cutting out ½ cup of sugar. But the flavor of the cake remained flat. Unlike juice, finely grated zest can be added without affecting texture, so I added increasing amounts of both lemon and lime zest until I'd topped off at 1 tablespoon of each. The zest lent a fragrant quality, but the cake still lacked conviction. Realizing I'd need to add fresh (highly acidic) lemon and lime juice despite the troubles they might cause, I gradually added each until I'd settled on ¼ cup between the two in place of an equal amount of 7UP. Now the cake tasted great, but as I'd feared, the texture had taken a turn for the worse. A perfect pound cake hinges on a fragile emulsion of butter and eggs. The extra acid (from the juice) was causing the batter to curdle, resulting in a tough, gummy cake.

The test kitchen has had success using melted butter in acidic cake batters. While softened butter provides an uneven coating that exposes the batter to the structure-wrecking acid, melted butter readily coats and therefore protects the gluten. To put this to the test, I simply melted the butter and, using a technique the test kitchen has liked in the past, pulled out the food processor. (The brawn of the machine ensures the emulsification.) Once the sugar and wet ingredients were combined, I slowly poured the melted butter down the feed tube. I stirred in the flour, baked and cooled the cake, then helped myself to a slice. This big, buttery cake had a fine, even crumb plus a forceful lemon-lime flavor that warranted the 7UP name.

UP POUND CAKE Serves 12

...esh, not flat, 7UP is essential for the best ...exture and rise. You can also bake the ...ake in a 12-cup nonstick Bundt pan.

...AKE

2½ cups granulated sugar
5 large eggs, room temperature
½ cup 7UP, room temperature
  (see note)
1 tablespoon grated zest plus
  2 tablespoons juice from 1 lemon
1 tablespoon grated zest plus
  2 tablespoons juice from 2 limes
½ teaspoon salt
20 tablespoons (2½ sticks) unsalted
  butter, melted and cooled slightly
3¼ cups cake flour

...LAZE

1 cup confectioners' sugar
1 tablespoon lemon juice
1 tablespoon lime juice

1. MIX Adjust oven rack to lower-middle position and heat oven to 300 degrees. Grease and flour 12-cup nonstick tube pan. Process sugar, eggs, 7UP, lemon zest and juice, lime zest and juice, and salt in food processor until smooth. With machine running, slowly pour in butter and process until incorporated. Transfer to large bowl. Add flour in three additions, whisking until combined.

2. BAKE Spread batter in prepared pan. Gently tap pan on counter. Bake until toothpick inserted in center comes out clean, 75 to 90 minutes. Cool cake in pan 10 minutes, then turn out onto wire rack set inside rimmed baking sheet to cool completely, about 2 hours.

3. GLAZE Whisk confectioners' sugar, lemon juice, and lime juice in bowl until smooth. Pour glaze over cooled cake. Let glaze set 10 minutes. Serve. (Cake can be wrapped in plastic and held at room temperature for 3 days.)

NOT-SO-SECRET INGREDIENT 7UP
Curious if other clear sodas could stand in for 7UP, we compared cakes made with Sprite, Fresca, Mountain Dew, and ginger ale with one using 7UP. The 7UP cake was indistinguishable from all but one—the Fresca cake, which was pale and tough. Blame it on the artificial sweeteners, and be sure to avoid Diet 7UP for the same reason. We also tried playing soda jerk by creating our own soda from seltzer water, lemon, and lime to equal the pH of 7UP. Our homemade soda worked fine but made for slightly less sweet cake.

The original, but not the only soda for the job.

ON THE SIDE Raspberry Lime Rickeys

...all us picky, but a raspberry lime rickey should taste of raspberries and lime, right? BY MEGHAN ERWIN

...rozen raspberries cost less than fresh, and they work just fine ...this soda fountain classic.

THIS PRETTY, PINK beach-shack drink, made of raspberry syrup, fresh lime juice, club soda, and lots of ice, is a variation of a plain lime rickey (nix the raspberry syrup), itself an offshoot of a gin rickey (nix most of the lime, add gin). But a good rickey is hard to find. The drink is often watered down and spoiled by "raspberry flavored" drink mixer. I decided to develop a berry-bursting rickey with a decidedly lime-y base.

We've learned that a combination of lime juice and zest is the path to bold lime flavor. I made a lime simple syrup by simmering 1 cup each of water and sugar, plus a tablespoon of grated lime zest. After replacing half the water with an equal amount of lime juice and increasing the zest by 1 teaspoon, I had a tart, invigorating base ready to combine with homemade raspberry syrup.

To begin, I simmered 3 cups of frozen raspberries (chosen over expensive fresh berries) with 1 cup of sugar until the mixture had thickened slightly. But as I was doing so, it occurred to me it was silly to make the raspberry and lime syrups separately. The next time, I combined all of the sugar with the raspberries, and then added the lime juice, zest, and water to the raspberry mixture just as the berries started to break down. I cooked everything together until the syrup was deep pink and potent. I strained and cooled it, measured 2 tablespoons of the syrup into a glass, mixed it with ¾ cup of seltzer, added ice, and took a long, cool sip.

RASPBERRY LIME RICKEY Makes 20 drinks
For an adult libation, add 1½ ounces of vodka or gin to each glass with the seltzer. You will need one 12-ounce package of frozen raspberries for this recipe; fresh berries will also work.

3 cups frozen raspberries (see note)
2 cups sugar
½ cup water
4 teaspoons grated zest and ½ cup juice
  from 4 limes
  Seltzer or club soda, chilled
  Ice

1. MAKE SYRUP Heat raspberries, sugar, and water in saucepan over medium heat until raspberries begin to release their juices, about 5 minutes. Mash with potato masher until berries break down, then stir in lime zest and juice. Simmer until mixture is slightly thickened, about 5 minutes.

2. STRAIN AND SERVE Pour raspberry mixture through fine-mesh strainer set over bowl, pressing on solids to extract liquid (you should have about 2½ cups). Discard berry solids. Refrigerate syrup until completely cool, at least 30 minutes or up to 1 week. To serve, combine ¾ cup seltzer and 2 tablespoons syrup in tall, ice-filled glass.

Equipment Review Paper Plates

Slip, rip, buckle, and spill. Can any paper plate take the heat and the weight? BY MEREDITH BUTCHER

COME SUMMER, meals head outdoors—and so does your tableware. But paper plates can spell trouble. Some are so flimsy you have to use several stacked together. Others become sodden or even rip when you cut into barbecued chicken or grilled steak. Newfangled paper plates with soakproof shields and cut-resistant surfaces promise a less eventful dining experience. The name, by the way, is a misnomer. These days, disposable plates may be made from crushed stone, sugar-cane fibers, clay, even potatoes and corn. (That's the plate, not the meal.) Whatever the material, we wanted one large enough to hold food without crowding, strong enough to not buckle, substantial enough to keep moisture and grease at bay, and tough enough to prevent knives from shredding it. We put seven brands to the test.

TAKING THE PRESSURE We loaded each plate with a pound of picnic fare: hot chicken, baked beans, potato salad, and coleslaw. Holding the plate in one hand, we walked around the test kitchen to simulate mingling at a party. (We ignored funny looks from colleagues.) A few plates buckled immediately. Others weakened at spots directly under hot food. We pressed a fork into the food as if eating standing up. The best plates held firm. One brand, EarthShell Premium Strength, was so weak its edges cracked and broke—there went dinner.

CUTTING EDGE Knives should cut through steaks or chicken, not plates. Using five strokes of equal force, we cut chicken into bite-sized pieces using plastic, silverware, and steak knives. Even the sharp steak knife left no mark in the Vanity Fair Dinner Premium plates and Solo Heavy Duty, while even a dull plastic knife cut through some brands.

SIZING UP We measured the angle of each plate's lip, and then compared them by tilting plates with a slice of pizza on each. The slice stayed put on plates with steeper angles and—whoops—slipped to the floor on plates with lower-angled sides. Solo Heavy Duty plates had a shallow well at the base of the rim that prevented runnier foods like baked beans from running over. While thinking about design, we also looked at how crowded each plate was when loaded with food. All of the plates were marketed as more than 9 inches in diameter. In reality, the largest plate had 8⅛ inches of space for

food, the smallest just 6¼ inches. The rest of the diameter was taken up by rim.

GREASE TRAP Greasy pizza usually makes an oily stain on paper plates, not something you want to soak through to your table or your pants. We ordered the cheesiest pizza in town and set a slice on each plate. Within minutes, the grease had soaked through some plates, and condensation

from the hot pizza left a triangular "shadow" on the table. Recognizing that people also use paper plates indoors on occasion, we microwaved pizza-filled plates for 30 seconds. Plates that hadn't already become greasy remained dry.

SUMMING UP Like so many other kitchen products, paper plates have entered the 21st century. Our testing showed that

the right material (hint: not paper) is the key to excellence. Our top two performers were Vanity Fair Dinner Premium, made from crushed stone and polypropylene plastic, and Solo Heavy Duty, made from paperboard coated with clay, printed with water-based inks, and finished with a food-safe plastic soak-proof shield. Both were sturdy enough to handle themselves with aplomb in any outdoor social situation.

HIGHLY RECOMMENDED

	CRITERIA		TESTERS' NOTES
VANITY FAIR Dinner Premium, 11 inches **Usable Size** (measured from inside of rim to inside of opposite rim): 8⅛ inches **Price:** $3.79 for 14 plates (27 cents each) 	Weight Bearing Cut Resistance Spill Prevention Sogginess Protection	★★★ ★★★ ★★ ★★★	**Comments:** Made from crushed stone and plastic, this plate was the sturdiest of the lot, but also the most expensive. Loaded with food it didn't bend or crack, and with the largest surface area, it would be welcome at a buffet. One minor complaint: Shallow sides let pizza slide over the edge.
SOLO Heavy Duty, 10 inches **Usable Size:** 7½ inches **Price:** $3.19 for 22 plates (15 cents each) 	Weight Bearing Cut Resistance Spill Prevention Sogginess Protection	★★ ★★★ ★★★ ★★★	**Comments:** Sturdy enough to hold a pound of food easily, this plate began to bend with the press of a fork. Made from paperboard covered with clay and coated with a food-safe plastic varnish, it stopped knife cuts at the surface. We particularly liked a shallow well at the plate's perimeter, which stopped moist foods from sloshing out; steep angles also kept food on the plate.

RECOMMENDED WITH RESERVATIONS

	CRITERIA		TESTERS' NOTES
DIXIE Ultra, 10 inches **Usable Size:** 7⁹⁄₁₆ inches **Price:** $3.99 for 40 plates (10 cents each) 	Weight Bearing Cut Resistance Spill Prevention Sogginess Protection	★★ ★★ ★★★ ★	**Comments:** No major catastrophes, but not many dazzling successes, either. This plate bent slightly under weight, especially under hot baked beans, and a steak knife made inroads. Pizza grease and condensation soaked through fast, especially after the slice was reheated on the plate. Steeply angled sides prevented spills.

NOT RECOMMENDED

	CRITERIA		TESTERS' NOTES
DIXIE 10¼ inches **Usable Size:** 7¾ inches **Price:** $2.99 for 24 plates (13 cents each) 	Weight Bearing Cut Resistance Spill Prevention Sogginess Protection	★ ★★ ★ ★	**Comments:** Dixie's cheaper, flimsier plate did not perform as well as Dixie Ultra. When we did our lap around the test kitchen holding a loaded plate, it buckled. Also, we blame the angle of the plate's lip, as well as the slick coating, for the pizza slice that fell to the floor.
STALKMARKET Heavy Duty, 10 inches **Usable Size:** 7⅞ inches **Price:** $2.60 for 15 plates (17 cents each) 	Weight Bearing Cut Resistance Spill Prevention Sogginess Protection	★ ★★ ★ ★	**Comments:** Engineered from the cellulose fibers of processed sugarcane, these plates are completely biodegradable. Good for the earth, not so good for your party: They leaked and tore, buckled under hot food, and soaked through with pizza grease and condensation.
CHINET Dinner, 10⅜ inches **Usable Size:** 7¾ inches **Prices:** $3.49 for 15 plates (23 cents each) 	Weight Bearing Cut Resistance Spill Prevention Sogginess Protection	★ ★ ★ ★★	**Comments:** Made from 100 percent unused milk-carton stock, this plate held coleslaw and potato salad with ease, but as soon as we introduced hot food, it buckled. Knives and forks stressed the plate, and bits of paper stuck to the tines of the fork.
EARTHSHELL Premium Strength, 9 inches **Usable Size:** 6¼ inches **Price:** $4.25 for 25 plates (17 cents each) 	Weight Bearing Cut Resistance Spill Prevention Sogginess Protection	★ ★★ ★ ★	**Comments:** Made from potatoes, corn, and limestone, this plate—the smallest in our lineup—was designed to biodegrade. However it was so brittle it started disintegrating the minute we put food on it. (Can't the environment wait until after dinner?)

Taste Test Canned Baked Beans

A sweet discovery helped us see which baked beans are best. BY SCOTT KATHAN

SINCE THEY ARE SO MILD, white beans are often cooked with plenty of salt, sugar, and pork—the alchemy that makes baked beans so popular. And while baked beans are a staple of backyard gatherings, few of us bother to make them from scratch. Canned baked beans deliver convenience, especially in the heat of summer. But are they any good?

We gathered cans from industry leaders B&M, Bush's, and Van Camp's, and three vegetarian-style brands (B&M, plus organic brands Amy's and Eden). We rounded out our lineup with an outlier, Campbell's Pork & Beans, which aren't technically baked beans but were deemed close enough (through pretasting). All the beans were heated in saucepans and sampled plain by our panel of 22 tasters. Our preferences quickly fell into line: We liked sweet, slightly firm beans.

Surprisingly, a meatless product, B&M Vegetarian Baked Beans, came out on top, just ahead of Bush's and Van Camp's. Tasters rated these three brands the sweetest, and a check of the ingredient list confirmed that they did indeed contain the most sugars. The top three brands were also judged to have the best texture, which makes sense when you consider that sugar slows the softening process (our tasters liked beans with a little bite).

More important, the type of sweetener had a big impact on flavor. Our top four brands—B&M Vegetarian, Bush's, Van Camp's, and B&M Original—all contain molasses (Bush's beans contain brown sugar, which is made with molasses), a classic baked bean seasoning that adds complexity and depth. Our three least-favorite brands, Campbell's, Amy's, and Eden, rely on high fructose corn syrup, evaporated cane juice and maple syrup, and sorghum (respectively) instead. Finally, the three lowest-ranked brands contain tomato puree, which made the beans taste inappropriately "ketchup-y"; the recommended brands are not made with any tomato product.

RECOMMENDED

		TASTERS' NOTES
B&M Vegetarian Baked Beans **Price:** $2 for 28 ounces **Sugars:** 12g per serving		**Comments:** Tasters loved the "very molasses-y" flavor of these beans, calling them "slightly sweet, complex, with a slow-cooked feeling." "Richer than the others" was a common refrain. Their "firm" and "pleasant" texture was another big plus.
BUSH'S BEST Original Baked Beans **Price:** $2 for 28 ounces **Sugars:** 12g per serving		**Comments:** Bush's came in a close second overall, and were given the highest scores for their texture, which was described as "creamy" but "firm." Tasters deemed these beans the sweetest of the lot, and praised their "smoky, rich flavor," which had a "nice balance of salty and sweet."
VAN CAMP'S Original Baked Beans **Price:** $1.89 for 28 ounces **Sugars:** 11g per serving		**Comments:** These "very smoky" (they contain natural smoke flavor) beans received solid scores across the board. "Nicely complex, with a texture that is soft but not mushy," said one taster. But there was no mistaking this brand for homemade beans, with a few tasters picking up a range of (not unpleasant) flavors from "cola" to "salad dressing."

RECOMMENDED WITH RESERVATIONS

		TASTERS' NOTES
B&M Original Baked Beans **Price:** $2 for 28 ounces **Sugars:** 10g per serving		**Comments:** These beans have fewer total sugars than their vegetarian cousins. Tasters liked the "nice molasses" flavor, but were none too keen on the "refried-bean-like" (and lowest-scoring) texture, which was "thick and sludgy" and "sticky."

NOT RECOMMENDED

		TASTERS' NOTES
CAMPBELL'S Pork & Beans **Price:** $1.69 for 15.75 ounces **Sugars:** 8g per serving		**Comments:** To be fair, these are labeled pork and beans and not baked beans, but their ingredients line up with the other contenders. Tasters found them "bland," "runny," and "entirely unremarkable." "I feel no compulsion to keep eating them."
AMY'S ORGANIC Vegetarian Baked Beans **Price:** $2.69 for 15 ounces **Sugars:** 9g per serving 		**Comments:** Ironically, tasters likened the flavor of this relatively wholesome brand to highly processed foods like "SpaghettiOs" and "Chef Boyardee." "Tastes like grade school," said one. Another thought these "ketchup-y" beans tasted of "tinny tomato, chemicals, and shoe polish." Enough said.
EDEN Organic Baked Beans **Price:** $1.99 for 15 ounces **Sugars:** 6g per serving		**Comments:** With just half as much sugars as our winners, tasters found these beans to be "mushy" (as sugar retards softening, less sugar usually means softer beans) and "bitter." Tasters disliked the "clove-y," "burnt," and "metallic" flavors. "I couldn't even swallow these" sums things up.

All About Inexpensive Steaks

How tender a steak is depends on how active the muscle once was. Meat cut from a steer's spine (tenderloin) or rib cage (prime rib, rib eye) never moved around much, so it's very tender (ergo, expensive), while meat cut from the shoulder or rump is chewy (and cheap).

Except in the case of flap meat, overcooking inexpensive steaks will make them inedibly tough. Also, it is key to slice cheaper cuts against the grain (those visible striations in the meat); this shortens the tough muscle fibers, thus ensuring more tender meat.

TOP BLADE

This surprisingly tender steak is cut from a steer's shoulder, or chuck, where most other cuts are quite tough. The line of gristle that runs through its middle accounts for the low price. But the clever cook can quickly remove it (halve the steak lengthwise, then trim and discard the gristle) for flavorful strips of meat that are perfect for kebabs, stir-fries, or stews.
- **ALTERNATE NAMES:** Flat-Iron Steak, Blade Steak

TOP SIRLOIN

The sirloin is cut from the back of a steer near the hind legs. Top sirloin, sometimes labeled New York sirloin (careful—it's not the same as New York strip), is a large cut with good beefy flavor. It makes for both a good steak and an excellent roast. The test kitchen usually grills it whole and then slices it thin.
- **ALTERNATE NAME:** Sirloin Butt Steak

FLAP MEAT

Flap meat is a large, rectangular, coarse-textured steak cut from a steer's back nearest its hind legs. Unlike most other steaks, it will be most tender when cooked medium to medium-well. Flap meat has a pronounced beefy flavor and substantial chew. It takes especially well to marinades; we like soy sauce–based marinades, which add flavor and help keep the meat juicy.
- **ALTERNATE NAMES:** Sirloin Tips, Steak Tips

FLANK

This large, thin, very flavorful steak is cut from the underside of a cow in the area nearest the hind legs. We like to grill and pan-sear it or cut it into thin strips and stir-fry it. To season, marinate the meat before cooking. For even more flavor, let the flank steak sit in some reserved marinade for a few minutes after cooking and then slice it.
- **ALTERNATE NAME:** Jiffy Steak

Test Kitchen Cooking Class How to Grill Chicken Parts

Smoky, succulent grilled chicken sounds wonderful, but it's not always easy to achieve. Flare-ups (and the resulting ashy char), sticking, and uneven cooking are problems that vex even seasoned grillers. Avoid vexation (and inedible chicken) by boning up on the basics.

Before You Begin Understand Your Grill

Many backyard cooks think their grill has one temperature only—hot. But if you cook chicken parts over this kind of fire, you'll wind up with nicely crisp skin disguising meat that's raw at the bone. We suggest you create two separate cooking zones on the grill. One area should have no direct heat, hence a much lower temperature. The chicken will spend most of the time in this cool zone, where you can safely "roast" it with no danger of flare-ups. The other zone should have plenty of heat, so just before serving, you can sear the chicken, glaze it, and crisp its skin.

GAS GRILL

Creating two cooking zones on a gas grill is simple. Preheat the grill with the lid down and all burners turned to high for 15 minutes. Leave the primary burner on high and turn off the other burners.

HOT ZONE
PRIMARY BURNER
ON HIGH

COOL ZONE
OTHER BURNERS
TURNED OFF

CHARCOAL GRILL

Arrange the coals to create two cooking zones. Spread the lit coals over just half of the grill. Use long-handled tongs to grab and move any stray coals. Once the lit coals are properly arranged, set the cooking grate in place and let the grill heat, uncovered, for 5 minutes.

HOT ZONE
COALS

COOL ZONE
NO COALS

Does This Look Familiar? 4 Common Problems and 4 Easy Solutions

Dry Breast Meat

CAUSE: White meat. Chicken is lean, especially the breast meat, which tends to dry out.

SOLUTION: Brine, Then Rinse

1. BRINE To brine 4 pounds of chicken, dissolve ½ cup table salt in 2 quarts of cold water in large bowl. Add chicken, cover bowl, and refrigerate for up to 1 hour. The brine also flavors the meat.

2. RINSE After you've brined it, rinse the chicken well to remove excess salt. The salt has already done its job, changing the molecular structure of the meat to help it retain its juices when cooked.

Sticking Skin

CAUSE: Moisture. Wet skin sticks to the grill. And if the grates are dirty, forget about saving the skin.

SOLUTION: Dry Skin, Oil Grate

1. BLOT DRY Shrink-wrapped packaging makes chicken skin very wet. Brining and rinsing make matters worse. Blot the chicken dry with paper towels before cooking it.

2. CLEAN GRATE Brush the hot grill grate clean. Next, dip a wad of paper towels in vegetable oil and use a pair of long-handled tongs to grease the clean grate.

Flabby Skin

CAUSE: Anxiety. Sure, indirect heat is safe (no towering infernos), but it won't ever get that skin crisp.

SOLUTION: Render, Then Sear

1. START LOW Arrange the chicken skin-side down on the cooler side of the grill. Cook, covered, until the fat has rendered and the skin is crisp and golden, about 20 minutes.

2. GO HIGH Move the chicken to the hot side of the grill, and continue to cook, turning occasionally, until both sides are well browned and the white meat registers 160 degrees (175 for dark meat).

Charred Skin

CAUSE: Twofold. The fat drips down and causes big flare-ups, or sweet sauces burn.

SOLUTION: Grill, Then Glaze

1. TAKE TEMP Only when the chicken is nearly done (150 degrees for white meat, 165 for dark) is it ready to glaze.

2. GLAZE LAST Apply the sauce, flip the chicken skin-side down, and grill it until it's completely done (160 degrees for white meat; 175 for dark meat) and the skin is crisp, 2 to 3 minutes more.

Notes from the Test Kitchen

Smoking with Wood Chips

Adding wood chips to a grill gives meats, fish, and even vegetables an appealing smoky taste. In the test kitchen, we've come up with three simple steps that guarantee slow, steady smoke and will work with both gas and charcoal grills. First, soak the wood chips in water for at least 15 minutes. Where dry chips would ignite and burn, soaked chips smolder and smoke, spelling the difference between food with no smoky flavor and mellow, pleasantly smoky eats. Second, place the soaked, drained chips on a large rectangle of heavy-duty aluminum foil and fold into a packet. Finally, use a paring knife to cut small slits in the top of the packet to let the smoke escape.

WRAP CHIPS IN FOIL FOR A SLOW BURN

Premium Oil

We can always tell when the test kitchen has run out of peanut oil. Foods deep-fried in other oils just don't taste the same. We got to thinking about this while developing our recipe for **Beer-Battered Onion Rings** (page 22). In researching it, we found little consensus about the best oil for frying, so we burned the midnight oil to test the most commonly used ones. All have high smoke points, which means you can heat them to at least 375 degrees without their burning or breaking down.

We had no trouble recruiting tasters to eat beer-battered onion rings. In order of preference, tasters picked peanut oil (crisp, greaseless rings, neutral taste), shortening (a surprise runner-up, slightly waxy rings), vegetable oil (acceptable, although the rings were a tad greasy), and canola oil (they hated it; somebody thought the onion rings tasted like fish).

Dill Seed or Weed?

We love the bright, herbal flavor that a finishing touch of fresh dill adds to our **Dilly Beans** (page 15), but we found its flavor fleeting in our pickling liquid. Most pickle brines are flavored with spices (mustard seeds, peppercorns, cloves, etc.), so we headed to the spice aisle seeking extra dill flavor. Dill weed, the dried fronds of the dill plant, disappeared in the assertive brine, but dill seeds added earthy depth and structure. Dill seeds, which look like small lentils, can also be used in rustic breads, dressings, and coleslaws—much like caraway or celery seeds.

Cucumbers Compared

You've probably seen them in stores: long, skinny cucumbers wrapped tightly in plastic. They're sold as seedless cucumbers (they contain small seeds), or sometimes English or European cucumbers. Maybe you noticed the price and walked on by. In fact, after peeling and seeding both English and standard American cucumbers while testing **German Potato Salad** (page 11), a test cook observed that the American kind generated a bigger pile of kitchen scraps. Curious, we held a before and after weighing-in. Seeded, the American cucumbers shed about 45 percent of their weight, the English cucumbers about 30 percent. Taking that into account, the price difference is small. Yeah, but how do they taste? The flesh was about the same, tasters said. But the skin of the American cucumber—coated with food-safe wax to prevent moisture loss—was tough and virtually inedible; the skin of the English variety tasted much better. So we'll be paying a bit more for the English variety when recipes call for seeding cucumbers. Less waste, plus we won't have to peel them.

ENGLISH   **AMERICAN**
English cukes have fewer seeds and softer skin.

Malt Vinegar

We raided the English larder while making our **Beer-Battered Onion Rings** (page 22) for a beloved condiment: malt vinegar. Britons douse fish and chips with the stuff, and given that it's produced from sprouted barley grains, which are also used to make beer, it made a certain amount of sense for beer-battered rings. Malt vinegar gave the batter a faint, pleasantly malty, yeasty taste. But if you don't have it, don't worry. Cider and white wine vinegars are fine substitutions. Avoid balsamic and rice vinegars (tasters found them too sweet for beer batter) as well as red wine and distilled white vinegars (too harsh).

"Paper" Plate Perils

The biggest surprise that emerged from our **Equipment Review: Paper Plates** (page 28) is that the best way to keep food on your plate and off your sandals at a picnic is to—avoid paper plates! The only plate we tested that was 100 percent paper was a dud, buckling under the weight of our 1-pound picnic lunch and becoming slick with grease in our pizza test. Manufacturers now make far sturdier disposable plates that combine paper with such unlikely materials as clay and stone.

100% PAPER
Can't handle the weight.

PAPER PLUS
Pile it on.

Test Kitchen Technique Halving Chickens

Our recipe for **Huli Huli Chicken** (page 21) calls for chicken halves, but for many home cooks, the prospect of cutting them in half is scary. Don't fret. You don't need a butcher's skill. You do need poultry shears (or any heavy-duty shears that can be thoroughly cleaned), a chef's knife, and these simple instructions. An added bonus? Freeze the backbone and use it to make stock later.

1. Using shears, cut along both sides of the backbone to remove it. Trim any excess fat or skin at the neck.

2. Flip the chicken over and, using a chef's knife, cut through the breastbone to separate the chicken into halves.

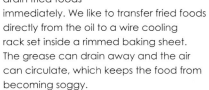

Looking for a Recipe

READER TO READER

Did you misplace a favorite recipe? Can you almost taste a chocolate cake from childhood, but the bakery—and the recipe—is long gone? Ask a reader. While you're at it, answer a reader. Visit the *Cook's Country* website both to post your requests and to answer those of fellow readers. Go to **CooksCountry.com** and click on **Looking for a Recipe**. We'll share all your submissions on the website (check it out—hundreds are already posted!) and print as many as we can fit in the magazine (see box at right). You may also write to us at Looking for a Recipe, Cook's Country, P.O. Box 470739, Brookline, MA 02447. Please include your name and mailing address with each request.

Repickled Pickles
Kristin Weaver, San Francisco, Calif.

I am looking for a recipe that my grandmother used to make called Repickled Pickles. Cinnamon sticks were added to the pickling jar, but I don't recall any of the other ingredients. Could you help? I would really appreciate it!

Pyttipanna
Elaine Hays, Exeter, N.H.

I had a vegetarian pyttipanna (a Swedish hash made from leftovers) the other day and it was incredibly good. I wondered if anyone has a good recipe for it. It seems like a great idea for leftovers during these rough economic times. I have found several recipes that include meat but I'm looking for a veggie-only version.

Bugs Bunny's Carrot Cake
Janie Olmos, Donna, Texas

I'm looking for a special recipe I found in a magazine more than 15 years ago for a carrot cake in honor of Bugs Bunny's birthday. It called for a combination of wheat and white flours, crushed pineapple, and pecans. Over the years I've collected and tried other carrot cake recipes, but none has been as good.

Duck Egg Pound Cake
Charlene Harding, Omaha, Neb.

In the 1970s we rented a farmhouse in central Nebraska where we raised various animals, including ducks. Since we had plenty of duck eggs, I was always on the lookout for recipes that called for them and found one for pound cake. It was the best cake ever! Unfortunately, I can no longer find the recipe or remember where it came from.

White Chocolate Raspberry Scones
Tracy French, King George, Va.

I'm in search of a white chocolate raspberry scone recipe that is sweet and cakey instead of a biscuit version. I've tried making scones in the past, but they end up tasting like nothing more than a sweet biscuit. Can you help?

Black Forest Cupcakes
Pat Konrad, via e-mail

I'm looking for a recipe for black forest cupcakes for an Oktoberfest gathering at our church. Anyone have a recipe? I picture them with cherry pie filling, but I'm open to trying anything.

Dressel's Chocolate Cake
Pat Skic, Davis, Ill.

I would appreciate receiving a recipe for the chocolate cake from Dressel's Bakery in the Chicago area. My children had this cake for all of their birthday celebrations, and I'd love to make it myself.

Dick's Bakery Burnt Almond Cake
Virginia Dunn, San Jose, Calif.

There is a fantastic bakery called Dick's Bakery in San Jose that makes the best burnt almond cake I have ever tasted. I've tried several recipes but none have come close. Can you help?

Butter Toffee Popcorn
Dina Cerchione, Culver City, Calif.

I am looking for a recipe for butter toffee popcorn similar to Crunch 'n Munch or Harry & David's Moose Munch. All of the recipes I've found claim to be toffee popcorn, but they're really more like caramel corn. I want a light, buttery popcorn rather than a dark, intensely flavored version.

Nut Rolls
Gaylene Greenwood, Roy, Utah

My great aunt used to make the most wonderful nut rolls. Unfortunately, none of us has her recipe. I've found and tried plenty of other recipes, but none of them are right—I've had a hard time coating the taffylike mixture with the caramel and nuts without making a huge mess.

Sweet French Bread
Adam J. Bolton, O'Fallon, Mo.

I'm looking for a recipe for a sweet French bread that I first had while working at a bakery several years ago. The bakery manager said the bread was made by adding 1 cup of white sugar to French bread dough. I've attempted this several times and have yet to achieve the same combination of soft texture, browned crust, and sweet flavor. Does anyone have a recipe for this bread?

FIND THE ROOSTER!

A tiny version of the rooster depicted on the cover has been hidden somewhere in the pages of this issue. If you find it, write to us with its location (plus your name and address) and you will be entered into a random drawing. The first correct entry drawn will receive an Anolon Advanced Double Burner Griddle (our top-rated stovetop griddle) and the next five will each receive a complimentary one-year subscription to *Cook's Country*. To enter the contest, visit **CooksCountry.com/emailus** or write to us at Rooster, Cook's Country, P.O. Box 470739, Brookline, MA 02447. Entries are due by July 31, 2009.

Did you find the rooster in the February/March 2009 issue? It was hidden in the Boneless Buffalo Chicken photo on page 25. Carolyn Hunter of Dunedin, Fla., spotted it and won a Michael Graves Design Hamilton Beach 4-Slice Toaster.

Our Favorite Recipe Finds

ANGEL PIE Serves 8
Audrey Holland, Horseheads, N.Y.

"My soon-to-be mother-in-law gave me this recipe while I was awaiting the return of her son Byard (my fiancé) from World War II. Despite its rich appearance, this pie is actually very light and is per[fect] after a heavy meal." The crust for this unusual pie is made of meringue.

- 4 large egg whites, room temperature
- ⅔ cup plus 2 tablespoons granulated sugar
- ⅓ cup confectioners' sugar
- 1 cup heavy cream, chilled
- ½ teaspoon vanilla extract
- 2 ounces bittersweet chocolate, finely chopped

1. Adjust oven rack to middle position and heat oven to 350 degrees. Grease 9-inch pie plate. With electric mixer on medium-high speed, whip egg whites until frothy. With mixer running, slowly add ⅔ cup granulated sugar and beat until soft peaks form. Fold confectioners' sugar into whipped egg white mixture until just inco[rpo]rated. Transfer to prepared pie plate and bake until golden, 35 to [?] minutes. Refrigerate until cool. (Pie shell will sink slightly in center.)

2. In clean bowl, whip cream, vanilla, and remaining granulate[d] sugar to stiff peaks. Fold chocolate into whipped cream. Spoon whipped cream mixture over chilled pie shell. Serve.

CHOCOLATE ZUCCHINI CAKE Serves 16
Tamara Anderson, Barrington, R.I.

"I take advantage of the abundance of summer zucchini by shred[ding] and freezing it in recipe-ready portions. Simply thaw and strain it be[fore] mixing into the batter."

- 2½ cups all-purpose flour
- ¼ cup Dutch-processed cocoa powder
- 1 teaspoon baking soda
- ½ teaspoon baking powder
- ½ teaspoon salt
- ½ teaspoon ground cinnamon
- ¼ teaspoon ground cloves
- 8 tablespoons (1 stick) unsalted butter, softened
- ½ cup vegetable oil
- 1¾ cups sugar
- 2 large eggs
- 1 teaspoon vanilla extract
- ½ cup buttermilk
- 2 medium zucchini, seeded and shredded
- ¾ cup semisweet chocolate chips

1. Adjust oven rack to middle position and heat oven to 325 degrees. Grease 13- by 9-inch baking pan. Combine flour, cocoa, baking soda, baking powder, salt, cinnamon, and cloves in bowl. With electric mixer on medium speed, beat butter, oil, and sugar u[ntil] smooth. Add eggs, vanilla, and buttermilk and mix until incorporat[ed]. Stir in flour mixture until combined. Stir in zucchini, then pour mixture into prepared pan.

2. Top batter with chocolate chips and bake until toothpick inserted in center comes out clean, about 45 minutes. Cool on wire rack. Serve.

Stained Glass Cake

A 1950s advertisement for Jell-O made Stained Glass Cake famous. Also known as Crown Jewel Cake or Broken Glass Cake, this easy, child-friendly icebox cake looks just as pretty today as it did then.

To make this cake you will need:

- 12 graham crackers, crushed to fine crumbs (about 1½ cups)
- ¾ cup sugar
- 5 tablespoons unsalted butter, melted and cooled slightly
- 3 (3-ounce) boxes Jell-O (2 red, such as Strawberry, and 1 blue, such as Berry Blue)
- 4½ cups boiling water
- ¾ cup pineapple juice
- 1 envelope unflavored gelatin
- 2 cups heavy cream
- 1 teaspoon vanilla extract
- ⅛ teaspoon salt

For the crust: Adjust oven rack to middle position and heat oven to 325 degrees. Stir cracker crumbs, ¼ cup sugar, and butter in bowl until crumbs resemble wet sand. Press into bottom of 9-inch springform pan and bake until edges are golden brown, 12 to 15 minutes. Cool on wire rack.

For the filling: In 3 separate large bowls, whisk each box Jell-O with 1½ cups boiling water until dissolved. Pour into 3 loaf pans or pie plates and refrigerate until set, about 4 hours. Once Jell-O has solidified, cut into ½-inch cubes and keep chilled. Combine ¼ cup pineapple juice and unflavored gelatin in bowl. Microwave, stirring occasionally, until gelatin is dissolved, 1 to 3 minutes. Slowly whisk in remaining pineapple juice. With electric stand mixer set on medium-high speed, whip cream, vanilla, salt, and remaining sugar until stiff peaks form, about 3 minutes. Reduce speed to low and slowly add juice mixture until combined. Gently fold Jell-O cubes into cream mixture. Scrape into prepared pan and refrigerate until set, at least 4 hours or up to 2 days. Serve.

Recipe Index

RC = Recipe Card

Cook's Country

AUGUST/SEPTEMBER 2009

Ultimate Grilled Steaks
With Serious Steakhouse Crust

Crispy Oven French Fries
Taste Deep-Fried, Really!

Make-Ahead Blueberry Pie
Fresh Flavor from Your Freezer

St. Louis BBQ Pork Steaks
Beer, Smoke, and Spice

Rating Vacuum Sealers
Do Any Really Work?

Batter-Fried Chicken
Reviving an Heirloom Recipe

Grilled Pork Tenderloin
Orange Juice Wakes Up Roast

Angel Food Cake
Sky High, Every Time

BBQ Sauce Taste-Test
No Sugar? No Thanks!

Carolina Shrimp Boil
Summer's Best One-Pot Meal

Skillet Chicken Tacos
30 Minutes to Taquería Flavor

-Minute Recipe Cards Inside

house Smothered Steak • Spicy Grilled Shrimp Skewers • Green Chicken Enchiladas
Medallions with Madeira and Sage • Spicy Spaghetti Pie • BBQ Chicken Sandwiches
-Seared Chicken Breasts with Olives and Feta • Chinese Glazed Pork Tenderloin

$4.95 U.S./$6.95 CANADA

Cook's Country

Dear Country Cook,

I find that folks like to paint the past in bright colors. For my money, the boy in the photo below is a tad too good-looking, the slice of watermelon is a bit too large, and the blue jeans seem to be perfectly worn; plus he is wearing high-tops, which most likely were not the footgear of choice for a farm kid 65 years ago.

So why do so many people feel that the past needs to be embellished? Isn't it the small things that resonate, the last piece of apple pie eaten on a Sunday morning before church, the first burst of chives from the herb garden in late April, or a bale of hay tossed skyward from wagon to barn? The past is about day-to-day familiarity, not grand themes or the types of things used to sell boxes of cereal.

A story told by farmer, writer, and educator E. R. Eastman goes this way: A teacher once told a student to avoid flights of fancy when writing, and to just write "what is in you." The young boy then wrote, "In me is my stomach, lungs, hart, liver, two apples, one piece of pie, one stick of lemon candy and my dinner." That's how I feel about the past—just stick to the facts of the matter and the rest will take care of itself.

The same is true of food writing. Test the recipes until they shine and then let them speak for themselves. Good food doesn't need flights of fancy—it creates its own memories all by itself.

Christopher Kimball
Founder and Editor, Cook's Country Magazine

Cook's Country

Founder and Editor Christopher Kimball
Editorial Director Jack Bishop
Executive Editor Peggy Grodinsky
Deputy Editor Bridget Lancaster
Senior Editors Scott Kathan, Lisa McManus, Jeremy Sauer
Test Kitchen Director Erin McMurrer
Associate Editors Cali Rich, Diane Unger
Test Cooks Lynn Clark, Kris Widican
Assistant Editors Meredith Butcher, Peggy Chung Collier
Assistant Test Cooks Meghan Erwin, María del Mar Sacasa
Assistant Test Kitchen Director Matthew Herron
Copy Editor Amy Graves
Editorial Assistant Abbey Becker
Executive Assistant Meredith Smith
Senior Kitchen Assistant Nadia Domeq
Kitchen Assistants Maria Elena Delgado, Ena Gudiel
TV Producer Melissa Baldino
Contributing Editor Eva Katz
Consulting Editor Meg Ragland
Science Editor Guy Crosby, Ph.D.

Online Managing Editor David Tytell
Online Editor Kate Mason
Online Associate Editor Leaya Lee
Online Editorial Assistant Mari Levine

Design Director Amy Klee
Art Director, Magazines Julie Bozzo
Designers, Magazines Jay Layman, Lindsey Timko
Deputy Art Director, Marketing and Web Christine Vo
Staff Photographer Daniel J. van Ackere

Director, Information Technology Rocco Lombardo
Systems Administrator S. Paddi McHugh
Web Production Coordinator Evan Davis
IT Support Technician Brandon Lynch

Production Director Guy Rochford
Traffic & Projects Manager Alice Carpenter
Production & Imaging Specialists Judy Blomquist, Lauren Pettapiece
Color & Imaging Specialist Andrew Mannone

Vice President Marketing David Mack
Circulation Director Doug Wicinski
Fulfillment & Circulation Manager Carrie Horan
Partnership Marketing Manager Pamela Putprush
Marketing Assistant Megan Cooley
Direct Mail Director Adam Perry
Senior Database Analyst Marina Sakharova
Products Director Steven Browall
Product Promotions Director Randi Lawrence
E-Commerce Marketing Director Hugh Buchan
E-Commerce Marketing Manager Laurel Zeidman
Marketing Copywriter David Goldberg
Customer Service Manager Jacqueline Valerio
Customer Service Representatives Jillian Nannicelli, Kate Sokol

Chief Financial Officer Sharyn Chabot
Human Resources Director Adele Shapiro
Controller Mandy Shito
Senior Accountant Aaron Goranson
Staff Accountant Connie Forbes
Accounts Payable Specialist Steven Kasha
Office Manager Tasha Bere
Receptionist Henrietta Murray

Sponsorship Sales Director Marcy McCreary
Retail Sales & Marketing Manager Emily Logan
Corporate Marketing Associate Bailey Vatalaro
Publicity Deborah Broide

COLOR FOOD PHOTOGRAPHY: Keller + Keller
STYLING: Mary Jane Sawyer
ON THE COVER: Watermelon, Deborah Ory

ILLUSTRATION: Russell Brocklehurst
Greg Stevenson (cover illustration)

Cook's Country magazine (ISSN 1552-1990), number 28, published bimonthly by Boston Common Press Limited Partnership, 17 Station Street, Brookline, MA 02445. Copyright 2009 Boston Common Press Limited Partnership. Periodicals Postage paid at Boston, Mass., and additional mailing offices. Publications Mail Agreement No. 40020778. Return undeliverable Canadian addresses to P.O. Box 875, Station A, Windsor, Ontario N9A 6P2. POSTMASTER: Send address changes to Cook's Country, P.O. Box 8382, Red Oak, IA 51591-1382. Customer Service: It's easy to subscribe, give a gift subscription, change your address, and manage your subscription online. Visit www.americastestkitchen.com/customerservice for all of your customer service needs or write to us at Cook's Country, P.O. Box 8382, Red Oak, IA 51591-1382.
PRINTED IN THE USA

AUGUST/SEPTEMBER 2009

Contents

EASY CHICKEN TACOS, 15   SOUTH CAROLINA SHRIMP BOIL, 20   ANGEL FOOD CAKE, 24

Features

In Every Issue

Lost Suppers Found

Remember when a from-scratch dinner brought everyone to the table? Whether your family gathered around a rosy-pink roast beef with gravy or a homey tamale pie steamed in a Dutch oven, nothing beat the flavor and comfort of a homemade meal. We sought your help to preserve these old-fashioned meals by asking for your favorite dinnertime recipes and the stories behind them. You raided family recipe boxes—and memories—and sent us more than 1,000 recipes for delicious dinners. We're publishing some 100 of our favorites in our new cookbook, *Cook's Country Best Lost Suppers,* coming out in September. To preorder a copy of the book, visit **www.CooksCountry.com/Suppers.** And look for the winning five recipes, including our $10,000 Grand Prize winner (Grandma's Enchiladas, pictured), in the next issue of *Cook's Country.*

America's TEST KITCHEN

America's Test Kitchen is a 2,500-square-foot kitchen located just outside of Boston. It is the home of Cook's Country and Cook's Illustrated magazines and is the workday destination for more than three dozen test cooks, editors, and cookware specialists. Our mission is to test recipes until we understand how and why they work and arrive at the best version. We also test kitchen equipment and supermarket ingredients in search of brands that offer the best value and performance. You can watch us work by tuning in to Cook's Country from America's Test Kitchen (CooksCountryTV.com) and America's Test Kitchen (AmericasTestKitchen.com) on public television.

Kitchen Shortcuts

HANDY TIP
Slider Lids
Chris McKernan, Sterling, Mass.

Mini hamburgers are the perfect size for either a casual cocktail or kid's birthday party, but I can never find buns in the supermarket to fit my burgers. I cut hot dog rolls into thirds to create three smaller hamburger "buns." I then shape and cook burgers to fit.

EASY CLEANUP
Cool Trash Trick
Marta Pasos, Key Biscayne, Fla.

My community only has trash pickup once a week. Whenever I have raw chicken or fish trimmings or bones to throw away, they inevitably stink up the house or garage until trash day (especially in hot and humid southern Florida). To solve this, I seal the trash in a plastic zipper-lock bag and stick it in the freezer. On trash day, I pop it in my garbage bag and put it outside. No more smells!

DOUBLE DUTY
Using the Old Bean
Whitney Pollett, Los Angeles, Calif.

When I use a vanilla bean to make custard, and then strain out the pod, I don't just throw it away. It's still so fragrant and filled with vanilla flavor. Instead, I stick it in the filter of my coffeemaker and let the coffee drip through. It makes delicious vanilla-flavored coffee, and I'm getting twice as much use out of an expensive ingredient.

KITCHEN EFFICIENCY
Old Dog, New Trick
Steven J. Guzman, Sumter, S.C.

Come summertime, I'm grilling almost every night—often burgers for my wife and me and hot dogs for the kids. The problem is my kids won't eat grilled hot dogs. They only like them boiled. Instead of boiling the hot dogs on the stove, I put them in a disposable aluminum pie plate, add water, and set it on the grill next to the burgers. The hot dogs simmer, the burgers sizzle, and I don't have to run back and forth from the grill to the kitchen while I'm getting supper ready.

KITCHEN EFFICIENCY
Storage Solutions
Pat Reitz, La Plata, Md.

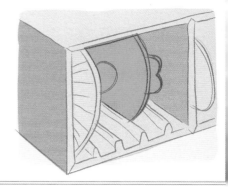

Digging in a cluttered kitchen drawer for a matching lid for my Tupperware was a nuisance. I discovered that I could use a CD storage rack laid on its side. There are more than enough slots to store my lids by size, and now I can grab one as I need it without going on a treasure hunt.

BETTER BAKING
Squeeze Play
Jill Fisher, Charleston, S.C.

I make mini muffins with my kids just about every weekend. I used to make a mess trying to portion the batter into the tiny tins until I came up with this trick. It's neater, faster, and easier if I load the batter into a zipper-lock bag, cut the end off (big enough for berries to fit through) and squeeze the batter into the tins. And the kids can help.

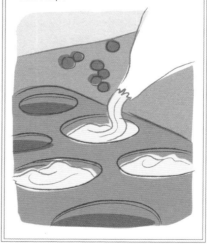

DOUBLE DUTY
Quick Onion Cooker
Mary Fountain, Kalamazoo, Mich.

In potato or pasta salad, I like the crunch of a raw onion, but not its pungent taste. While the potatoes or pasta is cooking, I chop the onion and place it in the bottom of my colander. I then pour the hot potatoes or pasta into the colander over the onion. In the few moments that the water is draining away, it cooks the onion just enough to mellow it yet not turn it soft or soggy.

HANDY TIP
Don't Hold the Mayo
Susan Frisby, St. Louis, Mo.

When I'm making grilled cheese sandwiches, I spread mayonnaise on the outside of the bread instead of waiting for butter to soften. It sounds strange, but when you think about it, mayonnaise is mostly oil anyway. It's spreadable (a thin coating will do), it's always ready to go, and it browns and crisps even better than butter. Don't try it with low-fat or nonfat mayonnaise, as these stick to the pan.

If you'd like to submit a tip, please e-mail us by visiting **CooksCountry.com/kitchenshortcuts** or send a letter to Kitchen Shortcuts, Cook's Country, P.O. Box 470739, Brookline, MA 02447. Include your name, address, and phone number. If we publish your tip, you will receive a free one-year subscription to Cook's Country.

Ask Cook's Country

One of my older cookbooks calls for using a pie bird. What is this?
Olivia Angel, Nashville, Tenn.

Pie birds evolved from utilitarian 19th-century kitchen gadgets variously called pie funnels, vents, whistles, or chimneys, which were used to prevent double-crust pies from cracking and leaking. By the 1930s, the funnels were often sold in the whimsical shapes of birds; blackbirds were common. The hollow, ceramic "birds" were nestled in the filled pie and pressed snugly through the top crust. In theory, the steam from the filling escapes through the bird's beak as the pie bakes. Plus, the bird whistles while it works! Although most pie birds today are antiques or collectibles, we bought the most widely available one still on the market and baked it in a blueberry pie. After 30 minutes, the top crust split at the perimeter, letting hot berry filling spill into the oven. And so much for that whistle—the bird didn't let out a peep. A little research revealed that back in the day, pie birds were mostly used for deep dish pies, often meat pies. Also, well-designed birds had wide "shoulders" (the birds' wings) to keep the crust from sagging onto the moist filling; ours did not. Sometimes, we learned, cooks poured extra gravy or cream through the funnel into the pie after it was partly baked. By 1948, the birds were

PIE BIRD
Inserting this hollow bird into a filled pie is supposed to allow steam to escape.

novelty items; one advertisement touted 1 dozen for $1.10: "A perfect pie-vent every woman wants, and ALSO makes a dandy miniature candlestick, bud vase, party favor, or knickknack." We're sticking with cutting slits, or decorated shapes, into the top crust to let steam escape. It's less charming, but more reliable.

LEAKY PIE
Although quaint, this pie bird didn't live up to its billing.

I buy natural peanut butter with no added sugar. Recipes often call for the sweetened stuff. Can I substitute?
Katie Campos, Via e-mail

To see how natural peanut butter would compare to the winning test kitchen brand, Skippy, we baked our favorite peanut butter cookie recipe with each.

Most tasters noticed a stronger, slightly savory peanut flavor in the natural peanut butter cookies, which several preferred. An even exchange of natural for processed peanut butter produced perfectly fine results, but to mimic the sweetness of processed peanut butter, add 1 tablespoon of white sugar per 1 cup of natural peanut butter. Because natural peanut butter is usually not homogenized, the oil from the peanuts floats to the top of the jar; be sure to stir the peanut butter thoroughly before using it to bake.

What "all-purpose" wines do you recommend for cooking?
John Whitney, Bryan, Ohio

We recommend medium-bodied, dry white wines such as Sauvignon Blanc or unoaked Chardonnays. Avoid oaky wines, which turn bitter with cooking. For red, we like fruity blends such as Côtes du Rhône, or medium-bodied, single varietals like Pinot Noir or Merlot. We compared wines of varying price points in slow-cooked braises and quick pan sauces and found that the average $10 bottle worked fine. It performed better than

WINE-NO
Don't cook with "cooking wine." (Don't drink it either.) It is a poor, salty stand-in.

cheaper wines, yet just as well as costlier ones. Anyway, who wants to pour their $30 Pinot Noir into a stew? Don't be tempted by supermarket "cooking wines." There's a reason these cost so little: They are low in alcohol and high in salt and acidity.

How do fresh and frozen salmon compare?
Heather Bauman, Burlington, Vt.

Some sources argue that salmon's high fat content keeps it moist and flavorful, even after freezing and cooking. To test that, we grilled, baked, and poached both commercially frozen and fresh salmon. Most tasters found fresh and frozen salmon tasted similar no matter how they were cooked. The frozen fish was slightly drier than fresh when baked and grilled, but tasters found it acceptable. Poaching made for moist fish all around.

Our advice? Commercially frozen salmon can substitute for fresh, but counter dryness with a sauce, salsa, or relish. And, as with fresh fish, the quality of frozen varies depending on how the fish was caught, handled, and stored. To avoid buying low-quality fish that's been defrosted and then re-frozen, choose packages that have airtight seals and few ice crystals.

If a recipe uses just a teaspoon or two of chipotle chiles, how should I store the rest of the can?
Roberta A. Kelly, Voorhees, N.J.

Canned chipotle chiles are jalapeños that have been ripened until red, smoked, and packed in a tangy tomato-based adobo sauce. Since the size of chipotles varies, in the test kitchen we measure them by minced teaspoons. Could we store leftovers in the freezer, or would they lose their potency? To see, we pureed several cans and froze teaspoon measures on a plastic wrap–covered plate. Once our "chipotle chips" were hard, we peeled them off the plastic and transferred them to a zipper-lock freezer bag.

Weeks later we made a salsa and a casserole with the frozen chipotles and compared them with the same dishes made with chiles from a newly opened can. Most tasters couldn't tell the two apart. The chipotles will keep for up to two months in the freezer and should be thawed before you use them. The chiles will also last for two weeks in the refrigerator.

I almost always brine pork and chicken. Why not brine beef?
Ben Seigal, Watertown, Mass.

We've found that soaking delicate, lean white meat, like pork, chicken, turkey, and even shrimp, in a salted water solution, or brine, before cooking results in moist, well-seasoned meat. So why not give beef the same treatment? In general, beef has a higher fat content than lean white meat, so it doesn't need the brine to remain juicy. Secondly, quick-cooking, tender beef cuts such as strip steaks or tenderloin roasts should ideally be cooked only to about 125 degrees (for medium-rare). In comparison, pork and chicken require a higher cooking temperature (145 for pork, 160 for white meat poultry and 170 for dark meat poultry) and are, therefore, in greater danger of drying out. Tougher cuts of beef, such as chuck roast or brisket, are cooked to more than 200 degrees, but their extensive marbling of fat and collagen melts and acts as a natural moisturizer.

I've seen recipes that specify dried Mexican oregano. Do I need to keep two types of oregano around?
Taryn Zarrillo, New York, N.Y.

Most oregano found in the grocery store is grown in Turkey or Greece. It may be labeled "Turkish," "Greek," "Mediterranean," or just plain "oregano." These varied labels encompass several slightly different varieties of oregano (genus: *Origanum*) that all come from the same family of plants. Mexican oregano,

however, is from an entirely different plant family (*Verbenaceae*), which happens to be high in carvacol, the essential oil that gives Turkish oregano its characteristic flavor and aroma. Earthy and slightly sweet, real oregano is said to have a milder flavor than the robust, almost spicy Mexican "oregano." Which brings us to your question. To see if we could really taste the difference, we prepared Italian dressing and marinated chicken kebabs using each. The Mexican oregano was stronger in both, but the difference was minimal. Go ahead and use either. No need to run to the store.

My favorite pound cake recipe calls for tapping the batter-filled pan on the counter before baking. Why?
Wendy Yackel, Reston, Va.

When it comes to cake baking, some oldtime advice is more folklore than fact (our favorite: don't slam doors, jump, or yell in the kitchen when a cake is in the oven), but like you, we've wondered if lightly rapping the pound cake batter actually does anything. The theory is that mixing thick pound cake batter creates air bubbles that remain trapped, leaving the baked cake dotted with holes. We baked two pound cakes, tapped and untapped. It turns out your favorite recipe is right. The cake that hadn't been tapped was indeed dotted with holes, while the cake we'd rapped against the counter had a neat, even crumb. Next time you make pound cake, gently tap the pan a few times on the counter before baking the cake.

HOLE-Y POUNDCAKE, BATMAN!
Trapped air bubbles in the thick batter cause holes in the finished cake.

ON TAP
For a neat, even crumb, tap the batter-filled pan on the counter before baking the cake.

To ask us a cooking question, visit **CooksCountry.com/emailus**. You can also write to Ask Cook's Country, P.O. Box 470739, Brookline, MA 02447. Just try and stump us!

Recipe Makeover Creamy Dips

No thanks, tasters said, when we doctored dips with surprise calorie-cutters like cauliflower and tofu. Sometimes the remedy lies right in front of your nose.

When the solution (low-fat cottage cheese) turns into the problem (grainy texture), what then? BY KRIS WIDICAN

WHAT'S IN A TYPICAL creamy dip? Most begin with a base of sour cream, for tang, and mayonnaise, for rich, velvety texture, with various flavorings (cheese, onions, vegetables, spices, etc.) mixed in. But did you know that an average dip contains more than 400 calories and 40 grams of fat per serving? (And that's without factoring in the fat and calories of the item you're dipping.) Concerned, I made several "healthy" dip recipes and put them out on the counter in the test kitchen. After an initial, obligatory nibble, my tasters politely declined to put chips or celery sticks within dipping distance of the concoctions of pureed tofu, cauliflower, or water chestnuts that cookbook authors offered as substitutes for sour cream and mayonnaise. As one taster disdainfully said, these dips were "just wrong."

I wanted to knock down the fat and calories in a creamy dip without sacrificing flavor or texture. First, I needed a rich-tasting, creamy base. Low-fat sour cream and mayonnaise were obvious starting points. When I substituted these for the full-fat versions, tasters found the low-fat sour cream acceptable, but the low-fat mayonnaise imparted unpleasantly sweet, artificial flavors. I tried every low-fat dairy product I could

think of—cottage cheese, yogurt, cream cheese—but none gave the dip the same silky texture as mayonnaise.

Backed into a corner, I tried blending in a few of the wacky ingredients I'd dismissed during my first round of testing: pureed hearts of palm and summer squash, potato flakes, and rice cereal for babies. Tasters complained they gave the dip a tinny, acidic flavor or the texture of gruel. I went back to the low-fat cottage cheese. We'd always liked its neutral dairy flavor, and if I could just fix the grainy texture, I might finally have my answer. Whirling the cottage cheese in the blender did little, but whirling it with some boiling water solved the problem. Like magic, the blended cottage cheese supplied the creamy texture and taste that had been missing from my dip base.

The combination of low-fat sour cream and pureed low-fat cottage cheese provided such a huge savings in fat and calories, I had some wiggle room to add flavorful, higher calorie ingredients to the base. Lots of sweet caramelized onions, assertive Parmesan, creamy blue cheese, and silken olive oil each gave the dip base full-fat flavor and texture. Tasters agreed: These were dips worth dipping into again and again.

REDUCED-FAT FRENCH ONION DIP

Makes about 2 cups, enough for 6 servings
You'll need two small- to medium-sized onions. Avoid red onion, which will turn the dip murky brown.

- 2 tablespoons olive oil
- 2 cups finely chopped onion (see note)
  Salt and pepper
- 1 cup low-fat cottage cheese
- ¼ cup boiling water
- 1 cup low-fat sour cream
- ½ teaspoon Worcestershire sauce
- ¼ teaspoon garlic powder

1. CARAMELIZE ONIONS Heat oil in nonstick skillet over medium-high heat until shimmering. Add onion, ½ teaspoon salt, and ¼ teaspoon pepper and cook until golden, about 5 minutes. Reduce heat to medium and cook, stirring frequently, until onions are deep golden brown and tender, about 20 minutes.
2. BLEND CHEESE Puree cottage cheese and boiling water in blender until no lumps remain. Add half of caramelized onions and blend until completely smooth. Transfer to medium bowl, then whisk in sour cream, Worcestershire, garlic powder, and remaining caramelized onion. Season with salt and pepper. Refrigerate at least 1 hour or up to 3 days. Serve.

REDUCED-FAT CREAMY PESTO DIP

Makes about 2 cups, enough for 6 servings
Cherry tomatoes pair beautifully with the bright basil flavor in this dip.

- 1 cup low-fat cottage cheese
- ¼ cup boiling water
- 1 cup low-fat sour cream
- ¼ cup finely chopped fresh basil
- 1 garlic clove, minced
- 5 tablespoons grated Parmesan cheese
- 1 tablespoon olive oil
  Salt and pepper

Puree cottage cheese and boiling water in blender until completely smooth. Transfer to medium bowl, then whisk in sour cream, basil, garlic, Parmesan, and oil. Season with salt and pepper. Refrigerate at least 1 hour or up to 3 days. Serve.

REDUCED-FAT CREAMY BLUE CHEESE DIP

Makes about 2 cups, enough for 6 servings
Precrumbled blue cheese is often too dried out; buy a piece of cheese and crumble it yourself.

- 1 cup low-fat cottage cheese
- 5 tablespoons crumbled blue cheese (see note)
- ¼ cup boiling water
- 1 cup low-fat sour cream
- 1 tablespoon olive oil
- 2 tablespoons finely chopped fresh chives
  Salt and pepper

Puree cottage cheese, 3 tablespoons blue cheese, and boiling water in blender until completely smooth. Transfer to medium bowl, then whisk in sour cream, oil, chives, and remaining blue cheese. Season with salt and pepper. Refrigerate at least 1 hour or up to 3 days. Serve.

Slow Cooker Meatballs and Marinara

The meatballs crumbled. The sauce lost its savor. A favorite dinner fell very short. Aren't slow cookers supposed to simplify things? BY LYNN CLARK

SLOW-COOKER RECIPES for meatballs and marinara are plentiful and, judging by the half dozen I prepared, underwhelming. Those that call for simply dumping raw meatballs and sauce ingredients into the slow cooker produced broken-down meatballs floating in thin, greasy marinaras. The few that called for baking or searing the meatballs first and simmering the sauce before adding everything to the appliance were better, but required so much prep they defeated the whole point: convenience. Surely I could find a happy medium: thick marinara; tender, flavorful meatballs that held their shape; and a reasonable amount of advance work.

Normally, marinara (a robust tomato sauce) gets complexity and heft from an hour-long simmer on the stove, which concentrates the flavors and texture. Slow cookers, however, don't allow for evaporation. To account for that, my sauce would need to be thick and well seasoned at the outset. Among various tomato products that I tested, tasters selected crushed tomatoes. Unfortunately, they lacked the body to coat a plate of pasta. For my next test, I added a small can of tomato paste, which sufficiently thickened the sauce. Sautéing the paste for several minutes—a proven test kitchen technique—bloomed its flavors, giving it

an almost meaty quality. In the same pot, I sautéed the onions and garlic—roughly double the number of cloves as in our favorite stovetop recipe for meatballs with marinara. I added everything to the slow cooker and waited. Hours later, it proved a satisfying foundation of flavor, if a little bland. The next time I made the sauce, I doubled the amount of dried oregano and upped the red pepper flakes, too. At the end I stirred in fresh basil, and then watched as happy tasters devoured a sauce that was more than a match for stovetop versions.

Our stovetop recipe for meatballs uses Parmesan and some of the aromatics from the sauce to flavor the meatballs, and sweet Italian sausage in addition to ground beef because, well, isn't it obvious? Sweet Italian sausage is delicious. To bind and moisten the meatballs, the recipe calls for eggs and a panade—a paste of milk and bread. The meatballs bake for 30 minutes to render the fat and simmer in the sauce for an additional 15 minutes. They're fantastic, but would they translate to the slow cooker? To reduce the front-end time, I tried microwaving the meatballs instead. About five minutes on high power rendered enough fat (which I discarded) to ensure the sauce wouldn't be greasy.

Unfortunately, after four hours in the slow cooker, the meatballs broke apart. The bread in the panade was absorbing too much liquid, becoming slimy, and losing its binding power. Eliminating the bread eliminated the sliminess, but also made the meatballs dry and crumbly. I tried replacing the milk with cream, which added moisture and richness. But the meatballs still needed a binder that could withstand prolonged cooking. Extra egg made the meatballs so wet they collapsed under their own weight. Dried bread crumbs made them chalky. Leafing through meatloaf recipes for ideas, I noticed a test kitchen recipe that uses shredded Monterey Jack as a binder. Since my meatballs "spoke" Italian, I tried mozzarella instead. A few tests showed that ½ cup was enough to bind and enrich the meatballs without making them taste more like cheese than meat. These slow-cooker meatballs and marinara could hold pride of place in any red-sauce restaurant in Little Italy, or on any Italian grandmother's table.

TEST KITCHEN TECHNIQUE
Microwaving Meatballs

Most recipes recommend browning the meatballs in the oven or on the stovetop. Microwaving the meatballs for just five minutes set the exterior, which kept them from falling apart in the slow cooker. The precooking also rendered some of the fat, minimizing the grease in our marinara sauce.

Our meatballs are big and meaty, so you probably can't guess what holds them together—cheese!

SLOW-COOKER MEATBALLS AND MARINARA Serves 6

Microwave the meatballs on a large plate or in a casserole dish to contain the rendering fat. You will need two 4.5-ounce tubes or one 6-ounce can of tomato paste. This recipe makes enough sauce to coat 1½ pounds of pasta. Use a garlic press to mince the 8 cloves quickly.

- 2 tablespoons olive oil
- 2 onions, chopped fine
- ⅔ cup tomato paste (see note)
- 8 garlic cloves, minced (see note)
- 1 tablespoon dried oregano
- ½ teaspoon red pepper flakes
     Salt
- ½ cup red wine
- 2 (28-ounce) cans crushed tomatoes
- 1 cup grated Parmesan cheese
- ½ cup shredded mozzarella cheese
- ¼ pound Italian sausage, casings removed
- 2 large eggs
- 1¼ pounds 85 percent lean ground beef
- 3 tablespoons heavy cream
- 2 tablespoons finely chopped fresh basil

1. COOK AROMATICS Heat oil in Dutch oven over medium-high heat until shimmering. Add onions, tomato paste, 6 garlic cloves, oregano, pepper flakes, and

¼ teaspoon salt and cook until golden, about 8 minutes.

2. MAKE SAUCE Transfer half of onion mixture to large bowl; set aside. Add wine to pot with remaining onion mixture and cook until slightly thickened, about 2 minutes. Stir in tomatoes, then transfer to slow cooker.

3. FORM MEATBALLS Add ½ cup Parmesan, mozzarella, sausage, eggs, ¾ teaspoon salt, and remaining garlic to bowl with reserved onion mixture. Mash with potato masher until smooth. Add beef and cream to bowl and knead with hands until well combined. Form mixture into twelve 2-inch meatballs.

4. COOK MEATBALLS Microwave meatballs on large plate until fat renders and meatballs are firm, 4 to 7 minutes. Nestle meatballs in slow cooker, discarding rendered fat. Cover and cook on low until meatballs are tender and sauce is slightly thickened, 4 to 5 hours. Skim fat. Stir in basil and remaining Parmesan. Season with salt. Serve over pasta.

MAKE AHEAD Raw meatballs and sauce can be refrigerated separately up to 24 hours in advance. When ready to cook, add sauce to slow cooker and microwave meatballs before adding them to the slow cooker. Continue with recipe as directed.

The crust split. Blueberries burned on the oven floor. The soupy filling required a spoon to eat. How could freezing an unbaked pie cause so much aggravation?

BY DIANE UNGER

Unlike many fresh pies, our freezer-to-oven blueberry pie slices cleanly.

THE LAST TIME I made blueberry pie, I made two and froze one for later. I used my favorite recipe, packing two rounds of pie dough with juicy, plump berries, lightly sweetened and thickened with just enough cornstarch to bind.

A few weeks later, I pulled out the frozen pie and put it in the oven. It smelled terrific as it baked, and after about an hour it looked just like my freshly baked pie. That's when things started to go wrong. The filling bubbled feverishly around the edges as the center remained cold. The top crust tore open near its edge, flooding my oven with burning blueberries. When it came time to eat, the pie was soupy and the crust sodden. I loved the idea of pulling a pie from the freezer at a moment's notice, but not the results.

If I could fix the soupy filling, I figured that would solve the drenched crust at the same time. The cornstarch, which ought to be thickening the pie, clearly wasn't doing the job. Minute tapioca emerged the clear winner among the thickeners I tested, including all-purpose flour, instant flour, potato starch, and rice starch. Our science editor explained that during the process of freezing and thawing, water is squeezed out of the starch gel, causing soupy filling and, consequently, soggy

crusts. Different starches have varying freeze-thaw stability properties, he said, and tapioca survives the process best. Two tablespoons—any more turned the pie gummy—wasn't perfect, but it was my best option. I turned to the berries.

Since the tapioca wasn't working full-bore, I tried adding grated apple to the filling. Its high pectin content makes it useful to thicken jams and pies. Sadly, the freezer rendered the pectin useless. I'd have to concentrate the blueberry juices before they got within striking distance of the crust. I simmered the berries for a few minutes, mashing them slightly. The pie I made, froze, and baked a week later looked and tasted like blueberry jam. The next time, for fresher taste and texture, I left 2 cups of berries raw, stirring them in at the end with the sugar and tapioca. The whole berries greatly improved the filling without making it significantly runnier. Unfortunately, the bottom crust was no better than at the start of my testing, and the top had steamed into a translucent mess.

I considered other ways to make the filling absorb more moisture so that the crust wouldn't. The test kitchen has occasionally used dried fruit in baked goods to absorb fruit juices. I tracked down a

bag of dried blueberries and stirred them into the simmering fresh berries. This pie sliced nicely (at last!) and had seriously delicious blueberry flavor. But the dried blueberries had been expensive and difficult to find. I turned to easier-to-find dried cranberries, adding one 6-ounce bag (1¼ cups) to the blueberries as I cooked them down. This pie, too, sliced cleanly, and the cranberries added a faint tart complement without calling any attention to themselves. But to my great frustration, my crust was barely improved.

Pie lore suggests brushing the bottom crust with egg white or melted butter to prevent a soggy bottom. The egg whites did nothing. The melted butter helped a little and added flavor, but didn't solve the problem. A recipe I'd seen called for sprinkling the bottom crust with graham cracker crumbs. I had a sudden inspiration to sprinkle them on top of the filling, too. Both bottom and top crust emerged from the oven flaky and tender, plus the crumbs had melded into the filling and disappeared.

But I still wasn't done! As the frozen pie slowly defrosted from the edge to the middle, the top crust was melting along the perimeter, then tearing from prolonged exposure to the steam from the filling. Apparently, I needed to reinforce the edge of the crust to insulate it against

the extra time in the oven; my frozen pie needed 1 hour and 20 minutes to bake, 20 minutes more than a fresh pie. Whatever you do, don't defrost the pie before baking it—that guarantees a soggy crust. Instead of crimping top and bottom crust together (the usual technique), I folded the bottom crust in over the filling and set the top crust over that. In addition to the usual steam vents in the middle of the pie, I cut several vents at its edge.

I baked, cooled, and sliced the pie and nervously took a bite. At last—a terrific from-the-freezer blueberry pie that was indistinguishable from freshly baked.

STEP-BY-STEP **A Crust That's Fit for the Freezer**

If you freeze an unbaked blueberry pie without adjusting a standard recipe, chances are the top crust will rupture and both crusts will become soggy. For a crisp, flaky, intact crust, follow these steps:

1. Brush the dough with melted butter and sprinkle with absorbent graham cracker crumbs. Sprinkle more crumbs over the filling to absorb moisture.

2. To prevent the dough from cracking around the edges of the pie, fold the bottom crust over the filling before topping with the top crust.

3. A frozen pie thaws from the outside in. To allow steam to escape at the edge, cut six slits near the edge and four more in the center of the pie.

MAKE-AHEAD BLUEBERRY PIE
Serves 8

Both fresh and frozen berries will work, but frozen berries will need to cook a few minutes longer in step 2. Go to CooksCountry.com for our Double-Crust Pie Dough, or use one 15-ounce box Pillsbury Just Unroll! pie crust.

- 1 recipe Double-Crust Pie Dough (see note)
- 4 tablespoons unsalted butter, melted
- 4 whole graham crackers, crushed to fine crumbs
- 6 cups blueberries (see note)
- 1¼ cups dried cranberries
- ¾ cup sugar
- 2 tablespoons Minute tapioca
- 2 teaspoons lemon juice
- ¼ teaspoon salt

1. PREPARE CRUSTS On lightly floured surface, roll 1 dough into 12-inch circle (if using store-bought dough, you do not need to roll either crust). Transfer to 9-inch pie plate. Brush crust with 2 tablespoons melted butter and sprinkle with half of cracker crumbs. Cover with plastic and refrigerate 30 minutes. Roll second dough into 12-inch circle and brush with remaining butter, leaving 1-inch border around edge. Refrigerate, covered, on large plate for 30 minutes.

2. MAKE FILLING Heat 4 cups blueberries and cranberries in saucepan over medium heat, stirring occasionally and mashing slightly, until blueberries break down and mixture is thickened, 8 to 10 minutes (mixture should measure 1¼ cups). Let cool slightly, then stir in sugar, tapioca, lemon juice, salt, and remaining blueberries. Refrigerate until cool, about 15 minutes.

3. ASSEMBLE PIE Transfer filling to dough-lined pie plate. Sprinkle remaining cracker crumbs over filling. Following photo 2, fold lip of bottom crust inward over filling. Brush border of dough with water, then arrange top crust, buttered-side down, over pie. Crimp edges of pie. Cut six 1-inch slits about 1 inch from crust and four 1-inch slits near center of pie. Allow pie to firm in freezer for 1 hour. Once pie is firm, wrap it tightly with plastic, then aluminum foil. Freeze for up to 2 months.

4. BAKE PIE Adjust oven rack to lowest position and heat oven to 375 degrees. Bake until juices are bubbling and crust is golden brown, about 80 minutes. Let cool on wire rack at least 2 hours. Serve.

You'll never guess how we doubled the tomato flavor. (Hint: Waste not, want not.)

BY JEREMY SAUER

ALL TOO OFTEN, cherry tomato salads are watery and bland. In the test kitchen, we've devised a few simple steps to address these problems and make cherry tomato salads appealing.

First, we quarter the cherry tomatoes, toss them with salt, and let them sit in a bowl for 30 minutes to draw out their excess moisture. Because the wee tomatoes are rarely as sweet as we'd like, we add a pinch of sugar with the salt. While the amount of sugar is small, its impact isn't. After 30 minutes, we gently spin the salted tomatoes in a salad spinner to loosen and separate the seeds and juices.

Depending on the season and the quality of the cherry tomatoes, the quantity of juice will vary. Whatever the amount, don't throw it away! When reduced and concentrated, it's a font of pure tomato flavor (trendy restaurants used to put it on the menu as "tomato water"). In the test kitchen, we're not big on trends, but we are keen on flavor. We strain the juices (to remove the seeds) and simmer them in a saucepan with vinegar and garlic, just a few minutes of work. The mixture makes a potent base for vinaigrette and gives our salad double the tomato flavor. We cool the mixture for a few minutes, whisk in good quality extra-virgin olive oil, and season.

Cheese and herbs play supporting roles. Toss them with the tomatoes and vinaigrette for a salad that captures summer. Variations abound. Simply play around with the vinegar, cheese, and herbs you use. We offer five of our favorite cherry tomato salads here.

CHERRY TOMATO CAPRESE SALAD Serves 4 to 6
You can substitute grape tomatoes for the cherry tomatoes.

- 2 pints cherry tomatoes, quartered (see note)
- ½ teaspoon sugar
  Salt and pepper
- 1 tablespoon balsamic vinegar
- 1 garlic clove, minced
- 2 tablespoons extra-virgin olive oil
- 8 ounces fresh mozzarella cheese, cut into ½-inch cubes and patted dry
- 1 cup chopped fresh basil

We cube the mozzarella so that it's about the same size as a quartered cherry tomato.

1. SALT TOMATOES Toss tomatoes, sugar, and ¼ teaspoon salt in large bowl. Let stand 30 minutes. Transfer tomatoes and any accumulated liquid to salad spinner and spin to remove seeds and liquid. Return tomatoes to bowl. Pour tomato liquid through fine-mesh strainer set over saucepan, pressing on solids to extract juice. (You should have about ½ cup liquid.)

2. MAKE DRESSING Add vinegar and garlic to pan with tomato liquid and simmer over medium heat until reduced to 3 tablespoons, about 5 minutes. Cool to room temperature, then whisk in oil.

3. DRESS SALAD Add cheese, basil, and cooled dressing to bowl with tomatoes and toss to combine. Season with salt and pepper. Serve.

ALL-AMERICAN CHERRY TOMATO SALAD
Prepare Cherry Tomato Caprese Salad, substituting 1 tablespoon cider vinegar for balsamic, 1 minced shallot for garlic, 8 ounces cheddar cheese, cut into ½-inch cubes, for mozzarella, and 3 tablespoons finely chopped fresh parsley for basil. Stir in 1 tablespoon maple syrup and 6 slices cooked and crumbled bacon before serving.

TUSCAN CHERRY TOMATO SALAD
Prepare Cherry Tomato Caprese Salad, substituting 1 tablespoon red wine vinegar for balsamic, ½ cup shaved Parmesan cheese for mozzarella, and 1 tablespoon minced fresh rosemary for basil. Stir in 1 cup drained, rinsed canned cannellini beans before serving.

NIÇOISE CHERRY TOMATO SALAD
Prepare Cherry Tomato Caprese Salad, substituting 1 tablespoon white wine vinegar for balsamic, 1 minced shallot for garlic, 1 cup crumbled goat cheese for mozzarella, and 2 tablespoons minced fresh tarragon for basil. Stir in ½ cup pitted and chopped niçoise olives before serving.

SPANISH CHERRY TOMATO SALAD
Prepare Cherry Tomato Caprese Salad, substituting 1 tablespoon sherry vinegar for balsamic, 1 minced shallot for garlic, 1 cup crumbled blue cheese for mozzarella, and 1 tablespoon minced fresh oregano for basil. Stir in 1 cup peeled and chopped orange slices before serving.

Batter-Fried Chicken

There are dozens of ways to fry a chicken—from brines to flour dredges, from honey-dipped to double-dunked. But one appealing method has practically disappeared: batter-frying. In the 19th century, recipes for it were common. Chicken parts were dipped in a batter not unlike pancake batter and shallow-fried in lard. On occasion, the chicken was cooked first, then battered and deep-fried, apparently to keep the batter from burning before the chicken was cooked through. Whatever the specifics, merely reading about batter-fried chicken made me very hungry. Recipes promised a delicate, fantastically crunchy coating encasing moist, nicely seasoned chicken. BY DIANE UNGER

This unusual, old-fashioned technique had piqued my interest, and so I was pleased when I found a few modern recipes to test. The batters sounded simple enough—flour, salt, eggs, and milk or buttermilk. Depressingly, the coatings these recipes produced were a disappointment. They were soft, doughy, and doughnutlike, and just as in some of the old recipes I'd been reading about, the batter burned before the chicken was cooked through.

But before I solved any of those problems, I needed to settle on a technique. Recipes were divided between deep- and shallow-frying. I tried both methods, and there was no contest: With shallow-frying, the batter consistently burned on the bottom.

Deep-frying method in hand, I turned to textural issues. I had a hunch the egg in the batter was contributing to the soft texture, which was just flat-out wrong for fried chicken. After all, these were basically pancake batters, so naturally they'd be soft and fluffy. Taking out the egg did make the coating less soft, but it still darkened too quickly. I tried batters made with whole milk, skim milk, and buttermilk, all to no avail. Were the milk sugars in the dairy causing the batter to burn, I wondered? I put in a call to our science editor, who confirmed my suspicions. It turns out that when wet batter hits hot frying oil, the moisture in the batter vaporizes, leaving behind the solids that adhere to the chicken. In this case, the sugars in the milk solids were browning too fast.

Obviously, I needed liquid of some sort to turn my flour mixture into batter. I tried beer, club soda (which is sometimes used in tempura batter), and, finally, plain old water. Wouldn't you know it? Ordinary water worked best, bringing to mind some of the Civil War–era batter-fried chicken recipes I'd researched. They'd called for water, too; presumably, times were hard and water was free.

Based on lots of test kitchen experience, I made an executive decision to soak the chicken parts in a salt/sugar/water brine to keep them moist and flavorful as they fried. Then I stirred together a very simple batter of flour, water, salt, and plenty of black pepper. I really wasn't sure how thick the batter was supposed to be, so I opted for the consistency of pancake batter to be sure it would stick. I dunked the pieces in batter and slipped them gently into the hot oil so that it wouldn't spatter. The results were promising. After 10 minutes, the batter hadn't burned (always a good sign), and by the time the chicken was cooked through, the exterior was a pretty golden brown. But the texture was more of a thick carapace than the thin, crispy coating I'd set my heart on.

I thinned the batter down with more water than I had used before. For crispiness, I turned to cornstarch, an ingredient the test kitchen has had luck using in the past. After testing varying amounts, I replaced half of the flour in the batter with an equal amount of cornstarch. It occurred to me that baking powder might add lift and lightness without doughiness. Along with this leavener, I stirred in black pepper, paprika, and cayenne for simple but unambiguous flavor, then dried off the brined chicken parts and put them into the batter to coat them thoroughly. I lifted out the pieces with tongs, let the excess batter drip off (now the coating was so thin you could see through it), and lowered them carefully into the deep, hot fat.

Some 15 minutes later, I marveled at my own handiwork. The chicken looked amazing, and a single bite confirmed I'd hit the mark. The meat was juicy yet cooked through. The picture-perfect, golden-brown crust snapped and crackled, and tasters loved its pleasant peppery bite. Just as I'd hoped, batter-fried chicken was incredibly easy, crispy as all get-out, and indisputably delicious.

But that's not the end of the story. Hard as it was to stop my colleagues from gobbling up all the chicken, I set aside a few pieces in the refrigerator. Two days later, I placed them on a wire rack set inside a baking sheet and warmed them in a 450-degree oven for about 10 minutes. Guess what? They were as good as the day I'd fried them.

BATTER-FRIED CHICKEN Serves 4 to 6

Halve breasts crosswise and separate leg quarters into thighs and drumsticks.

BRINE
- 1 quart cold water
- ¼ cup salt
- ¼ cup sugar
- 4 pounds bone-in, skin-on chicken pieces (see note)

BATTER
- 1 cup all-purpose flour
- 1 cup cornstarch
- 5 teaspoons pepper
- 1 teaspoon paprika
- ½ teaspoon cayenne pepper
- 2 teaspoons baking powder
- 1 teaspoon salt
- 1¾ cups cold water
- 3 quarts peanut or vegetable oil

1. MAKE BRINE Whisk water, salt, and sugar in large bowl until sugar and salt dissolve. Add chicken and refrigerate for 30 minutes or up to 1 hour.

2. MAKE BATTER Whisk flour, cornstarch, pepper, paprika, cayenne, baking powder, salt, and water in large bowl until smooth. Refrigerate batter while chicken is brining.

3. FRY CHICKEN Heat oil in large Dutch oven over medium-high heat to 350 degrees. Remove chicken from refrigerator, pour off brine, and pat dry with paper towels. Rewhisk batter. Transfer half of chicken to batter. One piece at a time, remove chicken from batter (allowing excess to drip back into bowl) and transfer to oil. Fry chicken, adjusting burner as necessary to maintain oil temperature between 300 and 325 degrees, until deep golden brown and white meat registers 160 degrees (175 degrees for dark meat), 12 to 15 minutes. Drain chicken on wire rack set inside rimmed baking sheet. Bring oil back to 350 degrees and repeat with remaining chicken. Serve.

The American Table Fried Chicken Junction

Looking for a living after the Civil War, newly freed slaves in Gordonsville, Virginia, hit on the idea of feeding hungry train passengers passing through town. Back then, trains had no dining cars, among the reasons train travel was grueling. As John T. Edge describes in *Fried Chicken: An American Story* (2004), the group of enterprising African-American women began selling batter-fried chicken (brined, dunked in a plain flour-water batter, and fried in lard), coffee, and pie to passengers through the windows of idling trains. They carried trays laden with food from their homes to the tracks. Edge quotes essayist George Bagby, who in 1869 dubbed the town "the chicken-leg centre of the universe." The informal concession continued for some 60 years. Today a historical marker honors the women as "Gordonsville's Legendary Chicken Vendors" and the town itself as the "Fried Chicken Capital of the World."

A 19th-century drive-thru window.

STEP-BY-STEP **Best Batter-Fried Chicken**

1. A crisp crust starts by whisking together a thin batter made from water, flour, baking powder, spices, and cornstarch.

2. After you've dipped the chicken in the batter, let the excess drip off (back into the bowl) to avoid a doughy coating.

3. To prevent the chicken pieces from sticking together in the oil, don't crowd the pot. Fry the chicken in two batches.

RATING BOTTLED ICED TEAS WITH LEMON

Americans' love of tea has blossomed in recent years, bringing new bottled iced varieties onto shelves and prompting familiar brands to revamp their formulas. We tasted seven top-selling brands of sweetened black teas with lemon, and not surprisingly, iced teas that actually tasted like tea (and real lemon) received the highest marks. The top performers extract flavor from concentrated tea leaves. Several brands we liked less use instant tea and seemed muddled. Tasters also liked balance. Our results didn't correlate with the total amount of sugar; rather, teas with too little citric acid came across as "lemon candy" and teas with too much as "too acidic." BY MEREDITH BUTCHER

RECOMMENDED

LIPTON PureLeaf Black Tea with Lemon **Price:** $1.89 for 16-ounce bottle
Comments: Tasters appreciated its "mellow tea flavor" and "good balance of flavor" and praised it as "bright" yet not "tart." Even the aroma won points for smelling like real tea leaves.

GOLD PEAK Lemon Flavored Tea **Price:** $2.09 for 16.9-ounce bottle
Comments: Some tasters liked the "lavender," "floral," and "refreshing honey undertones." Others faulted this tea's "minty finish" as slightly medicinal.

RECOMMENDED WITH RESERVATIONS

ARIZONA Original Lemon Tea **Price:** $1.89 for 20-ounce bottle
Comments: This tea got mixed reviews. Some tasters praised it as "tangy and bright"; others criticized it as "vegetal," even "smoky." A few tasters complained it was "unbalanced between astringency and sweetness."

SNAPPLE Lemon Iced Tea **Price:** $1.89 for 16-ounce bottle
Comments: Snapple's brand-new formula got similarly mixed reviews. Its "strong lemon punch" spelled overload for many tasters, including one who assessed the tea as "bitter with a bile taste." Others, however, noted its successful balance between sweet and tart.

NOT RECOMMENDED

LIPTON Iced Tea, Lemon **Price:** $1.25 for 16.9-ounce bottle
Comments: The low price failed to make up for a drink that tasted "like hay steeped in tea." Although the actual sugar content was comparatively low, the extremely sweet, "medicinal" flavor prompted comparisons to "cough syrup" and "lemon candy."

LIPTON Brisk Lemon Iced Tea **Price:** $1.89 for 20-ounce bottle
Comments: "Cloying" and "fizzy," tasters complained, finding that its "artificial" and "overpowering" sweetness masked any other flavors, including that of tea. One taster compared it to "sweet, brown water."

NESTEA Iced Tea with Natural Lemon Flavor **Price:** $1.89 for 20-ounce bottle
Comments: Tasters compared this tea to "flat cola" and faulted it as strangely "bubbly." It lost points for its "medicinal," "fermented" taste. A few tasters said they'd never have known they were drinking tea if they hadn't been told.

We peeled more potatoes than a soldier on KP duty to prove that baked doesn't have to mean bad when it comes to fries.

Crispy Baked French Fries

Does the phrase "crispy baked French fries" have to be an oxymoron? BY KRIS WIDICAN

ON WEEKNIGHTS WHEN I was growing up, my mom often reached for a bag of frozen French fries and baked them to serve with burgers or steak. Though convenient, they're usually pumped with chemicals to enhance their color, and taste more of the freezer than a potato. I wanted a crisp exterior, fluffy interior, and fresh taste that approached that of real French fries—minus the deep-fryer. The recipes I tried were simple: Cut russet potatoes into fries, toss with a little oil, and bake in a hot oven (usually 400 degrees) until crisp. Most batches tasted OK, but all of them—variously heavy, patchy, inconsistent, or limp—stopped several problems short of awesome.

Classic French fries are fried twice: The interior gets a head start cooking the first time. During the second dunk in hot oil, the outside crisps and the inside finishes.

Could I mimic that process with a baked fry? I tried steaming peeled, cut potatoes for three minutes in the microwave before putting them into the oven to finish. The texture was now fluffy and light. Our science editor explained that as the water in the microwaved potato turns to steam and escapes, the potato's starch granules absorb some of the moisture, causing them to swell and force the potato cells apart, resulting in a fluffy texture.

I turned to browning and crisping, knowing that finding the right shape was key. Shoestrings were fragile and tended to overcook. Extra-thick fries never lost the heavy texture of a baked potato, even when I tried my microwave trick. The best shape resembled a miniature two-by-four, about a half-inch wide by a half-inch thick. Although these fries browned, they managed (strange as it sounds) to remain limp. Figuring the hotter the oven, the crisper the fries, I increased the oven temperature to 500 degrees. Ultimately, I settled on 450 degrees. Any hotter and the edges of the fries incinerated before the centers browned and crisped. My fries were better than before, but still no match for fries from the deep-fryer.

I tried sprinkling cornstarch over the fries before baking them, hoping it would absorb moisture. A tablespoon of oil helped the cornstarch adhere. An improvement, yes, but all-over crispiness continued to elude me.

I had been tossing four russet potatoes with 2 tablespoons oil total, the quantity given in a number of recipes I'd tested. I eventually tripled the amount of oil. Now the fries didn't stick and weren't soggy, either. But the real key turned out to be getting both the oil and the pan good and hot ahead of time. I continued to mix 1 tablespoon oil with the cornstarch, then coated the baking pan with the remaining 5 tablespoons oil, and preheated pan and oil. The potatoes sizzled impressively the moment they touched the hot pan, but emerged from the oven lacking crispiness.

How could four ingredients cause so much trouble? It dawned on me that the potatoes came out of the microwave somewhat moist. I tested a few more batches, meticulously blotting them dry. Crispy! Happy and exhausted, I put down my peeler.

CRISPY OVEN FRIES Serves 4

You need a heavy-duty rimmed baking sheet for this recipe; see page 31 for our winning brand.

- **4 russet potatoes (6 to 8 ounces each),** peeled and cut into ½-inch-thick fries
- **6 tablespoons vegetable oil**
- **1 tablespoon cornstarch**
- **1 teaspoon salt**

1. MICROWAVE POTATOES Adjust oven rack to lowest position and heat oven to 450 degrees. Place potatoes in bowl, wrap tightly with plastic, and microwave until translucent around edges, 3 to 5 minutes, shaking bowl to redistribute potatoes halfway through cooking. Transfer potatoes to cooling rack and thoroughly blot dry with paper towels.

2. HEAT OIL Coat rimmed baking sheet with 5 tablespoons oil. Transfer to oven and heat until just smoking, 5 to 7 minutes. Meanwhile, whisk remaining oil, cornstarch, and salt in large bowl. Add potatoes to bowl and toss to coat.

3. BAKE POTATOES Arrange in single layer on hot baking sheet and bake until deep golden brown and crisp, 25 to 35 minutes, flipping potatoes halfway through cooking time. Transfer to paper towel–lined plate and blot with additional paper towels. Serve.

STEP-BY-STEP **Baked Fry Bliss**

1. For a fluffy interior, start the potatoes in the microwave.

2. Wet fries won't crisp, so blot them dry with paper towels.

3. Toss the fries with oil, cornstarch, and salt. The cornstarch absorbs moisture.

4. For deep-fried crispness, arrange the fries on an oiled, sizzling-hot baking sheet.

Super-Crusty Grilled Steaks

Why do steakhouse steaks taste so much better than those you grill at home? In a word, crust. BY LYNN CLARK

THE BEST STEAKS are salty, sizzling, and almost singed on the outside and juicy, red, and almost buttery within. It's the contrast that makes for perfect steak. Steakhouses achieve formidable crust with industrial-strength grills and broilers (some push temperatures into quadruple digits!) that instantly evaporate surface moisture on the meat, leaving a dry surface upon which to build a substantial caramelized crust. Home rigs can't get that hot (500 degrees is all you can ask for), so you can kiss good crust goodbye.

I wanted to use any old backyard grill to get that same delicious charred crust on our favorite tender (and expensive) cuts: strip, filet mignon, and rib eye. Most of us buy prepackaged supermarket steaks, which sit in a pool of juices on a Styrofoam tray. The obvious first step was to dry them. I blotted them with paper towels, heated the grill, seasoned the steaks with salt and pepper, and cooked them to medium-rare over a hot fire. They were pretty good eating, but the exteriors stayed pale and moist.

Many steakhouses dry-age beef for weeks to tenderize the meat (enzymes in the meat slowly break down) and concentrate flavor (through dehydration). I wondered if a byproduct of that dehydration—less moisture to be exuded during cooking, thus a drier surface—could help me develop a steakhouse-worthy crust. So I tried quickly "aging"

my steak overnight in the refrigerator (uncovered on a wire rack). It worked, but was too much advance work for a simple grilled steak.

Aware that salt draws moisture out of foods, I salted the steaks and let them sit on paper towels for an hour before cooking. The paper towels became soggy, but the grilled steaks still failed to form a respectable crust. Moving on, I sprinkled the steaks with sugar with the idea it might caramelize into a crusty coating. The sugar burnt, the steaks tasted sweet—a complete nonstarter.

In the test kitchen, we often talk about how the freezer robs food of moisture. The freezer's intensely dry environment causes rapid evaporation. Nine times out of 10, it's an effect we're trying to counteract, but could it work in my favor here? I froze unwrapped steaks for an hour and placed them on a hot grill. It did the trick! Since the steaks had been frozen for just an hour, the interiors remained tender and juicy, but the exteriors were sufficiently dehydrated to develop a first-class crust. (Starting out with cold meat also bought me almost a minute of extra grill time to develop char.)

Next, I tried salting the steaks before partially freezing them, which not only assured a well-seasoned steak but also drew moisture to the surface, where it evaporated. For one final test, I mixed the salt with a teaspoon of cornstarch—a champ at absorbing moisture. That allowed me to cut the freezing time in

half—to just 30 minutes—and still achieve a bone-dry exterior. My own house might not have the swagger and mahogany of a steakhouse, but I had what I wanted most: a perfect grilled steak.

CHAR-GRILLED STEAKS Serves 4
To minimize flare-ups, trim excess fat and gristle from the steaks before grilling.

- 1 teaspoon salt
- 1 teaspoon cornstarch
- 4 strip, rib-eye, or tenderloin steaks, about 1½ inches thick
  Pepper

1. CHILL STEAKS Combine salt and cornstarch. Pat steaks dry with paper towels and rub with salt mixture. Arrange on wire rack set inside rimmed baking sheet and freeze until steaks are firm and dry to touch, at least 30 minutes or up to 1 hour.

2. GRILL STEAKS Season steaks with pepper. Grill, covered, over hot fire until well browned and cooked to desired doneness, 4 to 8 minutes per side. Transfer to plate, tent with foil, and let rest 5 minutes. Serve.

CLASSIC STEAK SAUCE
Makes 1¼ cups
Raisins may seem unusual, but they add depth and sweetness.

- ⅓ cup raisins
- ½ cup boiling water
- ¼ cup ketchup
- 3 tablespoons Worcestershire sauce
- 2 tablespoons Dijon mustard
- 2 tablespoons white vinegar
  Salt and pepper

Combine raisins and water in bowl and let sit, covered, until raisins are plump, about 5 minutes. Puree raisin mixture, ketchup, Worcestershire, mustard, and vinegar in blender until smooth. Season with salt and pepper. (Sauce can be refrigerated in airtight container for 1 week.)

Visit Us Online!
For Garlic-Parsley and Spicy Red Pepper steak sauce recipes, visit **CooksCountry.com** and click on **Cook's Country Extras.**

We discovered an easy trick that lets the average backyard grill produce a charred, gorgeous crust.

TEST KITCHEN TECHNIQUE **Keys to Crust**
For steak with a steakhouse crust, freeze the steaks for 30 minutes before grilling.

1. Rubbing the steaks with salt and cornstarch before freezing accelerates drying.

2. Ready to grill? Remove the steaks from the freezer and season with pepper.

St. Louis BBQ Pork Steaks

Get invited to a backyard barbecue in St. Louis and chances are you'll soon be eating a grilled pork steak. The cut—from a bone-in Boston butt—is little known in other parts of America, but in St. Louis, it's so popular that pork steaks are on permanent sale in family packs at the supermarket. Schnucks, a local supermarket chain, claims to have originated the cut in the 1950s, using band saws to cut pork shoulders into steaks. The steaks are seared and then simmered over the grill in an aluminum pan brimming with a mix of Maull's, a locally famous barbecue sauce (tomato-based, thinned with vinegar, sweet and spicy) and another local product with a wider reputation: Budweiser. They emerge deliciously meaty, a tad chewy, and doused in the boozy sauce.

BY MEGHAN ERWIN

Growing up in St. Louis, I ate pork steaks every summer, so when my family and friends back home heard that I planned to write about them, they bombarded me with advice and recipes. Aside from the range of cooking times (from 20 minutes to two hours), the instructions and ingredients were all pretty much the same: Sear pork steaks, then simmer in sauce and beer. My mom shipped some Maull's sauce to the test kitchen, and I got busy looking for pork steaks in Boston. I managed to find a few. The sauce arrived. I lit the test kitchen grill, and a few hours later, invited my colleagues to try them.

Talk about ingrates! "These steaks are too chewy." "They taste baked, not grilled." "We don't have Maull's sauce." "We can't find pork steaks." I refused to be discouraged. The recipe had all the right elements: pork, barbecue sauce, and beer. With some polishing, how could it miss?

The next time I was in St. Louis, I asked a well-aged, well-known butcher about substitutes for pork steak. He eyed me coldly: There are none.

Humph. Since bone-in pork shoulder steaks are hard to find elsewhere, I'd just figure out how to cut my own. It's the rare kitchen that's equipped with a band saw, so I ordered five boneless Boston butts. I cut crosswise and lengthwise, I pounded and I tied. With knots of gnarly fat and an odd shape from being deboned, my steaks were consistently inconsistent. Many butts later, I hit on a method: cutting the pork butt in half crosswise and then turning each piece on end to slice 1-inch-thick steaks. (See photos on page 13; the technique is easier than it sounds.)

For the kind of barbecue with a pit, Boston butt is cooked until it nearly falls apart. St. Louisans,

however, like some chew. I found a happy medium after the steaks had simmered for 1½ hours, long enough for the connective tissue and fat pockets to melt yet not so long that the steaks fell apart. But the pork tasted braised. Where was the char and caramelization of a hot grill? A test kitchen recipe for brats and beer helped me out. Its method of sear, simmer, and sear again was untraditional, but it gave the steaks grill markings; nice char; addictive, candylike edges; and succulent, slightly chewy interiors.

Thus far, I'd been testing with Maull's. To reproduce it, I set out some likely ingredients. Tasters chose dark brown sugar over molasses, hot sauce over cayenne, and ketchup, cider vinegar, and garlic powder. A slug of piquant, peppery A.1. steak sauce added depth and balance. My colleagues were satisfied, and so was I—if a little homesick.

ST. LOUIS BBQ PORK STEAKS
Serves 6 to 8

In step 3, check the sauce after it has been on the grill for about an hour. If it looks thick and dry, add water to adjust the consistency. You can use any light-bodied American-style beer.

- 1½ cups ketchup
- 2 cups beer (see note)
- ¼ cup A.1. sauce
- ¼ cup packed dark brown sugar
- 2 tablespoons cider vinegar
- 2 tablespoons Worcestershire sauce
- 1 teaspoon garlic powder
- 1 teaspoon hot sauce
- 1 teaspoon liquid smoke
- 1 (5- to 6-pound) boneless pork shoulder roast, cut into steaks according to photos 1 to 3
  Pepper

1. MAKE SAUCE Whisk ketchup, beer, A.1., sugar, vinegar, Worcestershire, garlic powder, hot sauce, and liquid smoke in large bowl. Transfer to large disposable aluminum pan.

2. HEAT GRILL Heat all burners on high, covered, for 15 minutes. (For charcoal grill, light about 100 coals. When covered with fine gray ash, spread evenly over bottom of grill. Set cooking grate in place and heat covered, with lid vent open halfway, for 5 minutes.) Scrape and oil cooking grate.

3. SEAR AND SIMMER Season pork steaks with pepper and grill until well-browned, 5 to 7 minutes per side. Transfer steaks to pan with sauce, cover with foil, and place pan on grill. Turn all burners to low and cook, covered, until steaks are tender and sauce is slightly thickened, about 90 minutes.

4. FINAL SEAR Using potholders, remove pan from grill and turn all burners to high. (For charcoal grill, light about 50 coals. When covered with fine gray ash, remove grill grate and scatter evenly over spent coals.) Remove steaks from pan and grill until lightly charred around edges, 2 to 4 minutes per side. Skim fat from sauce and serve with steaks.

STEP-BY-STEP Butchering Boneless Pork Butt

Boneless Boston butt (a.k.a. shoulder) steaks can fall apart on the grill if you don't use our novel—and easy—technique to cut your own steaks from a 5- to 6-pound boneless roast.

1. Slice the pork crosswise in half and remove any large pieces of fat.

2. Rotate and stand each half of the pork butt on its cut end.

3. Cut each half into three or four 1-inch-thick steaks.

Butcher Shop

If you find bone-in pork butt steaks at the market, snap them up. Look for steaks that are about 1 inch thick. Alternately, a boneless Boston butt makes for steaks that are just as good, but you have to cut them yourself (see photos at left).

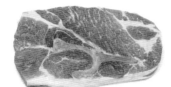
THE REAL DEAL
Bone-In Pork Butt Steaks

DO IT YOURSELF
Boneless Boston Butt

ON THE SIDE Creole Sautéed Corn

For variety, we stripped the cobs and spiced things up. BY JEREMY SAUER

BY LATE SUMMER, I've eaten so much corn on the cob that I'm ready for a fresh approach. That's when I take out my skillet. Sautéed corn takes beautifully to any number of flavors; I had Creole flavors in mind.

I softened green bell pepper in a skillet with a pat of butter, along with garlic and some scallions, which are lighter and better suited to summer than storage onions, reserving the scallion greens to stir in at the end. I added the corn kernels, browned them lightly for a pleasant nutty quality, and tasted. The dish was less than the sum of its parts.

To meld it, I turned to the test kitchen technique for extracting pulp and milk from corn cobs: Run the back of a knife down the stripped cobs and collect the juices. From six ears, I got ⅓ cup of corn pulp, which I added to the skillet with the kernels. Instantly, my sauté seemed creamy, and individual ingredients came together as a dish.

On the long-held theory that everything's better with bacon, I went back to the beginning and started the sauté with bacon. Instead of butter, I cooked the vegetables in 1 tablespoon of smoky bacon fat (I set aside the crisped bacon), which gave every bite a deep porky taste. When the vegetables were tender, I sprinkled them with the crumbled bacon and seasoned the dish with thyme, parsley, and the scallion greens I'd saved. One hit of hot sauce later, and the dish was done.

CREOLE SAUTÉED CORN Serves 4

We like Tabasco here for heat and authentic Creole flavor.

- 6 medium ears corn
- 4 slices bacon, chopped fine
- 5 scallions, white parts chopped fine, green parts sliced thin
- 1 green bell pepper, seeded and chopped fine
- 1 garlic clove, minced
- 1 tablespoon chopped fresh parsley
- 2 teaspoons minced fresh thyme
- 1 teaspoon hot sauce (see note)
  Salt and pepper

1. PREPARE CORN Following photos 1 and 2, cut kernels from cobs over large bowl and scrape remaining pulp into bowl with kernels. Set aside.

2. CRISP BACON Cook bacon in large skillet over medium-high heat until crisp, about 5 minutes. Using slotted spoon, transfer bacon to paper towel–lined plate. Pour off all but 1 tablespoon fat from skillet. Cook scallion whites and bell pepper in bacon fat until just softened, about 2 minutes. Add garlic and cook until fragrant, about 30 seconds.

3. BROWN CORN Add corn and corn pulp to skillet and cook until lightly browned, about 3 minutes. Off heat, stir in scallion greens, parsley, thyme, hot sauce, and bacon. Season with salt and pepper. Serve.

STEP-BY-STEP Get an Earful

For creamy texture and extra corn flavor, we use both kernels and pulp.

1. To keep the kernels from scattering, cut them off the cobs into a large bowl.

2. For maximum flavor and creaminess, scrape the pulp from the cobs.

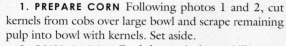
Hot sauce, garlic, bacon, and bell pepper add Creole cred to sautéed corn.

ON THE SIDE Southwestern Black Bean Salad

This is typically a no-cook salad, but we found 5 minutes in the skillet was time well spent. BY KRIS WIDICAN

STARTING IN THE 1990s, it seemed no picnic was complete without a bowl of black bean salad. Most recipes instruct the cook to open a couple cans of black beans, add a combination of Southwestern ingredients (avocado, corn, tomatoes, bell peppers, onion, and chiles), and dress the mix with a lime-cilantro vinaigrette. Sounds like a winner, but too many recipes I tried piled on the ingredients, resulting in a mishmash of competing flavors and textures. The dressing, on the other hand, was dull as dishwater. Clearly, for black bean salad, it was important to know what would fit—and when to quit.

Two 16-ounce cans of black beans would serve six to eight. I quickly edited out harsh onion (replacing it with scallions); bland bell pepper followed right behind. Creamy avocados stayed—they gave the salad richness. Tomatoes lent juicy freshness, while corn added welcome sweetness. To draw out its flavor, I sautéed the corn (both fresh and frozen work well) in a skillet until it was toasty and just starting to brown.

Dressing recipes typically use a ratio of 1 part acid (lime juice) to 3 parts oil (olive). But this salad needed a wake-up call. After gradual experimentation, I turned that ratio nearly upside down. A teaspoon of honey balanced the citrus kick, and throwing the scallions into the dressing mellowed them nicely. Rather than concoct a complicated mix of spices and chiles, I found that a tablespoon of minced canned chipotle chiles did the job. Then I combined the vegetables, beans, and dressing and took a tentative bite. Suddenly, black bean salad was great.

BLACK BEAN SALAD Serves 6 to 8

You will need 3 to 4 cobs to yield 2 cups of fresh kernels. If using frozen corn, be sure to thaw and drain it.

- 4 scallions, sliced thin
- 1 tablespoon minced canned chipotle chiles in adobo sauce
- 1 teaspoon honey
- ⅓ cup lime juice from 3 limes
    Salt and pepper
- ¼ cup olive oil
- 2 cups fresh or frozen corn kernels (see note)
- 2 (16-ounce) cans black beans, drained and rinsed
- 2 ripe avocados, pitted, skinned, and chopped
- 2 medium tomatoes, cored and chopped
- ¼ cup finely chopped fresh cilantro

1. **MAKE DRESSING** Combine scallions, chipotle, honey, lime juice, ½ teaspoon salt, and ½ teaspoon pepper in large bowl. Slowly whisk in 2 tablespoons oil. (Dressing can be refrigerated, covered, for 1 day.)

2. **TOAST CORN** Heat remaining oil in large skillet over medium-high heat until shimmering. Cook corn until spotty brown, about 5 minutes.

3. **TOSS SALAD** Add beans, avocados, tomatoes, cilantro, and toasted corn to bowl with dressing and toss to combine. Season with salt and pepper. Serve. (Salad can be refrigerated in airtight container for 2 days. Bring to room temperature and toss before serving.)

Toasted corn elevates our bean salad above the ordinary.

ON THE SIDE Thick and Chunky Salsa

Thick salsa or fresh salsa. It shouldn't have to be either/or. BY MEGHAN ERWIN

We wanted it all, and we got it. Salting the tomatoes and making our own fresh tomato puree prevented watery salsa.

PERUSE THE SUPERMARKET snack aisle and you'll find countless variations of jarred and bottled salsa, "Thick and Chunky" among them. I've always liked the chunky texture and the cohesive sauce that binds the chunks, but it's hard to get past that cooked-to-death flavor. Maybe fresh ingredients could perk up this style.

Most recipes called for chopping tomatoes, onions, and jalapeños into large pieces and tossing them with lime juice and cilantro. The freshness was there, and so were a few new problems. The tomatoes shed their juice and diluted the salsa; the big pieces of crunchy onions and jalapeños were unappealing, to say the least. Plus, with no binder, the salsa (literally "sauce" in Spanish) seemed more like a chopped salad.

The watered-down texture was easy to fix: I used the proven test kitchen techniques of seeding and salting the chopped tomatoes. After seeding and chopping 2 pounds of ripe tomatoes (keeping them on the chunky side), I placed them in a colander, sprinkled them with salt (which draws out their liquid), and let the juices (a good ¼ cup) drip away for 30 minutes.

I finely chopped the onions and jalapeño, mixed them with cilantro and lime juice, then added chili powder, which gave the salsa depth. To bind the salsa, I tested an idea I'd found in a recipe that called for stirring in canned tomato sauce. The texture was right, but, just like the supermarket salsas, the cooked tomato flavor was disappointing. I moved on to other tomato products: juice,

then pureed canned tomatoes. Nope and nope. Wait a minute. What if I made my own binder? I blended some of my fresh, already diced tomatoes in the food processor and stirred the puree into the rest of the ingredients. Now the salsa was thick, chunky, *and* fresh.

THICK AND CHUNKY SALSA Makes about 3 cups

If time allows, let the salsa sit at room temperature for 1 hour to develop flavors before serving.

- 2 pounds ripe tomatoes, cored, seeded, and chopped
- 2 teaspoons salt
- ½ small red onion, chopped fine
- 1 jalapeño chile, seeded and minced
- ¼ cup chopped fresh cilantro
- ¾ teaspoon chili powder
- 1 tablespoon lime juice

1. **SALT TOMATOES** Place tomatoes in strainer set over bowl and sprinkle with salt; let drain 30 minutes. Discard liquid. Meanwhile, combine remaining ingredients in medium bowl.

2. **COMBINE SALSA** Process one-third of drained tomatoes in food processor until smooth. Transfer puree to bowl with onion mixture. Add remaining drained tomatoes to bowl and toss to combine. Serve. (Salsa can be refrigerated in airtight container for 2 days.)

Easy Chicken Tacos

The road to authentic taco flavor in just 30 minutes (or less) took some astonishing turns. BY MARÍA DEL MAR SACASA

CHICKEN SOFT TACOS are everywhere, from forgettable 99-cent offerings at mall food courts to deeply satisfying versions at Mexican restaurants. At the mall, bland, underseasoned white meat is seared, chopped, and stuffed into a factory-made taco. At the other end of the spectrum, a whole chicken is broken down and poached in seasoned liquid to moist, fall-off-the-bone, deeply flavored perfection. Unfortunately, the tastier taco takes hours to make and requires a mile-long list of hard-to-find, exotic ingredients. For a fast weeknight dinner, I hoped to combine speed with quality.

I tested a variety of recipes, from Tex-Mex to Southwestern to regional Mexican, and quickly crossed off those calling for 24-hour marinades and obscure ingredients. Some of the quick-cooking recipes briefly marinated boneless chicken breasts in lime juice, cilantro, garlic, and spices like chili powder and cumin; cooked them over high heat; chopped the meat; and then stuffed it in a tortilla and piled on toppings. To begin my testing, I made such a marinade. The flavors needed work, but I wanted to pick the best cooking method first.

I knew the fast sear was out. In my initial testing, that method had yielded leathery, desiccated meat. Boneless, skinless breasts may be convenient, but they are so lean that an unsuitable cooking method guarantees they'll wind up dry and rubbery. In the test kitchen, we often brine chicken in saltwater to keep it juicy, but this extra step (about an hour in brine) didn't fit into my time frame. I considered another test kitchen technique: reserving a few tablespoons of marinade to toss with the seared and chopped chicken, almost like a dressing. It's meant to add extra flavor, but I figured the dressing would moisten the chicken, too, disguising any textural flaws. Unfortunately, it didn't work out that way.

I reconsidered the elaborate Mexican recipes that slowly simmer whole chickens in flavored broths and wondered if I could borrow the technique (poaching) for chicken breasts. I simmered chicken broth in a skillet, added the breasts, and cooked them, covered, for 10 minutes. The chicken emerged tender and moist. Unfortunately, it was also insipid.

Might a more flavorful solution be as near as my marinade? I added the marinade ingredients (garlic, lime juice, fresh jalapeños, and lots of cilantro) to the poaching liquid, but on my first try, the flavors were out of balance. While bright, the chicken was aggressively tart. I discarded the lime and reached for a carton of orange juice. While I was at it, I eliminated the chicken broth altogether and used ½ cup of the OJ instead. A touch of sweetness now tempered the vivid acidity. For smokier, more full-bodied flavor, I replaced the jalapeños with 2 teaspoons of chipotle chiles. Better, but not perfect.

But even with all these adjustments, I had to concede the white meat lacked robustness. It was time to call in the reinforcements. I was raised in Latin America, where—those from the U.S. may be surprised to learn—Worcestershire sauce and yellow mustard are pantry staples. In my home, these everyday items went into many basic chicken and beef marinades. I added some Worcestershire to the poaching liquid to mimic the more complex flavor of dark meat. A squirt of mustard pulled everything together, adding sharpness that balanced the sweet juice and smoky chipotle.

A pool of flavorful liquid remained in my skillet after the chicken was poached. It struck me that I could improve my taco by reducing it to make a sauce. As I was making the tacos again, this time sautéing the garlic and chipotle chiles in oil to build a base for the sauce, a colleague suggested I use butter instead of oil. "Tacos made with butter? Really?!" But she was on to something: A few pats of creamy butter added richness to the very lean breast meat.

I held back the mustard until the chicken was poached and the liquid reduced, about 15 minutes later. Whisking the mustard in at the end helped thicken and emulsify the sauce. Finally, I shredded the chicken (a side-by-side test showed shreds absorbed more sauce than cubed chicken) and tossed it with the sauce along with a final sprinkling of fresh cilantro. I reached for a steamy tortilla, piled it with chicken and toppings, and eagerly tucked into my easy, delicious chicken taco.

Poached chicken in a taco? We didn't believe it, either. And that's only half of the story.

EASY CHICKEN TACOS Serves 6

To warm the tortillas, wrap them in foil and heat in a 350-degree oven for 15 minutes. Top the tacos with shredded lettuce, grated cheese, diced avocado, tomato, and sour cream.

- 3 tablespoons unsalted butter
- 4 garlic cloves, minced
- 2 teaspoons minced canned chipotle chiles in adobo sauce
- ½ cup orange juice
- 1 tablespoon Worcestershire sauce
- ¾ cup chopped fresh cilantro
- 4 boneless, skinless chicken breasts (about 1½ pounds)
- 1 teaspoon yellow mustard
   Salt and pepper
- 12 (6-inch) flour tortillas

1. POACH CHICKEN Melt butter in large skillet over medium-high heat. Add garlic and chipotle and cook until fragrant, about 30 seconds. Stir in orange juice, Worcestershire, and ½ cup cilantro and bring to boil. Add chicken and simmer, covered, over medium-low heat until meat registers 160 degrees, 10 to 15 minutes, flipping chicken halfway through cooking.

Transfer to plate and tent with foil.

2. SHRED AND SAUCE Increase heat to medium-high and cook until liquid is reduced to ¼ cup, about 5 minutes. Off heat, whisk in mustard. Using 2 forks, shred chicken into bite-sized pieces and return to skillet. Add remaining cilantro to skillet and toss until well combined. Season with salt and pepper. Serve with tortillas.

Getting to Know Cherry Tomatoes

Cherry tomatoes aren't just round and red anymore. They've gone from garden variety to exotic, offering both new types and heirlooms such as the following 12. Buy cherry tomatoes that have been ripened on the vine, if you can find them.

Red Cherry
ALL-AROUND STAR

As cherry tomatoes go, this common supermarket variety is large—nearly 1½ inches in diameter—and "quite firm" with a "pleasant, balanced acidity." Widely available and reliably good throughout the year, the Red Cherry is good raw or cooked.

Pink Cherry
PRETTY IN PINK

Large, olive-shaped, and pink, the Pink Cherry won few fans among tasters, who found it "mealy and mushy" with "watered-down sweetness" and "almost no acidity." An heirloom, the Pink Cherry can be difficult to track down. Don't bother.

Green Grape
STRIPED MELON

This plump tomato looks like a miniature watermelon, a fact that may have influenced tasters' comments. They described it as "juicy and melonlike" and compared it to "sweet cucumbers." Thin-skinned and tender, the Green Grape is delicious raw.

Sweet 100's
TOMATO CANDY

At just ¾ inch in diameter, this small tomato packs a punch. It's very sweet, "like a grape or raisin," with a mildly acidic balance. Bite into it and the relatively thick skin and dense flesh yield an "audible, juicy pop." Alas, it's also seedy and turns "mushy" when cooked.

Juliet
COOK'S CHOICE

Large and oblong, the Juliet tapers elegantly at its non-stem end. Its skin is tough, its texture "very firm, almost crunchy," and its dense flesh "sweet," "mild," and "tomatoey." The Juliet's firm texture makes it a good choice for cooking.

Sun Gold
GARDENER'S CHOICE

Tasters loved this variety, which is popular among home gardeners, finding it perfectly poised between "sweet as candy" and "fruity and tart, like an apricot." Its soft, juicy flesh makes it good to eat raw or to toss with hot pasta for a quick raw tomato sauce.

Black Cherry
BLACK BEAUTY

The round and relatively large Black Cherry was a favorite among our tasters. "Not nearly as sweet" as the other tomatoes we tasted, it made up for that with complexity, "earthy, winey" notes, and "assertive acidity." A "near perfect" balance between juiciness and firmness makes it an excellent all-purpose cherry tomato.

Teardrop
CRY ME A RIVER

Both yellow and red varieties are "dull and bland," said tasters, who were unimpressed with their "thick, chewy skin" and "mealy flesh." Also known as "pear" tomatoes (both names refer to their shape), Teardrop varieties are available in gourmet stores, but they are not at the top of our list.

Super Snow White
POP CHART-TOPPER

Despite the name, this heirloom tomato is lemon yellow, not snow white. Its taut skin "pops" when you bite it, revealing "fruity, mildly acidic flesh" with a "grapy aftertaste—like white wine." Eat out of hand or add to salads.

Red Grape
MEATY, NOT MIGHTY

Tasters liked the Red Grape's "meaty, nearly seedless" flesh, but not its "lack of both acidity and sweetness." Cooking brings out its flavor, making it suitable for pasta dishes. Alternatively, toss with an assertive vinaigrette. Red Grapes are widely available in supermarkets.

Currant
TART CUTIE

This tomato measures just ½ inch in diameter and offers "nice acidity" but "little sweetness." Its "surprisingly thick," "tannic" skin made it even more tart. When cooked, it deflates into a pile of skins, so eat raw or skip altogether.

Sweet Gold
WORTH ITS WEIGHT

This one is as tasty as it is brightly colored. Tasters praised its "complex" flavor ("lemony" and "mangolike") and "perfect" texture ("firm" and "super juicy"). Excellent eaten out of hand, tossed into salads, or cooked briefly.

FIREHOUSE SMOTHERED STEAK

PORK MEDALLIONS WITH MADEIRA AND SAGE

SPICY GRILLED SHRIMP SKEWERS

GREEN CHICKEN ENCHILADAS

PORK MEDALLIONS WITH MADEIRA AND SAGE Serves 4

WHY THIS RECIPE WORKS: Cutting the tenderloin into medallions exposes more surface area, allowing the pork to develop a deeply flavored crust.

- 2 pork tenderloins (1½ to 2 pounds total), cut crosswise into 1½-inch pieces
  Salt and pepper
- 3 tablespoons vegetable oil
- 8 ounces white mushrooms, quartered
- 1 shallot, minced
- 1 garlic clove, minced
- ¼ teaspoon red pepper flakes
- ¾ cup Madeira wine (see note below)
- 3 tablespoons unsalted butter
- 1 tablespoon finely chopped fresh sage

1. Pat pork dry with paper towels and season with salt and pepper. Heat 2 tablespoons oil in large skillet over medium-high heat until just smoking. Cook pork until well browned, about 4 minutes per side. Reduce heat to medium and, using tongs, stand each piece of pork on its side, turning as necessary, until sides are browned and meat registers 145 degrees, about 6 minutes. Transfer to platter and tent with foil.

2. Heat remaining oil in empty skillet over medium-high heat until shimmering. Cook mushrooms and shallot until browned, about 5 minutes. Add garlic and pepper flakes and cook until fragrant, about 30 seconds.

3. Off heat, add Madeira and any accumulated pork juices to skillet. Return to heat and cook until slightly thickened, about 5 minutes. Off heat, whisk in butter and sage. Season with salt and pepper. Pour sauce over pork. Serve.

TEST KITCHEN NOTE: Madeira is a Portuguese fortified wine. You can substitute an equal amount of Marsala or brandy.

FIREHOUSE SMOTHERED STEAK Serves 4

WHY THIS RECIPE WORKS: Cooking the salted vegetables covered helps to draw out their juices, which forms a sauce for the steak.

- 1 flank steak (about 1½ pounds)
  Salt and pepper
- 2 tablespoons vegetable oil
- 10 ounces white mushrooms, quartered
- 1 red bell pepper, seeded and sliced thin
- 1 onion, halved and sliced thin
- ¼ teaspoon red pepper flakes
- 2 tablespoons tomato paste
- 1 tablespoon Worcestershire sauce
- 2 tablespoons unsalted butter

1. Pat steak dry with paper towels and season with salt and pepper. Heat 1 tablespoon oil in large skillet over medium-high heat until just smoking. Cook steak until well browned and cooked to desired doneness, 4 to 6 minutes per side. Transfer to cutting board and tent with foil.

2. Heat remaining oil in empty skillet over medium-high heat until shimmering. Add mushrooms, bell pepper, onion, pepper flakes, and ¼ teaspoon salt. Cover and cook until vegetables have softened and released their juices, about 3 minutes. Stir in tomato paste and cook until beginning to brown, about 2 minutes. Off heat, stir in Worcestershire, butter, and any accumulated meat juices.

3. Slice beef thinly on bias and against grain. Transfer to platter and smother with vegetable mixture.

TEST KITCHEN NOTE: Slicing the flank steak thinly against the grain shortens the muscle fibers, ensuring tender meat.

GREEN CHICKEN ENCHILADAS Serves 4 to 6

WHY THIS RECIPE WORKS: Pureed fresh cilantro gives canned enchilada sauce a bright herbal flavor.

- 2 (10-ounce) cans green enchilada sauce
- 1¼ cups chopped fresh cilantro
- 1 rotisserie chicken, skin discarded, meat shredded into bite-sized pieces (about 3 cups)
- 2½ cups shredded Mexican cheese blend (see note below)
  Salt and pepper
- 12 (6-inch) corn tortillas

1. Adjust oven rack to middle position and heat oven to 400 degrees. Grease 13- by 9-inch baking dish. Puree enchilada sauce and 1 cup cilantro in blender. Combine 1 cup enchilada sauce mixture, chicken, and 1½ cups cheese in large bowl and toss to combine. Season with salt and pepper.

2. Wrap tortillas in clean kitchen towel and microwave until pliable, 30 to 90 seconds. Top each tortilla with ¼ cup chicken mixture and roll tightly. Arrange, seam-side down, in prepared baking dish. Spray lightly with cooking spray, then top with additional 1 cup enchilada sauce mixture and remaining cheese. Bake until cheese is melted and enchiladas are heated through, 15 to 20 minutes. Sprinkle with remaining cilantro. Serve, passing remaining sauce at table.

TEST KITCHEN NOTE: You can use shredded mild cheddar cheese in place of the Mexican blend.

SPICY GRILLED SHRIMP SKEWERS Serves 4

WHY THIS RECIPE WORKS: Acidic fresh lime juice cuts through the spice and sugar of hot pepper jelly for a tangy, balanced glaze.

- 1½ pounds extra-large shrimp, peeled and deveined
- 4 tablespoons unsalted butter, melted
- ¼ teaspoon cayenne pepper
  Salt
- ½ cup hot pepper jelly (see note below)
- 1 teaspoon grated zest and 2 tablespoons juice from 1 lime

1. Pat shrimp dry with paper towels. Thread shrimp on skewers and brush with 1 tablespoon butter. Season with cayenne and salt.

2. Heat jelly in saucepan over medium heat until bubbling. Off heat, whisk in remaining butter, lime zest, and lime juice. Cover and keep warm.

3. Grill shrimp over hot fire until lightly charred, about 2 minutes per side. Brush with glaze. Serve.

TEST KITCHEN NOTE: You will need four 12-inch skewers for this recipe. Reese hot pepper jelly is the test kitchen's top-rated brand.

CHINESE GLAZED PORK TENDERLOIN

BBQ CHICKEN SANDWICHES WITH BUTTERMILK SLAW

PAN-SEARED CHICKEN BREASTS WITH OLIVES AND FETA

SPICY SPAGHETTI PIE

BBQ CHICKEN SANDWICHES WITH BUTTERMILK SLAW
Serves 4

WHY THIS RECIPE WORKS: Cooking the chicken in butter instead of oil adds depth and richness to the sauce.

- 4 boneless, skinless chicken breasts (about 1½ pounds)
  Salt and pepper
- 3 tablespoons unsalted butter
- ¾ cup barbecue sauce
- ½ cup plus 1 tablespoon cider vinegar
- 1 tablespoon hot sauce
- ½ cup mayonnaise
- ½ cup buttermilk
- 1 (16-ounce) bag shredded coleslaw mix
- 4 hamburger buns

1. Pat chicken dry with paper towels and season with salt and pepper. Melt butter in large skillet over medium-high heat. Add chicken and cook until lightly browned, about 2 minutes. Stir in barbecue sauce, ½ cup vinegar, and hot sauce and bring to boil. Reduce heat to medium-low and simmer, covered, until cooked through, about 10 minutes, flipping chicken halfway through cooking. Transfer chicken to large bowl and tent with foil. Continue to simmer sauce until thickened, about 3 minutes; cover and keep warm.

2. Combine mayonnaise, buttermilk, and remaining vinegar in large bowl. Stir in coleslaw mix and season with salt and pepper.

3. Using two forks, shred chicken into bite-sized pieces. Add to skillet with sauce and toss to combine. Serve on buns topped with coleslaw.

TEST KITCHEN NOTE: Serve with bread-and-butter pickles, extra hot sauce, and plenty of napkins.

CHINESE GLAZED PORK TENDERLOIN Serves 4 to 6

WHY THIS RECIPE WORKS: To develop flavor, we sear the tenderloins, simmer them in a bold sauce, then reduce the sauce to a thick glaze while the pork rests.

- ½ cup water
- ¼ cup ketchup
- ¼ cup dry sherry
- 3 tablespoons hoisin sauce
- 2 tablespoons light brown sugar
- 2 teaspoons grated fresh ginger
- 2 pork tenderloins (1½ to 2 pounds total)
- 1 teaspoon Chinese five-spice powder (see note below)
  Salt and pepper
- 1 tablespoon vegetable oil

1. Whisk water, ketchup, sherry, hoisin, sugar, and ginger in medium bowl. Pat pork dry with paper towels and season with five-spice powder, salt, and pepper. Heat oil in large nonstick skillet over medium-high until just smoking. Cook tenderloins until well-browned all over, 5 to 7 minutes.

2. Reduce heat to medium. Add sauce mixture and cook covered, rolling tenderloins occasionally, until meat registers 145 degrees, about 10 minutes. Transfer pork to cutting board, tent with foil, and let rest 5 minutes.

3. Simmer sauce and any accumulated pork juices until thickened, about 3 minutes. Slice pork and transfer to platter. Pour sauce over pork. Serve.

TEST KITCHEN NOTE: Chinese five-spice powder is a combination of cinnamon, clove, fennel seed, star anise, and Sichuan peppercorns.

SPICY SPAGHETTI PIE Serves 4 to 6

WHY THIS RECIPE WORKS: For bolder flavor, we replaced the mild mozzarella and plain ground beef typically used in this recipe with Mexican cheese blend and pepperoni. Use a spatula to press the pasta into the pie plate in step 3 to ensure the finished pie slices neatly.

- 12 ounces vermicelli (see note below)
  Salt
- 4 ounces sliced deli pepperoni, chopped fine
- 1 onion, chopped
- 3 (14.5-ounce) cans diced tomatoes
- ¼ teaspoon red pepper flakes
- ¾ cup heavy cream
- ½ cup chopped fresh basil
- 2 cups shredded Mexican cheese blend

1. Adjust oven rack to upper-middle position and heat oven to 475 degrees. Spray 9-inch pie plate with cooking spray. Bring 4 quarts water to boil in large pot. Add pasta and 1 tablespoon salt to boiling water and cook until al dente. Drain pasta and return to pot.

2. Meanwhile, cook pepperoni in large skillet over medium-high heat until crisp, about 2 minutes. Add onion and cook until softened, about 2 minutes. Stir in tomatoes, pepper flakes, and ¼ teaspoon salt and bring to boil. Reduce heat to medium and simmer until sauce is thickened and reduced to 4 cups, about 10 minutes; cover and keep warm.

3. Transfer 2 cups tomato sauce to pot with hot pasta, with cream, basil, and cheese and toss to combine. Transfer mixture to prepared pie plate and press with spatula to flatten surface. Bake until golden brown and bubbling, 10 to 15 minutes. Let cool 5 minutes. Serve, passing remaining sauce at table.

TEST KITCHEN NOTE: Thin spaghetti can be used in place of the vermicelli.

PAN-SEARED CHICKEN BREASTS WITH OLIVES AND FETA
Serves 4

WHY THIS RECIPE WORKS: Cooking the chicken skin-side down for the entire cooking time ensures well rendered and beautifully bronzed skin.

- 4 bone-in, skin-on split chicken breasts (about 3 pounds), halved crosswise
  Salt and pepper
- 1 tablespoon vegetable oil
- 1 small red onion, halved and sliced thin
- 4 garlic cloves, minced
- 1 teaspoon dried oregano
- ¾ cup low-sodium chicken broth
- ½ cup pitted kalamata olives, halved
- 2 tablespoons chopped fresh parsley
- ½ cup crumbled feta cheese (see note below)

1. Pat chicken dry with paper towels and season with salt and pepper. Heat oil in large skillet over medium-high heat until just smoking. Cook chicken skin-side down until well browned, about 5 minutes. Reduce heat to medium, cover, and cook until chicken registers 160 degrees, about 15 minutes. Transfer chicken to platter and tent with foil.

2. Pour off all but 1 tablespoon fat from skillet. Add onion and cook until softened, about 3 minutes. Add garlic and oregano and cook until fragrant, about 30 seconds. Stir in broth, olives, and any accumulated chicken juices and simmer, scraping up any browned bits, until slightly thickened, about 3 minutes. Off heat, stir in parsley. Pour sauce over chicken. Sprinkle with feta. Serve.

TEST KITCHEN NOTE: We recommend using shrink-wrapped or brine-packed feta rather than precrumbled. You will need 2 ounces.

Raspberry Cream Cheese Brownies

Many brownies are raspberry in name only. We asked the berry to earn its keep, no matter how fudgy the brownie. BY CALI RICH

THERE'S NOTHING WRONG with classic raspberry cream cheese brownies topped by a marble swirl, but my idea of these brownies was recently turned on its head when I tasted a version that put the cream cheese in the middle. Protected from drying out by brownie batter both above and below, the cream cheese layer was luscious. I decided to employ this unusual construction in building my own raspberry cream cheese brownie. My main challenge was clear from the start—finding balance. The cream cheese, chocolate, and fruity raspberry kept fighting each other for control, with the delicate fruit flavor the frequent loser. As one taster said after taking a bite, "Where's the raspberry?"

My testing began with a fabulously moist, fudgy brownie recipe developed in the test kitchen. As per usual for brownies, the chocolate and butter are melted together and then the sugar, eggs, and vanilla are mixed in, followed by the flour, baking powder, and salt. I added a standard-issue creamy layer made from cream cheese, sugar, vanilla extract, and egg yolk, then swirled in raspberry jam. I quickly realized that to balance the extra sugar in this recipe (from both the jam and cream cheese mixture), I'd probably need to use unsweetened chocolate; a test of brownie batters made with unsweetened versus semisweet chocolate proved me right.

I then turned to the raspberry part of the equation. Most recipes for raspberry cream cheese brownies swirl a little jam into the top cream cheese layer. That's good if what you're looking for is raspberry lite. Not us. To pump up the berry flavor, I tried scattering the cream cheese layer with fresh berries. After tasting this version, I filed the recipe in my Seemed Like a Good Idea at the Time file. Instead of the bright berry flavor I'd envisioned, I got a pan full of soggy, seedy brownies.

What if I added raspberry jam to the brownie batter? I tried it, and these brownies baked up with a winning raspberry depth. On the down side, the jam made them somewhat wet. Knowing that sugar adds moisture as well as sweetness, I wondered if reducing the sugar would reduce the sogginess. I cut the sugar by ¼ cup (exactly the amount of jam I had added) and baked a new batch. I was thrilled to find that I'd not only repaired the brownie's texture but also boosted the raspberry flavor—with less sugar, the flavor popped and more than held its own against the chocolate.

RASPBERRY CREAM CHEESE BROWNIES Makes 25 brownies

We used Smucker's, the test kitchen's top-rated seedless jam. Preserves will also work. Because the brownies are so rich, almost like truffles, we cut them in small squares.

FILLING
- 1 (8-ounce) package cream cheese, softened
- ¼ cup sugar
- 1 large egg yolk
- ¾ teaspoon vanilla extract

BROWNIES
- ⅔ cup all-purpose flour
- ½ teaspoon baking powder
- ½ teaspoon salt
- 8 tablespoons (1 stick) unsalted butter, cut into pieces
- 4 ounces unsweetened chocolate, chopped
- ½ cup raspberry jam
- 1¼ cups sugar
- 3 large eggs
- 1½ teaspoons vanilla extract

1. PREPARE FILLING Adjust oven rack to middle position and heat oven to 350 degrees. Line 8-inch square baking pan with foil, allowing excess to hang over pan edges. Grease foil. Process cream cheese, sugar, egg yolk, and vanilla in food processor until smooth.

2. MIX BATTER Combine flour, baking powder, and salt in small bowl. Microwave butter and chocolate in large bowl, stirring occasionally, until smooth, about 1 minute. Whisk in ¼ cup jam and let cool slightly. Add sugar, eggs, and vanilla to chocolate mixture, stirring until combined. Whisk in flour mixture until incorporated.

A novel construction technique made our filling remarkably creamy. It mostly hid the raspberries from sight, but their taste is unmistakable.

3. LAYER FILLING Microwave remaining jam until warm, about 30 seconds; stir until smooth. Scrape half of batter into prepared pan. Following photos 1 to 3, dollop filling over batter and spread into even layer. Dollop warm jam over filling and, using tip of knife, swirl jam through filling. Spread remaining batter evenly over filling.

4. BAKE BROWNIES Bake until toothpick inserted in center comes out with few dry crumbs attached, 50 to 60 minutes. Cool in pan on wire rack for at least 2 hours. Using foil overhang, lift brownies from pan and cut into 1½-inch squares. Serve. (Brownies can be refrigerated in airtight container for 2 days.)

STEP-BY-STEP Building a Better Raspberry Cream Cheese Brownie
Many recipes call for topping brownie batter with a cream cheese mixture, but we love this ultra-smooth filling sandwiched between layers of batter.

1. Top half of brownie batter with dollops of cream cheese filling and spread into even layer.

2. Dollop jam over cream cheese filling, then use tip of knife to swirl into filling.

3. Spread remaining brownie batter evenly over jam.

Grilled Orange-Glazed Pork Tenderloin

To get a zingy, bittersweet glaze on a moist, mild cut, concentrate! BY ADAM RIED

Don't apply the glaze until the pork has spent some alone time on the grill. The delay will prevent burning and let the tenderloin develop appealing grill marks.

IN THE TEST KITCHEN, we love to grill pork tenderloin. This convenient cut cooks quickly, thanks to its small, cylindrical shape, is tender, and tastes mild enough to take on many flavor accents. This time we wanted to grill our tenderloin with an orange-flavored glaze, and that presented two challenges. Most glazes we've tried are overly sweet and taste only faintly of orange, so first and foremost ours had to have a forthright, sweet-tart orange flavor. Second, the glaze had to be thick and sticky enough to give the meat an impressive lacquered sheen.

The tenderloins' compact size and shape make them easy to grill. Simply get the fire hot, oil and season the meat, and cook directly over the flame, turning them every few minutes to make sure they brown evenly. The only pitfall is drying out the meat by overcooking it, which is easy to avoid by taking its internal temperature with an instant-read thermometer. Cook the tenderloin to about 140 degrees and let it rest; the internal temperature will continue to rise to between 145 and 150 degrees. Slice into the tenderloin and it will still be juicy.

A good glaze starts with a sweetener, be it sugar (granulated or brown), molasses, maple syrup, or honey. Looking for a sweetener that would complement orange flavor, I tested all of the above, as well as orange marmalade. The marmalade was the runaway winner because it was sweet yet unobtrusive and contained strips of orange zest, which boosted the orange flavor. I wasn't crazy for the chewy texture of those strips, but running the marmalade through the food processor easily took care of that problem.

To build more potent orange flavor, I tried reducing fresh orange juice in a pan on the stove to concentrate the flavor; it worked, but why squeeze lots of oranges when you can buy a product that's done the work for you? Three tablespoons of frozen orange juice concentrate stirred into the marmalade worked nicely, providing a powerful burst of citrus flavor. A little grated lemon zest and juice further brightened the glaze. Finally, modest amounts of fresh thyme and garlic deepened its flavor and added interest.

The glaze tasted great, but it was too thin to cling to the meat on the grill. It had to be thicker from the get-go. My first thought was to thicken it with cornstarch, but a number of tests showed that no matter how little cornstarch I added, it gave the glaze a pasty quality that our tasters did not appreciate. Simmering the glaze down briefly on the stovetop gave me better results, as long as I watched for over-reducing. I started by simmering the glaze for 5 minutes. Though it looked right while it was still warm, as it cooled it became too thick to brush onto the meat easily. Shaving a minute off the simmering time helped, and shaving off two minutes was ideal. When cooled, it was thick enough to form a lacquer on the pork as it cooked, yet loose enough to brush onto the meat easily.

Last, I fine-tuned the glazing procedure. Allowing the glaze to cook on the meat for the entire grilling time resulted in a burnt mess, so I halved the amount of time the glaze spent over the heat. By grilling the tenderloin au naturel for the first few minutes, it developed light grill marks and got a nice head start in the cooking. At the eight-minute mark, I brushed on the glaze, reapplying it every two minutes until the pork reached 140 degrees internal temperature, which took four to eight minutes longer. By that time, the glaze on the tenderloin was thick, shiny, and caramelized.

I had a little leftover glaze, which I put to good use as a bath for the grilled tenderloins as they rested. This allowed the pork juices and the glaze to mingle and gave one last blast of orange flavor.

ORANGE-GLAZED GRILLED PORK TENDERLOIN Serves 4 to 6

Lean pork tenderloin tends to stick on the grill. For an easy release, heat the grill, covered, on high for 15 minutes (5 minutes for charcoal) and scrape and oil the grate before grilling.

- ½ cup orange marmalade
- 3 tablespoons orange juice concentrate
- 1 teaspoon grated zest and 1½ tablespoons juice from 1 lemon
- 1 teaspoon minced fresh thyme
- 1 garlic clove, minced
- 2 pork tenderloins (1½ to 2 pounds total)
- 2 teaspoons vegetable oil
  Salt and pepper

1. SIMMER GLAZE Process marmalade, concentrate, lemon zest, lemon juice, thyme, and garlic in food processor until smooth. Simmer marmalade mixture in saucepan over medium heat until slightly thickened, about 3 minutes. Transfer ⅓ cup glaze to 13- by 9-inch pan; set aside.

2. GRILL PORK Pat pork dry with paper towels, then rub with oil and season with salt and pepper. Grill pork, covered, over hot fire until browned all over, about 8 minutes. Brush pork all over with half of remaining glaze and continue grilling, turning and glazing every 2 minutes, until meat registers 140 degrees, 4 to 8 minutes longer. Transfer pork to baking dish with glaze and roll to coat. Tent with foil and let rest 5 minutes. Slice and serve.

KEY INGREDIENTS Enhancing Orange Flavor
Orange juice alone isn't up to the task. For pork with bold orange flavor, we rely on a triple-citrus whammy.

LEMON ZEST AND JUICE ADD A BRIGHT, FRESH TASTE.

CONCENTRATE ADDS INTENSE ORANGE FLAVOR.

MARMALADE HELPS THE GLAZE CLING.

ON THE SIDE Easy Stuffed Zucchini

Looking for a fast route to savory stuffed zucchini, we found inspiration in the Mediterranean. BY KRIS WIDICAN

I LIKE STUFFED ZUCCHINI that contrasts tender, mild cooked squash with an assertive, well-seasoned filling. Regrettably, the effort of hollowing out the zucchini, making the stuffing, stuffing the squash, and baking it until the squash is tender and the filling browned usually stops me cold. I hoped to simplify the process, embolden the stuffing, and bring stuffed zucchini into my weeknight repertoire.

Few recipes call for precooking the zucchini. But raw squash are crisp, making them prone to snap as you hollow them out, and take up to an hour to cook through once stuffed. Boiling made them mushy; broiling required close attention to avoid incineration. The microwave proved my best bet for precooking. In about six minutes, the zucchini were soft enough to scoop out.

Because it takes only minutes to prepare, nutty couscous was an obvious choice as the filling base: Boil some broth, stir in the couscous, turn off the heat, and cover. For more flavor, I sautéed a shallot before adding the broth and stirred in feta and olives, a combination beloved in the Mediterranean, where stuffed vegetables are themselves beloved. Chopped fresh basil added a pungent, licorice-like note. Just 10 minutes in a very hot oven sufficed to finish cooking the stuffed zucchini shells, warm the filling, and lightly brown the extra feta I'd crumbled on top.

EASY STUFFED ZUCCHINI Serves 4
Zucchini between 6 and 8 inches long work best here.

- 4 medium zucchini (see note), stem ends removed
- 2 tablespoons extra-virgin olive oil
- 1 shallot, minced
- ¾ cup low-sodium chicken broth
- ⅔ cup plain couscous
- ¾ cup crumbled feta cheese
- 3 tablespoons finely chopped pitted kalamata olives
- 2 tablespoons finely chopped fresh basil
  Salt and pepper

1. **MICROWAVE ZUCCHINI** Adjust oven rack to upper-middle position and heat oven to 475 degrees. Slice off top third of each zucchini lengthwise and discard. Arrange shells cut-side down in microwave-safe baking dish. Microwave until cut side of zucchini can be easily pierced with tip of knife, 4 to 8 minutes. Set aside.

2. **COOK COUSCOUS** Heat oil in small saucepan over medium-high heat until shimmering. Cook shallot until softened, about 1 minute. Add broth and bring to boil. Quickly stir in couscous, ½ cup feta, olives, and basil. Remove from heat and let sit, covered, until liquid is absorbed and couscous is tender, about 5 minutes. Fluff couscous with fork and season with salt and pepper.

Stuffed squash do not have to be a big project. Ours take about 20 minutes from cutting board to dinner table.

3. **SCOOP, STUFF, AND BAKE** Working with 1 zucchini at a time, carefully scoop out and discard seeds, leaving ¼-inch-thick shell. Arrange zucchini cut-side up in empty baking dish, season with salt and pepper, and stuff with couscous mixture. Sprinkle with remaining feta and bake until cheese is slightly browned, about 10 minutes. Serve.

ON THE SIDE Poppy Seed Coleslaw

We wanted more from this sweet-and-sour classic than a sugar rush and seeds between our teeth. BY MEGHAN ERWIN

I RECENTLY CAME ACROSS an old-fashioned recipe for poppy seed coleslaw, made from shredded cabbage in a honey and vinegar dressing and studded with poppy seeds. It was once an elegant dish, from a time when ladies lunched, and I didn't see why it should disappear just because times change. I decided to try reviving it in the test kitchen. Although the crunchy seeds won fans, the honey-heavy dressing tasted more like candy than slaw. It was time to rethink this recipe.

To begin, I used a technique the test kitchen employs for all its slaws—salting and draining shredded cabbage. This softens the cabbage and draws out moisture that otherwise would dilute the dressing. I rinsed off the salt, dried the softly wilted cabbage, and proceeded.

My dressing started with a base of vinegar and oil—olive is the test kitchen's favorite for vinaigrette. Tasters preferred bright lemon juice to harsher white or cider vinegar. I knew this dressing should be somewhat sweet, but the ½ cup of honey in some recipes was overkill. Even when I reduced the amount by half, honey still played the bully. After a few tests, I ended up using 3 tablespoons of granulated sugar and 1 tablespoon of honey.

Minced shallot fit the slaw's dainty personality, and Dijon mustard added tang and creaminess. Wondering if toasting the poppy seeds might draw out their flavor, I heated them in a skillet and soon savored a pleasant nutty aroma. I let the seeds cool for a few minutes in the pan, then whisked in the other dressing ingredients,

poured them over the cabbage, and chilled it all for half an hour. At last the slaw had a perfect tangy-sweet balance. Even if the occasional poppy seed stuck between my teeth, the toasty taste and pleasing crunch made it worthwhile.

POPPY SEED COLESLAW Serves 6 to 8
In step 1, the salted, rinsed, and dried cabbage can be refrigerated in a zipper-lock bag for 24 hours. Two tablespoons of minced red onion can be substituted for the shallot.

- 1 medium head green cabbage, quartered, cored, and shredded
- 2 teaspoons salt
- 1 teaspoon poppy seeds
- 1 shallot, minced (see note)
- 3 tablespoons lemon juice
- 2 tablespoons olive oil
- 2 teaspoons Dijon mustard
- 3 tablespoons sugar
- 1 tablespoon honey

1. **SALT CABBAGE** Toss cabbage and salt in colander set over bowl. Let stand until wilted, about 1 hour. Rinse cabbage under cold water, drain, dry well with kitchen towel, and transfer to large bowl.

2. **MAKE DRESSING** Toast poppy seeds in skillet over medium-high heat, shaking skillet (or stirring) frequently, until fragrant, about 2 minutes. Let pan cool 5 minutes,

An old-fashioned recipe shows there's more than one way to make a slaw.

then add remaining ingredients and whisk to combine.

3. **DRESS SLAW** Pour dressing over cabbage and toss to coat. Cover with plastic and refrigerate until chilled, about 30 minutes. Serve. (Slaw can be refrigerated in airtight container for 1 day.)

South Carolina Shrimp Boil

New England has its clambakes. New Orleans, its crawfish boils. In the coastal hamlet once known as Frogmore, South Carolina, and surroundings, they've got Frogmore stew—and let's be clear, it has no frogs and it's not stew. It's a South Carolina shrimp boil by another (very charming) name. Frogmore stew is made by simmering local shell-on shrimp, smoked sausage, corn on the cob, and potatoes in a broth seasoned with Old Bay. When it's time to eat, the broth is discarded and the shrimp and vegetables are heaped, higgledy-piggledy, onto newspaper-covered picnic tables cluttered with paper towels and "waster" buckets for spent cobs and shells. The dish is equally popular at backyard picnics and casual seaside restaurants along the Carolina coast.

BY CALI RICH

Yet as a Carolina native, I can attest that the one-pot appeal of Frogmore stew is often its downfall. Home cooks are apt to add everything to the pot at the same time, or let everything boil away madly while they tend to other dishes. In those instances, the fresh, summery charm of Frogmore stew vanishes, replaced with a mishmash of blown-out potatoes, mealy corn, and rubbery shrimp. The recipes I tested added the potatoes first and the shrimp last, but didn't agree on the sausage and corn. The Old Bay dominated some versions; in others, it was just a rumor.

The best recipe I tested began by browning smoky, spicy andouille sausage to render fat and boost flavor. The cook was then instructed to set the sausage aside and add 16 cups of water and 1 tablespoon of Old Bay to the now-empty pot. Halved red potatoes and quarters of corn on the cob went into the pot, simmering until the potatoes were barely tender. Next, the browned sausage and, five minutes later, the shrimp. The staggered cooking ensured intact potatoes, plump corn, and nicely cooked sausage and shrimp (as long as you watched closely). Unfortunately, the flavors were washed out.

You don't eat the broth in Frogmore stew, but if it has no flavor, the stuff you do eat won't either. I tested adding garlic, onion, celery, and bell pepper to the broth, but they didn't add much given the short cooking time. Instead of emptying a canister of Old Bay into the water, I attempted to get the same effect by subtraction. I reduced the water to 5 cups, barely enough to cover the 1½ pounds of potatoes, four ears of corn, 1½ pounds of sausage, and 2 pounds of shrimp I was using. For yet more flavor, I replaced a cup of the water with an equal amount of clam juice, or chicken broth, or beer. Tasters preferred the clam juice, which reinforced the taste of the sea. Some recipes call for tomato. I tried it. We liked it.

I had been adding the shrimp to the simmering liquid during the last few minutes of cooking, but that gave them scant time to soak up flavor. I tossed them with additional Old Bay before adding them to the pot, but the spice washed right off. Duh. To get it to adhere, I'd have to get the shrimp out of the broth. Might a metal steamer basket be the answer? I tossed the shrimp with 2 teaspoons Old Bay and placed them in the basket, which I set directly on the simmering vegetables and sausage. With the shrimp elevated above the liquid, the seasoning stayed put. Ten minutes later, they were juicy and much more flavorful. Plus, cooking them this way was more forgiving, so I could relax, right in spirit with a casual seafood boil.

SOUTH CAROLINA SHRIMP BOIL

Serves 8

This dish is always made with shell-on shrimp, and we think peeling them is half the fun. If you prefer peeled shrimp, use only 1 teaspoon of Old Bay in step 3. Can't find andouille? Substitute kielbasa sausage and add ¼ teaspoon cayenne pepper to the broth in step 2.

1½ pounds andouille sausage, cut into 2-inch lengths (see note)
2 teaspoons vegetable oil
4 cups water
1 (8-ounce) bottle clam juice
1 (14.5-ounce) can diced tomatoes
5 teaspoons Old Bay seasoning
1 bay leaf
1½ pounds small red potatoes, scrubbed and halved
4 ears corn, husks and silks removed, cut into 2-inch rounds
2 pounds extra-large (21 to 25 per pound) shrimp (see note)

1. BROWN SAUSAGE Heat sausage and oil in Dutch oven over medium-high heat until fat renders and sausage is browned, about 5 minutes; using slotted spoon, transfer sausage to plate.

2. SIMMER VEGETABLES Bring water, clam juice, tomatoes, 3 teaspoons Old Bay, bay leaf, potatoes, and corn to boil in empty pot. Reduce heat to medium-low and simmer, covered, until potatoes are barely tender, about 10 minutes.

3. STEAM SHRIMP Return browned sausage to pot. Toss shrimp with remaining Old Bay and transfer to collapsible steamer basket. Following photo 4 (below), nestle steamer basket into pot. Cook, covered, stirring shrimp occasionally, until cooked through, about 10 minutes. Strain stew and discard bay leaf. Serve.

TEST KITCHEN TECHNIQUE Layered Cooking

Our staggered cooking method develops flavor and guarantees that each ingredient is perfectly cooked.

1. Browning the sausage renders fat and builds flavor, giving the stew a spicy base of flavor.

2. The potatoes and corn get a head start, giving them time to soak up flavors and become tender.

3. For tender sausage, return the browned sausage to the pot for the last 10 minutes of cooking.

4. Steam the seasoned shrimp over the simmering stew to ensure they are just tender and well seasoned.

WHAT TO DO WITH LEFTOVERS Jambalaya

When a test cook began slurping the broth from our shrimp boil with a spoon, we thought she was crazy. Then we decided she was on to something. BY CALI RICH

Broth from our South Carolina Shrimp Boil gets a new lease on life as stock for jambalaya.

STRICTLY SPEAKING, the broth from a seafood boil like our South Carolina Shrimp Boil isn't left over. Almost by definition, a seafood boil is strained; the liquid it cooks in is thrown out, while the big pot of sausage, corn, potato, and shrimp is unceremoniously dumped out on a picnic table for messy enjoyment. Our broth included clam juice and Old Bay, and it had soaked up additional briny flavor from the shell-on shrimp. Pour it down the drain? Not on your life!

Jambalaya is a flavor-packed Cajun medley of rice, sausage, chicken, bell peppers, tomatoes, and spices that's often cooked in a seafood stock. We didn't have any seafood stock lying around (who does?), but we did have more than a quart of briny broth. We froze some for later, and then used 2 cups of it in place of stock in a favorite test kitchen recipe for jambalaya.

JAMBALAYA Serves 4 to 6

2 boneless, skinless chicken breasts (about 12 ounces)
 Salt and pepper
8 ounces andouille sausage, halved lengthwise and sliced thin
4 teaspoons vegetable oil
1 onion, chopped fine
1 celery rib, chopped fine
1 red bell pepper, seeded and chopped fine
1½ cups long-grain rice
5 garlic cloves, minced
½ teaspoon minced fresh thyme
2 cups leftover South Carolina Shrimp Boil broth

1. BROWN MEAT Pat chicken dry with paper towels and season with salt and pepper. Cook sausage in 2 teaspoons oil in large nonstick saucepan over medium-high heat until browned, about 5 minutes. Transfer sausage to plate. Cook chicken in sausage fat until browned on one side, about 4 minutes. Transfer to plate with sausage.

2. SAUTÉ AROMATICS Add onion, celery, bell pepper, and remaining oil to empty pan and cook until softened, about 5 minutes. Stir in rice, garlic, and thyme and cook until rice turns translucent, about 2 minutes. Add broth and browned sausage, scraping up any browned bits, and bring to boil. Nestle chicken, browned-side up, into rice. Reduce heat to low and cook, covered, until chicken is cooked through, about 10 minutes.

3. FINISH JAMBALAYA Transfer chicken to cutting board and tent with foil. Stir rice and continue to cook, covered, until liquid is absorbed, about 15 minutes. Cut chicken into ½-inch pieces and stir into rice. Remove from heat and let sit, covered, until chicken is heated through, about 5 minutes. Season with salt and pepper. Serve.

Juicy summer tomatoes make—and often break—tomato pie. We employed many tricks to ensure their full cooperation.

Summer Tomato Pie

James Beard himself loved this unusual combination of tomatoes, cheddar, and mayonnaise. He dubbed the pie American quiche. BY DAN ZUCCARELLO

MOST PEOPLE HEAR the words "tomato pie" and think pizza, or maybe green tomato pie, but we like a version that's neither. It's a homey, double-crust pie heaped with slices of summer tomatoes and slathered with mayonnaise and cheddar cheese. In *American Cookery* (1972), James Beard described tomato pie as a version of quiche, "an original." (The dairy forms a sort of custard that probably reminded him of quiche.) When food columnist Laurie Colwin revived it some 20 years later in the pages of *Gourmet*, she noted, "It would be hard to describe how delicious it is."

I made their recipes, plus several more, and found myself at a fork in the road. Some used biscuit dough, others pie dough. Tasters preferred the latter for the contrast of crisp shell and yielding interior. Make that imagined contrast. In reality, my first round of tests made it clear that while juiciness is the strength of a good tomato, it's the enemy of tomato pie. The wet tomatoes created a soaked, doughy bottom crust. Meanwhile, the mayonnaise curdled in the heat of the oven, looking more like cottage cheese than custard. I'd

fix that later. First, I'd deal with the crust.

I may have exacerbated the problem by opting for juicy beefsteak tomatoes, which I liked for their large size (less to slice) and full flavor. I left the skin on—tasters couldn't tell the difference, so why do extra work? To draw out their juice, I salted the tomatoes

and let them sit for 30 minutes. After the slices drained, I pressed them firmly with paper towels, layered them in the pie, and cut large vents in the top crust for steam to escape.

Despite all my effort, this pie, while much improved, still failed the crispiness test. The next time, I sprinkled cheese over the bottom crust before layering the other ingredients, hoping it would act as a protective barrier. Closer. My last idea was to place the pie on a very hot preheated baking sheet in a very hot oven. At 450 degrees, the crusts quickly browned.

Alas, the high heat worsened the curdling. The test kitchen always starts custard pies at high heat in order to set the crust, then lowers the temperature to protect the custard. Following suit, I kept the oven at 450 for 10 minutes, then lowered the temperature to 325 degrees for another 40 minutes. Good, not perfect. Could cornstarch, which helps prevent egg proteins in cooked custard from clumping, help? Four teaspoons added to the mayonnaise and cheese mixture produced a creamy pie.

For my final testing, I fine-tuned flavors. I'd found recipes calling for corn, zucchini, bacon, and cheeses of all stripes. Although I preferred the straightforward flavors of the classic, I put a few herbs to the test. Basil, thyme, and dill were all delicious, but scallions seemed the right fit for this homey tomato pie.

STEP-BY-STEP **Keys to Crispy Crust**
As they cook, juicy summer tomatoes expel so much moisture they turn pie shells sodden. Prevent slush with our three-step plan.

1. Salt the tomatoes and let them drain for 30 minutes. Then press on them firmly with paper towels to dry them.

2. Before filling the pie, sprinkle ½ cup of cheese over the bottom of the pie shell to protect the crust from the wet tomatoes.

3. Cut oval vent holes in the top crust so steam can escape. Place on a preheated baking sheet to set the bottom crust.

TOMATO PIE Serves 8

Visit CooksCountry.com for our Double-Crust Pie Dough, or use your own recipe or store-bought dough. If using store-bought dough, bake the pie for 30 minutes after turning down the heat in step 4.

- 2 **(9-inch) pie dough rounds (see note)**
- 2 **pounds beefsteak tomatoes (about 4 large), cored and cut into ¼-inch slices**
- ½ **teaspoon salt**
- ¼ **cup mayonnaise**
- 4 **teaspoons cornstarch**
- 1½ **cups shredded sharp cheddar cheese**
- 4 **scallions, sliced thin**

1. ROLL DOUGH On lightly floured surface, roll 1 dough round into 12-inch circle (if using store-bought dough, you do not need to roll either crust). Transfer to 9-inch pie plate, letting excess hang over edge. Cover with plastic and refrigerate 30 minutes. Roll second round into 12-inch circle and refrigerate for 30 minutes.

2. DRAIN TOMATOES Arrange tomatoes on paper towel–lined baking sheet and sprinkle with salt. Let drain 30 minutes, then press tomatoes with additional paper towels until very dry.

3. ASSEMBLE PIE Adjust oven rack to lowest position, place empty rimmed baking sheet on rack, and heat oven to 450 degrees. Mix mayonnaise, cornstarch, and 1 cup cheese in bowl until well combined. Sprinkle remaining cheese over bottom of dough-lined pie plate. Arrange third of tomatoes over cheese. Spread half of mayonnaise mixture over tomatoes and sprinkle with half of scallions. Layer with another third of tomatoes, remaining mayonnaise mixture, and remaining scallions, then top with remaining tomatoes.

4. CRIMP CRUST Arrange top crust on pie. Press crusts together, then trim, fold, and crimp edges. Cut four 2- by 1-inch oval vent holes in top. Place pie on heated baking sheet, bake for 10 minutes, then lower oven temperature to 325 degrees and bake until crust is golden brown, about 40 minutes. Cool on wire rack at least 3 hours. Serve at room temperature.

Hushpuppies

We didn't want to reinvent these fried cornmeal dumplings. We just wanted a recipe we could count on. BY DIANE UNGER

That hushpuppies got their name by hushing barking dogs, as legend goes, is doubtful. That they are hard to stop eating is not.

HUSHPUPPIES ARE CRISPY on the outside, fluffy on the inside, fried cornmeal dumplings served throughout the South with fried fish and barbecue. They were born out of thrift in a hardscrabble time, perhaps from leftover bits of cornmeal batter used to fry catfish. In the beginning, hushpuppies were made with no fat (or very little), no dairy, no flour, and were seasoned with nothing but salt. They were fried in whatever was on hand, usually lard. Early recipes produced hard, dense hushpuppies—I know because I tested a few. As time went on, cooks added eggs, dairy (milk or buttermilk), and seasonings such as pepper and grated onion.

To lighten the hushpuppies, some cooks began replacing a portion of the cornmeal with flour, adding baking powder or soda, and folding in whipped egg whites. (If you ask me, those whipped whites turned what should be a homespun fried bread into a fluffy, almost froufrou fritter, plus they required more work than a humble food should.) I didn't want to reinvent the hushpuppy. I wanted to cherry-pick from the many recipes I'd researched to get the very best hushpuppy—flavorful, crisp on the outside, and tender within—for the least effort.

Working with a basic batter that whisked together cornmeal and flour, whole eggs, baking powder, water, and salt, I started by testing varying ratios of cornmeal and flour. Obviously, the more cornmeal in the batter, the deeper the corn flavor, but more cornmeal also made for dense, gritty hushpuppies. At the other end of the scale, some recipes skewed so heavily toward flour that the hushpuppies turned out more like cakey, fluffy doughnuts than genuine hushpuppies. After a handful of tests, with the help of my tasters, I determined that ¾ cup cornmeal and ½ cup flour produced a hushpuppy that nicely balanced the two extremes.

For the liquid component of the batter, I tested water, milk, and finally buttermilk, always combined with eggs. (One recipe I found called for beer, but the flavor was strong and seemed way off base.) My tasters preferred the buttermilk for its slight tang. Once I'd settled on buttermilk, it made sense to add baking soda. Not only would soda react with acidic buttermilk to produce a lighter hushpuppy, but it would also help brown it for the requisite crunchy crust. In my next test, ½ teaspoon soda performed admirably, yielding hot, crusty, golden-brown hushpuppies with a striking yellow interior.

Still, with nothing but salt to season them, the hushpuppies tasted, thus far, pretty plain. I added cayenne pepper and finely minced onion (grating, called for in some recipes, was a hassle), both fairly typical additions based on my research and both befitting a classic. (I'd seen other recipes that variously called for such oddball ingredients as oregano, lemon zest, garlic, even chopped pickles.) While the batter sat for a few minutes to thicken, I heated the oil—far more likely to be on hand these days than lard. Then I dropped tablespoons of the batter into the bubbling oil and fried the hushpuppies. One recipe I'd come across said the hushpuppies would "roll over on their backs" when they were done. Right on call, a number of my fritters did just that, flipping over all on their own in the hot fat just like a good dog should.

RECIPE TESTING
Bad Dog, Good Dog

OLD YELLER
All-cornmeal hushpuppies are dense and dry as a bone.

A TENDER PUP
A combination of flour and cornmeal produces hushpuppies that are crisp on the outside and tender within.

HUSHPUPPIES Makes about 25

Avoid coarsely ground cornmeal, which will make the hushpuppies gritty. If you don't have buttermilk, whisk 1½ teaspoons lemon juice into ¾ cup milk and let it stand for 10 minutes.

- ¾ cup cornmeal (see note)
- ½ cup all-purpose flour
- 1½ teaspoons baking powder
- ½ teaspoon baking soda
- ¾ teaspoon salt
- ¼ teaspoon cayenne pepper
- ¾ cup buttermilk (see note)
- 2 large eggs
- ¼ cup minced onion
- 2 quarts peanut or vegetable oil

1. MAKE BATTER Combine cornmeal, flour, baking powder, baking soda, salt, and cayenne in large bowl. Whisk in buttermilk, eggs, and onion until combined. Let batter sit at room temperature for 10 minutes or up to 1 hour.

2. FRY HUSHPUPPIES Heat oil in large Dutch oven over medium-high heat to 350 degrees. Drop half of batter into oil in heaping tablespoons and fry until deep golden brown, 2 to 3 minutes, turning hushpuppies halfway through cooking. Transfer to wire rack set over rimmed baking sheet and repeat with remaining batter. Serve. (Hushpuppies can be refrigerated in airtight container for 2 days. Reheat in 450-degree oven for about 10 minutes.)

CORN AND RED PEPPER HUSHPUPPIES

Prepare Hushpuppies, adding 1 cup corn kernels (fresh or frozen, thawed), ½ red bell pepper, seeded and chopped fine, and 2 thinly sliced scallions to batter in step 1.

CRAB AND CHIVE HUSHPUPPIES

Prepare Hushpuppies, adding ½ pound crabmeat (picked over for shells), 2 tablespoons Dijon mustard, and 2 tablespoons minced fresh chives to batter in step 1.

HAM AND CHEDDAR HUSHPUPPIES

Prepare Hushpuppies, adding 4 ounces finely chopped deli ham, 1 cup shredded sharp cheddar cheese, 2 tablespoons Dijon mustard, and 2 thinly sliced scallions to batter in step 1.

Angel Food Cake 101

Angel food cake has a very short ingredient list—mostly egg whites, sugar, and flour. As with so many simple recipes, the devil is in the details. To name a few, if you don't sift the flour, separate the egg whites with tremendous care, and fold with a gentle touch, the majestic, snowy-white cake turns out depressingly dense, squat, and wet. Over seven weeks in the kitchen, we baked more than 100 angel food cakes to discover, once and for all, what matters, what doesn't, and how to achieve perfection. That's a tall order, and we rose to the challenge.

BY LYNN CLARK

Unlike most other cakes, angel food cake uses no butter or oil—you don't even grease the cake pan. It doesn't call for baking soda or baking powder, either, relying solely on beaten egg whites for its dramatic height. It's cooled in the pan it is baked in, upside down and suspended in the air! To make angel food cake, you whip egg whites with sugar and cream of tartar until white peaks form, fold in flour and flavorings, and bake.

Given the brevity of the recipe and the constancy of ingredients and basic method, it's puzzling how widely the outcomes can vary. Several experienced test cooks recently baked angel food cakes from nearly identical recipes on the same day in the same kitchen with the same equipment. Some of the cakes were tender and statuesque with a delicate crumb, others misshapen and heavy. Why?

Even I, an experienced baker, grew intimidated by the many dire warnings I read while researching recipes.

But through testing I discovered several steps that made no difference or could be streamlined. To begin with, cold egg whites will whip to the same volume as room-temperature eggs (they'll just take a few minutes longer). And don't panic if you slightly under- or over-beat them. We tried both, several times, and our cakes turned out respectably regardless. Next, you do indeed need to sift the flour—but not nearly as much as you think. While your cake is baking, have a ball! Jump up and down in front of the oven or open the door to take a peek. Several times. Your cake won't fall.

Some steps do matter. The key to angel food cake lies in voluminous, stable egg whites. The merest speck of yolk precludes them from whipping to peaks. Hurrying spells disaster. Cream of tartar offers some insurance against deflated whites. It's acidic, which helps stabilize egg whites, as would lemon juice or vinegar, but you'll be able to taste those.

Angel food cake, I would come to learn, isn't that difficult, nor does it require the skills of a professional. But it is exacting. That's why, while you almost never see a recipe in *Cook's Country* that calls for odd measurements or weights, we call for both here (1 cup plus 2 tablespoons cake flour, or 4½ ounces). No matter what I tried, my cake was slightly wet and spongy when I used 1 cup of flour. In despair, I added just 2 tablespoons additional flour and produced flawlessly tender texture time after time.

After almost two months of baking as many as six cakes a day, I finally had what I thought was the perfect recipe. But would it produce consistently good results for everyone? I gave it to several inexperienced bakers. Each produced identical tall, sweet stunners. I couldn't rest until I found out if they'd run into any problems. Their answer was better than angels singing: "Piece of cake!"

ANGEL FOOD CAKE Serves 10 to 12

Do not use all-purpose flour. Our tasters unflatteringly compared a cake made with it to Wonder Bread. If your angel food cake pan does not have a removable bottom, line the bottom of the pan with parchment paper. In either case, do not grease the pan (or the paper).

- 1 cup plus 2 tablespoons (4½ ounces) cake flour (see note)
- ¼ teaspoon salt
- 1¾ cups (12¼ ounces) granulated sugar
- 12 large egg whites
- 1½ teaspoons cream of tartar
- 1 teaspoon vanilla extract

1. PROCESS SUGAR Adjust oven rack to lower-middle position and preheat oven to 325 degrees. Whisk flour and salt in bowl. Process sugar in food processor until fine and powdery, about 1 minute. Reserve half of sugar in small bowl. Add flour mixture to food processor with remaining sugar and process until aerated, about 1 minute.

2. BEAT WHITES With electric mixer on medium-low speed, beat egg whites and cream of tartar until frothy, about 1 minute. Increase speed to medium-high. With motor running, slowly add reserved sugar and beat until soft peaks form, about 6 minutes. Add vanilla and mix until incorporated.

3. SIFT AND FOLD Sift flour mixture over egg whites in 3 additions, folding gently with rubber spatula after each addition until incorporated. Scrape mixture into 12-cup ungreased tube pan.

4. BAKE Bake until toothpick inserted into center comes out clean and cracks in cake appear dry, 40 to 45 minutes. Cool, inverted, to room temperature, about 3 hours. To unmold, run knife along interior of pan. Turn out onto platter. Serve.

LEMON–POPPY SEED ANGEL FOOD CAKE

Prepare Angel Food Cake, adding 2 tablespoons grated zest and 2 tablespoons juice from 2 to 3 lemons along with vanilla extract in step 2. Fold 1 tablespoon poppy seeds into batter along with flour in step 3.

CHOCOLATE-ALMOND ANGEL FOOD CAKE

Prepare Angel Food Cake, replacing ½ teaspoon vanilla extract with ½ teaspoon almond extract in step 2. Fold 2 ounces finely grated bittersweet chocolate into batter along with flour in step 3.

CAFÉ AU LAIT ANGEL FOOD CAKE

Prepare Angel Food Cake, adding 1 tablespoon instant coffee or espresso powder to food processor along with flour in step 1. Replace ½ teaspoon vanilla with 1 tablespoon coffee liqueur in step 2.

RATING TUBE PANS

Tube pans are not just for looks—the tube helps these very tall cakes bake faster and more evenly. After testing six brands, baking angel food and yellow sponge cakes in each, we learned that what matters most is heft, finish (dark is better), and a removable bottom. Our favorite pan also had feet on its rim, handy for elevating the upturned pan as the cake cooled. Our top three picks follow.

BY ELIZABETH BOMZE AND PEGGY CHUNG COLLIER

HIGHLY RECOMMENDED

CHICAGO METALLIC
Professional Nonstick Angel Food Cake Pan with Feet
Price: $19.95, **Model:** 69184
Source: www.cooking.com
Weight: 1 pound 6.5 ounces
Feet: Yes **Removable Bottom:** Yes
Browning: ★★★

TESTERS' NOTES
Dark, heavy, and nonstick, this pan, which is made of aluminized steel, yielded tall, evenly browned cakes. The removable bottom does not leak, and feet on its rim elevate the cake while it cools (so we don't need to turn it upside down over a bottle). For all those reasons, this pan is our favorite.

RECOMMENDED

CALPHALON
Classic Nonstick Bakeware Angel Food Cake Pan
Price: $19.95, **Model:** BW 6510
Source: www.cooking.com
Weight: 1 pound 5.75 ounces
Feet: No **Removable Bottom:** No
Browning: ★★★

TESTERS' NOTES
This sturdy, dark pan produced golden, evenly browned cakes. The sides of the cakes released easily, but because the pan lacks a removable bottom, we had to line it with parchment paper, an extra step we'd just as soon avoid.

RECOMMENDED WITH RESERVATIONS

BRIDGE KITCHENWARE
16-cup Tube Pan
Price: $43.60, **Model:** ABTP
Source: www.bridge kitchenware.com
Weight: 13.5 ounces
Feet: No **Removable Bottom:** No
Browning: ★

TESTERS' NOTES
This substantial pan holds 16 cups (compared to about 12 for the other pans we tested). The pan looks impressive, but would we ever bake a cake this gigantic? Also, given its price, we expected feet and a removable bottom. It has no feet, the bottom isn't removable, and the cakes we baked in it were pale.

Rise to the Challenge 7 Things That Matter

When making angel food cake, small mistakes can have big consequences, for example the cake below on the left. Here are the key steps to ensure your cake looks like the one on the right instead. (The short version? Don't deflate the whites!)

WHAT YOU'VE GOT
Dense, Squat Cake

WHAT YOU WANT
Delicate, Sky-High Cake

1. GRIND THE SUGAR EXTRA-FINE: Granulated or confectioners' sugar will make acceptable but somewhat heavy cakes. For an extraordinary angel food cake, process granulated sugar in the food processor until powdery. It'll be fine, light, and clump-free, so it won't deflate the egg whites.

2. FLUFF WITH FLOUR: Some recipes call for sifting the flour and/or sugar as many as eight times. What a pain! We tried skipping sifting altogether, but the resulting cake was squat. Ultimately, we figured out that by processing the flour (with half the sugar) in the food processor to aerate it, we could get away with sifting just once.

3. KEEP YOLKS AT BAY: We stirred ½ teaspoon egg yolk into 1 dozen whites, just to see. The eggs turned white and frothy with whipping, but even after 25 minutes, they failed to form peaks. Lesson learned: Separate eggs with care! For a failsafe method, see Notes from the Test Kitchen, page 31.

4. STABILIZE THE WHITES: Add cream of tartar to the egg whites at the start of whipping. Once the egg whites become foamy, add half the sugar—gradually. Don't dump it in all at once! Both help stabilize the egg whites, making them less likely to deflate.

5. SIFT FLOUR IN BATCHES: Gently sift the flour-sugar mixture over the beaten egg whites in three additions to avoid putting too much weight on the whites. If you're impatient or rough and tumble, the egg whites are certain to deflate.

6. FOLD GENTLY: Use a rubber spatula to gently turn or "fold" the flour and egg whites over one another until they are thoroughly combined. If you simply stir the two mixtures together, the abrupt motion can cause the egg whites to deflate.

7. COOL UPSIDE DOWN: Invert the cooked cake until it is completely cool, about 3 hours. If you don't have a pan with feet, invert it over the neck of a bottle. Angel food cakes cooled right-side up can be crushed by their own weight. To unmold the cooled cake, run a knife along the inside of the pan. Because you can't grease the pan, the cake sticks a bit.

Blackberry Roly Poly

In Beatrix Potter's "The Tale of Samuel Whiskers" (1908), rats roll the foolish Tom Kitten into a "roly-poly pudding" (he survives the ordeal). At the time, the jam-filled dessert was regarded as a child-friendly, economical treat, especially in winter, when fresh fruit was costly. Early versions were made by brushing suet dough with jam, rolling it into a cylinder, and boiling or steaming it wrapped in cloth. By Tom Kitten's time, the widespread use of stoves and the invention of baking powder and baking soda had given birth to a new style of roly poly. Made from biscuit dough and baked, this buttery, flaky, jam-filled roll soon eclipsed its precursors. The English still bake it. I wondered how something so good got lost in the States. BY CALI RICH

I couldn't resist testing the original versions, despite my colleagues' skepticism. I tripled a biscuit recipe, making dough from flour, water, and shortening (suet, or kidney fat, was nowhere to be found), rolled out three rectangles, brushed them with blackberry jam, and shaped three scrolls. I wrapped one in cheesecloth and submerged it in boiling water, steamed a second, and baked a third. A few hours later, I knew why the charmingly named "roly poly" is sometimes called, alarmingly, "dead man's arm"—the boiled cylinder was rigid, pallid, and oozing with jam. It was sodden and stodgy. The steamed dough was only a marginal improvement. Ah, but the baked version! Resembling a jumbo jammy biscuit, it was a hit, and not merely by comparison. There were just two problems: The interior was a tad soggy and the biscuit lean.

I tried some standard biscuit doughs: drop (all-butter biscuits are "dropped" onto a baking sheet), cream (made with cream instead of butter), and a favorite test kitchen version that uses both chilled butter and shortening. The drop biscuit was too wet to roll. The cream biscuit dried out and crumbled during the prolonged baking a roly poly requires. And why bother with shortening at all, tasters said of the combo biscuit.

So I replaced the shortening with butter, which I pulsed in a food processor with flour, sugar, salt, and baking powder. I added milk to bind the dough. It was richer, but still a little lean for a roly poly—it's a dessert, after all. Four tablespoons of butter per cup of flour is the test kitchen standard for biscuits. One extra tablespoon per cup produced an exceptionally flaky, buttery roly poly. Unfortunately, the added fat made the dough too soft to roll out easily, and it slumped in the oven. Borrowing a cookie-making technique, I refrigerated the dough for an hour to firm it. Perfect! Next, I tried freezing the dough to speed matters. Just 20 minutes later, it was ready to roll.

I hadn't yet solved my initial problem: The interior near the jam remained slightly wet. I'd been brushing the dough with ½ cup store-bought jam, but it thinned while the roly poly baked, making the inside soggy. Commercial jams are often thickened with pectin, which thins when heated. I decided to make a quick, thick homemade jam without pectin: I cooked 2 cups of berries with ¼ cup sugar until the berries had broken down. When the jam cooled, I brushed it on the roly poly, rolled it, brushed the cylinder with butter, sprinkled it with sugar (two last-minute improvements), baked, and waited.

In the test kitchen, we're used to the smell of good things cooking. Still, the scent of baking butter, blackberries, and sugar was heady stuff. After 45 minutes, I pulled the roly poly from the oven and waited impatiently for it to cool. When I sliced it, I admired my own handiwork—it was rustic and golden with an even swirl of fresh, bright jam. And let me assure you, nobody who tasted it could forget this roly poly anytime soon.

BLACKBERRY ROLY POLY Serves 8

Both fresh and frozen blackberries will work. Like a biscuit, roly poly tastes best on the day it's baked. Use a serrated knife to slice it.

- 2 cups blackberries (see note)
- ⅔ cup sugar
- ½ teaspoon grated lemon zest
- 3 cups all-purpose flour
- 1 tablespoon baking powder
- 1 teaspoon salt
- 16 tablespoons (2 sticks) unsalted butter, cut into ½-inch pieces and chilled
- 1 cup whole or low-fat milk

1. MAKE JAM Cook berries and ¼ cup sugar in saucepan over medium-low heat until berries begin to release juice, about 3 minutes. Increase heat to medium-high and cook, stirring frequently, until berries break down and mixture is thick and jam-like, about 10 minutes (mixture should measure ½ cup). Transfer jam to bowl, stir in zest, and cool to room temperature.

2. PROCESS DOUGH Pulse flour, baking powder, salt, additional ⅓ cup sugar, and all but 1 tablespoon butter in food processor until mixture resembles coarse meal. Transfer to large bowl and stir in milk until combined.

3. SHAPE DOUGH Adjust oven rack to middle position and heat oven to 375 degrees. Line baking sheet with parchment paper. Turn dough out onto lightly floured surface and knead until smooth, 8 to 10 times. Pat dough into 6-inch square, wrap with plastic, and freeze until

STEP-BY-STEP Rolling the Poly

Here's how we produce an even jam pinwheel and prevent jam from leaking out of our Blackberry Roly Poly.

1. On a lightly floured surface, roll the chilled dough into a 12- by 10-inch rectangle.

2. Spread the jam evenly over the dough, leaving a ½-inch border around the edges.

3. Starting with the long edge, roll the dough into a cylinder. Pinch to seal the seam and ends.

4. Carefully transfer the rolled dough, seam-side down, to a prepared baking pan.

just firm, about 20 minutes. Following photos 1 to 4, roll dough into 12- by 10-inch rectangle, spread with jam, roll into tight cylinder, and arrange seam-down on prepared baking sheet.

4. BAKE Melt remaining butter and brush over dough. Sprinkle with remaining sugar and bake until golden brown, about 45 minutes. Let cool 10 minutes on sheet, then transfer to wire rack. Serve warm or at room temperature.

MAKE AHEAD Roly poly can be prepared through step 3, then covered with plastic wrap and refrigerated on prepared baking sheet for 24 hours. To serve, remove plastic wrap and proceed with step 4, increasing baking time to 50 minutes.

Roly Poly Rolls Along

The jam-filled roly poly made its print debut in *Eliza Acton's Modern Cookery for Private Families* (1845). (Cooks were probably making it earlier; printed recipes usually lagged behind what was happening in the kitchen.) Acton tells cooks to boil the pudding, but notes that people with "modern tastes" may prefer steaming it. Eventually, both those cooking methods disappeared as cooks moved to a jam-filled biscuit dough they baked in the oven. After tasting all three versions, we are not pining for days of yore.

BOILED IS BRUTAL   **STEAMED IS SOGGY**   **BAKED IS BEST**

RECIPE REVIVAL Fruit Cocktail

Step away from the can, man. BY JEREMY SAUER

THE FDA DEFINES fruit cocktail as a mixture of 30 to 50 percent peaches, 25 to 45 percent pears, 6 to 16 percent pineapple, 6 to 20 percent grapes, and 2 to 5 percent cherries. Ingredients aside, its history is hotly debated. Was it first made in the canneries of Campbell, California, or in nearby Sunnyvale, home of a mural-ed water tower called the "World's Largest Can of Fruit Cocktail"? Was it invented by U.C. Berkeley Professor William Vere Cruess, or the pioneering canner J.C. Ainsley? What we know for certain is that the concept originated in California in the first half of the 20th century. Another non-negotiable fact is this: Canned fruit cocktail is nothing more than a poor diced fruit salad. Straight from the can, it's sweet as heck and has no distinct texture. Still, I couldn't help wondering what fruit cocktail might be with fresh fruit.

Fruit salad typically starts with simple syrup. The syrup, made by dissolving sugar in water, adds sheen and sweetens the fruit. For balance, I substituted lime juice for the water. Its tang was a plus, and using brown sugar in place of white sugar provided caramel undertones.

But after tossing the fruits with the syrup, the juices began to seep, turning the fruit cocktail into chunky sangria. In the test kitchen, we often salt juicy tomatoes or cucumbers to extract excess liquid. Would the idea work with sugar? I gave it a shot, combining the fruit with the

brown sugar, then draining it for 30 minutes. The salad was less watery, but all those flavorful juices had drained away. Next, I tried reserving the juices and cooking them down into the syrup with the lime juice. Finished with a nip of vanilla extract, this intensely flavored fruit cocktail might not resemble the fruit cocktail of old, but let's be honest, that's a good thing.

FRUIT COCKTAIL Serves 4 to 6

Add the cherries last or they'll discolor the salad.

- 2 ripe peaches, pitted and chopped
- 2 ripe pears, cored and chopped
- ½ small pineapple, peeled, cored, and cut into ½-inch pieces
- 1 cup red seedless grapes, halved
- 3 tablespoons light brown sugar
- ¼ cup juice from 2 limes
- ⅛ teaspoon vanilla extract
- ½ cup cherries, pitted and halved (see note)

1. SUGAR FRUIT Toss peaches, pears, pineapple, grapes, and 2 tablespoons sugar in colander set over large bowl. Let drain 30 minutes.

2. MAKE DRESSING Transfer drained fruit juices in bowl to saucepan. Stir in remaining sugar and lime juice

Fresh cherries, not maraschino, freshen our cocktail.

and simmer over medium heat until syrupy and reduced to ¼ cup, about 5 minutes. Off heat, stir in vanilla and cool.

3. TOSS SALAD Combine drained fruit and dressing in large bowl. Gently stir in cherries. Serve. (Fruit cocktail can be refrigerated in airtight container for 2 days.)

Equipment Review Vacuum Sealers

Do they save food from freezer burn, or simply suck your wallet dry? BY PEGGY CHUNG COLLIER

KEY **Good ★★★**   **Fair ★★**   **Poor ★**

IF YOU PICK bushels of berries, buy steaks in bulk, or return from a fishing trip with unexpected bounty, you have more than you can immediately eat. But though you freeze your stockpile with the notion of feasting all winter, just one month later you have food that is encrusted with fine white crystals. Should you buy a vacuum sealer, a device that promises to keep food fresher in the freezer ("up to five times longer," swears one brand) by creating an airtight wrap? We tested eight models with prices ranging from $18 to a whopping $470.

As food freezes, moisture migrates to the surface and forms ice crystals. Over time, the food dehydrates, discolors, and loses flavor. A good supermarket zipper-lock freezer bag can stave off these problems for a few weeks. But in our tests, food stored in freezer bags was covered with frost after a month. Would vacuum sealers work better for longer-term storage?

AN AIRTIGHT CASE

We assembled ground coffee, fresh strawberries, 50 pounds of raw steak and chicken breasts, and a fully cooked Thanksgiving dinner, then sealed and froze all of it. Our sealers ranged from handheld models to countertop devices. Most of the latter were about the size of a shoebox; one was larger.

The two handheld models seemed dummy-proof: We zipped the food into a plastic bag that has a valve, where we pressed the motorized device to suck out air. All was well until a few coffee grounds or a smear of mashed potatoes got in the way of the zipper. Suddenly, the bags refused to become airtight. Countertop models, which use heat for a tight seal, were more reliable. Most came with both premade bags and rolls made of two layers of plastic already sealed along the sides. We preferred the rolls, which let us create custom-sized bags.

To use the roll, you cut a piece to size, insert one open end into the machine to seal it, add the food, and then close the remaining open side, activating both vacuum and seal. All but two of the models required that you press firmly on them while sealing. One cumbersome model required that we press on different corners while simultaneously flattening the bag. Our favorite models all had sensors to detect overflowing liquids.

We pulled out the frozen packages after two weeks. We weren't surprised that the food in the Oliso Frisper and Deni models was coated in ice crystals, the first

sign of freezer burn. Those models had failed to form tight seals from the start, especially around the curvy contours of strawberries. Handheld models by Zip Vac and Reynolds had formed seemingly airtight seals, but at the two-week mark, bricks of coffee were limp sacks.

After one month, our top four continued to hold up. Pragotrade alone was frost-free; tiny air pockets filled with frost surrounded the others. After two months, the Pragotrade-wrapped steak remained bright red with just a little frost, while the remaining three contenders showed early-stage freezer burn.

It turns out that jagged ice crystals can poke pinholes through plastic, letting air and moisture seep in. At 0.05 mm thick, the Pragotrade bags were 0.02 mm thicker than Rival and FoodSaver bags, and 0.03 mm thicker than a standard zipper-lock bag. Small as it may seem, that extra protective bulk made a lot of difference and pushed Pragotrade to the top.

IT'S A WRAP

Are vacuum sealers economical? It depends how much food you freeze. Each vacuum sealer works only with its own plastic, and cheaper models didn't

necessarily come with cheaper plastic. A quart bag costs 26 cents with the $470 model and nearly three times that with the $30 model. The others averaged 45 to 55 cents per bag or foot.

Without a doubt, the Pragotrade Pro 2300 did the best job of getting an airtight seal and keeping food fresh in the freezer. But it requires lots of counter space, a little muscle, and a very large budget ($470 plus bags). For most people, the FoodSaver V2240 ($100) is a better choice. It was the easiest to use and kept a respectable seal after a month. It's our Best Buy.

HIGHLY RECOMMENDED

	CRITERIA	TESTERS' NOTES
PRAGOTRADE Vacuum Sealer Pro 2300 *(MILLIONAIRES ONLY)* **Price:** $469.95 at www.cooking.com **Roll (per foot):** 38 cents **Quart bag:** 26 cents	Frost-free: ★★★ Easy to Use: ★★	**Comments:** The Rolls-Royce of vacuum sealers. It was the only model with bags strong enough to keep frozen food perfectly sealed and frost-free after two months. But it was expensive, large, and heavy (26.5 pounds), and you must press on the lid during vacuuming. Only for the devoted freezer-owner.

RECOMMENDED

	CRITERIA	TESTERS' NOTES
FOODSAVER V2240 Vacuum Sealer Kit *(BEST BUY)* **Price:** $99.99 at www.foodsaver.com **Roll (per foot):** 56 cents **Quart bag:** 55 cents	Frost-free: ★★ Easy to Use: ★★★	**Comments:** Intuitive and easy to use, this hands-free model was much smaller and lighter than our heavyweight winner, sealing food tightly and quickly. After a month, tiny air pockets formed around food, but packages stayed sealed with minimal frost. At two months: early signs of freezer burn.
RIVAL Seal-A-Meal VS107 Food Saver with Hold Release **Price:** $63.02 at www.seal-a-meal.com **Roll (per foot):** 50 cents **Quart bag:** 45 cents	Frost-free: ★★ Easy to Use: ★★	**Comments:** This relatively lightweight model was harder to use than the FoodSaver V2240; we had to push on the lid during vacuuming, but it sealed as tightly. After a month, we saw tiny air pockets and frost, but packages stayed sealed. At two months: early signs of freezer burn.

RECOMMENDED WITH RESERVATIONS

	CRITERIA	TESTERS' NOTES
FOODSAVER V3840 Vacuum Sealer Kit **Price:** $173.97 at www.foodsaver.com **Roll (per foot):** 50 cents **Quart bag:** 45 cents	Frost-free: ★★ Easy to Use: ★	**Comments:** This model sealed as tightly as the other FoodSaver model, but its bells and whistles didn't justify the extra $73. Sitting vertically to save space, it's still wider than other models. The sealing slot is too narrow, and we found no difference between "dry" and "moist" food functions.

NOT RECOMMENDED

	CRITERIA	TESTERS' NOTES
REYNOLDS Handi-Vac Vacuum Sealer **Price:** $18.35 at supermarkets **Quart bag:** 35 cents	Frost-free: ★ Easy to Use: ★★★	**Comments:** As long as food didn't get caught in the zipper, this handheld device made a tight seal at first. But after one month, bags of coffee that had been brick-hard were loose, and other foods were covered in frost.
ZIP VAC Portable Food Storage System **Price:** $29.99 at www.zip-vac.com **Quart bag:** 67 cents	Frost-free: ★ Easy to Use: ★★★	**Comments:** This handheld model sealed tightly, but broke after just six uses. (A backup unit had similar problems.) If food got near the zipper, it wouldn't seal. After a month in the freezer, bags lost their seal. And while the device is cheap, its bags are not.
OLISO FRISPER Vacuum Sealer **Price:** $59.99 at www.oliso.com **Quart bag:** 60 cents	Frost-free: ★ Easy to Use: ★★	**Comments:** This model works by puncturing a hole in a reusable bag to draw out air, then heat-sealing around the hole. But its vacuum was too weak for a tight seal, especially around curvy strawberries, and was so loud we wanted earplugs.
DENI FRESHLOCK Turbo II Vacuum Sealer **Price:** $97.99 at www.target.com **Roll (per foot):** 62 cents **Quart bag:** 75 cents	Frost-free: ★ Easy to Use: ★	**Comments:** Between pressing on different corners and having to seal three sides of a roll to make a bag, this model is a hassle. Bags felt cheap, the thin melting wire almost broke after three uses, and its weak vacuum struggled mightily.

Taste Test Bottled Barbecue Sauces

The sweeter, the better—as long as molasses is in the mix. BY SCOTT KATHAN

WHETHER YOU USE it to baste, dip, or slather, chances are you have a bottle of barbecue sauce tucked into the door of your refrigerator. But is it the best-tasting brand? To find out, we gathered eight national brands (drawn from a list of top sellers from Information Resources, Inc., a Chicago-based market research firm) and asked 21 tasters from America's Test Kitchen to sample each sauce cooked (broiled on chicken thighs) and raw (on its own and as a dip for chicken nuggets).

Barbecue styles vary greatly by region, but we'd argue there's an all-American supermarket style. It's on the sweet side and balances tang, smoke, and tomato flavor. You can use it like ketchup. The sauces that fit that profile rated better than those closer to authentic regional barbecue styles. The latter failed, in part, because they weren't sweet enough. Lacking sugar, they struck our tasters as out of whack.

Total sugars proved the determining factor in our tasting. As a group, the sauces with more total sugars rated better than the sauces with less. (It is possible to have too much of a good thing; to wit, Sweet Baby Ray's Award Winning Barbecue Sauce.) And not all sugars are created equal. Our top picks, Bull's-Eye and KC Masterpiece, are the only two in our lineup that list molasses as their third ingredient; other brands contain it, but in lower relative concentrations. When the robust, distinct flavor of molasses was in short supply, the sauces fell flat.

Moreover, our winner, Bull's-Eye, contains no high-fructose corn syrup (HFCS). White sugar is its primary sweetener. The absence of HFCS was a distinct advantage for broiling: Because sugar caramelizes more slowly than HFCS, it was easy to get a thick, glossy glaze from Bull's-Eye without it burning. Admittedly, the only other sauce without any HFCS, Texas Best, finished last in our tasting (it is a spicy, Texas-style sauce with very low total sugars). But it reached its personal best in the broiled chicken test.

Taken as a group, these sauces underwhelmed us and in the main failed to make food taste better. Our advice? Make barbecue sauce yourself—it's not that hard. If you're rushed and must buy, however, avoid HFCS and look for molasses.

RECOMMENDED

	TASTERS' NOTES
 **BULL'S-EYE** Original Barbecue Sauce **$2.39 for 18 ounces** **Total Sugars:** 11g (per 2 tablespoon serving)	**Comments:** This "robust," "spicy" sauce won points for its "great, sticky crust" in the broiled chicken tasting. It also finished first as a dip for chicken nuggets. Tasters praised it as "fresh-tasting, smoky, and tomatoey," "tangy," and with a "good balance of smoky and sweet." "Almost perfect," one noted.

RECOMMENDED WITH RESERVATIONS

	TASTERS' NOTES
KC MASTERPIECE Original Barbecue Sauce **$3.69 for 28 ounces** **Total Sugars:** 12g	**Comments:** This "potent" sauce has "a pleasant kick" that one taster described as "very sweet and tangy with a smoky hook." A second taster "could eat this one right out of the bottle," but several others detected distasteful hints of "raisins" and "prunes." Everybody, however, liked its "velvety" texture.
SWEET BABY RAY'S Award Winning Barbecue Sauce **$1.67 for 18 ounces** **Total Sugars:** 16g	**Comments:** Tasters said the burn and spice were nice, but the high sugar content ("way too sweet") was not. In sum, as one taster put it, "spicy, but totally flat otherwise." This sauce has the most total sugars by far, and lists high-fructose corn syrup first.
HUNT'S Original Barbecue Sauce **$1.25 for 21.6 ounces** **Total Sugars:** 11g	**Comments:** Tasters thought this "thin," middle-of-the-road sample tasted like "sweet and sour sauce," "melted fruit roll-ups," and "barbecue Jolly Ranchers." "Middling potency and sweetness, not a standout but fine" and "solid if uninspiring."
KRAFT Original Barbecue Sauce **$1.89 for 18 ounces** **Total Sugars:** 10g	**Comments:** Tasters were divided. Some appreciated the fact that this sauce "packs a punch" and liked its deep smoky flavor. Others judged that same smoke flavor as "overwhelming" and "harsh."

NOT RECOMMENDED

	TASTERS' NOTES
JACK DANIEL'S Original No. 7 Recipe Barbecue Sauce **$2.99 for 19 ounces** **Total Sugars:** 8g	**Comments:** We heard a chorus of complaints. "Robitussin," "juniper," "nail polish remover," "rancid beer," and "sweat socks" were among the unpleasant flavors tasters detected. Tasters also found it "way too smoky." "Tastes so awful I spit it out."
STUBB'S Original Bar-B-Q Sauce **$4.49 for 18 ounces** **Total Sugars:** 4g	**Comments:** "I wouldn't call this barbecue sauce," one taster observed about this "peppery," "sour," and "acidic" sauce. The "tomato and vinegar flavors are not balanced or united," said another. Several thought it resembled "spicy ketchup or marinara sauce," not barbecue sauce.
TEXAS BEST Barbecue Sauce **$4.99 for 17.5 ounces** **Total Sugars:** 3g	**Comments:** With drastically less total sugars than our winner, it's no surprise that tasters found this Texas-style sauce "an apple among oranges" and "not balanced with sweetness." We liked it in a previous tasting, but the formula has changed twice in recent years. This was the only brand with no molasses whatsoever, and our tasters missed it. They complained loudly about this "very acidic," "tomato-heavy" sauce.

All About PORK RIBS

Pork ribs have a lot of fat and sinew, so they require long, slow cooking to go from tough to tender. For the same reason, they're relatively inexpensive. Different cuts come from different areas of the pig's ribcage. Here are the four most common cuts with notes on how we cook them.

SPARERIBS
Whole racks of pork spareribs (cut from the underside of the pig, near the belly) contain the brisket bone and surrounding meat. They weigh 4 to 5 pounds. Their large size and irregular shape make them bulky and unwieldy (large racks don't fit on some smaller grills), which is why we prefer St. Louis cut ribs.

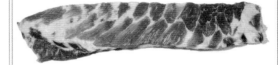

ST. LOUIS CUT SPARERIBS
These are pork spareribs trimmed of the brisket bone and surrounding meat. They are uniformly rectangular and weigh about 3 pounds per rack. We like to smoke St. Louis spareribs on the grill for a few hours at a low temperature (about 275 degrees), then wrap the ribs tightly in foil to seal in moisture and finish them in a 250-degree oven for two hours. The method is much faster than cooking them on the grill from start to finish.

BABY BACK RIBS
Baby back ribs, also called back ribs, loin ribs, or loin back ribs, are cut from the area of the ribs closest to the backbone (above the spareribs) of mature hogs. They can be cooked like spareribs, but watch the clock: They will become tender more quickly because they are smaller and leaner. Depending on how the animal was butchered, racks of baby back ribs can contain anywhere from eight to 15 bones.

COUNTRY-STYLE RIBS
Country-style ribs, like baby backs, are cut from near the backbone, but they come from the blade-end of the pig, nearest the shoulder. They contain less connective tissue than other ribs, with plenty of meat and considerable fat, and thus cook to tenderness comparatively quickly. We like to sear and then braise country-style ribs.

Test Kitchen Cooking Class How to Grill Hamburgers

Nothing says summer in America like hot, juicy backyard burgers. Unfortunately, backyard grillers all too often turn out shrunken, domed, dry burgers—sorry specimens that no amount of ketchup can save. Avoid burger heartbreak by mastering this lesson.

AMERICAN HERO

Shop Smart

Beef A good burger starts at the supermarket. Be sure to read the label or listen to your butcher. In the test kitchen, we're fans of burgers made with ground chuck, a shoulder cut with big, beefy flavor. By comparison, ground round and the generically labeled "ground beef" can be gristly and livery. And play the percentages—buy 80 to 85 percent lean beef or your burger will dry out.

Bun It's not a burger without the bun. We like big burgers (6 ounces each), so we need buns to match. Soft yet sturdy Pepperidge Farm Premium Bakery Rolls, with a generous 4½-inch diameter and hearty, wheaty taste, are the test kitchen favorite.

The Works These are the test kitchen's preferred brands.
★ **KETCHUP** Hunt's
★ **MUSTARD** Gulden's
★ **PICKLES** Cascadian Farm Bread and Butter Chips

CHOOSE CHUCK

PICK PREMIUM

Temperature Guide

Many of us depend on thermometers when we're grilling expensive steaks, but when we grill (cheap) burgers, we think we needn't bother. Wrong. For consistently delicious burgers cooked to just the right degree of doneness, don't guess. Take the temperature in the center of each burger with an instant-read thermometer.

MEDIUM-RARE BURGER
125 to 130 degrees, 2 to 3 minutes per side

MEDIUM BURGER
135 to 140 degrees, 3 to 4 minutes per side

MEDIUM-WELL BURGER
145 to 160 degrees, 4 to 5 minutes per side

WELL-DONE BURGER
160 degrees and up, 5 minutes and up per side

Well-Done Burgers Done Well

There's no way around it: Burgers cooked medium-well to well done are less juicy than those cooked less—even if you follow our lesson to the letter. But some folks love well-done burgers, or are worried about food safety and don't want to risk eating rare ground meat. We've found they can have their burgers and eat them too, if they add a panade to their meat mixture. A paste made from bread and milk, a panade adds moisture to meatballs and meatloaf. (And what's a burger but a meatball by another name?) For 1½ pounds of ground beef, combine 1 slice of hearty white sandwich bread, torn in pieces, with 2 tablespoons milk. Let it sit about 5 minutes, until the bread is soaked, then mash to a paste with a fork; you'll have about ¼ cup. Gently mix the panade into the meat before forming burgers.

BREAD + MILK = PANADE

Keys to Success

Don't Underseason
Just dusting salt on the exterior of shaped patties doesn't cut it. Put the ground beef in a bowl. Lightly break up the meat with your hands and sprinkle evenly with salt. Use 1 teaspoon of table salt for 1½ pounds of ground beef, the amount you will need for four burgers.

Don't Overwork
Ground beef is not Play-Doh. The more you handle it, the denser and more rubbery it will become when cooked. After you've seasoned the meat, divide it into individual portions and, with lightly cupped hands, shape into patties. As soon as the patties hold together, stop!

Don't Press
Flip the burgers just once—after they've developed deep brown grill marks—and don't be tempted to press on them. Pressing down on the burgers as they cook squeezes out the flavorful juices, which end up in your grill (causing flare-ups) instead of in your burgers.

Fight the Battle of the Bulge
The collagen, or connective tissue, in ground meat shrinks when heated. This causes the bottom and sides of the meat to tighten like a belt, which forces the surface of the burger to expand. To prevent a bubble burger, press a ¼-inch divot, or indentation, in the center of each patty. The collagen will still tighten, but the indented meat won't bulge.

FLAT PATTY = BULGING BURGER

DIVOTED PATTY = FLAT BURGER

Avoid a Sticky Situation
Be sure your grill is both hot and clean before you set the burgers down. Otherwise the crust of the burger will stick and rip

1. SUPER-HEAT The self-cleaning function in your oven blasts away stuck-on gunk. You can get your grill to do the same. A sheet of aluminum foil traps heat and gets the grill grate super-hot.

2. SCRAPE CLEAN Standard wire bristles wear down after just a few uses and are useless. We prefer the sturdy stainless scrubby pad on the Grill Wizard BBQ Brush. It's tough—and replaceable.

3. SLICK DOWN Grab a wad of paper towels with a pair of long-handled tongs and dip them in a bowl of vegetable oil. When the towels have absorbed the oil, run them over the cleaned grill grate.

4. BUILD UP SEASONING The oil will burn off at first. Continue to dip the towels into oil and slick down the grate; it will become "nonstick." When the grate turns black and glossy, your grill is good to go.

Notes from the Test Kitchen

Versatile Rimmed Baking Sheets

In the test kitchen, our heavy-duty rimmed baking sheets are indispensable. Whether we're baking cookies, biscuits, or our **Crispy Oven Fries** (page 10), we rely on them for even browning and crisping. This 18- by 13-inch pan is 1 inch deep, so it can comfortably accommodate a rack for roasting or broiling meat and catch crumbs from a freshly baked cake on a cooling rack. Look for a thick pan that resists warping at high temperatures. Our favorite, the Lincoln Foodservice Half-Size Heavy Duty Sheet Pan ($15.99), is sturdy and durable.

ONE PAN, MANY USES

Boost Bean Flavor

When making salads such as **Black Bean Salad** (page 14), we prefer to use canned beans processed with salt. Why? Easy—they taste better. Many "natural" or "organic" brands containing little or no salt can be quite bland, especially in recipes where the canned beans are not cooked. If all you've got in your pantry are unsalted beans, here's a neat trick for improving their flavor: Marinate them in the dressing for your salad for about 10 minutes.

Deveining Shrimp

You don't have to remove the "vein" that runs down the back of shrimp; it's flavorless and harmless. But lots of eaters can't get past the yuck factor, as in, "It's the shrimp's intestinal tract—yuck!" For that reason, shrimp are typically deveined. We use a paring knife for shelled shrimp, but when preparing shell-on shrimp for our **South Carolina Shrimp Boil** (page 21), we found the knife couldn't muscle through the shell. We reached for a pair of small scissors, which cut through the shell to expose the underlying vein. The tip of the scissors freed the vein.

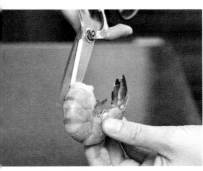

SHELL ON, VEIN OUT

Basic Technique Separation Anxiety

Most of the time when we're separating eggs, if a stray bit of yolk finds its way into the whites, we scoop it out with the eggshell. We've always wondered why that works so well, so we phoned our trusty science editor. He explained that the shell membrane is coated with the protein keratin, which has an affinity for the protein that is in yolks. When you try the same trick with a metal spoon, he continued, the yolk usually skitters to the other side of the bowl. The yolk contains water and lipoproteins that, in nonscientific terms, just don't like metal. Some experts caution against using the eggshell to "de-yolk," as it could contaminate the whites with salmonella. But if the whites will be heated to more than 165 degrees, don't worry about the bacteria. Our **Angel Food Cake** (page 25) depends entirely on whipped egg whites for lift, and here even the barest trace of yolk spells ruin, so we are extra careful. When we make this cake or meringues, we separate the eggs with a three-bowl method. Should a yolk break, it won't spoil the entire bowl of whites.

1. Crack the egg over the first bowl and let the white fall into the bowl.

2. Drop the yolk into the second bowl.

3. Pour the whites from the first bowl into the third bowl, and repeat the entire process.

Salt Your Vegetables

Here at the test kitchen, we sometimes instruct you to salt vegetables before you make salsas, coleslaws, salads, and certain other dishes. We aren't just making extra work. Salting draws moisture from plant cell walls to the outside of the vegetables (vegetables are 75 percent to 90 percent water). In recipes where, say, watery tomatoes would mar the results, salting is an easy, handy fix. With some of the moisture gone, the texture of the vegetables improves: Cabbage becomes crunchier, cucumbers crisper, and eggplant firmer and meatier.

We toss cut vegetables with ½ to 1 teaspoon of table salt for each pound of vegetables and drain them in a colander for at least 30 minutes. Then we sandwich the vegetables between paper towels and press on them or spin them in a salad spinner until they're dry. Salting vegetables can—no surprise—make them taste slightly salty. If you plan to dress them with a salty condiment like mayonnaise or soy sauce, rinse them under cold running water (to wash away any salt on the surface), then dry. Say what? Won't the vegetables absorb all the water you just worked to get rid of? No, they won't. Salting vegetables draws out water from the interior (the salt actually penetrates the cell walls of the vegetables). Vegetables rinsed under running water will not absorb moisture, and they can be easily dried before cooking.

When Is Your Steak Done?

Judging whether red meat is done is not an exact science, even with an instant-read thermometer. That's because as meat rests, the temperature continues to climb. We recommend pulling our **Char-Grilled Steak** (page 11) off the grill just before it reaches the desired temperature. Hold the steak with tongs and insert the thermometer through the side of the meat. Use the chart below to know when to take your steak off the grill. Let the cooked steaks rest on a platter—covered loosely with foil to keep them warm—for 5 minutes so the juices can distribute evenly.

	RARE	MEDIUM-RARE	MEDIUM
PULL THE STEAK	120	125	135
SERVING TEMPERATURE	125	130	140

Gadgets & Gear Grilling

There's more to grilling than just heading out to the backyard to turn on the gas grill (and drink a beer). Before you get started, here are a few must-haves.

GRILL BRUSH

The wire bristles on a standard grill brush work well removing gunk from the grates—for a few weeks. But we've found that after several uses the bristles wear down and the brush is useless. Our favorite is the Grill Wizard, which replaces bristles with a sturdier stainless steel "scrubby pad."

★ **TEST KITCHEN WINNER**
GRILL WIZARD BBQ Brush, $12.99

LONG-HANDLED TONGS

To stay as far away as possible from the hot fire yet still maintain control, we use long-handled grilling tongs. Look for sturdy tongs that are at least 12 inches long with nonslip handles and scalloped—not serrated—pincers.

★ **TEST KITCHEN WINNER**
OXO 16-inch Stainless Steel Kitchen Tongs, $13.95

GRILL SPATULA

The defining characteristic of a grill spatula is a few extra inches of handle to keep the cook's hand safely away from the heat—look for handles at least 12 inches long. We don't love our winning model's chintzy grill scraper, but do like the wide surface and the built-in bottle opener.

★ **TEST KITCHEN WINNER**
CHARCOAL COMPANION'S Mr. BBQ 4-in-1 Spatula, $9.95

INSTANT-READ THERMOMETER

We take the guesswork out of grilling by using an instant-read thermometer to check the temperature of grilled meats. A large digital face, accurate reading, and long probe are essential.

★ **TEST KITCHEN WINNER**
MAVERICK Redi-Check Professional Chef's Digital Thermometer, DT-01, $12.99

BASTING BRUSH

The worst basting brushes are nearly impossible to clean and leave bristles behind on your dinner. We like silicone brushes, which clean up easily and don't lose bristles. Look for long (8 to 12 inches) rubber or plastic handles, which keep heat at bay.

★ **TEST KITCHEN WINNER**
ELIZABETH KARMEL'S GRILL FRIENDS Super Silicone Angled BBQ Basting Brush, $9.95

Looking for a Recipe

READER TO READER

Did you misplace a favorite recipe? Can you almost taste a chocolate cake from childhood, but the bakery—and the recipe—is long gone? Ask a reader. While you're at it, answer a reader. Visit the *Cook's Country* website to both post your requests and answer those of fellow readers. Go to **CooksCountry.com** and click on **Looking for a Recipe**. We'll share all your submissions on the website (check it out—hundreds are already posted!) and print as many as we can fit in the magazine (see recipes at right). You may also write to us at Looking for a Recipe, Cook's Country, P.O. Box 470739, Brookline, MA 02447. Please include your name and mailing address with each request.

Gottlieb's Chewy Chocolate Cookie
Kathy Haspel, Los Angeles, Calif.

I'm looking for a recipe for a chewy chocolate cookie that I used to get at Gottlieb's Bakery in Hilton Head Island, S.C. Unfortunately, the bakery has closed. If anyone knows the recipe, please let me know.

Cheesy Pickle Meatloaf
Christine Tufts, Boise, Idaho

This recipe appeared in a magazine in the mid-1980s and made the best meatloaf I've ever had. It may have been part of a Vlasic pickle advertisement since it called for pickles. I also remember that Monterey Jack cheese was mixed into the meat. I can't believe I lost the recipe, but I would be so grateful if someone else had it!

Mincemeat Cookies
Karen Lester, Philadelphia, Pa.

When I was a child, every Christmas I would help my mom make sugar cookies filled with mincemeat. She didn't actually care for them but knew that they were my dad's favorite. Mom doesn't bake anymore, but I sure would love to make these cookies for Dad. Does anyone have a similar recipe?

Strickland's Pecan Pie
John Sides, St. Louis, Mo.

I'm looking for a recipe for a pecan pie I had at Strickland's in Jacksonville, Fla., in 1976. Unlike other pecan pies, it didn't have a sugary, gooey layer, just nuts and a small amount of sugar. The restaurant wouldn't give me the recipe, and I've never been able to figure out how the filling held together. It was truly delicious.

Pumpkin-Pecan Bread Pudding
Anne Williams, Danville, Va.

I recently saw (but forgot to set aside) a recipe for a Pumpkin-Pecan Bread Pudding. The custard mixture included pureed pumpkin and chopped pecans. Also, the recipe called for croissants instead of bread and was baked in a loaf pan, sitting in a water bath. Sound familiar?

Rouladen
Lacy Peterson, Dallas, Texas

I recently received a quarter of a cow so I have a lot of round steak on hand. I discussed different recipes that call for round steak with my mother, and she mentioned stuffed and rolled thin strips of beef called Rouladen. It sounds like something I would like to try. Does anyone have a recipe that is worth giving a shot? Thank you!

Vermont Common Cracker
Rebecca Killough, Grand Isle, Vt.

I've only lived in Vermont for five years, and before that I'd never tasted (or even heard of) a Vermont common cracker. Now, of course, my husband and I are addicted to them. I've searched the Internet but I can't find a reliable-looking recipe for them. Any suggestions?

Banana Salad
Tammy Mason-Bailey, Hillsboro, Ohio

My great aunt used to make a banana salad in the late 1960s with finely chopped nuts, banana pudding, and bananas, but I know there were a few other ingredients that I am forgetting. I would love to know what I am missing. Thank you and happy eating.

Coconut Rice Krispies Balls
Wendy C. Griffin, Bonney Lake, Wash.

My grandmother used to make a cookie at Christmas that had Rice Krispies and dates in the dough. I remember that they were rolled in coconut before they were baked. For the last 10 years, she has been ill and unable to make them. Unfortunately, I can't find the recipe. I would love to make the cookies for her, because I know they would bring back happy memories for both of us. Please help me find this recipe.

Gina Lollobrigida's Kebabs
Carol Snowden, Ellensburg, Wash.

I'm looking for a recipe that appeared in a women's magazine during the 1960s. It was actress Gina Lollobrigida's recipe for a shish kebab marinade. I've lost the recipe and can only remember that it called for Worcestershire sauce and bay leaves.

FIND THE ROOSTER!

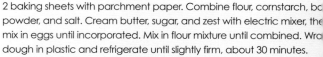

A tiny version of this rooster has been hidden somewhere in the pages of this issue. If you find it, write to us with its location (plus your name and address), and you will be entered into a random drawing. The first correct entry drawn will receive a FoodSaver V2240 (the "best buy" vacuum sealer from this issue), and the next five will each receive a complimentary one-year subscription to *Cook's Country*. To enter the contest, visit **CooksCountry.com/emailus**, or write to us at Rooster, Cook's Country, P.O. Box 470739, Brookline, MA 02447. Entries are due by September 30, 2009.

Did you find the rooster in the April/May 2009 issue? It was hidden in the Sweet and Sour Broccoli Rabe photo on page 22. Clare Moss of Locust Fork, Alabama, spotted it and won a Michael Graves Design Hamilton Beach 4-Slice Toaster.

Readers to the Rescue

MIDNIGHT CAKE Serves 16
Julie Stone, San Diego, Calif.

"I used to make this cake with my grandmother, and it was the recipe I added to the recipe box I began compiling in grade sch... The recipe uses mayonnaise in place of eggs and butter (or oil) cocoa instead of chocolate; it doesn't require a mixer. For all reasons, it's very easy to make. Avoid Dutch-processed cocoa po... here. Dust with confectioners' sugar to serve.

- 2 cups all-purpose flour
- ¼ cup cocoa powder
- 2 teaspoons baking soda
- 1 cup mayonnaise
- 1 cup sugar
- 1 teaspoon vanilla extract
- 1 cup water

1. Adjust oven rack to middle position and heat oven to 350 degrees. Grease and flour 13- by 9-inch baking pan. Combine flour, cocoa, and baking soda. Whisk mayonnaise, sugar, and vanilla until smooth. Whisk flour mixture into mayonnaise mixture in 3 additions, alternating with 2 additions of water, until incorporated.

2. Scrape batter into prepared pan and bake until toothpick inserted in center comes out with few crumbs attached, about 25 minutes. Cool on wire rack. (Cake can be wrapped in plastic and stored at room temperature for 2 days.)

ALFAJORES Makes about 1½ dozen cookies
Adriana Milner, Brussels, Belgium

"I found this recipe in an Argentinean newspaper about 40 years and I've kept my handwritten copy all this time. This version has a h... ratio of flour to cornstarch than other recipes so it has a slightly c... texture." Dulce de leche, a Latin American caramel of sorts, is so... the baking aisle of most supermarkets.

- 2 cups all-purpose flour
- 1 cup cornstarch
- 1 tablespoon baking powder
  Pinch salt
- 14 tablespoons (1¾ sticks) unsalted butter, softened
- 1 cup sugar
- 1 tablespoon grated lemon zest
- 2 large eggs
- 1¼ cups dulce de leche (see note)
- 1 cup sweetened shredded coconut, toasted

1. Adjust oven racks to upper-middle and lower-middle positions and heat oven to 375 degrees. Line 2 baking sheets with parchment paper. Combine flour, cornstarch, b... powder, and salt. Cream butter, sugar, and zest with electric mixer, the... mix in eggs until incorporated. Mix in flour mixture until combined. Wra... dough in plastic and refrigerate until slightly firm, about 30 minutes.

2. Roll level tablespoons of dough into balls. Place balls 2 inche... apart on prepared baking sheets. Bake until edges are just golden... about 12 minutes, switching and rotating sheets once. Cool 5 minu... on sheets, then transfer cookies to wire rack to cool completely. Repeat with remaining dough.

3. Spread 1 tablespoon dulce de leche on half of cookie botto... Top with remaining cookies to form sandwiches. Roll sides of cooki... coconut. Serve. (Cookies can be stored in airtight container at roo... temperature for 3 days.)

Peach Melba Ice Cream Cake

This frozen interpretation of the legendary French dessert, peach Melba, combines fresh peach puree, ice cream, and raspberry sorbet with a decorative layer of sliced raspberry jellyroll cake.

To make this cake you will need:

- 1 **pint raspberry sorbet**
- 1½ **pounds ripe peaches, peeled, pitted, and chopped**
- ⅓ **cup sugar**
- 1 **raspberry jellyroll cake, cut into ¾-inch-thick slices ***
- 2 **pints peach or vanilla ice cream**

* Go to **CooksCountry.com** for our Easy Jellyroll Cake or use your favorite recipe. If using a store-bought cake, buy one that is at least 10 inches long.

For the sorbet: Line 1-quart bowl with plastic wrap, letting ends of wrap overhang bowl. Scoop sorbet into large bowl and mash with wooden spoon until softened. Scrape sorbet into prepared 1-quart bowl and smooth top. Wrap with plastic wrap and freeze until firm, at least 3 hours.

For the peach puree: Cook peaches and sugar in large skillet over medium heat until peaches begin to break down and liquid has evaporated, about 8 minutes. Let cool slightly, then puree in food processor until smooth. Refrigerate until cold, about 30 minutes.

To assemble: Line 3-quart bowl with plastic wrap, letting ends of wrap overhang bowl. Line bowl with cake slices, packing gently to ensure there are no spaces between slices. Scoop ice cream into large bowl and mash with wooden spoon until softened. Stir in peach puree, then scrape into cake-lined bowl. Working quickly, unmold sorbet, discard plastic, and press into ice cream mixture until flush with level of ice cream. Wrap with plastic and freeze until completely firm, about 6 hours (or up to 1 week). Unmold and discard plastic. Let sit at room temperature for 5 minutes before slicing and serving.

Recipe Index

RC = Recipe Card

Cook's Country

OCTOBER/NOVEMBER 2009

America's Best Lost Suppers
$10,000 Prize-Winning Recipe

Roast Turkey 101
Perfect Bird Guaranteed

Manicotti with Meat Sauce
Start with No-Boil Noodles

Hearty Breakfast Casserole
Wake and Bake!

Old-Fashioned Pecan Pie
Corn Syrup Sent Packing

Soft & Chewy Rolls
Spuds Add Tenderness

Sausage-Cornbread Dressing
Simple, and from Scratch

Rating Chicken Noodle Soup
We're Sticking with Mom's

Best Garlic Bread
Slice, Then Bake

Baked Apple Dumplings
New Classic for 21st Century

Sloppy Joes Makeover
Keep the Beef, Not the Fat

Watch Our Show on TV
Cook's Country from America's Test Kitchen is back. Watch our second season on public television for the foolproof recipes and reliable results you've come to count on. From Old-Fashioned Roast Beef with Gravy to Tunnel of Fudge Cake, we make classic American food easy. To learn when the show airs on your station, go to **CooksCountryTV.com**.

$4.95 U.S./$6.95 CANADA

0 74470 05251 7

1 1>

Cook's Country

Dear Country Cook,

My wife and I still have a range just like the one in the photo below. It was a family hand-me-down that is now used only occasionally, but it is a constant, friendly reminder that great food often comes from small, frugal kitchens. In fact, the charm of American cooking is its thrifty beginnings, when preserving food was more important than cooking it, when fireplaces were both ovens and stovetops, and when food was seasonal, local, and expensive. Everything in a pig was used, as the saying goes, except the squeal.

I remember the first time I walked into Julia Child's kitchen in Cambridge in the early 1980s. Her husband, Paul, had put up Peg-Board, painted it white, and then used a black marker to outline all the pots and pans that hung there so they would always be put back correctly—hardly the sort of kitchen decoration promoted in fancy magazines. The center of the room contained a dining table with a plastic tablecloth: This is where the great Julia Child usually entertained. It was small, intimate, and well-used.

As Lord Byron once wrote, "Much Depends on Dinner," and meeting that necessity by making do, by using one's hands to produce something that matters, is the joy of cooking. Don't let anyone tell you that "the easier the better" is the secret of life; that road leads straight to perdition. Name one American or personal hero who took the easy road. Thought you couldn't!

So here's to all of you who may not have the most expensive cookware, the latest ovens, or the biggest kitchens. You make do and you are better cooks for it. You know that more depends on you, the cook, than the cookware. Good home cooking may, in the end, be the final triumph of man over machine.

Christopher Kimball
Founder and Editor, Cook's Country Magazine

Cook's Country

Founder and Editor Christopher Kimball
Editorial Director Jack Bishop
Executive Editor Peggy Grodinsky
Deputy Editor Bridget Lancaster
Senior Editors Scott Kathan,
Lisa McManus, Jeremy Sauer
Test Kitchen Director Erin McMurrer
Associate Editors Cali Rich, Diane Unger
Test Cooks Lynn Clark, Kris Widican
Assistant Editors Meredith Butcher, Peggy Chung Collier
Assistant Test Cooks Meghan Erwin
Maria del Mar Sacasa
Assistant Test Kitchen Director Matthew Herron
Copy Editor Amy Graves
Editorial Assistant Abbey Becker
Executive Assistant Meredith Smith
Senior Kitchen Assistant Nadia Domeq
Kitchen Assistants Maria Elena Delgado, Ena Gudiel
TV Producer Melissa Baldino
Contributing Editors Erika Bruce, Eva Katz
Consulting Editor Meg Ragland
Science Editor Guy Crosby, Ph.D

Online Managing Editor David Tytell
Online Editor Kate Mason
Online Editorial Assistant Mari Levine

Design Director Amy Klee
Art Director, Magazines Julie Bozzo
Designers, Magazines Jay Layman, Lindsey Timko
Deputy Art Director, Marketing and Web Christine Vo
Staff Photographer Daniel J. van Ackere

Director, Information Technology Rocco Lombardo
Lead Developer Scott Thompson
Web Developer Robert Martinez
Web Production Coordinator Evan Davis
Web Production Assistant Jennifer Millet
Systems Administrator S. Paddi McHugh
IT Support Technician Brandon Lynch

Production Director Guy Rochford
Traffic & Projects Manager Alice Carpenter
Traffic & Production Coordinator Laura Collins
Production & Imaging Specialists
Judy Blomquist, Lauren Pettapiece
Color & Imaging Specialist Andrew Mannone

Vice President Marketing David Mack
Circulation Director Doug Wicinski
Fulfillment & Circulation Manager Carrie Horan
Partnership Marketing Manager Pamela Putprush
Marketing Assistant Megan DeFilippo
Direct Mail Director Adam Perry
Senior Database Analyst Marina Sakharova
Products Director Steven Browall
Product Promotions Director Randi Lawrence
E-Commerce Marketing Director Hugh Buchan
E-Commerce Marketing Manager Laurel Zeidman
E-Commerce Search Manager Elizabeth Dillon
E-Commerce Marketing Coordinator Tia Freeman
Marketing Copywriter David Goldberg
Customer Service Manager Jacqueline Valerio
Customer Service Representatives
Jillian Nannicelli, Kate Sokol

Chief Financial Officer Sharyn Chabot
Human Resources Director Adele Shapiro
Controller Mandy Shito
Senior Accountant Aaron Goranson
Staff Accountant Connie Forbes
Accounts Payable Specialist Steven Kasha
Office Manager Tasha Bere
Receptionist Henrietta Murray

Sponsorship Sales Director Marcy McCreary
Retail Sales & Marketing Manager Emily Logan
Corporate Marketing Associate Bailey Vatalaro
Publicity Deborah Broide

COLOR FOOD PHOTOGRAPHY: Keller + Keller
STYLING: Mary Jane Sawyer
ON THE COVER: Sage, Devereux Imagery

ILLUSTRATION: Ross MacDonald
Greg Stevenson (cover illustration)

ook's Country magazine (ISSN 1552-1990), number 29,
ublished bimonthly by Boston Common Press Limited
tnership, 17 Station Street, Brookline, MA 02445.
pyright 2009 Boston Common Press Limited Partnership.
iodicals Postage paid at Boston, Mass., and additional
iling offices. Publications Mail Agreement No. 40020778.
urn undeliverable Canadian addresses to P.O. Box
, Station A, Windsor, Ontario N9A 6P2. POSTMASTER:
d address changes to Cook's Country, P.O. Box
2, Red Oak, IA 51591-1382. Customer Service: It's
sy to subscribe, give a gift subscription, change your
dress, and manage your subscription online. Visit www.
ericastestkitchen.com/customerservice for all of your
tomer service needs or write to us at Cook's Country,
. Box 8382, Red Oak, IA 51591-1382. PRINTED IN THE USA

OCTOBER/NOVEMBER 2009

Contents

GRANDMA WOOLY'S BEEF BARBECUE, 26

CRANBERRY SAUCE, 7

SWEET POTATO CASSEROLE, 10

Features

In Every Issue

A Taste of American Cooking

In response to our contest, you sent us more than 1,000 heirloom recipes. Each told a story about family suppers past and present, and together they wove a tapestry of American eating over the past century. You'll find our five prize-winners, including our $10,000 Grand Prize Winner, starting on page 24. Many more of your recipes were too good to keep to ourselves. We collected more than 100, put them through their paces in the test kitchen, and have published them in our newest cookbook, *Cook's Country Best Lost Suppers*. Pick up a copy at bookstores nationwide or visit our online bookstore at **CooksCountry.com.**

America's Test Kitchen is a 2,500-square-foot kitchen located just outside of Boston. It is the home of *Cook's Country* and *Cook's Illustrated* magazines and is the workday destination for more than three dozen test cooks, editors, and cookware specialists. Our mission is to test recipes until we understand how and why they work and arrive at the best version. We also test kitchen equipment and supermarket ingredients in search of brands that offer the best value and performance. You can watch us work by tuning in to *Cook's Country from America's Test Kitchen* (CooksCountryTV.com) and *America's Test Kitchen* (AmericasTestKitchen.com) on public television.

Kitchen Shortcuts

BETTER BAKING
Grease Is the Word
Jennifer English, Manchester, N.H.

It used to be that whenever I made bread in my mixer using the dough hook, the dough would climb the hook and never get properly kneaded. Recently I figured out a neat trick: I grease the mixer's dough hook very lightly with cooking spray before I begin.

TIME SAVER
Easy-Bake Potatoes
Serena Brown, Medford, Mass.

For me, an hour is too long to wait for a baked potato. To bake potatoes fast, I used to "bake" them in the microwave, first pricking them all over with a fork. They were quick, all right, but the skin was soggy. Then I got the idea to toast them. After the potatoes come out of the microwave, I place them in the toaster oven for one cycle of toast on high (or brownest). The insides are fluffy and tender, and the skin crisps up as though I'd baked them in the oven the entire time.

DOUBLE DUTY
Handle with Care
Louise Wood, Highlands Ranch, Colo.

At this time of year, my wine glasses make frequent appearances at holiday parties and such. I used to stress about washing them, as they're so fragile, until I figured out a nifty way to protect them. I line my stainless steel sink with a silicone baking mat before I begin washing. It provides a cushion to keep my fine glassware from shattering.

HANDY TIP
Old News, New Use
Ruth Hallows, Mesa, Ariz.

Paper towels are among my favorite tools in the kitchen, but I don't like to waste them. When I need to drain food over paper towels (fried chicken, doughnuts), I first place a thick layer of newspaper on a baking sheet, then lay one or two paper towels over the newspapers. I'm not only saving towels, I'm recycling papers.

DOUBLE DUTY
Avoiding an Oil Spill
Judith Shea, Chardon, Ohio

I often brown roasts on the stovetop in my cast-iron skillet before transferring them to the oven to cook through. To avoid grease or oil splattering all over the stovetop, I place a large metal colander upside down over the skillet. The holes let the steam escape, and the domed shape of the colander has room for the height of the roast. Easy cleanup makes me a happy cook!

KITCHEN EFFICIENCY
Easy Butter Dot
Judy Burke, Peterborough, N.H.

When you need to "dot" butter on a casserole, a cobbler, or baked fish, gently slide a cheese plane along the length of a frozen stick of butter to get a nice thin strip of butter. It's easy to break that strip into pieces to "dot" the top of whatever you're baking.

HANDY TIP
Sharp Shears
Frederick Earl, Seattle, Wash.

Few things are more frustrating than trying to cut with dull scissors. To give scissors a sharper edge, fold a piece of aluminum foil three or four times and cut through it a few times. I'm not sure why, but it works!

HANDY TIP
For Polishing, Think Condiment
Cheryl Locke, San Francisco, Calif.

I'd rather not use chemical cleaners to polish my silver. Luckily, I found I could do the job just as well with Worcestershire sauce. Remarkably, it actually works as a cleaner! I use a soft cloth to rub the Worcestershire on silverware or silver serving platters, then I rinse and dry them thoroughly. They look just like new.

EASY CLEANUP
An Oven Cleaner Worth Its Salt
Eduardo Canto, Coral Gables, Fla.

When I have a greasy oven spill, I carefully pour table salt over it while the oven is still hot and let the salt absorb the mess. Once the oven has cooled, I scoop up the salt (and the mess) with a spatula. A clean oven again!

Ask Cook's Country

Does flour stored in the freezer make yeast doughs rise more slowly?
Jenna Rounds, Watertown, Mass.

To find out, we made two batches of bread dough: one with room-temperature flour (70 degrees) and one with flour from the freezer (15 degrees). We placed both doughs in a warm place, monitoring their temperatures for an hour while they rose. The batch made with room-temperature flour was consistently about 10 degrees warmer, and it doubled about 30 minutes faster. The doughs even looked different. The room-temperature batch was soft, light, and airy during the initial 40 minutes of rise; the frozen flour batch appeared firm and taut.

We suggest that if you store your flour in the freezer, bring it to room temperature before you make your dough. To save time, you can microwave it at 10-second intervals, stirring after each stint. It took us just 20 seconds to warm up 2 cups of flour.

THE BOTTOM LINE: Bring frozen flour to room temperature before using or be patient while your dough slowly rises.

COLD FLOUR
Impeded rise

ROOM-TEMPERATURE FLOUR
High rise

When making gravy, should the broth I add to the roux be hot?
Michael Zimmer, Marco Island, Fla.

Roux, a mixture of flour and fat, is used to thicken gravy. After the roux has cooked for a few minutes into a paste, broth is gradually whisked in. It used to be said that the broth must be cold or the gravy will turn out lumpy. We made three gravies, one with gently simmering broth, one with room-temperature broth, and one with cold broth. Adding the warm broth shaved a few minutes off the cooking time, but there was no discernible difference in quality. Do, however, add the liquid gradually, whisk consistently, and always whisk out any lumps before adding more liquid.

THE BOTTOM LINE: Hot broth is quicker but doesn't make a better roux.

Is using a rolling pin cover and pastry cloth to roll out dough better than dusting a counter with flour?
Sue Emerson, West Friendship, Md.

Yes and no. Rolling pin covers are usually made from stretchy cotton and fit snugly around rolling pins. They protect the pins from nicks during storage and keep dough from sticking—or so it's said. Pastry cloths, which are made from heavy, durable materials like canvas, go on the counter. The idea is that because these coverings absorb excess flour, they prevent the dough from sticking.

We rolled out pizza and pie doughs with both a flour-dusted rolling pin cover and pastry cloth and a floured rolling pin on a counter liberally sprinkled with flour (lifting the dough and reflouring the surface as needed). Both methods worked equally well.

The upside: In a hot kitchen, pastry cloths allow easy transfer of dough from countertop to refrigerator and keep counters and tables clean. The downside: Manufacturers recommend that pastry cloths and covers be washed between uses to avoid picking up off-flavors from traces of fat left on the cover and cloth.

THE BOTTOM LINE: While pastry covers and cloths may save on countertop cleanup, they don't help with the laundry.

Can I use arrowroot in place of cornstarch?
Kiri Miller, Providence, R.I.

Arrowroot is both a tropical plant and the name of the edible starch that comes from it. It's used to thicken sauces and salad dressings, and when pastry chefs want crystal-clear candies and sauces (cornstarch makes them cloudy). Both starches need to come to a boil (or near boil for arrowroot) for their thickening power to kick in. Almost 1½ teaspoons of arrowroot thickens the same amount of liquid as 1 teaspoon cornstarch.

We substituted arrowroot for cornstarch in three of our recipes: General Tso's Chicken, Mile-High Lemon Meringue Pie, and Butterscotch Pudding. The arrowroot performed about as well as cornstarch as a coating for the chicken, and some tasters liked its sweet flavor better than that of "chalkier" cornstarch. The arrowroot also made for a clearer pie filling. In the pudding, however, tasters described it as slimy. Our science editor explained that arrowroot forms a "mucilaginous substance" when combined with liquid, an effect that may be exaggerated when the liquid is dairy.

THE BOTTOM LINE: Arrowroot costs more than cornstarch, so save it for translucent sauces and fillings and avoid it in recipes with dairy.

I've read that celery leaves have more flavor than the stalks. True?
Jimmy Demer, Atlanta, Ga.

To compare the two, we tasted stalks and leaves by themselves as well as in our recipe for Waldorf Salad with chicken and in a creamy celery soup, substituting an equal measure of leaves for some of the chopped stalks. On their own, the leaves tasted stronger than the stalks, "grassy" and "slightly metallic," according to tasters, and on occasion quite bitter. Naturally, if used raw, the leaves change the texture of dishes. The difference in flavor is subtle at best.

THE BOTTOM LINE: As long as you've got them, go ahead and toss the leaves in. But taste first in case they're bitter.

LEAF IT ON
Leaves enhance the flavor of celery slightly in some recipes.

Do the new shortenings without trans fats work as well as the old ones for pie crust?
Leslie Munson, Ashland, Va.

Shortenings tenderize and create an appealing crumbly, flaky texture in baked goods, especially pie doughs. They are semisolid fats at room temperature and melt into liquid oil when heated. Until recently, some brands contained an unhealthy type of fat known as trans fat, a byproduct of the process (partial hydrogenation) that was used to make the oil solid.

In response to public concern, manufacturers such as Crisco reformulated their product to get rid of trans fats. Others came out with new types of shortening that never had trans fat in the first place—Spectrum Naturals Organic All Vegetable Shortening, for one, which is made with palm oil.

We made batches of our double-crust pie dough with the Crisco and with the Spectrum shortening. We used them for pecan pies and also baked them unfilled. Some tasters found the Spectrum crusts slightly tougher and tasting faintly tropical. But without a side-by-side comparison, we doubt we could have told them apart. (Be aware, though, that experts continue to study the health impacts of these new formulations.)

THE BOTTOM LINE: Shortenings without trans fats work just fine in pie crusts.

Can you brine boneless chicken breasts, then freeze them for later?
Joyce Hegner, San Antonio, Texas

We brine chicken breasts both to season them and to help keep them moist during cooking. While considering your question, we began to ponder which is better: brine first, then freeze, or freeze first, then brine? To see, we brined, froze for two weeks, defrosted, and then cooked several boneless chicken breasts. We compared them with breasts we froze plain for the same two weeks, defrosted, and then brined and cooked. We pitted both of these frozen versions against chicken breasts that we freshly brined and cooked.

The result? There were slight textural differences, but all three were moist and juicy, and we'd happily use any in our cooking.

THE BOTTOM LINE: Go for it—brine and freeze. Or freeze, then brine.

My market sells several types of dried sage. Are they interchangeable?
A.F. Merrit, Wilmington, N.C.

The terms "whole," "rubbed," and "ground" refer to the processing of the sage plant. The leaves of whole sage are removed from the stem, dried, and packaged with minimal processing. Rubbed sage is made from dried, crumbled leaves, while ground sage may include both finely ground leaves and stems. We tried each of them in our recipes for Bread Stuffing, Crispy Bacon-Sage Pork Cutlets, and Sage-Vermouth Sauce.

In every recipe, the herb's distinctive woodsy flavor came through clearest when we used whole sage. Rubbed sage, slightly milder than whole leaves, was the runner-up. Ground sage was tasteless in the stuffing and pork cutlets, and it turned the sauce murky brown. To approximate the flavor of whole sage, increase the amount of rubbed sage by half.

THE BOTTOM LINE: Whole sage is best, rubbed is acceptable, but steer clear of ground sage.

SAGE SAMPLES
Whole leaves (above), rubbed (above right), and ground (right).

To ask us a cooking question, visit **CooksCountry.com/emailus.** You can also write to Ask Cook's Country, P.O. Box 470739, Brookline, MA 02447. Just try to stump us!

Brimming with fat and calories, this childhood favorite was due for a diet. But would a slimmed-down Sloppy Joe lose its charm? BY KRIS WIDICAN

Many "healthy" recipes try to fool you by replacing beef with odd ingredients such as tofu or wheat berries. We preferred sautéed mushrooms.

RECENTLY, I RAN into a friend from my past: good old Sloppy Joe, a childhood favorite. Biting through the squishy bun and the tangy, candy-sweet meat filling, orange grease staining my lips, I was 10 years old again. Too bad the nagging adult in me counted each one of the 570 calories and 30 grams of fat. Maybe it was time to put away childish things, but not before I tried giving Joe a makeover—and a second chance.

A Sloppy Joe gets its heft from onions browned with fatty ground beef; the mixture is then simmered in a high-calorie combo of ketchup, bottled chili sauce, and scoops of sugar. I started instead with low-calorie recipes I found in diet cookbooks and on the Web, which included a catalogue of nontraditional ingredients: chewy wheat berries, ground vegetable protein, tofu, and not a whit of sugar. My tasters didn't even recognize these sandwiches as Sloppy Joes. Most were too vegetal, and the imitation meat fooled no one. I changed course and reverted to the traditional recipe, hoping to cut calories where I could.

I began with the sauce. Instead of cups of ketchup, I was able to reduce the amount to ¼ cup, as long as I fortified it with either canned tomato sauce or puree

(tasters chose the former for its slightly sweeter edge). Sautéed minced onion and just a teaspoon of brown sugar (which has more robust flavor than granulated) added enough sweetness, and a teaspoon of cider vinegar gave the sauce its trademark tang.

Many recipes cut fat and calories by using ground chicken or turkey. I wanted to keep the beefy flavor, and after crunching the nutritional numbers was happy to find that 93 percent lean ground beef was comparable in calories and fat. But the

browned lean beef was chewy and tough. No matter how long I simmered it in the sauce, it never became tender. I ruled out browning and began testing when best to add the beef to the pan. Unexpectedly, I found that by stirring it into the cooked sauce and simmering the mixture for only minutes, the meat stayed very tender.

Although the Sloppy Joes were leaner, the pound of beef necessary for four sandwiches still pushed the nutritional numbers too high. Cutting back on the portion size (skimpy Joes?) was a no go, so I tried the time-honored technique of "stretching" the beef with various grains, like oatmeal and barley. Unfortunately, they gave the filling a weird, nutty taste and a slippery feel. Might mushrooms, which are often described as "meaty," work? Unlike the meat, these I browned; then I chopped them in the food processor to get the appearance and texture of ground meat. A few tests showed that I could switch out 6 ounces of the beef (which contains 260 calories and 12 grams of fat) with an equal amount of mushrooms (35 calories and zero fat!) before anyone caught on. Adding a splash of Worcestershire sauce to the tomato sauce boosted the sandwich's meaty flavor at the expense of only a few calories.

Tasters gave the thumbs-up to my overhauled Joes, which had mild spice, sweet tang, and a tender, almost dissolving texture—not to mention 270 fewer calories and about one-third the fat of the original sandwich. Skinny Joe never tasted so good.

KEY INGREDIENTS
Slimmer Sandwich Without Slimmer Flavor
Supplementing lean ground beef with browned white mushrooms gave us the same meaty flavor with fewer calories and less fat than traditional versions.

WHITE MUSHROOMS
Mushrooms have no fat and few calories. We browned, then ground them to bring out their beefy qualities.

LEAN BEEF
Ninety-three percent lean ground beef cuts the fat, but not the meatiness.

The Numbers
All nutritional information is for a single serving (including bun).

Traditional Sloppy Joe
CALORIES **570**
FAT **30g** • SATURATED FAT **10g**

Cook's Country Reduced-Fat Sloppy Joe
CALORIES **300**
FAT **9g** • SATURATED FAT **3g**

REDUCED-FAT SLOPPY JOES
Serves 4
If the mixture becomes too dry during cooking, add water a tablespoon at a time to reach the desired consistency.

- 2 teaspoons vegetable oil
- 6 ounces white mushrooms, sliced thin
- 1 small onion, minced
- 1¼ teaspoons chili powder
- 1 (8-ounce) can tomato sauce
- ¼ cup ketchup
- 1 tablespoon Worcestershire sauce
- 1 teaspoon brown sugar
- ¼ cup water
- 1 teaspoon cider vinegar
- 10 ounces 93 percent lean ground beef
  Salt and pepper
- 4 hamburger buns

1. PROCESS MUSHROOMS Heat 1 teaspoon oil over medium-high heat in large nonstick skillet until shimmering. Add mushrooms and cook until browned, about 5 minutes. Transfer to food processor and pulse until mushrooms are finely ground.

2. MAKE SAUCE Heat remaining oil in empty skillet over medium heat until shimmering. Cook onion and processed mushrooms, covered, stirring occasionally, until tender, 8 to 12 minutes. Stir in chili powder and cook until fragrant, about 30 seconds. Add tomato sauce, ketchup, Worcestershire, sugar, water, and vinegar. Simmer over medium-low heat until vegetables are completely tender and sauce is slightly thickened, about 15 minutes.

3. SIMMER BEEF Add beef and simmer, breaking up meat with wooden spoon, until no longer pink, about 5 minutes more. Season with salt and pepper. Divide mixture among buns. Serve.

Slow Cooker White Chicken Chili

By definition, chili equals heat and liveliness. The slow cooker sure put a damper on things.

BY MARÍA DEL MAR SACASA

WHITE CHILI is a simple yet flavorful stew of shredded chicken and white beans. It's spiked with vibrant, spicy green chiles and earthy spices like cumin and coriander, then finished with a shower of fresh cilantro. I figured it would make a good candidate for the slow cooker: The chicken would cook gradually and flavor the broth, the beans would turn creamy, and the chiles would lace the dish with heat.

Many slow-cooker recipes dump chicken, beans, canned green chiles, onions, garlic, spices, and chicken broth into the slow cooker and let it go for hours. This hands-off approach had ease in its favor, but not much else. I found the results to be more like soup than stew, and by the end of cooking, the dish had no chile flavor—or any flavor at all, no matter how potent the spices were at the start. I resigned myself to doing a little work up front, with the hope that the results would justify the effort.

I identified the best features of the recipes I'd tested and set out to combine them. First, I sautéed the onions, garlic, chiles, and spices before putting them in the slow cooker, a classic cooking technique that builds a foundation of flavor and did indeed give the chili some backbone. Canned green chiles were squishy, rubbery, and had zero heat—and that was before they had cooked for hours. Fresh jalapeños improved the stew considerably. To build another layer of flavor, I reserved some of the sauté to stir in at the end of cooking.

I'd been adding boneless, skinless chicken breasts directly to the slow cooker but suspected that bone-in, skin-on thighs would add deeper flavor, especially if I browned them first. I browned the chicken, then removed and discarded its skin and used the rendered fat to sauté the onion mixture. The chili was notably better—the dark-meat thighs held up better to the long cooking time and weren't in as much danger of drying out.

The flavor was much improved, but the texture remained problematic. In the test kitchen, we know from experience that slow cookers don't allow for evaporation, and so I cut back the chicken broth. I also upped the amount of beans, from the two cans used in many recipes to three cans. The chili was now significantly less soupy and became even better when I pureed one can of beans with some of the broth. The texture was good, but the flavor needed reinforcing.

The idea of corn crossed my mind, and after that there was no turning back. If you didn't grow up in the South or Southwest, you might not know about hominy. I had a hunch that hominy would puree nicely and add flavor, too. I emptied a can into the food processor with the beans. It made for a velvety-smooth chili base with a hearty note of toasted corn. Perfect.

To finish, I stirred in the usual cilantro and was about to add a squeeze of lime when I spied a jar of pickled jalapeños. I chopped a few tablespoons and stirred them in instead. They gave the chili just the right kick and sweetness.

We like to serve this warming chili with diced avocado and lime wedges.

STEP-BY-STEP Building Flavor

The slow cooker has a reputation for washing out flavors. Here's how we fight that.

1. Puree hominy (with beans and chicken broth) to give the broth heft, velvety texture, and subtle corn flavor.

2. Brown the chicken parts, then sauté onions, jalapeños, garlic, and spices in the rendered fat to add layers of flavor.

3. To brighten the flavors, stir in minced pickled jalapeños and half the sautéed aromatics just before serving.

SLOW-COOKER WHITE CHICKEN CHILI Serves 6 to 8

Four bone-in, skin-on split chicken breasts will work in place of the thighs.

- 3 (16-ounce) cans cannellini beans, drained and rinsed
- 1 (16-ounce) can white hominy, drained and rinsed
- 3 cups low-sodium chicken broth
  Salt and pepper
- 6 bone-in, skin-on chicken thighs (about 3 pounds, see note), fat trimmed
- 1 tablespoon vegetable oil
- 2 onions, chopped fine
- 4 jalapeño chiles, seeded and chopped fine
- 6 garlic cloves, minced
- 1½ tablespoons ground cumin
- 2 teaspoons ground coriander
- ¼ cup finely chopped fresh cilantro
- 2 tablespoons drained jarred pickled jalapeños, minced

1. BLEND BASE Puree 1 can beans, hominy, broth, and ¾ teaspoon salt in blender until completely smooth. Pour into slow cooker.

2. BROWN CHICKEN Pat chicken dry with paper towels and season with salt and pepper. Heat oil in large skillet over medium-high heat until just smoking. Cook thighs, skin-side down, until skin is well browned and fat has rendered, about 5 minutes. Remove and discard skin, then add thighs to slow cooker.

3. COOK AROMATICS Pour off all but 2 tablespoons fat from skillet. Cook onions, chiles, and ½ teaspoon salt until golden brown, stirring occasionally, about 8 minutes. Add garlic, cumin, and coriander and cook until fragrant, about 30 seconds. Transfer half of onion mixture to slow cooker; reserve remaining mixture in refrigerator.

4. FINISH CHILI Add remaining beans to slow cooker. Cover and cook on low until chicken is tender, about 4 hours. Transfer chicken to bowl. When cool enough to handle, discard bones and shred chicken into bite-sized pieces. Stir cilantro, pickled jalapeños, shredded chicken, and reserved onion mixture into slow cooker and let warm. Serve.

SECRET INGREDIENT **Hominy**
A can of pureed hominy (dried corn kernels soaked in lye or slaked lime to remove the hull and germ) added body and rich corn flavor that tasters loved.

Make Ahead Breakfast Casserole

All you have to do in the morning is pop this hearty casserole into a hot oven.

Breakfast casserole is convenient for a crowd, but if it's so bland and mushy no one wants to eat it, that's no help for the host. BY KRIS WIDICAN

ON BUSY MORNINGS when you have to feed a crowd, few things are easier than popping a breakfast casserole into the oven. The beauty of it is, of course, that you make it the day before—combining dried cubes of bread with browned sausage in a casserole dish, scattering that with cheese, pouring on eggs mixed with milk or cream, and letting it soak overnight. The next morning, the casserole bakes into puffy, golden, savory goodness.

Not so fast. The recipes I tried had a host of problems: Some were the texture of baby food, others tasted of little but sausage, and too many slanted toward heavy and greasy. I was looking for a flavorful breakfast casserole with a crisp top and a soft, custardy inside.

I tackled the texture first. Many recipes call for cubed white sandwich bread, but even when I gently staled the cubes in the oven first, the bread drank up too much custard and turned to mush after an overnight stay in the refrigerator. Sturdier Italian bread, sliced not cubed, held up better. I experimented with leaving the slices in the oven until they were toasted, not merely dry. The texture and flavor of the casserole improved.

Most recipes use a dozen eggs for casseroles made in 13- by 9-inch dishes, about right to meld with one loaf of sliced Italian bread. The 6 cups of milk or cream, however, was too much by far. Even the toasted bread practically dissolved in so much liquid. A few tests showed that 4 cups was ideal. In further side-by-side tests, tasters preferred whole milk to either cream or half-and-half; the latter were too heavy and rich. A glug of hot sauce added a touch of vinegary heat.

Recipes vary widely on the amounts of sausage and cheese they call for. To determine the right ratios for heft without heaviness, I subjected tasters to more breakfast casseroles than most people eat in a lifetime. When I used a lot of sausage, its seasoning tyrannized and the casserole was greasy; too little and it seemed like an afterthought. One pound of breakfast sausage, crumbled and browned with onion, struck the right balance. I wrested more flavor by using extra-sharp cheddar in place of the typical sharp cheddar.

Building the casserole with care helped ensure every bite had flavor: I shingled the bread in two layers, and layered the sausage-onion mixture and the cheese. But the casserole was dry in spots; the custard wasn't soaking in evenly. I tried wrapping the casserole with plastic wrap, then placed a spare baking dish—loaded with cans on top to compress it. Problem solved. Brunch was never so easy.

MAKE-AHEAD BREAKFAST CASSEROLE Serves 8 to 10

You can find unsliced loaves of Italian bread in the bakery section of your supermarket. Frank's RedHot is the test kitchen's top-rated hot sauce. If using a spicier sauce such as Tabasco, reduce amount to 1½ teaspoons.

- 1 (14-inch) loaf Italian bread (see note), ends trimmed
- 1 pound bulk pork sausage
- 1 small onion, chopped fine
- 3 cups shredded extra-sharp cheddar cheese
- 12 large eggs, lightly beaten
- 4 cups whole milk
- 1½ teaspoons salt
- 1 teaspoon pepper
- 1 tablespoon hot sauce (see note)

1. TOAST BREAD Adjust oven racks to upper-middle and lower-middle positions and heat oven to 400 degrees. Slice bread in half lengthwise, then slice each half crosswise into ½-inch-thick pieces. Spread bread in single layers on 2 rimmed baking sheets and bake until golden, 15 to 20 minutes, flipping bread and switching and rotating sheets halfway through. Let cool 15 minutes.

2. BROWN SAUSAGE Cook sausage in large skillet over medium heat until no longer pink, about 5 minutes. Add onion and cook until golden, about 5 minutes.

3. ASSEMBLE CASSEROLE Grease 13- by 9-inch baking dish. Shingle half of bread in prepared pan so that edges overlap slightly. Top with half of sausage mixture and 1 cup cheese. Repeat with remaining bread, remaining sausage mixture, and remaining cheese.

4. SOAK AND WEIGHT Whisk eggs, milk, salt, pepper, and hot sauce in large bowl. Pour evenly over casserole. Wrap casserole with plastic and weight according to photos below. Refrigerate for at least 1 hour and up to 24.

5. BAKE CASSEROLE Adjust oven rack to middle position and heat oven to 350 degrees. Let casserole stand at room temperature while oven is heating. Remove weights, unwrap casserole, and bake until the edges and center have puffed and top is golden brown, about 1 hour. Let cool 10 minutes. Serve.

BREAKFAST CASSEROLE WITH CHORIZO AND PEPPER JACK

Prepare Make-Ahead Breakfast Casserole, replacing bulk pork sausage with 1 pound chorizo sausage, halved lengthwise and sliced thin, and cheddar with 3 cups shredded pepper Jack cheese. In step 2, add ¼ cup chopped fresh cilantro to sausage mixture once it has been removed from heat.

BREAKFAST CASSEROLE WITH ITALIAN SAUSAGE AND FONTINA

Prepare Make-Ahead Breakfast Casserole, replacing bulk pork sausage with 1 pound hot or sweet Italian sausage, casings removed, and cheddar with 3 cups shredded Fontina cheese. In step 2, add ¼ cup chopped fresh basil to sausage mixture once it has been removed from heat.

TEST KITCHEN TECHNIQUE **Weight While You Wait**

To make sure the toasted bread fully absorbs the custard, we weight our casserole, first covering the assembled casserole with plastic wrap. Both of the following methods ensure a uniform casserole.

CANNED GOODS
Place a spare 13- by 9-inch pan on top of the wrapped casserole and set canned goods on top for extra weight.

BOXES OF BROTH
Haven't got a spare 13- by 9-inch pan? Wrap the casserole, then carefully place boxes of broth (or boxes of sugar) on top.

---

5 Easy Recipes Cranberry Sauce

Only 10 minutes stand between you and great homemade cranberry sauce. BY CALI RICH

FOR ALL THE PLANNING, preening, and preparation necessary to pull off the perfect Thanksgiving meal, we've never understood why so many hosts give up when they get to the cranberry sauce and just grab the can. Candy-sweet and jiggly, the canned cranberry sauce doesn't taste like cranberries. Real cranberry sauce, on the other hand, is soft and jammy, tart and sweet, and a gorgeous glistening ruby-red. Amazingly, it's just 10 minutes of work, if that. In the test kitchen, we start with one bag of cranberries and a back-of-the-bag recipe, and with a few modest changes, we make it shine.

Most "bag" recipes simmer a 12-ounce bag of whole cranberries (both fresh and frozen work equally well) with 1 cup each granulated sugar and water. We agree—1 cup sugar balances the sour berry. But cranberries contain a lot of juice, and we find that the standard 1 cup water makes the sauce too loose. We use ¾ cup instead. Also, just a pinch of salt—an ingredient missing from most recipes—makes the cranberry flavor pop!

Speaking of popping, the best cranberry sauce features just-softened whole berries. Simmering the berries for 10 minutes, as the "bag" suggests, produces a mushy red mash. We reduce the simmering time by half. You'll know that the sauce has reached the right texture when most (but not all) of the berries have popped.

BASIC CRANBERRY SAUCE
Makes about 2 cups

Fresh and frozen cranberries work equally well. If you are using frozen, add one to two minutes to the cooking time.

- ¾ cup water
- 1 cup granulated sugar
- ¼ teaspoon salt
- 1 (12-ounce) bag cranberries (see note), picked through

Bring water, sugar, and salt to boil in medium saucepan over medium heat. Add cranberries and simmer until slightly thickened and two-thirds of berries have burst, about 5 minutes. Transfer to serving bowl and cool completely, at least 1 hour. Serve. (Sauce can be refrigerated for 1 week.)

APPLE-RAISIN CRANBERRY SAUCE
Slightly sweet apples such as Golden Delicious or Gala work best for this recipe. Shred the apple on the large holes of a box grater.

Prepare Basic Cranberry Sauce, replacing water with ¾ cup apple cider and granulated sugar with ¾ cup packed light brown sugar. Add 1 apple, peeled, cored, and shredded; ¼ cup golden raisins; and ¼ teaspoon ground cinnamon along with cranberries.

ORANGE-MAPLE CRANBERRY SAUCE
Go to CooksCountry.com to view our tips for easy citrus segmenting. Be sure to use real maple syrup, not the maple-flavored stuff.

Prepare Basic Cranberry Sauce, replacing water with ¾ cup orange juice and granulated sugar with ½ cup maple syrup. Add pinch of cayenne pepper along with cranberries. After transferring sauce to serving bowl, stir in 1 orange, peeled, segmented, and chopped.

PEAR-GINGER CRANBERRY SAUCE
Ginger ale can be substituted for the ginger beer, though the ginger flavor will be less pronounced.

Prepare Basic Cranberry Sauce, replacing water with ¾ cup ginger beer and reducing granulated sugar to ¾ cup. Add 1 firm pear, peeled, cored, and shredded, and 1 teaspoon grated fresh ginger along with cranberries.

RASPBERRY-LEMON CRANBERRY SAUCE
Fresh or thawed frozen raspberries can be used in this recipe. Sprite and 7UP are both good soda choices here. Don't use diet soda.

Prepare Basic Cranberry Sauce, replacing water with ¾ cup lemon-lime soda and reducing granulated sugar to ¾ cup. After transferring sauce to serving bowl, stir in 1 cup raspberries and ½ teaspoon grated lemon zest.

Looks a lot prettier than the canned stuff, right? It tastes better, too.

FIVE EASY RECIPES FOR LEFTOVERS
Our recipe for Cranberry Sauce is a jack-of-all-trades. With a little doctoring, it's equally at home on a salad, in a sandwich, on grilled pork or chicken, or drizzled over ice cream. Here are five simple stir-in recipes to transform your leftover cranberry sauce into something new and surprising. Not to mention delicious.

TO MAKE CRANBERRY VINAIGRETTE: Whisk 1 minced shallot, 1 tablespoon Dijon mustard, ¼ cup red wine vinegar, and ⅓ cup olive oil into ½ cup of leftover cranberry sauce. Season with salt and pepper and use to dress green salads or try it drizzled over steamed green beans or Brussels sprouts.

TO MAKE SPICY CRANBERRY MUSTARD: Whisk 2 tablespoons dry mustard, 2 tablespoons Dijon mustard, and 2 teaspoons white vinegar into ½ cup of leftover cranberry sauce. Serve with sausages, on sandwiches, or as a dipping sauce for soft pretzels.

TO MAKE TANGY CRANBERRY SANDWICH SPREAD: Whisk ½ cup mayonnaise, 2 tablespoons Dijon mustard, and 2 tablespoons honey into ½ cup of leftover cranberry sauce. This spread will inject new life into leftover-turkey sandwiches. Or try it with sharp cheddar on a grilled cheese sandwich.

TO MAKE CRANBERRY BBQ SAUCE: Whisk 6 tablespoons ketchup, 3 tablespoons cider vinegar, ¼ teaspoon salt, 2 tablespoons brown sugar, ½ teaspoon pepper, ⅛ teaspoon cayenne pepper, and ⅛ teaspoon liquid smoke into ½ cup of leftover cranberry sauce. Brush on grilled chicken, pork, or beef during the last few minutes of grilling or serve as a dipping sauce.

TO MAKE CRANBERRY-ORANGE DESSERT SAUCE: Whisk ¼ cup orange juice concentrate, 3 tablespoons honey, and 1 tablespoon orange liqueur into ½ cup of leftover cranberry sauce. Drizzle over ice cream or cake, or use to fill thumbprint cookies.

Turkey 101

This year, we went back to basics. No herb swirl, no cheesecloth soak, no flavored butter under the skin. Nothing but a big ol' buttered bird. BY LYNN CLARK

Our foolproof cooking method ensures perfectly bronzed skin. And that's not all. It ensures perfectly cooked white and dark meat, too.

MOST OF US roast turkey just once a year, and for the next 364 days we get rusty, forgetting the basics of turkey cookery—assuming we knew them in the first place. The biggest challenge? The white and dark meat cook at different rates. If you can't figure out how to mesh the requirements of each, the lean breast meat will overcook long before the dark leg meat is done. Relax. In 15-plus years, the test kitchen has found a trick to solve that problem (see "Test Kitchen Technique: Learn to Turn" on page 9), and through obsessive testing, we've answered plenty of other turkey cooking questions, too. Following are seven of the most frequently asked—and most important—questions about roasting a turkey.

➤ What's the best way to thaw a frozen turkey?
Defrost the turkey in the refrigerator, calculating 1 day of defrosting for every 4 pounds of turkey. Say you're cooking a 12-pound turkey. The frozen bird should be placed in the refrigerator on Monday so that it's defrosted and ready to cook on Thanksgiving Day. If you plan on brining your bird the night before the big day (see question below), start thawing that 12-pound bird on Sunday.

➤ What if I don't thaw the turkey ahead of time?
Don't panic. You can still save the situation. Fill a large bucket with cold water. For a 12-pound bird, thaw the turkey (still in its original wrapper) in the bucket for 6 to 8 hours (or 30 minutes per pound). Change the cold water every half hour to guard against bacteria growth.

➤ How should I brine a turkey?
We sometimes brine turkey to make it moist and flavorful; for details on when, see "Shopping: Talking Turkey," page 9. Our overnight brine (12 to 14 hours) uses half a cup of table salt per gallon of cold water. For a quicker brine (4 to 6 hours), we use a whole cup of table salt

per gallon of water. Depending on the size of the bird and your brining bucket, you will need 2 to 3 gallons of water. Keep the turkey in the refrigerator while brining to keep it at a safe temperature. If your refrigerator is full, use a big cooler and ice packs. Don't leave the turkey in the brine longer than we suggest or it will be too salty. At the recommended hour, rinse off the salty water and pat the turkey dry with paper towels.

➤ Is it better to stuff the turkey or serve dressing?
In the test kitchen, we prefer to cook the stuffing, or dressing, separately. Cooking the stuffing inside the bird to a safe internal temperature takes too long: By the time the stuffing is safe to eat, the meat is overcooked. Instead we bake our

dressing in a dish alongside the turkey, or while the turkey rests. The crisp crust is an added bonus. Still, we recognize that every family has its own Thanksgiving traditions. If yours demands a stuffed bird, take the turkey out of the oven when the meat is done, scoop out the stuffing, and finish baking it in a dish while the turkey rests. Stuffing should reach a minimum temperature of 165 degrees.

➤ Do I need to truss the bird?
To prevent the legs from splaying open, which could make them cook unevenly, we tuck them into the pocket of skin at the tail end. Not all turkeys have such a pocket. If yours doesn't, simply tie the ankles together with kitchen twine. There is no need to fuss with trussing.

➤ What about basting?
Despite what you've been told, basting does nothing to moisten dry breast meat. The liquid simply runs off the turkey, meanwhile turning the skin chewy and leathery. Also basting requires that you incessantly open and close the oven, which means you won't be sitting down for Thanksgiving dinner anytime soon.

➤ Does the turkey really need to rest before I carve it?
Yes. Thirty minutes or so gives it time to reabsorb the meat juices; otherwise they'll dribble out when you slice, and the meat will be dry. Don't tent the turkey with foil to keep it warm while it's resting; it will make the skin soggy and is unnecessary. As long as the turkey is intact, it will cool quite slowly.

ROASTED TURKEY

Serves 10 to 22, depending on turkey size

If you are roasting a large (18- to 22-pound) bird and are reluctant to rotate it, don't line the V-rack with foil and roast the bird breast-side up for the full time, following the temperature guidelines in this recipe.

1 (12- to 22-pound) turkey, fully thawed if frozen, brined if desired (see page 8)
4 tablespoons unsalted butter, melted
Salt and pepper

1. PREPARE BIRD Adjust oven rack to lowest position and heat oven to 400 degrees (425 degrees if roasting 18- to 22-pound turkey). Remove neck and giblets from cavity and reserve for gravy (see page 30). Pat turkey dry with paper towels. Tuck legs into pocket of skin at tail end (alternatively, tie legs with kitchen twine) and tuck wings under bird.

2. BUTTER AND SEASON Line V-rack with foil and poke several holes in foil. Set rack inside large roasting pan and spray foil with cooking spray. Brush breast and legs of turkey with half of butter and season with salt and pepper. Arrange turkey, breast-side down, in rack. Brush remaining butter over back of turkey and season with salt and pepper. Roast turkey for 1 hour.

3. FLIP TURKEY Remove turkey from oven. (If roasting 18- to 22-pound turkey, reduce oven temperature to 325 degrees and do not flip.) Tip juices from cavity of turkey into pan. Using clean pot holders or kitchen towels, carefully flip turkey breast-side up. Roast until breast meat registers 160 degrees and thigh meat registers 175 degrees, 1 to 1½ hours (2 to 2½ hours for 18- to 22-pound turkey). Transfer to carving board and let rest, uncovered, for 30 minutes. Carve and serve.

For our Make-Ahead Turkey Gravy recipe, see Test Kitchen Cooking Class on page 30.

TEST KITCHEN TECHNIQUE
Learn to Turn

Our favorite method for roasting a turkey calls for roasting the bird breast-side down for the first hour and then flipping it onto its back until it's done. We developed this unusual technique through much trial and error (and literally dozens of turkeys) to ensure the dark and white meat get done at the same time, thus preventing chalky, dry breast meat. The dark meat, exposed to the high heat of the oven at the start, gets a head start while the leaner breast is afforded some protection. We freely admit our technique adds a step, also that the cook will have to briefly tussle with a hot, cumbersome turkey. But the payoff is very much worth the effort. The method guarantees a moist, juicy turkey from tip to tail or, more accurately, breast to thigh. And did we mention the golden, crackling skin? One word of caution: The bigger the bird, the harder it is to flip. Make sure to insulate your hands with clean pot holders or kitchen towels.

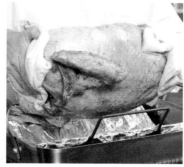

Tip the turkey so the juices in the cavity run into the pan. Then, with kitchen towels or potholders, flip the turkey and set breast-side up on the rack.

SHOPPING Talking Turkey

Natural, frozen, heirloom, kosher—which is best? It depends. We recommend a "self-basting" turkey or a kosher turkey for cooks who don't want to brine. "Self-basting" turkeys—available at any supermarket—are enhanced with a salty broth meant to keep the meat moist and juicy. Read labels if you have any doubts. If you see an ingredient list, the bird has been enhanced and is self-basting. Kosher turkeys, prepared in accordance with Jewish law, are soaked in water, salted, and rinsed. A byproduct of that process is tender, moist, deeply seasoned meat. Finally, if you prefer a natural or heirloom turkey, be prepared to brine. Natural turkeys are flavorful but can be dry. Brining ensures moist meat. Here are three brands that have done well in our taste tests—one for every kind of cook.

NATURAL TURKEY
Bell & Evans
Fresh Turkey

KOSHER TURKEY
Empire Kosher

SELF-BASTING TURKEY
Frozen Butterball
Premium "Prebasted"

COOKING TIMES
A Rough Guide

Even a substantial 22-pound bird takes only 3½ hours, at most, to cook through, following the oven temperatures and method in our recipe. Follow the chart below to determine approximate serving sizes and roasting times. Remember, the times are merely guidelines. For perfectly done turkey, always—repeat, always—temp the turkey with an instant-read thermometer.

RAW WEIGHT	NUMBER OF SERVINGS	APPROXIMATE ROASTING TIME
12 TO 14 POUNDS	10 TO 12	2–2½ HOURS
15 TO 17 POUNDS	14 TO 16	2½–3 HOURS
18 TO 22 POUNDS	20 TO 22	3–3½ HOURS

A Precise Guide

To determine when the turkey is done, take its temperature in at least two places with an instant-read thermometer. Never rely on the (highly inaccurate) pop-up timers embedded in many supermarket turkeys. They temp the breast only and inevitably "pop" right about the time the turkey is overcooked.

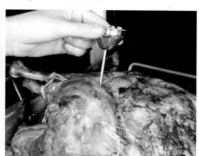

1. TO TEMP THE BREASTS Insert the thermometer into the deepest part of each, holding it parallel to the bird at the neck end. The breasts should reach 160 degrees.

2. TO TEMP THE THIGHS Insert the thermometer between the breasts and drumsticks and into the thickest part of each thigh, steering clear of the bone. The thighs should reach 175 degrees.

ESSENTIAL GEAR Pan and Rack

For roasting, we like a pan that is sturdy enough to support the weight of a large turkey and that has well-designed, easy-to-use handles. Plus, we depend on a V-rack. The rack holds the bird steady—you wouldn't want it to tip and splash hot drippings when you remove it from the oven. More important, it allows air to circulate so the turkey browns (but doesn't burn) on the bottom. Our favorite roasting pan is the Calphalon Contemporary Stainless Steel Roasting Pan ($129.95). It has all the features you'll need, plus it comes with its own solid V-rack.

If you dust off your roasting pan only once a year for the Thanksgiving turkey, it may not be worth the investment. In that case, roast your turkey in a disposable aluminum foil pan. Be sure to place the pan on a rimmed baking sheet; otherwise it'll buckle under the weight of the turkey—very dangerous. You'll still need a V-rack. Either way, line the V-rack with aluminum foil so that the bars won't leave tracks in the meat, spray foil with cooking spray to prevent sticking, and poke the foil with holes so the fat and juices can drain; eventually, you'll add those to the gravy.

OUR FAVORITE
Calphalon Contemporary
Stainless Steel Roasting Pan

IN A PINCH
An inexpensive and perfectly serviceable substitute

COOK'S EXTRA How to Carve a Turkey

For step-by-step instructions on how to carve your Thanksgiving turkey, visit **CooksCountry.com** and click on **Cook's Extras**.

Sweet Potato Casserole

Every year between October and December, 35 million pounds of marshmallows are sold in America. A single dish—sweet potato casserole—accounts for much of the tonnage. The casserole was popularized by a recipe booklet that the Campfire marshmallow company printed in 1930, "How Famous Chefs Use Campfire Marshmallows," in which solemn chefs in imposing toques touted marshmallows as a way to dress up dinner. The booklet includes some half dozen recipes for mashed sweet potatoes with toasted marshmallow crusts (not to mention a recipe for Campfire Marshmallow Mayonnaise—don't ask). Mercifully, the latter has disappeared into the mists of time. But sweet potato casserole has earned an enduring place in our hearts, and on our Thanksgiving tables.

BY LYNN CLARK

Sadly, over the years, sweet potato casserole has lost its early glamour and become something of an embarrassment. Have you ever noticed, though, that the guests who make the most fun of it are the same ones you'll find discreetly eating second helpings? After testing a handful of recipes, I could see both sides. The marshmallow topping was visually stunning and tasted irresistibly good. The nostalgia factor was huge with my tasters, many of whom remembered the dish from their childhoods. But many casseroles emerged from the oven watery, too sweet, and so dolled up with spices, you might mistake them for dessert—and that was before they donned their marshmallow caps. Also, with so much going on, the flavor of the sweet potatoes got lost. My goal: Restore the reputation of a venerable—if often mistreated—casserole. After all, it wouldn't be Thanksgiving without it.

Sweet potato casserole is made by roasting or boiling sweet potatoes until tender (or, heaven forbid, reaching for the syrupy canned ones); mashing them with butter, cream, sugar, and spices; spooning them into a baking dish; topping them with mini marshmallows; and broiling until brown. But boiling the sweet potatoes made the casserole watery and washed out their flavor, while roasting took too long. I wondered if an unusual method the test kitchen had developed in the past for mashed sweet potatoes might work. Following that recipe, I simmered 5 pounds of peeled and cubed sweet potatoes, covered, in ½ cup of cream and 12 tablespoons of melted butter (as they simmer, moist sweet potatoes produce steam that helps cook them), then took them off the heat and mashed them. They weren't firm enough for a casserole. I decreased the butter and cream to 6 tablespoons each—any less

and the potatoes burned. They were still soggy. Since I was mashing them in the pot anyway, I tried leaving the heat on medium-low while I mashed. Pouf! The excess moisture vanished.

Unfortunately, by cutting back on the cream and butter, I'd inadvertently dialed back on the richness that befits a holiday dish. To restore it, I tried adding eggs (they altered the texture and turned the casserole into a soufflé), then evaporated milk (it made the casserole taste too lean). Mentally ticking off other dairy products in my effort to add fat, I hit on cheese. Cheese with marshmallows? Yuck. I changed my mind when a colleague suggested tangy (but otherwise neutral) cream cheese. Just 2 ounces made the casserole richer without making it wetter. Even better, its tang tempered the sweetness of the casserole.

It sure needed tempering. Some recipes add as much as 3 cups of sugar. I eliminated all of it. Suddenly, tasters missed the sugar, never mind their previous complaints. I added back 2 teaspoons, just enough to gently reinforce the sweet potatoes' natural sweetness. In such a small amount, brown sugar added no discernible flavor, so I stuck with white. Next, I tested spices. Tasters rejected ginger, nutmeg, and cinnamon on the grounds they turned what should be a side dish into a pie. In the end, I stopped at salt and pepper. The marshmallows made enough of a statement on their own; I needn't go crazy with the spices.

I felt I'd restored dignity and deliciousness to the bottom half of the casserole, so I turned a critical eye on the topping. If you're thinking it was just a matter of sprinkling on a few handfuls of mini marshmallows, think again. Cranky tasters grumbled that the roasted marshmallows were chalky and dried out. I did some checking and found that mini marshmallows, unlike full-sized ones, are coated with cornstarch to keep them from sticking to each other in the bag. I ditched the minis and instead topped the casserole with large marshmallows that I cut in half through the equator (if left uncut, the large marshmallows were too thick and gooey). The golden brown topping was creamy, crispy, and starch-free. I'd put this sweet potato casserole up against that of any famous chef, however tall his hat.

SWEET POTATO CASSEROLE
Serves 8 to 10

If you prefer silky-smooth potatoes, use a hand mixer to beat the potatoes in step 3. Use sharp, clean scissors sprayed with cooking spray (to prevent sticking and make cleanup easier) to snip the marshmallows in half through the equator.

- 5 pounds sweet potatoes, peeled and cut into 1-inch chunks
- 6 tablespoons heavy cream
- 6 tablespoons unsalted butter, cut into 6 pieces
- 2 teaspoons sugar
- 1 teaspoon salt
- ½ teaspoon pepper
- 2 ounces cream cheese
- 1 (10-ounce) bag marshmallows, halved crosswise

1. COOK POTATOES Combine potatoes, cream, butter, sugar, salt, and pepper in Dutch oven. Cook covered, stirring occasionally, over medium heat until potatoes begin to break down, 20 to 25 minutes.

2. SIMMER POTATOES Reduce heat to medium-low and continue to cook, covered, until liquid has been absorbed and potatoes are completely tender, 15 to 20 minutes. Meanwhile, adjust oven rack to upper-middle position and heat oven to 450 degrees.

3. MASH POTATOES Add cream cheese to pot. Using potato masher, mash until cream cheese is fully incorporated and sweet potatoes are smooth. Continue to cook, stirring constantly, until potatoes are thickened, about 5 minutes.

4. TOAST MARSHMALLOWS Transfer potato mixture to 2-quart baking dish and top with single layer marshmallows. Bake until marshmallows are browned, about 5 minutes. Serve.

MAKE AHEAD: After transferring sweet potato mixture to baking dish, mixture can be refrigerated, covered, up to 2 days. Microwave until warm for 4 to 7 minutes before topping with marshmallows and baking as directed.

The American Table
Marshmallow's Roots

In 2000 B.C., Egyptians made marshmallows by boiling sugar with the root of the mallow plant, which grew in marshes (get it? marsh mallow). Egyptian royals gobbled them up. Fast forward to the mid-19th century, when French candy makers combined mallow sap with egg whites and sugar, whipping and molding marshmallows by hand and selling them at a handsome price. As marshmallows became more popular, new recipes and cheaper ways to make them developed. By the early 1900s, U.S. manufacturers had replaced mallow root with gelatin and were selling marshmallows as penny candy. These days, they've come full circle with handmade, artisanal marshmallows selling for as much as $4 apiece.

From ancient treat to campfire favorite.

ON THE SIDE Skillet Green Beans with Walnuts
For the holidays, we wanted to dress green beans in their Sunday best. BY MARÍA DEL MAR SACASA

Easy spiced walnuts give green beans a kick in the pants.

ON WEEKNIGHTS, I sometimes steam green beans and top them with a pat of butter and a handful of chopped walnuts. For Thanksgiving, I hoped to dress up the dish. To begin with, steaming—a fine technique for a weeknight—would taste like spa cuisine alongside holiday fare. Instead, I sautéed the beans in butter in a skillet for about eight minutes until they turned spotty brown and developed toasty flavors. I added a little water and covered the pan to briefly steam them to crisp tenderness. In the last few minutes of cooking, I uncovered the pan to let any remaining water evaporate.

The beans were delicious, but the sprinkling of raw nuts tasted like an afterthought. Since I was dirtying a skillet anyway, I toasted the nuts in it, which I stirred into a new batch of the green beans. The dish still lacked pizzazz. What if I added warm spices in this season of spiced nuts? I started anew, this time adding a knob of butter to the skillet after the nuts had toasted. I let it brown, a technique that gives it a faintly nutty flavor. I stirred in 1 tablespoon of brown sugar, hoping it would caramelize lightly and help the spices adhere. Tasters nixed cinnamon; it tasted like dessert. But they liked ground ginger (for warmth and kick) and a combination of black and cayenne peppers for two layers of lingering heat. And they loved the finished dish.

SKILLET GREEN BEANS WITH WALNUTS Serves 8

- ⅔ cup walnuts, chopped
- 4 tablespoons unsalted butter, cut into 4 pieces
- 1 tablespoon brown sugar
- ¾ teaspoon ground ginger
   Pinch cayenne pepper
   Salt and pepper
- 2 pounds green beans, stem ends trimmed
- ¼ cup water

1. TOAST NUTS Toast walnuts in large skillet over medium-low heat until golden, about 5 minutes. Add 2 tablespoons butter and cook, stirring constantly, until butter is nutty brown, about 2 minutes. Stir in sugar, ginger, cayenne, ¼ teaspoon salt, and ¼ teaspoon pepper and cook until fragrant, about 30 seconds. Transfer walnut mixture to bowl and reserve. Wipe out skillet.

2. COOK BEANS Melt remaining butter in empty skillet over medium-high heat. Cook beans, stirring occasionally, until spotty brown, about 8 minutes. Add water and cook, covered, over medium-low heat until beans are nearly tender, about 3 minutes. Remove lid and cook until liquid evaporates, about 1 minute. Off heat, add reserved walnut mixture. Season with salt and pepper. Serve.

Soft and Chewy Dinner Rolls

Some rolls are as squishy as a teddy bear, others as rustic as rawhide. We wanted a happy medium for our holiday table. BY LYNN CLARK

We were on a roll, so we developed variations with a range of add-ins. But Soft and Chewy Rolls are also delicious dressed in nothing but butter.

FLUFFY, SOFT AMERICAN-STYLE rolls and chewy, crusty European rolls both begin with flour, yeast, and salt, but the remaining ingredients and the technique make all the difference. American rolls include milk, butter, and egg for tenderness. European rolls use water, the barest amount of fat (usually olive oil), and a lengthy rise and a very hot oven for a sturdy crust. Although I like both styles, I longed for something in the middle—a roll with a soft crumb and hearty chew.

Since the test kitchen's Fluffy Dinner Roll recipe is relatively quick and straightforward in both technique and ingredients (no specialty bread flour, just all-purpose), I decided to start there and work toward something leaner. Out went the full stick of butter and the egg, and I replaced the milk with water. This roll wasn't rich anymore, but it wasn't chewy, either: It was tough, like bad pizza dough. Clearly, it needed some fat. As little as 2 tablespoons of butter made it too much like a soft dinner roll, but an equal amount of olive oil yielded the right amount of chew—though I still wanted more tenderness.

Potato bread has a soft, moist crumb, thanks to the inclusion of a boiled, mashed, and cooled potato in the dough. I added just such a potato to my dough and baked the rolls in a 400-degree oven (the right temperature for good browning). These rolls had both pleasing chew and supple softness. To skip the step of making real mashed potatoes, I tried replacing the russet I'd used with instant potato flakes (reconstituted with water). This dough produced the same tender, chewy rolls without the extra work.

From there, it was easy to create a few variations. Chopped olives, sun-dried tomatoes, herbs, nuts, and dried fruit added rustic appeal, while a brush of beaten egg and a sprinkling of salt gave the basic rolls extra crunch and shine.

SOFT AND CHEWY ROLLS
Makes 12 rolls

- 1¼   cups water, heated to 110 degrees
- 2   tablespoons extra-virgin olive oil
- 1   tablespoon sugar
- 1   envelope (2¼ teaspoons) rapid-rise or instant yeast
- 3   cups all-purpose flour
- ½   cup instant potato flakes
      Salt
- 1   egg, lightly beaten

1. WARM OVEN Adjust oven rack to middle position and heat oven to 200 degrees. When oven reaches 200 degrees, turn it off. Line baking sheet with parchment paper. Grease large bowl.

2. MAKE DOUGH Whisk water, oil, sugar, and yeast in liquid measuring cup until yeast dissolves. In bowl of stand mixer fitted with dough hook, mix flour, potato flakes, and 1½ teaspoons salt until combined. With mixer on low, add water mixture in steady stream and mix until dough comes together, about 1 minute. Increase speed to medium and knead until dough is smooth and comes away from sides of bowl, about 6 minutes.

3. LET RISE Turn dough onto lightly floured counter and knead briefly to form smooth, cohesive ball. Transfer dough to prepared bowl and turn to coat. Cover with plastic wrap and place in turned-off oven until dough has doubled in size, about 45 minutes.

4. SHAPE ROLLS Punch down dough on lightly floured work surface. Divide dough into quarters and cut each quarter into 3 equal pieces. On clean surface, form each piece into rough ball by pinching and pulling the edges under so that the top is smooth. Then cup each round with your palm and move in a circular motion on an unfloured surface to shape a smooth ball. Transfer to prepared baking sheet. Cover loosely with plastic wrap and return to turned-off oven until doubled in size, about 20 minutes. (Or refrigerate rolls for up to 24 hours.)

5. BRUSH AND BAKE Remove rolls from oven and discard plastic wrap. Heat oven to 400 degrees. Brush rolls with egg and sprinkle evenly with ½ teaspoon salt. Bake until golden brown, about 15 minutes, rotating sheet halfway through cooking. Cool rolls on sheet 10 minutes. Serve.

MAKE AHEAD: Bake as directed until rolls are just beginning to brown and outside is set, about 5 minutes. Cool completely and freeze in zipper-lock bag. When ready to reheat, defrost at room temperature for about 1 hour and bake 10 minutes in 400-degree oven.

TO MAKE WITHOUT A MIXER: In step 2, whisk water, oil, sugar, and yeast in liquid measuring cup. Mix flour, potato flakes, and salt in large bowl. Make well in flour, then add water mixture to well. Stir until dough becomes shaggy and difficult to stir. Turn out onto floured work surface and knead until dough is smooth and forms cohesive ball, about 10 minutes. Proceed as directed.

CRANBERRY-PECAN ROLLS
Prepare Soft and Chewy Rolls, adding 1 cup dried cranberries and 1 cup pecans, toasted and chopped, along with flour.

ROSEMARY-OLIVE ROLLS
Prepare Soft and Chewy Rolls, reducing salt in step 2 to 1 teaspoon. Add 1 tablespoon olive brine along with water. Add ¾ cup pitted kalamata olives, chopped and patted dry, and 2 tablespoons minced fresh rosemary along with flour.

SUN-DRIED TOMATO AND BASIL ROLLS
Prepare Soft and Chewy Rolls, adding ½ cup sun-dried tomatoes packed in oil, rinsed, patted dry, and minced, and 2 tablespoons finely chopped fresh basil along with flour.

Sausage and Cornbread Dressing

Most dressing recipes start with store-bought cornbread or a mix: Don't do it! Making your own cornbread is worth the trouble. BY CALI RICH

CORNBREAD AND SAUSAGE dressing is gutsier than its buttoned-up bread-based sibling, and it's not difficult to make: Cube stale cornbread. Combine it with sautéed onion, celery, and seasonings. Add cooked sausage. Moisten with broth and eggs. Bake. Straightforward enough, but the recipes I tried had one huge problem: store-bought cornbread. Whether I bought prepared cornbread or made it from a mix, it was too sweet to use in dressing. Its tender, fluffy texture also spelled trouble, greedily soaking up the broth and eggs, and turning the dressings to mush.

After several abortive attempts, I concluded I'd have to make the cornbread myself. I began my testing with the test kitchen's all-purpose cornbread, which stirs together equal amounts of cornmeal and flour, leavener, salt, and sugar (which I omitted), then whisks in eggs, buttermilk, milk, and melted butter. I baked, cooled, and cubed the cornbread, and let it stale overnight. Using a ratio I'd gleaned from my early tests—16 cups of dried cornbread (one 13- by 9-inch pan's worth), 4½ cups of chicken broth, and 2 beaten eggs—I soaked the cubes, added 1 pound of browned sausage, a few shakes of poultry seasoning, some sautéed onion and celery, and baked it.

Not bad, but since the dressing would be so flavorful, I wondered if I could pare down the cornbread before fine-tuning everything else. The combination of milk and buttermilk seemed redundant for a cornbread that I didn't intend to eat on its own. Sure enough, when I eliminated the buttermilk, tasters couldn't detect the difference in the finished dressing. Likewise, replacing the melted butter with vegetable oil simplified things, and tasters were none the wiser. And if I forgot to stale the cubed cornbread overnight, I found I could get the same results in under an hour in a gentle 250-degree oven.

Cornbread finished, I turned to the dressing. My tasters objected to the "dusty" quality of the poultry seasoning and were happy when I replaced it with dried sage and thyme. Adding four cloves of minced garlic to the onions and celery did wonders for the flavor. Things were

coming together nicely, but the dressing wasn't rich enough.

I first added an extra ½ pound of sausage, then doubled the eggs to four. I replaced 1 cup of the chicken broth with the same amount of half-and-half. For good measure, I drizzled melted butter over the dressing before baking it. That not only added richness but also helped to crisp the top, creating that essential contrast between crust and what lies beneath. In the end, making my own cornbread added 15 minutes of kitchen work. For that, I got a side dish with flavors that shouted celebration.

HOMEMADE CORNBREAD DRESSING Serves 10 to 12

The baked cornbread can be left in its pan up to two days before making the stuffing. Instead of oven-drying in step 2, stale the cubed cornbread overnight at room temperature. Use fine or coarse cornmeal.

CORNBREAD
- 2⅔ cups milk
- ½ cup vegetable oil
- 4 large eggs
- 2 cups cornmeal (see note)
- 2 cups all-purpose flour
- 4 teaspoons baking powder
- 1 teaspoon salt

DRESSING
- 1½ pounds bulk pork sausage
- 2 onions, chopped fine
- 3 celery ribs, chopped fine
- 6 tablespoons unsalted butter
- 4 garlic cloves, minced
- 1 teaspoon dried sage
- 1 teaspoon dried thyme
- 3½ cups low-sodium chicken broth
- 1 cup half-and-half
- 4 large eggs
- ½ teaspoon salt
- ⅛ teaspoon cayenne pepper

1. PREPARE CORNBREAD Adjust oven racks to upper-middle and lower-middle positions and heat oven to 375 degrees. Grease and flour 13- by 9-inch baking pan. Whisk milk, oil, and eggs in bowl; set aside. Combine cornmeal, flour,

baking powder, and salt in large bowl. Add milk mixture, whisking until smooth. Pour batter into prepared pan and bake on lower-middle rack until golden and toothpick inserted in center comes out clean, about 30 minutes. Cool in pan on wire rack, about 2 hours. (Cornbread can be prepared up to 2 days in advance.)

2. DRY CORNBREAD Heat oven to 250 degrees. Cut cornbread into 1-inch squares. Divide cornbread between two rimmed baking sheets and bake until dry, 50 to 60 minutes, switching and rotating baking sheets halfway through baking. Cool cornbread completely on sheets, about 30 minutes.

3. SAUTÉ AROMATICS Cook sausage in large nonstick skillet over medium-high heat until no longer pink, about 5 minutes. Transfer sausage to paper towel–lined plate and pour off all but 2 tablespoons fat from pan. Add onions, celery, and 2 tablespoons butter to fat in pan and cook until softened, about 5 minutes. Add garlic, sage, and thyme and cook until fragrant, about 30 seconds. Stir in broth, remove from heat, and let cool 5 minutes.

4. SOAK CORNBREAD Whisk half-and-half, eggs, salt, and cayenne in large

bowl. Slowly whisk in warm broth mixture until incorporated. Fold in dried cornbread and reserved sausage and let sit, tossing occasionally, until saturated, about 20 minutes.

5. BAKE DRESSING Heat oven to 375 degrees. Grease 13- by 9-inch baking pan. Transfer soaked cornbread to prepared pan. Melt remaining butter and drizzle evenly over top. Bake on upper-middle rack until surface is golden brown and crisp, 30 to 40 minutes. Let cool 15 minutes. Serve.

We cook our dressing outside the turkey. Otherwise, the bird will overcook before the dressing is done.

Old-Fashioned Pecan Pie

Long before cloying Karo syrup was a gleam in the eye of its inventors, 19th-century homemakers were setting "transparent pies" to cool on windowsills. Made with sugar, butter, and eggs and sweetened with molasses, maple, cane, or sorghum syrup, these pies resembled pecan pie without the nuts. Then manufacturers came up with a flavorless, cheap liquid sugar made from highly processed cornstarch. In 1902, the Corn Products Refining Company of New York and Chicago aggressively marketed it as Karo corn syrup: "Great spread for daily bread, a table delight, appreciated morning, noon, or night." Three decades later, the wife of a Karo executive baked a transparent pie with the newfangled syrup and added pecans. The company printed her recipe in a promotional booklet, pie history was made, and Karo took off.

BY DIANE UNGER

In truth, I've never entirely understood the popularity of pecan pie, or Karo pie, as it's sometimes called in the South. Flavorless Karo syrup brings nothing but undifferentiated, over-the-top sweetness. I wanted to return the pie to its roots—at least what I imagined them to be. And I wanted to actually taste the pecans rather than smothering them in tooth-aching sweetness. As I'd never tasted cane syrup or sorghum syrup (the latter is made from a cereal grass), I mail-ordered a few bottles from the mostly small, local southern companies that still produce them.

When these old-fashioned syrups arrived in the test kitchen, I tried them on their own and baked in pies. Tasters were delighted by their range, from full-bodied and molasses-y to light and buttery to honeyed—and everything in between. The darker syrups overwhelmed the pecan pies, but the more delicate ones were sensational, with far more flavor than I'd ever managed to coax from either light or dark corn syrup. Now that I knew what I was missing, I set out to approximate it using ordinary pantry ingredients.

As a reference point, I started with the original 1930s Karo recipe, which has changed little since that time: 3 eggs, 1 cup sugar, 1 cup light or dark Karo syrup, 2 tablespoons butter or margarine, and 1¼ cups pecans. The pie is baked at 350 degrees in an unbaked pie shell. I started my experimenting with granulated sugar, which, like cane syrup, is made from sugarcane. My idea was to make my own faux sugarcane syrup out of sugar and water. I found a recipe online that purported to do so, and following its instruction, I caramelized sugar in a skillet, added water, and boiled until the syrup thickened slightly. Along the way, I burned the caramel twice and lacquered the stove in bubbling syrup. Even when I got it right, the results didn't much resemble the cane syrups I'd tasted. Even the mildest variety of honey tasted like, well, honey; no one thought it suited pecan pie. Maple syrup came the closest to the syrups we'd tasted, but the maple flavor was too pronounced. Many sugar tests later, I discovered I could mellow the maple and achieve the flavors I sought by combining it with light brown sugar and just a single tablespoon of molasses.

I heated the sugars briefly, which dissolved the brown sugar, thus eliminating graininess. I stirred in the butter. My working recipe called for 2 tablespoons. Other recipes I'd tested use as many as 8 tablespoons. I settled on 4 for appreciable buttery flavor without greasiness. Now, the filling tasted as good as I imagined it had before Karo syrup hijacked it nearly 80 years ago. When I was researching the

history of pecan pies, I'd repeatedly run across a close cousin to transparent pies: sirop (syrup) pies. They were made in almost the same way, but usually added cream to the filling. How could that be bad? For the heck of it, I added in ½ cup cream with the sugars for my pie. Tasters loved the creamy, custardy transformation it wrought. Unfortunately, the cream made the filling looser. The maple syrup, I learned, was also partly to blame; it has a higher water content than corn syrup. To better bind the filling and get a sliceable pie, I replaced the three whole eggs with six yolks, which have less water than whites, so bind more firmly.

All that was left was the nuts. Bringing out their flavor was as simple as toasting them before they went into the pie. Five to 10 minutes in a 350-degree oven gave them enough crunch and flavor to hold their own in the filling.

Most recipes suggest simply pouring the filling into an unbaked pie shell. But when I did so, the bottom crust came out soggy and undercooked. Apparently, as soon as the pie went into the oven, the uncooked bottom crust soaked up the uncooked liquid filling. Some recipes solve the problem by prebaking the crust, a tiresome extra step. Up to this point I'd been baking the pie at a steady 350 degrees on the middle rack of the oven. What if I started it at a high temperature (450 degrees), then immediately turned down the dial to a gentle 325 degrees? I hoped the initial high heat would give the bottom crust a head start, and the subsequent low temperature (it took 15 minutes for the temperature inside the oven to come down to 325) would prevent the eggs from curdling. At the same time, I lowered the oven rack. The intense heat from below would help set the crust. The result was just as I'd hoped: a crisp, golden bottom crust.

To the dismay of my tasters, pecan pie needs to completely cool before you can eat it. Otherwise, as I learned through gluttony and error, the filling won't firm to the proper consistency, so the pie won't slice nicely. Cooling took about four hours, at which point the filling was silky yet firm; the flavor a mild caramel with hints of molasses; and the nuts a toasty, crunchy counterpoint. The other thing that happened after four hours? My tasters threatened to kill me if I didn't let them have a piece.

OLD-FASHIONED PECAN PIE
Serves 8 to 10

Regular or mild molasses tastes best in this pie. Use your favorite pie dough or go to CooksCountry.com for our Single Crust Pie Dough recipe.

- 1 cup maple syrup
- 1 cup packed light brown sugar
- ½ cup heavy cream
- 1 tablespoon molasses
- 4 tablespoons unsalted butter, cut into ½-inch pieces
- ½ teaspoon salt
- 6 large egg yolks, lightly beaten
- 1½ cups pecans, toasted and chopped
- 1 (9-inch) unbaked pie shell (see note), chilled in pie plate for 30 minutes

1. MAKE FILLING Adjust oven rack to lowest position and heat oven to 450 degrees. Heat syrup, sugar, cream, and molasses in saucepan over medium heat, stirring occasionally, until sugar dissolves, about 3 minutes. Remove from heat and let cool 5 minutes. Whisk butter and salt into syrup mixture until combined. Whisk in egg yolks until incorporated.

2. BAKE PIE Scatter pecans in pie shell. Carefully pour filling over. Place pie in hot oven and immediately reduce oven temperature to 325 degrees. Bake until filling is set and center jiggles slightly when pie is gently shaken, 45 to 60 minutes. Cool pie on rack for 1 hour, then refrigerate until set, about 3 hours and up to 1 day. Bring to room temperature before serving.

RECIPE TEST DRIVE

We asked readers to make our Old-Fashioned Pecan Pie recipe before it was published. Here's what we learned from the 75 home cooks who did.

Help, There's Salt in My Butter

"I used salted butter. I know—a sin against cooking, but it's what I had."

OUR ADVICE We prefer unsalted butter because different brands of salted butter contain different amounts of salt, which makes recipe development tricky. We also think unsalted butter tastes better. That said, if you keep salted butter on hand, you can get a rough approximation of unsalted butter by removing ⅜ teaspoon salt for every stick of butter in a recipe. Our pie filling calls for half a stick of butter and ½ teaspoon salt, so reduce the salt to a bit more than ¼ teaspoon if you use salted butter. If you're going to bake with salted butter, you better like math.

Browner Is Not Better

"I found, at the last moment, that I had dark brown sugar and not light brown sugar and that I only had blackstrap molasses in my cupboard. Interestingly, most thought there was chocolate in the pie! If I was making again (OK, when I make it again!), I'll find some lighter molasses."

OUR ADVICE Our tasters thought dark brown sugar made the pie too molasses-y. If you use dark brown rather than light brown sugar, we suggest omitting the molasses altogether. As for using other types of molasses, bottles labeled "robust" or "full-flavored" will yield a stronger but not unpleasant molasses flavor. However, avoid using blackstrap molasses in this pie. It's very potent. If all you have on hand is blackstrap molasses, just use the light brown (or dark brown) sugar and maple syrup and omit the molasses.

Toast Those Nuts

"Toasting the pecans? Seemed a bit much—they are great just out of the shell."

"We loved the taste of the toasted pecans, which I haven't done in the past."

"My husband had trouble with toasting the pecans. He had to do it a second time after burning the first batch."

OUR ADVICE Toasted nuts have more flavor. And while our pie is in the oven for nearly an hour, the nuts are coated with the sticky custard and can't really toast. You can toast nuts in a dry skillet over medium heat or on a baking sheet in a 350-degree oven. Don't walk away. When you can smell the nuts, they're done. This will take 3 to 5 minutes in a skillet, or 5 to 10 minutes in the oven.

BOURBON WHIPPED CREAM
Makes about 2 cups

Although any style of whiskey will work here, we like the smokiness of bourbon. As bourbon is both American and southern, it fits right in.

- 1 cup heavy cream
- 2 tablespoons bourbon
- 1½ tablespoons light brown sugar
- ½ teaspoon vanilla extract

With electric mixer on medium speed, beat cream, bourbon, sugar, and vanilla until stiff peaks form, about 2 minutes. (Whipped cream can be refrigerated for 4 hours.)

Getting to Know Dried Fruit

Almost any fruit can be dried (the process concentrates flavor and sugar), and these days, most of them are—from blueberries to cranberries to mangos. But should you buy dried fruit sugared or unsweetened? Unsulfured or not? And what the heck is a dried currant, anyway? (See page 31 for information on plumping dried fruit for cooking and baking.)

Raisins
GRANDPA GRAPE

Raisins, the granddaddy of dried fruits, start life as green Thompson (or Sultana) grapes. They've been eaten for thousands of years: Phoenicians traded them, Roman emperors feasted on them, Hannibal snacked on them. Astoundingly, they are largely still dried the old-fashioned way—in the sun for two to four weeks.

Golden Raisins
CLOSE KIN

Golden raisins come from the same grape as ordinary black raisins, but are dried mechanically and treated with sulfur dioxide to preserve their color. Curious if anyone could tell them apart, we blindfolded tasters. Some could, describing golden raisins as "tart and lemony." Some couldn't. Use the two interchangeably.

Cranberries
SALAD FIND

Fresh, naturally tart cranberries are infused with sweetened cranberry juice in the process of being dried. Dried cranberries, which are sometimes sold as "Craisins," have "papery skins." We like to add them to salads and pilafs.

Mangos
NO SUGAR NEEDED

Dried mangos are most readily available candied (pictured), but unsweetened dried mangos can be found in natural foods stores. We found candied dried mangos too sweet. We enjoy the unsweetened variety eaten out of hand or chopped and added to baked goods.

Currants
MINI MISNOMER

Name aside, currants are made from black Corinth grapes, not currant berries. Often called Zante currants (after the Greek island where the grape grows), these "intensely flavored" fruits are smaller than raisins. Brits like to bake them into scones and Christmas cakes. We like them in green and grain salads, too.

Cherries
SWEETIE PIE

We've always wondered where all the fresh sour cherries go. Now we know. Ninety percent of dried cherries are made from sour cherries, because their tart flavor stands up to the drying process. We use dried cherries in both sweet and savory recipes.

Pineapples
DOUBLE TROUBLE

Dried pineapples come as either dehydrated, brown slices or fruit juice–soaked or sugared bright-yellow slices. We didn't like either. The former were "chalky," "chewy," and "burnt," while the sweet variety "lacked all pineapple tang" and had the taste and texture of "gumdrops."

Wild Blueberries
BERRY BLAST

These small, dark, "fleshy" berries were a hit with tasters, who loved their "insanely concentrated blueberry flavor." Use in muffins, scones, or pancakes for intense blueberry flavor without blueberry bleed.

Prunes
PLUM ALIAS

In the U.S., prunes are best known for their, ahem, health benefits (although old cookbooks offer a plethora of prune whips, stewed prunes, and cakes). In recent years, prune promoters have renamed them "dried plums" and infused them with cherry and orange. Eat in sweet or savory dishes or as a snack.

Calimyrna Figs
PLUMP PACKAGE

The Calimyrna is the California version of the Turkish Smyrna fig. Tasters described them as "seedy and chewy" with "caramel notes," like a "fresh Fig Newton." Add them raw to salads, serve with cheese, or cook in sauces or stuffings for chicken or pork.

Apricots
GOLD MEDALS

Most supermarket apricots are treated with sulfur dioxide to preserve their sunny color and extend shelf life. Eaten out of hand, these plump sulfured apricots have "citrus and honey" flavors. Unsulfured apricots were drier, chewier, and "mud-colored" raw, but revealed "bright, true apricot" flavor when baked.

Apples
BAKER'S BUDDY

Mass-market dried apples had "little or no real apple flavor," tasters said. By contrast, organic varieties were "tart and sweet" with "fresh, just-picked" flavor. Both are "spongelike" and "rubbery," which is why we like them for baking, not snacking. Add finely chopped dried apples to fruit pies to soak up moisture and keep crusts crisp.

SEARED FLANK STEAK WITH CHIMICHURRI SAUCE

GRILLED APPLE-GLAZED PORK CHOPS

SPINACH- AND TARRAGON-STUFFED CHICKEN BREASTS

SWEET AND SPICY VEGGIE STIR-FRY

GRILLED APPLE-GLAZED PORK CHOPS Serves 4

WHY THIS RECIPE WORKS: The combination of sliced apples, apple jelly, and cider vinegar gives these grilled chops a triple dose of apple flavor.

- 2 tablespoons unsalted butter
- 2 Granny Smith apples, peeled, cored, and cut into ½-inch wedges
- 1 shallot, minced
- 1 cup apple jelly
- ¼ cup cider vinegar
- ½ teaspoon minced fresh thyme
- ⅛ teaspoon cayenne pepper
- 1 tablespoon Dijon mustard
- 4 bone-in rib or center-cut pork chops, about 1 inch thick (see note below)
  Salt and pepper

1. Melt butter in large saucepan over medium-high heat. Cook apples and shallot until golden and beginning to soften, about 5 minutes. Add jelly, vinegar, thyme, and cayenne and bring to boil. Reduce heat to medium and simmer, stirring occasionally, until mixture is thickened and apples are tender, 5 to 7 minutes. Off heat, whisk in mustard; cover and keep warm.

2. Pat chops dry with paper towels and season with salt and pepper. Grill over hot fire until well browned and meat registers 145 degrees, about 6 minutes per side. Brush with ¼ cup apple mixture and cook 1 minute longer. Transfer to platter and pour remaining apple mixture over chops. Serve.

TEST KITCHEN NOTE: To prevent the chops from curling as they cook, cut two slits about 2 inches apart through the fat around the outside of each chop.

SEARED FLANK STEAK WITH CHIMICHURRI SAUCE Serves 4

WHY THIS RECIPE WORKS: We avoid a harsh, oniony flavor in the sauce by using mild scallions instead of raw onion.

- 2 garlic cloves, unpeeled
- ½ cup chopped fresh parsley
- 2 scallions, chopped
- 1 tablespoon red wine vinegar
- ¼ teaspoon red pepper flakes
- 5 tablespoons olive oil
  Salt and pepper
- 1 flank steak (about 1½ pounds)

1. Toast garlic in large skillet over medium-low heat, shaking pan occasionally, until fragrant and spotty brown, about 5 minutes. When cool enough to handle, peel garlic and transfer to blender with parsley, scallions, vinegar, and pepper flakes. With blender running, slowly drizzle in 4 tablespoons oil until smooth and emulsified. Season with salt and pepper.

2. Pat steak dry with paper towels and season with salt and pepper. Heat remaining oil in empty skillet over medium-high heat until just smoking. Cook steak until well browned, 5 to 7 minutes per side. Transfer to cutting board, tent with foil, and let rest 5 minutes. Slice steak thinly against grain. Serve, passing sauce at table.

TEST KITCHEN NOTE: Chimichurri sauce also tastes delicious on chicken and fish. The sauce can be refrigerated in an airtight container for 3 days.

SWEET AND SPICY VEGGIE STIR-FRY Serves 4

WHY THIS RECIPE WORKS: Draining the tofu and dredging it in cornstarch before frying helps it hold its shape and texture.

- 1 (14-ounce) block firm tofu, cut into 1-inch cubes
- ¼ cup honey
- 3 tablespoons soy sauce
- 1 tablespoon Asian chili-garlic sauce
- 1 tablespoon grated fresh ginger
- ½ cup cornstarch
- ½ cup vegetable oil
- 1 pound salad bar vegetables, cut into bite-sized pieces (see note below)

1. Place tofu on paper towel–lined plate and let drain 15 minutes. Whisk honey, soy sauce, chili-garlic sauce, ginger, and 1 teaspoon cornstarch in medium bowl.

2. Spread remaining cornstarch in shallow plate. Pat tofu dry with additional paper towels and dredge in cornstarch, shaking off excess. Heat oil in large nonstick skillet over medium-high heat until shimmering. Cook tofu, turning occasionally, until golden brown and crisp, 6 to 8 minutes. Using slotted spoon, transfer tofu to plate lined with fresh paper towels.

3. Pour off all but 1 tablespoon oil from pan. Add vegetables and cook until softened, about 5 minutes. Stir in honey mixture and cook until slightly thickened, about 2 minutes. Add tofu and toss to combine. Serve.

TEST KITCHEN NOTE: We like a mixture of broccoli, snow peas, bell peppers, baby corn, and red onion from the supermarket salad bar. Make sure to use firm, not soft, tofu. Serve over rice.

SPINACH- AND TARRAGON-STUFFED CHICKEN BREASTS
Serves 4

WHY THIS RECIPE WORKS: Cutting a neat pocket into the chicken eliminates the usual hassle of pounding, rolling, and tying the stuffed chicken breasts.

- 2 slices hearty white sandwich bread, torn into pieces
- 2 tablespoons chopped fresh tarragon
- 1 (10-ounce) box frozen chopped spinach, thawed and squeezed dry
- ¾ cup crumbled goat cheese (see note below)
- 2 garlic cloves, minced
  Salt and pepper
- 4 boneless, skinless chicken breasts (about 1½ pounds) (see note below)
- 1½ tablespoons mayonnaise

1. Adjust oven rack to lower-middle position and heat oven to 425 degrees. Pulse bread and 1 tablespoon tarragon in food processor until coarsely ground. Combine remaining tarragon, spinach, cheese, garlic, ¼ teaspoon salt, and ¼ teaspoon pepper in medium bowl.

2. Pat chicken dry with paper towels and season with salt and pepper. Using paring knife, cut deep pocket in thickest part of chicken, extending into most of breast. Spoon spinach mixture into pocket and seal by threading toothpick through chicken about ½ inch from opening.

3. Arrange stuffed chicken breasts in 13- by 9-inch baking dish. Brush top of chicken with mayonnaise and top with bread crumb mixture, pressing gently to adhere. Bake until crumbs are golden brown and chicken is cooked through, 20 to 25 minutes. Serve.

TEST KITCHEN NOTE: Avoid using chicken breasts that weigh more than 6 ounces each, as the crumbs may burn before the chicken is cooked through. You'll need 3 ounces of crumbled goat cheese.

TURKEY TETRAZZINI PASTA

STEAK WITH CRISPY SPICED POTATOES

QUICK CROQUE MONSIEUR

CHICKEN TOSTADAS WITH SPICY CABBAGE SLAW

STEAK WITH CRISPY SPICED POTATOES Serves 4

WHY THIS RECIPE WORKS: Four strip steaks don't easily fit in a large skillet so we use 2 extra-thick steaks and cut them into 4 portions total.

- 1 pound small red potatoes, quartered
- 2 tablespoons vegetable oil
- 2 strip steaks, about 1½ inches thick, trimmed of fat and halved crosswise
  Salt and pepper
- 2 tablespoons unsalted butter
- ½ teaspoon dried oregano
- ½ teaspoon paprika (see note below)
- ½ teaspoon onion powder
- ¼ teaspoon garlic powder
- ⅛ teaspoon cayenne pepper (see note below)

1. Toss potatoes and 1 tablespoon oil in large bowl. Wrap tightly with plastic and microwave until edges of potatoes are translucent, 4 to 7 minutes, shaking bowl (without removing plastic) to redistribute potatoes halfway through cooking.

2. Pat steaks dry with paper towels and season with salt and pepper. Heat remaining oil in large nonstick skillet over medium-high heat until just smoking. Cook steaks until well browned, 4 to 6 minutes per side. Transfer to plate and tent with foil.

3. Drain potatoes and cook in empty skillet until browned and crisp, about 5 minutes. Add butter, oregano, paprika, onion powder, garlic powder, cayenne, ½ teaspoon salt, and ¼ teaspoon pepper and cook until fragrant, about 30 seconds. Serve.

TEST KITCHEN NOTE: We developed this recipe using sweet paprika (often just labeled "paprika"). If using hot paprika, omit the cayenne.

TURKEY TETRAZZINI PASTA Serves 4

WHY THIS RECIPE WORKS: Grated Parmesan adds cheesy depth to this simplified version of the classic leftovers casserole.

- 2 tablespoons unsalted butter
- 10 ounces white mushrooms, sliced thin
  Salt and pepper
- 2 garlic cloves, minced
- 1 cup heavy cream
- 1 tablespoon dry sherry
- 1½ cups grated Parmesan cheese
- 1 pound spaghetti
- 3 cups cooked turkey meat, cut into bite-sized pieces (see note below)
- 2 cups frozen peas, thawed

1. Bring 4 quarts water to boil in large pot. Melt butter in large skillet over medium-high heat. Cook mushrooms, ¼ teaspoon salt, and ¼ teaspoon pepper until golden brown, about 10 minutes. Add garlic and cook until fragrant, about 30 seconds. Stir in cream and sherry and simmer until slightly thickened, about 2 minutes. Off heat, stir in Parmesan. Cover and keep warm.

2. Add 1 tablespoon salt and pasta to boiling water and cook until al dente. Reserve 1 cup pasta cooking water, drain pasta, and return to pot. Add mushroom sauce, turkey, and peas, and ½ cup reserved pasta water to pot and toss to combine, adding additional reserved pasta water as needed. Season with salt and pepper. Serve.

TEST KITCHEN NOTE: We use leftover Thanksgiving turkey here, but at other times of the year we substitute the meat of one rotisserie chicken.

CHICKEN TOSTADAS WITH SPICY CABBAGE SLAW Serves 6

WHY THIS RECIPE WORKS: We use the liquid from the cans of beans to give our "refried" beans a creamy texture.

- 12 (6-inch) corn tortillas
- ⅓ cup vegetable oil
- 2 (16-ounce) cans pinto beans (see note above)
- 1 tablespoon finely chopped jarred pickled jalapeños, plus 5 tablespoons jalapeño brine
  Salt and pepper
- 1 (16-ounce) bag coleslaw mix
- 1 cup crumbled queso fresco (see note below)
- 1 rotisserie chicken, skin discarded, meat shredded into bite-sized pieces (about 3 cups)
- ½ cup sour cream
- 3 tablespoons juice from 2 limes

1. Adjust oven racks to upper-middle and lower-middle positions and heat oven to 450 degrees. Brush tortillas with 3 tablespoons oil and arrange in single layer on two baking sheets. Bake until lightly browned and crisp, about 10 minutes, switching and rotating sheets halfway through baking.

2. Heat remaining oil in large skillet over medium heat until shimmering. Add beans and their liquid, pickled jalapeños, and 1 tablespoon jalapeño brine and cook, mashing with potato masher, until mixture is thickened, about 5 minutes. Season with salt and pepper. Cover and keep warm.

3. Toss coleslaw mix, ¼ teaspoon salt, ¼ teaspoon pepper, and remaining jalapeño brine in large bowl until combined. Spread bean mixture over crisp tortillas and top with cheese, chicken, and slaw. Whisk sour cream and lime juice in bowl, then drizzle over tostadas. Serve.

TEST KITCHEN NOTE: Queso fresco is a fresh, soft Mexican cheese available in many markets. If you can't find it, use crumbled feta cheese instead.

QUICK CROQUE MONSIEUR Serves 4

WHY THIS RECIPE WORKS: This grilled ham sandwich is dressed up with a cheese sauce. Instead of cooking 1 or 2 sandwiches at a time in a skillet, we use a rimmed baking sheet and a hot oven to cook all 4 sandwiches simultaneously.

- 3 tablespoons butter, softened
- 2 tablespoons all-purpose flour
- 1 cup whole milk
- 2½ cups shredded Gruyère cheese (see note below)
  Salt and pepper
- 8 slices hearty white sandwich bread
- 2 tablespoons Dijon mustard
- 6 ounces thinly sliced deli ham

1. Adjust oven rack to upper-middle position and heat oven to 475 degrees. Melt 2 tablespoons butter in saucepan over medium heat. Whisk in flour and cook until golden, about 2 minutes. Slowly whisk in milk and simmer until slightly thickened, 3 to 5 minutes. Off heat, stir in ½ cup cheese, ¼ teaspoon salt, and ¼ teaspoon pepper. Cover and keep warm.

2. Spread remaining butter over 4 slices of bread. Arrange, buttered-side down, on rimmed baking sheet. Spread each slice with mustard, then divide ham, 1 cup cheese, and ½ cup sauce over mustard-topped slices and top with remaining bread. Top with remaining sauce and cheese. Bake until cheese is golden brown and bubbling, 8 to 10 minutes. Serve.

TEST KITCHEN NOTE: Gruyère is a Swiss cow's milk cheese with a nutty flavor. If you can't find Gruyère, use deli Swiss cheese instead. You will need 10 ounces of cheese.

Cream of Mushroom Soup

Surely it didn't have to be bland sludge. We wanted a velvety soup that pulled deep, earthy flavor from ordinary supermarket mushrooms. BY DIANE UNGER

WHEN MOST PEOPLE think of cream of mushroom soup, they picture the pasty, flavorless glop in the iconic red and white can (we don't remember it fondly). But when it's made from scratch with flavorful (read: expensive) wild mushrooms, the soup can be so much more. I wanted that deep, woodsy flavor and creamy texture without having to forage in the supermarket aisles. The trouble was, the less expensive (at least comparatively speaking) supermarket mushrooms also have less flavor.

None of the handful of recipes I tried was inspiring. The worst added sautéed mushrooms to white sauce (butter, flour, and milk or cream) and called the results soup. They were better than the canned stuff, but not by a heck of a lot. More successful, but not perfect, were a few recipes that sautéed onions and mushrooms, sprinkled in flour to thicken, cooked the mixture in broth, then pureed and added

cream at the end. These soups were lighter and had better mushroom flavor. Blueprint in hand, I went to work on the details.

My jumping-off point was a recipe calling for 1½ pounds of sliced mushrooms, 1 onion, 5 cups of chicken broth, and 2 cups of cream. I browned batches of white button, cremini, and a combination of both with the chopped onion in butter, stirred in 3 tablespoons of flour, added the broth, and left each pot to simmer. When the vegetables were tender, I pureed each soup, stirred in the cream, and gathered my tasters. The type of mushrooms, I learned, matters less than the quantity: All three versions were acceptable, but the mushrooms had cooked down so dramatically, every batch was thin and wan.

I immediately doubled the mushrooms in my recipe. A big improvement, provided the water they released had time to evaporate—mushrooms are 90 percent water. It took about 15 minutes for them to brown and concentrate. Given their volume, I found it much faster to break them up with my hands than to slice them: What's the point of neat slices anyway, when I was only going to puree them at the end? A bit of Madeira (dry sherry and brandy are also delicious) lent complexity, as did giving the butter a chance to brown slightly before sautéing the mushrooms. Garlic and thyme rounded out the flavor. To accentuate the meatiness of the mushrooms, I used beef instead of chicken broth and reduced the cream from 2 cups to 1—the oversupply had been masking everything else.

The extra pureed mushrooms had added bulk, not merely depth. I no longer needed the flour for thickening, which pleased me, as it had been making my soup pasty. Alas, though lighter, the soup still wasn't silky. What I was looking for, I thought, was that exquisite velvety texture of potato-leek soup. A lightbulb went on. For my next batch, I replaced the onion with leeks, a swap that worked wonders, then finished the soup with fresh lemon juice. Field, forest, the heft of velvet, and the brightness of lemon—I had everything but the red and white can, which was no loss at all.

A garnish of croutons and chopped chives adds texture and color to this creamy soup.

CREAMY MUSHROOM SOUP
Serves 6 to 8

Since this soup is pureed, don't waste time slicing mushrooms. Just break them into rough pieces with your hands. Use the blender, not the food processor, for the smoothest possible soup. You can use brandy or dry sherry in place of the Madeira. Be sure to use low-sodium beef broth: Pacific beef broth is the test kitchen's top-rated brand.

- 4 tablespoons unsalted butter
- 3 pounds white or cremini mushrooms, broken into rough pieces (see note)
- 2 leeks, white and light green parts only, halved lengthwise and chopped (see page 31)
  Salt and pepper
- 4 garlic cloves, minced
- 2 teaspoons chopped fresh thyme
- 5 cups low-sodium beef broth (see note)
- ½ cup Madeira (see note), plus additional for serving
- 1 cup heavy cream
- 2 teaspoons lemon juice

1. COOK MUSHROOMS Melt butter in large Dutch oven over medium-high heat, stirring constantly, until butter is golden brown and has a nutty aroma, about 3 minutes. Add mushrooms, leeks, ½ teaspoon salt, and ¼ teaspoon pepper and cook, covered, until mushrooms release their liquid, about 5 minutes. Remove lid and cook, stirring occasionally, until liquid has evaporated, about 15 minutes. Remove ⅔ cup mushroom mixture, chop fine, and reserve.

2. SIMMER SOUP Add garlic and thyme to pot with remaining mushroom mixture and cook until fragrant, about 30 seconds. Stir in broth and Madeira and bring to boil. Reduce heat to medium-low and simmer, covered, until mushrooms and leeks are completely tender, about 20 minutes.

3. FINISH SOUP Puree soup in blender in batches until smooth. Return pureed soup to pot, stir in cream, lemon juice, and chopped mushrooms and return to simmer. Season with salt and pepper. Serve, drizzling individual portions with additional Madeira.

It's not just for pizza anymore. Ground pepperoni makes our sauce meaty and spicy.

Baked Manicotti with Meat Sauce

We spent hours in the kitchen, but our manicotti was still mediocre. Could we make it faster—and better?

BY CALI RICH

STUFFED MANICOTTI is a labor of love. It takes time and effort to brown ground beef, build a tomato sauce, cook and cool pasta tubes, pipe in the ricotta filling, sauce the stuffed pasta, and bake the ensemble. The reward is a hearty, homey, knockout dish—or at least it should be. I painstakingly prepared a number of recipes, only to discover the harsh realities of bland fillings, sauce and meat that never melded, and shredded pasta tubes. Where was the love?

Manicotti was originally made by rolling sheets of fresh pasta around a filling. This sounded easier than grappling with dried manicotti tubes, but making fresh pasta was out of the question for a weekday supper. What about no-boil lasagna noodles? Could giving them a quick soak to make them pliable save me trouble? After soaking 16 noodles (enough to fill a 13- by 9-inch dish) in hot water, I patted them dry, portioned out the filling, and started rolling. I filled these noodles much more quickly than dried tubes, and with no ripping. In a finished casserole, they were indistinguishable.

One and a half pounds of ground beef and two 28-ounce cans of crushed tomatoes made enough sauce to cover the filled tubes. But the beef flavor was faint. If I had all day, I'd let the sauce simmer and develop flavor. I remembered that a colleague had used the food processor to jump-start his Bolognese sauce: Once the ground beef was broken down, its flavor permeated the tomatoes. This technique worked just as well for my manicotti sauce. For rounder flavor, I tested using meatloaf mix and ground pork in combination with the ground beef, but they didn't contribute much. Hot Italian sausages were a modest improvement, and pepperoni—I know it sounds odd—was even better. When I ground pepperoni slices with the beef, tasters couldn't identify the new addition but loved the spicy, meaty taste it imparted.

The standard filling of equal parts ricotta and mozzarella (plus an egg for binding) tasted flat. I exchanged 1 cup of the mozzarella for more assertive Parmesan. While the taste improved, the texture took a nosedive. Provolone fixed both. A taster suggested adding meat to the filling. I reserved 1 cup of the sautéed meat mixture and stirred it into the ricotta mixture. Now the dish tasted meaty to its core. My manicotti isn't effortless. But the method is easy, and the robust, flavorful payoff is worth a little exertion.

BAKED MANICOTTI WITH MEAT SAUCE Serves 6 to 8

You will need 16 no-boil lasagna noodles. The test kitchen's preferred brand, Barilla, comes 16 to a box, but other brands contain only 12. It is important to let the dish cool for 15 minutes after baking.

MEAT SAUCE

- 1 onion, chopped
- 6 ounces sliced deli pepperoni
- 1 pound 85 percent lean ground beef
- 1 tablespoon tomato paste
- 5 garlic cloves, minced
- ¼ teaspoon red pepper flakes
- 2 (28-ounce) cans crushed tomatoes
  Salt and pepper

MANICOTTI

- 3 cups ricotta cheese
- 2½ cups shredded mozzarella cheese
- 1½ cups shredded provolone cheese
- 1 large egg, lightly beaten
- ½ teaspoon salt
- ½ teaspoon pepper
- ¼ cup finely chopped fresh basil
- 16 no-boil lasagna noodles (see note)

1. GRIND MEAT Adjust oven rack to upper-middle position and heat oven to 375 degrees. Pulse onion and pepperoni in food processor until coarsely ground. Add beef and pulse until thoroughly combined.

2. MAKE SAUCE Transfer beef mixture to large saucepan and cook over medium heat, breaking up mixture with wooden spoon, until no longer pink, about 5 minutes. Using slotted spoon, transfer 1 cup beef mixture to paper towel–lined plate and reserve. Add tomato paste, garlic, and pepper flakes to pot with remaining meat mixture and cook until fragrant, about 1 minute. Stir in tomatoes and simmer until sauce is slightly thickened, about 20 minutes. Season with salt and pepper. (At this point, sauce can be refrigerated in airtight container for 3 days.)

3. PREPARE FILLING Combine ricotta, 2 cups mozzarella, 1 cup provolone, egg, salt, pepper, basil, and reserved meat mixture in large bowl. Pour 2 quarts boiling water into 13- by 9-inch baking dish. Soak noodles until pliable, about 5 minutes. Drain noodles on kitchen towel. Pour off water and dry baking dish.

4. ASSEMBLE DISH Spread half of meat sauce over bottom of baking dish. Following photos below, top each soaked noodle with ¼ cup cheese filling, roll, and arrange, seam-side down, over sauce in baking dish. Spread remaining sauce over manicotti. Cover with foil and bake until bubbling around edges, about 40 minutes. Remove foil and sprinkle with remaining mozzarella and provolone. Bake until cheese is melted, about 5 minutes. Let cool 15 minutes. Serve.

TEST KITCHEN TECHNIQUE
Thinking Outside the Tube

Manicotti shells are hard to fill without tearing. For easy-to-fill manicotti, we reinvented the noodle.

1. Soak the no-boil lasagna noodles briefly in hot water. With the short side facing you, spread the filling across the bottom of each and roll into a tube.

2. Arrange the rolled manicotti, seam-side down, over the sauce in the baking dish.

ON THE SIDE Italian Broccolini

It may look like broccoli. But that doesn't mean you can cook it just the same. BY MEGHAN ERWIN

THE JUST-CRISP yet tender stalks and delicate tips of broccolini—a cross between broccoli and *kai-lan* (Chinese broccoli)—convinced us to give heftier broccoli a break, if just for a moment. But a few forays in the kitchen showed that pan-steaming, a proven test kitchen method for cooking broccoli, was ill-suited to its cousin. The method starts with sautéing broccoli florets and sliced stalks in oil until they start to brown, then adds a little water. Immediately, the pan is covered with a lid. The broccoli steams in minutes.

The delicate broccolini tips, however, scorched during the sauté, so I skipped step one. Instead, I brought water (⅓ cup was enough to steam 1 pound of broccolini), and ½ teaspoon of salt to a boil in a skillet. In went the broccolini, on went the cover, and five minutes later, tender, emerald-green broccolini stalks emerged. With the lid off and the heat still on, any remaining trace of water was able to evaporate—which took all of 30 seconds.

The process was a keeper, but there were inconsistencies from test to test. Broccolini is usually cooked intact, but because some stalks were twice as fat as others, they were cooking unevenly. To solve the problem, I halved the bottom 2 inches of the thicker stalks lengthwise, in effect creating two slender stalks.

Not many people are familiar with broccolini. Since I was introducing a new vegetable, I decided on classic, familiar flavors. I combined olive oil, garlic, and red pepper flakes and tossed them with the hot broccolini. A shower of grated Parmesan cheese topped it off.

You'll recognize the flavors—olive oil, garlic, and Parmesan—but the vegetable may be something new.

GARLICKY BROCCOLINI Serves 4
Broccolini is also sold as baby broccoli or asparation. Serve with lemon wedges.

- ⅓ cup water
- ½ teaspoon salt
- 2 bunches broccolini (about 1 pound), trimmed (see note)
- 2 tablespoons olive oil
- 2 garlic cloves, minced
- ⅛ teaspoon red pepper flakes
- 2 tablespoons grated Parmesan cheese

1. STEAM BROCCOLINI Bring water and salt to boil in large skillet. Add broccolini and cook over medium-low heat, covered, until bright green and tender, about 5 minutes. Remove lid and cook until liquid evaporates, about 30 seconds.

2. ADD SEASONINGS Stir in oil, garlic, and pepper flakes and cook until fragrant, about 30 seconds. Transfer to platter and sprinkle with Parmesan. Serve.

TEST KITCHEN TECHNIQUE Splitting Stems

Starting about 2 inches from the base of the stalk, use a paring knife to slice through any broccolini stems that are ½ inch thick or larger.

ON THE SIDE Crispy Garlic Bread

A few small tricks separate adequate from awesome. BY MEGHAN ERWIN

Just ¼ teaspoon sugar brings out garlic's sweet side.

BRUSHING SLICES OF BREAD with melted butter, garlic, and salt makes serviceable garlic bread. But the crisp, toasty edges don't compensate for the greasy, soggy center, and the garlic can taste unpleasantly pungent. For garlic bread with balanced garlic flavor and crunch from edge to edge, I'd have to try something different.

Sandwich bread was wimpy, baguette slices too dainty, but hearty Italian loaf, which yielded 12 inch-thick slices, offered plenty of room to develop crunch. Melted butter soaked into the bread, so instead I spread slices with softened butter on both sides and baked them on a baking sheet in a 425-degree oven. The toasty tops and crispy centers were a plus, but the bottoms got a little soggy before I could flip the bread. Maybe a pre-heated baking sheet would give them a running start? Sure enough, the slices sizzled upon contact with the hot sheet. After 8 minutes, the tops were beautifully browned and the bottoms just toasted. A flip and 5 minutes more—now the second side was seriously crisp.

The test kitchen sometimes precooks garlic to tame its raw bite, but speed and ease were my bywords. A colleague recommended using a rasp-style grater to turn the garlic into a paste (mincing the garlic super fine works, too). That helped disperse it through the butter, but failed to tame it. Thinking of the sweet flavor of roasted garlic, I added a touch of sugar to the butter mixture. I hadn't thought I needed a recipe for something as simple as garlic bread. These slices convinced me otherwise.

CRISPY GARLIC BREAD Makes 12 slices
For the smoothest texture, grate the garlic cloves on a rasp-style grater.

- 12 tablespoons (1½ sticks) unsalted butter, softened
- 4 garlic cloves, grated (see note) or minced
- ¼ teaspoon sugar
- ¼ teaspoon salt
- ¼ teaspoon pepper
- 12 (1-inch) slices Italian bread

1. MAKE PASTE Adjust oven rack to middle position, place rimmed baking sheet on rack, and heat oven to 425 degrees. Using fork, beat butter, garlic, sugar, salt, and pepper in small bowl until combined. Spread butter mixture evenly over both sides of bread.

2. TOAST BREAD Arrange buttered bread on heated baking sheet and bake until golden brown on first side, 8 to 10 minutes. Flip and bake until golden brown on second side, about 5 minutes. Serve.

Freezer-Ready Garlic Bread
After spreading the bread with the butter mixture in step 1, freeze the slices on a large plate until firm, about 15 minutes. Transfer bread to zipper-lock freezer bag and freeze for up to 1 month. To serve, bake as directed, adding 2 to 5 minutes to cooking time.

Baked Apple Dumplings

Apple dumplings are a home-spun combination of warm pastry, concentrated apple flavor, raisins, butter, and cinnamon. In the 19th century, every homemaker could toss off a biscuit or pie dough and deftly wrap it 'round the stuffed apples. They tied up the dumplings in cheesecloth, boiled or steamed them, and served them with sauce; latter-day cooks prefer to bake them. The dumplings were so loved that in the animated 1937 classic film, Snow White's ability to make them persuaded the Seven Dwarfs to let her stay. Somehow they've fallen off our collective radar screen, but we say if a Disney cartoon character could make apple dumplings, surely the modern American cook can.

BY DIANE UNGER

In fact, successfully sealing an apple in dough isn't easy. And baking produced crunchy apples inside over-cooked crusts, apples that turned to mush, and gummy dough at folds and crimps. Finally, because most dumplings are baked in sauce, their bottoms get soggy.

I made some dumplings using store-bought pie dough, a shortcut many recipes take. While acceptable in a pie, where the filling stars, it was a letdown in dumplings. No question I'd be making my own dough. I also knew I'd bake my dumplings. Boiling and steaming couldn't produce crust worthy of the word. My first real decision, then, was pie versus biscuit dough. Raw pie dough tore, and baking ruptured it at the seams and sent it sliding down the shoulder of the fruit like an unzipped dress. Meanwhile, steam from the baking apple had turned the dough gluey.

Moving on to biscuit dough, I gradually increased the fat in a favorite test kitchen recipe from 8 tablespoons butter (for flavor) and 4 tablespoons shortening (for tenderness) to 10 and 5 tablespoons, respectively.

Mixed with 2½ cups flour, 2 teaspoons baking powder, and ¾ cup buttermilk, they yielded a sturdy yet tender dough. I wrapped the dumplings with ease. This dough formed tender, fluffy biscuits that absorbed the apple juices everywhere but where the dumplings had been sitting in sauce. Given the inevitable soggy results, why bake them in syrup, anyway? I'd make the sauce separately and save it for serving.

I set the dough-wrapped apples on a baking sheet and baked them at 450 degrees—our favored temperature for biscuits. Now, the bottom crusts were crisp. Alas, so were the apples. I'd been using Granny Smiths, because the test kitchen likes them for baking. Were they to blame? In any event, tasters complained they were too tart. After a series of tests, tasters picked sweeter Golden Delicious, which held up during baking. Held up too well…they were still crisp.

An old recipe came to the rescue. It had suggested using three-quarters of each apple if the apples were big. I adapted the idea, cutting the apples in half for

simplicity's sake. I seeded and cored them and filled the hollows with cinnamon sugar, raisins, and butter. I wrapped each half, cut a hole in the tops to let steam escape, brushed the dumplings with beaten egg white, and sprinkled them with cinnamon sugar.

Twenty-five minutes later, after the apple juices had started to bubble and the kitchen smelled fantastic, I pulled the dumplings from the oven. The apples were tender, the biscuits tender and buttery, and tasters could even finish a serving.

On the stovetop I boiled a syrup of sugar and water, alongside several variations. The winning sauce used equal parts apple cider and water, to which I added sugar, cinnamon, butter, and lemon. I drizzled the dumplings with sauce and sighed in contentment. I was remembering something I'd read in an 1888 *Good Housekeeping* article on apple dumplings: "This time-honored dish does not appear on our tables as often as its excellent qualities would warrant." My recipe could have changed that.

BAKED APPLE DUMPLINGS Serves 8

Use a melon baller or a metal teaspoon measure to core the apples. We like to serve the dumplings warm with vanilla ice cream and Cider Sauce (recipe below). Other sweet, moderately firm apples, such as Braeburns or Galas, can be used in this recipe.

DOUGH

- 2½ cups all-purpose flour
- 3 tablespoons sugar
- 2 teaspoons baking powder
- ¾ teaspoon salt
- 10 tablespoons (1¼ sticks) unsalted butter, cut into ½-inch pieces and chilled
- 5 tablespoons vegetable shortening, cut into ½-inch pieces and chilled
- ¾ cup cold buttermilk

APPLE DUMPLINGS

- 6 tablespoons sugar
- 1 teaspoon ground cinnamon
- 3 tablespoons unsalted butter, softened
- 3 tablespoons golden raisins, chopped
- 4 Golden Delicious apples (see note)
- 2 egg whites, lightly beaten

1. MAKE DOUGH Process flour, sugar, baking powder, and salt in food processor until combined. Scatter butter and shortening over flour mixture and pulse until mixture resembles wet sand. Transfer to bowl. Stir in buttermilk until dough forms. Turn out onto lightly floured surface and knead briefly until dough is cohesive. Press dough into 8-by 4-inch rectangle. Cut in half, wrap each half tightly in plastic, and refrigerate until firm, about 1 hour.

2. PREP APPLES Adjust oven rack to middle position and heat oven to 425 degrees. Combine sugar and cinnamon in small bowl. In second bowl, combine butter, raisins, and 3 tablespoons cinnamon sugar mixture. Peel apples and halve through equator. Following photos 1 and 2, remove core and pack butter mixture into each apple half.

3. ASSEMBLE DUMPLINGS On lightly floured surface, roll each dough half into 12-inch square. Cut each 12-inch square into four 6-inch squares. Working one at a time, lightly brush edges of dough square with egg white and place apple, cut-side up, in center of each square. Following photo 3, gather dough one corner at a time on top of apple, crimping edges to seal. Using paring knife, cut vent hole in top of each dumpling.

4. FINISH APPLES Line rimmed baking sheet with parchment paper. Following photo 4, arrange dumplings on prepared baking sheet, brush tops with egg white, and sprinkle with remaining cinnamon sugar. Bake until dough is golden brown and juices are bubbling, 20 to 25 minutes. Cool on baking sheet 10 minutes. Serve with Cider Sauce.

STEP-BY-STEP **Dumpling Assembly Line**

According to an 1888 *Good Housekeeping* article on apple dumplings, King George III (1738–1820) had been "sadly puzzled to know how the apple came inside the dumpling." (Is it any wonder that he lost the American colonies?) Here's how, Your Highness:

  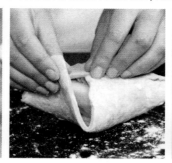 

1. Scoop out the core and seeds, taking care not to pierce the bottom of the apple halves.

2. Divide the butter mixture among the apple halves, filling the hollows.

3. Fold the corners of the dough up to enclose the apple halves, overlapping and crimping to seal.

4. Arrange dumplings on baking sheet, brush with egg white, and sprinkle with cinnamon sugar.

CIDER SAUCE Makes about 1½ cups

To make this sauce up to 2 days in advance, reduce the cider mixture until it measures 1½ cups, then refrigerate. When ready to serve, return mixture to simmer and whisk in butter and lemon juice off heat.

- 1 cup apple cider
- 1 cup water
- 1 cup sugar
- ½ teaspoon ground cinnamon
- 2 tablespoons unsalted butter
- 1 tablespoon lemon juice

Bring cider, water, sugar, and cinnamon to simmer in saucepan and cook over medium-high heat until thickened and reduced to 1½ cups, about 15 minutes. Off heat, whisk in butter and lemon juice. Drizzle over dumplings to serve.

BAD FOOD **Two Rotten Apples**

HEATSTROKE
Some apples, such as McIntosh, can't take the heat. They turn into applesauce before the pastry is baked.

EXTRA CRUNCHY
Whole apples are barely cooked when the pastry is done. To avoid that, we use halved Golden Delicious.

RECIPE TEST DRIVE

We asked readers to prepare our Baked Apple Dumplings recipe before it was published and send us feedback. Here's what we learned from the 70 home cooks who did.

That's a Weird Way to Core an Apple

"The whole business of how to cut the apples was confusing. You can't cut out the stem or the leafy crud at the bottom without letting the butter drain out."

OUR ADVICE We admit that our coring method is odd. But when we halved the apples through the stem and blossom ends, the rounded pieces wobbled and the filling spilled out. Yes, our method means you're leaving the blossom end intact. (Pull off any stems.) We don't mind, but if this bothers you, cut out the blossom when you're coring the apples and plug the bottom of the holes with apple slivers.

The Dough Is Too Soft

"Despite being chilled for 2 hours, the dough was difficult to roll and would not hold its shape. It sloughed off a few apples."

OUR ADVICE All the fat and buttermilk in our dough make it tasty—and soft. The rolled dough should be tender enough to pinch the seams together, but it shouldn't fall off the apples. Make sure your butter, shortening, and buttermilk are cold. Heavily flouring your work surface will help, as will refrigerating the dough, especially on warm days. Also, measure flour using the dip-and-sweep method. If you spoon flour into a dry measuring cup, you will end up with 10 to 20 percent less, which will make this rich dough really soft. Finally, use a light hand with the egg wash on the inside of the dough squares.

The Apples Weren't Fully Cooked

"The top half of my apples did not cook all the way through. Twenty-five minutes in the oven does not seem long enough. I used Granny Smith apples instead of Golden Delicious because that's what I had on hand."

OUR ADVICE Halved medium-sized Golden Delicious apples will be tender by the time the pastry is nicely browned. If you buy very large Golden Delicious apples (more than 7 ounces each) or use firmer apples, like Grannies, don't despair. Once the pastry is browned, test the apples for doneness. If a skewer meets with significant resistance, cover the dumplings with a sheet of foil and continue baking. The foil will keep the pastry from overbrowning, and an additional 10 or 15 minutes of baking time should soften even the biggest or firmest apples.

ON THE SIDE Caraway Egg Noodles

A sprinkling of seeds was a step in the right direction, but most recipes considered that the end of the road. BY MEGHAN ERWIN

Caraway seeds and browned butter spiff up plain buttered noodles.

BUTTERED EGG NOODLES are an easy, versatile side dish, but no one would call them exciting. I'd seen recipes that perked up the noodles with a sprinkling of caraway seeds, but this seemed more like a passing thought than a fully conceived dish. To bring out more of their distinctive taste, I chopped the caraway seeds lightly, then toasted them in a skillet. I stirred these now-fragrant seeds into the noodles. The noodles definitely tasted of caraway, tasters agreed, but not much else.

I'd been tossing the cooked noodles with cold butter, which formed a creamy coating. I wondered what the flavor of browned butter would contribute. I heated 4 tablespoons of butter (enough for a 12-ounce bag of noodles) over medium-low heat and watched the color deepen to golden brown. The butter took on the pleasant nutty flavor I'd hoped for, but melting it made the noodles greasy. For my next test, I browned only 3 tablespoons and stirred it into the noodles along with 1 tablespoon of cold butter. Now the noodles were creamy again. It occurred to me that I could eliminate a step if I added the raw caraway seeds to the butter and toasted them together. This proved both tasty and time-saving.

I helped myself to a bowl of these buttered noodles and was pleased. The caraway was aromatic, the browned butter added an extra dimension of flavor, and a generous sprinkling of herbs lent freshness and color.

EGG NOODLES WITH CARAWAY AND BROWN BUTTER Serves 6

Give the caraway seeds a gentle chop with a chef's knife; it brings out their flavor and helps disperse them throughout the dish. The test kitchen's favorite egg noodles are Light'n Fluffy Wide Egg Noodles. Do not use dried dill or chives in this recipe; their dusty flavor spoils the noodles.

- 1 (12-ounce) bag egg noodles (see note)
  Salt
- 4 tablespoons unsalted butter, cut into 4 pieces
- 1 teaspoon caraway seeds, chopped (see note)
- 2 tablespoons finely chopped fresh dill or chives

1. COOK NOODLES Bring 4 quarts water to boil in Dutch oven. Add noodles and 1 tablespoon salt to boiling water and cook until al dente. Drain noodles and return to pot.

2. TOAST CARAWAY Meanwhile, melt 3 tablespoons butter in small saucepan over medium-low heat. Add caraway seeds and cook, swirling pan occasionally, until butter is nutty brown and fragrant, about 5 minutes. Add browned butter mixture, herbs, and remaining butter to pot with noodles and toss to combine. Season with salt. Serve.

ON THE SIDE Roasted Cabbage

Can a vegetable usually destined for coleslaw thrive in the heat of the oven? BY MEGHAN ERWIN

POTATOES AND CARROTS may be the usual suspects for roasting, but the test kitchen has found that time spent in a very hot oven can draw out the best in broccoli and cauliflower, too; the sweet, deep flavors they develop could charm even an avowed vegetable loather. I wondered if wedges of cabbage would fare as well. Cabbage is in the same cruciferous family, after all.

I started with a straightforward approach—brushing cabbage wedges with oil, salt, and pepper; arranging them on a baking sheet; and roasting them in a 400-degree oven. Despite the heat, the wedges seemed almost steamed; their soggy state wasn't going to win any converts. Next time, I set the dial to 450 and preheated the baking sheet, hoping to give the oiled, seasoned wedges an initial blast of heat. Big improvement.

Most vegetables need only the occasional shake of the pan to brown and roast evenly, but to brown both sides of the cabbage wedges, I'd have to flip them one by one. Inevitably, some (or most) of the delicate wedges flopped apart during the flip, and I ended up with cabbage shreds. These shreds were never going to brown evenly—not before they burned, anyway. To fix this, I cut the cabbage very carefully, making sure to leave the core intact. Now each wedge had something to hold on to.

As I was flipping the wedges, I had an epiphany. I remembered that cabbage, like broccoli, is low in natural sugars. So when the test kitchen roasts broccoli, we add a smidge of sugar to the salt and pepper seasoning. Maybe if I did the same here, it would help caramelize the tops of the wedges and let me skip the flip altogether. I sugared, preheated, roasted, and I neither flipped nor flopped: The cabbage wedges had a wonderful nutty flavor and were tawny brown on both the top and bottom. A final drizzle of balsamic vinegar ensured that tasters and I went back for seconds—quite a feat for cabbage.

With roasting, cabbage shows its better side.

ROASTED CABBAGE WEDGES Serves 4 to 6

- 1 teaspoon salt
- ¼ teaspoon pepper
- 1 teaspoon sugar
- 1 medium head green cabbage
- 3 tablespoons vegetable oil
- 2 teaspoons balsamic vinegar

1. PREP CABBAGE Adjust oven rack to upper middle position. Place rimmed baking sheet on rack and heat oven to 450 degrees. Combine salt, pepper, and sugar in small bowl. Quarter cabbage through core and cut each quarter into 1-inch wedges, leaving core intact. You'll have about 16 wedges. Brush cabbage wedges all over with oil and sprinkle with salt mixture.

2. ROAST WEDGES Arrange cabbage on hot baking sheet and roast until cabbage is tender and lightly browned around edges, about 25 minutes. Drizzle cabbage with vinegar. Serve.

TEST KITCHEN TECHNIQUE Wedge Cut

To keep cabbage wedges together so they brown evenly, quarter the cabbage, taking care to cut directly through the core. Cut each quarter through the core into 1-inch-thick wedges.

Chicken Paprikash

How do you load up on paprika flavor while keeping grit to a minimum? BY KRIS WIDICAN

GENTLY COOK BONE-IN chicken pieces and some well-chosen vegetables in a broth that's ruddy and fragrant from sweet paprika. Swirl in sour cream for tang and body, and you've got chicken paprikash, a classic Hungarian dish that has been popular in this country for decades. It features tender chicken in a velvety sauce with flavor as deep as paprika is red—or at least that's how I imagined it. In reality, I couldn't find one problem-free recipe. Some produced bland, flabby-skinned chicken mingling with limp vegetables. Others had sauce that was harsh, gritty, greasy, or curdled or tasted nothing like paprika. I was determined to get this dish back on track.

The first round of testing confirmed that bone-in, skin-on chicken pieces were key. Searing the skin and then scraping up the browned bits in the pot gave the sauce a rich chicken taste. The bones added body to the sauce and kept the chicken moist. But braising turned the skin flabby and the sauce greasy. An astute taster pointed out that since the chicken would be served coated in sauce, the skin could be removed once it had contributed its flavor. Indeed, no one missed it, and removing it meant the grease was history.

Next, I tackled the vegetables. Mushrooms turned slimy, carrots added unwanted bulk, and green bell peppers were unpopular. All detracted from the sweetness of the paprika and the creaminess of the sauce. I tested different combinations of vegetables until tasters agreed on lightly caramelized onions and red bell peppers.

Preventing the sauce from curdling proved to be a simple matter of stirring in the sour cream off the heat. The real challenge, I realized, would be to enhance the paprika flavor yet keep the sauce silky. As expected, when I increased the amount of paprika from the meager 2 teaspoons called for in some recipes to the ¼ cup used by others, we could actually taste it. Paprika is made by drying red peppers, either sweet or hot, then grinding them to a powder. In small amounts, the sweet variety (traditional in chicken paprikash) is mild, but in larger quantities, it tastes harsh and gritty. Nonetheless, my tasters and I thought the dish should taste like its namesake spice, so I used the full ¼ cup and determined to figure out how to counter the bitterness and grit.

I unearthed a recipe for goulash (Hungarian beef stew) that called for pureeing cooked, jarred red peppers in the sauce. In theory, this would allow me to reduce the amount of paprika yet retain a sweet roasted pepper flavor. I got out the blender. Although I was on the right track with texture, the jarred peppers tasted processed; I nixed them. Next, I pureed the onions and peppers in the sauce. The puree gave the sauce a pleasant sweetness. Unfortunately, it also turned the sauce the pastel color of a fruit smoothie.

Maybe the sauce would benefit from a different vegetable puree—or, better yet, a ready-made paste. Just 1 tablespoon of sweet, smooth tomato paste offset the bitterness. Two tablespoons gave the sauce enough body to mask the grittiness (and didn't turn it an objectionable color). I finally understood why the Hungarians have eaten chicken paprikash for generations.

We use a generous ¼ cup of sweet paprika in this recipe—make sure yours is fresh.

STEP-BY-STEP Secrets to Silken, Flavorful Sauce

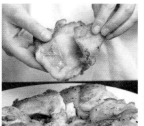

1. Chicken skin turns flabby when braised, plus it makes the sauce greasy. Brown the skin to add flavor, then discard.

2. Paprika makes the sauce gritty. Two tablespoons of tomato paste lend sweetness and body—and mask the grit.

3. For a velvety sauce that won't curdle, stir in the sour cream after the pot is off the heat.

CHICKEN PAPRIKASH Serves 4

Use any combination of white and dark meat. For even cooking, halve breasts crosswise and separate leg quarters into thighs and drumsticks. Reduced-fat sour cream can be used in this recipe. We like to serve this chicken over egg noodles (see recipe on preceding page) or rice.

- 3 pounds bone-in, skin-on chicken pieces (see note)
  Salt and pepper
- 1 tablespoon vegetable oil
- 2 onions, chopped fine
- 2 red bell peppers, stemmed, seeded, and sliced thin
- 1 garlic clove, minced
- 2 tablespoons tomato paste
- ¼ cup paprika (see box at right)
- 2 tablespoons all-purpose flour
- 1 cup low-sodium chicken broth
- ¾ cup sour cream (see note)

1. BROWN CHICKEN Pat chicken dry with paper towels and season with salt and pepper. Heat oil in Dutch oven over medium-high heat until just smoking. Cook chicken until well browned all over, about 10 minutes; transfer to plate. When chicken is cool enough to handle, remove and discard skin.

2. COOK VEGETABLES Pour off all but 1 tablespoon fat from pot. Add onions and bell peppers and cook until softened, 6 to 8 minutes. Stir in garlic, tomato paste, paprika, and flour and cook until fragrant, about 1 minute. Slowly stir in broth and bring to boil.

3. SIMMER CHICKEN Add browned chicken and any accumulated juices to pot. Reduce heat to low and simmer, covered, until white meat registers 160 degrees (or dark meat registers 175 degrees), 20 to 25 minutes. Off heat, stir in sour cream until incorporated and season with salt and pepper. Serve.

INGREDIENT Paprika

There is no single paprika pepper. The powdered spice we call paprika comes from a variety of peppers that range in intensity and flavor from the sweetest bells to the hottest chiles to smoked peppers. Use sweet paprika in our Chicken Paprikash for the most authentic flavor.

AMERICA'S BEST LOST SUPPERS

WE ASKED HOME COOKS across America to submit their favorite old-fashioned recipes—and the memories they evoke. More than 1,000 cherished recipes poured in. As we paged through them, a theme emerged: grandmas. We learned about one who fried chicken for coal miners in the middle of the last century ("and never had a pair of new shoes until she was in her 40s") and another who toiled in the late 19th-century kitchen of Kaiser Wilhelm II. A grandchild recalled her first cooking lesson: Her grandmother showed her how to make strudel, "measuring by the handful and adding just enough water until the dough felt right." That sounds daunting, but apparently not if you've got a grandmother at your (flour-dusted) elbow.

Of course there were plenty of aunts, fathers, grandfathers, and others, too. Your recipes and stories gave us renewed appreciation for our melting-pot nation and made us more evangelical than ever about the importance of the family dinner. Picking our five favorite recipes was difficult (and involved weeks of cooking and tasting). Technically, our five prize-winning recipes are presented on the following pages, but to be honest, we think they're all blue-ribbon material. We've gathered more than 100 of our favorite reader recipes in *Cook's Country Best Lost Suppers*. This just-published book is available in bookstores nationwide or through our online bookstore at CooksCountry.com.

Aunt Nina's Breadballs

DONNA BARDOCZ, HOWELL, MICH.

With no meat on hand, a mother used a heaping helping of ingenuity to put a delicious, thrifty dinner on the table for her 12 hungry kids.

DONNA'S AUNT NINA learned how to make this simple, satisfying comfort food—"meatless meatballs"—from her own mother. Grandma Coppola, as she came to be called, fed her 12 children breadballs whenever her husband came home empty-handed from hunting. "If you have to feed that many kids, you have to be inventive," Donna said. (Italians have a long and delicious tradition of using bread creatively to stretch meals.) Donna inherited the recipe several years ago in a booklet of treasured recipes that were collected and printed up for a family reunion. A very old photograph of Grandma Coppola making the passage from Italy to America is on its cover.

These "Poor Man's Meatballs," as Donna called them, are prepared just like ordinary meatballs but without the meat: bread crumbs, eggs, cheese, and herbs are stirred together and rolled into balls, which are then browned and simmered in tomato sauce. Although these days the family can afford to buy meat whenever they like, the breadballs remain a favorite. Aunt Nina's daughters continue to make them, and so does Donna, although she admits to one ironic change in tradition: She serves them with sausages! "My husband is a big carnivore," she explained, laughing.

AUNT NINA'S BREADBALLS AND SAUCE Serves 6 to 8
Let the breadballs form a good crust during frying or they will fall apart when simmered. To keep them from sticking to the pan, make sure the oil is shimmering before you start cooking and don't move them for the first few minutes of browning.

BREADBALLS
- 1 cup water
- 1 large egg
- 3 garlic cloves, minced
- 1 tablespoon chopped fresh parsley
- 1 tablespoon chopped fresh basil
- ¼ teaspoon pepper
- 1 (16-ounce) loaf Italian bread, torn into small pieces
- 1½ cups grated Parmesan cheese
- 6 tablespoons olive oil

SAUCE
- 1 onion, minced
- Salt and pepper
- 2 (6-ounce) cans tomato paste
- 1 tablespoon sugar
- 3 garlic cloves, minced
- 2 teaspoons dried oregano
- ⅛ teaspoon red pepper flakes
- 2 cups water
- 1 (28-ounce) can diced tomatoes
- 1 (15-ounce) can tomato sauce
- 1 tablespoon chopped fresh parsley
- ½ cup grated Parmesan cheese

A loaf of Italian bread stands in for the ground meat in these surprising "meatballs."

1. ASSEMBLE BREADBALLS Combine water, egg, garlic, parsley, basil, and pepper in large bowl. Add bread and Parmesan and mix with hands until well combined. Using wet hands, form mixture into 1½-inch breadballs (you should have about 30).

2. BROWN BREADBALLS Heat ¼ cup oil in Dutch oven over medium-high heat until shimmering. Cook half of breadballs without moving until well browned on bottom, 2 to 4 minutes. Continue to cook, turning gently, until well browned all over, about 5 minutes longer. Transfer to bowl. Repeat with remaining oil and breadballs.

3. MAKE SAUCE Pour off all but 1 tablespoon oil from pot. Add onion and ½ teaspoon salt and cook over medium heat until softened, about 5 minutes. Stir in tomato paste, sugar, garlic, oregano, pepper flakes, and ¼ teaspoon pepper and cook until tomato paste begins to brown, 2 to 4 minutes. Add water, tomatoes, and tomato sauce and bring to boil. Reduce heat to medium-low and simmer covered, stirring occasionally, for 1 hour.

4. SIMMER AND SERVE Carefully add browned breadballs to pot and continue to simmer, covered, until sauce is slightly thickened and breadballs are tender, about 30 minutes. Off heat, stir in parsley and season with salt and pepper. Serve, sprinkling with Parmesan (and additional parsley, if desired).

RUNNER UP

Granny's Tamale Pie

BETTY HESTERBERG, BOZEMAN, MONT.

Some 70 years ago, the elderly wife of a sheep rancher bestowed this unusual recipe on Betty's family. Now Betty is sharing it.

"MY MOTHER GOT this recipe from the elderly wife of a sheep rancher, who would make this dish and heat it up over the fire at herding camps. We always made it with pheasants, which were plentiful in the area when I was a child, but as the pheasant population grew slim we turned to ducks or geese. Now we use chicken, ideally dark meat for more flavorful broth. This dish was always made on my father's birthday in November, a tradition started in the late 1930s and continued until his death in 1990. Now I serve it on special occasions and whenever I get to see my brothers."

Granny's Tamale Pie caught our attention immediately because it is a far cry from the cheese-heavy casserole-style versions we usually see. (You won't find a single shred of cheese here—don't worry, you won't miss it.) This old-fashioned tamale pie is baked in a Dutch oven set in a roasting pan filled with simmering water, a method that mimics the way tamales are steamed. And instead of mixing in a sauce before baking, Betty makes a flavorful, spicy tomato sauce to serve on the side.

RUNNER UP

TEST KITCHEN TIP
Water Bath Baking
A water bath moderates the temperature and results in gentle, even cooking. When we tried baking this tamale pie without it, the sides dried out and the interior was gluey and heavy. Baking the pie in a "tub" of boiling water solved these problems.

GRANNY'S TAMALE PIE
Serves 6 to 8
To make the pie with white meat, use bone-in, skin-on split breasts and reduce the cooking time in step 2 by 20 minutes.

TAMALE PIE
- 3 pounds bone-in, skin-on chicken thighs, trimmed (see note)
  Salt and pepper
- ½ cup vegetable oil
- 3 cups low-sodium chicken broth
- 8 slices bacon, chopped
- 1 onion, minced
- 2 garlic cloves, minced
- 2 (14.5-ounce) cans diced tomatoes, drained
- 1 (15-ounce) can creamed corn
- 1 (6-ounce) can pitted black olives, drained and chopped
- 2 cups yellow cornmeal
- 1 cup whole milk
- 3 large eggs
  Boiling water

SAUCE
- 3 tablespoons all-purpose flour
- 1 tablespoon chili powder
- 1 teaspoon ground cumin
- 1 teaspoon ground coriander
- 1 (8-ounce) can tomato sauce
  Salt and pepper

1. BROWN CHICKEN Pat chicken dry with paper towels and season with salt and pepper. Heat 1½ teaspoons oil in large Dutch oven over medium-high heat until just smoking. Cook half of chicken until well browned, about 5 minutes per side. Transfer chicken to plate and discard skin. Repeat with additional 1½ teaspoons oil and remaining chicken.

2. BRAISE CHICKEN Stir broth into pot, scraping up any browned bits. Add browned chicken, along with any accumulated juices, and bring to boil. Reduce heat to medium-low and simmer, covered, until chicken is fork-tender, about 1 hour. Transfer chicken to plate. When cool enough to handle, shred chicken into bite-sized pieces; set aside. Strain broth, reserving 1½ cups for sauce. (Save any remaining broth for another use.)

3. COOK VEGETABLES Meanwhile, adjust oven rack to lower-middle position and heat oven to 325 degrees. Cook bacon in Dutch oven over medium heat until crisp, about 8 minutes. Using slotted spoon, transfer bacon to paper towel–lined plate. Cook onion and ½ teaspoon salt in bacon fat until softened, 5 to 7 minutes. Stir in garlic and sauté until fragrant, about 30 seconds. Add tomatoes, corn, olives, ½ teaspoon pepper, and remaining oil and bring to boil.

4. MAKE BASE Whisk cornmeal, milk, and eggs in medium bowl until smooth. Slowly pour cornmeal mixture into pot, stirring constantly to prevent clumping, and cook until mixture is slightly thickened, about 1 minute. Off heat, stir in reserved bacon.

5. ASSEMBLE AND BAKE Carefully pour half (about 4 cups) of cornmeal mixture into large bowl and reserve. Smooth surface of remaining corn-meal mixture in pot, then top with shredded chicken. Pour reserved cornmeal mixture evenly over chicken and smooth surface. Arrange pot inside large roasting pan. Place roasting pan on oven rack and carefully pour enough boiling water into the pan to reach one-third of way up sides of Dutch oven. Bake until cornmeal mixture is firm, dry, and lightly browned, 1½ to 2 hours. Carefully remove from oven and let cool 10 minutes.

6. MAKE SAUCE While pie cools, toast flour in dry skillet over medium heat, stirring frequently, until golden, 3 to 5 minutes. Stir in chili powder, cumin, and coriander and cook, stirring continually, until fragrant, about 30 seconds. Stir in tomato sauce and reserved chicken broth and bring to boil. Reduce heat to medium-low and simmer until thickened, about 3 minutes. Season with salt and pepper. Serve, passing sauce at table.

Two cups of cornmeal and a can of creamed corn give this cheeseless tamale pie plenty of satisfying corn flavor.

Cheese Frenchees

PAM PATTERSON, LEON, KAN.

A breaded, deep-fried grilled cheese with mayo inside? You bet.

"DINING OUT WAS a rare and special occasion when I was a child during the '60s in Lincoln, Nebraska. A local favorite family restaurant was King's Food Host. The novelty of this restaurant was the telephone situated at each booth. You placed your order by picking up the phone and giving it to the hostess over the phone. In a time when many households had only one phone in the entire house, having a telephone tableside was very thrilling! The kids' indisputable favorite was King's take on the grilled cheese sandwich, a deep-fried grilled cheese sandwich with a side of French fries or onion rings." A Frenchee has even more to recommend it. The sandwich is made with a touch of mayonnaise. It's cut into triangles, which are battered and rolled in a crunchy coating before they're deep fried. Exactly who invented the sandwich is unclear, but it is clear that it won King's restaurants hordes of devoted patrons. King's Food Host USA, founded in Lincoln, began as King's Drive-In, and at its peak had about 160 restaurants in 17 states, mostly in the Midwest.

Adds Pam: "After having children of my own and King's Food Host was a distant memory, I came across a recipe that attempted to replicate this childhood treat. It remains a family favorite to this day!"

CHEESE FRENCHEES Serves 4

Pam's recipe didn't specify a brand of cracker, but we like Ritz here. Try dipping the sandwiches in ketchup—a Frenchee fanatic told us that's how she ate them growing up in Oklahoma.

- 1½ sleeves Ritz crackers (50 crackers), pulsed in food processor to coarse crumbs
- ⅔ cup milk
- 2 large eggs
- ½ cup mayonnaise
- 8 slices hearty white sandwich bread
- 6 slices deli American cheese
- 3–4 quarts peanut or vegetable oil

1. ASSEMBLE SANDWICHES Line rimmed baking sheet with parchment paper. Spread cracker crumbs in shallow dish. Whisk milk and eggs in medium bowl. Spread mayonnaise on 1 side of each slice bread. Arrange 1½ slices cheese on 4 slices bread and top with remaining 4 slices bread, mayonnaise side facing cheese. Cut each sandwich diagonally into quarters. One at a time, dip sandwich quarters into egg mixture, then coat with cracker crumbs, pressing to

After tasting this deep-fried classic from the Great Plains, you might never go back to ordinary grilled cheese.

adhere. Refrigerate on prepared baking sheet until set, about 1 hour.

2. FRY SANDWICHES Pour oil into large Dutch oven until it measures 2 inches deep. Heat oil to 375 degrees over medium-high heat. Fry half of chilled sandwich quarters until golden brown, 1 to 2 minutes per side. Transfer to paper towel–lined plate and repeat with remaining sandwich quarters. Serve.

Grandma Wooly's Beef Barbecue

CHARLES WOOLEVER, ROCHESTER, N.Y.

Some barbecue is served with a side of pickles. Grandma Wooly tossed pickling spices right in with the meaty beef chuck.

"THIS RECIPE COMES from my paternal grandmother, Dorothy Woolever, 'Grandma Wooly,'" Charles wrote us. "It's remarkable in that the simplicity of the ingredients belies the deep flavors of the finished dish. This recipe is, indeed, way more than the mere sum of its parts!"

We agree. Grandma's saucy shredded beef barbecue, which is served on buns, is in a league of its own. When you take a bite, you'll know there's something different about these sandwiches, but you may not be sure exactly what. Grandma's secret? A combination of pickling spice, dry mustard, and cider vinegar. It's tangy, sweet, and sets off the tender meat nicely.

"My father and his siblings ate this for dinner during the week when they were growing up," Charles Woolever continued. "They passed the tradition along to their children, and we all enjoy making—and eating—it today."

GRANDMA WOOLY'S BEEF BARBECUE Serves 8

- 1 tablespoon pickling spice
- 2 pounds boneless beef chuck-eye roast, trimmed and cut into 1½-inch cubes
  Salt and pepper
- 2 tablespoons vegetable oil
- 2½ cups water
- 1½ cups ketchup
- 1 tablespoon cider vinegar
- 1 teaspoon dry mustard
- 8 hamburger buns, toasted

1. BROWN BEEF Adjust oven rack to lower-middle position and heat oven to 300 degrees. Tie pickling spice in cheesecloth to make sachet. Pat beef dry with paper towels and season with salt and pepper. Heat 1 tablespoon oil in large Dutch oven over medium-high heat until just smoking. Cook half of beef, turning occasionally, until well browned all over, about 8 minutes. Transfer to large bowl. Repeat with the remaining oil and beef.

2. BRAISE BEEF Stir water into pot, scraping up any browned bits. Add beef, along with any accumulated juices, to pot and bring to boil. Transfer pot to oven and cook covered, stirring occasionally, until meat is

This barbecued beef finishes cooking in a sauce made from ketchup, dry mustard, and vinegar.

nearly tender, about 1 hour. Stir ketchup, vinegar, and mustard into pot. Add pickling spice sachet and continue to cook, covered, until meat is fork-tender, about 1 hour longer.

3. SHRED AND SERVE Discard sachet. Using slotted spoon, transfer beef to plate. When cool enough to handle, shred beef into bite-sized pieces. Return beef to pot and stir until coated with sauce and warmed. Season with salt and pepper. Serve on hamburger buns.

Grandma's Enchiladas

JOSIE LANDON, IDAHO FALLS, IDAHO

The smells of a Mexican kitchen delight a little girl, who grows up to cook what she remembers.

The beefy, tomatoey braising liquid becomes the sauce for these hearty enchiladas.

MANY AMERICAN-STYLE enchiladas are made with ground meat, so Josie's filling—deliciously tender, slow-cooked shredded chuck roast—made her recipe an immediate standout. Josie adapted it from the Mexican grandmother of her childhood friend Elena. We were surprised to get the recipe from a part of the country, Idaho, we don't usually associate with Mexican cooking, but Josie told us that the state is home to a long-standing Mexican-American population.

Elena's family had a huge garden, and as a girl, Josie was impressed that her friend's grandmother would pick tomatoes and onions and then head straight for the kitchen. "What's that smell?" Josie would ask her friend as the girls were playing and the house filled with tantalizing scents. "We *have* to go see what your grandmother is doing." Happily ensconced in the kitchen on many an afternoon, Josie learned from Elena's grandmother not only to make enchiladas but also to roast and then grind whole spices; her own family simply opened jars of preground spices. Josie also credits her love of cooking to her own beloved great-grandmother, who died a few years ago at the age of 102 after a lifetime of feeding her family memorable meals. "She would measure everything with her hand. That fascinated me. I've definitely had the good luck to learn from accomplished cooks."

GRANDMA'S ENCHILADAS Serves 6
Serve with chopped cilantro and lime wedges.

- 3   pounds boneless beef chuck-eye roast, trimmed and cut into 1½-inch cubes
  Salt and pepper
- 2   tablespoons vegetable oil
- 2   onions, minced
- 3   tablespoons chili powder
- 2   teaspoons ground cumin
- 2   teaspoons ground coriander
- ¼   teaspoon cayenne pepper
- 4   garlic cloves, minced
- 2   (15-ounce) cans tomato sauce
- ¼   cup red wine
- 2   cups shredded cheddar cheese
- 12 (6-inch) corn tortillas

1. BROWN BEEF Adjust oven rack to lower-middle position and heat oven to 300 degrees. Pat beef dry with paper towels and season with salt and pepper. Heat 1 tablespoon oil in large Dutch oven over medium-high heat until just smoking. Cook half of beef, turning occasionally, until well browned all over, about 8 minutes. Transfer to large bowl. Repeat with remaining oil and beef.

2. COOK AROMATICS Pour off all but 1 tablespoon fat from pot. Add onions and ½ teaspoon salt and cook over medium heat until softened, about 8 minutes. Stir in chili powder, cumin, coriander, cayenne, and ¼ teaspoon pepper and cook until spices darken, about 2 minutes. Add garlic and cook until fragrant, about 30 seconds. Stir in tomato sauce and wine and bring to boil.

3. BRAISE BEEF Add browned beef, along with any accumulated juices, to pot. Transfer pot to oven and cook, covered, until meat is fork-tender, 2 to 2½ hours. Transfer beef to large bowl. Strain sauce through fine-mesh strainer, discarding solids, and set aside. (You should have about 2 cups sauce.)

4. MAKE FILLING Increase oven temperature to 375 degrees. Spread ¾ cup sauce over bottom of 13- by 9-inch baking dish; set aside. When beef is cool enough to handle, shred into bite-sized pieces. Add 1 cup cheese and additional ¼ cup sauce and toss to combine.

5. ASSEMBLE Spray tortillas on both sides with cooking spray and arrange on rimmed baking sheet. Bake until they are warm and pliable, about 1 minute. Arrange warm tortillas on work surface. Place ⅓ cup beef mixture in center of each tortilla. Roll tightly and arrange, seam-side down, in prepared baking dish.

6. BAKE Pour remaining sauce evenly over enchiladas and sprinkle with remaining cheese. Cover with foil and bake until cheese is melted and enchiladas are heated through, 20 to 25 minutes. Serve.

STEP-BY-STEP Assembling Enchiladas
Sandwiching the filled, rolled tortillas between layers of sauce is a key to an integrated, well-seasoned dish.

1. Spread ¾ cup of sauce evenly over bottom of dish.

2. Fill tortillas, roll tightly, and place seam-side down over sauce in baking dish.

3. Pour remaining 1 cup sauce over enchiladas to coat evenly.

4. Sprinkle enchiladas with cheese and cover dish tightly with foil before baking.

Equipment Review Dish Towels

Don't throw in the towel! One cloth does it all. BY MEREDITH BUTCHER

MANY DISH TOWELS can't handle the smallest kitchen mishap. Some have zero absorbency, while others wipe up spills easily but stain just as readily. Then there are towels that shrink to the size of a tissue in the dryer or break delicate stemware with their bulk. We tested eight towels, from $2.50 to $8.99, in our search for a dish towel that would soak up liquid, dry dishes without streaks or destruction, and look good as new after washing.

SOAKING IT UP
Our dish towels came in fabrics from microfiber to cotton, bamboo to rayon. Microfiber—a synthetic made by splitting polyester and polyamide fibers—felt horrible, sticking like Velcro to fingertips and fabrics. Cotton and cotton-blend towels differed radically, depending on the weave (flour sack, ribbed, or terry cloth). Bamboo felt cushy as a baby blanket. The most unusual was rayon, which promised to pick up 12 times its weight in water.

We suspended each towel over a measured bucket of water, letting one end dangle in the liquid. After 15 minutes, you could see a rising line as towels soaked up water, except for a few towels (cotton weaves of herringbone and flour sack), which simply floated. The MU Microfiber towel was the thirstiest, drinking a full cup. But when we wiped up spilled water, it dried no better than other materials, more or less pushing the spill around. Overall, the ribbed cotton NOW Designs Ripple Towel performed best; its ribs created extra surface area to dry every last drop.

DELICATE TOUCH
We dried glass and metal bowls, wine glasses, and delicate champagne flutes. Thick, high-pile cotton towels couldn't fit into narrow flutes, while flour sack and bamboo towels were so big and cumbersome (nearly 5 square feet), we were afraid we'd drop glassware. The most useful size was 3 square feet: The MU Microfiber towel was just undersized, and the NOW cloth just oversized, but both were thin enough to maneuver in tight spots.

STAIN REMOVAL
To simulate messy spills, we stained each towel with mustard, wine, soy sauce, beet juice, and oil, and let them sit over a weekend. On Monday we found a dry, caked-on mess. After one laundry cycle, the only towel that was completely stain-free was NOW Designs Ripple Towel. Despite seven more laundry cycles, no other towels ever came clean.

SHRINKING VARIABLES
Every towel shrank a little after eight cycles of washing and drying. But bamboo towels underwent a sea change: They emerged from the machine curled, tattered, and truly miniature, with one brand shrinking by a whopping 53 percent. Microfiber towels, at 9 percent, shrank the least.

SUMMING UP
Innovative materials such as microfiber and bamboo promised better absorption but often failed to deliver in the kitchen. While microfiber performed well, we couldn't get past its uncomfortably prickly texture. In the end, we preferred the feel and absorbency of cotton, but terry cloth was too bulky, and flimsy herringbone and flour sack towels couldn't stand up to demanding kitchen work. Only the NOW Designs Ripple Towel passed all our tests with near perfect scores. It's the towel we've been waiting for. Now, we have no excuse for not drying the dishes.

RECOMMENDED

Product		CRITERIA		TESTERS' NOTES
NOW DESIGNS Ripple Towel, Set of 3 $10 at www.cookware.com ($3.33 per towel) **Material:** 100% ribbed cotton **Original Size:** 30 by 20½ inches **Shrinkage:** 17%		Absorption ★★ Stain Resistance ★★★ Drying Delicacy ★★★ Durability ★★★		A champion at soaking up spills, this well-proportioned towel left glassware streak-free and easily slipped into the smallest champagne flute. While it shrank slightly, its shape didn't distort, and just one trip through the washer and dryer got the stains out.
CALPHALON Kitchen Towel Ensembles $6.99 at www.bedbathandbeyond.com **Material:** 100% combed cotton terrycloth **Original Size:** 29¼ by 16 inches **Shrinkage:** 18%		Absorption ★★ Stain Resistance ★★★ Drying Delicacy ★ Durability ★★★		Extremely sturdy, this towel remained almost stain-free and new-looking, even after multiple washes. However, the thick material made drying champagne flutes and wine glasses treacherous.

RECOMMENDED WITH RESERVATIONS

Product		CRITERIA		TESTERS' NOTES
MU Microfiber Dish Towel $8.99 at www.cheftools.com **Material:** microfiber; 80% polyester, 20% polyamide **Original Size:** 24 by 16 inches **Shrinkage:** 9%		Absorption ★★ Stain Resistance ★★ Drying Delicacy ★★ Durability ★★		Testers hated the feel of this towel. It soaked up 1 cup of water, more than any other towel tested, in the dangling towel test, but didn't do as well with an actual spill. Mustard stains remained visible.
BAMBOO Kitchen Towel, Set of 3 $25.99 at www.ecokitchen.com ($8.66 per towel) **Material:** 100% bamboo **Original Size:** 31 by 20 inches **Shrinkage:** 35%		Absorption ★★ Stain Resistance ★ Drying Delicacy ★★ Durability ★★		Stains left their mark and its large size was cumbersome, but this towel absorbed ⅔ cup of water. Soft as a baby blanket, it was an odd choice for a kitchen towel but proved gentle enough to dry delicate items.

NOT RECOMMENDED

Product		CRITERIA		TESTERS' NOTES
A.R.E. NATURALS Bamboo Kitchen Towel, Set of 3 $24.99 at www.arenaturals.com ($8.33 per towel) **Material:** 60% bamboo, 40% cotton **Original Size:** 29 by 17½ inches **Shrinkage:** 53%		Absorption ★★ Stain Resistance ★ Drying Delicacy ★★ Durability ★		While it absorbed fairly well, this towel shrank by more than 50 percent. By the end of testing, it was extremely distorted and was discolored by stains—more of a rag than a dish towel.
MOPPINE Oven Mitts by Rachael Ray, Set of 3 $22.95 at www.cooking.com (Item # 647453), ($7.65 per towel) **Material:** 100% cotton **Original Size:** 27 by 17½ inches **Shrinkage:** 27%		Absorption ★★ Stain Resistance ★ Drying Delicacy ★ Durability ★		This unusual towel–oven mitt combination sounded like a great idea, but it performed poorly. Although quite absorbent, the towel stained and quickly became frayed, with curled edges. As a mitt, it was unstable and slippery. If the towel gets wet, you can't use it as an oven mitt because heat transfers through.
NOW DESIGNS Floursack Teatowel Collection, Set of 3 $14.99 at www.cookware.com ($4.99 per towel) **Material:** 100% cotton **Original Size:** 35 by 23½ inches **Shrinkage:** 18%		Absorption ★ Stain Resistance ★ Drying Delicacy ★★ Durability ★		Towel or tablecloth? Giant and awkward, this towel got in the way during every test. The thin material struggled to absorb, with the towel simply floating on top of liquid. By the end of testing, the material was stained and thinning.
SHAMWOW! Set of 4 large and 4 small $19.99 at www.target.com ($2.50 per towel) **Material:** rayon **Original Size:** 24 by 19½ inches **Shrinkage:** 13%		Absorption ★★ Stain Resistance ★ Drying Delicacy ★ Durability ★		Despite the infamous infomercials, the gimmicky Shamwow! was all sham and no wow. Not only did it not soak up "12 times its weight in liquid" as promised, it practically disintegrated by the end of testing. Following instructions, we avoided the dryer, but the shoddy material pilled and shredded after the first wash.

Taste Test Canned Chicken Noodle Soup

Our winners had two things in common: plenty of salt and MSG. BY SCOTT KATHAN

EVEN "GOURMET" CANNED chicken noodle soups can't match the long-cooked goodness of what Mom or Grandma could make with fresh chicken, plenty of vegetables, and half a day. But when the need for soup hits quickly, today's busy cooks often reach for the canned stuff. We wanted to determine which canned soups, if any, were worth buying.

We heated eight nationally available canned soups (including expensive "gourmet" and healthier choices) and called in our tasters—24 cooks and editors from America's Test Kitchen. The keys to good canned soup, we learned, are no off-flavors or troubling textures and plenty of salt—our top

four soups had the most sodium (a cup serving has almost half the American Heart Association's recommended daily intake). But salt alone isn't the answer; when we added enough salt to a low-sodium entry to match the level of the winner, tasters still disliked it.

The soups we rated highest fell into two distinct camps: meaty soups with good flavor and texture (the two soups from Progresso) and brothy, inexpensive soups whose scores seemed to be inflated by nostalgia (the two condensed soups from Campbell's). As one taster noted about the latter, "Not great, but familiar."

Our top four soups also contain MSG, or monosodium glutamate,

which enhances meaty, savory flavor. By contrast, our "Not Recommended" soups contain no MSG. Leaving no stone unturned, we strained out the solids in three cans of each soup to calculate the average relative weights of the chicken, noodles, and vegetables inside. Our top soup did contain the highest percentage of chicken, but more chicken alone couldn't propel other brands to the winner's circle. And the amounts of vegetables and noodles were less important than their texture; bloated veggies and mushy pasta torpedoed several brands. Only one brand is recommended, and none received our top rating ("highly recommended"). For that, we suggest Mom.

RECOMMENDED	TASTERS' NOTES
PROGRESSO Traditional Chicken Noodle $2.50 for 19 ounces **Sodium:** 950 mg per 1 cup serving **MSG:** Yes **Percentage of Chicken (out of total soup— broth and solids—weight, 3 cans averaged):** 9.6%	This "salty, but in a really good way" and "robust" soup with "meaty-tasting broth" received the highest scores for both flavor and texture. The noodles "still have some bite," and it contained the highest percentage of chicken that "actually seemed real."
RECOMMENDED WITH RESERVATIONS	**TASTERS' NOTES**
PROGRESSO Traditional Hearty Chicken & Rotini $2.50 for 19 ounces **Sodium:** 960 mg **MSG:** Yes **Percentage of Chicken:** 7.2%	While some tasters questioned the "weird noodle choice," most praised the "good chicken-y flavor" and "full-bodied," "rich, savory broth." A few tasters, however, found the broth "gummy" and "viscous."
CAMPBELL'S Condensed Homestyle Chicken Noodle $1.89 for 10.75 ounces (makes 21.72 ounces when reconstituted) **Sodium:** 940 mg **MSG:** Yes **Percentage of Chicken:** 1.6%	"I know this is ghetto, but I love it," one taster said about this "kid-friendly" soup. The miniscule amount of chicken was deemed "mushy." "Nice and salty and not complex."
CAMPBELL'S Condensed Chicken Noodle Soup $1.49 for 10.75 ounces (makes 21.72 ounces when reconstituted) **Sodium:** 890 mg **MSG:** Yes **Percentage of Chicken:** 1.3%	Even with its "squishy" chicken and "bloated" noodles (and no vegetables), most tasters thought this familiar soup had a "nicely balanced" if "somewhat bland" broth. "It goes down easy," one taster summed up.
NOT RECOMMENDED	**TASTERS' NOTES**
MUIR GLEN Organic Chef Inspirations Chicken Noodle Soup $3.29 for 18.8 ounces **Sodium:** 880 mg **MSG:** No **Percentage of Chicken:** 5.1%	Tasters were not excited about the "overly vegetal," "very herby" flavor. The "tough and chewy," "hard and dry" meat didn't help matters, nor did the "wobbly," "mushy" noodles.
CAMPBELL'S Select Harvest Healthy Request Chicken with Egg Noodles $3.19 for 18.6 ounces **Sodium:** 480 mg **MSG:** No **Percentage of Chicken:** 4.5%	According to the label, the soup is "98% fat-free" and "lower sodium." Tasters didn't need the label to notice the reduced salt, which made for a "flat" and "flavorless" soup. Tasters also identified an unappetizing "metallic," "aluminum" flavor.
HEALTHY CHOICE Old Fashioned Chicken Noodle Soup $2.50 for 15 ounces **Sodium:** 480 mg **MSG:** No **Percentage of Chicken:** 7.9%	While tasters liked the texture ("full-bodied broth, firm noodles"), they disliked the "sour, oniony, vegetal" taste, and they really missed the salt. "No flavor, no seasoning." "Tastes flat."
WOLFGANG PUCK Organic Chicken with Egg Noodles Organic Soup $2.59 for 14.5 ounces **Sodium:** 760 mg **MSG:** No **Percentage of Chicken:** 4.6%	This "murky," "funky," "scary-looking" brew scored last for both flavor and texture. Tasters were especially put off by the "nasty" bits of dark chicken meat. "Tastes exactly as it looks: like mud."

All About Pork Sausage

The test kitchen likes to use highly seasoned pork sausages to add meaty, spicy depth to soups, stews, stuffings, casseroles, pasta, rice dishes, and even meatballs and meatloaf. Here are the four types we use the most.

ANDOUILLE
Born in France, this very spicy smoked and cured sausage immigrated to Louisiana, finding wide acceptance in its new home. Today, it wouldn't be gumbo or jambalaya without it. This sausage is seasoned with garlic, dried hot pepper, and herbs. It doesn't need to be cooked (although cooking augments its flavor). Sautéed andouille adds lots of flavor to soups, stews, and stuffings.

CHORIZO
The most common chorizo in American markets (pictured) is sold fully cooked and is seasoned with garlic and chili powder. We use it  to lend kick to casseroles, potatoes, eggs, and any dishes with Latin origins. Less common in this country are Spanish- and Mexican-style chorizos. The former is a hard, smoky cured sausage with the texture of pepperoni; it is often served as an appetizer with cheese. The latter is made from fresh pork seasoned with garlic, paprika, and chili powder and must be fully cooked.

ITALIAN
Italian sausages are either hot or sweet. Both are made with coarsely ground 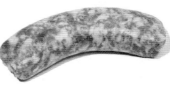 fresh (not cured or smoked) pork flavored with garlic and fennel seed. The hot variety is also seasoned with red pepper flakes. Both need to be cooked. Grill or sauté whole sausages or remove the casing and crumble the meat into pastas or stews.

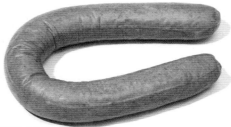

KIELBASA
Kielbasa, a smoked sausage, hails from Poland. Although its main seasoning is garlic, it's neither hot nor assertive. Kielbasa is sold fully cooked, but a good sear improves both flavor and texture. Some brands are much saltier than others, so always taste for seasoning when you cook with kielbasa. Smithfield Naturally Hickory Smoked Polska Kielbasa is our top-rated brand.

Test Kitchen Cooking Class Make-Ahead Turkey Gravy

If you follow our turkey cooking instructions on page 9, a bronzed, evenly cooked bird is manageable. But with multiple side dishes commanding your last-minute attention just as guests are arriving, you don't want to worry about the gravy too. By following these easy steps, you can start the gravy as many as three days in advance, so all you have to do day-of is heat and add the drippings.

MAKE-AHEAD TURKEY GRAVY

Makes about 6 cups

This recipe makes enough gravy for a 12- to 14-pound turkey, with leftovers. Leftovers can be refrigerated for up to three days or frozen for up to two months. Dried thyme may be substituted for the fresh.

- 1 tablespoon vegetable oil
  Reserved turkey neck and giblets, minus the liver (see box at right)
- 1 onion, chopped
- 4 cups low-sodium chicken broth (see box at right)
- 2 cups water
- 4 sprigs fresh thyme (see note)
- 1 bay leaf
- 4 tablespoons unsalted butter
- 6 tablespoons all-purpose flour
  Salt and pepper

1. SAUTÉ AND SOFTEN Heat oil in large saucepan over medium-high heat and brown giblets (minus the liver) and neck for 5 minutes. Add onion and cook until softened, about 3 minutes, then reduce heat to low, cover, and simmer for 20 minutes.

2. SIMMER AND SKIM Turn heat to high, add chicken broth and water, scrape pan bottom, and bring to boil. Reduce heat to low, add herbs, and simmer for about 30 minutes, skimming if needed.

3. STRAIN AND COOL Pour broth through fine-mesh strainer. Discard solids. Broth can be made in advance and stored in the refrigerator for 2 days.

4. MAKE ROUX Melt butter in large saucepan over medium heat. Whisk in flour. Cook, whisking constantly, until honey-colored and fragrant, about 4 minutes.

5. ADD BROTH Bring reserved turkey broth to simmer and add to pan, a little at a time, whisking constantly. Simmer gravy, whisking occasionally, until thickened, about 5 minutes. Set aside, covered, until turkey is done. (Gravy can be refrigerated, covered, for 1 day.)

6. DEFAT AND FINISH Scrape up bits in roasting pan and pour drippings into fat separator. Reheat gravy over medium heat until bubbling. Add defatted drippings. Simmer for 2 minutes until the gravy thickens. Season with salt and pepper. Serve with turkey.

STEP-BY-STEP Foolproof Make-Ahead Gravy

1. Brown, then sweat the onion, neck, heart, and gizzard (but not the liver) to build a deep base of flavor.

2. Deglaze with chicken broth and water, scraping the flavorful brown bits from the bottom of the pan.

3. Strain out (and discard) giblets and onion; the broth can be refrigerated until ready to use.

4. Stir flour into melted butter, whisking constantly, to make a roux, which thickens the gravy and adds nutty flavor.

5. Slowly add broth to roux, whisking constantly, until fully incorporated. This mixture can be made a day in advance.

6. While the turkey rests, pour defatted drippings from the roasting pan into gravy for extra richness.

Don't Fear the Bag

The turkey's cavities contain the neck, heart, gizzard (part of the bird's stomach), and liver. Although it might look scary, conquer your fears—the heart, neck, and gizzard are flavor powerhouses that can greatly enhance your gravy. We brown, then sweat and discard them to extract meaty flavor. The liver, however, has a potent, unpleasant flavor that can ruin a good gravy: Do not use it.

TURKEY LIVER
Don't use the liver! Its strong flavor will overpower your gravy. The other items in your giblets bag—the neck, heart, and gizzard—add delicious depth.

Notes from the Test Kitchen

Turkey Pepperoni

We typically take a pass on low-fat, turkey-based products such as turkey bacon and turkey jerky, but we wondered if garlicky, highly seasoned turkey pepperoni might pass muster in the test kitchen. Put to the test in our **Baked Manicotti with Meat Sauce** (page 18), the turkey pepperoni was indistinguishable from the standard beef and pork blend and, at 70 percent less fat, a smart substitute. Further taste tests—in sandwiches and on pizza—showed that turkey pepperoni lacks some of the pleasingly greasy qualities of the real stuff. But if you're looking to cut some fat and calories, it's a good place to do it.

FLAVOR WITHOUT THE FAT
A turkey-based product worth trying.

Plumping Dried Fruit

In testing dried fruit for our **Getting to Know** roundup (page 16), we found that many of them benefit from a hot liquid soak, especially any that have been sitting in the cupboard for a while, shriveling and turning hard. The technique, known as "plumping," is often used for dried fruits that will be baked. Place the fruit in a bowl and just cover with water. Wrap tightly with plastic wrap and microwave until the water begins to boil, about 1 minute. Let stand until the dried fruits are soft, about 5 minutes.

Depending on the flavors in your recipe, you can experiment with broth, wine, spirits, tea, or coffee in place of the water. They'll flavor the fruit as well as soften it.

Cider Substitute

Unlike most other fruit juices, apple cider contains residual solids from the pressing process. These solids make the cider cloudy but also give it a full, rich apple flavor. (Clarified apple juice, by contrast, is usually clear and less flavorful.) In Massachusetts, where America's Test Kitchen is located, we're blessed with a year-round supply of apple cider, but since many of you aren't so lucky, we developed an easy substitution that can be used in any cider-centric recipe, such as our **Cider Sauce** on page 21. For each cup of cider, substitute a combination of ¾ cup apple juice and ¼ cup unsweetened applesauce.

Browning Butter

Long a chef's secret, browned butter gives nutty depth to both sweet and savory dishes. We use it often in the home kitchen. The process is seemingly simple (melt butter on the stovetop until it turns brown), but it's important to pay attention or the butter will go from brown to burnt. Always work in a light-colored pan, so you can judge the color of the butter. The stovetop temperature doesn't matter much; it can range from low to medium-high heat, although cooking times will differ significantly. Foaming, which happens when the water boils off from the butter, is your clue that the butter is nearly done. Once the foaming subsides, don't wander off! Almost immediately, you'll see tiny specks settling to the bottom of the pan. These are the milk solids—particles of protein and carbohydrates—that give the browned butter its characteristic color and flavor. Do not strain them out. As soon as the butter turns chestnut brown and smells toasty, remove the pan from the heat. Use browned butter immediately or transfer it to another container. Otherwise, the residual heat from the hot pan may burn it. Browned butter is very versatile. It tastes fantastic in cakes, on noodles, and with fish.

Test Kitchen Technique
Prepping and Washing Leeks

Leeks grow in sandy soil, where their many layers capture and hold the dirt and grit. The classic technique for cleaning them is to split them lengthwise (not through the root), rinse them in running water to remove the trapped dirt, and pat dry before slicing. In prepping leeks for our **Creamy Mushroom Soup** (page 17), however, we were determined to figure out an easier way, and we did.

Swish the cut leeks in a salad spinner, drain, and spin dry.

Gadgets & Gear Mashed Potatoes

Mashed potatoes are as easy as side dishes get, provided you have the right tools. Here's what we use:

DUTCH OVEN

For most occasions, you can boil potatoes in any old saucepan. But when the holiday crowds congregate, we break out the big gun. With a 6.5-quart capacity and tight-fitting lid, here is yet another job for a heavy-duty Dutch oven.

★ **TEST KITCHEN WINNER**
TRAMONTINA 6.5-Qt. Cast Iron Dutch Oven, $44.97

VEGETABLE PEELER

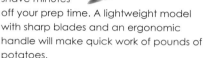

A good vegetable peeler can shave minutes off your prep time. A lightweight model with sharp blades and an ergonomic handle will make quick work of pounds of potatoes.

★ **TEST KITCHEN WINNER**
MESSERMEISTER Swivel Peeler, $5.95

COLANDER

To drain anything from chunky potatoes to tiny lentils, stick with a fine-meshed colander. A footed, oversized bowl and large handles are nice features.

★ **TEST KITCHEN WINNER**
ENDURANCE Stainless Steel Colander/Strainer, $27.95

POTATO MASHER

Wire-looped mashers will never yield smooth potatoes no matter how much you mash. What's more, their awkward shape makes it nearly impossible to reach the curved edges of the pot. Stick with a perforated mashing disk—it's all about efficiency.

★ **TEST KITCHEN WINNER**
PROFI PLUS
Masher, $15.99

POTATO RICER

Even with a good hand masher, no amount of elbow grease can approximate the luxuriously silky texture that a potato ricer affords. A large hopper and interchangeable disks (to vary the texture of puree) make this model our winner.

★ **TEST KITCHEN WINNER**
RSVP INTERNATIONAL Classic Kitchen Basics Potato Ricer, $11.99

Test Kitchen Technique Ready, Set, Roll

Roll cakes, like our **Pumpkin Roll** (inside back cover) or any jellyroll cake, are easier than they look. Here's a step-by-step guide to rolling and filling.

1. After baking, run a knife around the edge of the cake and flip it onto a large sheet of parchment paper dusted with confectioners' sugar. Peel off and discard the parchment paper that was baked onto the cake.

2. Starting from the short side, roll the cake and fresh parchment into a log to "train" it into shape so that it will roll easily once it has cooled and been spread with jam or filling. Let cool, seam-side down, for 1 hour.

3. Unroll the cake. Spread the filling over the cake, leaving a 1-inch border at the edges. If you spread the filling to the edge, it will leak out the ends when you roll it up again.

4. Re-roll the cake gently but snugly around the filling, leaving the parchment behind as you roll. Wrap the cake in plastic and refrigerate until well chilled, at least 1 hour or up to 2 days.

Looking for a Recipe

READER TO READER

Did you misplace a favorite recipe? Can you almost taste a chocolate cake from child-hood, but the bakery—and the recipe—is long gone? Ask a reader. While you're at it, answer a reader. Visit the Cook's Country website to post your requests and answer those of fellow readers. Go to **CooksCountry.com** and click on **Looking for a Recipe**. We'll share all your submissions on the website (check it out—hundreds are already posted!) and print as many as we can fit in the magazine (see recipes at right). You may also write to us at Looking for a Recipe, Cook's Country, P.O. Box 470739, Brookline, MA 02447. Please include your name and mailing address with each request.

Dolley Madison Coconut Cake
Kimberly Alexander, Visalia, Calif.

My cousins and I remember the square Dolley Madison Coconut Cake our grandmother used to serve for Sunday dinners—it was delicious. We've searched in vain for a similar recipe. Does anyone have one?

Funeral Pie
Dean Treadway, Knoxville, Tenn.

Years ago, my grandmother used to make a pie with raisins that she called Funeral Pie. Remembering this wonderful dessert brings back fond memories, and I would love to make it for my own grandkids.

Art Linkletter's Ham
Jean Comeau, Springbrook, Wis.

Years ago, I had a recipe for (TV personality) Art Linkletter's ham. I lost it in a move. The ham was wrapped in a rolled-out pie crust and baked. I don't know what was in the crust, but it was delicious.

Onion Pie (Calzone alla Cipolle)
Lorraine Sardone, Spotswood, N.J.

I am looking for a recipe for an onion-filled pie featured in a DuPont company magazine in the 1940s. It was one of my husband's favorites, but he never had his mom (who used to make it) write it down.

42nd Street Diner Bread Pudding
William Dean Butler, Via e-mail

The 42nd Street Diner in New York used to serve a bread pudding with a wonderful flavor and custardy texture. The restaurant is now closed. I'd love to have the recipe.

Wyatt's Cafeteria Eggplant Casserole
Karen Samartan, Los Angeles, Calif.

Forty-plus years ago I recall eating at a Wyatt's Cafeteria in Texas and having their Eggplant Casserole. I've lost the recipe and would love to make it again. It's economical and pure comfort food.

Pickled Beet Eggs
Anna Gayheart, Mayfield Heights, Ohio

I'd like to make pickled eggs for my husband as a surprise. He grew up in rural Ohio, where pickled eggs were in every home and also available in a huge jar at every corner bar. I'd like to find a basic (NOT rubbery) pickled egg recipe that uses beet juice for that distinctive reddish-purple color.

Horn & Hardart Chocolate Glace
Maryanne Morone, Las Vegas, Nev.

My mom was a waitress at Horn & Hardart in Philadelphia for many years. I've been searching for a recipe for my favorite H&H dessert, which was called Chocolate Glace. They resembled cupcakes, and they were the BEST! What a special treat when my mom brought them home. I would love to have this recipe so I can re-create a childhood favorite.

"APIE" Cookies
Meg van Meter, Ambler, Pa.

My grandmother used to make what she called APIE cookies. I was told they might have originated with A&P supermarkets, hence their name. They were large, very white, and they contained a little wine. I have not been able to come close to duplicating her lost recipe.

German Pork Chops in Vinegar
Kristine Dahlstedt, Wausau, Wis.

I'm looking for a vinegar pork chop recipe my husband's mom used to make in the 1950s and '60s. The pork chops were marinated in vinegar overnight, then breaded and fried. He thinks they were called "ving en dosh" (spelled phonetically).

Dilly Bread
Marsha Dahl-Huff, Kansas City, Mo.

I'm looking for a recipe for Dilly Bread that my grandmother used to make a lot.

Grape-Nuts Banana Bread
Sally Trachsel, Portland, Ore.

Years ago, my aunt made a delicious banana bread that had Grape-Nuts cereal in it. I've lost the recipe and would really love to make this bread again. Can you help?

FIND THE ROOSTER!

Our Favorite Recipe Finds

In response to reader queries, Margaret Kerbrat sent us a recipe for Goody Goody Bars, and Marti Thevenin sent us one for Tomato Butter.

GOODY GOODY BARS Makes 24 bars
Margaret Kerbrat, Mission Viejo, Calif.

"I've always called these 'Like Baby Ruth Bars,' but they sound just like what Phyllis Nichols is looking for." Melt the chocolate by micro-waving the chips in a bowl until smooth, 30 to 60 seconds.

- 1 cup packed light brown sugar
- 1 cup light corn syrup
- 1 cup peanut butter
- 1 cup salted dry-roasted peanuts, chopped
- 6 cups cornflakes
- 1 cup semisweet chocolate chips, melted (see note)

1. Grease 13- by 9-inch baking pan. Bring sugar and corn syrup to simmer in large pot. Off heat, add peanut butter and peanuts, stirring until smooth. Add cornflakes and stir until incorporated.

2. Scrape mixture into prepared pan and press into bottom and corners with greased spatula. Drizzle melted chocolate over top and spread to cover. Let cool completely, about 30 minutes. Slice and serve. (Bars can be stored in airtight container for 2 days.)

TOMATO BUTTER Makes about 3 cups
Marti Thevenin, London, Ohio

"My mother used to make this recipe, and after I got married, we always had it on salt-rising bread (made with an old-fashioned fermentation technique, instead of yeast), which made for a nice contrast of tastes." We also love this jamlike spread on biscuits or sandwiches. To peel the tomatoes, use a vegetable peeler with a serrated blade.

- 3 pounds tomatoes, peeled, cored, seeded, and chopped
- 1 onion, grated on large holes of box grater
- 2 cups packed light brown sugar
- 2 teaspoons ground ginger
- 1 teaspoon turmeric
- 1 teaspoon paprika
- 1/8 teaspoon cayenne pepper
- 1/4 cup juice from 2 lemons
  Salt and pepper

1. Simmer tomatoes, onion, sugar, ginger, turmeric, paprika, and cayenne in large saucepan over low heat until thick and jamlike, 2 to 2½ hours.

2. Stir in lemon juice and season with salt and pepper. Transfer to medium bowl, cover with plastic wrap, and refrigerate at least 2 hours and up to 1 week. Serve.

Pumpkin Roll

This simple pumpkin sponge cake with fluffy cream cheese filling needs no more than a dusting of powdered sugar. For details on rolling it, see page 31.

To make this cake, you will need:

- 1 **cup cake flour, sifted**
- 2 **teaspoons pumpkin pie spice**
- ½ **teaspoon baking soda**
- ½ **teaspoon salt**
- 5 **large eggs**
- 1 **cup sugar**
- 1 **cup canned pumpkin puree**
- 3 **cups cream cheese frosting***
  Confectioners' sugar and store-bought spiced nuts, for garnish

* Go to **CooksCountry.com** for our cream cheese frosting recipe.

For the cake: Adjust oven rack to middle position and heat oven to 350 degrees. Grease 18- by 13-inch rimmed baking sheet and line with greased parchment paper. Whisk flour, spice, baking soda, and salt in medium bowl; set aside. With electric mixer on medium-high speed, beat eggs and sugar until pale yellow and thick, 6 to 10 minutes. Add pumpkin and mix on low until incorporated. Fold in flour mixture until combined. Spread batter evenly in prepared pan. Bake until cake is firm and springs back when touched, about 15 minutes. Before cooling, run knife around edge of cake to loosen, and turn out onto clean sheet of parchment paper that has been dusted with confectioners' sugar. Gently peel off parchment attached to cake and discard. Roll cake and fresh parchment into log and cool completely, about 1 hour.

To assemble: Gently unroll cake and spread with frosting, leaving 1-inch border at edges. Re-roll cake snugly, leaving parchment behind. Wrap cake firmly in plastic wrap and chill completely, at least 1 hour or up to 2 days. Remove plastic, dust with confectioners' sugar, and garnish with spiced nuts.

Recipe Index

RC = Recipe Card

Cook's Country

DECEMBER/JANUARY 2010

Herbed Roast Beef
Cheap Cut, Big Flavor

Divine Duchess Potatoes
Dressing Up Mashed Spuds

Holiday Cookie Contest Winners
Spumoni Wins the Day!

Slow-Cooker Short Ribs
Secret Is in the Bones

Swiss Steak
Sprucing Up an Old Favorite

Skillet "Carbonara"
All-New American Classic

Pie Dough Primer
Roll Without Fear or Failure

Cider-Braised Chicken
With 4-Way Apple Flavor

Hand-Mixer Showdown
Can $50 Buy You $300 Performance?

Wellesley Fudge Cake
With Real Fudge Frosting

Rating Creamy Italian Dressings
2 Brands OK in a Pinch

$4.95 U.S./$6.95 CANADA

0 1>

0 74470 05251 7

Tune In, Tune Up Your Cooking
Cook's Country from America's Test Kitchen has begun its second season on public television. Learn to sharpen a knife, bake a Red Velvet Cake, grill a pork loin, and much more. In our Vermont farmhouse kitchen, we make classic American food easy. Go to CooksCountryTV.com to see when the show airs in your area.

Dear Country Cook,

I like to think of history as a progression, that things get better, that we learn from our mistakes, and that the past is a pale reflection of the present, holding the promise of what's to come but none of the benefits.

Looking at the photo below, I am reminded that in the 1950s and '60s, one part of "progress" meant counters built around the perimeter of the kitchen with overhanging cabinets. In Vermont just 50 years ago, when I was growing up, the cooking was done on a table in the middle of the room. The same table was used to serve the noontime dinner. In the 19th century, a Victorian kitchen would also have used a central table for the preparation of food. It was a vastly superior setup. This is one case of progress setting us back.

But the modern kitchen may yet hold promise. The "Material Feminists" of the late 1800s wanted to free themselves from the bondage of cooking and housekeeping in an effort to unlock their creativity and potential. Cooking was neither an art nor a pleasure, in part because women spent six hours per day standing at a hot stove. This was the beginning of the end of American cooking—it was tagged as inconvenient and menial.

Today, however, science and industry have removed most of the drudgery from cooking, and we are left with an opportunity to fulfill the dreams of our ancestors—to be creative and also fulfilled. It's an invitation that millions of us have accepted with great enthusiasm. Baking cookies is not the occupation of the oppressed or unenlightened. It is one of the great joys of life, a gift from mother to son, from father to daughter.

Let the baking begin.

Christopher Kimball

Christopher Kimball
Founder and Editor, Cook's Country Magazine

Cook's Country

Founder and Editor Christopher Kimball
Editorial Director Jack Bishop
Executive Editor Peggy Grodinsky
Deputy Editor Bridget Lancaster
Food Editor Karen Berner
Senior Editors Scott Kathan,
Lisa McManus, Jeremy Sauer
Test Kitchen Director Erin McMurrer
Associate Editors Cali Rich, Diane Unger
Test Cooks Lynn Clark, Kris Widican
Assistant Editors Meredith Butcher, Peggy Chung Collier
Assistant Test Cooks Meghan Erwin
Maria del Mar Sacasa
Assistant Test Kitchen Director Matthew Herron
Copy Editor Amy Graves
Editorial Assistant Abbey Becker
Executive Assistant Meredith Smith
Senior Kitchen Assistant Nadia Domeq
Kitchen Assistants Maria Elena Delgado, Ena Gudiel
TV Producer Melissa Baldino
Contributing Editors Erika Bruce, Eva Katz
Consulting Editor Meg Ragland
Science Editor Guy Crosby, Ph.D.

Online Managing Editor David Tytell
Online Editor Kate Mason
Online Editorial Assistants Eric Grzymkowski, Mari Levine

Design Director Amy Klee
Art Director, Magazines Julie Bozzo
Designers, Magazines Jay Layman, Lindsey Timko
Deputy Art Director, Marketing and Web Christine Vo
Designer, Marketing Beatrice Keng
Staff Photographer Daniel J. van Ackere

Director, Information Technology Rocco Lombardo
Lead Developer Scott Thompson
Web Developer Robert Martinez
Web Production Coordinator Evan Davis
Web Production Assistant Jennifer Millet
Systems Administrator S. Paddi McHugh
IT Support Technician Brandon Lynch

Production Director Guy Rochford
Traffic & Projects Manager Alice Carpenter
Traffic & Production Coordinator Laura Collins
Production & Imaging Specialists
Judy Blomquist, Lauren Pettapiece
Color & Imaging Specialist Andrew Mannone

Vice President Marketing David Mack
Circulation Director Doug Wicinski
Fulfillment & Circulation Manager Carrie Horan
Partnership Marketing Manager Pamela Putprush
Marketing Assistant Megan DeFilippo
Direct Mail Director Adam Perry
Senior Database Analyst Marina Sakharova
Products Director Steven Browall
Product Promotions Director Randi Lawrence
E-Commerce Marketing Director Hugh Buchan
E-Commerce Marketing Manager Laurel Zeidman
E-Commerce Search Manager Elizabeth Dillon
E-Commerce Marketing Coordinator Tia Freeman
Marketing Copywriter David Goldberg
Customer Service Manager Jacqueline Valerio
Customer Service Representatives
Jillian Nannicelli, Kate Sokol

Chief Financial Officer Sharyn Chabot
Human Resources Director Adele Shapiro
Controller Mandy Shito
Senior Accountant Aaron Goranson
Staff Accountant Connie Forbes
Accounts Payable Specialist Steven Kasha
Office Manager Tasha Bere
Receptionist Henrietta Murray

Sponsorship Sales Director Marcy McCreary
Retail Sales & Marketing Manager Emily Logan
Corporate Marketing Associate Bailey Vatalaro
Publicity Deborah Broide

COLOR FOOD PHOTOGRAPHY: Keller + Keller
STYLING: Mary Jane Sawyer
ON THE COVER: Cranberries, Keller + Keller

ILLUSTRATION: Ross MacDonald
Greg Stevenson (cover illustration)

Cook's Country magazine (ISSN 1552-1990), number 30, published bimonthly by Boston Common Press Limited Partnership, 17 Station Street, Brookline, MA 02445. Copyright 2009 Boston Common Press Limited Partnership. Periodicals postage paid at Boston, Mass., and additional mailing offices. Publications Mail Agreement No. 40020778. Return undeliverable Canadian addresses to P.O. Box 875, Station A, Windsor, Ontario N9A 6P2. POSTMASTER: Send address changes to Cook's Country, P.O. Box 8382, Red Oak, IA 51591-1382. Customer Service: It's easy to subscribe, give a gift subscription, change your address, and manage your subscription online. Visit www.americastestkitchen.com/customerservice for all of your customer service needs or write to us at Cook's Country, P.O. Box 8382, Red Oak, IA 51591-1382. PRINTED IN THE USA.

DECEMBER/JANUARY 2010

Contents

HERBED ROAST BEEF, 14

DUCHESS POTATOES, 12

SPUMONI BARS, 4

Features

In Every Issue

One Smart Cookie

Michigan resident **Donna Bardocz** is on a roll. Last month, her recipe for Aunt Nina's Bread Balls was a finalist in our Lost Suppers Recipe Contest. This month, her **Spumoni Cookies** took the $1,000 Grand Prize in our annual Holiday Cookie Contest. To break the ice when we called her about the cookie, we asked if she cooked often. "That's all I do besides work." You could hear the smile in her voice as she added, "Well, there's my grandkids!" It's not too soon to enter next year's contest. Send your original holiday cookie recipes to **CooksCountry.com/emailus** or Holiday Cookie Contest, Cook's Country, P.O. Box 470739, Brookline, MA 02447. Recipes are due May 31, 2010.

America's TEST KITCHEN

America's Test Kitchen is a 2,500-square-foot kitchen located just outside of Boston. It is the home of Cook's Country and Cook's Illustrated magazines and is the workday destination for more than three dozen test cooks, editors, and cookware specialists. Our mission is to test recipes until we understand how and why they work and arrive at the best version. We also test kitchen equipment and supermarket ingredients in search of brands that offer the best value and performance. You can watch us work by tuning in to Cook's Country from America's Test Kitchen (CooksCountryTV.com) and America's Test Kitchen (AmericasTestKitchen.com) on public television.

Kitchen Shortcuts

KITCHEN EFFICIENCY
I Can See Clearly Now
Margaret Brown, Loxley, Ala.

I store my spices in a clear hanging shoe rack on the back of my kitchen door. No more rummaging through cabinets looking for curry powder when I'm in the middle of cooking. All the spices are in sight, so it's easy to keep track of what I need to replace.

DOUBLE DUTY
Oil Doily
Don Blake, Denver, Colo.

My bottles of olive and vegetable oil used to leave greasy rings on the shelves of my pantry and refrigerator. It seemed like I was always wiping up. Now I place them in cupcake liners to contain the grease—the sturdier foil-lined ones are especially good for the job—and my days of cleaning up oil slicks are over. I replace the liners when they start to look grungy.

SMART PREP
Cuts Like a Charm
David Hedrick, Centennial, Colo.

Winter squashes like acorn and butternut are hard as nails. I've tried using a mallet to tap the knife in so I can cut them in half more easily, but that technique often leaves me with uneven halves, plus it's still a tough job. I've found that putting the squash in the microwave for 1 to 2 minutes softens the skins just enough to make even, easy cutting possible.

HANDY TIP
Slick Spritz
Bonnie Johnson, Kempner, Texas

Concern about cost and trying to avoid a throwaway lifestyle inspired me to improvise an oil mister. I bought a small nonaerosol pump at the hardware store and filled it with oil. I use it for greasing skillets and baking sheets or to spray food before browning or baking. It's become a favorite, indispensable kitchen tool.

If you'd like to submit a tip, please e-mail us by visiting CooksCountry.com/kitchenshortcuts or send a letter to Kitchen Shortcuts, Cook's Country, P.O. Box 470739, Brookline, MA 02447. Include your name, address, and phone number. If we publish your tip, you will receive a free one-year subscription to *Cook's Country.*

MAKE AHEAD
Single-Serving Savvy
Sharon Mathers, Pioneer, Calif.

Recently, I had to bring food to a friend who was recovering from surgery. Rather than bringing over large, unwieldy casseroles, I made individually sized meals of mac and cheese and breakfast strata: I lined muffin tins, filled them with the food I'd made, froze them, and put the casserole "muffins" in a gallon freezer bag. Depending on how my friend feels, two "muffins" should be enough for a meal. For a final touch, I wrote the microwave instructions right on the bag.

HANDY TIP
Chop Chop!
Marisa Hill, Lilburn, Ga.

To make quick work of chopping hard-cooked eggs for egg salad, I use a potato masher in the same bowl I'll be mixing and serving the egg salad in. I can dispense with a knife and cutting board, which means that cleanup is fast and easy, too. Once the eggs are "chopped," I add the mayonnaise, pickles, and seasonings.

SMART PREP
Easy Clean
June Shen-Epstein, South Burlington, Vt.

I usually buy new and fingerling potatoes in mesh bags at the supermarket. One day, it occurred to me I could use the bag to wash them. Instead of scrubbing each little potato individually, I loosen the bag and then run the whole thing under water, using the coarse mesh to rub the potatoes clean. It is the easiest way I've found to wash small potatoes.

BETTER BAKING
Butter Up!
Neil Guercio, Highland Lakes, N.J.

When I need softened butter to grease a baking pan and I don't feel like waiting for the butter to come to room temperature, I place the pan in the oven for a few minutes while the oven is preheating. Then I move the warm pan to a wire rack or trivet and rub it with cold butter. The butter melts slightly, so I get complete coverage, even on Bundt pans with hard-to-reach nooks and crannies.

What does it mean to "cut across the grain" of meat, and why should I?
Pat Berrigan, Edmonton, Alberta, Canada

If you look closely at a piece of meat, you'll notice little bundles of closely packed muscle fibers that run parallel to one another. This pattern of fibers is known as the grain. Recipes recommend slicing across the grain—perpendicular to the fibers—to shorten them and thereby make the meat tender and easier to chew. To be sure this wasn't merely convention, we made our recipe for Pan-Roasted Flank Steak and sliced the cooked steak into pieces cut both with and across the grain. Tasters unanimously agreed the slices cut with the grain were chewier and stringier than those cut against it. It's equally important to cut across the grain when you're cutting up raw flank steak for a stir-fry.

THE BOTTOM LINE For easier eating, cut against the grain.

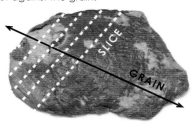

TENDER NOT TOUGH
Slice against the grain (unless you have very strong teeth).

You often mention freezing leftover egg whites; can they be whipped after defrosting?
Louise Mill, Prescott, Ontario, Canada

Custards or other recipes that call for thickening with egg yolks often leave the cook with leftover egg whites. We've recommended freezing individual whites for later use in recipes. But do they whip to the same volume and consistency as fresh whites?

We compared frozen egg whites that had been defrosted overnight in the refrigerator to fresh whites in two recipes: our Angel Food Cake and the meringue topping for our Mile-High Lemon Meringue Pie. In both instances, the frozen whites reached the desired consistency (soft peaks for the angel food cake and stiff peaks for the meringue topping) a few seconds faster than the fresh. A little research revealed that freezing the egg whites begins the process of unwinding their proteins, which the mechanical action of the whip continues. That was the only difference. Otherwise, frozen and fresh whites performed equally well.

THE BOTTOM LINE Use either frozen (defrosted) whites or fresh; they whip to the same volume and consistency, but be mindful that frozen whites will reach full volume a little more quickly.

Can I reconstitute evaporated milk and use it in place of ordinary milk in recipes?
Erin Lalime, Baltimore, Md.

Who hasn't run out of milk at an inconvenient time? We knew that substituting reconstituted evaporated milk (1 part water to 1 part evaporated milk) for whole milk wouldn't matter in small amounts but wondered if it would make a difference in recipes where milk was a primary ingredient. We compared these milks in recipes for vanilla pudding and vanilla cake as well as in a béchamel (white) sauce. The reconstituted evaporated milk performed reasonably well in all of these, though it did result in deeper, toastier colors and slightly sweeter, faintly caramelized flavors. Well and good in the pudding and the cake, but some tasters found the sweetness off-putting in the béchamel.

THE BOTTOM LINE Reconstituted evaporated milk is ok for desserts. For savory sauces and soups, go to the store and buy fresh milk.

Can you make a proper pan sauce in a nonstick skillet?
Andia Wecht, Hopatcong, N.J.

Unlike sauces that take hours to become concentrated and develop flavor, pan sauces take just a few minutes and are made in the same skillet in which the meat or poultry is cooked. These sauces typically rely on fond (the browned bits that get stuck to the bottom of the pan) for added flavor. The fact that nonstick skillets don't allow much fond to develop made us suspect that sauces made in them would have less flavor. To find out, we cooked chicken breasts in nonstick and stainless steel skillets, then made a vermouth pan sauce in each. Sure enough, the sauces made in nonstick skillets were pale compared to those made in stainless steel. Also, we noticed a striking difference in the flavor of the sauces. The sauce made in stainless steel had robust chicken flavor, while the sauce made in a nonstick skillet was watery and weak.

THE BOTTOM LINE For best flavor and color, stick with stainless steel.

DEEP FLAVOR
Pan sauce made in a stainless steel skillet is dark and rich.

MEEK FLAVOR
The same sauce made in a nonstick skillet lacks flavor.

Should I remove bay leaves from stew before refrigerating it? I've heard their flavor can take over.
Lauralee Gunby, Dallas, Texas

To find out, we made two pots of the test kitchen's Hearty Beef Stew, left the bay leaves in one pot and removed them from the other, and then tasted both the next day. Tasters commented that the stew with the bay leaves left in overnight tasted more "herbal," while the stew without the leaves tasted "sweeter." The bolder bay leaf flavor bothered a few tasters, who deemed it "medicinal," but most liked both stews. We repeated the test with our recipe for Four Vegetable Soup, which is more delicately flavored. Again, the bay flavor was more pronounced in the version that had the bay leaves left in it overnight. Although a few tasters found it "somewhat harsh," most considered it fine.

THE BOTTOM LINE Unsurprisingly, the flavor of bay leaves is more pronounced if you leave them in after cooking. But whether you like that flavor or not is a matter of personal preference.

Will soaking dried beans longer than overnight affect their texture?
Martha Willey, Lyndonville, Vt.

To determine how a long soak affects dried beans, we soaked 2-cup batches of Great Northern beans (each in a quart of water) in the refrigerator for five, four, three, and two days and compared them to beans we had soaked overnight. Each batch of beans absorbed about the same amount of water while soaking, and all looked about the same. The cooking time varied by up to 15 minutes from batch to batch. After cooking, tasters found small variations in texture, but deemed all batches acceptable. We were not able to tell if these small differences were attributable to the length of soaking time or to variations among the beans themselves.

THE BOTTOM LINE Beans soaked for up to five days can be used interchangeably with beans soaked overnight. Keep them in the refrigerator to protect against foodborne bacteria.

Does flouring fruit or nuts really keep them from sinking in batter?
Kate O'Connor, Amherst, Wis.

Many recipes call for tossing berries or nuts with a few teaspoons of flour before folding them into cake or muffin batter. The flouring is supposed to prevent sinking. Your question made us wonder if those few spoonfuls of flour really did anything. Curious, we tested floured fruit and nuts

against unfloured in a muffin batter, a delicate butter-rich coffee cake, and a sturdier fruit-and-nut loaf. After the first round of testing, we couldn't believe our eyes: The muffins, cake, and loaves with floured and unfloured ingredients were virtually identical. We tried the test again. And again. And again with frozen berries. The results? Flouring did not keep the berries or nuts from sinking in any of the batters. (We did notice, however, that nuts and berries folded into thicker batters sink less overall than those mixed into thinner batters.) What about tossing the fruit and nuts with, say, ¼ cup flour? Would that work? Only if you don't mind nasty spots of unincorporated flour in your cakes and muffins.

THE BOTTOM LINE Forget the flour, and for thinner batters, save a few berries to sprinkle on top. Some will sink to the middle during baking for even layers of berries throughout.

CAN YOU SEE A DIFFERENCE?
We couldn't. The blueberries in the muffin on the left were floured, then stirred into the batter; the blueberries in the muffin on the right were unfloured.

Can I substitute the basil herb pastes I see in the supermarket for fresh herbs?
Laura Bean-Kelly, Scarborough, Maine

We tested two brands of frozen chopped basil, and one brand of refrigerated basil paste, against fresh basil in our recipe for Quick Tomato Sauce. Tasters overwhelmingly preferred the fresh basil for its—surprise!—freshness, and assertiveness, too.

Compared to fresh basil, the two brands of frozen chopped basil were muted and dull. We were surprised, however, by the assertive flavor of the refrigerated basil paste both plain and in the sauce. Some tasters loved it, others found it grassy and medicinal. A look at the ingredient list helped explain some of its additional flavor: Dextrose, fructose, whey, and salt all appear on the label.

THE BOTTOM LINE Stick with fresh basil for the best and brightest herbal flavor; avoid frozen brands; and if you don't mind a laundry list of ingredients, the refrigerated basil paste might be worth considering.

To ask us a cooking question, visit **CooksCountry.com/emailus.** You can also write to Ask Cook's Country, P.O. Box 470739, Brookline, MA 02447. Just try and stump us!

Holiday Cookie Contest

Lemon Crunch Cookies, Sunbeam Cookies, Anise Drops—the names alone made us eager to head into the kitchen and bake. We asked for your favorite holiday cookies and got more than 200 treasured recipes. How lucky are we! Narrowing down our selection to just five may have been the toughest job we faced all year. Also the sweetest.

SPUMONI BARS
Donna Bardocz, Howell, Mich.

Makes 4 dozen cookies
Donna says: "These pretty tricolored cookies are somewhat time-consuming to make, but oh so worth your efforts!"

- 2 cups all-purpose flour
- ¼ teaspoon baking powder
- ⅛ teaspoon salt
- 12 tablespoons (1½ sticks) unsalted butter, softened
- ⅔ cup sugar
- 3 large egg yolks
- 1 teaspoon vanilla extract
- 12 maraschino cherries, drained, stemmed, and chopped fine
- ¼ cup walnuts, toasted and chopped fine
- ¼ cup semisweet chocolate chips, melted and slightly cooled

1. MAKE DOUGH Combine flour, baking powder, and salt in bowl. With electric mixer on medium-high speed, beat butter and sugar until light and fluffy, about 2 minutes. Add egg yolks and vanilla and mix until incorporated. Reduce speed to low, add flour mixture, and mix until just combined. Divide dough into thirds and transfer each third to separate bowl.

2. FLAVOR DOUGH Add cherries to first bowl and mix until incorporated. Add walnuts to second bowl and mix until incorporated. Add melted chocolate to third bowl and mix until incorporated. Refrigerate until doughs are slightly firm, about 10 minutes.

3. ROLL ROPES Adjust oven racks to upper-middle and lower-middle positions and heat oven to 375 degrees. Line 2 baking sheets with parchment paper. Divide each dough in half. On lightly floured surface, roll each dough half into 12-inch rope. Place 1 rope of each color side-by-side on floured surface and gently press together. Refrigerate until slightly firm, about 10 minutes, then roll dough into 24- by 3-inch rectangle. Cut crosswise into 1-inch cookies and place ¾ inch apart on prepared baking sheet. Repeat with remaining dough. Chill for another 10 to 15 minutes.

4. BAKE COOKIES Bake until just set but not browned, 12 to 14 minutes, switching and rotating sheets halfway through baking. Cool 5 minutes on sheets, then transfer to wire rack and cool completely. (Cookies can be stored in airtight container for 1 week.)

$1,000 GRAND PRIZE WINNER

Our winner offers three cookies in one—cherry, vanilla-walnut, and chocolate.

STEP-BY-STEP **Spumoni Cookie Assembly**
For picture-perfect tricolored cookies, follow these simple steps.

1. Roll each dough into ropes, gently press them together, and chill.

2. Use a rolling pin to roll a single long rectangle.

3. Cut the rolled dough crosswise into 1-inch cookies.

CHERRY CHEESECAKE COOKIES
Stephanie Matthews, Tempe, Ariz.

Makes about 4½ dozen cookies

Stephanie says: "I love to bring these to parties and potluck dinners. They go well on a Christmas dessert table, too." To make graham cracker crumbs, process 8 whole graham crackers in a food processor until finely ground.

- 3½ cups all-purpose flour
- 2 teaspoons baking powder
- 1 teaspoon salt
- 2 (8-ounce) packages cream cheese, softened
- 20 tablespoons (2½ sticks) unsalted butter, softened
- 1½ cups sugar
- 2 large eggs
- 2 teaspoons vanilla extract
- 1 cup graham cracker crumbs (see note)
- 3 (20-ounce) cans cherry pie filling, drained

1. MAKE DOUGH Combine flour, baking powder, and salt in bowl. With electric mixer on medium-high speed, beat cream cheese, butter, and sugar until smooth and creamy, about 2 minutes. Add eggs and vanilla and mix until incorporated. Reduce speed to low, add flour mixture, and mix until just combined. Refrigerate dough until firm, at least 30 minutes.

2. HEAT OVEN Adjust oven racks to upper-middle and lower-middle positions and heat oven to 350 degrees. Line 2 baking sheets with parchment paper. Place graham cracker crumbs in shallow dish.

3. ASSEMBLE COOKIES Roll dough into 1½-inch balls, then roll in crumbs. Place balls 2 inches apart on prepared baking sheets. Using tablespoon measure, make indentation in center of each ball. Place 3 cherries in each dimple. Bake until golden around edges, 12 to 14 minutes, switching and rotating sheets halfway through baking. Cool 5 minutes on sheets, then transfer to wire rack to cool completely. (Cookies can be stored in airtight container for 2 days.)

BOOZY BISCOTTI
Nicole Mitchell, Sacramento, Calif.

Makes about 2 dozen cookies

Nicole says: "My family is Italian, hence the biscotti cookie. The grits are my husband's grandmother's touch." We like these cookies dipped in melted chocolate (heat 8 ounces bittersweet chocolate and ½ cup heavy cream until smooth; stir in rum reserved from plumping cherries).

- 1 cup dried cherries
- ¼ cup spiced rum
- 1¼ cups instant grits
- 1¼ cups all-purpose flour
- ½ teaspoon baking powder
- 1 teaspoon salt
- 8 tablespoons (1 stick) unsalted butter, softened
- 1 cup sugar
- 1 tablespoon grated orange zest
- 2 large eggs
- 1 cup macadamia nuts, chopped

1. PLUMP CHERRIES Adjust oven rack to middle position and heat oven to 350 degrees. Line rimmed baking sheet with parchment paper. Microwave cherries and rum in bowl, covered, until bubbling, about 1 minute. Let sit until cherries have plumped, about 5 minutes. Drain cherries, reserving rum to stir into chocolate.

2. MAKE DOUGH Combine grits, flour, baking powder, and salt in bowl. With electric mixer on medium-high speed, beat butter, sugar, and zest until light and fluffy, about 2 minutes. Add eggs and mix until incorporated. Reduce speed to low and add flour mixture, nuts, and plumped cherries; mix until just combined. Form dough into two 7-by 3-inch logs and transfer to prepared baking sheet. Bake until light golden and just beginning to crack on top, about 35 minutes. Let cool on sheet 10 minutes.

3. FINISH BISCOTTI Using serrated knife, cut logs crosswise into ½-inch slices. Place slices ½ inch apart on baking sheet and bake until golden, about 10 minutes, flipping each slice halfway through baking. Transfer to wire rack to cool completely. (Cookies can be stored in airtight container for 1 week.)

PECAN TRIANGLES
Karen Kuhn, Bloomington, Ill.

Makes 32 cookies

Karen says: "These cookies were adapted from a 1970s White House recipe." In step 2, add the cream with care, as the mixture will bubble vigorously.

- 20 tablespoons (2½ sticks) unsalted butter, softened
- ¼ cup granulated sugar
- 1 large egg
- 1¼ cups all-purpose flour
- ⅓ cup packed light brown sugar
- ⅓ cup honey
- 2 tablespoons heavy cream
- 1½ cups pecans, toasted and chopped

1. MAKE CRUST Adjust oven rack to middle position and heat oven to 375 degrees. Line 8-inch square baking pan with foil, allowing excess foil to hang over pan edges. Grease foil. With electric mixer on medium speed, beat 6 tablespoons butter and granulated sugar until light and fluffy, about 2 minutes. Add egg and mix until incorporated. Reduce speed to low, add flour, and mix until just combined. Press mixture into prepared pan, dock with fork, and bake until light golden, about 15 minutes. Cool on wire rack 20 minutes.

2. PREPARE CARAMEL Melt remaining butter in large saucepan over medium heat. Add brown sugar and honey and cook, stirring constantly, until sugar dissolves, about 2 minutes. Slowly whisk in cream and cook for 30 seconds. Off heat, stir in pecans.

3. BAKE BARS Pour caramel mixture over cooled crust. Bake until bubbly and deep golden brown, about 20 minutes. Cool completely on wire rack, about 1 hour. Using foil overhang, lift cookies out of pan. Cut into 2-inch squares, then cut each square into 2 triangles. (Cookies can be stored in airtight container for 3 days.)

GINGERY MAPLE THINS
Diane Nemitz, Ludington, Mich.

Makes about 2 dozen cookies

Diane says: "I live just down the road from a maple syrup farm. You can't beat the taste of the real thing. A friend turned me on to crystallized ginger cookies, so I combined the two flavors." We second Diane—be sure to use pure maple syrup, not pancake syrup.

- 1½ cups all-purpose flour
- 1 teaspoon baking soda
- 1 teaspoon ground ginger
- 8 tablespoons (1 stick) unsalted butter, softened
- ½ cup packed light brown sugar
- 1 large egg
- ¼ cup maple syrup (see note)
- 1 teaspoon maple extract
- 3 tablespoons minced crystallized ginger
- ¼ cup granulated sugar

1. MAKE DOUGH Adjust oven racks to upper-middle and lower-middle positions and heat oven to 350 degrees. Line 2 baking sheets with parchment paper. Combine flour, baking soda, and ground ginger in bowl. With electric mixer on medium-high speed, beat butter and brown sugar until light and fluffy, about 2 minutes. Add egg, maple syrup, and maple extract and mix until incorporated. Reduce speed to low, add flour mixture and crystallized ginger, and mix until just combined.

2. COAT WITH SUGAR Place granulated sugar in bowl. Moisten hands with water and roll dough into 1½-inch balls, then roll in sugar. Place sugared balls 2 inches apart on prepared baking sheets. Using flat-bottomed glass, press each ball to ½ inch thickness. Bake until golden, 12 to 14 minutes. Cool 5 minutes on sheets, then transfer to wire rack to cool completely. (Cookies can be stored in airtight container for 1 week.)

VISIT US ONLINE

For two more cookie recipes (Aysha Schurman's **Deluxe Peanut Butter and Banana Chocolate Chip Cookies** and Terry Ann Moore's **Apple Cobbler Bars**), visit our website at **CooksCountry.com.** You can also find information on upcoming recipe contests.

How do you cut the fat yet preserve the creamy richness? To find out, we tried everything from soy milk to soufflés. BY KRIS WIDICAN

Finally, a bread pudding you can feel good about.

CUBES OF BREAD, a pour of cream, a touch of sugar, a few egg yolks. Combine and bake and you've got bread pudding: a borderline minimalist dessert. But don't be fooled. The calories and fat are hardly negligible. Each slice averages 800 calories and almost 50 grams of fat—and that's before it gets a drop of sauce or dollop of whipped cream.

At the opposite end of the calorie spectrum, "light" recipes would scare away all but the most desperate dieter. Some I tried were made from reduced-calorie bread that dissolved into the custard. Tasters complained these versions were gummy and pasty. Others had no fat whatsoever, relying on whipped egg whites and nonfat milk to moisten bits of lean, flavorless bread. They were ropey, wet, and they curdled as they cooled—I could barely round up a taster. Without fat to carry flavor, the puddings were depressingly bland. My tasters and I imagined a silken yet sturdy makeover pudding, fluffy enough to fill out a baking dish—but not the eater. Heady vanilla and warm cinnamon would flavor it from the inside out, and it would be just sweet enough to call dessert.

Back to reality, it was obvious that none of the diet bread puddings came close, so I thought it best to carve away calories from a fully loaded test kitchen recipe we loved for its floral vanilla scent and crunchy cinnamon-sugar topping. I immediately reduced the number of egg yolks from eight to four for a savings of almost 35 calories and over 3 grams of fat per portion. But the yolks both thicken the custard and bind the casserole, so when I removed half of them, the pudding collapsed in a mushy heap. To support it, I tried toasting the bread, but that turned the pudding soggy and heavy. A better solution was to swap the four yolks for three whole eggs. The whites added structure to the pudding, plus I saved a few extra calories and fat grams.

Finding a replacement for the silken, rich heavy cream was a bigger—but necessary—task, as the 2 cups in the original recipe contributed over 100 calories and 15 grams of fat per serving. I rounded up potential replacements: whole milk, evaporated milk, coconut milk, fat-free half-and-half, buttermilk, sour cream, yogurt, and vanilla soy milk, and all of these in various combinations. All were too thin, too tangy, or too caloric.

I settled on "too thin" (skim milk) and looked for a way to thicken the custard without adding oodles of calories. Flour made the pudding pasty and dull. Next, I whisked a couple of tablespoons of cornstarch into the milk, poured it over the bread cubes, and baked the pudding as usual. Although the pudding lacked the sweet, buttery flavor of cream, its texture improved. Still, it felt achingly lean. When a colleague commented that I'd effectively turned my custard into vanilla pudding, I got an idea. Instead of cornstarch, I added 3 tablespoons of instant pudding mix to the custard. The mix's combination of cornstarch and milk powder transformed my bread pudding, which finally tasted rich and creamy. At the same time, the mix reinforced the bread pudding's fragrant vanilla flavor. To offset the sugar in the pudding mix, I reduced the sugar in my working recipe by 3 tablespoons.

I had slashed so many calories, I gave myself permission to add a few back: Surely I could do better than the humdrum sandwich bread I'd been using. French, Italian, brioche, and other bakery-fresh breads had promise, but the calorie and fat contents varied widely from bakery to bakery. In any case, a more flavorful solution was in the bread aisle at the grocery store. At an increase of only 15 calories per slice, the cinnamon swirl bread perfumed the pudding with its warm spice and added a hint of extra sweetness. Not one taster could believe this pudding had been reduced by 500 calories and more than 40 grams of fat per serving.

The Numbers

All nutritional information is for a single serving.

Full-Fat Bread Pudding
CALORIES **780**
FAT **48g** • SATURATED FAT **29g**

Cook's Country Reduced-Fat Bread Pudding
CALORIES **300**
FAT **7g** • SATURATED FAT **1.5g**

REDUCED-FAT BREAD PUDDING

Serves 6

Both instant and "cook and serve" pudding mixes work here, but avoid sugar-free, which will give the bread pudding a chemical aftertaste. Look for any brand of cinnamon swirl sandwich bread that has about 80 calories per slice.

- 2 cups skim milk
- 3 large eggs
- 5 tablespoons sugar
- 3 tablespoons vanilla pudding mix (see note)
- 2 teaspoons vanilla extract
- ¼ teaspoon salt
- 12 ounces cinnamon swirl sandwich bread (about 12 slices), cut into ¾-inch pieces (see note)
- ¼ teaspoon ground cinnamon

1. MAKE CUSTARD Adjust oven rack to middle position and heat oven to 375 degrees. Whisk milk, eggs, 4 tablespoons sugar, pudding mix, vanilla, and salt in large bowl until combined. Stir in bread. Let stand, tossing occasionally, until liquid is absorbed, about 10 minutes.

2. BAKE PUDDING Combine cinnamon and remaining sugar in small bowl. Grease 8-inch-square baking dish. Transfer soaked bread mixture to prepared pan and sprinkle with cinnamon sugar. Bake until pudding is just set and surface is golden brown, 35 to 40 minutes. Let cool 30 minutes. Serve.

KEY INGREDIENTS **Not Your Usual Diet Duo**

With drastically reduced fat, diet bread puddings are bland and disappointingly lean. These two ingredients gave ours plenty of creaminess and flavor.

BOXED VANILLA PUDDING
Pudding mix adds richness and flavor but few calories.

CINNAMON SWIRL BREAD
Cinnamon swirl bread gives the pudding warmth and spice.

Make Ahead Sweet and Sour Cocktail Meatballs

Recipes for this 1960s party classic sacrificed taste for speed. We wanted both. BY DIANE UNGER

IN THEIR DAY, cocktail meatballs were as popular as the avocado-green Crock-Pots or the Salton hot trays used to serve them. The sweetness usually came from grape or cranberry jelly (as in "Tangy Grape BBQ Meatballs" from Welch's, circa 1968) while the tang came from vinegar and chili sauce or ketchup (think Heinz's "Ultimate Party Meatballs"). Sweet and Sour Cocktail Meatballs are easy to serve for a crowd, and the sugary sauce is a guilty party pleasure. That's what I remembered from my childhood, anyway.

After testing a few versions, I figured outh had clouded my judgment. Browning dozens of meatballs in a skillet was a headache. The sauce was sickly sweet. I froze the meatballs in order to void much last-minute work; made vith all-beef and filler, they turned hard nd dry. Tasters compared the results to "beef-flavored grape Popsicles"; still, I vas determined to bring sweet and sour meatballs into the 21st century with a ast, easy, tangy, delicious version that I ould freeze without compromise.

Meatballs intended for the freezer need at to keep them moist. I tested various neats and percentages before landing on 35 percent lean ground beef combined vith ground pork, for tenderness. I also lected to use two egg yolks in place of whole egg. A gamut of binders—bread rumbs, cracker crumbs, and cornflake rumbs—made the meatballs dry, so I urned to panade. The word is French for paste made from bread softened in liquid in this case, milk). My reformulated

meatballs didn't dehydrate in the freezer.

Some of the recipes I'd tested seasoned the meatballs with a heavy hand. But the herbs and spices either disappeared into the sweet and sour sauce or clashed with it. In the end, salt and lots of pepper, garlic, and chopped parsley proved that less was more. To form the meatballs quickly, I shaped them with a small melon baller. To brown them easily, I set them on a rimmed baking sheet in a 450-degree oven—the meatballs were done in 15 minutes. After they cooled, I froze them in zipper-lock bags.

I lined up a selection of jams, jellies, and condiments, and went to work on the sauce; thus far, I'd been testing with a very basic mix of chili sauce (spicy ketchup at heart) and jellied cranberry sauce. First, I pitted the jams and jellies against one another. Tasters liked tangy apricot preserves best. Nobody liked the "shrimp cocktail" flavor the chili sauce evoked. They preferred ordinary tomato sauce. With the basic components in place, tasters demanded complexity, so I sautéed an onion, then stirred in the tomato sauce and apricot preserves. Still flat. The (unsweetened) tomato sauce gave me some leeway with the sugar, and ¼ cup of dark brown sugar contributed a pleasing molasses-y undertone. Dijon mustard and red pepper flakes helped balance the flavors, and Worcestershire sauce added much-needed depth.

I emptied the frozen meatballs into the bubbling sauce and waited just 10 minutes for them to warm. Finally, I'd hit the mark.

Open the freezer, turn on the stove, and in no time your guests will be enjoying homemade meatballs.

STEP-BY-STEP Make-Ahead Magic

To reheat, the baked and frozen meatballs can go straight from the freezer into the simmering sauce, which can also be made ahead and frozen separately.

1. Bake the meatballs, cool them on the counter, and refrigerate.

2. Place the chilled meatballs in zipper-lock bags and freeze.

3. To reheat, dump the frozen meatballs directly into the simmering sauce.

MAKE-AHEAD SWEET AND SOUR COCKTAIL MEATBALLS Serves 20

Use a 1¼-inch melon baller or a 1 tablespoon measuring spoon to form the meatballs.

MEATBALLS

4	slices hearty white sandwich bread, torn into pieces
½	cup whole milk
2	large egg yolks
½	pound ground pork
½	cup finely chopped fresh parsley
2	garlic cloves, minced
1	teaspoon salt
2	teaspoons pepper
2½	pounds 85 percent lean ground beef

SAUCE

1	tablespoon vegetable oil
1	onion, minced
1	(28-ounce) can tomato sauce
2½	cups apricot preserves
¼	cup packed dark brown sugar
3	tablespoons Worcestershire sauce
2	tablespoons Dijon mustard
¼	teaspoon red pepper flakes

1. MAKE MEATBALLS Adjust oven racks to upper-middle and lower-middle positions and heat oven to 450 degrees.

Using fork, mash bread, milk, and egg yolks in large bowl until smooth. Add pork, parsley, garlic, salt, and pepper and mix until incorporated. Add beef and knead gently until combined.

2. BAKE MEATBALLS Form mixture into 1¼-inch meatballs (you should have about 80). Bake meatballs on 2 rimmed baking sheets until cooked through and beginning to brown, 12 to 15 minutes, switching and rotating sheets halfway through cooking. Let cool to room temperature, then refrigerate until firm, about 30 minutes. Transfer to large zipper-lock freezer bag and freeze for up to 1 month.

3. MAKE SAUCE Heat oil in Dutch oven over medium-high heat until shimmering. Cook onion until softened, about 5 minutes. Whisk in tomato sauce, preserves, sugar, Worcestershire, mustard, and pepper flakes and bring to boil. Reduce heat to medium-low and simmer until sauce is thickened, about 15 minutes. Let cool to room temperature. Transfer to airtight container and freeze for up to 1 month.

4. TO SERVE Reheat sauce, covered and stirring occasionally, in Dutch oven over medium-low heat. Once sauce reaches simmer, stir in frozen meatballs and cook until heated through, 10 to 15 minutes. Serve.

Slow Cooker Red Wine–Braised Short Ribs

Do a little upfront kitchen work. Walk away. Eight hours later, enjoy short ribs that are long on flavor.

The slow cooker yielded tender, fall-off-the-bone rib meat. Too bad about the (lack of) flavor.

BY MARÍA DEL MAR SACASA

SHORT RIBS ARE a tough cut of meat that requires a long, slow braise to achieve melting, fork-tender perfection. Recipes for wine-braised ribs have you brown the meat to render some of the fat, and then sauté onions, carrots, and celery in the pot. Next, you stir in tomato paste, red wine, and broth (scraping up the flavorful browned bits known as fond) before returning the ribs to the pot to simmer. Given the usual three-hour cooking time, it's no surprise that most slow-cooker cookbooks include a recipe.

What did surprise me was that none I tested was much good: In general, the ribs, though tender, tasted boiled and drab, and the sauce was watery and dotted with fat. The closed, moist environment of a slow cooker allows no evaporation, so the flavors couldn't become concentrated and deepened. Clearly, I'd have to work on developing flavor before the ingredients entered slow-cooker lockdown. I put together a basic sauce (figuring I'd refine it later), then turned to the meat.

In the test kitchen, we use English-style ribs for braises. Their single bone and thick layer of meat make for hefty, uniform portions. I knew browning the ribs in a skillet first was key. But the ribs' curved bones prevented the meat from lying flat in the pan, in turn preventing the full development of fond—and thus flavor (I'd need all the flavor I could get in the slow cooker). Since I'd be removing the meat from the bone before serving the short ribs anyway, I sliced it off the bone upfront, trimming some fat at the same time. This allowed for more browning, and more fond development, than with bone-in ribs.

I tossed the raw bones into the slow cooker with the browned meat, but they added surprisingly little flavor. I cooked them in the skillet first to enhance their taste, but that pesky curve inhibited proper browning, so they made a lackluster statement. Roasting the bones (as restaurant chefs do when making stock) took too much time. Wondering if I could "roast" the bones in the microwave, I laid them in a baking dish and hit start. After about 15 minutes, the bones looked like they'd spent hours in an oven, and indeed, they added unequivocal depth to the sauce.

Although the sauce was flavorful, it lacked enough acid to balance the rich, fatty beef. I doubled the red wine from 1 cup to 2 cups—with scant effect. Next, I reduced the 2 cups back to 1 cup on the stovetop to concentrate the flavors and found that this gave the sauce real muscle. Two tablespoons of balsamic vinegar added a subtle sweetness that pulled the dish together.

For a glossy, velvety consistency, I rejected cornstarch (gluey) and flour (starchy) in favor of instant tapioca, which I added with the broth. Only one problem remained: Short ribs ooze fat as they cook. To remedy this, many recipes chill them overnight so that the gelled fat can be scraped from the cooking liquid and discarded. I didn't want to add a day to my cooking, so I simply fished out the ribs and set them aside, discarded the bones, strained the sauce, and then reached for the fat separator—an easy fix. At last my sauce had sheen, body, and layers of flavor.

STEP-BY-STEP Fifteen Minutes to Unlocking Beefy Flavor

Separating the meat from the bones—and "roasting" the bones in a surprising way—yields the most flavorful dish.

1. Insert a knife between the rib and meat and, staying as close to the bone as possible, saw the meat off the bone.

2. Microwave the bones for 10 to 15 minutes and add them to the slow cooker to add rich, roasted flavor.

SLOW-COOKER RED WINE– BRAISED SHORT RIBS Serves 4

For this recipe, we prefer English-style ribs, each of which contains a single, large rib bone and a thick piece of meat, rather than thinner, flanken-style ribs.

    5 pounds beef short ribs (6 to 8 English-
       style ribs), trimmed of excess fat
       (see note)
       Salt and pepper
    2 tablespoons vegetable oil
    2 onions, chopped
    1 carrot, peeled and chopped
    1 celery rib, chopped
    2 tablespoons tomato paste
    1 teaspoon dried thyme
    2 cups red wine
    2 tablespoons balsamic vinegar
    2 cups low-sodium chicken broth
    2 tablespoons Minute tapioca
    2 bay leaves
    2 tablespoons chopped fresh parsley

1. MICROWAVE BONES Following photo 1, cut meat from bones and set aside. Arrange bones in 13- by 9-inch baking dish and microwave until well browned, 10 to 15 minutes. Transfer to slow cooker.

2. BROWN MEAT Pat meat dry with paper towels and season with salt and pepper. Heat oil in large skillet over medium-high heat until just smoking. Cook meat until well browned, about 5 minutes per side. Transfer to slow cooker.

3. COOK AROMATICS Cook onions, carrot, and celery in now-empty skillet over medium heat until browned, about 8 minutes. Stir in tomato paste and thyme and cook until beginning to brown, about 1 minute. Stir in wine and vinegar and simmer, scraping up any browned bits, until reduced to 1 cup, about 5 minutes. Stir in broth, tapioca, and bay leaves and return to boil. Transfer to slow cooker.

4. BRAISE AND FINISH Cover slow cooker and cook on low until meat is fork-tender, about 8 hours (or cook on high for 4 to 5 hours). Transfer meat to serving platter. Strain and defat cooking liquid and discard solids. Stir parsley into sauce and season with salt and pepper. Pour 1 cup sauce over meat. Serve, passing remaining sauce at table.

As much as we adore butter, egg whites make a better binder for glueing spice to nut.

BY MARÍA DEL MAR SACASA

NUTS ARE EXPENSIVE, so it's especially disappointing when you make a batch of spiced nuts for the holidays that just doesn't measure up. The best recipes produce nuts that are crisp and evenly coated with spices, and they don't turn soggy after a day or two. In the test kitchen, we've had plenty of chances to perfect our technique. We've also developed a favorite recipe that calls for sugar, cinnamon, ginger, and coriander. This year, we reprised our easy method, and we rummaged through our spice rack to come up with some habit-forming variations.

Since you're going to flavor the nuts yourself and bake them for close to an hour, it makes no sense to use toasted, salted, or dry-roasted nuts. Start with a blank canvas: raw, unsalted nuts. You can use a single type or mix and match whichever nuts strike your fancy.

Different recipes use different tricks to get the spices to adhere. Some rely on oil or melted butter, but we've found spiced nuts made this way have spotty coatings and leave fingers slick and greasy. Other recipes use simple syrup (made by boiling sugar and water), which essentially makes for chewy nut candy, not a savory snack and not what we were looking for. Mixing the nuts with corn syrup or maple syrup turns the nuts soft and gooey within a couple of days—we wanted something that would hold through the holiday season.

We took a fourth approach, using egg whites to help the spices adhere. The whites are too thick to coat the nuts evenly, however, so we add a splash of water (to dilute them) and salt (which helps keep the egg proteins apart, thus preventing them from coagulating). As an extra precaution against the whites leaving rubbery clots on the nuts as they bake, we drain the nuts thoroughly in a colander, letting any excess whites drip away. Only then do we toss the nuts with sugar and spices, for an even, delicate "shell" around each baked nut.

Turn your oven to a moderate 300 degrees. Slow and low, the nuts bake long enough for both nut and coating to crisp. Higher temperatures scorch the coating before the nuts are toasted; use lower temperatures and Christmas will be over before you're enjoying the nuts. To prevent them from sticking, we line a baking sheet with parchment paper and spray it with baking spray.

Don't go crazy with the spices. Too heavy a hand and you'll think you're eating potpourri. Our master recipe uses a cinnamon, ginger, and coriander blend. To spice things up (sorry, we couldn't help ourselves), we developed variations with a hot-and-tart chili powder–lime coating (we like it with cashews, almonds, and peanuts); floral cardamom and orange zest (try almonds and pistachios); caramel-y Coca-Cola and five-spice powder (tropical macadamia nuts and cashews go nicely); and, should your fancy turn toward Italy, rosemary and lemon (use hazelnuts, almonds, and walnuts, all of which grow there).

CRUNCHY SPICED NUTS

Makes about 5 cups
You can use any variety of unsalted raw nuts. To double the recipe, adjust oven racks to upper-middle and lower-middle positions and bake the nuts on 2 baking sheets, switching and rotating sheets halfway through baking.

- 1 **large egg white**
- 1 **tablespoon water**
- 1 **teaspoon salt**
- 1 **pound unsalted nuts (see note)**
- ½ **cup granulated sugar**
- 2 **teaspoons ground cinnamon**
- 1 **teaspoon ground ginger**
- 1 **teaspoon ground coriander**

1. COAT NUTS Adjust oven rack to upper-middle position and heat oven to 300 degrees. Line baking sheet with parchment paper and coat with cooking spray. Whisk egg white, water, and salt in large bowl. Add nuts and toss to coat. Drain in colander thoroughly, 4 to 5 minutes.

2. SEASON NUTS Mix sugar, cinnamon, ginger, and coriander in large bowl. Add drained nuts and toss to coat. Spread nuts evenly on prepared baking sheet and bake until dry and crisp, 40 to 45 minutes, rotating sheet halfway through baking time. Cool completely. Break nuts apart and serve. (Nuts can be stored in airtight container for 3 weeks.)

Once you understand the basic method, vary the nuts and the spices to your heart's content.

CHILI-LIME SPICED NUTS
Use a combination of cashews, peanuts, and almonds in this spicy-sweet variation.

Prepare Crunchy Spiced Nuts, replacing water with 1 tablespoon lime juice and adding 1 tablespoon grated lime zest to egg white mixture. Substitute 2½ teaspoons chili powder, 1 teaspoon ground cumin, and ½ teaspoon cayenne pepper for cinnamon, ginger, and coriander.

ORANGE-CARDAMOM SPICED NUTS
Almonds and pistachios are a good combination here.

Prepare Crunchy Spiced Nuts, replacing water with 1 tablespoon orange juice and adding 1 tablespoon grated orange zest and ¼ teaspoon vanilla extract to the egg white mixture. Substitute 1 teaspoon ground cardamom and ½ teaspoon pepper for cinnamon, ginger, and coriander.

ASIAN SPICED NUTS
We like macadamia nuts and cashews in this variation. The cola lends sweetness and depth of flavor.

Prepare Crunchy Spiced Nuts, replacing water with 1 tablespoon Coca-Cola. Decrease ginger to ½ teaspoon and substitute 1½ teaspoons five-spice powder for cinnamon and coriander.

ROSEMARY-LEMON SPICED NUTS
Try a combination of almonds, walnuts, and hazelnuts for this Italian-inspired variation.

Prepare Crunchy Spiced Nuts, replacing water with 1 tablespoon lemon juice and adding 1 tablespoon grated lemon zest to egg white mixture. Substitute ½ cup packed light brown sugar, 1 tablespoon minced fresh rosemary, and ¼ teaspoon red pepper flakes for granulated sugar, cinnamon, ginger, and coriander.

TEST KITCHEN TECHNIQUE
Achieve Adhesion
Recipes that use oil, butter, or sugar syrup as a binder for spiced nuts can be messy and greasy. We prefer to coat the nuts with an egg white (diluted with a little water) before tossing them with spices and baking. To avoid unappealing clumps of egg white on the baked nuts, drain the nuts thoroughly before adding the spices.

Cranberry Roast Pork

Cranberry-glazed pork roast sounds like a great idea—as long as the meat stays juicy and the cranberry is more than just a pretty color. BY DAVID PAZMIÑO

Don't limit cranberries to your Thanksgiving turkey. Here, they dress up a pork roast.

RECENTLY, A FRIEND served me glazed cranberry pork loin. She smeared a center-cut, boneless loin with canned cranberry sauce (that jiggly, jellied stuff), poured chicken broth over it, and roasted the meat in a 350-degree oven until it was done, a recipe she said she'd found on the Internet. The roast was ghostly beige and the sauce flavor seriously underdeveloped (don't tell her I said this). On the positive side, the meat was juicy and the cranberries imbued the meat itself, not merely the sauce, with their flavor. She'd overcome (well, sort of) the chief challenges of cooking pork loin: The cut is lean, so it can be bland and dry. I hoped to duplicate the dish, or rather improve on it, for the holidays.

I bought a center-cut loin with its fat cap intact, knowing from previous test kitchen experience that the fatty top would baste the meat during roasting to help moisten the pork further. To enhance the rendering, I scored the fat in a crosshatched pattern. Then I faced my first challenge: getting color on the roast. I tried browning it in a skillet before simply popping it into the oven. It worked fine, but I missed the simplicity of my friend's method. (Stick roast in oven. Walk away. Return when roast is done.) Next, I tried basting the roast with the canned cranberry mixture, thinking it would caramelize and brown the roast. That was a bust: The sauce ran off the roast as fast as I could spoon it back on. Amazingly, the simple step of boosting the oven temperature to 425 degrees browned and blistered the fat cap beautifully and let me skip the skillet sear. I didn't have to worry about the meat drying out at this higher temperature, because the sauce the pork was cooking in protected it.

For the glaze, tasters demanded more berry texture, so I replaced the jellied canned sauce with canned whole cranberry sauce. I also used cranberry juice in place of the chicken broth and simmered the mixture down to magnify its flavor. A little cornstarch gave the mixture cling. Now the sauce was too sweet, so for balance I turned to items I'd seen in other recipes for cranberry pork. Baking spices were overwhelming; tendrils of orange peel were too precious. Bottled barbecue sauce was too smoky, but a mix of ketchup, Dijon mustard, and vinegar cut through the sweetness nicely and gave the sauce some interest. Garlic and thyme rounded it out.

Still, something was missing. I tried stirring in fresh berries, but found them acerbic. Seeking a more pleasant pucker, I tossed in dried cranberries instead and waited to see what would transpire. The berries plumped in the simmering sauce and added bright pockets of tart chew. The sauce snapped into focus with a final addition of 2 tablespoons brown sugar. I placed the pork in a baking pan, poured the sauce around it, and roasted it until the top rendered and browned. I opened the oven just once, to spoon some of the thickened sauce over the top of the roast, and then continued to cook the pork through. After a 15-minute rest, the juicy, ruby-crusted pork was ready to slice and serve with its jammy, bejeweled sauce. It was fit for the finest holiday table.

CRANBERRY PORK LOIN Serves 6 to 8

Use whole berry cranberry sauce, not jellied. Avoid unsweetened cranberry juice in this recipe, but cranberry juice cocktail will work just fine. Look for a pork loin roast with about a ¼-inch cap of fat on the top; the fat helps keep this lean roast moist during cooking.

- 1 boneless pork loin roast (about 3 pounds)
  Salt and pepper
- 1 tablespoon unsalted butter
- 2 garlic cloves, minced
- 2 teaspoons minced fresh thyme
- 1 (16-ounce) can whole berry cranberry sauce (see note)
- 1½ cups plus 2 tablespoons cranberry juice (see note)
- 1 cup dried cranberries
- 3 tablespoons ketchup
- 1 tablespoon Dijon mustard
- 2 tablespoons light brown sugar
- 1 teaspoon white vinegar
- 1 tablespoon cornstarch

1. **PREP PORK** Adjust oven rack to upper-middle position and heat oven to 425 degrees. Pat pork dry with paper towels and season with salt and pepper. Using knife, score fat on top of roast at ½-inch intervals.

2. **MAKE SAUCE** Melt butter in large saucepan over medium-high heat. Cook garlic and thyme until fragrant, about 30 seconds. Stir in cranberry sauce, 1½ cups cranberry juice, dried cranberries, ketchup, mustard, sugar, and vinegar and bring to boil. Reduce heat to medium-low and simmer until slightly thickened, about 5 minutes. Whisk cornstarch and remaining cranberry juice in small bowl, then whisk into pot. Simmer until sauce is thickened, 1 to 2 minutes.

3. **ROAST PORK** Place pork, fat-side up, in 13- by 9-inch baking pan. Pour sauce around pork and roast until top of pork is golden brown, about 45 minutes. Carefully spoon sauce over pork and continue to cook until meat registers 145 degrees, 20 to 25 minutes. Transfer pork to carving board, tent with foil, and let rest 15 minutes. Transfer sauce to serving bowl, cover, and keep warm. Slice pork and serve, passing sauce at table.

KEY INGREDIENTS Triple Cranberry Whammy
The secret to more cranberry flavor? Cranberries every which way.

CRANBERRY SAUCE
Whole berry cranberry sauce provides the backbone for our sauce/glaze.

CRANBERRY JUICE
Cranberry juice reinforces the flavors.

DRIED CRANBERRIES
Dried cranberries hold their shape and add concentrated bursts of tartness.

Sweet Potato Biscuits

We faced a dilemma: adding sweet potato helped the flavor but hurt the texture. BY DIANE UNGER

IN THE SOUTH, where biscuits are king and sweet potatoes as common as Piggly Wiggly stores, it was only a matter of time before some inspired cook married the two. Made right, the sweet potato adds earthy sweetness and moist tenderness to a biscuit, setting it apart from the more familiar (at least to northerners) flaky buttermilk biscuit. I tested five recipes, and even mail-ordered biscuits to try. They all looked the part, tinged a pretty pale peach from the cooked, mashed sweet potato. But the taste and texture left much to be desired. As a group, the biscuits were wet, heavy, and didn't taste of sweet potatoes.

I cobbled together a biscuit recipe, basically a buttermilk biscuit to which mashed sweet potato is added. As with carrots in carrot cake, the sweet potato

---

TEST KITCHEN SECRET
Doubling the Sweet Potato Punch

MORE POTATOES
Our recipe calls for twice as many sweet potatoes as most others.

NUKE 'EM!
We microwave the sweet potatoes to concentrate their flavor and release moisture, making for lighter, more flavorful biscuits.

PURE PUREE
Our recipe uses a full 2 cups of sweet potato puree and no buttermilk whatsoever.

---

flavor should be in the background but not nonexistent. Most recipes add ½ to 1 cup of the mashed tuber to 3-plus cups of flour, so I started in the middle, at ¾ cup, gently kneading it into the dough. I inched my way up, losing buttermilk as I went along to compensate for the moist sweet potatoes, stopping at 2 cups of the potato mash and no buttermilk whatsoever. These biscuits had a lovely deep orange color and faint earthy flavor, which I accentuated by adding ¼ cup brown sugar.

Tasters missed the buttermilk tang, so I stirred 2 tablespoons cider vinegar into the sweet potato puree and liked the results. The acidic vinegar reacted with the alkaline baking soda to lighten the biscuits slightly. Thank goodness, as doubling the sweet potato had made the biscuits dense. Many southern cooks swear by soft wheat flour (such as White Lily) for tender biscuits. Lacking that, I switched from the all-purpose flour I had been using to cake flour, which is also made from softer wheat, and saw some improvement.

Naturally, how I was cooking the sweet potato was affecting the finished biscuit, so I tried every technique going, from boiling (wet) to baking (time-consuming) to stirring in raw, grated sweet potato (gross—strings of raw potato in my biscuit). Canned sweet potatoes were as easy as opening a can, but many brands were too sweet, too spicy, or both. I turned to the microwave, letting the potatoes cook for 10 minutes, when I remembered a bit of food wisdom I'd read in a George Washington Carver biography, *From Captivity to Fame* (1929): "A sweet potato cooked quickly is not cooked. Time is an essential element."

With that in mind, I microwaved the sweet potatoes for 20 minutes until they were so soft their skins peeled right off. The extra 10 minutes got rid of moisture and concentrated the flavor, producing the best flavor and texture in the biscuits yet. One last happy discovery awaited: Plain biscuits taste best minutes after they're baked, but Sweet Potato Biscuits have a leg up. The sweet potato protects the biscuit from drying out, and its flavor deepens as it sits, making the biscuits good as new when gently rewarmed.

We like to serve these biscuits with butter or jam, or sandwiched with ham and mustard.

SWEET POTATO BISCUITS

Makes 16 biscuits

You can substitute a combination of 3 cups all-purpose flour and 6 tablespoons cornstarch for the cake flour. If you halve the recipe, in step 1 reduce the microwave time to 10 to 15 minutes.

- 2½ pounds sweet potatoes (4 to 5 medium)
- 2 tablespoons cider vinegar
- 3¼ cups cake flour (see note)
- ¼ cup packed dark brown sugar
- 5 teaspoons baking powder
- ½ teaspoon baking soda
- 1½ teaspoons salt
- 8 tablespoons (1 stick) unsalted butter, cut into ½-inch pieces and chilled; plus 2 tablespoons unsalted butter, melted
- 4 tablespoons vegetable shortening, cut into ½-inch pieces

1. MICROWAVE POTATOES Prick potatoes all over with fork. Microwave on large plate until potatoes are very soft and surface is wet, 15 to 20 minutes, flipping every 5 minutes. Immediately slice potatoes in half to release steam. When cool enough to handle, scoop flesh into bowl and mash until smooth. (You should have 2 cups. Reserve any extra for another purpose.) Stir in vinegar and refrigerate until cool, about 15 minutes.

2. MAKE DOUGH Adjust oven rack to middle position and heat oven to 425 degrees. Line rimmed baking sheet with parchment paper. Pulse flour, sugar, baking powder, baking soda, salt, chilled butter, and shortening in food processor until mixture resembles coarse meal. Transfer to bowl with cooled potatoes and fold with rubber spatula until incorporated.

3. CUT BISCUITS Turn dough out onto floured surface and knead until smooth, 8 to 10 times. Pat dough into 9-inch circle, about 1 inch thick. Using 2¼-inch biscuit cutter dipped in flour, cut out biscuits and arrange on prepared baking sheet. Pat remaining dough into 1-inch-thick circle and cut out remaining biscuits.

4. BAKE BISCUITS Brush tops of biscuits with melted butter and bake until golden brown, 18 to 22 minutes. Let cool 15 minutes. Serve. (Biscuits can be stored at room temperature in an airtight container for 2 days.)

Duchess Potatoes

Duchess potatoes are an elegant, French-pedigreed classic in which mashed potatoes are enriched with egg, piped into decorative rosettes, and baked until golden brown. The egg lightens the potato, creating an almost weightless, dainty fluff that contrasts with the crispy, craggy exterior. In 1867, an article in Galaxy magazine lamenting the state of American cooking noted duchess potatoes on the menu of a rare good dinner. For the next century, the dish made regular appearances on the menus of country clubs, ocean liners, and fancy-pants restaurants, but by the 1970s, it seemed stuffy and out of step with the times, and it fell into culinary disrepute. Which is a shame, because duchess potatoes really are something very special. BY LYNN CLARK

I tested recipes dating back almost a century as well as modern versions; all had similar ingredients and technique. Recipes combined boiled, mashed russet potatoes (fluffy russets contribute to fluffy duchess) with butter, eggs, cream or milk, and a pinch of nutmeg. The mix is placed in a pastry bag, piped, and baked. The potatoes looked suitably impressive, and tasters liked the airiness of the little peaks, but they found the texture cottony and dry and the mash too lean for elegant party fare.

Baking was drying the mounds out (broiling won't cook the egg to a safe temperature, so I ruled it out). As a group, recipes skimped on cream and butter, which wasn't helping. But when I added more, the mixture slumped into puddles. My challenge was to make a puree firm enough to pipe, yet rich and creamy enough to be worth the effort.

Most recipes called for boiling the potatoes. Even drained and dried (by cooking on the stovetop for a minute), they remained too waterlogged to pipe. Baking added an hour to an already time-consuming recipe. Microwaving, however, took just 20 minutes or so, and since it used no liquid, I could safely mash 1 cup of cream into 3 pounds of potatoes—more than twice the cream in most recipes I'd tested.

Mashed into the hot potatoes, 6 tablespoons butter (the amount needed for a rich, buttery taste) melted, making the mixture too loose to pipe. So I cooled the mash before adding the butter in small chunks. I had no trouble piping, but the butter oozed out in the oven. I got the idea to add half of the butter while the potatoes were hot (the mash absorbed it) and the other half once they'd cooled (which, as I'd hoped, melted into buttery pockets in the oven but didn't leak out).

Unfortunately, weighed down with extra butter and cream, my duchess lacked the light, puffy texture that should distinguish her. That lift comes from the eggs. In my initial testing, recipes called for anywhere from one to four. More eggs made the potatoes taste (surprise!) eggy, so I settled on one whole egg and one yolk (for added richness), but that amount wasn't enough to lighten my creamy, buttery puree.

If lift was what I was after, might baking powder work? Admittedly, it was a weird idea, but in the test kitchen, we'll try anything once. I stirred ½ teaspoon into the potato puree, piped, baked, and hoped. About 20 minutes later, I had my answer: rich, buttery, yet practically weightless potatoes. Sure, piping duchess potatoes takes time. Good things do. Incidentally, the potatoes won't suffer any if you pipe them a day ahead, handy when company is coming.

DUCHESS POTATOES Serves 8

For the smoothest, most uniform texture, use a food mill or ricer to mash the potatoes.

- 3 pounds russet potatoes, scrubbed
- 1 cup heavy cream
- 6 tablespoons unsalted butter, cut into ¼-inch cubes and softened
- 1 large egg plus 1 egg yolk, lightly beaten
- 1¼ teaspoons salt
- ½ teaspoon pepper
  Pinch nutmeg
- ½ teaspoon baking powder

1. MICROWAVE POTATOES Adjust oven rack to upper-middle position and heat oven to 475 degrees. Meanwhile, prick potatoes all over with fork, place on plate, and microwave until tender, 18 to 25 minutes, turning potatoes over after 10 minutes.

2. MASH POTATOES Cut potatoes in half. When cool enough to handle, scoop flesh into large bowl and mash until no lumps remain. Add cream, 3 tablespoons butter, eggs, salt, pepper, nutmeg, and baking powder and continue to mash until potatoes are smooth. Let cool to room temperature, about 10 minutes. Gently fold in remaining butter until pieces are evenly distributed.

3. PIPE AND BAKE Transfer potato mixture to piping bag fitted with ½-inch star tip. Pipe eight 4-inch-wide mounds of potato on rimmed baking sheet. Spray lightly with cooking spray and bake until golden brown, 15 to 20 minutes. Serve.

MAKE AHEAD Once piped onto the baking sheet, the potatoes can be covered loosely with plastic wrap and refrigerated for 24 hours. Remove plastic and spray lightly with cooking spray before baking.

TEST KITCHEN TECHNIQUE Two Paths to Perfect Piping
With a pastry bag fitted with a star tip, making beautiful duchess potatoes is child's play. If you don't have a pastry bag, don't worry: There's another easy way.

WITH PASTRY BAG Start each portion by piping a 4-inch circle on the baking sheet. Continue to pipe upward in circles until you've made a 3-inch peak.

WITHOUT PASTRY BAG Scoop the potatoes into a zipper-lock bag, snip off a corner, and pipe as directed. Use tines of a fork to created rippled edges.

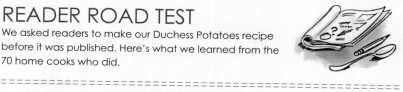

READER ROAD TEST

We asked readers to make our Duchess Potatoes recipe before it was published. Here's what we learned from the 70 home cooks who did.

==

Help! I can't get the hang of the fork.

"The fork just stuck to the potatoes."

"I found the mixture too firm to swirl with a fork to leave ridges."

OUR ADVICE To make decorative duchess without a pastry bag, pipe the potatoes with a zipper-lock bag and use the tines of a fork for texture (see Test Kitchen Technique at left). It's easier to trace the lines with the fork right (concave) side up; otherwise, the puree tends to pile up in the tines. Start at the bottom of each duchess mound and work your way up in a circular path. If the potatoes are too hot, the lines will look blurry and untidy. If the puree is too cold, it will be too firm to draw lines easily. Start decorating when the potatoes are at room temperature. Dip the fork occasionally into a glass of hot water to keep it clean and make for neat lines. We tried spraying the fork lightly with cooking spray, but found that made little difference.

==

Can I freeze Duchess Potatoes?

"I used four of the 'rosettes' that evening, and I sealed the other four and have them in the freezer for my own experiment."

OUR ADVICE Hey, maybe we can find you a job in the test kitchen! You're just the kind of curious, adventurous cook we like to hire. Yes, indeed, Duchess Potatoes freeze beautifully, which is handy, as they're ideal for a party. Pipe the mounds onto a rimmed baking sheet and then cover lightly with plastic wrap. Freeze for two hours until solid and transfer the potatoes to an airtight container (or leave them on the sheet pan if you've got the space). When you are ready to bake them, arrange on a rimmed baking sheet (or simply remove the plastic), spray lightly with cooking spray, and bake according to our recipe. They can go straight from freezer to oven, and they won't even need any extra time.

==

WANTED: Recipe Testers. Would you like to join the ranks of our volunteer recipe testers? Here's how it works: Periodically, we e-mail you a recipe that's under development in our test kitchen. We ask you to make it within the week and to send us your feedback—what's working, what isn't, would you make it again, and if not, why not. To sign up, visit **CooksCountry.com.**

ON THE SIDE Roasted Carrots with Sage and Walnuts

Baby carrots can deliver grown-up flavor. Fast. BY JEREMY SAUER

THESE CARROTS ARE PERFECT for when you're strapped for time but want a sophisticated side dish that's more than an afterthought.

Starting with baby carrots is a real time saver—prepping them consists of opening the bag and dumping them in a bowl. The baby carrots roast on a pre-heated baking sheet in about a half hour (but remember to shake the pan a few times to ensure even browning). While many recipes roast the walnuts on the same baking sheet with the carrots, we found that toasting the walnuts solo (away from the moisture of the carrots) kept them from getting soggy. Fresh sage adds a heady complexity, and a modest 2 tablespoons of honey not only draws more sweetness out of the carrots, but also cooks down into a sticky glaze that ensures plenty of seasoning in every bite.

ROASTED CARROTS WITH SAGE AND WALNUTS Serves 8

Toast the walnuts in a dry skillet over medium heat until fragrant, shaking occasionally, about 5 minutes.

- 3 tablespoons unsalted butter
- 2 tablespoons honey
- 2 (16-ounce) bags baby-cut carrots
- ⅓ cup walnuts, toasted and chopped
- 1 tablespoon finely chopped fresh sage
  Salt and pepper

1. HEAT BAKING SHEET Adjust oven rack to middle position and heat oven to 475 degrees. Heat rimmed baking sheet in oven 10 minutes. Microwave butter and honey in large bowl until butter melts, about 1 minute.

2. ROAST Toss carrots with butter mixture in bowl. Spread carrots on heated baking sheet. Roast, shaking pan occasionally, until carrots are browned and tender, about 30 minutes. Return carrots to empty bowl and toss with walnuts and sage. Season with salt and pepper. Serve.

Baby carrots require no prep and cook quickly.

Affordable Herbed Roast Beef

It's easy to impress with an expensive beef roast, but can you make an equally big splash with a cheap cut? BY KRIS WIDICAN

We stuff the inside of the roast with herbs, sear it for crust and color, then cook it at a low temperature for a moist, rosy interior.

PRICEY, LUXURIOUSLY TENDER prime rib and beef tenderloin make for impressive and imposing centerpieces on many a holiday table, but I hoped to dress up a cheaper cut of beef to look—and taste—as good. I hatched a plan to envelop a top sirloin, the test kitchen's favorite economical beef roast, in a flavorful herb crust.

The test kitchen has a fantastic recipe for beef tenderloin with an herb–bread crumb crust, so I started by patting that same crust—homemade fresh bread crumbs, Parmesan cheese, olive oil, and chopped parsley and thyme (the herb combination preferred by our tasters)—onto a 4-pound top sirloin. Using the test kitchen's low-temperature method (see Test Kitchen Technique, page 31) to ensure perfectly rosy meat, I cooked the roast to medium rare (1½ to 2 hours at just 275 degrees) before crisping the crust under the broiler. The crust looked amazing—until I attempted to cut the roast into thin slices. It promptly plopped onto the cutting board. The bread crumb and cheese crust was clearly better suited to an ultra-tender roast (such as the tenderloin it was designed for) that you can slice thickly. Since top sirloin must be sliced thinly to minimize chew, I had to find another way to add herb flavor.

Without the crumbs and Parmesan to serve as a binder, a "crust" of just herbs and oil wouldn't adhere—it slid right off the meat as fast as I could put it on. Then I thought back to my days as a restaurant chef, when we put butter in, around, and on top of everything, including steaks and roasts; I decided to roast the meat with nothing but salt and pepper, and then, when it came out of the oven, coat it liberally with a potent herb butter. I made a traditional herb butter by mashing together parsley, thyme, and minced shallot. As the flavored butter melted on the resting roast, it mingled with the meat juices and created an easy sauce that was tasty—as far as it went. The problem was, the butter failed to flavor every nook and cranny. For a roast this special, I needed a way to get maximum herb flavor in each and every bite.

It occured to me that I could put the herb butter inside the roast. I grabbed a raw roast from the refrigerator and butterflied it, making a single horizontal cut through the middle (stopping just before the edge) so I could open the meat like a book. I spread a thick layer of softened herb butter inside, folded the flap shut, and tightly tied the roast back into its original shape with kitchen twine (this process really is easier than it sounds: see photos 1 to 3 below left). After the meat was cooked through, I slathered more herb butter on top and gathered my tasters around. As soon as I sliced the roast open, the hot melted butter gushed from the interior—carrying the herbs with it. I needed a filling that would stay put, but I didn't want to fuss with both a sauce and a filling. Perhaps I could repurpose a few components of the sauce to make a flavorful filling?

I butterflied four more roasts, and set aside some of the herbs and shallot. Instead of butter, I tested adding roasted garlic, horseradish, goat cheese, Parmesan, and Dijon mustard to bind the filling. Tasters found even small amounts of roasted garlic and horseradish too dominant, and the cheeses overpowered the delicate flavor of the herbs. The mild, tangy bite of the Dijon mustard, however, set off the herbs perfectly, and did the work of binding the herbs in place. To make the finishing sauce, I blended the remainder of the herbs with butter, as before. With a flavorful vein of herb flavor within and a luscious herb-butter sauce to top it off, this roast was ready to impress on any holiday table. (Shhh. Don't tell anyone it's an inexpensive cut.)

STEP-BY-STEP **Herbs Galore**
Fresh parsley and thyme flavor both the interior and exterior of our roast.

1. Butterfly the roast by slicing horizontally through the middle of the meat. Leave about ½ inch of meat intact, then open it like a book.

2. After seasoning the meat, spread the herb-mustard mixture over the interior of meat.

3. Fold the meat back to its original position, then tie securely at 1-inch intervals with kitchen twine.

4. For a second hit of herb flavor after the roast is cooked, spread it with herb butter.

HERBED ROAST BEEF Serves 6 to 8

For even deeper seasoning, refrigerate the roast overnight after filling it with the herb mixture in step 2.

- ⅓ cup finely chopped fresh parsley
- 2 tablespoons minced fresh thyme
- 1 shallot, minced
- 1 tablespoon Dijon mustard
- 2 tablespoons olive oil
- 4 tablespoons unsalted butter, softened
- 1 (4-pound) top sirloin roast, fat trimmed to ¼ inch thick
- 1 tablespoon salt
- 1 tablespoon pepper

1. PREP HERBS Combine parsley, thyme, and shallot in bowl. Transfer 2 tablespoons herb mixture to another bowl and stir in mustard and 1 tablespoon oil until combined. Add butter to remaining herb mixture and mash with fork until combined.

2. PREP BEEF Following photos 1 and 2 on previous page, butterfly roast and rub inside and out with salt and pepper. Spread herb-mustard mixture over interior of meat and tie securely with kitchen twine at 1-inch intervals. Refrigerate at least 1 hour or up to 24 hours.

3. BROWN AND ROAST Adjust oven rack to middle position and heat oven to 275 degrees. Pat roast dry with paper towels. Heat remaining oil in large skillet over medium-high heat until just smoking. Brown roast all over, 8 to 12 minutes, then arrange on V-rack set inside roasting pan. Transfer to oven and roast until meat registers 125 degrees (for medium-rare), 1½ to 2 hours.

4. BUTTER AND REST Transfer roast to carving board, spread with herb-butter mixture, tent with foil, and let rest 20 minutes. Remove kitchen twine. Slice roast crosswise against grain into ¼-inch-thick slices. Serve.

RATING ELECTRIC KNIVES

Electric knives might seem like relics of the 1960s, but we wanted to see if these knives had any place in the modern kitchen. We selected four new models under $20 and tested them slicing roast beef, turkey breast, angel food cake, and apple pie. The results were clear: Contrary to manufacturer claims, electric knives are not adept at slicing meat neatly and thinly—all four models shredded beef roasts. Plus, they're aggravatingly loud; we prefer to carve with our favorite slicing knife. What their powered pairs of independently moving serrated blades do best is cut through delicate baked goods without crumbling and slice through crisp turkey skin without ripping. BY MEREDITH BUTCHER

Key **Good ★★★** **Fair ★★** **Poor ★**

RECOMMENDED WITH RESERVATIONS

	TESTERS' NOTES
OSTER Electric Knife Set **Price:** $19.99 **Blade Length:** 7 inches **Turkey Slicing:** ★★ **Roast Carving:** ★ **Dessert Slicing:** ★★ **Design:** ★★ 	This powerful model produced jagged meat slices. Turkey fared slightly better, and the skin remained intact. Pie slices came out clean. The handle was comfortable and easy to "choke up" on for increased control. This knife may be purchased solo or with a carving fork.
TOASTMASTER Electric Carving Knife **Price:** $10.79 **Blade Length:** 6¾ inches **Turkey Slicing:** ★★ **Roast Carving:** ★ **Dessert Slicing:** ★★ **Design:** ★★ 	This knife felt more balanced than other models, but was shaky when slicing through turkey skin and angel food cake. Slicing pie, however, was a breeze. While the instructions state to refrain from sawing, the knife wouldn't slice through meat without some action from testers.
ELITE CUISINE 2 Speed Electric Knife **Price:** $16.99 **Blade Length:** 7 inches **Turkey Slicing:** ★★ **Roast Carving:** ★ **Dessert Slicing:** ★★ **Design:** ★ 	While this knife sliced through cake, pie, and turkey skin with ease, it left unattractive striations on the meat and cake. Its noticeably weaker motor struggled to slice roast beef. The awkward top-mounted power button cramped testers' fingers throughout testing, and the two speeds were unnecessary.

NOT RECOMMENDED

	TESTERS' NOTES
BLACK & DECKER Slice Right Electric Knife **Price:** $16.95 **Blade Length:** 7¼ inches **Turkey Slicing:** ★ **Roast Carving:** ★ **Dessert Slicing:** ★★ **Design:** ★ 	This cumbersome knife stuttered through slicing, leaving ridges on meat. Turkey skin was pulled and tattered from the violent shaking of the motor. Being able to choke up on the handle helped control the blade's range of motion, which, in turn, helped us to cut even slices of pie. Inserting the blades was tricky, leaving us wondering if we had attached them correctly.

ON THE SIDE
Maple-Glazed Brussels Sprouts

Braised and glazed, sweet and sour. And good.

BY JEREMY SAUER

BRUSSELS SPROUTS GET a bad rap—deservedly so. Boiled to death, as is often their fate, they turn a little bitter and a lot stinky. But the test kitchen's braising method has won many converts. We simmer 2 pounds of halved Brussels sprouts in a covered skillet with ½ cup of chicken broth until just tender—a 10-minute wait at most. To finish, a couple of tablespoons each of butter and sugar glaze the leaves. This time, I would ask maple syrup to the party.

In what turned out to be a misguided attempt to get the maple syrup flavor to come through loud and clear, I used it in place of the chicken stock. I was hoping it would "season" the sprouts through and through. What I got instead was Brussels sprouts candy. (It won't give M&Ms a run for its money any time soon.) My boss reigned in my temporary insanity, insisting I pull back on the maple syrup tablespoon by tablespoon—until I was down to just 2, which I now added (in place of the sugar in the original recipe) after simmering the Brussels sprouts in the restored chicken stock.

To balance the sweetness of the syrup, I tested various vinegars and citrus juices, stirring them in with the butter after the sprouts were tender. All worked, but fruity cider vinegar had a definite edge. Fresh thyme and a dash of cayenne rounded out the flavors.

My Brussels sprouts were tasty, but I missed those browned, caramelized edges you get when you roast. To mimic that, the next time, I started the Brussels sprouts in 2 additional tablespoons butter, sautéing them for several minutes until browned. Only then did I add the

broth and, on a hunch, 1 tablespoon of the maple syrup, which gently seasoned the sprouts, as I'd originally planned.

Flavorful ingredients cook down into a glaze for this sometimes misunderstood vegetable.

MAPLE-GLAZED BRUSSELS SPROUTS Serves 6 to 8

Choose Brussels sprouts with small, tight heads, no more than 1½ inches in diameter. Use pure maple syrup, not pancake syrup.

- 4 tablespoons unsalted butter
- 2 pounds Brussels sprouts, trimmed and halved through core
- ½ cup low-sodium chicken broth
- 2 tablespoons maple syrup
- 1 teaspoon minced fresh thyme
- ⅛ teaspoon cayenne pepper
- 4 teaspoons cider vinegar
- Salt and pepper

1. BROWN SPROUTS Melt 2 tablespoons butter in large skillet over medium-high heat. Add Brussels sprouts and cook until browned, 6 to 8 minutes. Stir in broth, 1 tablespoon syrup, thyme, and cayenne and cook over medium-low heat, covered, until Brussels sprouts are nearly tender, 6 to 8 minutes.

2. FINISH COOKING Uncover and increase heat to medium-high. Cook until liquid is nearly evaporated, about 5 minutes. Off heat, stir in remaining butter, remaining syrup, and vinegar. Season with salt and pepper. Serve.

TEST KITCHEN TIP
Trimming Sprouts

To keep the halved sprouts intact, cut them through the stem (and remove any tough outer leaves).

Getting to Know Supermarket Italian Cheeses

Italy is second only to France in the variety of cheeses it produces, but many of the "Italian" cheeses sold in American supermarkets are produced here. Such cheeses are generally fine for everyday use in pastas, sandwiches, and casseroles; reserve expensive, imported-from-Italy cheeses for a cheese board. Below is a sampling of "Italian" cheeses regularly sold in supermarkets.

Mascarpone
DESSERT DARLING

Mascarpone is a rich, creamy cow's milk cheese with a short shelf life. Chances are you've tasted mascarpone in tiramisú—it's often flavored with coffee, chocolate, or liqueur and used in desserts. It's also delicious atop fresh berries. Our tasters described it as "sweet and fatty" with a pleasantly "mouth-coating" texture.

Smoked Mozzarella
SMOKE OUT

We're not fans of supermarket smoked mozzarella, which is usually made with "rubbery," low-quality block mozzarella. Its smoke flavor dominates and tastes "fake" and "acrid," according to our tasters. Buy the real deal from Italy or seek out a high-quality domestic brand.

Block-Style Mozzarella
PIZZA PAL

Pizzerias use this cheese for pies and calzones because it melts well and is pleasingly "mild" and "milky." Block mozzarella is sold in part-skim and whole-milk varieties; the two can be used interchangeably. Raw, both were unpleasantly "spongy," "bouncy" and "salty," but we liked both in lasagna and pizza. In sum, use them for cooking.

Fresh Mozzarella
BATHING BEAUTY

Originally, all mozzarella was made from the milk of water buffaloes; today, most is made from cow's milk. Fresh mozzarella is lighter, silkier, and more flavorful than block mozzarella. It's sold in spheres packaged in whey or water or shrink-wrapped. Our tasters loved its "creamy and mild," "clean and fresh-tasting" flavor. Fresh mozzarella is the only choice for salads.

Fontina
GOOD MELTER

The Italian original, Fontina Val d'Aosta, is a costly cheese prized for its rich, nutty flavor and excellent meltability. Other fontinas are not in the same league but can be good nonetheless—"bright," "firm," and "smooth and creamy," tasters said. Even at the supermarket, look for Italian-made fontina and use it in panini and baked pastas.

Pecorino Romano
SALTY CHARACTER

When they weren't expanding their empire or feeding Christians to the lions, Roman citizens made this aged sheep's milk cheese, hence its name. It shines in such boldly flavored dishes as *pasta alla carbonara*, but we often mix it with Parmesan to mitigate its sharp saltiness. Our tasters were split: Some praised it as "grassy and rich" and "strong but not bitter," while others found it disagreeably "gamey" and "sheep-y."

Ricotta
WHEY COOL

Ricotta means "re-cooked" in Italian, and this "pillowy," moist, fresh cheese is so named because it was traditionally made with leftover whey from the production of other cow's milk cheeses. (American ricotta, however, is made from milk, not whey.) Mass-market ricotta is fine in baked pasta, but for something extraordinary, buy ricotta without stabilizers, gums, or preservatives. It has a short shelf life but is so good it probably won't last anyway.

Gorgonzola
TRUE BLUE

Inexpensive, mass-produced domestic gorgonzola (the kind sold in most supermarkets) is "super-salty" and "sour," although passable in small quantities or if paired with other strong flavors. When it's the star of the show, seek out authentic imported Gorgonzola, a blue cheese that's creamy, rich, and assertive—even stinky, but in a good way. Precrumbled Gorgonzola is often dry and of poor quality; avoid it.

Provolone
SANDWICH FIXING

Authentic provolone cheese, which is usually aged for 2 to 3 months, is pear-shaped, nutty, and mildly assertive. Alas, the supermarket deli provolone we tasted was "bouncy and bland" and "mild," "like milk Jell-O," "nothing like the real deal." It does melt well, however, and is often used in sandwiches.

Parmesan
THE BIG CHEESE

Made in a northern region of Italy, the real deal, Parmigiano-Reggiano, can be found in many American supermarkets—at a price. It's nutty, buttery, and crystalline; Italians consider it the king of cheeses. The domestic stuff is cheaper (by as much as $10 per pound), younger, and less nuanced but wonderfully versatile for cooking. We use the rinds to add depth to soups, stews, and stocks.

Ricotta Salata
WORTH ITS SALT

Ricotta salata ("re-cooked and salted" in Italian) is made with leftover whey from the production of sheep's milk cheeses. It is almost exclusively imported from Italy. This firm, dry cheese is "very salty" and has a "barnyard-y" bite that complements fruit (try apples, pears, figs, or watermelon). It's also good in salad.

Asiago
PARM STAND-IN

Because of its lower price and nutty flavor, this firm, aged cow's milk cheese is a common substitute for Parmigiano-Reggiano. It is often grated over pasta, shaved for salads, or served with meats as antipasti. We found supermarket Asiago "tangy" and "like a combination of cheddar and Parmesan," with a strong, but not unpleasant, aftertaste.

PORK SCALOPPINI

CHICKEN AND RICE POT PIE

PAN-ROASTED CHICKEN WITH ROOT VEGETABLES

PASTA WITH SPICY TOMATO AND OLIVE SAUCE

CHICKEN AND RICE POT PIE Serves 6

WHY THIS RECIPE WORKS: Cooking the pastry topping and creamy filling separately puts this pot pie on the table in under 30 minutes.

- 1 (9½- by 9-inch) sheet puff pastry, thawed overnight in refrigerator
- 4 boneless, skinless chicken breasts (about 1½ pounds), cut crosswise into ½-inch pieces
   Salt and pepper
- 4 tablespoons unsalted butter
- 2 teaspoons all-purpose flour
- 1 cup instant white rice
- 1¾ cups low-sodium chicken broth
- ½ cup heavy cream
- 1 cup frozen peas and carrots
- 3 scallions, sliced thin

1. Adjust oven rack to middle position and heat oven to 400 degrees. Cut puff pastry in half, then cut each half into thirds. Bake on parchment-lined baking sheet until golden brown and crisp, about 15 minutes.

2. Meanwhile, pat chicken dry with paper towels and season with salt and pepper. Melt 1 tablespoon butter in large skillet over medium-high heat. Cook half of chicken until no longer pink, 1 to 2 minutes per side; cut into cubes and transfer to medium bowl. Repeat with additional 1 tablespoon butter and remaining chicken.

3. Add flour and remaining butter to empty skillet and cook until golden, 1 to 2 minutes. Stir in rice, broth, and cream and bring to boil. Reduce heat to medium and simmer, covered, until rice is nearly tender, 3 to 5 minutes. Stir in peas and carrots, scallions, and chicken, along with any accumulated juices. Simmer until sauce is thickened, about 3 minutes. Season with salt and pepper. Top with puff pastry. Serve.

TEST KITCHEN NOTE: Prepared puff pastry is sold frozen.

PORK SCALOPPINI Serves 4

WHY THIS RECIPE WORKS: For the best flavor and texture, we make our own cutlets with pork tenderloin rather than relying on packaged pork loin cutlets.

- 1 large pork tenderloin (about 1 pound), cut into 4 equal pieces and pounded ¼ inch thick
   Salt and pepper
- 5 tablespoons unsalted butter
- 2 garlic cloves, minced
- ¾ cup low-sodium chicken broth
- 2 tablespoons lemon juice
- 1 teaspoon brown sugar
- 1 tablespoon finely chopped fresh parsley (see note below)

1. Pat cutlets dry with paper towels and season with salt and pepper. Melt 1 tablespoon butter in large skillet over medium heat. Cook 2 cutlets until golden brown and cooked through, 1 to 2 minutes per side. Transfer to platter and tent with foil. Repeat with additional 1 tablespoon butter and remaining cutlets.

2. Add garlic and additional 1 tablespoon butter to empty skillet and cook until fragrant, about 30 seconds. Stir in broth, lemon juice, sugar, and any accumulated pork juices and simmer until slightly thickened, about 5 minutes. Off heat, whisk in parsley and remaining butter. Pour sauce over cutlets. Serve.

TEST KITCHEN NOTE: To vary the flavor, you can substitute an equal amount of fresh tarragon, chives, or basil for the parsley. Serve over egg noodles or with rice pilaf.

PASTA WITH SPICY TOMATO AND OLIVE SAUCE Serves 4

WHY THIS RECIPE WORKS: Sautéing the anchovies, garlic, and pepper flakes in olive oil for just 30 seconds blooms their flavors and adds depth to the sauce.

- 3 tablespoons extra-virgin olive oil
- 3 anchovy fillets, minced
- 5 garlic cloves, minced
- 1 teaspoon red pepper flakes
- 1 (28-ounce) can diced tomatoes
- ½ cup pitted kalamata olives, halved
- 3 tablespoons drained capers
- ¼ cup chopped fresh basil
   Salt
- 1 pound spaghetti or linguine

1. Bring 4 quarts water to boil in large pot. Heat oil in large saucepan over medium heat until shimmering. Add anchovies, garlic, and pepper flakes and cook until fragrant, about 30 seconds. Stir in tomatoes and simmer until slightly thickened, about 10 minutes. Off heat, add olives, capers, and basil.

2. Add 1 tablespoon salt and pasta to boiling water and cook until al dente. Reserve ½ cup cooking water. Drain pasta and return to pot. Stir in sauce and toss to combine, adding reserved pasta water as needed. Serve.

TEST KITCHEN NOTE: Top with grated Pecorino Romano or Parmesan cheese.

PAN-ROASTED CHICKEN WITH ROOT VEGETABLES Serves 4

WHY THIS RECIPE WORKS: Cooking the chicken breasts skin-side down for the entire cooking time ensures deep brown, crispy skin and moist meat.

- 4 bone-in, skin-on split chicken breasts (about 3 pounds), halved crosswise
   Salt and pepper
- 1 tablespoon vegetable oil
- 4 carrots, peeled and cut into ½-inch rounds
- 4 parsnips, peeled and cut into ½-inch rounds
- ¼ cup white wine
- ¼ cup low-sodium chicken broth
- 1 teaspoon minced fresh rosemary
- 2 tablespoons unsalted butter

1. Pat chicken dry with paper towels and season with salt and pepper. Heat oil in large skillet over medium-high heat until just smoking. Cook chicken skin-side down until well browned, about 5 minutes. Reduce heat to medium, cover, and cook until meat registers 160 degrees, about 15 minutes. Transfer chicken to platter and tent with foil.

2. Pour off fat from skillet. Stir in carrots, parsnips, wine, broth, and rosemary and simmer covered, stirring occasionally, until vegetables are tender and pan is nearly dry, about 8 minutes. Off heat, stir in butter and season with salt and pepper. Transfer to platter with chicken. Serve.

TEST KITCHEN NOTE: Buy parsnips and carrots that are no more than 1 inch in diameter. Thicker vegetables can be fibrous.

FLANK STEAK WITH SHALLOT-MUSTARD SAUCE

**HONEY-GLAZED PORK CHOPS
WITH SWEET AND TANGY SLAW**

OVEN-BAKED CHICKEN CHIMICHANGAS

QUICK BEEF BURGUNDY

HONEY-GLAZED PORK CHOPS WITH SWEET AND TANGY SLAW Serves 4

WHY THIS RECIPE WORKS: The sweetness of the honey glaze is balanced by the tartness of the vinaigrette used to dress the slaw.

- 6 tablespoons cider vinegar
- ¼ cup honey
- 4 teaspoons Dijon mustard
  Salt and pepper
- 3 tablespoons olive oil
- 1 (16-ounce) bag coleslaw mix
- 4 bone-in rib or center-cut pork chops (see note below), about 1 inch thick
- 2 teaspoons minced fresh thyme
- ⅛ teaspoon cayenne pepper

1. Combine 4 tablespoons vinegar, 2 tablespoons honey, 2 teaspoons mustard, ¼ teaspoon salt, and ¼ teaspoon pepper in large bowl. Slowly whisk in 2 tablespoons oil. Add coleslaw and toss to combine.

2. Pat chops dry with paper towels and season with salt and pepper. Heat remaining oil in large skillet over medium-high heat until just smoking. Cook chops until well browned, about 5 minutes per side. Transfer to plate and tent with foil.

3. Add thyme, cayenne, remaining vinegar, remaining honey, and remaining mustard to empty skillet. Cook over medium heat, scraping up any browned bits, until slightly thickened, about 2 minutes. Return chops and any accumulated juices to skillet and simmer, turning often, until glaze coats chops, about 1 minute. Serve with slaw.

TEST KITCHEN NOTE: To prevent the chops from curling as they cook, cut 2 slits about 2 inches apart through the fat and connective tissue around the outside of each chop.

FLANK STEAK WITH SHALLOT-MUSTARD SAUCE Serves 4

WHY THIS RECIPE WORKS: A touch of cream adds body and tames the mustardy bite in this pan sauce.

- 1 flank steak (about 1½ pounds)
  Salt and pepper
- 2 tablespoons vegetable oil
- 3 shallots, peeled and sliced thin
- ½ cup red wine
- ¾ cup low-sodium chicken broth
- 2 tablespoons heavy cream
- 1 tablespoon coarse-grain mustard (see note below)
- 1 tablespoon finely chopped fresh parsley

1. Pat steak dry with paper towels and season with salt and pepper. Heat 1 tablespoon oil in large skillet over medium-high heat until just smoking. Cook steak until well browned, 5 to 7 minutes per side. Transfer to cutting board and tent with foil.

2. Heat remaining oil in empty skillet over medium heat until shimmering. Cook shallots until softened, about 3 minutes. Add wine, broth, and any accumulated beef juices and simmer, scraping up any browned bits, until slightly thickened, about 5 minutes. Off heat, whisk in cream, mustard, and parsley. Slice steak thinly against grain. Spoon sauce over steak. Serve.

TEST KITCHEN NOTE: We prefer the texture of coarse-grain mustard, but smooth Dijon also works fine.

QUICK BEEF BURGUNDY Serves 4 to 6

WHY THIS RECIPE WORKS: The thorough marbling of the steak tips (a.k.a. flap meat) keeps the meat tender and moist as it simmers.

- 2 pounds sirloin steak tips, cut into 1-inch chunks
  Salt and pepper
- 4 slices bacon, chopped
- 8 ounces cremini or white mushrooms, quartered
- 1 cup frozen pearl onions, thawed
- 3 tablespoons unsalted butter
- ¼ cup all-purpose flour
- 2 cups red wine (see note below)
- 1 cup low-sodium chicken broth
- 2 teaspoons minced fresh thyme

1. Pat steak tips dry with paper towels and season with salt and pepper. Cook bacon in Dutch oven over medium-high heat until crisp, about 5 minutes. Using slotted spoon, transfer bacon to paper towel–lined plate. Cook steak tips in bacon fat until well browned all over, about 5 minutes. Transfer to plate and tent with foil.

2. Add mushrooms and onions to empty pot and cook until browned, about 5 minutes; transfer to medium bowl. Stir butter and flour into empty pot and cook until golden, 1 to 2 minutes. Stir in wine, broth, thyme, and beef along with any accumulated beef juices and bring to boil. Reduce heat to medium-low and simmer, covered, until sauce is slightly thickened, about 10 minutes. Stir in bacon, onions, and mushrooms. Serve.

TEST KITCHEN NOTE: Fruity, medium-bodied red wines, such as Côtes du Rhône or pinot noir, work best here.

OVEN-BAKED CHICKEN CHIMICHANGAS Serves 6

WHY THIS RECIPE WORKS: We mimic the crunch of authentic chimichangas (deep-fried burritos) by brushing the tortillas with oil and baking them on a preheated baking sheet.

- ¼ cup vegetable oil
- 1 onion, chopped fine
- 1 (16-ounce) can black beans, drained and rinsed
- 1 (8.8-ounce) package Uncle Ben's Ready Rice
- 1 rotisserie chicken, skin discarded, meat shredded into bite-sized pieces (about 3 cups)
- 2 teaspoons minced canned chipotle chiles in adobo
- 1 cup shredded Mexican cheese blend
- ½ cup finely chopped fresh cilantro
  Salt and pepper
- 6 large flour tortillas (see note below)

1. Place rimmed baking sheet in oven and heat oven to 450 degrees. Heat 2 tablespoons oil in large skillet over medium-high heat until shimmering. Cook onion until just softened, about 3 minutes. Stir in beans, rice, chicken, and chipotle and cook until heated through, about 3 minutes. Off heat, stir in cheese and cilantro. Season with salt and pepper.

2. Stack tortillas on plate and microwave, covered, until pliable, about 1 minute. Top warm tortillas with chicken mixture, leaving 2-inch border at bottom. Fold in sides and roll up tightly. Brush wrapped tortillas with remaining oil and arrange, seam-side down, on preheated baking sheet. Bake until crisp and golden, 8 to 10 minutes. Serve.

TEST KITCHEN NOTE: Use "burrito-sized" tortillas that are at least 10 inches in diameter.

Skillet Carbonara Casserole

We wanted the smoky bacon, silky sauce, and peppery bite of the original pasta in a more forgiving, single skillet supper. BY MARÍA DEL MAR SACASA

We admit it. We cheated. Our easy, one-pan casserole isn't authentic carbonara, but it's got all the same great flavors.

OUR FORAY INTO skillet suppers began about four years ago when we attempted to turn a meaty lasagna (a complicated, multistep casserole) into an easy one-pot dinner. We developed a method that revolutionized our thinking: First we built a meat sauce in a skillet, fortifying it with plenty of diced tomatoes. The loose, watery sauce was just what we wanted, as it allowed us to break dry lasagna noodles into pieces that we added to the pan and softened right in the juicy sauce. Dollops of ricotta and a handful of fresh basil made this dish a winner and led to a string of other delicious, streamlined skillet suppers: beef goulash with noodles, macaroni and cheese, spaghetti with meat sauce. So it was natural to turn our eye toward another favorite pasta dish: spaghetti carbonara.

The test kitchen's conventional recipe starts with boiling pasta in a big pot of water. Meanwhile, we reduce white wine on the stovetop with garlic and black pepper. We drain the pasta, toss it in the mixture along with bacon, eggs, a little cream, and lots of Pecorino Romano, and end up with a rich, creamy sauce that cooks from the heat of the noodles. It's a simple dish, but the final minutes can be cruel. If the mixture is too hot, the eggs curdle. If it's not hot enough, the cheese won't melt, and don't even think of letting this dish sit around while

diners gather. In the blink of an eye, velvety carbonara turns into a heavy, clumpy tangle. I wanted to spare the cook anxiety by parlaying carbonara into a more forgiving, skillet-friendly casserole.

The beginning recipe steps changed little: I crisped and rendered bacon and set it aside, then cooked garlic, pepper, and white wine until reduced to ¼ cup, per our original recipe. In order to cook a pound of pasta in a skillet (I used penne, which is better suited to a casserole), I found that I needed an additional 4½ cups of liquid. Unlike other pasta skillet casseroles, though, I didn't have an abundance of canned tomatoes to flavor the dish. I tried chicken broth, but the flavor was too distinct, so I stuck with water.

When the pasta was just about done, I got ready to add the eggs and cheese, but I faced the usual conundrum: The eggs couldn't cook for long or they'd curdle, but the cheese needed time to melt. My first step was to use two eggs instead of three. At the same time, I whisked 2 tablespoons of heavy cream into them (the cream diluted the eggs, preventing them from coagulating as quickly). Despite my efforts, the eggs curdled before the cheese melted. Stirring in additional heavy cream made the carbonara too rich, while milk separated in the last few moments of cooking. So I tried an ingredient that we'd used in other casseroles: evaporated milk. It worked beautifully and never separated (thanks to the fact that it's stabilized), but the sauce was a little thick for what should be a silken carbonara. Easy enough to fix: I cut the creamy canned milk with a little water.

It was almost a perfect casserole, save for one glaring omission: a crunchy bread-crumb topping. So I incorporated some of the casserole flavors—crumbled bacon, pepper, and more cheese—into bread crumbs, sprinkled the mixture over the pasta, and broiled it until golden brown. Tasters gave my carbonara casserole two thumbs up, and even a second helping remained rich and creamy. Although miles from the original carbonara, the flavors had survived the journey.

TEST KITCHEN TECHNIQUE
Skillet Pasta: Just Add Water

Stir pasta and water into skillet. Bring to a boil, cover, and simmer. It is done when most of the liquid is absorbed and the pasta is al dente.

SKILLET CARBONARA CASSEROLE Serves 4 to 6

Carbonara is defined in no small part by the peppery, sheep's milk bite of Pecorino Romano, so don't settle for preshredded cheese. Buy a 3-ounce wedge of Pecorino from the deli department and grate it yourself.

- 8   slices bacon, chopped fine
- 2   slices hearty white sandwich bread, torn into pieces
- 1¼ cups grated Pecorino Romano (see note)
     Salt and pepper
- 2   large eggs
- 1   cup evaporated milk
- 5¼ cups water
- 3   garlic cloves, minced
- 1   cup white wine
- 1   pound penne

1. FRY BACON Cook bacon in large nonstick skillet over medium-high heat until crisp, about 5 minutes. Transfer bacon to paper towel–lined plate. Pour off fat from pan, reserving 3 tablespoons.

2. PREPARE TOPPING Pulse bread, ¼ cup cheese, ½ teaspoon pepper, one-quarter of crisp bacon, and 2 tablespoons reserved bacon fat in food processor until coarsely ground. Whisk eggs, milk, remaining cheese, and ¾ cup water in medium bowl.

3. SIMMER PASTA Heat remaining bacon fat in empty skillet over medium-high heat until shimmering. Add garlic and 1 teaspoon pepper and cook until fragrant, about 30 seconds. Stir in wine and cook until reduced to ¼ cup, about 3 minutes. Stir in remaining water, penne, and ¾ teaspoon salt and bring to boil. Reduce heat to medium and simmer covered, stirring occasionally, until most of liquid is absorbed and pasta is al dente, 15 to 20 minutes. Adjust oven rack to upper-middle position and heat broiler.

4. ADD SAUCE Off heat, add egg mixture and remaining crisp bacon to pan and toss to combine. Top with bread-crumb mixture and broil until golden brown, about 2 minutes. Cool 5 minutes. Serve.

ON THE SIDE Braised Hearty Greens

We hoped to coax fabulous flavor from winter greens minus the pork and an hours-long simmer. BY DIANE UNGER

Agreed, these greens may not be the prettiest thing on the table, but they taste so good they'll disappear quickly.

MY GOAL? A COMPARATIVELY quick braise of winter greens (kale, mustard greens, collards) that would be lighter than usual—no pork products just this once—and yet as flavorful as any that had simmered for hours with a ham hock and a southern grandmother hovering.

To feed four, I stemmed and trimmed the ribs from 2½ pounds of raw greens and set 2 tablespoons butter to melt in a Dutch oven. To add flavor from the start, I began by sautéing a sweet red onion.

My pile of greens wouldn't fit into the pot, so after the onion softened, I added half of the greens, along with 1 cup of chicken broth. I covered the pot and wilted the leaves. Within one minute, they'd cooked down enough to allow me to heap in the remaining greens. In 40 minutes, the greens were tender, but swimming in liquid. The next time, I cut the simmering back to 30 minutes, uncovered the pot, and let the liquid that remained boil away for 10 minutes.

Flavored with only butter and onion, the greens tasted tame. I stirred in brown sugar (to counteract the bitterness of the greens) and cayenne pepper for zip and heat. For a creamy finish, I stirred in 2 more tablespoons of butter and added a sprinkle of vinegar for wake-me-up sweet-sour flavor. Lively and almost silky, these vegetables are the kind you'd be happy to eat without prodding.

BRAISED HEARTY GREENS Serves 4 to 6
Collards may need a few extra minutes in step 1.

- 4 tablespoons unsalted butter
- ½ red onion, sliced thin
- 2½ pounds hearty greens (kale, mustard, turnip, or collards), stemmed and chopped
- 1 cup low-sodium chicken broth
- 1 tablespoon brown sugar
- ½ teaspoon salt
- ¼ teaspoon cayenne pepper
- 2 tablespoons cider vinegar

1. **SIMMER GREENS** Melt 2 tablespoons butter in Dutch oven over medium heat. Cook onion until softened, about 5 minutes. Add half of greens, broth, sugar, salt, and cayenne. Cover and cook until greens are beginning to wilt, about 1 minute. Stir in remaining greens and cook, covered and stirring occasionally, over medium-low heat until completely tender, about 30 minutes.

2. **FINISH COOKING** Remove lid and cook over medium-high heat, stirring occasionally, until liquid is nearly evaporated, about 10 minutes. Off heat, stir in remaining butter and vinegar. Serve.

ON THE SIDE Cracklin' Cornbread

Could we make this cornbread crackle without the traditional cracklings?

BY MEGHAN ERWIN

SOUTHERNERS ARE PURISTS about cornbread. Flour and sugar are an abomination, and if you don't bake the batter in a hot, greased cast-iron skillet (for the crispest crust possible), you might as well wear a "Yankee" sticker on your forehead. Among the most beloved variations is cracklin' cornbread, which is speckled with crispy, salty bits of rendered pork skin. If you've got the time to render the skin yourself, you're in for a treat. Sadly, commercial cracklins, or pork rinds, are about as similar to homemade as plastic roses to a fragrant blossom. How could I duplicate the cornbread without the cracklings?

As a jumping-off point, I used the test kitchen recipe for skillet cornbread (cornmeal, leaveners, buttermilk, butter, eggs). Among my more bizarre (and least successful) mock cracklings were Fritos that I fried in bacon grease. Chopped salt pork was too salty and tough. Fried bacon, however, added flecks of chewy, salty pork throughout. My cornbread really started to crackle when I replaced ¼ cup of the butter with the same amount of bacon fat I'd rendered. Using flavorless vegetable oil for the remaining butter brought the smokiness to the forefront.

During testing, the batter sometimes stuck. (Hey, we don't all have perfectly seasoned skillets.) Then I discovered a neat trick: When the skillet and 1 tablespoon oil were good and hot, I dolloped in the batter. The oil no longer decamped to the pan's edges, which ensured the cornbread's easy release. I turned out the dark golden bread five minutes after it was done, so it wouldn't steam and soften in the skillet. There was really only one way to serve it: crunchy crust-side up.

CRACKLIN' CORNBREAD Serves 10
For the crunchiest crust, bake the cornbread in a cast-iron pan. See page 31 for information about seasoning cast-iron skillets. Avoid coarsely ground cornmeal, which will make the cornbread too gritty.

- 6 slices bacon, chopped fine
- 2¼ cups cornmeal (see note)
- 1 teaspoon baking powder
- 1 teaspoon baking soda
- ½ teaspoon salt
- 2 cups buttermilk
- ¼ cup vegetable oil
- 2 large eggs, lightly beaten

1. **COOK BACON** Adjust oven rack to middle position and heat oven to 450 degrees. Cook bacon in 10-inch heatproof skillet over medium heat until crisp, about 8 minutes. Transfer bacon to paper towel–lined plate. Pour off fat from pan, reserving ¼ cup.

2. **MIX BATTER** Combine cornmeal, baking powder, baking soda, and salt in large bowl. Whisk in buttermilk, 3 tablespoons oil, reserved bacon fat, eggs, and crisp bacon.

3. **BAKE CORNBREAD** Heat remaining oil in empty skillet over medium-high heat until just smoking. Spoon cornmeal mixture, ½ cup at a time, into skillet and bake until top begins to crack and sides are golden brown, 12 to 16 minutes. Cool in pan 5 minutes, then turn out onto wire rack. Serve.

Crispy bacon replaces the cracklings in this savory cornbread.

TEST KITCHEN TECHNIQUE
Do the Dollop
If you dump the batter in, the hot oil that's greasing the skillet gets pushed to the edge. Dolloping the batter guarantees the cornbread will release cleanly, even in an underseasoned skillet.

Quicker Hoppin' John

This hearty, humble dish of rice, black-eyed peas, and ham hocks takes hours to cook. Could we hop a little faster? BY CALI RICH

Southerners have a saying about eating hoppin' John for New Year's: "Eat poor that day, eat rich the rest of the year." We respectfully disagree. This one-pot meal makes for delicious eating.

IN THE LOWCOUNTRY of South Carolina and Georgia, eating hoppin' John at the start of the new year is said to bring 365 days of good luck. (On a related note, it's also said to help with hangovers.) Traditional recipes for this rib-sticking dish call for simmering fresh black-eyed peas (they're beans, despite the name) with smoked ham hocks until creamy and infused with meaty savor. Rice plumps in the broth toward the end of cooking.

Since fresh black-eyed peas can be hard to find if you live outside the South, most modern recipes rely on their dried counterpart, which can take hours to achieve the perfect creamy—but not mushy—state. I prepared a handful of recipes and found that while the extended cooking time helps give smoky, meaty flavor to both the rice and beans, it also makes the dish a bit starchy and gummy. I didn't want to cheat, as some recipes do, by cooking the rice and black-eyed peas

separately (I tried it, and it just wasn't as flavorful), but I also didn't want my hoppin' John to sit like a rock in my stomach. Plus, I hoped to reduce the cooking time considerably.

My first challenge was cooking the beans faster. Working from the most promising one-pot recipe I'd tried, I browned several slices of chopped bacon, removed them for stirring in at the end, and sautéed onion, celery, garlic, and thyme in the flavorful fat. Now that it was time to add the beans, I tested adding 2 pounds of canned black-eyed peas versus an equal amount of frozen—both cook much faster than dried—with water and a ham hock. The canned beans quickly blew apart, but the frozen ones held their shape and turned creamy after just 40 minutes. For my next test, I added 1½ cups of rice at the 20-minute mark. After 40 minutes, both components were evenly cooked, but the dish was too starchy, and, without enough time to draw out the ham hock's flavor, it lacked the smoky richness of slow-simmered versions.

I addressed the rice first. While flipping through recipes, I found an older one that rinsed the rice before cooking to remove excess starch and lighten the texture of the hoppin' John. Accordingly, I put the rice in a strainer, opened the tap, and watched the milky starch run off the grains. At the end of cooking, I removed the lid to find nicely toothsome rice amid creamy beans—the rinse made the difference.

To extract their flavor, smoked ham hocks require hours of simmering. Looking for another smoked pork product that would give up its flavor more quickly, I grabbed a small boneless ham at the grocery store. I sliced it into steaks, browned them in the bacon fat, and then stirred in the broth and beans, as before. I added the rice as usual and when it was done removed the ham steaks, chopped them, and stirred them back into the stew with the reserved bacon dice. Tasters loved the meatiness of the ham and the smoky pork flavor it contributed, but the chopped ham pieces were rubbery. Removing the steaks before adding the rice solved the problem. A sprinkle of scallions brightened the dish, and my quick and easy hoppin' John hopped to the table.

HOPPIN' JOHN Serves 8

Small boneless hams are available in the meat case at most supermarkets. An equal weight of ham steak can be used. To ensure that the rice cooks evenly, cover the surface with aluminum foil when cooking. Use low-sodium chicken broth or the dish will be too salty. Serve with hot sauce.

- 6 slices bacon, chopped
- 1 (1- to 1½-pound) boneless ham, cut into ¾-inch-thick planks (see note)
- 1 onion, chopped fine
- 2 celery ribs, chopped fine
- 4 garlic cloves, minced
- ½ teaspoon dried thyme
- 4 cups low-sodium chicken broth (see note)
- 2 (16-ounce) bags frozen black-eyed peas
- 2 bay leaves
- 1½ cups long-grain rice
- 3 scallions, sliced thin

1. BROWN PORK Cook bacon in Dutch oven over medium heat until crisp, about 8 minutes. Using slotted spoon, transfer bacon to paper towel–lined plate. Pour off all but 1 tablespoon fat from pot and brown ham, about 3 minutes per side. Transfer to plate with bacon.

2. COOK VEGETABLES Add onion and celery to pot and cook until softened, about 5 minutes. Stir in garlic and thyme and cook until fragrant, about 30 seconds. Add broth, peas, bay leaves, and browned ham and bring to boil. Reduce heat to low and simmer, covered, until beans are just tender, about 20 minutes. Transfer ham to cutting board and cut into ½-inch pieces.

3. SIMMER RICE Place rice in fine-mesh strainer set over large bowl. Rinse under running water until water runs clear, about 1 minute. Drain rice well and stir into pot. Place square of aluminum foil directly on surface of simmering liquid. Simmer covered until liquid is absorbed and rice is tender, about 20 minutes, stirring and repositioning foil twice during cooking. Remove from heat and let stand, covered, for 10 minutes. Fluff rice with fork. Stir in scallions, bacon, and ham. Serve.

Reviving Swiss Steak

In 1930, a Good Housekeeping cookbook, "Meals, Tested, Tasted, and Approved," featured a dish sometimes known as Swiss steak (the cookbook called it Tomato Steak). Round steaks were pounded, floured, browned, and then smothered in carrots, tomatoes, and turnips, which cooked down during a long oven braise to a savory, satisfying gravy; the steaks, meanwhile, became almost tender enough to eat with a spoon. The recipe enabled frugal housewives to transform a tough, cheap cut of meat and ordinary vegetables into a delicious and filling meal. Sadly, over the years, Swiss steak became the province of school cafeterias and the victim of midcentury convenience trends (onion soup mixes, etc.). But made right, it's an easy, inexpensive supper. We set out to restore and, better yet, perfect it. BY LYNN CLARK

I made that original recipe along with a handful of others, which variously added celery and bell peppers and used different cuts of meat, like cube steak and blade steak. The promise of the dish—its ease, economy, and tangy, beefy flavors—was evident. But none of the recipes lived up to it. Gravies were bland, pasty, or watery. The meat by turn was dry, mangled, gristly, or too thin to qualify as a meaty steak.

Starting with a basic gravy of onions, canned tomato sauce, and water, I began by testing different cuts of meat. It had to be economical, as befit Swiss steak. Tasters rejected the round steak as lean, dry, and livery; and cube steaks as mangled, shaggy, and too thin for Swiss steak. I moved on to blade steaks. In their favor: a thick shape and good beefy flavor. Against them: a line of gristle running down the middle. A deal breaker, tasters said.

The butcher suggested chuck roast, a well-marbled cut popular in stews. I carved the roast into steak-sized pieces—or tried to. But the same pockets of fat that made this cut juicy also prevented me from cutting it into neat steaks. This Swiss steak was moist, tender, and appropriately beefy—it just wasn't steak. Since I was going to the trouble of butchering, maybe I ought to butcher a blade roast into steaks. With a little ingenuity, could I trim the gristle? I cut a whole blade roast into four, turned the chunks on their sides, cut again, then sliced off the gristle. (See photos 1 to 3, next page).

Swiss steak doesn't come from Switzerland. Rather, the technique of pounding raw meat to tenderize it resembles swissing, a method of smoothing out cloth between two rollers. (A 1930s recipe instructed pounding flour into the steak "until it could take no

more.") Call me a heretic, but I skipped this step. Pounding doesn't actually tenderize meat (see page 31). Anyway, the slow braise made the meat plenty tender. As for the flour, stirring a tablespoon into the gravy to thicken it was simpler than dredging the meat.

Thus far, my gravy mix of tomato sauce, water, and raw onions tasted uninspired. I added, in turn, turnips, carrots, bell peppers, and celery. The tomato sweetened the sauce without carrots, and tasters insisted I eliminate the other vegetables. So I simply sautéed the onions in the fat from the browned steaks, then bolstered them with tomato paste, garlic, and thyme. Next, I replaced the water with chicken broth. After that, I discovered that diced tomatoes supplied more body than sauce. Swiss steak's original name, Tomato Steak, gave me the idea to stir in minced sun-dried tomatoes, which pulled the dish together.

SWISS STEAK WITH TOMATO GRAVY Serves 6 to 8

Top blade roast may also be labeled chuck roast first cut, top chuck roast, flat iron roast, or simply blade roast. Use low-sodium chicken broth or the gravy will be too salty.

- 1 (3½- to 4-pound) boneless top blade roast (see note)
  Salt and pepper
- 2 tablespoons vegetable oil
- 1 onion, halved and sliced thin
- 3 garlic cloves, minced
- ½ teaspoon dried thyme
- 2 tablespoons tomato paste
- 1 tablespoon all-purpose flour
- 1 (14.5-ounce) can diced tomatoes
- 1½ cups low-sodium chicken broth
- 1 tablespoon sun-dried tomatoes packed in oil, rinsed, patted dry, and minced
- 1 tablespoon finely chopped fresh parsley

1. BUTCHER ROAST Adjust oven rack to middle position and heat oven to 300 degrees. Following photos 1 to 3, cut roast crosswise into quarters and remove line of gristle to yield 8 steaks.

2. BROWN STEAKS Pat steaks dry with paper towels and season with salt and pepper. Heat 1 tablespoon oil in Dutch oven over medium-high heat just until smoking. Brown 4 steaks, about 3 minutes per side. Transfer to plate and repeat with remaining oil and steaks.

3. ADD AROMATICS Add onion to empty pot and cook until softened, about 5 minutes. Add garlic, thyme, tomato paste, and flour and cook until fragrant, about 1 minute. Stir in diced tomatoes and broth and bring to boil.

4. BRAISE STEAKS Return steaks and any accumulated juices to pan. Transfer to oven and braise, covered, until steaks are fork-tender, about 2 hours. Transfer steaks to platter, tent with foil, and let rest 5 minutes. Skim fat from sauce. Stir in sun-dried tomatoes and parsley. Season with salt and pepper. Pour sauce over steaks. Serve.

STEP-BY-STEP Blade Butchery

Top blade roast, a shoulder cut with great flavor, has a pesky line of gristle that runs horizontally through its center. Follow these simple steps to remove it and cut perfect Swiss steaks.

1. Place roast on cutting board and cut crosswise into four even pieces.

2. One piece at a time, turn meat on its side to expose the line of gristle that runs through its center.

3. Remove by slicing through meat on either side of gristle to yield two "steaks." Repeat with remaining pieces of blade roast to yield a total of eight steaks.

The American Table
Taste of Home

A frugal, tasty dish, Swiss steak was popular on the home front during World War II. Bob Dole, then a young soldier, later a U.S. senator, longed for it, and much more, in this letter home: "Send candy, gum, cookies, cheese, grape jelly, popcorn, nuts, peanut clusters, Vick's vapor rub, wool socks, wool scarf, fudge cookies, ice cream, liver and onions, chicken, banana cake, milk, fruit cocktail, Swiss steak, crackers, more candy, Life Savers, peanuts, piano, radio, living room suite, record player, and Frank Sinatra. I guess you might as well send the whole house if you can get it in a five-pound box."

Swiss steak in an ad from 1952.

WHAT TO DO WITH LEFTOVERS
Spicy Beef and Bean Enchiladas

With beans, tortillas, and a little spice, Swiss steak transforms itself. BY LYNN CLARK

I LOVE THE IDEA of a second-day dinner so different from its parent, it doesn't seem like leftovers. Case in point: from Swiss steak, an old-fashioned American braise with tomato gravy, to Spicy Beef and Bean Enchiladas, an oniony, chile-spiked Tex-Mex standard.

Swiss steak gravy has lots of onions and garlic, so I had a head start. I warmed up 1 cup of the leftover gravy with canned tomato sauce, cumin, and plenty of chili powder. The spices weren't emphatic enough, so I drew out their flavor by first sautéing them in oil. To make the filling, I reached for a can of creamy pinto beans, which stretched the meat so I could serve four. I brightened the filling with chopped cilantro and reinforced its Tex-Mex credentials with pepper Jack cheese. I stirred a few tablespoons of the sauce into the filling to help it hold together.

Once I'd microwaved the corn tortillas to soften them, assembly was the usual matter of filling, rolling, saucing, and sprinkling with cheese. I put the pan into the oven, and 30 minutes later Swiss steak had entirely disappeared. Like a magician pulling a rabbit out of a hat, I pulled enchiladas out of the oven.

Serve these hearty enchiladas with lime wedges and sour cream.

SPICY BEEF AND BEAN ENCHILADAS Serves 4
Use canned plain tomato sauce, not pasta sauce, in this recipe.

- 2 teaspoons vegetable oil
- 2 tablespoons chili powder
- 1½ teaspoons ground cumin
- 1 cup leftover Tomato Gravy, plus 3 leftover Swiss Steaks, shredded into bite-sized pieces
- ⅔ cup canned plain tomato sauce (see note)
- 1½ cups shredded pepper Jack cheese
- 2 tablespoons chopped fresh cilantro
- 1 (16-ounce) can pinto beans, drained and rinsed
- 8 (6-inch) corn tortillas

1. MAKE SAUCE Adjust oven rack to middle position and heat oven to 350 degrees. Heat oil in large saucepan over medium heat until shimmering. Cook chili powder and cumin until fragrant, about 1 minute. Stir in Tomato Gravy and tomato sauce and simmer until slightly thickened, about 4 minutes.

2. ASSEMBLE ENCHILADAS Combine Swiss Steaks, 2 tablespoons sauce, 1 cup cheese, cilantro, and beans in large bowl. Spread additional ½ cup sauce in 8-inch square baking dish. Stack tortillas on plate and microwave, covered, until softened, about 1 minute. One at a time, place heaping ⅓ cup beef mixture in center of each tortilla, roll tightly, and arrange seam-side down in prepared baking dish.

3. TOP AND BAKE Pour remaining sauce evenly over enchiladas, top with remaining cheese, and cover with foil. Bake until enchiladas are heated through, about 15 minutes. Remove foil and bake until cheese is lightly browned, 5 to 10 minutes. Serve.

TEST KITCHEN TIP
Microwaving Corn Tortillas

Corn tortillas are spongy and fragile out of the package and need to be warmed, which makes them elastic enough to roll without tearing. Most recipes call for toasting 1 or 2 tortillas at a time in a dry skillet (or over the open flame of your range or grill). To heat 8 tortillas at once, simply put them on a plate, cover with plastic wrap, and microwave for 1 minute.

Skillet Stuffed Onions

Does stuffing an onion have to take all afternoon?

BY MARÍA DEL MAR SACASA

Halved yellow onions hold about ½ cup of stuffing and cook through quickly.

WE SELDOM REGARD the onion as the main attraction. It's usually relegated to a supporting role. A rare exception is the stuffed onion. With its savory-sweet caramelized shell and complementary filling, the onion gets to strut its stuff. Unfortunately, stuffed onions are time-consuming to make (an average two-hour prep time), too big for a side dish, and judging by the recipes I tested, not always successful. I wanted delicious stuffed onions with a basic stuffing I could dress up or down. And I wanted them fast.

Existing recipes filled the onions with everything from leftover Thanksgiving dressing to sauerkraut and pineapple (I'm not making that up!) The common theme? Tedious instructions. Some recipes roast the onions whole for an hour or more before scooping, stuffing, and baking again. Others carve out raw onions and boil the shells before stuffing and baking. One recipe I tried stuffed the onions raw, a timesaver I really wanted to work. Sadly (and predictably), the shells were crunchy.

To begin, what type of onion best suits stuffing? White onions, which have high moisture content, turned soggy. Red onions turned mousy brown. But ordinary yellow onions held their shape, color, and were gently sweet. To make more reasonable portions, I split the onions in half across the equator, and to steady the round, rocking cups, I trimmed the ends. Hollowing the onions was a simple matter of popping out the cores with my fingers; I reserved the cores for the stuffing.

I baked my halved onions in a very hot oven for 15 minutes, expecting they'd cook faster than whole ones. Perhaps so, but they were still crunchy. A turn in the microwave left them shriveled and soggy. During initial tests, tasters had loved deeply sweet roasted onions, but they'd required 1½ hours of roasting. In the test kitchen we often "roast" vegetables in a skillet as a fast way to achieve the same effect. I melted butter in a skillet, seasoned my cups with a teaspoon of sugar to jump-start browning, and cooked them, cup-side down, for a few minutes to slightly caramelize. I poured in half a cup of flavorful chicken broth, covered the pan, and steamed the onions. The shells were tender, browned, and sweet in under 10 minutes!

I wanted a streamlined, bread-based stuffing with room for additions. I chopped then sautéed the reserved onion cores in butter, and mixed them with toasted bread crumbs (untoasted, the crumbs turned to mush). I stirred in broth and Parmesan cheese to flavor and bind, and finished with lemon zest and parsley. A final sprinkling of cheese and a few minutes under the broiler in the skillet gave the onions a crispy, golden top in just 30 minutes.

STUFFED ONIONS Serves 8

Fresh parsley is essential here: Don't even think about using dried, which tastes dusty and stale.

- 5 slices hearty white sandwich bread, torn into pieces
- 4 yellow onions (3½ to 4 inches each)
- 5 tablespoons unsalted butter
- 1 cup low-sodium chicken broth
- 2 tablespoons chopped fresh parsley (see note)
- ¼ teaspoon grated lemon zest
- ¾ cup grated Parmesan cheese
  Salt and pepper
- 1 teaspoon sugar

1. TOAST CRUMBS Adjust oven rack to middle position and heat oven to 350 degrees. Pulse bread in food processor until coarsely ground. Bake bread crumbs on rimmed baking sheet, stirring occasionally, until golden, about 15 minutes. Transfer to large bowl.

2. PREPARE ONIONS Following photos 1 to 3, trim ½ inch from both stem and root ends of onions, peel, halve through equator, and pop out center of each half, leaving outermost 3 rings intact. Chop onion centers finely to measure 1 cup (reserve any additional onion for another use).

3. MAKE STUFFING Melt 3 tablespoons butter in large ovenproof skillet over medium-high heat. Cook chopped onion until softened, about 5 minutes. Off heat, stir in ½ cup broth, parsley, zest, ½ cup cheese, ½ teaspoon salt, and ¼ teaspoon pepper. Transfer to bowl with bread crumbs and toss to combine.

4. BROWN ONIONS Sprinkle onion halves with sugar and season with salt and pepper. Melt additional 1 tablespoon butter in empty skillet over medium heat. Place 4 onion halves in skillet, wide ends down, and cook until browned, about 3 minutes. Transfer to plate and repeat with remaining butter and onion halves. Flip onions and return first batch to skillet, browned-side up. Add remaining broth and simmer, covered, until liquid evaporates and onions are softened, about 5 minutes.

5. STUFF ONIONS Heat broiler. Fill onion halves with bread-crumb mixture and sprinkle with remaining cheese. Broil until stuffing is golden brown and heated through, 2 to 4 minutes. Serve.

STEP-BY-STEP Making Onion Cups

Here's how to prep the onions so they cook quickly and don't wobble.

1. To keep the onions from tipping, create a flat surface by trimming the stem and root ends. Next, peel the onions.

2. Halve the onions through the equator to speed the cooking and create onion cups the right size for a side dish.

3. Push out center of each onion half, leaving outermost three rings intact. The filling will stay put despite the hole in the bottom.

VISIT US ONLINE

For Stuffed Onion variations— **Mushroom-Spinach, Smoky Apricot-Almond,** and **Sausage-Apple**—visit **Cooks Country.com** and click on **Cook's Extras.**

Cider-Braised Chicken

It takes more than cider to infuse chicken with to-the-bone apple flavor. BY ADAM RIED

A hybrid braising technique and a handful of apple products are the keys to this recipe's appeal.

BRAISING PORK CHOPS in fresh apple cider permeates them with apple flavor. I wanted to adapt the method for chicken, but my initial tests uncovered trouble.

Simply braising chicken in apple cider was a natural starting point. I browned chicken pieces until they were golden, set them aside, and then sautéed onions and garlic in the same pan. I returned the chicken to the pan, poured in cider until the meat was nearly submerged, and placed it in a low oven (we prefer the consistently gentle heat of the oven to the stovetop for braising). I left the cover off, knowing that a moist environment wouldn't allow the chicken skin to render and crisp. Well, the skin was still soggy and flabby, and the dish tasted nothing of apples; the chicken juices had diluted the cider, which clearly needed lots of support to deliver deep apple flavor.

First, I trained my attention on the chicken. Braised chicken skin is often rubbery because the fat hasn't been rendered correctly. Most recipes call for browning the chicken until "golden brown," usually about five minutes per side. I took the time to thoroughly render the skin—a full 10 minutes over medium-high heat until it had turned deep chestnut brown. (It took just five minutes to brown the skinless flip side.)

For even crisper skin, I ignored the "low and slow" rule of braising and tried cranking the heat up to 450 degrees. In just 10 minutes, the chicken was done and the skin was better, but still not perfect. Things really turned the corner when I re-thought the technique I'd been using of flipping the chicken pieces halfway through

their oven time. As long as I didn't over-cook the chicken, I found I could leave it skin-side up. At the same time, I reduced the amount of liquid in the pan so that it reached just halfway up the chicken pieces, leaving the skin exposed to the drier heat. The finish line was in sight.

Now I focused on the sauce. The extra browning of the chicken left plenty of fond in the pan, and the high heat roast-ing sans lid let the liquid evaporate in the oven, which helped concentrate the apple flavor. To give the braise more interest, I chopped up one apple and stirred it in after the onions. McIntosh turned to mush, Granny Smith were too tart and firm, but buttery Golden Delicious, Cortland, and Jonagold each retained its integrity when cooked.

I looked for more apple products to fortify the braising liquid. Applesauce gave the dish a grainy feel; apple butter was so intense it overwhelmed the deli-cate chicken, and both apple jelly and apple juice concentrate made the sauce too sweet. I thought that drier alcoholic hard apple cider could replace some (or all) of the fresh cider, but tasters missed the fruitiness of the fresh cider. The addi-tion of apple brandy, however, echoed the earthiness of the apples and gave the sauce depth.

To turn the braising liquid into a sauce, I browned 2 teaspoons of flour with the garlic at the start; it would thicken the final sauce. Fresh thyme provided warmth and herbal softness. To further under-line the dish's apple character, I added splashes of cider vinegar and additional apple brandy before serving.

TEST KITCHEN TECHNIQUE No More Flabby Skin
We avoid flabby skin with a hybrid technique that combines braising and pan roasting.

1. Brown the chicken, skin-side down, in a skillet for 10 minutes until deep brown. Brown the second side for 5 more minutes...

2. ...then finish it, skin-side up and uncov-ered, in a hot oven. Be sure the liquid does not submerge the chicken pieces.

APPLE CIDER CHICKEN Serves 4
Either white or dark meat (or a combina-tion) will work. To ensure even cooking, halve breasts crosswise and separate leg quarters into thighs and drumsticks before cooking. Plain brandy, cognac, or Calvados (a French apple brandy) can be used in place of the apple brandy.

- 3 **pounds bone-in, skin-on chicken pieces (see note)**
  Salt and pepper
- 2 **teaspoons vegetable oil**
- 1 **onion, chopped fine**
- 2 **garlic cloves, minced**
- 2 **teaspoons minced fresh thyme**
- 2 **teaspoons all-purpose flour**
- 1 **large Golden Delicious, Cortland, or Jonagold apple, peeled, cored, and cut into ¾-inch chunks**
- 1 **cup apple cider**
- ¼ **cup apple brandy (see note)**
- 1 **teaspoon cider vinegar**

1. BROWN CHICKEN Adjust oven rack to middle position and heat oven to 450 degrees. Pat chicken dry with paper towels and season with salt and pepper. Heat oil in large ovenproof skillet over medium-high heat until just smoking. Cook chicken, skin-side down, until well browned, about 10 minutes. Flip and brown on second side, about 5 minutes. Transfer to plate.

2. BUILD SAUCE Pour off all but 1 tablespoon fat from skillet. Cook onion in chicken fat until softened, about 5 minutes. Stir in garlic, thyme, and flour and cook, stirring frequently, until fragrant and flour is absorbed, about 1 minute. Add apple, cider, and 3 table-spoons brandy and bring to boil.

3. ROAST CHICKEN Nestle chicken, skin-side up, into sauce and roast until white meat registers 160 degrees (or dark meat registers 175 degrees), about 10 minutes. Transfer chicken to platter. Stir vinegar and remaining brandy into sauce. Season with salt and pepper. Serve, passing sauce at table.

Christmas Kringle

Most of Wisconsin has a reputation for dairy, brats, and beer, but in Racine, kringle is king. Recipes for this oval-shaped, supremely buttery danish arrived with the many Danish immigrants who settled in Racine in the 1800s. Kringle, often eaten at Christmas, combines the richness of sweet yeast dough with some of the flakiness of painstakingly made puff pastry. It's variously filled with jammy fruit, sweetened cream cheese, or sugared and spiced nuts, and is drizzled with a simple glaze. Aside from stunning amounts of butter, kringle requires one thing above all others: patience. Traditional kringle, as it is still made in Racine, takes three days and calls for bakers to fold the dough dozens of times, stopping repeatedly to let it chill and relax. Even I, an inveterate baker, wondered how would I ever chill and relax with so much work ahead. BY CALI RICH

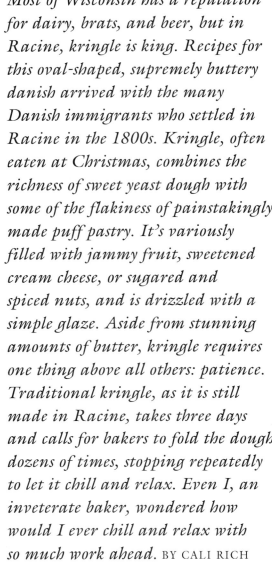

Fortunately, after I returned from visiting five bakeries in Racine and sampling plenty of kringle, I uncovered recipes that purported to cut down the time and labor. I settled on a pecan-butter filling, the most popular variation in Racine, then mixed, rolled, and shaped nine kringles. I baked them after their overnight rest. They looked impressive but tasted, well...some were heavy and cakey, others lean and bready. Many were greasy rather than buttery, and several were encased in stiff, achingly sweet frostings. I wanted a kringle that rivaled the real McCoy in every respect, except for the hours required to make it.

I stepped back to get a handle on the difference between authentic and quick (comparatively speaking) kringle. Authentic kringle is made with danish dough, a cousin of croissant and puff pastry dough that adds eggs to the mix of milk, flour, yeast, and sugar for an especially rich, tender texture. The dough is chilled, rolled out, wrapped around a slab of butter, rolled again, folded into thirds, and chilled again. This process forms layers of butter that melt and steam in the oven, making the dough puff and separate into thin, light-as-air pastry sheets. In quick versions of kringle, cubes of cold butter are cut into flour, sugar, and yeast, after which water, milk, cream, or sour cream and sometimes eggs are stirred in. The dough is simply rolled, filled, shaped into an oval, and rested.

One dough of my initial bunch stood out. It used 2 cups sour cream as its sole wet ingredient (with 2 cups butter, 4 cups flour, 2 tablespoons sugar, and 1 envelope yeast). The recipe yielded two kringles with a tender, just-flaky crumb. Our science editor explained that the acidic sour cream weakened the dough's gluten structure, in effect mimicking the flaky texture of an authentic kringle. Unfortunately, it was greasy. I reduced the amount of butter bit by bit to 1¼ cups—the greasiness disappeared. So did the tenderness. I experimented with using cornstarch (which has no gluten) for some of the flour, but it had little effect. Next, I replaced some of the butter with shortening, a known tenderizer. Restraint was key, as butter is the mark of any self-respecting danish. I hit the sweet spot at ¼ cup shortening and 1 cup butter.

During my visit to Racine, Eric Olesen, baker and co-owner of O&H Bakery, had told me, "The key to a light and tender kringle is letting the dough relax, and that takes time." But how much time? To speed my kringle along, I whittled down the overnight rest, ultimately reducing it to four hours with no ill effect.

I turned my attention to the filling and glaze. Bakeries in Racine layer on the brown sugar, butter, and cinnamon mix, which they top with ground pecans. To streamline the process, I pulsed everything in a food processor (toasting the pecans first to bring out their flavor) and spread the mixture over the dough in a single layer. My working recipe used an excessively thick glaze made from confectioners' sugar and milk. I thinned it, added vanilla extract, and applied it with a light hand.

Tender, buttery, flaky, and both easier and quicker to make, my kringle was ready for a showdown. I mail-ordered a kringle from O&H, king of kringle bakeries in the town that bills itself the Kringle Capital (granted, how much competition is there?) of the U.S. Nervously, I called tasters over for a side-by-side tasting. Mine more than held its own.

PECAN KRINGLE
Makes 2 kringles, each serving 8
To bake only one kringle, adjust the oven rack to the middle position. If the dough appears shaggy and dry after adding the sour cream in step 2, add up to 2 tablespoons ice water until the dough is smooth. If the capacity of your food processor is less than 11 cups, pulse the butter and shortening into the dry mixture in two batches at the beginning of step 2.

FILLING
- ¾ cup packed light brown sugar
- 1 cup pecans, toasted
- ¼ teaspoon ground cinnamon
- ⅛ teaspoon salt
- 4 tablespoons unsalted butter, cut into ½-inch pieces and chilled

DOUGH
- 4 cups all-purpose flour
- 2 tablespoons confectioners' sugar
- 1 envelope (2¼ teaspoons) rapid-rise or instant yeast
- ¾ teaspoon salt
- 16 tablespoons (2 sticks) unsalted butter, cut into ½-inch pieces and chilled
- 4 tablespoons vegetable shortening, chilled, cut into ½-inch pieces
- 2 cups sour cream
- 1 large egg, lightly beaten

GLAZE
- 1 cup confectioners' sugar
- 2 tablespoons whole or low-fat milk
- ½ teaspoon vanilla extract

1. MAKE FILLING Process sugar, pecans, cinnamon, and salt in food processor until pecans are coarsely ground. Add butter and pulse until mixture resembles coarse meal. Transfer to bowl.

2. MIX DOUGH Add flour, sugar, yeast, salt, butter, and shortening to empty food processor and pulse until mixture resembles coarse meal. Transfer to bowl and stir in sour cream until dough forms. Turn dough out onto lightly floured surface and divide in half. Pat each half into 7- by 3-inch rectangle and wrap in plastic.

Refrigerate dough for 30 minutes, then freeze until firm, about 15 minutes.

3. ROLL DOUGH Following photos 1 to 4 below, roll one dough half into 28- by 5-inch rectangle, cover bottom half of strip with half of filling, fold dough over filling, and pinch seams closed. Shape into oval, tuck one end inside of other, and pinch to seal. Transfer to parchment-lined, rimmed baking sheet, cover with plastic wrap, and refrigerate at least 4 or up to 12 hours. Repeat with remaining dough and filling.

4. BAKE KRINGLE Adjust oven racks to upper-middle and lower-middle positions and heat oven to 350 degrees. Discard plastic, brush kringles with egg, and bake until golden brown, 40 to 50 minutes, switching and rotating sheets halfway through baking. Transfer kringles to wire rack and cool 30 minutes.

5. MAKE GLAZE Whisk sugar, milk, and vanilla in bowl until smooth. Drizzle glaze over kringles. Let glaze set 10 minutes. Serve warm or at room temperature. (Kringle can be stored in airtight container at room temperature for 2 days.)

CREAM CHEESE FILLING
Prepare Pecan Kringle, omitting pecan filling. In step 1, combine 8 ounces softened cream cheese, ¼ cup granulated sugar, and ½ teaspoon lemon zest in bowl. In step 3, spread half of cream cheese mixture over bottom of dough and continue with recipe as directed. Repeat with remaining dough and cream cheese mixture.

DOUBLE BERRY FILLING
Do not substitute raspberry jam for the preserves; it will leach out of the kringle.

Prepare Pecan Kringle, omitting pecan filling. In step 1, combine ½ cup raspberry preserves and ¼ cup finely chopped dried cranberries in bowl. In step 3, spread half of preserves mixture over bottom half of dough and continue with recipe as directed. Repeat with remaining dough and preserves mixture.

RATING DECAFFEINATED COFFEES

Has grocery store decaf coffee improved as much as the high-octane stuff in recent years? Or is that asking for the moon? We tasted seven nationally distributed supermarket brands (the top five are shown here; visit CooksCountry.com for the full results), all of which are sold preground, to find out. Each coffee was sampled first black, and then with milk by our panel of tasters. We also sent the beans to an independent laboratory to confirm their caffeine content: All had even less caffeine than the U.S. government requirement that decaffeinated coffee be 97 percent caffeine-free.)

Our top-ranked brands contained only Arabica beans, a lower-caffeine varietal known for good flavor. The bottom-ranked brands blended Arabica with Robusta beans, a high-caffeine varietal that is faster and easier to grow—but doesn't taste as good. Manufacturers would not explain their decaffeination processes, but coffee experts told us that no matter the method, Robusta beans require more processing, which tends to diminish flavor and quality.

While we predicted that premium brands would do well, one of the cheaper ordinary supermarket brands actually edged them out to prevail in both tastings. Our tasters' favorite was Maxwell House Decaf Original Roast, at just 41 cents per ounce.

BY MEREDITH BUTCHER

RECOMMENDED

MAXWELL HOUSE Decaf Original Roast
Price: $0.41 per ounce **Bean:** 100% Arabica
Comments: Praised as "mellow and smooth," our top-ranked brand was neither acidic nor harsh. Tasters liked its "detectable complexity, with a slight nutty aftertaste," "like dark chocolate," describing it as "fruitier" than other coffees in the lineup.

PEET'S Decaf House Blend Ground
Price: $0.75 per ounce **Bean:** 100% Arabica
Comments: Tasters praised this "smoky and robust," full-bodied coffee for its "woody and chocolate" notes. Some enjoyed its "stronger, bitter flavors."

STARBUCKS COFFEE Decaf House Blend
Price: $0.75 per ounce **Bean:** 100% Arabica
Comments: "Decent toasted bean flavor" with a "slightly acidic, but rounded" profile, this coffee packed the strongest punch in our lineup. Several tasters liked that, calling it "sharper and more robust," but detractors faulted it for "bitterness and acidity."

RECOMMENDED WITH RESERVATIONS

DUNKIN' DONUTS Decaffeinated Original Ground
Price: $0.58 per ounce **Bean:** 100% Arabica
Comments: Some tasters liked the "chocolate notes" and "mellow nutty and vanilla" and "fruity" flavors; others found the coffee "astringent and sour."

NOT RECOMMENDED

CHOCK FULL O'NUTS Decaffeinated
Price: $0.38 per ounce **Beans:** Arabica and Robusta
Comments: "Cardboard, ashy, and tastes like yesterday's reheated brew," one despairing taster said. "Stale and bland, with an overall thin flavor," seconded another.

STEP-BY-STEP **Kringle Construction**
Working with one piece of chilled dough at a time, follow these steps to roll and shape the kringle.

1. Working on a lightly floured surface, roll the dough into a 28- by 5-inch strip with one long side closest to you. The dough will be about ¼ inch thick.

2. Leaving a ½-inch border around the bottom and side edges, spread half of the filling over the bottom half of the dough.

3. Brush the edge of the uncovered dough with water and fold the dough over the filling, pinching to close the long seam.

4. Fit one end of the folded dough inside the other to make an oval and press together to seal.

Wellesley Fudge Cake

Unbelievable as it may sound, roughly 100 years ago, fudge (yes, fudge) was a contraband treat coveted by Wellesley students. The girls were expected to stick to "plain" food and avoid sweets, as college founder Henry Fowle Durant held that "pies, lies, and doughnuts should never have a place in Wellesley College." But the students held secret fudge-making parties in their dorm rooms and, according to an undated newspaper article, "put on great airs over their skill in making fudge." Within 10 years, several tearooms in the town of Wellesley were known for their Wellesley Fudge Cake, with its luscious fudge frosting, and recipes for the cake proliferated.

BY DIANE UNGER

In its heyday, Wellesley Fudge Cake was a mild chocolate layer cake filled and frosted with an unusually thick layer of confectionery fudge frosting. The cake was made from unsweetened chocolate (Baker's brand, manufactured in nearby Dorchester, Massachusetts, was specified), brown sugar, pastry flour, and "thick, sour milk." The crumb was tender, spongy, and delicate. It was baked in two square pans, unusual for a layer cake. But it was the frosting that truly distinguished Wellesley Fudge Cake. Chocolate, milk, and sugar were boiled together to what candy makers call the soft ball stage. The warm fudge was spread on the cake and quickly (too quickly, ofttimes) set up.

Over the years, recipes called "Wellesley Fudge Cake" have become just another chocolate layer cake with just another chocolate buttercream frosting (shortening or butter and confectioners' sugar beaten together). I made the original recipe plus several other versions and was dismayed by cottony, pale cakes with marginal chocolate flavor topped with gritty, thin, or coal-black frostings. Nowadays, we're so accustomed to ramped-up chocolate flavor and silken ganaches (not to mention high-quality chocolate), the cake failed to make the impression it once did. Just as bad, slices fell apart. I wanted to honor the spirit of the original—its singular square shape, reputation as a special treat, and honest, barely granular fudge frosting—while adjusting it for modern expectations.

The thick frosting is spread so lavishly on Wellesley Fudge Cake that my cake had to be sturdier than the delicate original in order not to tear. I replaced the pastry flour with all-purpose flour, giving the cake more gluten formation, and therefore more structure. To simulate the "thick sour milk," I used buttermilk. Tasters preferred the deep flavor of cocoa powder to bar chocolate, and the hot water in the original recipe that had melted the chocolate now handily "bloomed" the cocoa, deepening its flavor. Finally, I replaced the brown sugar with granulated, which didn't interfere with the chocolate flavor.

On to the showstopper: the frosting. Straightaway, I eliminated any recipes that simply stirred together melted chocolate, confectioners' sugar, and milk— that's not fudge! But the true fudge icings I tested were alternately hard and grainy, thin and soupy, or too darn difficult. I was after the milky, nearly achy sweetness and slight crystalline crunch that marks real fudge. And I wasn't willing to wrestle with a candy thermometer.

In my research, I'd come across an old advertisement for evaporated milk that included a simple fudge recipe promising that "every single batch turns out mellow-rich and marvelous." Sold! I combined butter with granulated sugar and evaporated milk and boiled the mixture until it was caramel-like, some 4 to 8 minutes. I was encouraged, except that the granulated sugar crystallized unpredictably. Switching to brown sugar stabilized the base, but the minute I added the chopped chocolate, the mixture turned dry and grainy. I looked up the science and learned that the hot sugar mixture was causing the fat in the chocolate to separate. So after my next batch thickened, I took it off the heat. I added more butter and more evaporated milk to cool it slightly, only then stirring in the chopped chocolate. Problem solved.

Unlike fudge candy, I'd never let my frosting base reach the soft ball candy stage, which would have made it too hard to spread. Now, however, it was too loose, so I added confectioners' sugar (sifted, to eliminate lumps) and cooled the mixture for about an hour, stirring periodically. After I iced the cake, I chilled it in the refrigerator. One hour later, the cake sliced perfectly. The frosting was deeply fudgy with the luscious texture of barely softened butter and the faintest sugar crunch. It was also very sweet—but hey, it's fudge. All in all, Wellesley Fudge Cake tasted as satisfying to us as it must have to students a century ago.

WELLESLEY FUDGE CAKE Serves 12

We prefer the deep color and balanced flavor of Dutch-processed cocoa powder, but natural cocoa can be used. Although not traditional, two 9-inch round cake pans will work.

CAKE

- 2½ cups all-purpose flour
- 2 teaspoons baking soda
- 1 teaspoon baking powder
- ½ teaspoon salt
- ¾ cup hot water
- ½ cup Dutch-processed cocoa powder (see note)
- 16 tablespoons (2 sticks) unsalted butter, cut into 16 pieces and softened
- 2 cups granulated sugar
- 2 large eggs
- 1 cup buttermilk, room temperature
- 2 teaspoons vanilla extract

FROSTING

- 8 tablespoons (1 stick) unsalted butter, cut in half, and softened
- 1½ cups packed light brown sugar
- ½ teaspoon salt
- 1 cup evaporated milk
- 8 ounces bittersweet chocolate, chopped
- 1 teaspoon vanilla extract
- 3 cups confectioners' sugar, sifted

STEP-BY-STEP **Fearless Fudge Frosting**
True fudge frostings typically require a candy thermometer and precision timing—but not this one. We figured out how to simplify it.

1. Heat the frosting base of butter, brown sugar, and evaporated milk until small bubbles begin to appear around the edge of the saucepan, 4 to 8 minutes.

2. Reduce the heat and simmer until large bubbles form and the mixture has thickened and turned deep golden brown, about 6 minutes longer.

3. Transfer the frosting base to a bowl and stir in the remaining butter and evaporated milk until the mixture has cooled slightly, then add chocolate.

4. Whisk in the confectioners' sugar. Cool the frosting to room temperature, stirring occasionally, until it thickens to a spreadable consistency.

1. MAKE BATTER Adjust oven rack to middle position and heat oven to 350 degrees. Grease and flour two 8-inch-square cake pans. Combine flour, baking soda, baking powder, and salt in bowl; set aside. In a small bowl, whisk hot water with cocoa powder until smooth; set aside. With electric mixer on medium-high speed, beat butter and granulated sugar until light and fluffy, about 3 minutes. Add eggs, 1 at a time, and mix until incorporated. Add flour mixture in 3 additions, alternating with 2 additions of buttermilk, until combined. Reduce speed to low and slowly add cocoa mixture and vanilla until incorporated.

2. BAKE CAKES Scrape equal amounts of batter into prepared pans and bake until toothpick inserted in center comes out with a few crumbs attached, 25 to 30 minutes. Cool cakes in pans 15 minutes, then turn out onto wire rack. Cool completely, about 1 hour. (Cooled, wrapped cakes can be stored at room temperature for 2 days.)

3. MAKE FROSTING Heat 4 tablespoons butter, brown sugar, salt, and ½ cup evaporated milk in large saucepan over medium heat until small bubbles appear around perimeter of pan, 4 to 8 minutes. Reduce heat to low and simmer, stirring occasionally, until mixture has thickened and turned deep golden brown, about 6 minutes. Transfer to large bowl. Slice remaining butter into 4 pieces and stir in with remaining evaporated milk until mixture is slightly cool. Add chocolate and vanilla and stir until smooth. Whisk in confectioners' sugar until incorporated. Cool to room temperature, stirring occasionally, about 1 hour.

4. ASSEMBLE CAKE Place 1 cake square on serving platter. Spread 1 cup frosting over cake, then top with second cake square. Generously spread remaining frosting evenly over top and sides of cake. Refrigerate cake until frosting is set, about 1 hour. Serve. (Cake can be refrigerated, covered, for 2 days. Bring to room temperature before serving.)

READER ROAD TEST

We asked our readers to bake our Wellesley Fudge Cake before we published the recipe and to tell us what they thought. Here's what we learned from the almost 200 home cooks who did.

The frosting never thickened.

"The cake was very good, but the frosting was almost impossible to work with. I let it cool for two hours and it was still too runny to hold to the side of the cake."

OUR ADVICE Admittedly, our real fudge frosting is trickier than ordinary buttercream, which calls for simply creaming together butter, confectioners' sugar, and flavoring. But it's so luscious, it's worth a little extra effort. For starters, do NOT be tempted to use margarine instead of butter. Unlike butter, when margarine melts, it turns to oil, and when it cools again, it doesn't readily return to its solid state. Next, be sure to pack the brown sugar tightly—too little can translate to glaze rather than frosting. Likewise, it's important to measure the confectioners' sugar before you sift; otherwise, you may have significantly less sugar than the 3 cups the recipe calls for. Finally, keep an eye on the timing, and—even more important—watch for visual cues (see photos 1 and 2 above). You'll know when the frosting base is ready as it will be the consistency of honey and the color of a Kraft caramel; undercooking could be another factor in the frosting running off the cake.

How do you know when a chocolate cake is done?

"Cake = Dry (I followed the directions, but as I do not make cakes, maybe I messed it up somewhere.)"

"The cake was extremely dense, almost brownielike in consistency."

OUR ADVICE These problems could be the flip sides of the same coin. A dry cake may mean it's overbaked, while a sinking, dense cake may be underbaked. We can see why you might have problems, as it's tricky to tell when chocolate cake is done. Unlike white cakes, their color offers no guide. To begin, be sure your oven is properly calibrated (use an oven thermometer to check). To test whether the cake is done, insert a toothpick into its center. It should come out with a few crumbs clinging to it. Some recipes suggest waiting until the cake pulls away from the sides of the pan. Nonsense! That actually indicates the cake is overbaked. Finally, be sure the butter is softened before you begin mixing the cake. If it's too cold, it won't cream properly, which could be another reason your cake was dense.

WANTED: Recipe Testers. Would you like to join the ranks of our volunteer recipe testers? Here's how it works: Periodically, we e-mail you a recipe that's undergoing development in our test kitchen. We ask you to make it within the week and to send us your feedback—what's working, what isn't, would you make it again, and if not, why not. To sign up, visit **CooksCountry.com**.

Equipment Review Hand-Held Mixers

Do new, more powerful models make these the equal of stand mixers? BY PEGGY CHUNG COLLIER

WHEN IT COMES to heavy-duty baking, we favor stand mixers over hand mixers every time. Even the best hand mixers fail miserably at kneading bread dough, a task any decent stand mixer can handle while freeing the cook to do other things. But if you don't make bread (or if you knead it by hand), bake only on occasion, or have a small kitchen or budget, a hand mixer is a good alternative. It's compact, simple to clean, and compared to stand mixers, which cost upward of $250, it's cheap. Moreover, a hand mixer is good for lighter jobs such as beating egg whites, making whipped cream, and whisking ingredients that are warming over a double boiler (try that with a stand mixer!). It's also good for small jobs—whipping one egg white or ½ cup cream. But it's important to invest in a good one. In the past, we've found too many hand mixers with lousy designs and weak motors. We gathered seven, priced from $15.99 to $79.99, to see if any could meet our standards.

We beat egg whites to stiff peaks, creamed butter and sugar, whipped cream, and mixed flour and peanuts into thick peanut butter cookie dough. To gauge mixing efficiency, we put cooked potatoes in a bowl with yellow and blue food coloring and used the mixers to mash the potatoes, timing how long it took to turn them bright green. (Don't do this at home: It results in gluey potatoes.)

None could match the speed and convenience of a stand mixer. Still, all produced satisfactory results for light whipping tasks. It was our mashed potato test, the heavy mixing category, that separated the men from the boys. While two models performed adequately, most struggled. Two models, the Proctor Silex Plus Hand Mixer and Hamilton Beach 6-Speed Hand Mixer, strained their motors and emitted burning smells. Because this task took up to five minutes to complete, we began to appreciate mixers that weighed less. The heaviest in our group of seven, Oster's 6-Speed 250-Watt Hand Mixer, weighed 3 pounds and made our arms tired.

Most mixers had little variation between low and high speeds, a flaw that became apparent when we beat thick, heavy peanut butter cookie dough. The Black & Decker Power Pro 250-Watt Hand Mixer and the Oster mixer were powerful enough to whip cream almost as quickly as our stand mixer, but they didn't know the meaning of "low," spraying flour and ground peanuts all over the counter. We found two exceptions: the Cuisinart and

the KitchenAid mixers offered genuinely "low" speeds that let us gently incorporate ingredients without making a mess.

Beater style made a difference. Traditional hand-mixer beaters are flat, ribbon-shaped strips of metal around a center post. The trouble is, this style traps clumps of batter. We much preferred simple, slim wire beaters that lacked that central post and whipped with great efficiency. Some brands gave us both wire and flat beaters, plus extras: whisks,

dough hooks, and even disks for making milkshakes. Simple wire beaters could handle everything we wanted to mix.

A few mixers featured a "bowl rest" (a lip for resting the machine on the bowl rim). Good idea, bad execution: The feature prevented the beaters from reaching the batter in the bottom of the bowl. Quiet mixers won points—some models were deafening. We preferred digital displays to manual dials (which didn't always match speeds). Separate

buttons to eject beaters were safer than models that had you press the speed dial for release; with the latter, it was too easy to switch the mixer on by accident.

One mixer aced every test: Cuisinart's Power Advantage 7-Speed Hand Mixer offered excellent control with gentle low speeds and powerful high speeds that nearly matched those of a stand mixer. We liked its digital display and quiet motor. At $49.95, it's a fraction of the cost of a stand mixer.

HIGHLY RECOMMENDED

	CRITERIA	TESTERS' NOTES
CUISINART Power Advantage 7-Speed Hand Mixer, model HM-70 $49.95 at Cuisinart.com **Weight:** 2 pounds, 8 ounces	 Range of Speeds: ★★★ Design: ★★★ Light Whipping: ★★★ Heavy Mixing: ★★★ Mashed Potatoes: ★★	Powerful enough to whip and beat almost as quickly as a stand mixer, its extra-low speed also let us incorporate light ingredients without making a mess. The motor was quiet, and the simple digital controls, separate beater-release lever, and contoured handle made the mixer a pleasure to use. A swiveling cord helps left-handed users.
KITCHENAID Professional 9-Speed Hand Mixer, model KHM9P $79.99 at Cooking.com **Weight:** 2 pounds, 5⅜ ounces	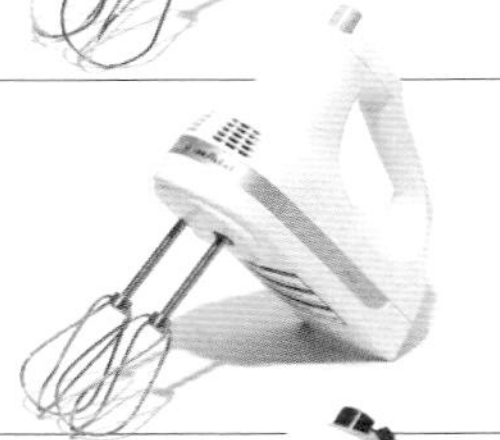 Range of Speeds: ★★★ Design: ★★★ Light Whipping: ★★★ Heavy Mixing: ★★★ Mashed Potatoes: ★★	This model has the low speeds needed for mess-free mixing. Its lightweight body, quiet motor, digital speed controls, and separate button for beater release contributed to its high score. But it cost $30 more than the Cuisinart, dropping it to second place.

RECOMMENDED WITH RESERVATIONS

	CRITERIA	TESTERS' NOTES
BLACK & DECKER Power Pro 250-Watt Hand Mixer, model MX300 $20.95 at HSN.com **Weight:** 2 pounds, 4⅝ ounces	 Range of Speeds: ★ Design: ★ Light Whipping: ★★★ Heavy Mixing: ★ Mashed Potatoes: ★	This turbo-charged mixer whipped and creamed at breakneck speed. But its lowest speed was way too fast—spraying flour, cream, and batter everywhere. Its motor was deafening, and its useless spatula attachment trapped batter before popping off.
SUNBEAM Heritage Hand Mixer, model 3156 $39.99 at Shopsunbeam.com **Weight:** 2 pounds, 7⅛ ounces	 Range of Speeds: ★ Design: ★ Light Whipping: ★★★ Heavy Mixing: ★ Mashed Potatoes: ★	Although it whipped and mixed quickly, there was little difference between low and high speeds. Even set to "low," it sprayed batter and flour. Large, circular vents provided retro style—but had nooks that trapped food.
OSTER 6-Speed 250-Watt Hand Mixer, model 2577 $34.15 at Amazon.com **Weight:** 3 pounds	 Range of Speeds: ★ Design: ★ Light Whipping: ★★★ Heavy Mixing: ★ Mashed Potatoes: ★	We liked the retractable cord, but even on "low," this souped-up mixer left more food outside than in the bowl. Its weight made our arms ache, and it should come with earplugs.

NOT RECOMMENDED

	CRITERIA	TESTERS' NOTES
HAMILTON BEACH 6-Speed Hand Mixer, model 62695V $29.99 at Hamiltonbeach.com **Weight:** 2 pounds, 8⅜ ounces	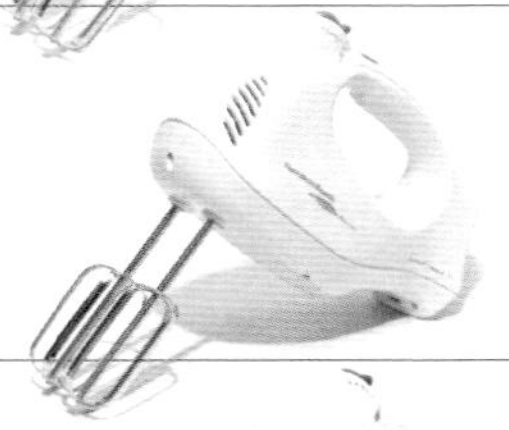 Range of Speeds: ★ Design: ★ Light Whipping: ★★ Heavy Mixing: ★ Mashed Potatoes: ★	Adequate for whipping, creaming, and mixing, but its fast "low" speed splattered ingredients. The cheap speed dial didn't match actual speeds. And a burning smell during the mashed potatoes test made us wonder how long this mixer would last.
PROCTOR SILEX Plus Hand Mixer, model 62545 $15.99 at Proctorsilex.com **Weight:** 1 pound, 14 ounces	 Range of Speeds: ★ Design: ★ Light Whipping: ★★ Heavy Mixing: ★ Mashed Potatoes: ★	This lightweight, inexpensive mixer with a handy snap-on storage case did a decent job of whipping, beating, and creaming. But it struggled with thick cookie dough. The strong burning smell as we mashed potatoes indicated a weak motor.

Taste Test Creamy Italian Dressings

Fat equals flavor—but only if it's the right fat. BY SCOTT KATHAN

HERE IN THE TEST KITCHEN, we always make our own salad dressing. But readers insist they like the convenience of bottled dressing on occasion. In the hopes of finding an acceptable supermarket creamy Italian dressing, we rounded up six top-selling brands (data courtesy of Information Resources, Inc., a Chicago-based market research firm), readied our industrial-sized salad spinner, and called 20 cooks and editors from America's Test Kitchen to taste each dressing plain and with iceberg lettuce.

The results? We still prefer homemade, and can't recommend any store-bought bottles more strongly than "with reservations." Two, Marzetti and Marie's, are acceptable. They have the least sodium per serving, aren't too sweet, and have no off-flavors. Most important, they have the most fat of those we tasted. The type of fat matters, too. Each dressing has vegetable oil as its primary fat source, but the fats listed next in the Marzetti dressing are egg yolk and buttermilk; in Marie's, sour cream, whole egg, and egg yolk. These rich, fatty ingredients give our winners creamy flavor and texture. The Wish-Bone and Kraft dressings get virtually all their fat from relatively flavorless oils. Newman's Own does have egg yolk, but it also has Romano and Parmesan cheeses, a combination our tasters found overpowering.

Ingredient lists don't tell the entire story. With the exception of Marie's (the lone refrigerated dressing here) and Newman's Own, the dressings contain chemical additives and preservatives, a fact that didn't correlate to our preferences. Top-ranked Marzetti, for example, contains high fructose corn syrup, preservatives, and artificial color. Newman's Own, which finished second to last, has none of those additives. While our top dressings are passable in a pinch, we still suggest you make your own (visit CooksCountry.com for our recipe).

RECOMMENDED WITH RESERVATIONS	TASTERS' NOTES
MARZETTI Creamy Italian Dressing with Cracked Peppercorns **$2.79 for 16 ounces** **Total Fat per 2-Tablespoon Serving:** 14g **Primary Sources of Fat:** Soybean oil, egg yolk, buttermilk. **Sodium:** 220 mg	Tasters thought the "spicy," "peppery" flavors lent a "nice bite" of "freshness." "Archetypical creamy Italian," said one taster about the "nice combo of spices and herbs." Some tasters were put off by a "tangy," "astringent," "vinegar-heavy" taste. But on the whole, we found Marzetti "very flavorful" and "decent all around."
MARIE'S Creamy Italian Garlic **$3.99 for 16 ounces** **Total Fat per Serving:** 19g **Primary Sources of Fat:** Soybean oil, sour cream, whole egg, egg yolk. **Sodium:** 135 mg	This refrigerated "homemade-tasting" dressing contains sour cream, making it much thicker than other samples. Some tasters liked that, others didn't. The sour cream made it either winningly "thick, rich, and buttery" or "too thick—almost like paste" and "better suited to a dip." One taster wished it had more herb flavor.
WISH-BONE Creamy Italian **$1.49 for 8 ounces** **Total Fat per Serving:** 10g **Primary Source of Fat:** Soybean oil **Sodium:** 240 mg	Our panel split on the "chunky bits," with some calling them "odd chewy bits" and others appreciating the "good crunch of veggies." "Like school cafeteria dressing, in a good way," said one, adding "I like it." Several tasters mentioned the "balanced" flavors, but others found it "sour" and didn't think much of the "slimy" texture, either.
KEN'S STEAK HOUSE Creamy Italian **$2.50 for 16 ounces** **Total Fat per Serving:** 13g **Primary Sources of Fat:** Vegetable oil (soybean and/or canola), sour cream solids (milk) **Sodium:** 300 mg	Tasters struggled to identify the distinctive seasoning, variously guessing nutmeg, caraway, oregano, allspice, dried basil, and "stale potpourri." (There's no way of knowing. The FDA requires only that "spice" be listed.) "Not bad, but not creamy Italian," observed one taster. "Sweet, but with good balanced acidity," said another. Naysayers compared it to "corn syrup mixed with mayo and oregano."

NOT RECOMMENDED	TASTERS' NOTES
NEWMAN'S OWN Creamy Italian **$3.49 for 16 ounces** **Total Fat per Serving:** 14g **Primary Sources of Fat:** Vegetable oil (soybean and/or canola), egg yolk, buttermilk powder, Romano cheese, Parmesan cheese **Sodium:** 270 mg	The fresh-looking ingredient list gave us high hopes—which were soon dashed. The "very cheese-heavy" flavor tasted "like the green can," one taster said. "Smells like funky cheese, tastes like unwashed socks," said another. The cheese was "gritty and dry," the dressing "one-dimensional" and "too salty."
KRAFT Creamy Italian **$3.29 for 16 ounces** **Total Fat per Serving:** 11g **Primary Source of Fat:** Soybean oil **Sodium:** 250 mg	Our tasters had almost nothing nice to say about this "inedibly sweet," "slimy" dressing, which finished dead last for flavor, texture, and perceived freshness. First impression: "Smells like Elmer's glue." Lasting impression: "Overly sweet fake flavor." Other comments included, "wet dog-y," "plasticky," and "I wouldn't let this touch my lettuce." "Italians would be ashamed."

Test Kitchen Cooking Class How to Roll a Single-Crust Pie Dough

Form meets function with pie shells: If your shell is misshapen, your pie won't be structurally sound or able to contain its filling properly. Don't fret—the fundamentals of rolling pie dough are within reach.

Three Common Mistakes—and How to Avoid Them

The thousands of pies we've baked over the years in the test kitchen have taught us a thing or three about what can go wrong when rolling the dough. Here are the three most common problems—and instructions for avoiding them.

UNEVEN, ASYMMETRICAL PIE "ROUND"

CAUSE: Poor rolling technique, or dough too cold to roll
SOLUTION: Roll, rotate, repeat—and let the dough warm up if necessary.

TORN DOUGH

CAUSE: Manhandling en route
SOLUTION: Use rolling pin to transfer dough to pie plate.

SHRUNKEN BAKED SHELL

CAUSE: Stretched or insufficiently chilled dough
SOLUTION: Support dough when fitting, and chill before baking.

Edge of Perfection Crimping Primer

Our easy crimping technique creates an edge sturdy enough to withstand baking and filling, and decorative enough to impress.

CUT OVERHANG

1. Use scissors to trim the overhanging dough to a uniform ½ inch.

TUCK DOUGH

2. Tuck the dough under to form a thick, even, stable edge on the lip of the pie plate.

FLUTE EDGE

3. For a fluted edge, pinch the dough into ridges around the rim between the index finger of one hand and the thumb and index finger of the other hand. Work your way around the perimeter of the pie, using gentle downward pressure to help the crust adhere to the lip of the pie plate.

Six Steps to Success Rolling Perfect Single-Crust Pie Dough

1. Lay the disk of chilled dough on a clean, dry, lightly floured work surface. Sprinkle disk lightly with flour if it is tacky. Starting in the center, roll once away from you. If the dough splits at the edge, it's too cold; cover it with plastic wrap and rest for 10 minutes at room temperature.

2. Rotate the dough one-quarter turn and repeat rolling. Continue to rotate and roll until the dough is the right size and thickness. Dust round with flour as necessary to prevent sticking, and flip the dough over halfway through. Adjust as necessary to make an even circle.

3. Transferring by hand can stretch and tear dough. Instead, place your pin at one end of the dough and loosely roll the dough around it. Then drape the hanging edge of the dough over one end of the pie plate and gently unroll it into place.

4. Stretched dough will shrink in the oven. Fit the dough by using one hand to support the overhang and the other to gently press the dough into the plate. Work your way around the pie.

5. Torn dough? Don't panic. To patch it, trim a little excess dough from the overhang, moisten this scrap with a bit of water, and press it into the fissure.

6. Refrigerate the shell for 40 minutes so the gluten in the flour can relax, thus minimizing shrinkage when baked. Freeze the dough for an additional 20 minutes to solidify the fat in the dough, giving the dough more time to set in the oven.

VISIT US ONLINE! For *Cook's Country*'s Single-Crust Pie Dough Recipe, visit **CooksCountry.com** and click on **Cook's Extras.**

Notes from the Test Kitchen

Surprise Anchovy Substitute

In the test kitchen we often use anchovies in pasta sauces (see our Recipe Card for **Pasta with Spicy Tomato and Olive Sauce**), stews, and even salad dressings to add a savory, indefinable flavor. We wondered if other pantry ingredients could substitute for anchovies in a pinch. We gathered soy sauce, dried porcini mushrooms, fish sauce, and canned tuna (selected for their similar meaty depth) and compared them to the anchovies in pasta sauce and Caesar salad dressing. The salty soy and intensely mushroom-y porcini missed in both the sauce and dressing. The fish sauce was acceptable in the cooked sauce, but it made the dressing thin. To our surprise, canned tuna was nearly indistinguishable from the anchovy in both sauce and dressing—if the tuna is finely minced. Use 1 tablespoon of finely chopped, water-packed tuna per teaspoon (about 2 fillets) of minced anchovy.

CANNED TUNA   ANCHOVY

Pound Foolish

Our **Swiss Steak with Tomato Gravy** (page 21) bucks tradition by skipping the "swissing," or pounding, of the meat. Why? Because it did nothing to tenderize it. The only way to tenderize a tough piece of meat is to physically shorten the muscle fibers. Consider cube steak. Cut from the round, cube steak is naturally tough. That's why the individual round steaks are fed through a machine that "cubes" the meat at multiple angles with needle-like blades. The blades sever the muscle fibers, rendering tough meat tender. Pounding meat only compresses the muscle fibers, ensuring a consistent thickness.

Seasoning Cast Iron

Most nonstick skillet coatings scratch off with wear and tear, but properly maintained cast iron keeps its seasoned, stick-free surface for a lifetime (and beyond—some cooks pass skillets down through generations as cherished treasures). After each use, wash the skillet lightly with water and a sturdy, non-abrasive brush. (Soap, metal brushes, and extended soaking will destroy the nonstick coating.) Thoroughly dry the skillet, return it to the stovetop, and heat 1 tablespoon vegetable oil over low heat. Using paper towels, rub the oil into the skillet, creating an even, shiny black patina. Repeat this step as needed, wiping out excess oil before storing.

Even if your cast iron has been neglected, you can restore it. Put the pan over low heat, add enough vegetable oil to cover its bottom by about ¼ inch, sprinkle in a generous handful of coarse kosher salt, and scrub with a wad of paper towels. The salt acts as an abrasive, helping you remove any rust or cooked-on food. Rinse the skillet under warm water and repeat as necessary until you've restored the pan to its former glory.

Halve or Halve Not

Since poor cooking technique can turn Brussels sprouts mushy and sulfurous, we paid close attention to detail when developing our recipe for **Maple-Glazed Brussels Sprouts** (page 15). Some recipes recommend cooking the sprouts whole, others halved, and many others with an X scored into the sprouts' stem end—that last, it's said, for even cooking. We put them to the test both in our recipe and by simply boiling average-sized sprouts (1 to 1½ inches in length) in salted water. The whole sprouts flunked. They took nearly 15 minutes to cook, and by the time the core was tender, the exterior was army green, mushy, and sulfurous. The halved sprouts not only cooked faster (in 6 to 8 minutes) and more evenly, but the exposed interiors soaked up seasoning from both the maple glaze and the salted water. So did X mark the spot? Not so much. While the scored sprouts cooked slightly faster (about 13 minutes) than the whole sprouts, again the exterior over-cooked before the inside was done.

TEST KITCHEN TECHNIQUE

Fast Sear, Slow Roast for Beef

To promote browning when roasting beef (like our **Herbed Roast Beef** on page 15), you want the oven to be very hot. Unfortunately, even if you remove the roast when the center is pink, you'll find a thick, unsightly band of gray, overcooked meat at its edge; a low temperature does a better job of cooking the meat evenly. So we brown most beef roasts on the stovetop to build a flavorful crust, then roast them gently for a uniformly rosy, juicy interior.

1. Searing the roast assures a flavorful, deep brown crust.

2. Roasting at a low temperature (275 degrees) keeps the meat moist and succulent.

Tuber Tutorial

Many grocery stores carry three varieties of sweet potatoes: Beauregards, Jewels, and Red Garnets. To see if we could detect any differences among the three, we tasted them in a simple mash as well as in our recipe for **Sweet Potato Biscuits** (page 11). Beauregards, the most common variety, made great biscuits—buttery-sweet and fluffy—and were tasty, albeit one-dimensionally sweet, as a plain mash. The flesh of the Jewels was less sweet than the Beauregards but with an equally firm texture. Red Garnets, decidedly more savory than the others, had an earthiness that tasters appreciated in the mash. Their loose, watery texture, however, made the biscuits slightly gummy.

BEAUREGARD	JEWEL	RED GARNET
Best for biscuits.	Less sweet, but fine for all applications.	Great on their own, but make for gummy biscuits.

Looking for a Recipe

READER TO READER

Did you misplace a favorite recipe? Can you almost taste a chocolate cake from childhood but the bakery—and the recipe—are long gone? Ask a reader. While you're at it, answer a reader. Visit the *Cook's Country* website both to post your requests and to answer those of fellow readers. Go to **CooksCountry.com** and click on **Looking for a Recipe.** We'll share all your submissions on the website (check it out—hundreds are already posted!) and print as many as we can fit in the magazine. You may also write to us at Looking for a Recipe, Cook's Country, P.O. Box 470739, Brookline, MA 02447. Please include your name and mailing address with each request.

Jamie's Spicy Pinto Beans
Cindy Stewart, Granbury, Texas

I am looking for the recipe for the wonderful spicy pinto beans that the restaurant Jamie's in Arlington, Texas, used to serve as an appetizer to everyone. They have been out of business for many years, and I still haven't come up with the secret to the beans. If you can, my family would love it.

Nabisco Brown Edge Wafers
Joanne Reed, Via e-mail

I remember fondly the old Nabisco Brown Edge Wafers, which seem to have disappeared. I would love to be able to re-create these yummy, buttery, crispy treats (at least that's how I remember them). Can anybody help? Thanks.

Tomato Pudding
Virginia Dunton, San Jose, Calif.

My childhood meals often included tomato pudding. The tomatoes were baked with bread, butter, and some brown sugar. This old-fashioned recipe was simple, and sure tasted great. Does anyone have a recipe?

North Jersey Texas Wiener
Todd Post, Arlington, Va.

I grew up on a North Jersey phenomenon called the "Texas Wiener," a deep-fried beef hot dog topped with spicy mustard, chopped onions, and a distinctive chili sauce. Not to be confused with a chili dog, the chili sauce on a Texas wiener is more fluid, more like a mild chili gravy than a thick chunky chili. I'd like to decipher the mystery of the Jersey Texas Wiener sauce so I can bring a little of it to Virginia!

Old-Fashioned Rock Candy
Lois Andrews, Washington, N.J.

Does anyone have a recipe to share with me for making Old-Fashioned Rock Candy on a string? Any help would be much appreciated.

Thomas' Date Nut Loaf
Michel Foster, Sedona, Ariz.

This is from the same company that makes the English muffins. Back in the late 1950s, they used to sell Date Nut Bread, and it was wonderful with cream cheese. It was a great quick bread, and they no longer sell it. Does anyone have a recipe for something similar?

Scottish Potato Scones
Jean Peacock,
Calgary, Alberta, Canada

I've tried again and again to duplicate my (Scottish) gran's potato scones, but I've never been able to do it. Hers were chewy and thinner than other scones. She would refry them in butter in a cast-iron skillet and serve them with bacon and eggs. The outside crisped up by the frying, but the inside stayed soft and chewy, and really tasted of potatoes. Yum.

Smackaroni Salad
Mark Allen Jones, Via e-mail

This has been around for a long time, maybe a mayonnaise jar recipe? It's a macaroni salad with bell pepper, olives, and tomatoes. We lost our copy when my mother moved. Anyone who has this recipe would be canonized in the Jones family Hall of Fame!

Orange Puffs with Foamy Orange Sauce
Katherine Stevens, Tunkhannock, Pa.

My mother used to make a recipe I've been looking for, for many, many years, called Orange Puffs with Foamy Orange Sauce. I would dearly love to have it to recapture a part of my childhood.

Zucchini Donuts
Midge Gwartney, Claremore, Okla.

Back in the 1970s, C & H brown sugar had a recipe for Zucchini Donuts on the side of the box. In a move, I lost the recipe. My little ones used to help cut the donuts, I deep-fried them, and the older ones got to shake them in bags of different toppings. It was fun having kids help fix foods they enjoyed so much.

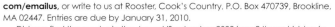

FIND THE ROOSTER!

A tiny version of this rooster has been hidden somewhere in the pages of this issue. If you find it, write to us with its location (plus your name and address), and you will be entered into a random drawing. The first correct entry drawn will receive a Cuisinart Power Advantage 7-Speed Hand Mixer (the winning model from this issue) and the next five will each receive a complimentary one-year subscription to *Cook's Country.* To enter the contest, visit **CooksCountry. com/emailus,** or write to us at Rooster, Cook's Country, P.O. Box 470739, Brookline, MA 02447. Entries are due by January 31, 2010.

Did you find the rooster in the August/September 2009 issue? It was hidden in the Easy Chicken Tacos photo on page 15. Linda Tekieniewiski of Munnsville, N.Y., spotted it and won a Foodsaver V2240 vacuum sealer.

Readers to the Rescue

TOURTIÈRE Serves 8
David Grant, Garland, Maine

"My French-Canadian mother has made this traditional meat and potato pie every Christmas Eve for as long as I can remember." Use leftover mashed potatoes or simmer 1½ pounds russet potatoes, peeled and cut into 1-inch chunks, until tender, about 15 minutes. Drain and mash.

- 2 pounds ground pork
- 1 onion, chopped fine
- 3 garlic cloves, minced
- 1 teaspoon dried thyme
- 1 teaspoon dried sage
- ¼ teaspoon ground nutmeg
- 1 cup low-sodium beef broth
- 2 cups mashed potatoes (see note)
- Salt and pepper
- 2 (9-inch) pie dough rounds

1. Adjust oven rack to middle position and heat oven to 425 degrees. Cook pork, onion, garlic, thyme, sage, and nutmeg in Dutch oven over medium-high heat until pork is lightly browned, about 10 minutes. Add broth and bring to boil. Reduce heat to medium-low and simmer, covered, about 10 minutes. Uncover, increase heat to medium-high, and cook until most of liquid evaporates, about 10 minutes. Off heat, stir in prepared mashed potatoes. Season with salt and pepper and let cool completely, at least 30 minutes.

2. Line pie plate with 1 dough round. Fill with pork and potato mixture and top with second round, crimping edges to seal. Cut 4 vent holes in top and bake until crust is golden brown, 35 to 40 minutes. Cool on wire rack 15 minutes. Serve.

U.S. POSTAL SERVICE STATEMENT OF OWNERSHIP, MANAGEMENT AND CIRCULATION

1. Publication Title: Cook's Country; 2. Publication No. 1552-1990; 3. Filing Date: 9/28/09; 4. Issue Frequency: Dec/Jan, Feb/Mar, Apr/May, Jun/Jul, Aug/ Sep, Oct/Nov; 5. No. of Issues Published Annually: 6; 6. Annual Subscription Price: $29.70; 7. Complete Mailing Address of Known Office of Publication: 17 Station Street, Brookline, MA 02445; 8. Complete Mailing Address of Headquarters or General Business Office of Publisher: 17 Station Street, Brookline, MA 02445; 9. Full Names and Complete Mailing Address of Publisher, Editor and Managing Editor: Publisher: Christopher Kimball, 17 Station Street, Brookline, MA 02445; Editor: Christopher Kimball, 17 Station Street, Brookline, MA 02445; Managing Editor: Jack Bishop, 17 Station Street, Brookline, MA 02445; 10. Owner: Boston Common Press Limited Partnership, Christopher Kimball, 17 Station Street, Brookline, MA 02445; 11. Known Bondholders, Mortgagees, and Other Securities: None; 12. Tax Status: Has Not Changed During Preceding 12 Months; 13. Publication Title: Cook's Country; 14. Issue Date for Circulation Data Below: October/November 2009; 15a. Total Number of Copies: 407,142 (Oct/Nov 2009: 415,997); b. Paid Circulation: (1) Mailed Outside-County Paid Subscriptions Stated on PS Form 3541: 294,827 (Oct/Nov 2009: 285,144); (2) Mailed In-County Paid Subscriptions Stated on PS Form 3541: 0 (Oct/Nov 2009: 0); (3) Paid Distribution Outside the Mails Including Sales Through Dealers and Carriers, Street Vendors, Counter Sales, and Other Paid Distribution Outside the USPS: 36,091 (Oct/Nov 2009: 41,102); (4) Paid Distribution by Other Classes of Mail through the USPS: 0 (Oct/Nov 2009: 0); c. Total Paid Distribution: 330,918 (Oct/Nov 2009: 326,246); d. Free or Nominal Rate Distribution: (1) Free or Nominal Rate Outside-County Copies Included on PS Form 3541: 2,134 (Oct/Nov 2009: 2,307); (2) Free or Nominal Rate In-County Copies Included on Form PS 3541: 0 (Oct/Nov 2009: 0); (3) Free or Nominal Rate Copies Mailed at Other Classes Through the USPS: 0 (Oct/Nov 2009: 0); (4) Free or Nominal Rate Distribution Outside the Mail: 65 (Oct/Nov 2009: 65); e. Total Free or Nominal Rate Distribution: 2,199 (Oct/Nov 2009: 2,372); f. Total Distribution: 333,117 (Oct/Nov 2009: 328,618); g. Copies Not Distributed: 74,025 (Oct/Nov 2009: 87,379); h. Total: 407,142 (Oct/Nov 2009: 415,997); i. Percent Paid: 99.34% (Oct/Nov 2009: 99.28%).

Eggnog Bundt Cake

Swirl warm eggnog spices into 1 cup of a rich, buttery cake batter. Spread a thin layer
of the spiced batter on top of the plain batter and marvel at the magical swirl it forms
as the cake bakes. Top off the finished cake with a heady rum glaze.
This year you'll be able to drink your eggnog and eat it too!

To make this cake you will need:

- 1   recipe yellow Bundt cake batter*
- 1   teaspoon ground nutmeg
- ¼   teaspoon ground cinnamon
- ¼   cup dark rum or brandy
- 1½   cups confectioners' sugar

* Go to **CooksCountry.com** for our Classic
Yellow Bundt Cake recipe or use your own.

For the cake: Adjust oven rack to middle position and heat oven to 350 degrees. Grease and flour 12-cup nonstick Bundt pan. Combine 1 cup cake batter, nutmeg, cinnamon, and 1 tablespoon rum or brandy in large bowl and stir until just combined. Spread remaining batter in even layer in prepared pan. Spoon spiced batter over top and spread gently in thin, even layer. Bake until toothpick inserted into center comes out with few crumbs attached, 50 to 60 minutes. Cool cake in pan 15 minutes, then turn out onto wire rack set inside rimmed baking sheet. Let cool completely, about 3 hours.

For the glaze: Whisk confectioners' sugar and remaining rum or brandy in bowl until smooth. Pour over cooled cake and let dry, about 30 minutes. Serve.

Recipe Index

(RC) = Recipe Card